COMPUTER SCIENCE SOURCE BOOK

THE McGRAW-HILL SCIENCE REFERENCE SERIES

Acoustics Source Book
Communications Source Book
Fluid Mechanics Source Book
Meteorology Source Book
Nuclear and Particle Physics Source Book
Optics Source Book
Physical Chemistry Source Book
Solid-State Physics Source Book
Spectroscopy Source Book

For more information about other McGraw-Hill materials, call 1-800-2-MCGRAW in the United States. In other countries, call your nearest McGraw-Hill office.

COMPUTER SCIENCE SOURCE BOOK

Sybil P. Parker, *Editor in Chief*

McGRAW-HILL BOOK COMPANY

New York   St. Louis   San Francisco
Auckland   Bogotá   Caracas   Colorado Springs   Hamburg
Lisbon   London   Madrid   Mexico   Milan   Montreal
New Delhi   Oklahoma City   Panama   Paris   San Juan
São Paulo   Singapore   Sydney   Tokyo   Toronto

Cover: Detail of graphical representation of a mathematical formula executed by the Calcomp digital plotter, colored by hand for added effect. (*California Computer Products, Inc.*)

This material has appeared previously in the McGRAW-HILL ENCYCLOPEDIA OF SCIENCE AND TECHNOLOGY, 6th Edition, copyright © 1987 by McGraw-Hill, Inc. All rights reserved.

COMPUTER SCIENCE SOURCE BOOK, copyright © 1988 by McGraw-Hill, Inc. All rights reserved. Printed in the United States of America. Except as permitted under the United States Copyright Act of 1976, no part of this publication may be reproduced or distributed in any form or by any means, or stored in a data base or retrieval system, without prior written permission of the publisher.

1 2 3 4 5 6 7 8 9 0 DOC/DOC 8 9 5 4 3 2 1 0 9 8

ISBN 0-07-045507-4

Library of Congress Cataloging in Publication Data:

Computer science source book / Sybil P. Parker, editor in chief.
    p.   cm.—(The McGraw-Hill science reference series)
  "This material has appeared previously in the McGraw-Hill encyclopedia of science and technology. 6th edition"—T.p. verso.
  Bibliography: p.
  Includes index.
  ISBN 0-07-045507-4
  1. Computers—Dictionaries. 2. Electronic data processing—Dictionaries. I. Parker, Sybil P. II. McGraw-Hill encyclopedia of science & technology. III. Series.
QA76.15.C633 1988
004—dc19   88-12773

For more information about other McGraw-Hill materials, call 1-800-2-MCGRAW in the United States. In other countries, call your nearest McGraw-Hill office.

TABLE OF CONTENTS

Introduction	1
Types of Computer	5
Architecture and Circuitry	49
Data Conversion and Output	119
Computation: Theory and Mathematics	151
Programming and Software	181
Computer Communications and Networks	225
Artificial Intelligence	245
Systems Applications	285
Contributors	357
Index	363

COMPUTER SCIENCE SOURCE BOOK

INTRODUCTION

A COMPUTER ia a device that receives, processes, and presents information. The two basic types of computers are analog and digital. Although generally not regarded as such, the most prevalent computer is the simple mechanical analog computer, in which gears, levers, ratchets, and pawls perform mathematical operations—for example, the speedometer and the watt-hour meter (used to measure accumulated electrical usage). The general public has become much more aware of the digital computer with the rapid proliferation of the hand-held calculator and a large variety of intelligent devices, ranging from typewriters to washing machines.

Analog computer. An analog computer uses inputs that are proportional to the instantaneous value of variable quantities, combines these inputs in a predetermined way, and produces outputs that are a continuously varying function of the inputs and the processing. These outputs are then displayed or connected to another device to cause action, as in the case of a speed governor or other control device.

The electronic analog computer is often used for the solution of complex dynamic problems. Electrical circuits, usually transistorized, perform the processing. Electronic amplifiers allow signals to be impressed upon cascaded circuits without significant electrical loss of attenuation through loading of prior stages, a feature absent in purely mechanical computers. Friction in a mechanical analog computer builds up and limits the complexity of the device.

Small electronic analog computers are frequently used as components in control systems. Inputs come from measuring devices which output an electrical signal (transducers). These electrical signals are presented to the analog computer, which processes them and provides a series of electronic outputs that are then displayed on a meter for observation by a human operator or connected to an electrical action device to ring a bell, flash a light, or adjust a remotely controlled valve to change the flow in a pipeline system. If the analog computer is built solely for one purpose, it is termed a special-purpose electronic analog computer.

General-purpose electronic analog computers are used by scientists and engineers for analyzing dynamic problems. A general-purpose analog computer receives its degree of flexibility through the use of removable control panels, each of which carries a series of mating plugs. Outputs from one component are routed to the input of another component by connecting an electrical conductor from one mating plug on the removable board (output) to another plug on the removable board (input). This process is called patching, and the removable panel is frequently called a patch board.

Thus, in any analog computer the key concepts involve special versus general-purpose computer designs, and the technology utilized to construct the computer itself: mechanical or electronic. In any case, an analog computer receives inputs that are instantaneous representations of variable quantities and produces output results dynamically to a graphical display device, a visual display device, or in the case of a control system a device which causes mechanical motion.

Digital computer. In contrast, a digital computer uses symbolic representations of its variables. The arithmetic unit is constructed to follow the rules of one (or more) number systems. Further, the digital computer uses individual discrete states to represent the digits of the number system chosen.

Electronic versus mechanical computers. The most prevalent special-purpose mechanical digital computers have been the supermarket cash register, the office adding machine, and the desk calculator. Each of these is being widely replaced by electronic devices allowing much greater logical decision making and greatly increased speed. For example, most products now carry a bar code, the Universal Product Code (UPC); in suitably equipped supermarkets, the code is scanned by a light-sensitive device, bringing information about each product into the point-of-scale (POS) terminal that has replaced the mechanical cash register. The POS terminal then computes total charges and provides a receipt for the customer. It may also communicate with a centralized computer system that controls inventory, accounts payable, salaries and commissions, and so on. While a mechanical cash register could carry out only a small number of operations each minute, and some electromechanical devices might handle several hundred operations per second, even a small general-purpose electronic computer can carry out its computations at speeds up to a million operations per second.

Stored program operation. A digital computer works with a symbolic representation of variables; consequently, it can easily store and manipulate numbers, letters, or graphical information represented by a symbolic code. Typically, a general-purpose electronic digital computer operates on numbers by using both decimal and binary number systems, and on symbolic data expressed in an alphabet. It contains both an arithmetic unit and a storage unit. As the digital computer processes its input, it proceeds through a series of discrete steps called a program. The storage unit serves to retain both the values of the variables and the program to process those variables. The arithmetic unit may operate on either variables or coded program instructions interchangeably, since both are usually retained in the storage unit in the same form. Thus, the digital computer has the capability to be adaptive because processing can be determined by the previously prepared program, by the data values supplied as input to the computation, and by the values generated during the course of the computation. Through the use of the stored program, the digital computer achieves a degree of flexibility unequaled by any other computing or data-processing devices.

Applications. Most digital computers are occupied with performing applications related to bookkeeping, accounting, engineering design, or test data reduction. On the other hand, applications that were once considered esoteric have led to industrial applications, such as the use of robots on manufacturing assembly lines. Many of the heuristic techniques employed by these robots are based on algorithms developed in such artificial-intelligence applications as chess playing and remotely controlled sensing devices. Modern chess programs are capable of defeating even excellent human players, and computer chess tournaments are held routinely at national and international computer conferences. Of lesser difficulty, perhaps, but illustrative of the kind of information that can be manipulated is the solution of algebraic equations in symbolic form, to provide general algebraic solutions instead of numeric instances of solutions.

Another area of major societal impact is the application of digital computers to word processing, including the entire concept of office automation. The ability of even modest computer systems to store, organize, and retrieve very large amounts of information has brought about radical change in the very nature of many business offices.

1

TYPES OF COMPUTERS

Analog computer	6
Digital computer	26
Microcomputer	38
Supercomputer	42

ANALOG COMPUTER
PER A. HOLST

A computer or computational device in which the problem variables are represented as continuous, varying physical quantities. An analog computer implements a model of the system being studied. The physical form of the analog may be functionally similar to that of the system, but more often the analogy is based solely upon the mathematical equivalence of the interdependence of the computer variables and the variables in the physical system. SEE SIMULATION.

COMPUTER TYPES

Analog computers can be classified in two ways: in accordance with their use, and in accordance with the type of components used to assemble them. In terms of use, there are general-purpose and special-purpose analog computers. The general-purpose computer is designed so that it can be programmed to solve many kinds of problems or permit the development of different simulated models as needed (**Fig. 1**). The special-purpose computer has a fixed program with a few or no permitted adjustments; it is generally built into or appended to the physical system it serves (**Fig. 2**).

In terms of the components with which computers are made, there are mechanical, hydraulic, pneumatic, optical, electrical, and electronic analog computers serving in various applications. Because of its ease of programming, flexibility of operation, and repeatable results, the general-purpose electronic analog computer has come into wide use. Therefore this article deals specifically with features and applications of electronic analog computers. The flexibility of the electronic analog computer has allowed it to be augmented with interface channels to the electronic digital computer, so that during the 1960s a third type of general computer, the hybrid computer, came into being. The characteristics of this computer are also described in this article.

Digital equivalents. Because of the practical difficulties of scaling, interconnecting, and operating an electronic analog computer, the equivalent of its powerful problem-solving capability has been sought and realized in other forms. Many digital computer programs have been developed which essentially duplicate the functions of analog computers via digital algorithms. Such programs as CSMP, DARE, SIMSCRIPT, CSSL, or CPSS are available for almost all widely used

Fig. 1. General-purpose electronic analog computer, model EA1-2000. (*Electronic Associates, Inc.*)

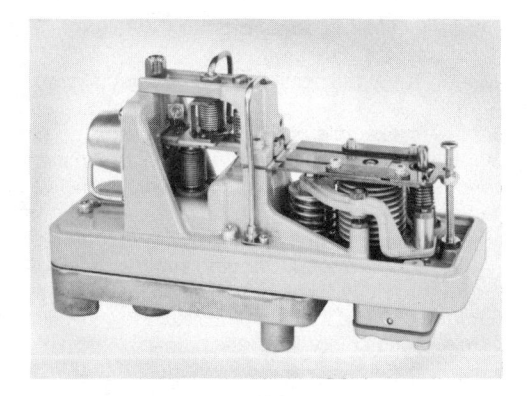

Fig. 2. Special-purpose pneumatic analog computer, model Foxboro 556. (*Foxboro Co.*)

digital computers; these programs approximate the parallel, continuous-time operation of the electronic analog computer by stepwise-incrementing a solution "time" and repeatedly solving the programmed dynamic equations. Digital equivalents to the electronic analog computer are free from scaling requirements and are convenient to run; on the other hand, no interaction within the dynamic response is possible, the solution speed is slower by a factor of a hundred times or more, and little or no on-line model building and exploring is possible.

Digital multiprocessor analog system. Another type of analog computer is the digital multiprocessor analog system (**Fig. 3**), in which the relatively slow speeds of sequential digital increment calculations have been radically boosted through parallel processing. In this type of analog computer it is possible to retain the programming convenience and data storage of the digital computer while approximating the speed, interaction potential, and parallel computations of the traditional electronic analogs.

The digital multiprocessor analog computer typically utilizes several specially designed high-speed processors for the numerical integration functions, the data (or variable) memory distributions, the arithmetic functions, and the decision (logic and control) functions. All variables

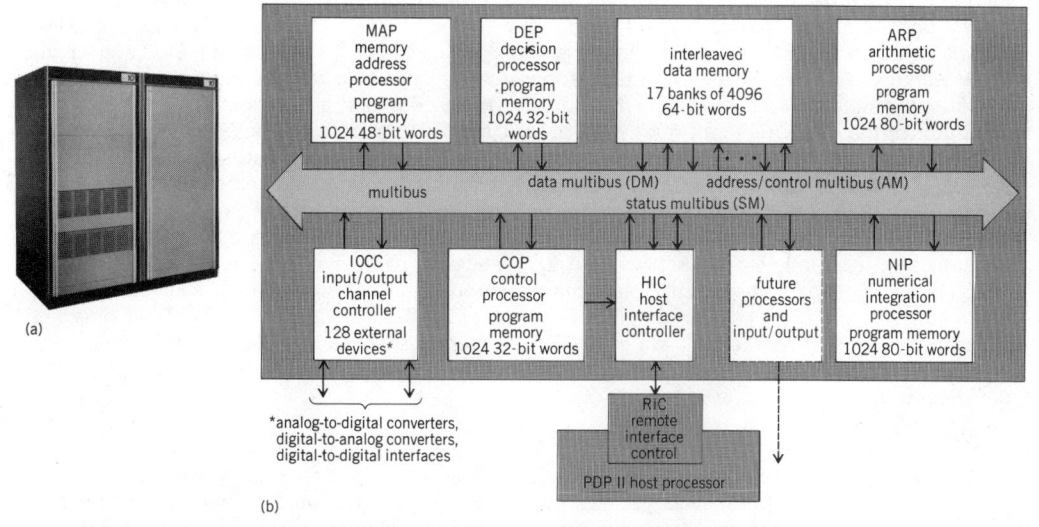

Fig. 3. Multiprocessor analog computer, model AD10. (*a*) Exterior. (*b*) Organization. (*Applied Dynamics International*)

remain as fixed or floating-point digital data, accessible at all times for computational and operational needs.

The digital multiprocessor analog computer achieves an overall problem-solving efficiency comparable to the very best continuous electronic analog computers, at a substantially lower price. An example of such a computer, the model AD10 (Fig. 3a), can solve large, complex, and multivariate problems at very high speeds and with the advantages of all-digital hardware. Its computation system (Fig. 3b) is based on five parallel processors working in a special computer architecture designed for high-speed operation. The various elements are interconnected by means of a data bus (MULTIBUS). A highly interleaved data memory of up to 10^6 words serves the data and program storage functions. The five processors working in parallel are: the control processor (COP), which controls all operations; the arithmetic processor (ARP), which runs the numerical calculations; the decision processor (DEP), which executes the logic parts of the program; the memory address processor (MAP), which makes sure that all data are fetched and stored efficiently; and the numerical integration processor (NIP), which carries out the integration functions that are crucially important in an analog computer.

HISTORY

The slide rule, which originated in the 17th century, represents the first analog computing aid to become a common engineering tool. In it a mechanical position represents the problem variable, and the computations take the form of adding or subtracting linear positional displacements.

Beginning approximately in 1825, several mechanical integrating devices were developed for measuring the area under a curve, and in 1876 William Thomson (later Lord Kelvin) presented a complete description of a process for solving a general ordinary differential equation by analog means. In 1881 the integraph was introduced by C. V. Boys and Abdank-Abakanowicz for drawing the integral curve of a given curve. The mechanical analog computer was greatly improved during World War I; in the succeeding years it was applied primarily to naval gunfire systems.

Significant advancements were made by Vannevar Bush and his colleagues at the Massachusetts Institute of Technology when they developed the first large-scale general-purpose mechanical differential analyzer in the early 1930s. The success of this machine led to the construction of similar machines in the United States and other countries and prompted the MIT group to construct a more elaborate machine, placed in operation in 1942.

The electronic analog computer had its origin in the dc network analyzer developed about 1925 by General Electric Company and Westinghouse Corporation; the dc network analyzer was followed in 1929 by the more versatile ac analyzer. The electronic differential analyzer, as it was called, had its fastest growth during World War II and soon displaced mechanical computers except for some special-purpose applications, such as jet-engine fuel controllers. C. A. Lovell and D. B. Parkinson of Bell Telephone Laboratories were responsible for the first published use of operational amplifiers as computer components. They used operational amplifiers in the real-time computer of the M9 antiaircraft-gun director built by Western Electric Company. J. B. Russell of Columbia University brought the circuits used in the M9 computer to the attention of J. R. Ragazzini, R. H. Randall, and F. A. Russell, who then built the first general-purpose electronic analog computer under contract with the National Defense Research Committee. This work led to the publication of the first article, in May 1947, describing the operational amplifier as a computer component. Meanwhile G. A. Philbrick had independently pioneered the use of high-gain direct-coupled amplifiers as components of fast-time electronic analog computers. The invention of the chopper-stabilized direct-coupled amplifier was primarily due to E. Goldberg of RCA Laboratories; it essentially eliminates the problem of drift in dc computation. In 1947 Reeves Instrument Corporation, under a Navy contract, developed a computer which was the forerunner of the present-day electronic analog computer.

DESCRIPTION AND USES

The typical modern general-purpose analog computer consists of a console containing a collection of operational amplifiers; computing elements, such as summing networks, integrator networks, attenuators, multipliers, and function generators; logic and interface units; control circuits; power supplies; a patch bay; and various meters and display devices. The patch bay is arranged to bring input and output terminals of all programmable devices to one location, where they can be conveniently interconnected by various patch cords and plugs to meet the requirements of a given problem. Prewired problem boards can be exchanged at the patch bay in a few seconds and new coefficients set up typically in less than a half hour. Extensive automatic electronic patching systems have been developed to permit fast setup, as well as remote and time-shared operation.

The analog computer basically represents an instrumentation of calculus, in that it is designed to solve ordinary differential equations. This capability lends itself to the implementation of simulated models of dynamic systems. The computer operates by generating voltages that behave like the physical or mathematical variables in the system under study. Each variable is represented as a continuously varying (or steady) voltage signal at the output of a programmed computational unit. Specific to the analog computer is the fact that individual circuits are used for each feature or equation being represented, so that all variables are generated simultaneously. Thus the analog computer is a parallel computer in which the configuration of the computational units allows direct interactions of the computed variables at all times during the solution of a problem.

An example of a general-purpose electronic analog computer, the model EAI-2000, is shown in Fig. 1. This analog/hybrid computer is controlled by digital means, and operator input/output is through a keyboard-equipped cathode-ray tube. Plug-in analog/digital converters and digital/analog multipliers quickly convert the computer for complete hybrid operation, discussed below. Computational speed is equivalent to 15,000,000 operations per second, or more.

Applications. The analog computer or its equivalent, the continuous system simulation by a digital computer, is employed in every area of science and technology. The range of applications is constantly increasing, from the social sciences, to economics, human relations, political problems and policy/decision-making, to ecology and environmental studies, medicine, health and welfare, up to the more traditional analog computer application areas: science, technology, and hardware and systems development and engineering.

The analog computer is used to gain better insight into research topics, to develop and test methods and equipment, to carry out the design of new processes, or to predict by trial-and-error methods the model responses of system applications beyond known boundaries as well as to improve the behavior of systems already in operation. Special-purpose analog computers are directly connected to or built into physical systems to serve such on-line tasks as immediate and continuous computation or data reduction, or as part of dynamic control. An example of this type is the pneumatic computer shown in Fig. 2. This computer uses standard (3–15 psi or 20–100 kilopascals) air-pressure signals, a mechanical flexure construction, and a readily interchangeable switch plate to perform any one of the following functions: multiplication, division, squaring, and square-root extraction.

The analog computer serves especially well in two categories of systems engineering. In the first, the inductive process of model building, an analytical relation between variables is hypothesized to describe the physical system of interest. Forcing functions identical to those in the physical system can then be applied to the hypothetical model, enabling a comparison of the response of the model with that of the actual physical system. This will often indicate improvements and extensions that should be made in the model to fit it to the system better and thus make it more valid. Because of the ease with which parameter variations and model changes can be accomplished, the analog computer is useful in conducting many trial-and-error experiments on the model to obtain the best fit to the physical system.

In the second category, the deductive process of systems analysis, mathematical statements describing the physical system to be studied are necessary. These mathematical statements (equations) are often supplemented by graphical information as well as by logic statements. Also, validity ranges for parameters are established for the study. Experiments are then performed, varying the inputs and parameters that describe the system, to obtain (finally) a set of optimum responses for the system, to develop a better understanding of the intrinsic nature of the system by studying input-output relations, or to lay a foundation for further investigations into the system.

Unique features. The unique features of the analog computer which are of value in science and technology are as follows:

1. Within the useful frequency bandwidth of the computational units and components, all

programmed computations take place in parallel and are for practical purposes instantaneous. That is, there is no finite execution time associated with each mathematical operation, as is encountered with digital computer methods.

2. The dynamics of an analog model can be programmed for time expansion (slower than real system time), synchronous time (real time), or time compression (faster than real time).

3. The computer has a flexible addressing system so that almost every computed variable can be measured, viewed with vivid display instruments, and recorded at will.

4. One control mode of the computer, usually called HOLD, can freeze the dynamic response of a model to allow detailed examination of interrelationships at that instant in time, and then, after such study, the computing can be made to resume as though no stop had occurred.

5. By means of patch cords, plugs, switches, and adjustment knobs the analog computer program or model can be directly manipulated, especially during dynamic computation, and the resultant changes in responses observed and interpreted.

6. Because of the fast dynamic response of the analog computer, it is easy to implement implicit computation through the use of problem feedback. (This important and powerful mathematical quality of the analog computer is discussed more fully below.)

7. The computer can be used for on-line model building; that is, a computer model can be constructed in a step-by-step fashion directly at the console by interconnecting computational units on the basis of one-for-one analog representation of the real system elements. Then, by adjusting signal gains and attenuation parameters, dynamic behavior can be generated that corresponds to the desired response or is recognizable as that of the real system. This method allows a skillful person to create models when no rigorous mathematical equations for a system exist.

8. For those applications to which it is well suited, the analog computer operates at relatively low cost, thus affording the analyst ample opportunity to investigate, develop, and experiment within a broad range of parameters and functions.

COMPONENTS

Manipulations of the signals (voltages) in the analog computer are based upon the fundamental electrical properties associated with circuit components. The interrelation of voltages for representing mathematical functions is derived by combining currents at circuit nodes or junctions.

Linear computing units. The simplest arrangement of components for executing addition would be to impress the voltages to be added across individual resistors (**Fig. 4**a). The resistors would then be joined (Fig. 4b) to allow the currents to combine and to develop the output voltage across a final resistor. Use of this simple configuration of elements for computation is impractical, because of the undesirable interaction between inputs. A change in one input signal (voltage) causes a change in the current that flows through the input resistor; this changes the voltage at the input resistor junction, and the change secondarily causes a different current to

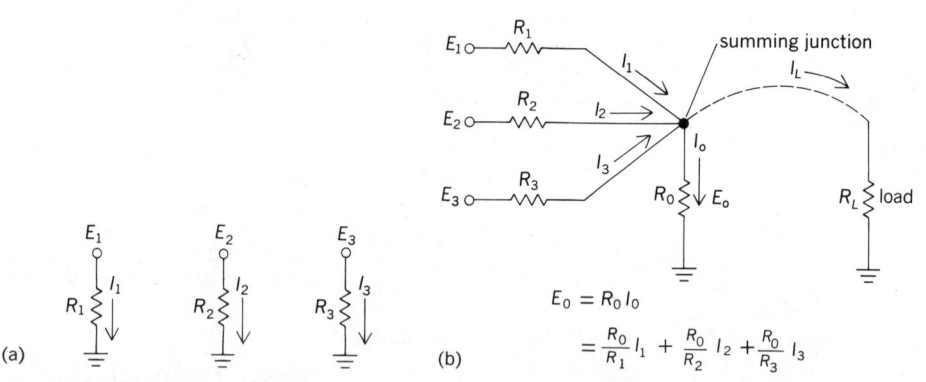

$$E_0 = R_0 I_0 = \frac{R_0}{R_1} I_1 + \frac{R_0}{R_2} I_2 + \frac{R_0}{R_3} I_3$$

Fig. 4. Addition of electric currents by using a passive network of resistors. (a) Individual voltages and resistors. (b) Voltages and corresponding currents summed into a common resistor.

flow in the other input resistors. The situation gets more interactive when another computing circuit is attached so that part of the summing current flows away from the summing junction. This interaction effect also prevents exact computing. If, in some way, each voltage to be summed could be made independent of the other voltages connected to the summing junction, and if the required current fed to other circuits could be obtained without loading the summing junction, then precise computation would be possible.

Function of operational amplifier. The electronic analog computer satisfies these needs by using high-gain (high-amplification) dc operational amplifiers. A symbol to represent a dc direct-coupled amplifier is shown in **Fig. 5**. According to convention, the rounded side represents the input to the amplifier, and the pointed end represents the amplifier output. A common reference level or ground exists between the amplifier input and output, and all voltages are measured with respect to it. The ground reference line is understood and is usually omitted from the symbol. The signal input network (consisting of summing resistors) connects to the inverting (or negative) amplifier input terminal. The noninverting (or positive) amplifier input terminal is normally connected to the reference ground. Generally the inverting input is called the summing junction (SJ) of the amplifier. Internal design of the amplifier is such that, if the signal at the summing junction is positive with respect to ground, the amplifier output voltage is negative with respect to ground. The amplifier has an open-loop voltage gain of $-A$; therefore an input voltage of E_s results in an output voltage of $-AE_s$. Gain of a commercial computing amplifier is typically 10^8; thus, an input voltage of less than 1 μV can produce several volts at the amplifier output.

Because the operational amplifier thus inverts the signal (changes its sign or polarity), it lends itself to the use of negative feedback, whereby a portion of the output signal is returned to the input. This arrangement has the effect of lowering the net gain of the amplifier signal channel and of improving overall signal-to-noise ratio and increasing computational accuracy.

Circuit operation (**Fig. 6**) can be viewed in the following manner. A dc voltage E_{in} applied to input resistor R_{in} produces a summing junction voltage E_s. The voltage is amplified and appears at the amplifier output as voltage E_o, (equal to $-AE_s$, where A is voltage gain of the amplifier). Part of output voltage E_o returns through feedback resistor R_f to the summing junction. Because the returned or feedback voltage is of opposite (negative) polarity to the initial voltage at the summing junction, it tends to reduce the magnitude of E_s, resulting in an overall input-output relationship that may be expressed as Eq. (1). In fact, the summing junction voltage E_s is so small

$$\frac{E_o}{E_{in}} = \frac{-A}{A+1} = \frac{-1}{1+1/A} \simeq -1 \qquad A > 10^8 \qquad (1)$$

that it is considered to be at practically zero, a condition called virtual ground.

To illustrate how the operational amplifier serves the needs of the computing network, consider the currents that flow and the corresponding algebraic expressions (**Fig. 7**). The operational amplifier is designed to have high input impedance (high resistance to the flow of current into or out of its input terminal); consequently the amplifier input current I_s can then be considered to be practically zero. The resulting current equation states that input current I_{in} is equal to feedback current I_f. Since the amplifier has a very high gain, the summing junction voltage is virtually zero. Voltage drop across R_{in} is thus equal to E_{in}; voltage drop across R_f is E_o. The equation in the box is the fundamental relationship for the amplifier. As long as the amplifier has such a high gain and requires a negligible current from the summing junction, the amplifier input and

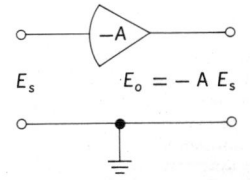

Fig. 5. Symbol for a high-gain direct-current amplifier, with one inverting input referenced to ground.

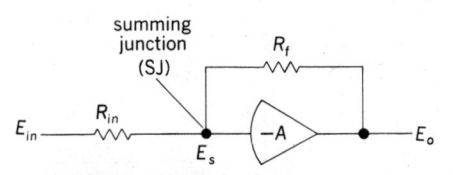

Fig. 6. High-gain amplifier which has been made into an operational amplifier through the inclusion of an input resistor and a feedback resistor tied together at the amplifier's summing junction (SJ).

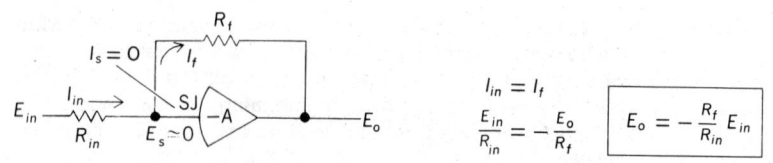

Fig. 7. Summing junction currents into an operational amplifier create the fixed gain function, determined by resistor values, as indicated in the box.

$$I_{in} = I_f$$
$$\frac{E_{in}}{R_{in}} = -\frac{E_o}{R_f}$$
$$E_o = -\frac{R_f}{R_{in}} E_{in}$$

output voltages are related by the ratio of the two resistors and are thus not affected by the actual electronic construction of the amplifier. If several input resistors are connected to the same summing junction and voltages are applied to them (**Fig. 8**), then because the summing junction remains at practically zero potential, none of the inputs will interfere with the other inputs. Thus all inputs will exert independent and additive effects on the output.

Because amplifier gain has a negative sign, output voltage equals the negative sum of the input voltages, weighted according to the values of the individual resistors in relation to the feedback resistor, as shown in the box in Fig. 8.

When a computing circuit is connected to the amplifier output, a demand for load current is introduced. Such a required output load current must be supplied by the amplifier without a measurable change in its output voltage. That is, the operational amplifier must act as a voltage controller, supplying whatever current is required within limits, while maintaining the net voltage gain established by the mathematical ratio of its input and feedback elements. The operational amplifier and network is a linear network because once the input-feedback ratios are adjusted, signal channel gains remain constant (a straight-line function) during computation.

Accessories with operational amplifier. The input and feedback elements that can be used with an operational amplifier are not restricted to resistors alone. A reactive feedback component such as a capacitor may also be used, resulting in mathematical operations analogous to integration with respect to time. The capacitor is a device that accumulates electric charge. The voltage that exists across it is related to its electrical size (capacitance in farads) and the quantity of charge (in coulombs) it contains. Should more charge flow into it (an electric current is actually equivalent to charge per unit time), the voltage across the capacitor would rise. To state this concept mathematically: the capacitor integrates electric current (flow of charge) with respect to time. An operational amplifier with a feedback capacitor (**Fig. 9**) will thus generate an output voltage that is the time integral of its input voltage.

To solve equations with specific numerical values, many different circuit gains are needed. Although it is possible to provide almost any desired gain by selecting appropriate resistances for the input-feedback ratio of operational amplifier channels, each one usually remains fixed once it has been established. In practice the choice of gain is limited to a few integer values (amplifier gains such as 1, 5, 10) which are obtained with high accuracy, using matched resistors, on the general-purpose analog computer.

Another linear computing element, called the attenuator, also known as the potentiometer

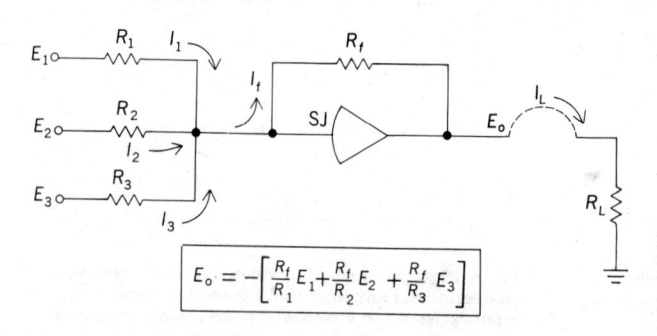

$$E_o = -\left[\frac{R_f}{R_1} E_1 + \frac{R_f}{R_2} E_2 + \frac{R_f}{R_3} E_3\right]$$

Fig. 8. Operational amplifier which has been made into a summer through the use of several input resistors connected to the summing junction. Output is equal to the inverted weighted sum of the inputs.

TYPES OF COMPUTERS 13

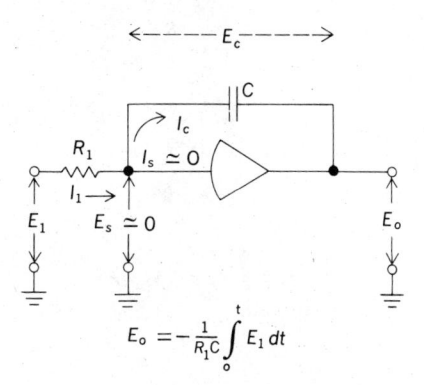

Fig. 9. Use of a capacitor as a feedback element to turn a high-gain amplifier into an integrator, with a time scale determined by the RC time constant.

$$E_o = -\frac{1}{R_1 C} \int_0^t E_1 \, dt$$

or pot, is used to adjust signal gains to desired fractional values. It thus allows parameters (coefficients in the problems) to be adjusted either manually or automatically, between or during computations. Traditionally, the attenuator is a three-terminal potentiometer consisting of a multiturn, resistive winding with a movable wiper (**Fig. 10**a). Output voltage is a fraction of the input, depending upon the position of the wiper (Fig. 10b). For manually adjusted potentiometers, a dial is mounted on the wiper shaft so that the actual pot position can be read out (Fig. 10c). Servo-set potentiometers are adjusted automatically, using individual dc motors in a measurement and control loop fashion; a desired attenuation coefficient value is entered via the console keyboard, and the corresponding potentiometer is set to that value in less than a second. The most modern attenuator is the digitally set one, in which the coefficient value is established via electronic multiplication techniques, making it possible for a digital computer (in a hybrid setup) to control at high speed the coefficients used in the analog computer program. An in-line circle symbol is used to represent the attenuator in analog circuit diagrams (Fig. 10d).

Because the classical potentiometer type is a passive element rather than an active one like the operational amplifier, it can only provide signal attenuations of less than unity. When it is connected to other circuits, including amplifier inputs, some current is drawn through its wiper arm. Therefore, for greatest accuracy in setting, the attenuator must be adjusted while measuring the voltage at the wiper arm when it is under load and with a steady, known reference voltage applied to the potentiometer input. This procedure compensates for such slight loading voltage drops as occur when input resistors of value commensurable with the potentiometer resistance are connected to the wiper. Otherwise the result is a dial reading that is higher than the electrical

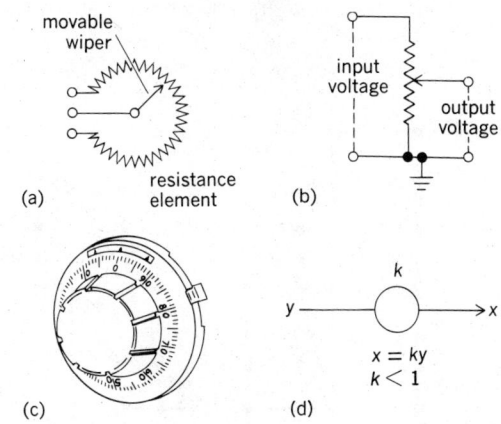

Fig. 10. Attenuators. (a) Traditional potentiometer voltage divider. (b) Circuit used in analog computers. (c) Typical manually adjusted dial with indication of mechanical position of wiper in 10-turn potentiometer. (d) Circuit symbol for attenuator with coefficient k.

$x = ky$
$k < 1$

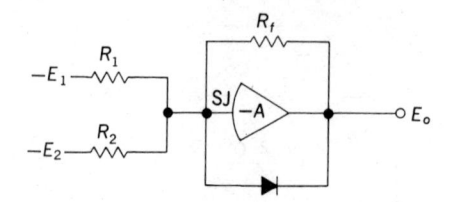

$R_1 = R_2 = R_f$
$E_0 = E_1 + E_2$ when $E_1 + E_2 > 0$
$E_0 = 0$ when $E_1 + E_2 \leq 0$

Fig. 11. Circuit containing one-way conducting diode that limits the output of an amplifier to positive signals (since a negative output would draw a short-circuit current from the summing junction through the diode).

attenuation. As will be described below, attenuators in conjunction with other elements allow the computer to be set up for any required problem value or analog model scale factor.

Nonlinear computing elements. In nature nearly all systems or processes exhibit nonlinear features in the form of constraints, discontinuities, and variable gains. If an analog computer is to be programmed and operated as a realistic system model, it must include devices with programmable nonlinear characteristics. The most versatile computing element for this service is the diode function generator.

The diode operates as an electrical one-way check valve, allowing current to flow one way but not the other. Electrically, a diode has two states or conditions: the ON or conducting condition and the OFF or nonconducting condition. Due consideration should be given to the fact that a diode operates solely according to the voltage across it. A diode will assume the ON condition whenever the anode (the positive terminal) is more positive than the cathode. For example, if the anode is at -6 V and the cathode is at -8 V, the diode is in a conducting (ON) condition; if the anode is at $+9$ V and the cathode is at $+15$ V, the diode will be in a nonconducting (OFF) condition.

Within various limitations, the diode may be used in the input, feedback, and output circuits of operational amplifiers to simulate nonlinear features that are functions of the variable voltages being computed. To illustrate diode action, the output of an amplifier (**Fig. 11**) might represent the computer altitude of a space vehicle above the lunar surface. Upon descent, the constraint is encountered at touchdown that no negative signal (and thus no negative altitude, meaning "flying underground") be allowed to occur, because such conditions obviously make the system equations invalid. Should the amplifier output signal attempt to go negative, the cathode of the diode would assume a lower potential than the anode at the summing junction's virtual ground, placing the diode in the ON condition. The result is to shunt the feedback resistor so that the effective R_f becomes nearly zero. When the amplifier output signal once again goes positive, the diode switches to its OFF condition and no further limiting occurs.

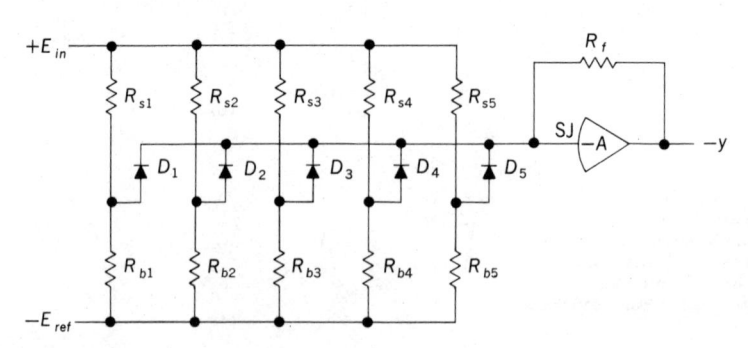

Fig. 12. Diode function generator with five diodes, each biased to a different voltage and contributing a specified current to the summing amplifier, to generate a desired function of the input signal.

TYPES OF COMPUTERS   **15**

$$\text{at } Q: -y = x \left[\frac{R_f}{R_{s1}} + \frac{R_f}{R_{s2}} + \frac{R_f}{R_{s3}} \right]$$

D_1, D_2, and D_3 on
D_4, D_5 off

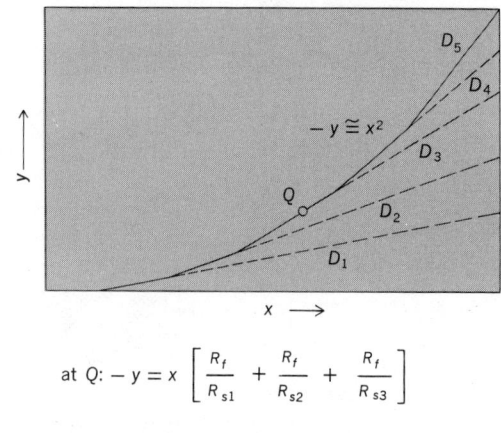

Fig. 13. Resultant function of diode function generator, made up of the sum of currents from the individual diodes; the desired function is approximated by a number of straight-line segments.

Diodes, in addition to being used to implement simulations of unique nonlinearities such as limits, backlash, and deadzones, can be combined with a network of resistors to produce particular nonlinear functions. A diode function generator (DFG) uses the one-way conducting property of diodes to selectively alter the resultant gain of an operational amplifier in accordance with a desired function of the input voltage. The amplifier input circuit of **Fig. 12** is adjusted so that the breakpoint resistors R_b permit individual diodes to conduct at successively higher values of the input signal E_{in}. The resultant input-output gain is determined by the sum of the ratios of feedback resistor R_f and output increment (or slope) resistors R_s, as illustrated by the equation for point Q on the curvature in **Fig. 13**. Specific resistor values for the set of R_b's and R_s's can be calculated to generate many mathematical functions, such as x, x^2, log x, e^x, cos x, or sin x. The DFG can be arranged to operate on either positive or negative input signals by choosing the orientation of diodes and reference voltage polarity. Further, by utilizing fully adjustable potentiometers for breakpoint and slope resistances, a variable diode function generator (VDFG) is established, permitting the programming of most analytic, arbitrary, and empirical functions, including functions with one or more inflections.

Multipliers. The principal device for multiplication of one variable by another (to yield a product of variables) is the electronic quarter-square multiplier. The mathematical function "mul-

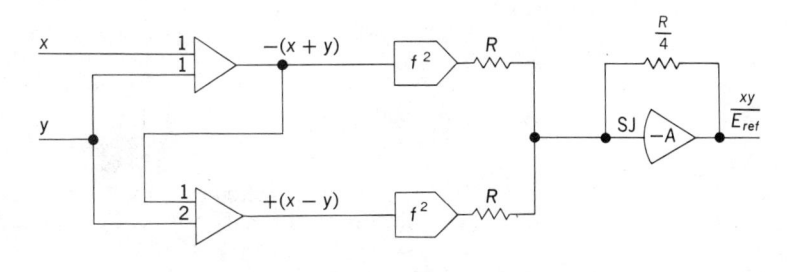

Fig. 14. Electronic quarter-square multiplier, which uses an algebraic identity to achieve the multiplication of variables.

$$xy = 1/4[(x + y)^2 - (x - y)^2]$$
$$= 1/4(x^2 + 2xy + y^2 - x^2 + 2xy - y^2)$$
$$= 1/4(4xy) = xy$$

when $x + w > 0$ $\begin{cases} m = \text{true} \\ z = -y \end{cases}$

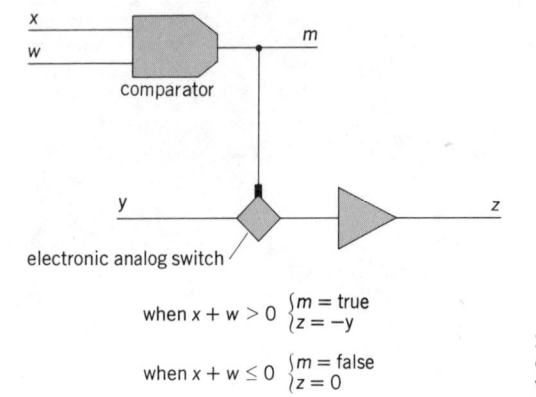

when $x + w \leq 0$ $\begin{cases} m = \text{false} \\ z = 0 \end{cases}$

Fig. 15. Comparator and electronic analog switch, combined to give signal and coefficient changes in the analog circuits based on the comparison results.

tiplication" corresponds to a nonlinearity in which one signal input is acted on through a second input, such as a variable gain. Traditionally, an electromechanical device, the servo-multiplier, accomplished this by dynamically positioning the wiper arm of a potentiometer through a motor drive that responded to the second input signal. Servo-multipliers are now infrequently used in electronic analog computers. However, they represent a type of computing unit having relatively low cost, great versatility, and low signal bandwidth.

The all-electronic quarter-square multiplier achieves the multiplication function to frequencies of several thousand hertz by implementing an algebraic identity (**Fig. 14**). The squaring operations are accomplished with high accuracy by two DFG circuits, as described earlier. Typically, 80 or more properly oriented diodes are employed to permit the accurate generation of the square-law terms of all polarity combinations required for complete four-quadrant multiplication. The simplified symbols which are used in the circuit diagram are more fully discussed below.

Signal-controlled programming. An electronic comparator–analog switch combination provides the analog computer with decision-making and preprogrammed automatic signal-rerouting capabilities (**Fig. 15**). These are nonlinear functions preset to take place at some particular point in a calculation run and to cause a change in coefficients or signals, that is, a branching in mathematical procedure or a change in the control of the run. The technique consists of using a comparator with two or three inputs, generating a logic output signal (TRUE-FALSE) which depends on whether or not the sum of the input signals is greater than zero. Basically the comparator responds to its input analog signals and abruptly shifts its output from one logic level (FALSE) to the other (TRUE) whenever there is a polarity change to positive at its summing junction, that is, whenever the sum of the input voltage goes through zero. The comparator must switch its output rapidly because there is no intermediate value assumed in the transition. The comparator output signal m may be used in logic units (AND gates, OR gates, flip-flops, and counters) to achieve complex logic functions and automatic (programmed) control of computations. SEE LOGIC CIRCUITS.

The electronic analog switch is an ON-OFF input network used in connection with an operational amplifier. The network is ON, permitting an analog input signal to propagate through it to the associated amplifier when, and only when, a logic high (TRUE) signal is applied to its command input. If the command input is logic low (FALSE) or absent, the signal switch network remains in its disconnected or shut-off mode, and no analog input signal will be conducted through it.

One or more of the comparator inputs can be dynamically variable inputs, so that the comparison function itself is a function of the analog computation. The analog signal switch can be used to alter the configuration of computing circuits or to change signal gains by switching between pairs of attenuator potentiometers set to different coefficient values. In modern computers, each comparator also applies power to its indicator light bulb on the console front panel to indicate the state of the comparison function.

PROGRAMMING

To solve a problem using an analog computer, the problem solver goes through a procedure of general analysis, data preparation, analog circuit development, and patchboard programming.

He or she may also make test runs of subprograms to examine partial-system dynamic responses before eventually running the full program to derive specific and final answers. The problem-solving procedure typically involves eight major steps, listed below:

1. The problem under study is described with a set of mathematical equations or, when that is not possible, the system configuration and the interrelations of component influences are defined in block-diagram form, with each block described in terms of black-box input-output relationships.

2. Where necessary, the description of the system (equations or system block diagram) is rearranged in a form that may better suit the capabilities of the computer, that is, avoiding duplications or excessive numbers of computational units, or avoiding algebraic (nonintegrational) loops.

3. The assembled information is used to sketch out an analog circuit diagram which shows in detail how the computer could be programmed to handle the problem and achieve the objectives of the study.

4. System variables and parameters are then scaled to fall within the operational ranges of the computer. This may require revisions of the analog circuit diagram and choice of computational units.

5. The finalized circuit arrangement is patched on the computer problem board.

6. Numerical values are set up on the attenuators, the initial conditions of the entire system model established, and test values checked.

7. The computer is run to solve the equations or simulate the black boxes so that the resultant values or system responses can be obtained. This gives the initial answers and the "feel" for the system.

8. Multiple runs are made to check the responses for specific sets of parameters and to explore the influences of problem (system) changes, as well as the behavior which results when the system configuration is driven with different forcing functions.

Symbols. A number of concepts and techniques are used to ease the process of programming an analog computer. For example, it usually is too tedious and cumbersome to show all of the wiring associated with the computing devices used in a program; therefore, simplified symbols are used to represent the various computer components (**Fig. 16**). These symbols are easy to draw, and they allow a complex program to be designed quickly, yet with sufficient clarity for unambiguous patching.

When an amplifier symbol is shown with a straight front, it is understood to have a standard feedback resistor; but when the front is curved, the feedback circuit is not included and must be explicitly programmed in the computer diagram. In the integrator, the constant of integration C is applied to a separate, special input terminal through a mode switching network of the integrator to provide for establishment of initial conditions. Function-generating networks as such do not show a polarity reversal because they represent characterized impedances (resistor-diode arrays), but they are usually permanently connected to one or two summing amplifiers. The multiplier normally comes with an output amplifier; thus it provides an inverted output.

Representation of variables. When equations are to be solved or a system is to be modeled on the analog computer, all individual parameters and variables must be fitted (scaled) to the available three dimensions of the computer: voltage range, input gains, and computing time. The voltage range spans from negative reference voltage, through zero (ground), to positive voltage reference. The range on large multiconsole analog computers often extends from -100 to $+100$ V; on most small desktop or single-console-type computers the range is -10 to $+10$ V. Reference voltages are carefully established and rigidly regulated to provide a means of generating accurate input signals and to ensure a reliable base against which computed variables can be measured.

The zero point is usually referred to as high-quality ground; it is wired separately from the standard electronic chassis ground and power return ground. All computing signals are referenced to the high-quality ground. The precision of the computing gain of an amplifier is dependent on carefully matching its input and feedback resistors to provide the desired ratio with great accuracy. To avoid errors due to ambient temperature variations, these resistors as well as the feedback capacitors used in the integrators are either specially compensated against thermal errors, or they are physically maintained at a constant temperature in an oven mounted immediately

COMPUTER SCIENCE SOURCE BOOK

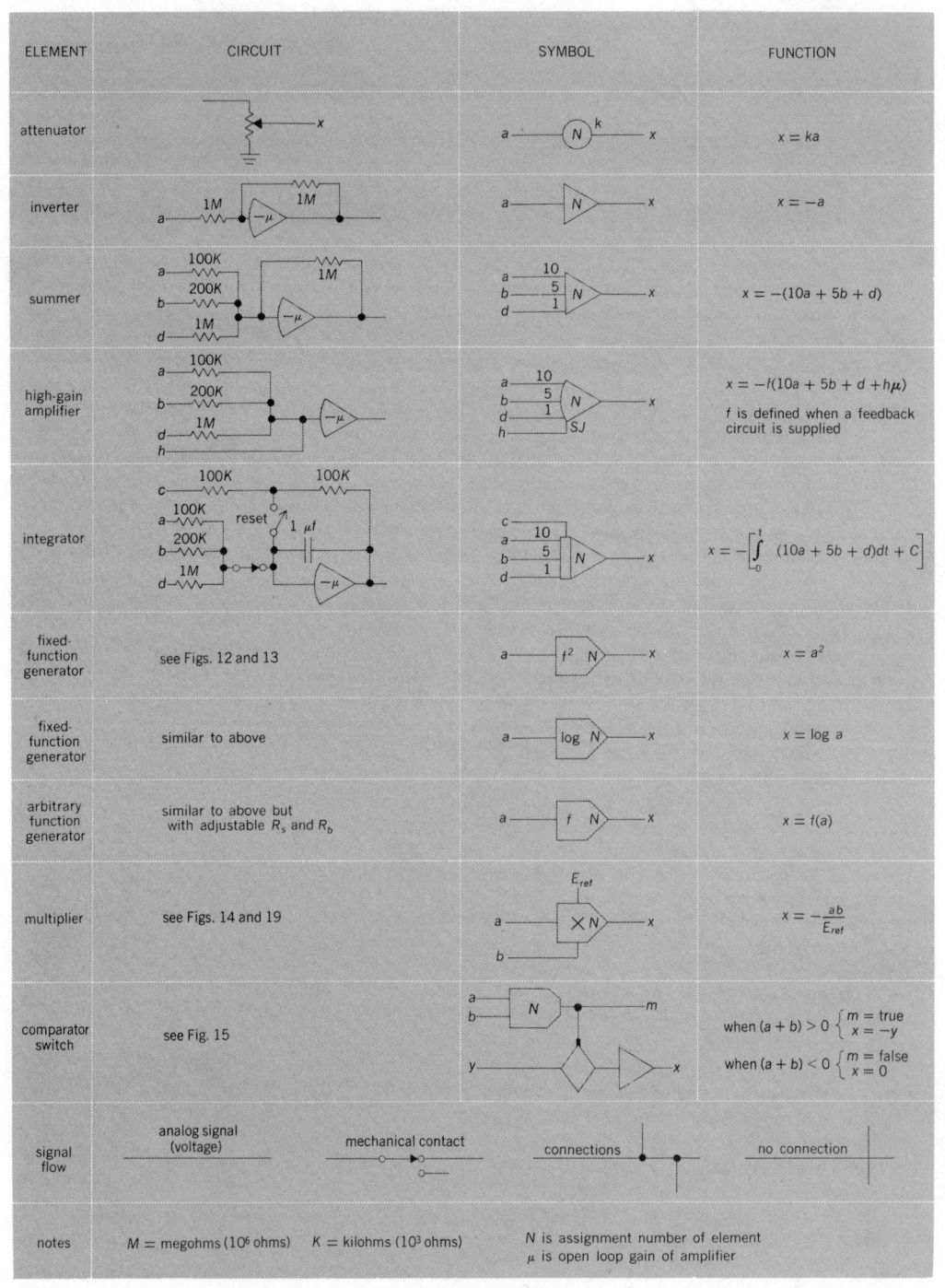

ELEMENT	CIRCUIT	SYMBOL	FUNCTION
attenuator		a —(N)^k— x	$x = ka$
inverter	a—1M—(−μ)—1M—	a —▷N— x	$x = -a$
summer	a—100K, b—200K, d—1M, feedback 1M, (−μ)	a—10, b—5, d—1, N— x	$x = -(10a + 5b + d)$
high-gain amplifier	a—100K, b—200K, d—1M, h—, (−μ)	a—10, b—5, d—1, h—SJ, N— x	$x = -f(10a + 5b + d + h\mu)$ f is defined when a feedback circuit is supplied
integrator	c—100K, a—100K, b—200K, d—1M, reset, 1 μf, 100K, (−μ)	c—10, a—10, b—5, d—1, N— x	$x = -\left[\int_0^t (10a + 5b + d)dt + C\right]$
fixed-function generator	see Figs. 12 and 13	a —[f^2 N]— x	$x = a^2$
fixed-function generator	similar to above	a —[log N]— x	$x = \log a$
arbitrary function generator	similar to above but with adjustable R_s and R_b	a —[f N]— x	$x = f(a)$
multiplier	see Figs. 14 and 19	a—, b—[×N] E_{ref} — x	$x = -\dfrac{ab}{E_{ref}}$
comparator switch	see Fig. 15	a—, b—N—m, y—▷— x	when $(a + b) > 0$ $\begin{cases} m = \text{true} \\ x = -y \end{cases}$ when $(a + b) < 0$ $\begin{cases} m = \text{false} \\ x = 0 \end{cases}$
signal flow	analog signal (voltage) ————	mechanical contact —o▶o—	connections •┼•	no connection ┼
notes	M = megohms (10^6 ohms) K = kilohms (10^3 ohms)	N is assignment number of element μ is open loop gain of amplifier	

Fig. 16. Symbols used in the programming of analog circuit diagrams.

behind the patch bay. By using multiturn potentiometers as attenuators, excellent resolution is obtained for coefficient adjustment. The maximum range of such coefficient adjustment, using the available input gains (including the combination of a potentiometer and an amplifier), may span approximately six decades (0.0001 to 100).

The time duration required for the dynamic response of a system model determines how long the computer must be programmed to run. A single run can be as short as 1 ms or as long as hours. The precision of the computational results is determined by how accurately all the computer circuits function and how well the operational amplifiers are stabilized against drift.

Just as the analog voltage range can be scaled to represent the range of any real system variable, so the analog time dimension can be used to represent a system dimension other than time. For example, the problem to be programmed might be the calculation of the temperature profile of a metal rod heated at one end and cooled at the other. The analog computer could be programmed to sweep continuously in time along the length of the rod, developing a varying analog voltage scaled to represent the temperature. Thus, the computer time dimension would correspond to the rod length dimension.

Inverse operations. The complementary nature of the input and feedback networks of the operational amplifier gives it one of its most flexible properties. If, for example, a squaring module in an amplifier input circuit is moved to the amplifier feedback circuit, the amplifier will compute the square root. In general, when a function is exchanged between the input and feedback positions of an operational amplifier, the inverse function is obtained. For example, the constant k in **Fig. 17**a becomes the reciprocal $1/k$ when relocated in the feedback circuit of Fig. 17b. Similarly, the log function exchange (**Fig. 18**a and b) provides the exponential function.

(a) $\quad y = -kx \quad$ (b) $\quad y = -\frac{1}{k}x$

Fig. 17. Movement of an attenuator from the input to the feedback network of an operational amplifier to create the inverse function: the coefficient changes from k in a to the inverse, $1/k$ in b.

No special device is needed in an analog computer to divide one variable by another. Division is achieved by placing a multiplier in the feedback path of an amplifier, as shown in **Fig. 19**. (For the division to be stable, the denominator W in Fig. 19b must always be negative and larger than zero, so that there is no positive feedback loop around the amplifier.) Similarly, the derivative of a function can be obtained by using this same principle. Since differentiation is the inverse mathematical operation of integration, the feedback circuit in **Fig. 20** incorporates an integrator to satisfy the requirement. The function of differentiation, due to its nature, exhibits

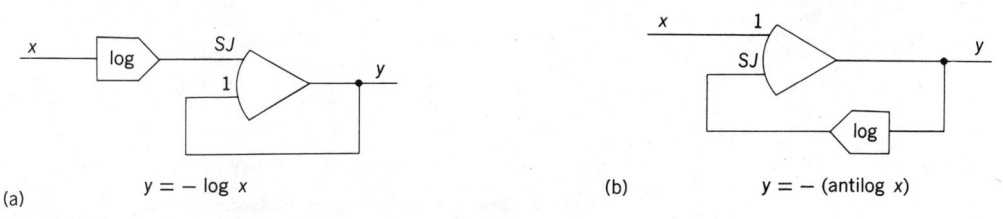

(a) $\quad y = -\log x \quad$ (b) $\quad y = -(\text{antilog } x)$

Fig. 18. Movement of a logarithm function generator from the input to the feedback network of an operational amplifier to change the amplifier function from (a) log x to (b) antilog x (exp x).

variable multiplication

$$y = -\left(\frac{xw}{E_{ref}}\right)$$

(a)

variable division

$$y = -\left(\frac{x\,E_{ref}}{w}\right)$$

$w < 0$

(b)

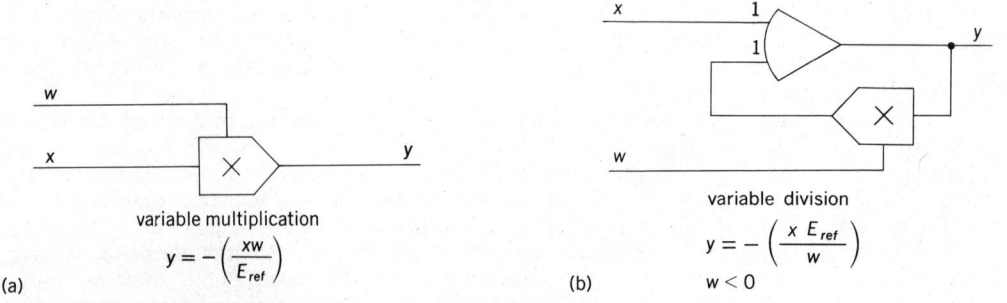

Fig. 19. Use of multiplier (*a*) to create the variable multiplication function, and (*b*) in the feedback path of an amplifier to create the variable division function.

higher gain at higher signal frequencies, a characteristic which may often lead to excessive amplification of high-frequency circuit noise; therefore, the addition of a feedback attenuator, indicated with a broken line in Fig. 20, is often useful to reduce the gain above a selected high-frequency roll-off corner.

Solution of algebraic equations. Programming an analog computer to solve an equation such as Eq. (2) can be described by referring to **Fig. 21**. Basically, a circuit is devised to

$$y = x^2 + 4x - 50 \qquad (2)$$

generate each term of the equation; the output of each is then summed algebraically by the final amplifier.

The first term results from a squaring function generator in the input circuit of amplifier 6 as defined previously in Fig. 12. The arithmetic for the second term is programmed by dividing the forward gain of amplifier 5 by its feedback gain, 20/5, to yield a net gain of 4. The third term derives from the reference voltage by an adjustment of attenuator 2. Each circuit of the program operates in parallel with all others and instantaneously, so that y is explicitly and immediately developed; thus the circuit will handle either varying or steady-state values of the input signal x.

Because the analog computer has a limited operational range and therefore resolution, the desired practical ranges of the various terms in a problem must be scaled to fit the analog voltage range. This requirement corresponds somewhat to that of keeping track of the decimal point when using the slide rule. The circuit of Fig. 21*b* is scaled for a specific range such that a signal voltage V is related to the numerical value N by a scale factor α. The maximum value of 80 for x can be directly accommodated within the 100-V range of the computer. Accordingly, its scale factor α_1 is set at unity. But the corresponding maximum value for y would exceed the unscaled computer range, necessitating an assignment of 0.01 for α_9 (meaning the y signal will not rise above 66.70 V). All the signals collected at the summing junction of amplifier 3 must have scales that are

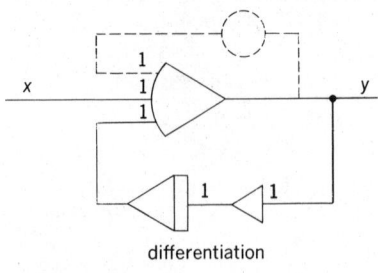

differentiation

$$y = -\frac{dx}{dt}$$

Fig. 20. Use of an integrator in the feedback path of an operational amplifier to achieve differentiation with respect to time, dx/dt.

TYPES OF COMPUTERS

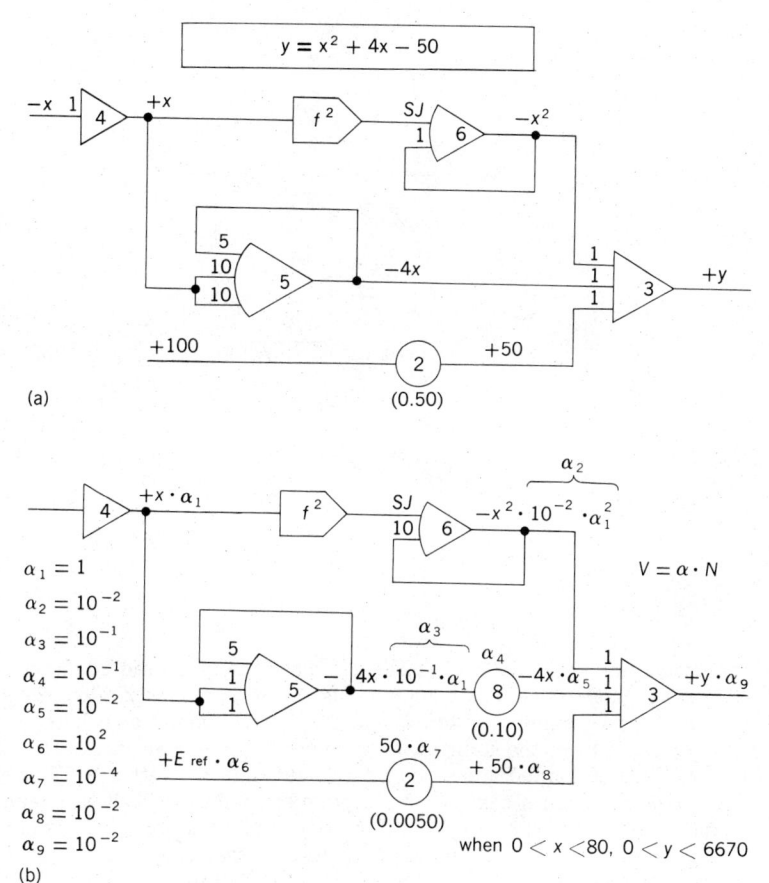

$$y = x^2 + 4x - 50$$

Fig. 21. Analog computer circuits for solving a problem in algebra. (*a*) Unscaled circuit reflecting the equation given in box. (*b*) Circuit scaled for computation in computer with 100-V range, with appropriate scale factors α_1-α_9.

$\alpha_1 = 1$
$\alpha_2 = 10^{-2}$
$\alpha_3 = 10^{-1}$
$\alpha_4 = 10^{-1}$
$\alpha_5 = 10^{-2}$
$\alpha_6 = 10^{2}$
$\alpha_7 = 10^{-4}$
$\alpha_8 = 10^{-2}$
$\alpha_9 = 10^{-2}$

$V = \alpha \cdot N$

when $0 < x < 80$, $0 < y < 6670$

compatible with the output variables; therefore α_2, α_5, and α_8 are matched to α_9. Taking into consideration the reference voltage and the choice of slope resistors used to establish the square function generator, a scale of 0.01 at amplifier 6 seems practical when a feedback gain of 10 is used. This scale factor relates directly with α_1^2 to yield the desired α_2 factor. To adjust the second-term circuit for α_5, the forward gain of amplifier 5 must be lowered by a decade to set α_3, and attenuator 8 was added to insert α_4 so that the product of α_3 and α_4 would produce the proper scale factor α_5. The necessary α_8 in the third circuit arises from the α_6 associated with a 100-V reference and a readjustment of attenuator 2, taking into account α_7 ($10^2 \times 10^{-4} = 10^{-2}$).

Use with calculus. Because of its fundamental ability to perform continuous integration, the analog computer is particularly well suited to solve ordinary differential equations, typically arising in the problems of calculus. Because of this ability, the analog computer has at times been referred to as the electronic differential analyzer. Significantly, the analog computer integrator will respond correctly to any simple or complex signal waveform presented at its input; it is not restricted to applications involving conventional classes of functions defined by analytic calculus.

The analog program for a third-order, nonlinear differential equation is illustrated in **Fig. 22**. The equation is nonlinear because the third term has a variable coefficient, 7x, operating on the first derivative. As a result, this equation has no known analytic solution in closed form. Nevertheless, the analog computer does generate the solution for x by virtue of its instantaneous, parallel structure, its inherent capability to carry out continuous integrations, its ability to multiply variables, and its feature of problem feedback permitting implicit computation. The first step in

22 COMPUTER SCIENCE SOURCE BOOK

$$4\frac{d^3x}{dt^3} + 5\frac{d^2x}{dt^2} + 7x\frac{dx}{dt} - 3x + 36 = 0$$

$$-\frac{d^3x}{dt^3} = \frac{5}{4}\frac{d^2x}{dt^2} + \frac{7}{4}x\frac{dx}{dt} - \frac{3}{4}x + 9$$

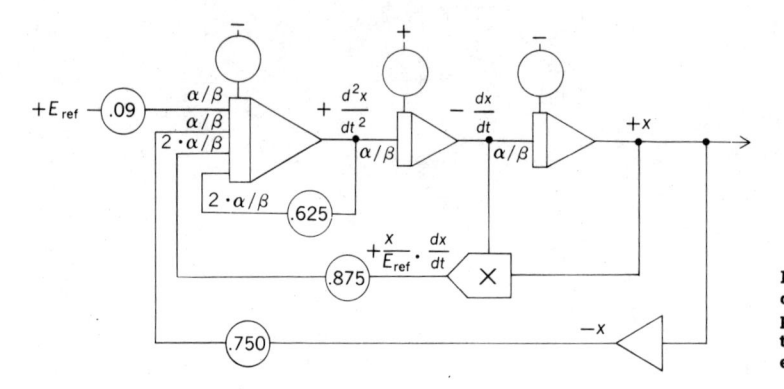

Fig. 22. Analog computer circuit for solving a problem in calculus, with third-order differential equation shown in box.

the programming procedure is to algebraically rearrange the equation so that the highest-order derivative stands alone on the left side, as shown in the second expression in Fig. 22. The second step in the programming is to assume that a condition of signals representing the highest time derivative exists in the form of the summed inputs of an integrator (this condition is justified below). Then, by integration, the next lower time derivative will appear at the output of this integrator. By using a cascade of integrators (composed of three integrators in this case), each derivative is developed in turn until the dependent variable finally is generated. Next, each term on the right side of the expression may now be assembled through separate analog components and circuits and then gathered at the input of the first integrator. Now, when the circuits are activated electronically, the signals that the expression equates as the highest derivative will exist in fact at the integrator, justifying the original assumption. The circuit configuration involves the feedback of problem variables; therefore it is said that an implicit rather than an explicit solution of the equation is being made.

The analog computer can only represent the independent variable as time (clock time or real time). That is, regardless of the nature of the independent dimension in the simulated system, all derivatives in the computer representation are taken with respect to time. Because the computer accommodates a practical but finite time span, time ranges must be scaled in a fashion similar to that for voltage amplitudes discussed earlier. Computer time T is related to real system time t by a scale factor β. Also, an integrator operates on a voltage with respect to time, so that the gain of an integrator is determined by the ratio α/β. When β is one, the computer calculates in real time; when β is greater than one, computer time is expanded (responses take place at speeds slower than real time); and when β is less than one, computer time is compressed (and responses occur faster than in real time). In arranging the time scales, it is mandatory that the β value be identical for all integrators within one interdependent system program. The potentiometer shown at the top of each integrator is used to preset the integrator to its proper initial condition (also called the constant of integration), as will be discussed later.

Use as simulator. The dynamic system in **Fig. 23**a is presented to illustrate how an analog computation can be built up block by block directly from the characteristics of a system. Each part of the automobile suspension system is treated as a black box containing a second-order response mechanism. These boxes are then strongly intercoupled to the main chassis member. The design objective would be to adjust the masses M_i, the spring constants K_i, and the

TYPES OF COMPUTERS 23

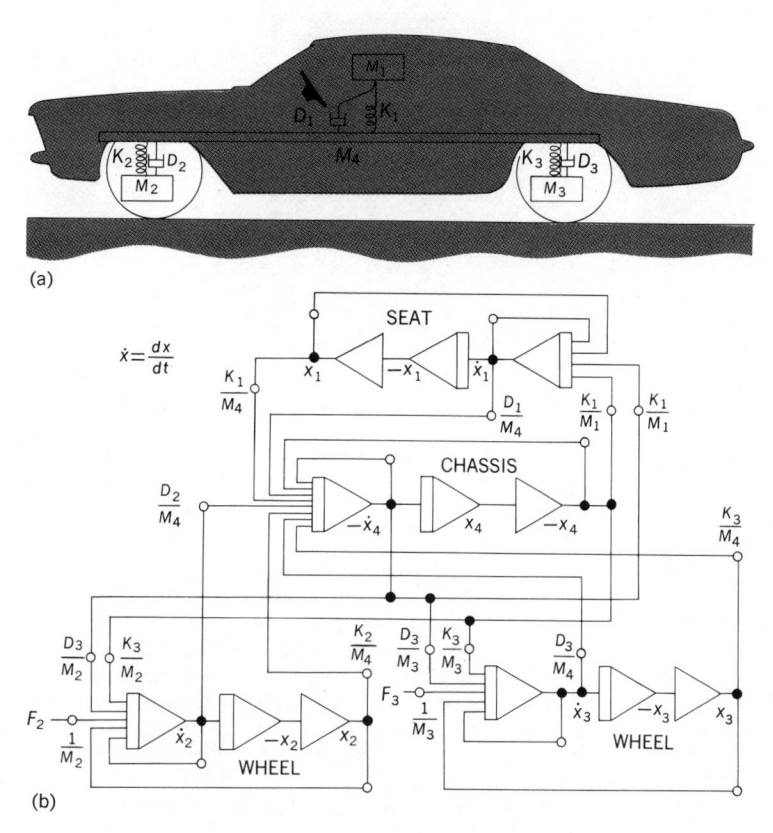

Fig. 23. Construction of an analog computer model. (a) Approximation of the suspension system of an automobile with damped second-order systems. (b) Diagram of corresponding analog computer model. (After T. H. Truitt and A. E. Rogers, Basics of Analog Computers, John F. Rider, 1960)

dampers D_i to minimize x_1, the seat displacement that the driver experiences under various road conditions. Figure 23b shows the assembled analog computer model, with its variables labeled.

Finding a single combination of parameter settings is difficult, because at different road speeds the forcing functions at the front and rear wheels, F_2 and F_3, reflect a shift in frequency content and a difference in the excitation delay time from front to back. Once the building block model has been assembled, it is possible to see that a set of four simultaneous differential equations could be extracted from the analog circuit configuration to represent the system mathematically.

OPERATION

After a program has been connected up on the patchboard in accordance with the foregoing programming procedures, the problem patchboard inserted in the patch bay, and the attenuators adjusted to their proper values, the analog computer is ready for a solution run. The mode of operation of the computer is governed by integrator controls, as shown in **Fig. 24**. The input to an integrator amplifier is connected to one of the four possible points: potset (PS) for adjusting potentiometers, in which the integrator is effectively short-circuited; the reset or initial condition (IC) mode, in which the capacitor is charged up to the initial value E_{IC}; hold (HD), which is a stop and freeze mode mainly for readout purposes; and operate (OP) mode, in which the intended continuous integration with respect to time takes place. The switching between these modes is done with high-speed electronic analog signal switches (older computers use relay contacts) controlled from the computer console or via logic command signals connected on the patchboard. At the beginning of a run, the computer is put in the reset or initial condition mode, energizing a bus circuit so that the integrators assume their initial conditions. Next, the computer is switched

24 COMPUTER SCIENCE SOURCE BOOK

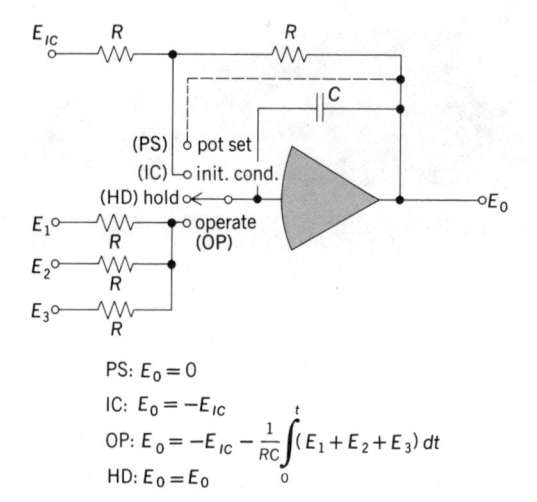

PS: $E_0 = 0$
IC: $E_0 = -E_{IC}$
OP: $E_0 = -E_{IC} - \frac{1}{RC}\int_0^t (E_1 + E_2 + E_3)\,dt$
HD: $E_0 = E_0$

Fig. 24. Integrator controls.

to the operate mode, removing the initial condition inputs and connecting the integrand inputs to the integrators. The generated and connected input signals are now integrated by the integrator according to its programmed time scale.

A study of the recorded responses in **Fig. 25** for the x, y, and w integrators reveals how each linear ramp function develops by the integration of its particular constant-voltage input signal. As the computer modes are exercised, each integrator behaves in accordance with its initial condition and the polarities and amplitudes of input signals imposed upon it. During the normal problem run, the integrators respond to rapidly varying, interacting signals, and many different dynamic results are generated.

In operating the computer, the user must be prepared to deal with many practical circumstances and to diagnose the troubles or errors that arise from the analog computer program. Mistakes in circuit patching, incorrect attenuator settings, wrong reference polarities, misapplication of ranges of computer units and display devices, and inappropriate time scale factor as-

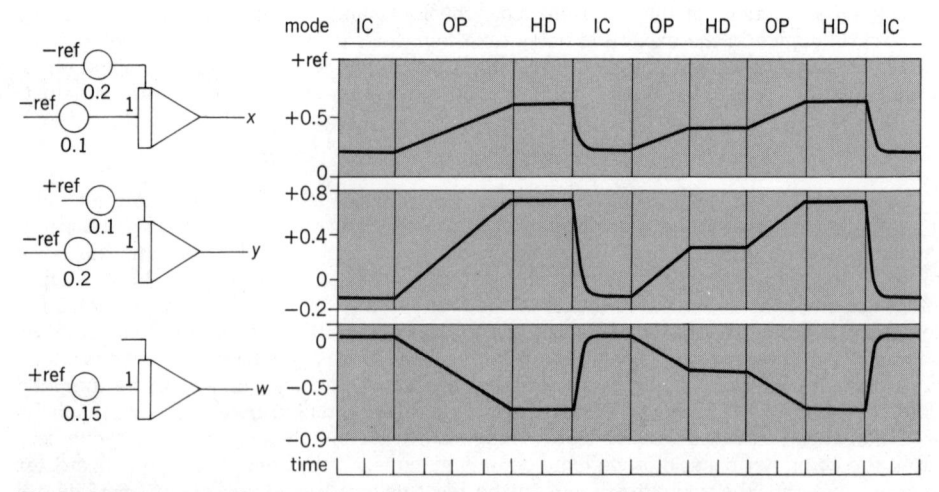

Fig. 25. Integrator control: outputs from three integrators are recorded with respect to time, showing how they depend on the computer control modes, integration initial conditions, and integrand inputs.

signments may occur, as well as a host of details associated with the electronic properties of the computer. A smooth-running program, however, returns an extremely large amount of problem insight and experience, well worth the effort required to get the problem running.

HYBRID COMPUTERS

The accuracy of the calculations on a digital computer can often be increased through double precision techniques and more precise algorithms, but at the expense of extended solution time, due to the computer's serial nature of operation. Also, the more computational steps there are to be done, the longer the digital computer will take to do them. On the other hand, the basic solution speed is very rapid on the analog computer because of its parallel nature, but increasing problem complexity demands larger computer size. Thus, for the analog computer the time remains the same regardless of the complexity of the problem, but the size of the computer required grows with the problem.

Interaction between the user and the computer during the course of any calculation, with the ability to vary parameters during computer runs, is a highly desirable and insight-generating part of computer usage. This hands-on interaction with the computed responses is simple to achieve with analog computers. For digital computers, interaction usually takes place through a computer keyboard terminal, between runs, or in an on-line stop-go mode. An often-utilized system combines the speed and interaction possibilities of an analog computer with the accuracy and programming flexibility of a digital computer. This combination is specifically designed into the hybrid computer.

A modern analog-hybrid console is depicted in **Fig. 26**. It contains the typical analog components plus a second patchboard area to include programmable, parallel logic circuits using high-speed gates for the functions of AND, NAND, OR, and NOR, as well as flip-flops, registers, and counters. The mode switches in the integrators are interfaced with the digital computer to permit fast iterations of dynamic runs under digital computer control. As shown in **Fig. 27**, data flow in many ways and formats between the analog computer with its fast, parallel circuits and the digital

Fig. 26. Analog-hybrid laboratory equipped with a HYSHARE 600 system. This system can include up to six analog computer consoles and one or more digital processors for multiuser, multitask applications. (*Electronic Associates, Inc.*)

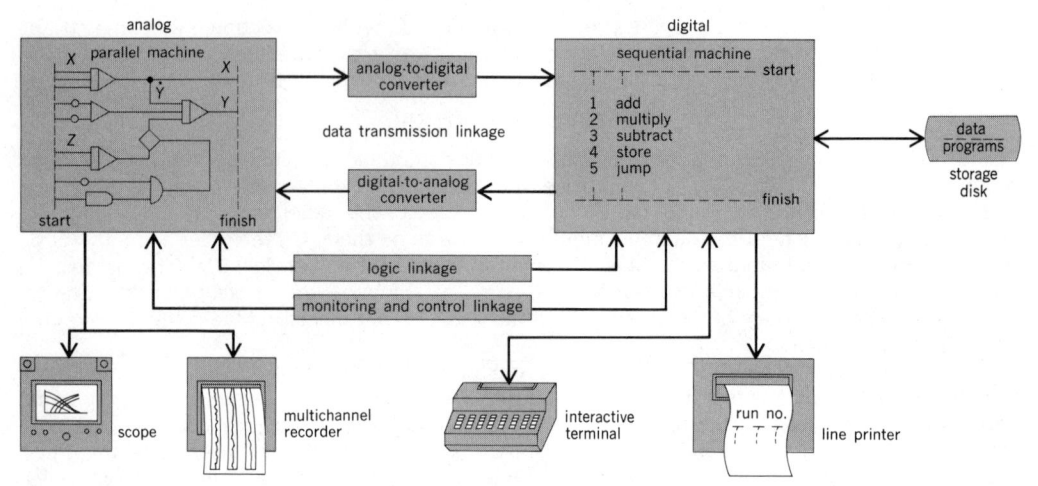

Fig. 27. Block diagram representation of a hybrid analog-to-digital computer.

computer with its sequential, logic-controlled program. Special high-speed analog-to-digital and digital-to-analog converters translate between the continuous signal representations of variables in the analog domain and the numerical representations of the digital computer. Control and logic signals are more directly compatible and require only level and timing compatibility. SEE ANALOG-TO-DIGITAL CONVERTER; BOOLEAN ALGEBRA; DIGITAL-TO-ANALOG CONVERTER.

The programming of hybrid models is a more complex challenge than described above, requiring the user to consider the parallel action of the analog computer interlaced with the step-by-step computations progression in the digital computer. For example, in simulating the mission of a space vehicle, the capsule control dynamics will typically be handled on the analog computer in continuous form, but interfaced with the digital computer, where the navigational trajectory is calculated.

DIGITAL COMPUTER
MONTGOMERY PHISTER, JR.

Any device for performing mathematical calculations on numbers represented digitally; by extension, any device for manipulating symbols according to a detailed procedure or recipe. The class of digital computers includes microcomputers, conventional adding machines and calculators, digital controllers used for industrial processing and manufacturing operations, store-and-forward data communication equipment, and electronic data-processing systems.

In this article emphasis is on electronic stored-program digital computers. These machines store internally many thousands of numbers or other items of information, and control and execute complicated sequences of numerical calculations and other manipulations on this information in accordance with instructions also stored in the machine. The first section of this article discusses digital system fundamentals, reviewing the components and building blocks from which digital systems are constructed. The following section introduces the stored-program general-purpose computer in more detail and indicates the characteristics by which system performance is measured. The final section traces the history of stored-program digital computer systems and shows how the requirements of new applications and the development of new technologies have influenced system design.

DIGITAL SYSTEM FUNDAMENTALS

A digital system can be considered from many points of view. At the lowest level it is a network of wires and mechanical parts whose voltages and positions convey coded information.

Table 1. Counting from 0 to 19 by decimal and binary numbers

Decimal number	Binary number
00	00000
01	00001
02	00010
03	00011
04	00100
05	00101
06	00110
07	00111
08	01000
09	01001
10	01010
11	01011
12	01100
13	01101
14	01110
15	01111
16	10000
17	10001
18	10010
19	10011

At another level it is a collection of logical elements, each of which embodies certain rules, but which in combination can carry out very complex functions. At a still higher level, a digital system is an arrangement of functional units or building blocks which read (input), write (output), store, and manipulate information.

Codes. Numbers are represented within a digital computer by means of circuits that distinguish various discrete electrical signals on wires inside the machine. Theoretically, a signal on a wire could be made to represent any one of several different digits by means of the magnitude of the signal. (For example, a signal from 0 to 1 V could represent the digit zero, a signal between 1 and 2 V could represent the digit one, and so on up to a signal between 9 and 10 V, the digit nine.) In practice, the most reliable and economical circuit elements distinguish between only two signal levels, so that a signal between 0 and 5 V may represent the digit zero and a signal between 5 and 10 V, the digit one. These two-valued signals make it necessary to represent numbers and symbols using a corresponding base-two or binary system. **Table 1** lists the first 20 binary numbers and their decimal equivalents. For a detailed discussion of binary numbers SEE NUMBER SYSTEMS.

Data are stored and manipulated within a digital computer in units called words. The binary digits (called bits), which make up a word, may represent either a binary number or a collection of binary-coded alphanumeric characters. For example, the two-letter word "it" may be stored in a 16-bit computer word as follows, making use of the code shown in **Table 2**:

0100100101010100

The computer word merely contains a binary pattern of alternating 1's and 0's, and it is up to the computer user to determine whether that word should be interpreted as the English word "it" or as the decimal number 18,772. SEE BIT.

Logical circuit elements. Two kinds of logical circuits are used in the design and construction of digital computers: decision elements and memory elements. A typical decision element provides a binary output as a function of two or more binary inputs. The AND circuit, for example, has two inputs and an output which is 1 only when both inputs are 1. A memory element stores a single bit of information and is set to the 1 state or reset to the 0 state, depending on the signals on its input lines. And because such a circuit can be caused alternately to store 0's and 1's from time to time, a memory element is commonly called a flip-flop. SEE SWITCHING THEORY.

These two basic logical elements are all that are required to construct the most elaborate

Table 2. American standard alphabetic code for binary representation of letters

11000001	A	11001110	N
11000010	B	01001111	O
01000011	C	11010000	P
11000100	D	01010001	Q
01000101	E	01010010	R
01000110	F	11010011	S
11000111	G	01010100	T
11001000	H	11010101	U
01001001	I	11010110	V
01001010	J	01010111	W
11001011	K	01011000	X
01001100	L	11011001	Y
11001101	M	11011010	Z

and complex digital arithmetic and control circuits. A simple example of such a circuit is shown in **Fig. 1**. Here the object is to perform a simple binary count, as shown in the table at the bottom of Fig. 1. As long as control signal C is equal to 1, the counting continues. When the control input is 0, the counter is to remain in whatever state it had last counted to. Two flip-flops are used, labeled Q1 and Q2, and will be made to count through the sequence 0,1,2,3,0,1, ... To understand the design, it is necessary to introduce one more concept, the complementary output of a flip-flop. Each flip-flop generally has two output wires, which are always of opposite polarity. Whe flip-flop Q1 is storing a 1, output Q1 is 1 and the complementary output (which is labeled $\overline{Q1}$ and pronounced Q1 bar) is 0. When the flip-flop contains a 0, the $\overline{Q1}$ output is 1 and the Q1 output is 0.

Binary count:

Q1	Q2
0	0
0	1
1	0
1	1
0	0
0	1
...	...

Logic equations:

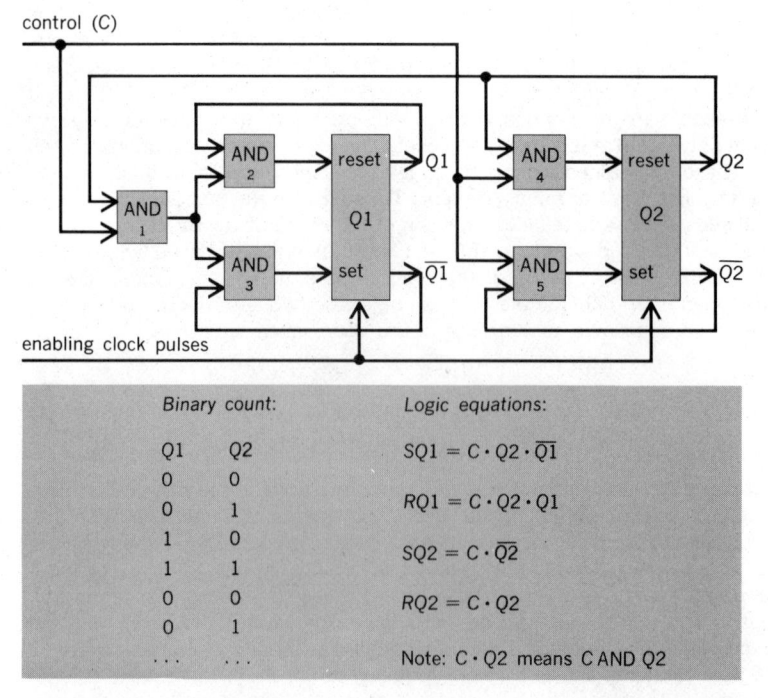

$SQ1 = C \cdot Q2 \cdot \overline{Q1}$

$RQ1 = C \cdot Q2 \cdot Q1$

$SQ2 = C \cdot \overline{Q2}$

$RQ2 = C \cdot Q2$

Note: $C \cdot Q2$ means C AND Q2

Fig. 1. Simple digital counting circuit.

To analyze the circuit, note first that, when control input C is 0, the outputs of all AND gates are 0 and, because the reset and set inputs to both flip-flops are 0, the flip-flops will remain in whatever state they last reached. Now suppose that Q1 and Q2 both contain 0 and that the control input becomes 1. While flip-flop Q2 contains a 0, its Q2 output is also 0 and AND gate number 1 (labeled AND 1) is effectively turned off so that the reset and set inputs to Q1 are both 0. Thus flip-flop Q1 will remain in the 0 state. For the same reason AND gate 4 will also be turned off, and the reset input to flip-flop Q2 will be 0. However, from flip-flop Q2 complementary output $\overline{Q2}$ will be in the 1 state, and (while the control input is 1) AND gate 5 will be turned on and the set input to Q2 will be 1. Flip-flop Q2 will thus be turned on by the first clock pulse to occur after C is turned on; and from one clock pulse time to the next the two flip-flops will change from the (0,0) state to the (0,1) state. A careful review of the indicated circuits will show that the counter will indeed go through the count sequence as shown, as long as the control input is 1. The logic equations in Fig. 1 represent another way of describing the circuit and may be used in place of the more cumbersome diagram. SEE DIGITAL COUNTER; LOGIC CIRCUITS.

Physical components. The logical elements described in the paragraphs above are the fundamental conceptual components used in virtually all digital systems. The actual physical components which were used to realize conceptual gates and flip-flops in some specific piece of equipment are dependent on the status of electronic technology at the time the equipment was designed. In the 1950s the earliest commercial computers used vacuum tubes, resistors, and capacitors as components. A flip-flop typically required a dozen or more such components in these first-generation computers. Between the late 1950s and middle 1960s, solid-state transistors and diodes replaced the vacuum tubes, and the resulting second-generation systems were considerably more reliable than their first-generation predecessors; they were also smaller and consumed less power. But the number of electronic components per conceptual logical component remained about the same—a dozen or more for a flip-flop.

Since the mid-1960s the integrated circuit (IC) has been the principal logical building block for digital systems. Early digital integrated circuits contained a single flip-flop or gate, and the use of these components permitted designers of the early third-generation systems to provide much more capability per component than was possible with the first- or second-generation technology. Since the mid-1960s integrated circuit technology has consistently improved, and typical large-scale-integration (LSI) circuits contain thousands of flip-flops and gates. SEE INTEGRATED CIRCUITS.

System building blocks. On a completely different conceptual level, a digital computer can be regarded as being composed of functional, system building blocks, containing (among other things) subassemblies of the fundamental logical components. A computer viewed at this level may be described in an oversimplified fashion by the diagram of **Fig. 2**. The computation

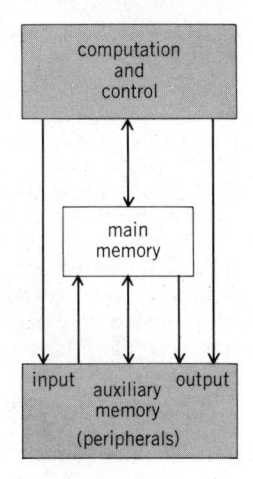

Fig. 2. Block diagram of a digital computer.

and control block (often called the central processing unit, or CPU) is constructed entirely of logical elements of the kind described above. The main memory, which may store from a few thousand to several million binary digits, and the input/output and auxiliary memory devices (the so-called peripheral equipment) are specialized devices available over a range of speeds and operating characteristics. SEE COMPUTER SYSTEMS ARCHITECTURE.

Main memory is a building block capable of storing data or instructions in bulk for use by the computation and control portion of the computer. The important characteristics of a memory are capacity, access time, and cost. Capacity is the amount of data that the computer can store. Access time is the maximum interval between a request to the memory for data and the moment when the memory can provide that data. Cost is measured by dividing total memory cost by the number of bits stored. For first-generation systems, designers used a variety of technologies in realizing main memory: mercury delay lines, electrostatic storage tubes, and magnetic drums all appeared in various products. But second- and third-generation systems were almost exclusively built using magnetic core main memories. Starting in the early 1970s, the integrated circuit memory was introduced, and is now the most widely used technology. SEE COMPUTER STORAGE TECHNOLOGY.

Input/output and auxiliary memory peripherals represent the other major computer building blocks. Equipment is now and has from the beginning been available for feeding information to the computer from paper tape and punched cards, and for receiving data from the computer and printing it, or punching it on tape cards. But in the intervening years, designers have provided additional output devices which record computer data on microfilm, or plot data on graphs, or use data to control physical devices such as valves or rheostats. They have also designed input equipment which feeds the computer data from laboratory instruments, and from devices which scan documents and "read" printed characters. Data can be transmitted to and from the computer over ordinary telephone lines, and a wide variety of devices generally called terminals, make it possible for people to send data to, or receive requested data from, a computer system located hundreds or thousands of miles away. SEE CHARACTER RECOGNITION; COMPUTER GRAPHICS; DATA COMMUNICATIONS; MULTIACCESS COMPUTER.

The earliest auxiliary memory equipment recorded data on reels of magnetic tape. Magnetic tape units are still very widely used, for although they are slow in comparison to the operating speeds of modern computers—it typically takes 2–30 min to read all the data on a 2400-ft (732-m) reel of tape, depending on the speed of the tape unit—they make it possible to store large volumes of data at low cost by virtue of the low cost of the tape itself. The other widely used auxiliary memory devices are the magnetic disk and drum, both of which provide faster access to data than do the tape units, but at higher cost per bit of data stored. SEE DATA-PROCESSING SYTEMS.

STORED PROGRAM COMPUTER

Components and building blocks described in the preceding paragraphs could be organized in a multitude of different ways. The first practical electronic computers, constructed during the latter part of World War II, were designed with the specific purpose of computing special mathematical functions. They did their jobs very well, but even while they were under construction, engineers and scientists had come to realize that it was possible to organize a digital computer in such a way that it was not oriented toward some particular computation, and could in fact carry out any calculation desired and defined by the user. The basic machine organization invented and constructed at that time was the stored-program computer, and it continues to be the fundamental basis for each of the hundreds of thousands of computing systems in use today. It has also become a system component, since the microcomputer is simply a stored program computer on a single integrated-circuit chip.

The concept of the stored-program computer is simple and can be described with reference to Fig. 2. Main memory contains, in addition to data and the results of intermediate computations, a set of instructions (or orders, or commands, as they are sometimes called); these specify how the computer is to operate in solving some particular problem. The computation and control section reads these instructions from the memory one by one and performs the indicated operations on the specified data. The instructions can control the reading of data from input or auxiliary memory peripherals, and (when the prescribed computations are completed) can send the result to auxiliary memory, or to output devices where it may be printed, punched, displayed, plotted, and so forth. The feature that gives this form of computer organization its great power is the ease with which instructions can be changed; the particular calculations carried out by the computer are determined entirely by a sequence of instructions stored in the computer's memory; that sequence can be altered completely by simply reading a new set of instructions into the memory through the computer input equipment.

Instructions. To understand better the nature of the stored-program computer, consider in more detail the kinds of of instructions it can carry out and the logic of the computation and control unit which interprets and implements the instructions. Because the instructions, like the data, are stored in computer words, one begins by examining how an instruction is stored in a word. As an example, assume one is looking at a small computer with words 16 bits long, and assume further that an instruction is organized as shown in **Fig. 3**. In this simple computer an instruction has two parts: the first 5 bits of the word specify which of the computer's repertoire of commands is to be carried out, and the last 11 bits generally specify the address of the word referred to by the command. A 5-bit command permits up to 32 different kinds of instructions in the computer, and an 11-bit address permits one to address up to 2048 different memory locations directly.

Typical instruction types for a computer of this kind are listed below.

Load. Load the number from the prescribed memory location into the arithmetic unit.

Store. Store the number from the arithmetic unit in the memory at the prescribed memory location.

Add. Add the contents of the addressed memory location to the number in the arithmetic unit, leaving the result in the arithmetic unit.

Subtract. Subtract the contents of the addressed memory location from the number in the arithmetic unit, leaving the result in the arithmetic unit.

Branch. If the number in the arithmetic unit is zero or positive, read the next instruction from the address in the next-instruction register as usual. If the number in the arithmetic unit is negative, store the address from the branch instruction itself in the next-instruction register, so that the next instruction carried out will be retrieved from the address given in the branch instruction.

Halt. Stop; carry out no further instructions until the operator presses the RUN switch on the console.

Input. Read the next character from the paper tape reader into the addressed memory location and then move the tape so a new character is ready to be read.

Output. Type out the character whose code is stored in the right-hand half of the addressed memory location.

With the exception of the branch command, the preceding instructions are easy to interpret and to understand. The load and store commands move data to and from the arithmetic unit, respectively. The add and subtract commands perform arithmetic operations, each using the number previously left in the arithmetic unit as one operand, and a number read from a designated memory location as the other. The halt command simply tells the computer to stop and requires intervention by the operator to make the computer initiate computation again. The input and output commands make possible the reading of information into the computer memory from a paper tape input device, and the printing out of the results from previous computations on an output typewriter.

To understand the branch command, consider how the computation and control unit of **Fig. 4** uses the instructions in the memory. To begin with, the instructions which are to be carried out must be stored in consecutive storage locations in memory. Assume that the first of a sequence of commands is in memory location 100. Then the "next-instruction address register" in the computation and control unit (Fig. 4) contains the number 100, and the following sequence of four events takes place: (1) read, (2) readdress, (3) execute, and (4) resume.

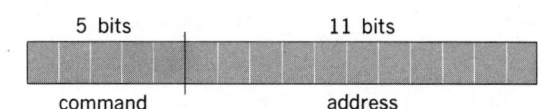

Fig. 3. Sixteen-bit instruction.

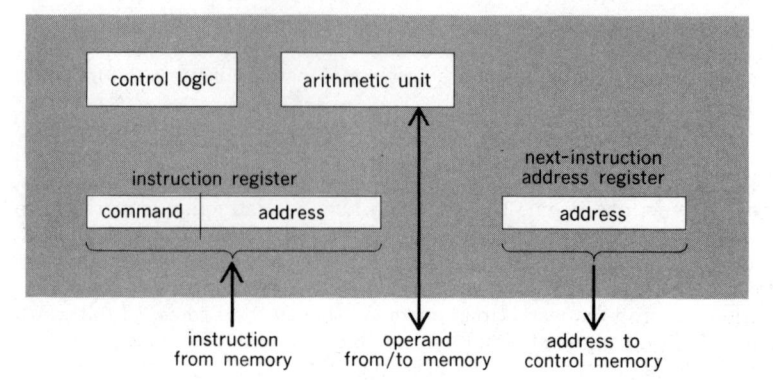

Fig. 4. Computation and control unit.

(instruction from memory; operand from/to memory; address to control memory)

Read. The control logic reads the next instruction to be carried out from the memory location whose address is given by the next-instruction address register. The instruction coming from memory is stored in another register called the instruction register. (In this example the next-instruction address register started out containing the number 100, and so the instruction in memory location 100 is transferred to the instruction register.)

Readdress. The control logic now adds unity to the number in the next instruction address register. (In the present example this changes the number in the next instruction address register from 100 to 101. The result is that, when the computer has interpreted and carried out the instruction from location 100, following the rules given in the third and fourth steps below, it will return to the read step above and next interpret and carry out the instruction from location 101.)

Execute. The instruction from location 100 is now in the instruction register and must be carried out. The control logic first looks at the command portion of the instruction in the left-hand 5 bits of the register and interprets or decodes it to determine what to do next. If the instruction is add, subtract, load, or output, the control logic first uses the address in the instruction register—the address associated with the command—and reads the word from that addressed location in memory; it then proceeds to load the word into the arithmetic unit, add it to or subtract it from the number in the arithmetic unit, or transfer it to the output typewriter, depending on the command. If the command is store or input, the control logic collects a number from the arithmetic unit or the paper tape reader and then transfers that number to a location in the memory whose address is given in the instruction register. If the command is halt, the control logic simply prevents all further operations, pending a signal from the operator console.

If the command is branch, the control logic begins by looking at the number in the arithmetic unit. If that number is zero or positive, the control logic goes on to the fourth step below. If the number is negative, however, the control logic causes the address in the instruction register to be transferred to the next-instruction address register before going on to the fourth step. The computer will then continue with one sequence of commands if the previous arithmetic result was positive, and with another if the result was negative. This seemingly simple operation is one of the most important features a computer possesses. It gives the computer a decision-making capability that permits it to examine some data, compute a result, and continue with one of two sequences of calculations or operations, depending only on the computed result.

Resume. As the fourth and final step in the sequence, when the command has been interpreted and carried out properly, the control logic returns to the read step and repeats the entire series of steps.

A sequence of instructions intended to carry out some desired function is called a program; collections of such programs are called software (as distinguished from the equipment, or hardware), and the act of preparing such programs is called programming. Because a computer can perform no useful function until someone has written a program embodying that function, the programming activity is an exceedingly important one and provides a basic limitation to the facility with which the computer can be applied to new areas. SEE DIGITAL COMPUTER PROGRAMMING.

TYPES OF COMPUTERS

Table 3. Typical computer characteristics

Characteristics	Typical systems	
	Large	Small
Memory cycle time	0.03 μs	0.90 μs
Add time	0.07 μs	2.84 μs
Main memory storage capacity	4,000,000 words	128,000 words
Word length	64 bits	16 bits

Computer characteristics A computer installation is complex. Consequently it is difficult to describe a system or to compare the characteristics of two systems without listing their instruction types and describing their modes of operation at some length. Nevertheless, certain important descriptors are commonly used for comparison purposes and are shown in **Table 3**, where salient characteristics of two typical systems are shown. Definitions of these characteristics can be stated as follows.

Memory cycle time is the time required to read a word from main memory. Most modern computers have integrated-circuit memories with cycle times in the ranges shown in Table 3. Add time is the time required to perform an addition, including the time necessary to extract the addition instruction itself and the operand from memory. Main memory storage capacity is the number of words of storage available to the computation and control unit. Typically, a computer manufacturer gives the buyer some choice; the buyer can purchase enough memory to meet the needs of the expected application. This internal capacity refers to the high-speed internal storage only, and does not include disks, drums, or magnetic tape.

Word length is the number of bits in a computer word.

System cost may vary over a range of 5 or even 10 to 1 for a particular computer because of the great variety of options offered the buyer by the manufacturer—options such as memory size, special instructions for efficiency in certain calculations, and number and type of peripheral devices.

There are obviously a number of other measures which may be used to describe a computer. They include such characteristics as multiplication time, transfer rates between input/output equipment and memory, physical size, power consumption, and the availability of a variety of computing options and special features.

EVOLUTION OF CAPABILITIES

The process by which new circuit and peripheral equipment technologies led to the development of a series of generations of computers was discussed above. But simultaneous with the changes in technology, there came changes in the structure or architecture of computers. These changes were introduced to improve the capability and efficiency of systems, as designers came to understand how computers were actually used.

Computer efficiency. One way of looking at system efficiency is indicated in **Fig. 5**, where the operation of a computer is shown broken down into the following four parts. (1) Operator time includes such activities as inserting cards into a card reader, loading magnetic tapes onto a tape unit, setting up controls on a computer operator's panel, and reviewing printed results. (2) Input comes to the computer from peripheral devices or from auxiliary memory. The inputs include instructions from the operator, inputs of programs to be run, and inputs of data. (3) Computation, being the principal activity, should occupy relatively much of the total time. (4) Output includes storage of intermediate and final results in auxiliary memory, and printing of results along with instructions or warnings to the computer operator.

First-generation computer. In the first generation of computer equipment only one of these activities could be carried out at a time. Between jobs the computer was idle while an operator made ready for the next task. When the operator was ready, the program was read into the computer from some input device and the input data were then loaded. The program operated

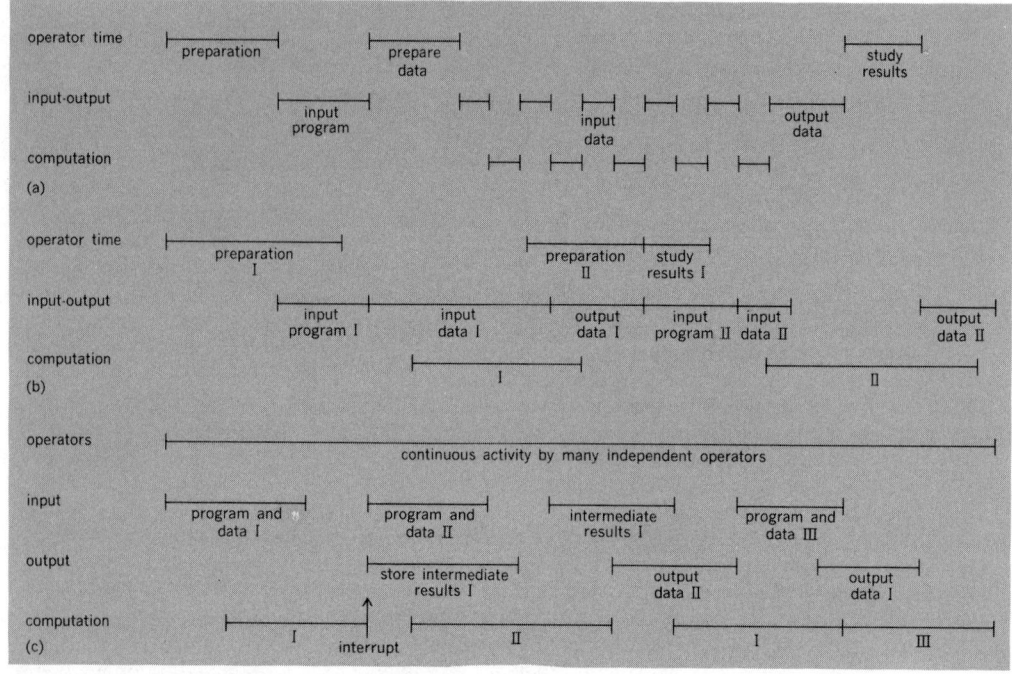

Fig. 5. Comparison of efficiency for three generations of computers: (a) first, (b) second, and (c) third.

upon the data and performed necessary calculations. When the calculations were complete, the computer printed out answers, and the operator took steps to set up the next problem.

Second-generation computer. This series of operations was inefficient, and the designers of second-generation equipment removed some of the inefficiency by arranging input and output operations to be performed directly between the input/output peripherals and the computer memory without interfering with computations. As a result, second-generation computers were able to perform computations while reading in data and printing out replies, and efficiency was greatly enhanced. **Figure 6** indicates schematically the organizational change between generations of computers.

First-generation equipment was most efficient while performing tedious and lengthy computations. The input/output capabilities of the second generation made them useful in applications where large volumes of data had to be handled with relatively little computation—applications such as billing, payroll, and inventory control. At the same time, the great capability and increased reliability of second-generation systems encouraged engineers to apply them to situations where the computer acts as a control element. In military aircraft, in oil refineries and chemical plants, in research laboratories, and in factories, the computer received data directly from measuring instruments, performed appropriate calculations, and as a result made adjustments in the aircraft engine thrust, the flow of raw materials in the plant or factory, or the experimental setup in the laboratory. These new application areas led to two important developments in computer design. The first was a new set of input/output equipments that could be connected to process instruments, converting instrument signals into digital quantities and back again. SEE ANALOG-TO-DIGITAL CONVERTER; DIGITAL-TO-ANALOG CONVERTER.

The second development, which evolved from the use of the computer in second-generation control applications, was the interrupt. The processes or activities under control provided data to, and required action from, the computer at random times. These random requests to the computer required rapid response, either because the process required quick control action on

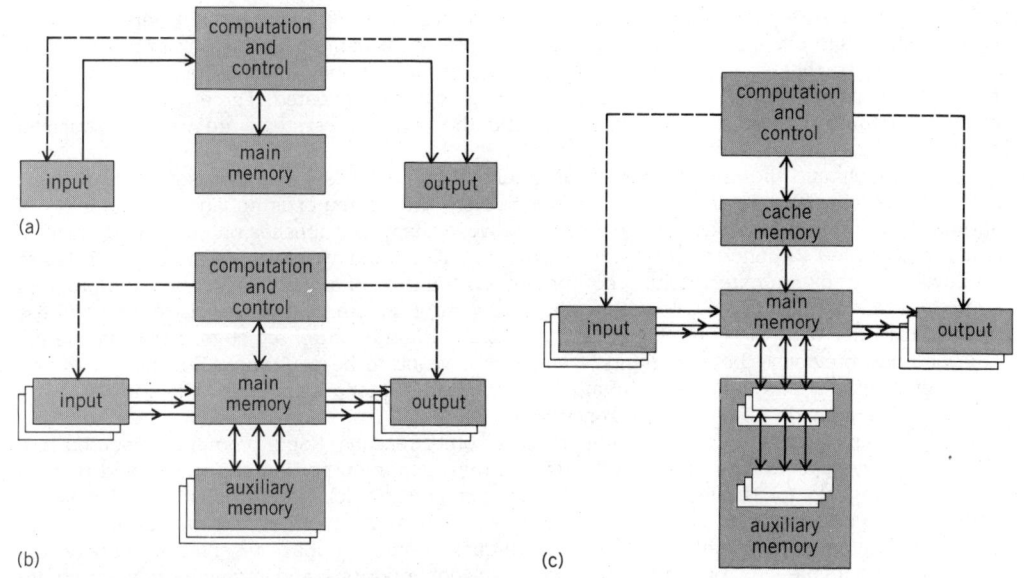

Fig. 6. Evolution of organization for four generations of computers: (a) first; (b) second and third; (c) fourth.

the part of the computer or because the process data supplied by instruments were rapidly changing and had to be stored before the data were lost. The interrupt feature, built into the computation and control unit, solved these problems by providing circuits that could stop the computer after any given instruction, enable it to carry out some special program in response to the external interrupt, and finally permit it to return to precisely the position in the program where it had originally been interrupted.

The logic to achieve these ends is quite simple. When an interrupt signal is received from an external device, the logic circuitry waits until the computer has completed the current instruction and then stores the next instruction address in a specially reserved storage location. The logic substitutes a standard predetermined address in the next instruction address register and continues. The computer of course next executes the instruction at the standard address, and the rest is up to the programmer. The programmer must have inserted a special program at this standard address, and the program must respond to the conditions that caused the interrupt (by inputting data from instrumentation or by taking previously specified control action, for example) and then must return control to the original program at exactly the same place where the program was interrupted. Though the interrupt was originally used largely in control applications, it is now employed in virtually all systems to notify the computer when transfers to and from peripheral equipment are completed.

Third-generation computer. In the mid-1960s a new set of trends in computer applications was becoming apparent, and a third generation of computer systems became available to cope with those trends. The usefulness and flexibility of the stored-program computer, together with its improved cost-performance ratio, made it apparent that the computer had the basic power to perform a great variety of small and large tasks simultaneously. For example, the speed and capability of a computer were such that it could simultaneously collect data from a test run or experiment; maintain a file of inventory records on a disk memory; answer inquiries on status of specific items in inventory, such as inquiries entered at random from a dozen different cathode-ray-tube display devices; and assemble or compile programs for users at numerous terminals, all remote from the computer and all working independently on different problems.

A computer system which serves a number of users in this way is called a time-sharing system. To perform in such complex applications, third-generation computers required elaborations of the features found in second-generation computers (Fig. 6). Main and auxiliary memories became bigger and cheaper, more input/output equipments became available, input/output channels improved so that a larger number of simultaneous operations were possible, and interrupt structures grew more flexible. In addition, many new features appeared. Three of them, memory protection circuitry, rapid context switching, and the operating system, are worth discussing briefly.

To understand the implications of third-generation computers and the usefulness of these new features, consider the last portion of Fig. 5. Here the computer is engaged in a variety of different tasks, and it switches back and forth between them as it finishes one portion of a job or as it is interrupted to perform some high-priority job. This rapid switching from job to job led to the development of context-switching equipment. At the time of a changeover from one program to another, the programmer is able with a single instruction to interchange the instruction address register, together with the contents of various arithmetic and control registers, between the job he or she had previously been working on and the new job to be performed. Second-generation computers, without this context-switching feature, require a long sequence of commands every time a change is made from one task to another.

The memory protect feature is important for other reasons. Some programs executed in a time-sharing system such as that depicted by the third-genration portion of Fig. 6 would be new programs being run for the first time. Errors are common in such new programs, and it is the nature of the computer that such errors could have serious effects on system operation. For example, a user's program might accidentally store data in memory space reserved for supervisory or monitor programs—the programs that determine job priorities and reconcile conflicting input/output requirements. To keep such critical memory areas from being destroyed or modified by unchecked programs, designers have made it possible for the user to designate certain areas of memory as protected, and have ensured that only the monitor or supervisory programs can access these particular areas.

The operating system is the set of supervisory programs which manages the system, keeps it operating efficiently, and takes over many of the scheduling and monitoring functions which had previously been the function of the computer operator. It is typically supplied by the computer hardware manufacturer, and was first used with some second-generation systems, where it included little more than interrupt processing and error-handling routines, together with programs to control input/output operations for the user. Its size and importance have both grown with time, and it currently includes those early functions, as well as facilities for accessing compilers and utilities, scheduling jobs to maximize system throughput, managing data-communication facilities, controlling user access to protected data, maintaining records on system usage, and so forth.

Fourth-generation systems. Computer memory has become increasingly important with the passing generations, as users have found it useful to store more and more business, government, engineering, and scientific data in machine-readable form. Starting with the third generation, but increasingly with computers introduced in the early 1970s, computer system architects have provided a hierarchy of memory devices to improve system performance and give the user access to very large memory capacities. Figure 6c shows how a very large system may make use of such a hierarchy. A so-called cache memory has been interposed between the central processing unit and the main memory, and auxiliary memory has been split into two parts.

The cache is a relatively small but very high-speed memory which stores the data and programs currently being used by the central processing unit. When the central processing unit needs an instruction or data, it sends a main memory address to the cache memory. If the requested information is stored in the cache, it is immediately delivered to the central processing unit; if it is not in the cache, special cache memory hardware requests a block of information from main memory, and that block, which includes the data requested by the central processing unit, is delivered to the cache and displaces another block stored there. Because programs contain many branches, a typical program may repeatedly access a relatively small portion of the main memory, and so a small fast cache can be very effective in increasing the central processing unit's instruction-processing rate. (The cache's great speed makes it correspondingly expensive, and therefore not economical for use as main memory.)

A typical large fourth-generation system may make use of a similar hierarchical arrangement between main and auxiliary memory. Main memory in a large system may contain 750,000 words. But a system equipped with a virtual storage translator can give the user-programmer the illusion of working with 16,000,000 words. This is done by supplying the 750,000 words of real memory with temporary virtual addresses, and transferring data automatically from auxiliary to main storage as it is needed. For example, suppose the central processing unit needs a program which starts at address 2,500,000. The virtual storage translator may assign the virtual memory address 2,500,000 to the real address 700,000, and then transfer a block of (say) 1000 words from auxiliary memory to the main memory locations starting with 700,000. Now when the central processing unit next requests, for example, information from location 2,500,001, the translator locates it in real memory location 700,001, and sends it off to the cache.

Finally, in some very large systems there may also be an auxiliary memory hierarchy, in which a very large, cheap, but relatively slow auxiliary memory delivers data or programs as required to the primary auxiliary memory.

In all these hierarchical arrangements, the guiding principle is that the larger, slower, cheaper memory supplies data as needed to the smaller, faster, more expensive memory. The various levels of memory are invisible to the user; the hardware and, where necessary, the operating system make the various hierarchical levels deliver data and programs to the user without the necessity for any special action on his or her part.

Fifth-generation systems. In 1981 the Japanese government announced a 10-year program intended to encourage the development of "intelligent" computers. Japanese industry is participating in the program, whose object is to offer, in the 1990s, machines which can learn and reason, can "talk" to humans in everyday language, and can understand speech and pictures. The Japanese have called these machines fifth-generation computer systems. The American and European responses to Japan's ambitious project have been fragmented and disjointed, although the United States and many European countries continue to conduct research on all of the topics included in the Japanese study. SEE ARTIFICIAL INTELLIGENCE; SPEECH RECOGNITION; VOICE RESPONSE.

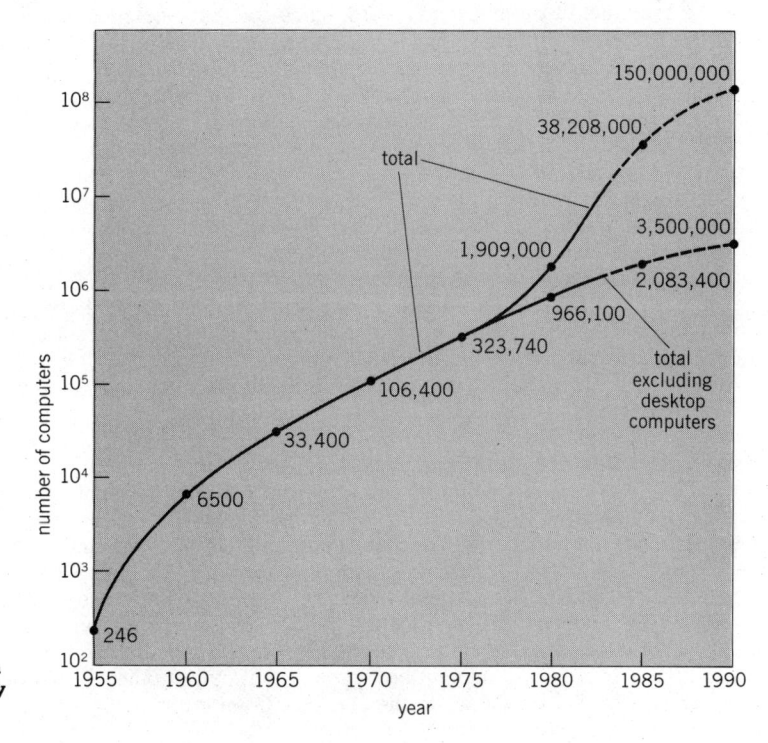

Fig. 7. Worldwide growth in the number of computers (measured on a logarithmic scale) made by United States companies.

Industry growth. The versatility of the digital computer has led to its application in a wide variety of industries and activities. The evolution of the integrated circuit has made it possible for designers to provide ever-cheaper systems, and as a result, since the mid-1970s the desktop computer has become economical for use in small organizations, at the office worker's desk, and even in the home, where it can supply entertainment, educational, record-keeping, and computing capabilities. The net result of these developments is indicated in **Fig. 7**, which shows the growth in the number of computers in use each year, and forecasts how that growth will continue.

The influence of the digital computer is extending far beyond the realm of computing. The microcomputer has become a component in a variety of apparently noncomputing applications, being used in games, toys, robots, automobiles, appliances, tools, and many other artifacts. SEE MICROCOMPUTER; MICROPROCESSOR; ROBOTICS.

Bibliography. T. C. Bartee, *Digital Computer Fundamentals*, 6th ed., 1985; P. Bishop, *Fifth Generation Computers: Concepts, Implementations, and Uses*, 1986; G. G. Bitter, *Computers in Today's World*, 1984; G. Brookshear, *Computer Science, An Overview*, 1985; H. C. Lucas, Jr., *Introduction to Computers and Information Systems*, 1985; D. H. Sanders, *Computer Concepts and Applications*, 1987; Special issue on tomorrow's computers, *IEEE Spectrum*, vol. 20, no. 11, November 1983.

MICROCOMPUTER
LARRY D. TINDELL

A digital computer whose central processing unit (CPU) resides on a single semiconductor integrated circuit chip. The development of the microcomputer is of such historical significance that the event may be compared to the invention of the Gutenberg printing press. Just as the printed word made knowledge available on an unprecedented scale, so has the microcomputer made unprecedented computational power widely available. Indeed, the potential for the microcomputer far exceeds that of the published word, since the machine offers a much more intimate mode of interaction with information.

The microcomputer has had an extraordinary impact upon technology and society since its introduction in 1975. The "computer on a chip," a product of large-scale integration of digital circuits, has evolved from a special-purpose dedicated device to a general-purpose system. Microcomputers control machines of all kinds, from home appliances to Earth satellites. The general-purpose implementations, in the form of personal and professional computers, support a variety of applications, from video games to business reports to laboratory analysis.

Hardware. The microcomputer is an electronic device consisting of a microprocessor central processing unit, memory input/output (I/O) capabilities, and a power supply. This self-contained unit provides all that is needed for digital data processing. The term microcomputer is often used as a synonym for the heart of the unit, the microprocessor. The microprocessor resides on a single chip of silicon and provides the computational and control capabilities of the system. The microcomputer itself usually consists of a printed circuit (PC) board upon which are mounted the microprocessor and other large-scale integrated (LSI) chips for memory and input/output. All of these devices are connected by metal circuits printed on the board. SEE INTEGRATED CIRCUITS; MICROPROCESSOR.

Architecture. The microprocessor central processing unit consists of the same components as most digital computers: a control unit (CU), an arithmetic and logic unit (ALU), special memory units called registers, high-frequency clocks, and input/output devices. The control unit is responsible for fetching and decoding programmed instructions and managing the system. The arithmetic and logic unit performs computations and data manipulations such as addition, subtraction, comparison, and logical (boolean) AND and OR operations. The registers are very fast memory units which store data for the central processing unit and the arithmetic and logic unit and for input/output. The clock is needed to provide a continuous pulse which triggers and synchronizes events for the computing device. Input/output devices, or drivers, are needed to communicate with the world outside the chip. SEE COMPUTER SYSTEMS ARCHITECTURE.

Word size. The size of a microcomputer is usually measured in terms of the width of its registers in units of bits (binary digits capable of storing either a 1 or a 0). Some devices have 4-bit registers, while others have 32 or more. The first generation of personal computers was based upon 8-bit devices. Since it requires 8 bits to represent a single character, or byte, the register size (or word size) is an important measure of the speed and power of a central processing unit. SEE BIT.

Clocks. Another important measure of the microcomputer's power is the clock rate. Just as the register size measures how much data the device can process at a time, so the clock frequency determines how fast the device can process the information. Commercial microprocessors operate in the range of 1 to 25 MHz. This high level of activity is maintained by a quartz crystal oscillator made to vibrate with great consistency by using the piezoelectric effect. Outside the central processing units, other clocks are used for timing [such as the programmable interval timer (PIT)] and for input/output.

Data bus. Input/output between the microprocessor and the rest of the microcomputer system is performed over a bus. This is simply a data path. A data bus connects all components of the system, while an address bus is used to determine where data are located, and a control bus is used to monitor and manage the system. The bus width is yet another measure of the power of a microcomputer. It is quite common for the bus to be half the width of the register (word) size; for example, 16-bit registers may be used with an 8-bit bus. The control bus may consist of 100 or more lines of communication to the components of the system. Multiplexing is often used to allow both data and status codes to be simultaneously passed along a bus.

Data storage. The memory available to the microcomputer is also an important determination of its power. Memory is available in several forms, including random-access memory (RAM) chips and read-only memory (ROM) chips. The total amount of memory permitted for a particular machine is its address space. This is a function of the register size of the central processing unit and the overall design of the machine. A 16-bit device, for example, may be able to address more than 64 k (1 k = 1024) bytes (characters) of memory. Various programming schemes are available which allow a device to access memory beyond its hardware limit, up to millions of bytes. SEE SEMICONDUCTOR MEMORIES.

In addition to the general-purpose memory available to the central processing units, there are various kinds of special-purpose memories. The ROMs are preprogrammed with commonly used instructions such as the bootstrap program for initializing the sytem, the nucleus of the operating system, input/output routines, and even interpretive computer languages. The RAMs may be configured to provide for buffers and caches for quick access to data retrieved from or transmitted to slower devices. Both RAMs and magnetic bubble memories are used to provide high-speed bulk storage for data as electronic disks. SEE MAGNETIC BUBBLE MEMORY.

For larger stores of data, more economical (in cost per bit) secondary storage devices are used. These include floppy disks and hard disks. The floppies are useful for smaller quantities of related data, such as word-processing text files. The hard disks, which have a capacity of several megabytes, are suitable for larger data bases of information. A microcomputer can support several secondary storage units or drives. Often a cassette tape unit is used to archive data which is not currently needed from the active storage units. Work on such technologies as laser disks promises even more economical mass storage with extremely large storage capacities. SEE COMPUTER STORAGE TECHNOLOGY; DATA-BASE MANAGEMENT SYSTEMS; WORD PROCESSING.

Input and output. The impression the microcomputer makes upon the user is closely related to the mechanisms used for input and output. Unlike its cumbersome predecessors, the microcomputer offers a very rich selection of input and output mediums. For general character and numeric data, the keyboard remains an important source of input, but it is accompanied by such devices as the optical mouse, the light pen, the joystick, and the graphics tablet. All of these pointing devices rely upon software to communicate with the system. For certain printed material, optical character recognition is available. Voice input can be very effective, although the vocabulary of the machine is usually limited to a relatively small set of words spoken and passed by the user. SEE CHARACTER RECOGNITION; SPEECH RECOGNITION.

The output produced by the microcomputer can be especially impressive. One or more color graphics displays can be used to preset text and graphics in virtually limitless variations. The use of bit-mapped graphics memories and special-character and figure generation devices has made this possible. The bits of data stored in the memories are related directly to the picture elements (pixels) on the screen, permitting complex graphical manipulations simply by turning bits on and off and copying data into the memory. Multiple planes of video memory can be used to overlay one image upon another. The effect is especially dramatic when used with simulations, such as a flight simulator, but is also useful in business presentations. Voice output is also achievable with microcomputers although, like the voice input, the intelligble vocabulary is somewhat limited. Of course, hard-copy output devices such as printers and plotters remain an important part of the microcomputer system. SEE COMPUTER GRAPHICS; DATA-PROCESSING SYSTEMS; VOICE RESPONSE.

Additional devices. Modern microcomputers include several intellgent devices in addition to the primary central processing unit. For numerical computations, special floating–point microprocessors serve as a companion to the controlling processor. Memory access is managed by special devices which provide for direct memory access (DMA). Secondary storage is handled by satellite processors called device controllers. Each input/output device may have its own microprocessor, including viewing screens, keyboards, and printers. The microcomputer is developing into a network of microprocessors working together to perform one or more parallel or serial tasks.

Microprocessors and computing power. Among the most popular microprocessors are the Intel 8086 family of processors and the Motorola 68000 family. These 16-bit devices evolved from their 8-bit predecessors, the original micocomputers. The two families of chips have resulted in two rather different families of microcomputers. Both processors have advantages and disadvantages and can serve equally well in most applications. The original 8-bit chips, the Intel 8080 and Motorola 6502, are also still used in personal computers and in control applications. These, and many other popular devices, provide considerable computing power for many personal applications, while the 16-bit machines are more suitable for professional, business, and engineering use.

The generation of 32-bit microprocessors makes available as much computing power as was available in large mainframe computers at the time when the microcomputer was introduced. These desktop computers have the capacity to support several users performing concurrent programming, word processing, financial analysis, and data-base searches. Tied to computer networks, these systems make great resources available to the individual. The Motorola 68000–based systems and those using true 32-bit devices are fast enough to provide for multiprocessing and timesharing. These systems have provided a basis for implementations of the UNIX operating system. SEE LOCAL-AREA NETWORKS; MULTIACCESS COMPUTER; MULTIPROCESSING; OPERATING SYSTEM; WIDE-AREA NETWORKS.

At the other end of the spectrum are a variety of small briefcase- and notebook-size machines which make all of the power of the original microcomputers available in a conveniently transportable package. These devices serve for data collection, calculation, word processing, and on-the-spot computing. Their ability to communicate with larger machines permits them to be used as terminals for data input and retrieval in the field.

Software. Taken as is, the microcomputer may not appear to have much to offer. It can accept data in its own (machine language) form and manipulate it in rather basic ways at a very fast rate. It cannot, however, perform useful work without first being given a program. Ultimately this program must be a set of instructions in the form of binary code which directs the actions of the machine. Each device has its own instruction set of allowable operations. This concept of the stored-program computer is attributed to John Von Neumann, and is the basic form of most modern digital computers. With the appropriate program, and connections to the outside world, the computer exhibits a certain intelligence. It becomes an extension of the mind just as conventional machines become an extension of muscle power. The possibilities for programs are without limit. SEE DIGITAL COMPUTER PROGRAMMING.

Fortunately, microcomputers evolved at a time when a very substantial body of knowledge about programming was available. The techniques used to develop software for large mainframe computers and intermediate minicomputers have been applied to microcomputers. Not only has software been borrowed or converted, but much new code has been written as well. Microcomputers have provided an opportunity to greatly improve the software which is still used on most larger computers. This fresh start has resulted in a highly interactive and very productive kind of personal computing.

TYPES OF COMPUTERS

Levels. Microcomputers provide several levels of software that, together, can meet the needs of almost anyone. Many video game cartridges are programmed directly into machine code (microcode). For programmers and some engineers there are low-level assemblers which translate mnemonic instructions into machine code. These professionals along with business analysts and students take advantage of high-level compilers and interpreters that translate Englishlike syntax into machine code. Popular compilers include Pascal, C, Cobol, and Fortran. The most popular interpreter is BASIC. Compilers usually require a significant amount of memory and so are available ony for the larger machines. Programs written in assembly language usually run faster, but are more difficult to develop and to debug (correct). SEE PROGRAMMING LANGUAGES.

Application software. Many individuals and software vendors have used software tools such as compilers and assemblers to develop a vast range of application software to meet the needs of professional and personal users. General-purpose systems for word processing, spreadsheet calculations, graphics, communication, and other applications make the microcomputer a powerful tool for manipulating words, numbers, or symbols. General-purpose software for storing information in computer files on floppy or hard disks is available which rivals that available on mainframe computers. These file management and data-base management systems allow data to be stored in a convenient form and then sorted, searched, processed, and reported in a variety of ways. All of this general-purpose application software is complex and would require much time for an individual to develop. This software is a significant resource for the microcomputer user.

Integration. Although each of these software tools is powerful in itself, a quantum leap in utility has been achieved through their integration. Software for microcomputers has evolved beyond a collection of generally unrelated components to a unified set of tools where each application can share the data produced by any other application. This integration is usually based upon a common set of data definition and directory information referred to as a data dictionary. This concept, which was derived from the mainframe software environment, provides for the commonality of the application software available to the microcomputer user.

Applications. The continuation of the trend toward applying faster and more powerful machines to a broad range of problems presents profound implications for the future.

Education. In education, the microcomputer is available from grade school through graduate school. It serves as a replacement for the typewriter and calculator as essential tools for the college student, and it is likely to pervade education at all levels. In addition to their application to homework, the machines are providing the basis for interactive computer-assisted instruction (CAI). The language Logo was developed expressed to teach programming and to allow children to express themselves creatively.

Libraries. Although the machines are far too small to store the contents of an institution's books, they are powerful enough to process specific information garnered from the stacks. Research papers, statistical analysis, charts, and graphs can all be produced by using these library resources.

Home computers. Home computers have outgrown computer games and are being effectively applied to record keeping, financial management, word processing, and education. These machines can communicate with one another over telephone lines. As a result, hundreds of personal computer networks exist for exchanging information. Communication links also provide for access to a variety of information sources including financial data, government reports, airline schedules, current events, and abstracts of publications in many fields. With the advent of fiber-optic communications channels, Videotex systems are capable of providing a variety of two-way services as the home microcomputer communicates with a central system. Individual financial institutions established their own timesharing arrangements to permit their customers to conduct transactions from the convenience of their homes. SEE VIDEOTEX AND TELETEXT.

Business. Business organizations, both large corporations and small firms, find the microcomputer to be essential to growth and profitability. Each machine can send information to the company's large computers for storage and processing and can also receive information from virtually any other machine. The electronic mail capability of microcomputer networks has been one important reason for their success, since it allows messages, reports, and graphics to be transmitted at high baud rates to a given destination or broadcast to many terminal points. The machines are essential tools for financial analysts, and managers are able to control information much more directly than with centralized computing. SEE ELECTRONIC MAIL.

Engineering. For engineering organizations and engineers the microcomputer offers more power than many mainframe machines of the 1970s. Not only can analysis and design computations be perfomed, but interactive graphics as well. Computer-aided design (CAD) systems using microcomputers permit engineers to design and test a mathematical model of a new product in a fraction of the time required by traditional procedures. The machines can feed information directly into microprocessor controlled milling machines and robots for computer-aided manufacturing (CAM). SEE COMPUTER-AIDED DESIGN AND MANUFACTURING; COMPUTER-AIDED ENGINEERING; ROBOTICS.

Smart systems. Microprocessors and microcomputers not only are employed in the design and manufacture of products, but embedded (built-in) in the products as well. This created a new generation of intelligent machines, and smart systems for managing the environment at home, controlling office machines at work, and monitoring the functioning of communications, transportation, and energy systems. Although these systems are often inconspicuous, their contribution to society is considerable. SEE ARTIFICAL INTELLIGENCE; EMBEDDED SYSTEMS.

Military electronics. The microcomputer provides many advantages because of its small size, light weight, low power requirements, and capacity for adding intelligence to weapons systems and supporting equipment. Militarized microcomputers assist in the control of aircraft, surface vessels, and submarines. The microcomputer is responsible for the capabilities of military satellites as well. With the development of very high-speed integrated circuits (VHSIC) these systems will be able to perform even better in real-time environments. SEE DIGITAL COMPUTER.

Bibliography. M. Dahmke, *Microcomputer Operating Systems*, 1982; H. D'Angelo, *Microcomputer Structures*, 1981; I. Flores, *The Professional Microcomputer Handbook*, 1985; C. A. Holt, *Microcomputer Organization*, 1985; A. J. Khambata, *Microprocessors/Microcomputers: Architecture, Software, and Systems*, 2d ed., 1986; P. J. O'Connor, *Understanding Digital Electronics: How Microcomputers and Microprocessors Work*, 1984; N. Stern and R. A. Stern, *A User's Guide to Microcomputers*, 1986.

SUPERCOMPUTER
DAVID W. MIZELL

A computer which, among existing computers at any given time, is superlative, often in several senses: highest computation rate, largest memory, or highest cost. Predominantly, the term refers to the fastest "number crunchers," that is, machines designed to perform numerical calculations at the highest speed that the latest electronic device technology and the state of the art of computer architecture allows.

As of 1984, the fastest supercomputers built in the United States (**Fig. 1**) were capable of peak speeds of about 400 megaflops (million floating point operations per second). Japanese manufacture of supercomputers began in 1984: these machines were rated from 500 megaflops to 1.3 gigaflops (billion floating point operations per second). [The term floating point refers to a particular method of representing numerical values in a digital computer. A floating point number consists of an exponent and a mantissa, and is similar to the written form of numbers called scientific notation. A floating point operation is one of the common arithmetic operations, such as add, subtract, multiply, or divide, performed on floating point numbers.]

In the 1980s the term supercomputer also began to be applied to predicted future machines designed to perform symbolic, or artificial intelligence–oriented, computations. In 1984 the Department of Defense's Defense Advanced Research Projects Agency (DARPA) initiated its Strategic Computing Program, a five-year research and development program aimed at producing very high-speed, parallel computers especially for artificial intelligence applications. In Japan there are two government-funded research and development activities with goals of producing supercomputers: the National Superspeed Computer Project, oriented toward numerical computation; and the Fifth-Generation Computer System Project, aimed at producing a high-speed, artificial intelligence–oriented computer by the early 1990s. SEE ARTIFICIAL INTELLIGENCE.

Scientific applications. The demand for the ability to execute arithmetic operations at the highest possible rate originated in computer applications areas collectively referred to as scientific computing. Researchers in fields such as physics, structural mechanics, meteorology, and

Fig. 1. Two-processor Cray X-MP, which is capable of as many as 400 million arithmetic operations per second. (*Cray Research, Inc.*)

aerodynamics often need to do large-scale numerical simulations of physical processes. A technique common to several of these disciplines is to compute an approximate numerical solution to a set of partial differential equations which mathematically describe the physical process of interest, but are too complex to be solved by formal mathematical methods. The approximate numerical solution is obtained by first superimposing a grid on a region of space, with a set of numerical values attached to each grid point. Each of these values represents a physical quantity hypothetically measurable at that point in space, such as temperature, pressure, or velocity. Then, the physical process is computationally "simulated" by repetitively updating the values at each grid point according to a system of algebraic equations, derived from the defining partial differential equations, which specify the relationships between the values. Each repeated step might represent a span of time; that is, the simulated time is divided into a series of discrete steps, just as space is divided into a set of grid points. A more accurate solution requires a finer spatial grid and shorter time intervals. Large-scale scientific computations of this type often require hundreds of thousands of grid points with 10 or more values attached to each point, with 10 to 500 arithmetic operations necessary to compute each updated value, and hundreds of thousands of time steps over which the computation must be repeated before a steady-state solution is reached. Large problems in computational physics and aerodynamics sometimes require 100 h of computer time on current supercomputers. SEE NUMERICAL ANALYSIS; SIMULATION.

There is no foreseeable end to the demand for increased speed of numerical computation. Additional speed can always be exploited in two ways: first, problems which previously took hours can be executed in minutes, enhancing the user's ability to rely on the computer for assistance in an interactive manner; and second, new, larger problems can be attempted which were computationally infeasible on slower machines. An example of both kinds of opportunities is the effect of a 1000-times-faster supercomputer on the applications area of aerodynamics: First, an aeronautical engineer might repeatedly modify an aircraft design on a supercomputer-based design system, and be able to determine the aerodynamic implications of each design refinement in a few minutes, instead of 100 h. Second, such an increase in computational speed over current supercomputers would allow three-dimensional airflow simulations of a complete airplane design, whereas simulations of two-dimensional cross sections of parts of the aircraft (wing, engine nacelle) are now the rule.

There are two lines of technological advancement which have significantly contributed to what roughly amounts to a doubling of the fastest computers' speeds every year since the early 1950s—the steady improvement in electronic device technology and the accumulation of improvements in the architectural designs of digital computers.

Advances in electronics technology. The successive advancements in device technology are commonly summarized by the list of generations into which electronic digital computers of the past and present are categorized. The first-generation computers were constructed in the 1940s and early 1950s by using electromechanical relays and later vacuum tubes as switching devices. Second-generation computers of the early 1950s through the early 1960s employed transistors as switching devices and were the first to incorporate magnetic core memories. Third-generation computers were built from the early 1960s to the mid-1970s. They are characterized electronically by the use of small-scale integrated (SSI) and medium-scale integrated (MSI) circuits. Solid-state memories began replacing magnetic cores. Today's computers belong to the fourth generation. They incorporate large-scale integrated (LSI) circuits with tens of thousands of transistors per silicon chip for both logic and memory components.

Supercomputers generally employ a variant of silicon-based integrated circuitry known as emitter-coupled logic (ECL). It is less dense than other types of integrated circuits, offering at most a few thousand transistors per chip, but providing switching speeds in the range of a few nanoseconds. The next generation of supercomputers is expected to employ faster versions of emitter-coupled logic, complementary metallic oxide semiconductors (CMOS), or switching devices which are based on gallium arsenide (GaAs) semiconductor technologies instead of the silicon-based materials currently employed. SEE COMPUTER STORAGE TECHNOLOGY; INTEGRATED CIRCUITS; LOGIC CIRCUITS; SEMICONDUCTOR MEMORIES.

Advances in computer architecture. Increases in computing speed which are purely due to the architectural structure of a computer can largely be attributed to the introduction of some form of parallelism into the machine's design: two or more operations which were performed one after the other in previous computers can now be performed simultaneously. An explanation of techniques to increase parallelism requires the introduction of a few basic terms of computer architecture. A simple, general view of a digital computer divides it into two major components: the central processing unit (CPU) and the memory. Both data and programs are stored in the memory. The central processing unit contains the logic circuitry for repeatedly fetching program instructions, decoding them, fetching from memory the data items the instructions call to be operated upon, performing the arithmetic or logical operations required by each instruction, and returning the resultant data to the memory. SEE COMPUTER SYSTEMS ARCHITECTURE.

Pipelining. This is a technique which allows several operations to be in progress in the central processing unit at once. It is analogous to an assembly line, in the sense that operations which take several steps pass through a sequence of stages, each stage represents one step closer to completion of the entire operation, and already-passed stages can be simultaneously active, performing their respective steps of the operation on separate sets of operands.

The first form of pipelining used was instruction pipelining. Since each instruction must have the same basic sequence of steps performed, namely instruction fetch, instruction decode, operand fetch, and execution, it is feasible to construct an instruction pipeline, where each of these steps happens at a separate stage of the pipeline (**Fig. 2**). The efficiency of the instruction pipeline depends on the likelihood that the program being executed allows a steady stream of instructions to be fetched from contiguous locations in memory. If one instruction is a branch, that is, it orders the central processing unit to begin fetching instructions starting at a different memory location, then the instructions in the pipeline stages behind the branch instruction are no longer valid. They must be removed from the pipeline without being executed (flushed). Thus, each branch instruction causes a decrease in instruction execution speed until the pipeline is refilled with instructions from the new location. Variations of this problem are common to all pipelined architectures. The IBM STRETCH computer, built in the late 1950s, was the first computer to incorporate a pipelined architecture for the central processing unit.

Interleaved memory. The central processing unit nearly always has a much faster cycle time than the memory. This implies that the central processing unit is capable of processing data items faster than a memory unit can provide them. Interleaved memory is an organization of memory units which at least partially relieves this problem. Consecutive memory addresses are located in different memory units, allowing the central processing unit to initiate fetches from several units in sequence whenever the instructions of a program call for the fetching of the contents of each successive word from a contiguous block of memory words (**Fig. 3**). This happens often with the processing of matrices and vectors in scientific computations. The first com-

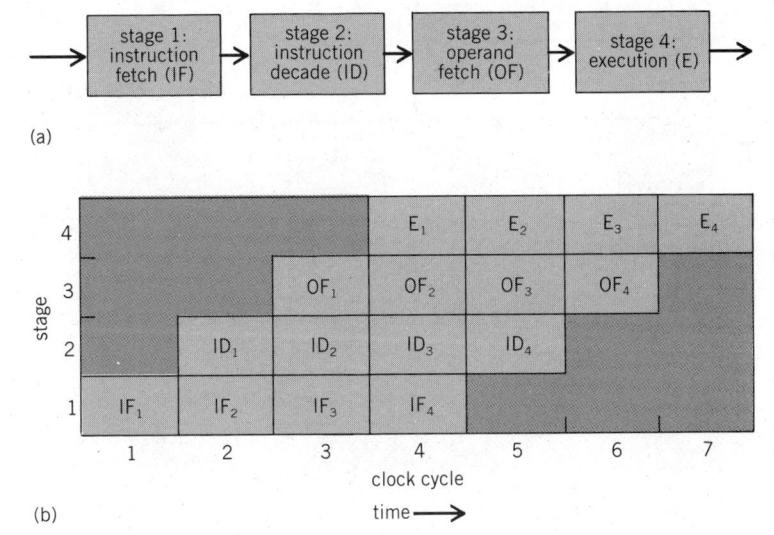

Fig. 2. Instruction pipeline. (a) Instruction processing stages. **(b)** Chart illustrating the overlapping of stages for four consecutive instructions.

puters to employ memory interleaving were the IBM STRETCH and the Illiac II, built in the late 1950s.

Circuitry. Parallelism within arithmetic and logical circuitry has been introduced in several ways. Adders, multipliers, and dividers now operate in bit-parallel mode, while the earliest machines performed bit-serial arithmetic. The Control Data Corporation 6600, designed in 1964, incorporated a higher level of parallelism: it had 10 independently operating parallel functional units within the central processing unit, each of which could perform an arithmetic operation such as add, multiply, or shift. The CDC 6600 and its follow-on, the 7600, were the highest-speed supercomputers of the 1960s and early 1970s.

Array processing. This is a form of parallelism in which the instruction execution portion of a central processing unit is replicated several times and connected to its own memory device

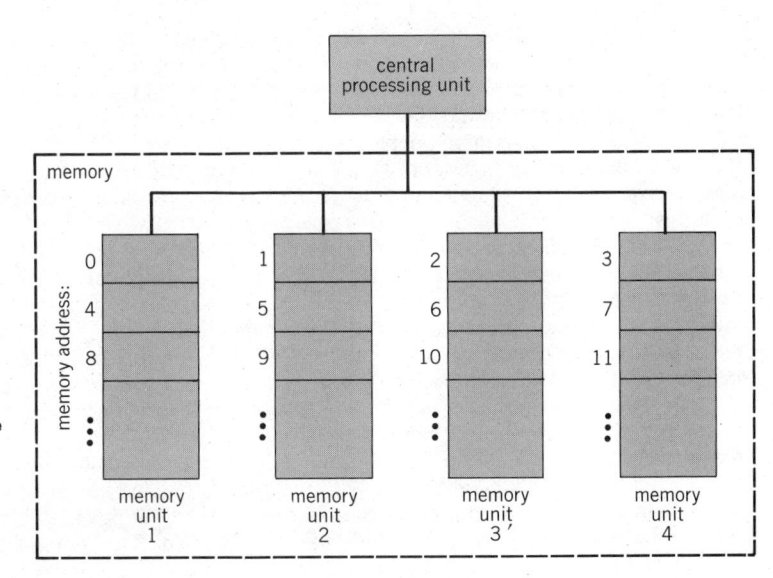

Fig. 3. Simplified diagram of memory interleaving. In this example, the memory is four-way interleaved, that is, the central processing unit can initiate the fetching of data values from four consecutive memory locations before having to wait for a memory unit to become idle.

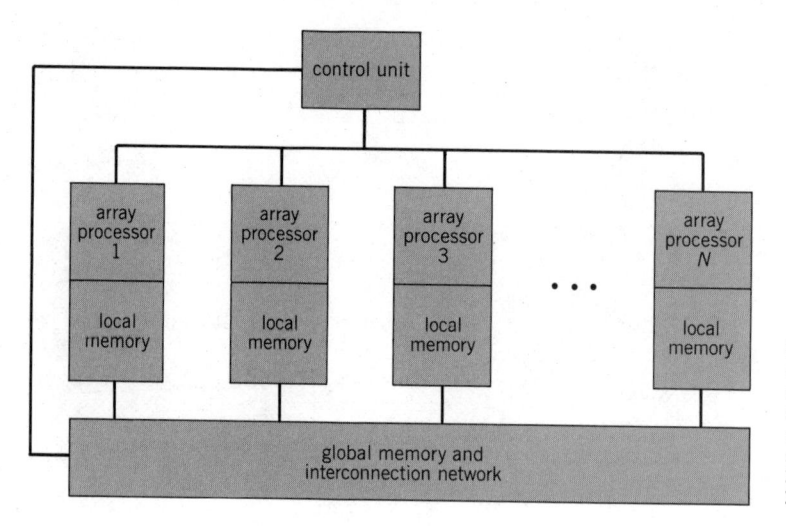

Fig. 4. Conceptual diagram of an array processor. The array processors simultaneously perform the same operation on separate sets of data stored in their local memories, as directed by the control unit.

as well as to a common instruction interpretation and control unit. In this way, a single instruction can be executed at the same time on each of several execution units, each on a different set of operands (**Fig. 4**). This kind of architecture is often referred to as single-instruction-stream, multiple-data stream (SIMD). The Illiac IV was the first array processor supercomputer. It contained an array of 64 processing units, which could be operated in the "lockstep" manner described above. The Illiac IV (only one was built) was operated from 1973 until 1982, and was the fastest supercomputer of its time on certain classes of problems.

Vector processing. This is the term applied to a form of pipelined arithmetic units which are specialized for performing arithmetic operations on vectors, which are uniform, linear arrays of data values. It can be thought of as a type of SIMD processing, since a single instruction invokes the execution of the same operation on every element of the array. The Cray-1 (1976) was the first supercomputer to contain vector pipelines, and the leading supercomputers are now vector processors. This necessitates that the programs they execute be heavily oriented toward vector operations, in order that the vector pipelines are kept full, and the maximum efficiency of the machine is realized.

It has been often pointed out that a supercomputer's speed should not be judged simply on its peak performance rating, that is, its highest possible instruction execution rate, assuming that the pipelines are full and all potential parallelism is completely exploited, but rather a means should be found for predicting the usable-instruction-throughput rate on certain classes of computer programs. The Livermore Loops are a well-known set of 14 programs designed by supercomputer users at Lawrence Livermore National Laboratory, which are intended to provide a uniform basis for comparison of supercomputer performance on a variety of different possible program structures.

One of the most important software components of a contemporary supercomputer is a compiler (an automatic translator of programs written in a high-level language, usually FORTRAN, into the supercomputer's low-level machine operation codes) which contains sophisticated techniques for vectorizing programs. That is, the compiler must detect as many instances as possible of segments of a program that can be expressed as vector operations, and translate them accordingly for machine execution. SEE DIGITAL COMPUTER PROGRAMMING; PROGRAMMING LANGUAGES.

Multiprocessing. This is a form of parallelism that has complete central processing units operating in parallel, each fetching and executing instructions independently from the others. This type of computer organization is called multiple-instruction, multiple-data (MIMD) stream. The Cray X-MP is a MIMD supercomputer with two processors and a shared memory.

As in the case of vector processing, the advent of multiprocessing raises software-oriented issues of how to effectively utilize this type of parallelism. One approach calls for compilers to

contain parallelization techniques analogous to the vectorization techniques now in use; that is, they will detect inherent parallelism in the input programming language and produce parallel code for the machine. Another approach argues that automatic detection of parallism will be found insufficient and that multiprocessors will be used efficiently only if they are programmed in languages which contain high-level, parallel constructs which a programmer can explicitly invoke.
SEE CONCURRENT PROCESSING; DATA FLOW SYSTEMS; DIGITAL COMPUTER; MULTIPROCESSING.

Bibliography. K. Hwang and A. F. Briggs, *Computer Architecture and Parallel Processing*, 1984; R. A. Jenkins, *Supercomputers of Today and Tomorrow: The Parallel Processing Revolution*, 1986; R. D. Levine, Supercomputers, *Sci. Amer.*, 246(1):118–134, January 1982; F. A. Matsen and T. Tajima (eds.), *Supercomputers: Algorithms, Architectures and Scientific Computation*, 1986; N. Metropolis et al. (eds.), *Frontiers of Supercomputing*, 1985; D. P. Siewiorek, G. Bell, and A. Newell, *Computer Structures: Principles and Examples*, 1982.

2

ARCHITECTURE AND CIRCUITRY

Computer systems architecture	50
Computer storage technology	55
Semiconductor memories	68
Magnetic bubble memory	72
Concurrent processing	75
Multiprocessing	77
Data flow systems	79
Fault-tolerant systems	82
Embedded systems	84
Optical computing	85
Microcomputer development system	86
Integrated circuits	87
Logic circuits	109
Microprocessor	115

COMPUTER SYSTEMS ARCHITECTURE
DENNIS J. FRAILEY

The discipline that defines the conceptual structure and functional behavior of a computer system. It is analogous to the architecture of a building, determining the overall organization, the attributes of the component parts, and how these parts are combined. It is related to, but different from, computer implementation. Architecture consists of those characteristics which affect the design and development of software programs, whereas implementation focuses on those characteristics which determine the relative cost and performance of the system. This division is necessary because of the existence of computer families. A family is a series of several computers (usually from the same manufacturer) that offers a variety of cost and performance options (different implementations) but can run the same software programs (that is, all have the same architecture).

The architect's main goal has long been to produce a computer that is as fast as possible, within a given set of cost constraints. This requires a strong background in electrical engineering. Over the years, other goals have been added, such as making it easier to run multiple programs concurrently or improving the performance of programs written in higher-level languages. Thus, the architect also needs a strong background in the software (programming) aspect of computing. SEE DIGITAL COMPUTER PROGRAMMING; PROGRAMMING LANGUAGES; SOFTWARE ENGINEERING.

A computer system consists of four major components (**Fig. 1**): storage, processor, peripherals, and input/output (communication). The storage system is used to keep data and programs; the processor is the unit that controls the operation of the system and carries out various computations; the peripheral devices are used to communicate with the outside world; and the input/output system allows the previous components to communicate with one another.

Storage. The storage or memory of a computer system holds the data that the computer will process and the instructions that indicate what processing is to be done. In a digital computer, these are stored in a form known as binary, which means that each datum or instruction is represented by a series of bits. Bits are conceptually combined into larger units called bytes (usually 8 bits each) and words (usually 8 to 64 bits each). SEE BIT.

A computer will generally have several different kinds of storage devices, each organized to hold one or more words of data. These types include registers, main memory, and secondary or auxiliary storage (**Table 1**).

Registers. These are the fastest and most costly storage units in a computer (**Table 2**). Normally contained within the processing unit, registers hold data that are involved with the computation currently being performed. Registers are also used to hold information describing the current state of the computing process. Implementation of registers may vary with different members of the same architecture family.

Main memory. This device holds the data to be processed and the instructions that specify what processing is to be done. Main memory consists of a sequence of words or bytes, each individually addressable and each capable of being read or written to. Two good measures

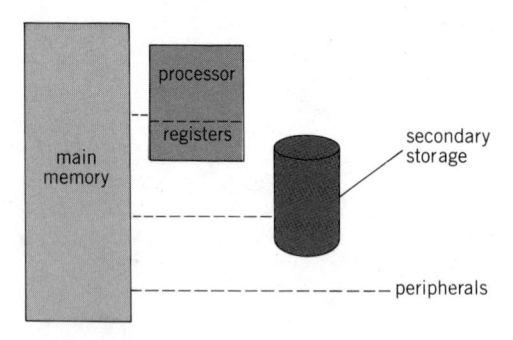

Fig. 1. Overview of a computer system. Storage is made up of registers, main memory, and secondary storage. Broken lines indicate input/output.

ARCHITECTURE AND CIRCUITRY

Table 1. Storage characteristics of typical computers

Storage type	Capacity (words)	Access time, s	Typical uses
Registers	1–128	10^{-8} to 10^{-6}	Computation
Main	4,096–16,000,000	10^{-7} to 10^{-6}	Storage of programs and data
Secondary	300,000–1,000,000,000	10^{-2} to 10^{-1}	Archival or long-term data and program storage

of a computer system are how much main memory it can have and how fast that memory can be accessed. A major goal of the computer architect is to increase the effective speed and size of a memory system without incurring a large cost penalty. Two prevalent techniques for increasing effective speed are interleaving and cacheing, while virtual memory is a popular way to increase the effective size.

Interleaving involves the use of two or more independent memory systems, combined in a way that makes them appear to be a single, faster system. In one approach, all words with even addresses come from one memory system and all words with odd addresses come from the other. When an even-numbered word is fetched, the next-higher odd-numbered word is fetched at the same time. If that odd-numbered word is requested next (a situation that occurs often), it has already been fetched and thus has an access time of zero. This nearly doubles the average access speed.

With cacheing, a small, fast memory system contains the most frequently used words from a slower, larger main memory. With careful design, cacheing can yield considerably improved average memory speeds.

Virtual memory is a technique whereby the programmer is given the illusion of a very large main memory, when in fact it has only a modest size. This is achieved by placing the contents of the large, "virtual" memory on a large but slow auxiliary storage device, and bringing portions of it into main memory, as required by the programs, in a way that is transparent to the programmer.

Auxiliary memory. This portion of memory (sometimes called secondary storage) is the slowest, lowest-cost, and highest-capacity computer storage area. Programs and data are kept in auxiliary memory when not in immediate use, so that auxiliary memory is essentially a long-term storage medium.

There are two basic types of secondary storage: sequential and direct-access. Sequential-access secondary storage devices, of which magnetic tape is the most common, permit data to be accessed in a linear sequence. Thus, in order to access the 100th datum on such a device, the first 99 must be "passed over." For processes where sequential access is suitable, such as printing

Table 2. Registers commonly found in computers

Register	Other names	Function
Instruction register	I register	To hold the instruction currently being executed by the processor
Accumulator	Arithmetic register	To hold the results of computation
Status register	State register	To indicate the results of tests, occurrence of unusual conditions, and status of certain activities
Program counter	Instruction pointer	To hold the address in main memory of the next instruction to be executed
Index register	Counter, B register	For counting (for example, number of times through a repeated computation)
Base register	Pointer register, address register	For pointing to (holding the address of) something in main memory

a list of names or merging two files of insurance records, sequential-access devices are very cost-effective.

A direct-access device is one whose data may be accessed in any order. Disks and drums are the most commonly encountered devices of this type, although certain low-speed semiconductor devices, such as bubble memory, are also used. Direct-access devices permit high-speed access to any block of data, regardless of its location on the device, and thus are well suited to situations where sequential access is not convenient, such as obtaining individual insurance records, at random, from a large file. SEE MAGNETIC BUBBLE MEMORY; SEMICONDUCTOR MEMORIES.

Memory mapping. This is one of the most important aspects of modern computer memory designs. In order to understand its function, the concept of an address space must be considered. When a program resides in a computer's main memory, there is a set of memory cells assigned to the program and its data. This is known as the program's logical address space. If several programs reside in memory at the same time, each has its own logical address space.

The computer's physical address space is the set of memory cells actually contained in the main memory. In the simplest case, where only one program resides in main memory, the logical and physical address spaces may be identical. A more common situation (**Fig. 2**) is where several programs, and thus several logical address spaces, reside within the same physical address space. In such a case, it is desirable to design the system so that the program does not need to know in which part of the physical address space it resides; this anonymity permits the program to be placed anywhere. It is also desirable for the computer to prevent one program from accidentally accessing data in another program's memory. These goals are achieved by means of memory mapping.

Memory mapping is simply the method by which the computer translates between the computer's logical and physical address spaces. The most straightforward mapping scheme involves use of a bias register (**Fig. 3**). Suppose the physical address space begins at location 0, but the program is placed in memory at location 10,000. With the bias scheme, the program is written as though it began at location 0, and the number 10,000 is placed in the bias register. Each time memory is referenced by the program, the contents of the bias register are added to the memory address, thus offsetting the program addresses by the bias amount. Assignment of a different bias value to each program in memory enables the programs to coexist without interference.

Another strategy for mapping is known as paging. This technique involves dividing both logical and physical address spaces into equal-sized blocks called pages. Mapping is achieved by means of a page map, which can be thought of as a series of bias registers (**Fig. 4**). Each logical address is divided into a page number and an offset; the offset is combined with the page map value to yield a physical address.

A simple extension of paging, known as demand paging, allows implementation of virtual memory. In this scheme, the page map includes a "presence" bit for each page, indicating whether that page actually resides in main memory. For a page that is located in main memory, the operation is identical to that of simple paging. If, however, the presence bit indicates that the page is not in main memory, a page fault occurs, causing the computer to obtain the desired page from secondary storage and copy it into main memory. The above procedure is carried out

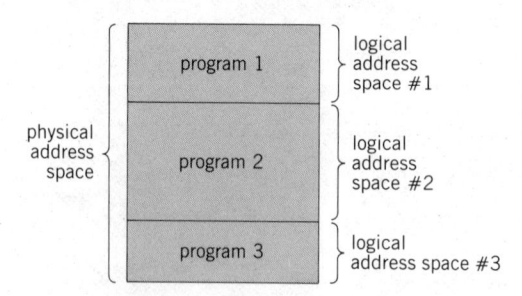

Fig. 2. Several logical address spaces within a physical address space.

ARCHITECTURE AND CIRCUITRY

logical address	+	bias	=	physical address
0 3 0 4		1 0 0 0 0		1 0 3 0 4

(a)

(b)

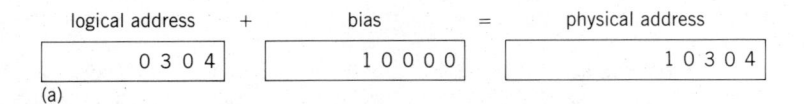

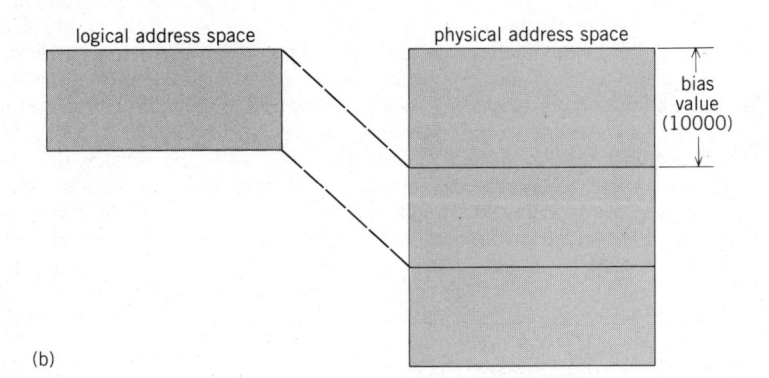

Fig. 3. Memory mapping by means of a bias register. (*a*) Translation formula. (*b*) Memory structure.

logical address

page number	offset
0 2	0 7 0 2

page map

0	3
1	1 2
2	1 7
3	4
4	5

| 1 7 | 0 7 0 2 |

physical address

| 1 7 0 7 0 2 |

(a)

logical address space   physical address space

(b)

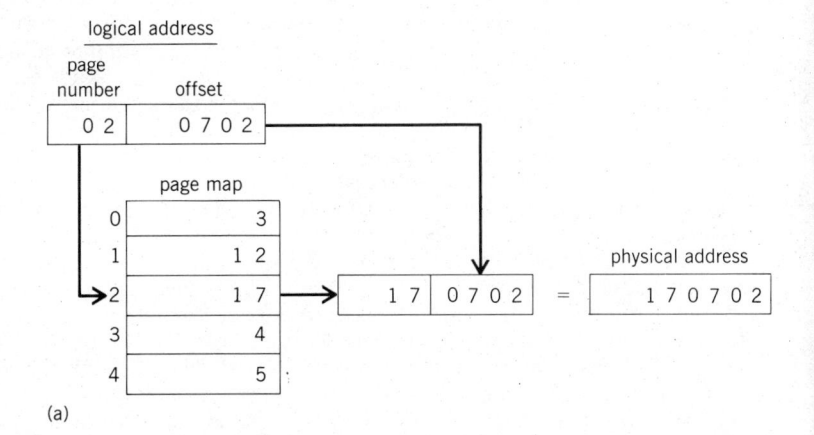

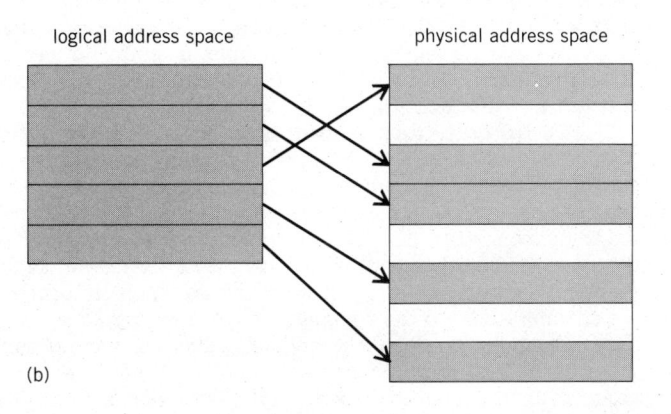

Fig. 4. Memory mapping by means of a page table. (*a*) Translation formula. (*b*) Memory structure.

by the operating system and is essentially unseen by the application program. *See* Computer storage technology.

Processing. A computer's processor (processing unit) consists of a control unit, which directs the operation of the system, and an arithmetic and logic unit (ALU), which performs computational operations. The design of a processing unit involves selection of a register set, communication paths between these registers, and a means of directing and controlling how these operate. Normally, a processor is directed by a program, which consists of a series of instructions that are kept in main memory. Each instruction is a group of bits, usually one or more words in length, specifying an operation to be carried out by the processing unit. The basic cycle of a processing unit consists of the following steps: (1) fetch an instruction from main memory into an instruction register; (2) decode the instruction (determine what it indicates should be done); (3) carry out the operation specified by the instruction; and (4) determine where the next instruction is. Normally, the next instruction is the one immediately following the current one.

Each instruction must indicate an operation to be performed and the data to which the operation should be applied. The assembly language reference manual for any computer system will contain a good illustration of its repertoire of instructions, including both their formats and their functions. There is considerable variation between instruction sets from different computers, and selection of a set of instructions is a major job of the computer architect.

Microprogramming. In the above discussion, it has been assumed that the process of decoding and executing instructions is carried out by logic circuitry. Although such is often the case, the complexity of instruction sets can lead to very large and cumbersome circuits for this purpose. To alleviate this problem, a technique known as microprogramming was developed. With microprogramming, each instruction is actually a macrocommand that is carried out by a microprogram, written in a microinstruction language. The microinstructions are very simple, directing data to flow between registers, memories, and arithmetic units. The microprograming cycle is similar to that described above for macroinstructions, except that the microinstructions are stored in a special microstore memory that cannot be used for storing regular programs and data.

The advantage of microprogramming is that the architect can create very complicated macroinstructions by simply increasing the complexity of the microprograms. The logic circuitry need not be made more complex, and the only cost is in providing a larger microstore to hold the increasingly complex microprograms.

It should be noted that microprogramming has nothing to do with microprocessors. A microprocessor is a processor implemented through a single, highly integrated circuit. *See* Microprocessor.

Parallelism. There are limits to the speed of circuitry, determined by the state of technology and ultimately by the laws of physics. Efforts to design a faster computer often depend on parallelism. Because most techniques used to exploit parallelism belong to the area of implementation, they will be discussed only briefly.

Parallelism can occur in many ways. Parallel computer architectures have been categorized into four groups, depending on whether the instructions or the data are being handled in parallel. An example of the former is a system that fetches one instruction before it finishes with the previous one. An example of the latter is a system whose instructions specify groups of data to be processed at the same time (as in "add this vector to that one"). Perhaps the most widespread technique for parallelism, called pipelining, is similar to an assembly line in which the execution of an instruction is divided into stages, and there is a different instruction at each stage. *See* Concurrent processing; Data flow systems.

Peripherals and communication. A typical computer system includes a variety of peripheral devices such as printers, keyboards, and displays. These devices translate electronic signals into mechanical motion or light (or vice versa) so as to communicate with people. For example, as a person strikes a key (say, the letter K), a particular sequence of signals is transmitted to the computer. This sequence is interpreted as a string of bits, which the computer sees as the letter K. The details of how a peripheral device works are in the realm of mechanical and electrical engineering. The computer architect is more concerned with how the electrical signals are communicated to the computer. *See* Data-processing systems; Electronic display.

There are two common approaches for connecting peripherals and secondary storage devices to the rest of the computer: the channel and the bus. A channel is essentially a wire or group of wires between a peripheral device and a memory device (either main memory or a register). An input operation occurs when the memory receives data from the peripheral device, and an output operation occurs when the contents of the memory are transmitted to the device. A multiplexed channel allows several devices to be connected to the same wire.

A bus is a form of multiplexed channel that can be shared by large number of devices. The overhead of sharing many devices means that the bus has lower peak performance than a channel; but for a system with many peripherals, the bus is more economical than a large number of channels.

A computer controls the flow of data across buses or channels by means of special instructions and other mechanisms. In addition to the wires used to move data, a channel or bus has one or more wires that control what happens when. The simplest scheme is known as program-controlled input/output (I/O). In this approach, the computer has an instruction such as "read from channel n" which causes the processor to send a control signal across a particular channel. That control signal is interpreted by the device as a sign to transmit a word or byte of data across the channel. The data will be deposited in some register, and subsequent instructions will process that data or store the data into main memory for later use.

Direct memory access (DMA) I/O is a technique by which the computer signals the device to transmit a block of data, and the data are transmitted directly to memory, without the processor needing to wait. This is also a form of parallelism, for the processor may carry out other functions while the data transfer is taking place. Memory mapped I/O is a similar technique, except that the computer places commands to the device in a designated portion of memory rather than executing a special instruction.

Interrupts are a form of signal by which a peripheral device notifies a processor that it has completed transmitting data. This is very helpful in a direct memory access scheme, for the processor cannot always predict in advance how long it will take to transmit a block of data. Architects often design elaborate interrupt schemes to simplify the situation where several peripherals are active simultaneously. For example, there might be a separate interrupt signal for each peripheral, or a priority scheme so that, if two peripherals send interrupts at the same time, the more important one is transmitted to the processor first. SEE DATA PROCESSING SYSTEM; DIGITAL COMPUTER.

Bibliography. P. J. Denning, Third generation computer systems, *ACM Computing Surveys*, 3(4):175–216, December 1971; M. J. Flynn, Very high-speed computing systems, *Proc. IEEE*, 54:1901–1909, December 1966; C. C. Foster and A. R. Iberall, *Computer Architecture*, 3d ed., 1985; C. V. Hamacher, Z. G. Vranesic, and S. G. Zaky, *Computer Organization*, 1984; G. J. Myers, *Advances in Computer Architecture*, 2d ed., 1982; Special issue on computer architecture, *Communications of the ACM*, vol. 21, no. 1, January 1978; W. Stallings, *Computer Organization and Architecture*, 1987.

COMPUTER STORAGE TECHNOLOGY
MICHAEL PLESSET AND DOUGLAS THEIS

The techniques, equipment, and organization for providing the memory capability required by computers in order to store instructions and data for processing at high electronic speeds. In early computer systems, memory technology was very limited in speed and high in cost. Since the mid-1970s, the advent of high-density, high-speed random-access memory (RAM) chips has reduced the cost of computer main memory by more than two orders of magnitude. Chips are no larger than ¼ in. (6 mm) square and contain all the essential electronics to store tens to hundreds of thousands of bits of data or instructions. An analogous increase in magnetic recording density has increased the capacity and reduced the cost per bit of secondary memory. Traditionally, computer stroage has consisted of a hierarchy of three or more types of memory storage devices (for example, RAM chips, disks, and magnetic tape units). SEE BIT.

MEMORY HIERARCHY

Memory hierarchy refers to the different types of memory devices and equipment configured into an operational computer system to provide the necessary attributes of storage capacity, speed, access time, and cost to make a cost-effective practical system. The fastest-access memory

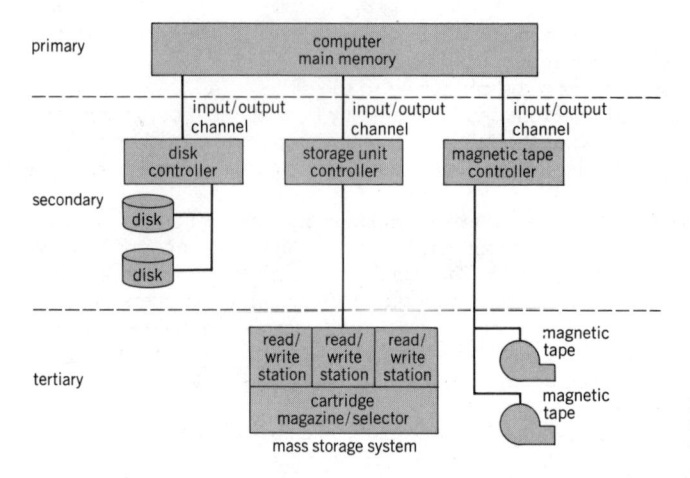

Fig. 1. Memory hierarchy levels and equipment types.

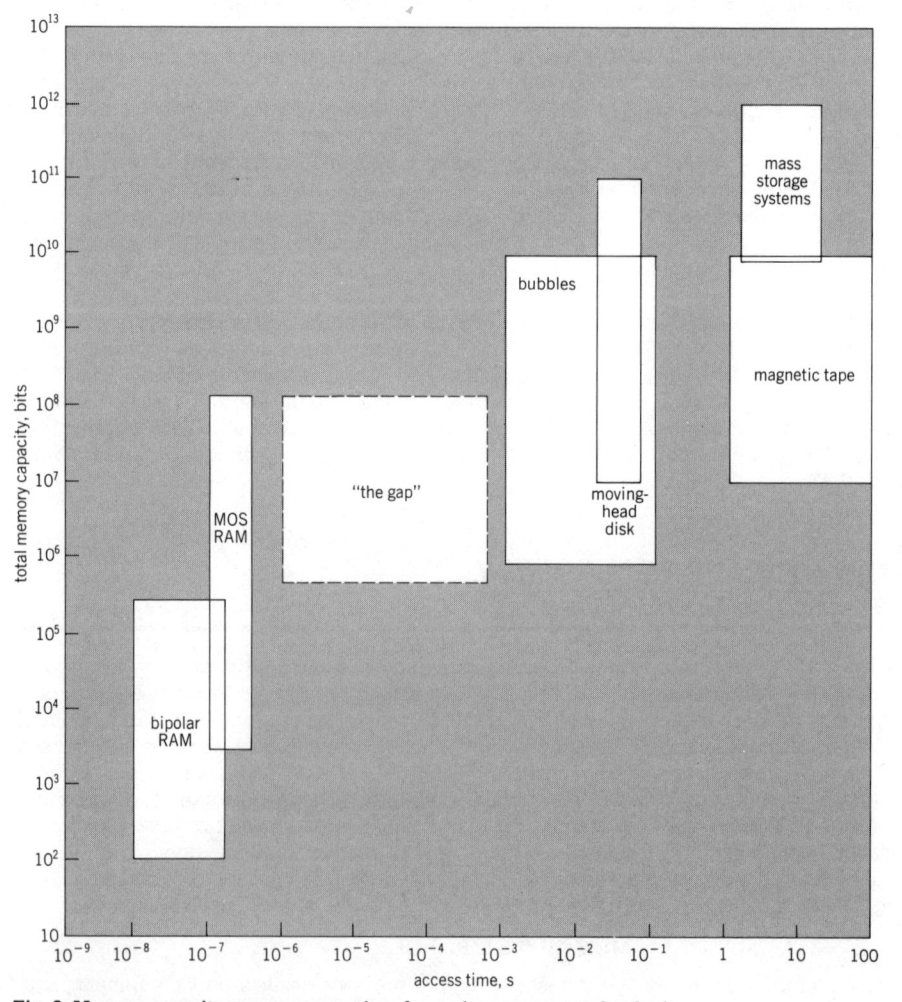

Fig. 2. Memory capacity versus access time for various storage technologies.

in any hierarchy is the main memory in the computer. In most computers manufactured after the late 1970s, RAM chips are used because of their high speed and low cost. Magnetic core memories were the predominant main-memory technology in the 1960s and early 1970s prior to the RAM chip. The secondary storage in the hierarchy usually consists of disks. Significant density improvements have been achieved in disk technology, so that disk capacity has doubled every 3–4 years. Between main-memory and secondary-memory hierarchy levels, however, there has always been the "memory gap."

The memory gap noted by J. P. Eckert (a developer of the ENIAC computer in the 1940s) still presents a problem for the data-processing system designer. The memory gap for access time is bounded on one side by a 1-microsecond typical computer main memory cycle time and on the other by the 30-millisecond typical disk-drive access time. Capacity is bounded on the one side by a maximum mainframe memory capacity of 64 megabytes and on the other by multiple disks, each with a capacity of 100 to 2500 megabytes.

The last, or bottom, level (sometimes called the tertiary level) of storage hierarchy is made up of magnetic tape transports and mass-storage tape systems (**Fig. 1**). Performance (**Fig. 2**) is usually measured by two parameters: capacity and access time. (Speed or data rate is a third parameter, but it is not so much a function of the device itself as of the overall memory design.) Capacity refers to the maximum on-line user capacity of a single connectable memory unit. Access time is the time required to obtain the first byte of a randomly located set of data.

MEMORY ORGANIZATION

The efficient combination of memory devices from the various hierarchy levels must be integrated with the central processor and input/output equipment, making this the real challenge to successful computer design. The resulting system should operate at the speed of the fastest element, provide the bulk of its capacity at the cost of its least expensive element, and provide sufficiently short access time to retain these attributes in its application environment. Another key ingredient of a successful computer system is an operating system (that is, software) that allows the user to execute jobs on the hardware efficiently. Operating systems are available which achieve this objective reasonably well. SEE COMPUTER SYSTEMS ARCHITECTURE.

The computer system hardware and the operating system software must work integrally as one resource. In many computer systems, the manufacturer provides a virtual memory system. It gives each programmer automatic access to the total capacity of the memory hierarchy without specifically moving data up and down the hierarchy and to and from the central processing unit (CPU). During the early years of computing, each programmer had to incorporate storage allocation procedures by determining at each moment of time how information would be distributed among the different hierarchic levels of memory, whenever the totality of information was expected to exceed the size of main memory. These procedures involved dividing the program into segments which would overlay one another in main memory. The programmer was intimately familiar with both the details of the machine and the application algorithms of the program. This all changed in the 1970s and was much improved in the 1980s, when sophisticated higher-level program languages and data-base management software became well established, to provide significantly greater problem-solving capability. Thus manufacturer-supported operating systems evolved, with complete built-in virtual memory support capabilities, which made it possible for the user to ignore the details of memory hierarchy internal software and hardware operations. SEE DATA-BASE MANAGEMENT SYSTEMS; DIGITAL COMPUTER PROGRAMMING; OPERATING SYSTEM; PROGRAMMING LANGUAGES.

In the area of memory organization, two types of memory augmentation have been employed in the more widely used computers to enhance the overall computer performance capabilities. These two memory organization techniques are the cache memory, which speeds up the flow of instructions and data into the central processing unit from main memory, and an intelligent disk controller memory that is used as a staging buffer memory to queue up instructions and data for more rapid access into main memory.

Cache memory. A cache memory is a small, fast buffer located between the processor and the main system memory. Data and instructions in current use are moved into cache, producing two benefits. First, the average access time for the processor's memory requests is reduced, increasing the processor's throughput. Second, the processor's utilization of the available memory bandwidth, is thereby reduced, allowing other devices on the system bus to use the memory without interfering with the processor. Cache memory is thus used to speed up the flow of instructions and data into the central processing unit from main memory. This cache function is important because the main memory cycle time is typically slower than the central processing unit clocking rates. To achieve this rapid data transfer, cache memories are usually built from the faster bipolar RAM devices rather than the slower metal oxide semiconductor (MOS) RAM devices.

Performance of mainframe systems is very dependent upon achieving a high percentage of accesses from the cache rather than main memory. In typical systems 80–95% of accesses are to cache memory, with a typical cache size of 8K bytes. (1K bytes is equal to 1024 bytes.) Since the cache contents are a duplicate copy of information in main memory, writes (instructions to enter data) to the cache must eventually be made to the same data in main memory. This is done in two ways: write-through cache, in which write is made to the corresponding data in both cache and main memory; and write-back cache, in which main memory is not updated until the cache page is returned to main memory, at which time main memory is overwritten.

Intelligent disk controller memory. This is used as a cache memory between disk and main memories. Typically it consists of MOS RAM chips which overlap the disk operations, with their longer access time, to mask out the disk access delays so that main memory can execute subsequent tasks more rapidly and efficiently. Intelligent disk controllers provide the latest techniques to fill the memory gap with the best practical memory organization techniques for high performance. Microprocessors are also an integral part of intelligent disk controllers, and carry out many central processing unit operating system functions necessary for disk operations. This off-loads the mainframe computer from doing this kind of overhead processing to a large extent. SEE MICROPROCESSOR.

MAIN SEMICONDUCTOR MEMORY

The rapid growth in high-density large-scale integrated (LSI) circuits has advanced to a point where only a few applications require the tens to hundreds of thousands of transistors that can now be placed on a chip. One obvious exception is computer main memory, in which there is a continual demand for higher and higher capacity at lower cost. SEE INTEGRATED CIRCUITS.

In the 1960s and early 1970s, magnetic core memories dominated computer main-memory technology, but these have been completely replaced by semiconductor RAM chip devices of ever-increasing density. This transition started with the introduction of the first MOS 1K-bit RAM memory in 1971. This was followed with the 4K-bit RAM chip in 1973, the 16K-bit RAM chip in 1976, the 64K-bit RAM chip in 1979, and 256K-bit chip in 1982. **Figure 3** shows the progression

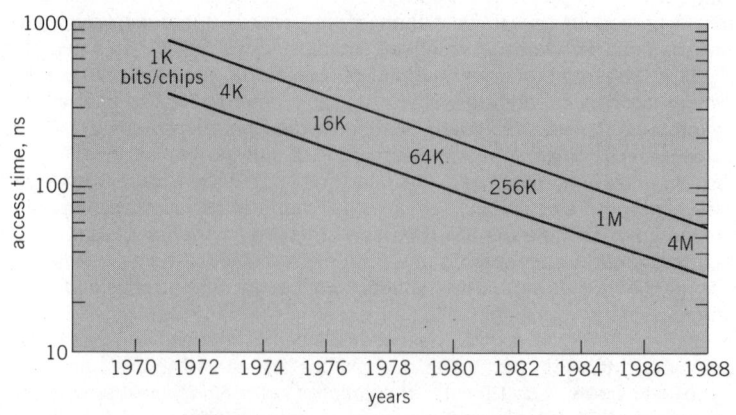

Fig. 3. Trends in performance and density (in bits per chip) of dynamic RAM chips. 1K = 1024 bits; 1M = 1024 × 1024 bits = 1,048,576 bits.

of RAM chips, which follows the "rule of four," according to which the cost of development of a new RAM device generation can be justified only by a factor-of-four increase in capacity. S‍ee S‍emiconductor memories.

256K-bit RAM chips. The 256K-bit MOS RAM has continued to push photolithographic fabrication techniques with feature sizes of 1 to 3 micrometers. For RAM chip densities of 256K bits or more per device, the integrated circuit industry has had to make a twofold improvement to maintain volume production and device reliability: better means, such as x-ray step-and-repeat equipment, to achieve features under 2 µm; and plasma-etching or reactive-ion-etching machines to achieve vertical profiles needed as horizontal dimensions decrease. Considerable progress has been made in the use of both x-ray and electron-beam techniques to achieve the submicrometer-size features needed to make even higher-density RAM chips. All 256K-bit RAMs are dynamic RAMs. The production techniques for dynamic and static RAM chips are identical. Therefore, the cost per unit quickly becomes the cost for mass-producing one chip. Since building costs per chip are about the same whether they store 4K bits or 256K bits, higher densities lead to lower costs per bit.

RAM chip types and technologies. RAM chips come in a wide variety of organizations and types. Computer main memories are organized into random addressable words in which the word length is fixed to some power-of-2 bits (for example, 4, 8, 16, 32, or 64 bits). But there are exceptions, such as 12-, 18-, 24-, 48-, and 60-bit word-length machines. Usually RAMs contain NK · 1 (for example, 64K · 1) bits, so the main memory design consists of a stack of chips in parallel with the number of chips corresponding to that machine's word length. There are two basic types of RAMs, static and dynamic. The differences between them are significant. Dynamic RAMs are those which require their contents to be refreshed periodically. They require supplementary circuits on-chip to do the refreshing and to assure that conflicts do not occur between refreshing and normal read-write operations. Even with those extra circuits, dynamic RAMs still require fewer on-chip components per bit than do static RAMs (which do not require refreshing).

Static RAMs are easier to design, and compete well in applications in which less memory is to be provided, since their higher cost then becomes less important. They are often chosen for minicomputer memory, or especially for microcomputers. Because they require more components per chip, making higher bit densities more difficult to achieve, the introduction of static RAMs of any given density occurs behind that of dynamic versions.

There is another trade-off to be made with semiconductor RAMs in addition to the choice between static and dynamic types, namely that between MOS and bipolar chips. Biopolar devices are faster, but have not yet achieved the higher densities (and hence the lower costs) of MOS. Within each basic technology, MOS and bipolar, there are several methods of constructing devices, and these variations achieve a variety of memory speeds and access times, as well as power consumption and price differences. Within the basic MOS technologies there are several types, such as the *n*-channel MOS referred to as NMOS and the complementary MOS solid-state structure referred to as CMOS. For bipolar there are several types such as transistor-to-transistor logic (TTL) and the emitter-coupled logic (ECL). S‍ee L‍ogic circuits.

Memory cycle and access times. The RAM memory cycle time in a computer is defined as that time interval required to read or write one word of data. Access time is defined as the time interval in which the data are available after the initiation of the read cycle. From the user's point of view, cycle time is also an important characteristic because it has more impact on overall computational speed of the system. A new data read-write cycle does not begin until the previous read cycle is completed. The specified timing, signal overlap, and tolerances allowed vary with each RAM main memory system.

Error checking and correction. Most computer main memories have a memory fault control consisting of a memory controller and a fault control subsystem which automatically corrects all single-bit errors and detects and reports all double-bit or three-bit errors. Each bit in a word is read from a separate RAM device. The fault control permits computer operation to continue even if a memory module is malfunctioning, and thus the computer will operate even if a memory chip is removed from the board. Failures are pinpointed to the specific chip by fault-indicating light-emitting diodes built into each array board.

FIFO and LIFO chips. As memory chips increased in storage density and designers attempted to minimize interconnection circuitry, specialty memory function organizations such as first-in first-out (FIFO) buffers and last-in first-out (LIFO) buffers became available as chips. These kinds of chips are readily used in memory buffering applications to accommodate varying data rates between one element and another. The other complementary feature of FIFO and LIFO chips is the dual data paths (called ports) to allow simultaneous transfer of data into and out of these memory buffer chips. These chip types are commonly used on microcomputer boards and in the computer's peripheral interface and controller electronics.

Gallium arsenide memory chips. All the memory chips discussed above are based on the predominant silicon technology. Reliable gallium arsenide (GaAs) intergrated circuits have been produced: 1K-bit and 4K-bit static RAM (SRAM) devices with 1-nanosecond access times. Development of 16K-bit SRAMs has been undertaken for military applications. Considering the need for and emphasis on increasingly rapid computers, there is definite potential for high-speed gallium arsenide logic and memory devices.

ROMs, PROMs, and EPROMs. Microcomputers have evolved their own special set of semiconductor memory chips to suit their application needs. Whereas large, medium-size, and minicomputers primarily use only RAMs that have read-write capability, microcomputers have found significant use for read-only memory (ROM) chips and programmable read-only memory (PROM) chips. Data and program storage in most microcomputer applications is separately allocated between RAMs and ROMs. ROMs provide protection, since the contents are fixed or hard-wired and the chips are completely nonvolatile. During microcomputer program development, PROMs are typically used. A PROM can be written only once and involves the irreversible process of blowing polysilicon fuse links. These PROMs are neither erasable nor reprogrammable. Other kinds of devices, called an erasable PROM (EPROM), is cleared or rewritten by putting the EPROM chip under an ultraviolet light to zero out its contents and then using a PROM programmer to write in the new bit pattern for the modified program. After the microcomputer application program has completed final tests and acceptance, the final bit pattern in the EPROM can be put into ROMs or PROMs (using a chip mask) to facilitate quantity production. SEE MICROCOMPUTER; MICROCOMPUTER DEVELOPMENT SYSTEM.

EEPROMs. There are also memory chip devices called electrically erasable programmable read-only memories (EEPROMs). They have an internal switch on the chip to permit a user to electrically rewrite new contents into them. This means EEPROMs do not have to be removed from the circuit in order to clear their contents to put in the new or modified bit pattern representing another program of instructions. Therefore EEPROMs have met the requirement in microcomputer systems for a nonvolatile in-circuit reprogrammable random word access memory device.

EEPROMs use two distinctively different technologies. The more mature technology is metal nitride oxide semiconductor (MNOS), which is a very different gate insulator process technology from that used for MOS. The MNOS technology previously used the generic acronym EAROM (electrically alterable read-only memories) until EEPROMs became common in usage for both technologies. The other technology is floating-gate MOS (also called FAMOS). FAMOS technology was used for ultraviolet erasable EPROMs (UVPROMs) and was subsequently refined to provide an electrically erasable technology. Both technologies rely on Fowler-Nordheim tunneling to move the charge to be stored from the substrate to the gate. FAMOS stores the charge on the gate itself, whereas MNOS devices trap the charge in the nitride layer under the gate.

SECONDARY MEMORY

High-capacity, slower-speed memory consists of two major functional types: random-access, which has been provided primarily by disk drives, and sequential-access, which has been provided primarily by tape drives. Since tape drives provide removability of the medium from the computer, tape is used for the majority of off-line, archival storage, although some disks are removable also. The on-line random-access disk devices are classed as secondary, and tape-based systems are classed as tertiary.

Over the history of electronic computers, while the technology for processors and main memory has been evolving from vacuum tubes to transistors to very large-scale integration (VLSI) chips, the predominant technology for secondary memory has continued to be magnetic recording on tape and disk. This has not been due so much to the absence of competing alternatives as to the continuous and rapid progression in magnetic recording capability. The increase in recording density on disks is shown in **Fig. 4**. The scale of the figure is logarithmic, so the rate of improvement has been exponential.

The current magnetic-disk technology will be discussed, and also the potential of new magnetic recording techniques such as thin-film, vertical recording, and bubble-memory devices; and a nonmagnetic technology, optical recording.

Magnetic disk storage. Conventional magnetic-disk memories consist of units which vary in capacity from the small 250-kilobyte floppy disks (used with microcomputers) to 2500-megabyte disk drives used with large-scale computers. Hard-disk memories are characterized by access times in the 20–80-millisecond region (versus access times of hundreds of nanoseconds to 1 microsecond for RAMs). **Figure 5** shows the historical progression in several performance factors: capacity, transfer rate, and access time.

Capacity. The major area of development in disks has been the progressive and even spectacular increases in capacity per drive, particularly in terms of price per byte. There is a substantial economy of scale in storage capacity, in that the cost per byte goes down as the drive capacity goes up. Between small disks and top-end drives, the differences in access time and transfer rate may be only a factor of two to five, while the capacity difference is a factor of as much as 500, that is, from 5 megabytes to 2500 megabytes.

Transfer rate. The rotation rate of the disk platter, like the action of the head actuators, is limited by considerations of physical dynamics, and major increases over the 3600-rpm rate of present large drives are not currently achievable. Increases in transfer rate will come from greater linear bit density around the track. In an absolute sense, transfer rates are not as often a system performance bottle neck as is access time.

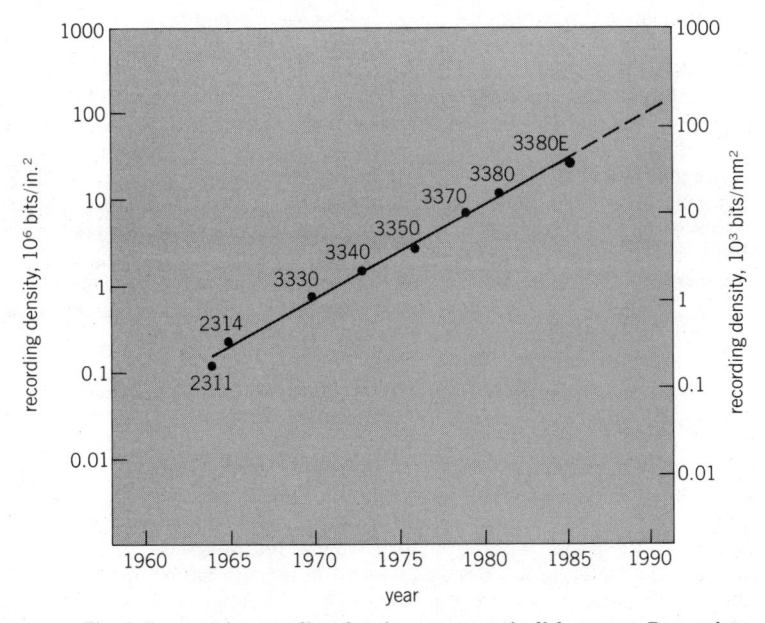

Fig. 4. Increase in recording density on magnetic disk storage. Data points represent IBM models, and model numbers are indicated.

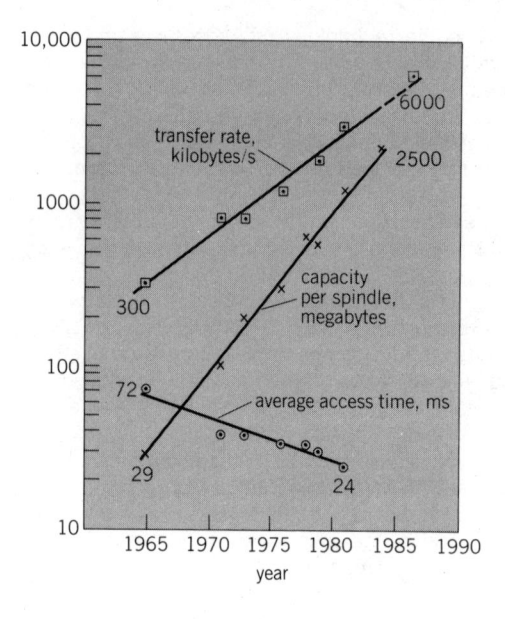

Fig. 5. Development of magnetic disk performance factors.

Average access time. Since the arm supporting the read-write head is one of the few moving mechanical parts in a computer system, it has not shown the multiple-orders-of-magnitude performance improvement over time that the electronic technologies have. Also, average access times for the highest-priced and lowest-prices disks do not vary by an enormous factor, being in the range of 40 to 80 milliseconds for a typical microcomputer hard (as opposed to floppy) disk, and 24 to 30 milliseconds for large disks on mainframe computers. There is nothing which indicates a breakthrough in the technology governing access time, even though greater capacities and transfer rates are still coming. Therefore, for random-access bottlenecks, the solution in the future will be the same as it is now: multiple smaller drives to allow overlapped seeks instead of a single large-capacity drive.

Basic disk technology. Many significant advances in the capabilities of commercially available disk memory technology were made during the late 1970s. One of the major trends was toward larger-capacity disks, progressing from 100 megabytes to 2500 megabytes per disk drive. The majority of technology improvements to provide higher capacities, lower costs, and better reliabilities resulted from the Winchester technology. Prior to this technology, removable disk packs established themselves as the most advanced technology for large-capacity disks. The Winchester technology is characterized by nonremovable, sealed disk packs, which inherently provide more reliability due to less handling and make more stringent alignment tolerances practical.

The head, or read-write transducer, has undergone substantial refinement. Central to the advance in increasing disk-packing density was the reduction in the flying height of the read-write head. Because flux spreads with distance, reduced separation between the read-write head and the magnetic surface will decrease the area occupied by an information bit. This obviously limits the number of bits that can be defined along an inch of track and increases the minimum spacing between tracks. The ideal would be a direct contact between head and surface, which is the case with magnetic tape. But this is not possible with a rigid aluminum disk whose surface is traveling at rates that can exceed 100 mi/h (45 m/s). By applying a load on the head assembly, proper spacing is maintained. All movable media memories utilize an air-bearing mechanism known as the slider or flying head to space the transducer in proximity to the relatively moving media. The slider, when forced toward the moving surface of the medium, rests on a wedge of air formed between it and the medium by virtue of their relative motion. The thickness of the wedge can be controlled by the applied force, and the wedge in effect is an extremely stiff pneumatic spring. Head-to-medium spacings were well under 10 μin. (0.25 μm) in 1982.

Some standards have been developed for interfaces between the drive and the controller, to permit compatibility among drives of various capacities and manufacturers. One is the Storage Module Device (SMD) interface. Also in use is an American National Standards Institute (ANSI) standard.

In addition to fixed Winchester-type disk units of various capacities, disk storage is used in several removable forms.

Cartridge disks. Removable storage cartridges containing single-disk packs are used extensively with minicomputer systems. The cartridge disk-drive unit has capacities ranging from 1 to 10 megabytes, depending on the recording density. Average access times range from 35 ro 75 milliseconds, and data transfer rates from 200 to 300 kilobytes per second. Physically, these plastic-encased cartridges are either top-loaded or front-loaded units. These units, besides having a removable disk, also have a fixed disk. The performance features of cartridge disks compete favorably with the larger-capacity disk pack storage equipment. A disadvantage of removable disk cartridges or disk packs is reduced reliability compared to fixed units.

Floppy disks. Floppy disks have become the widely used random-access secondary memory for microcomputer systems. The floppy disk was originally developed by IBM in 1965 for internal use on its large 370 computers. The disk was designed to be a permanent nonvolatile memory storage device, written at the factory. However, large numbers of new and varied applications evolved for these relatively small, compact disk systems. Floppy disks derive their name from the recording medium, an oxide-coated flexible disk (similar to, but more flexible than, plastic 45-rpm music records) enclosed within a protective plastic envelope. The Mylar flexible disk is 8 in. (200 mm) in diameter, 0.003 in. (0.075 mm) thick, and records 3200 bits per inch (125 bits per millimeter) and 48 tracks per inch (1.9 tracks per millimeter). The disk is permanently enclosed in a protective envelope, and this package is 8 in. (200 mm) square, hence the common reference to the size as 8-inch. The protective envelope contains alignment holes for spindle loading, head contact, sector-index detection, and write-protect detection. The capacity of this easily transportable medium is 8 megabits, commonly laid out on 77 tracks, each divided into 26 sectors.

The flexible-disk drive subassembly consists of the metal base frame, the disk-drive motor that rotates the spindle (360 rpm for 8-in. or 200-mm, 300 rpm for 5¼-in. or 133-mm) through a belt drive, and a stepping motor with an integral lead screw to form the head-positioning actuator. The read-write head is mounted on a carriage that the lead screw moves. Head load is achieved by moving a load pad against the disk and restraining the disk between the head and the load pad to accomplish the head-to-disk compliance.

The removable floppy disk, called a diskette, was originally 8 in. (200 mm), in both single and double densities, and single- and double-sided. A variety of incompatible formats exist, particularly in double density, as the majority of suppliers use a common (IBM) format in single density. The most conspicuous format difference is in sector boundaries, hard-sector referring to boundaries of physical holes in the diskette, and soft-sector to boundaries that are software-formatted. As recording density increased and packaging considerations for microcomputers became important, a smaller, 5¼-in. (133-mm) diskette was introduced in 1976 and has become dominant, with a similar proliferation of formats as in 8-in. (200-mm). Newer systems are using yet smaller sizes such as 3, 3¼, and 3½ in. (75, 81, and 87 mm).

Thin-film and vertical recording. Several technologies are in development for disk storage.

The recording technology for conventional magnetic disk recording has been based upon ferrite heads and a recording surface consisting of a coating embedded with ferrous oxide particles. One of the limiting factors is the thickness of the recording layer, which is 20 to 50 μin. (0.5 to 1.25 μm). With current products pushing the limits of recording density achievable with that approach, a successor technology has been developed, called thin-film.

The thin-film technique uses a continuous magnetic film of cobalt or nickel, applied by electroplating to a controlled thickness of as little as 1 μin. (25 nanometers). Either the head or the recording surface or both can use thin-film technology. Most of the major conventional large disks use thin-film heads and an oxide recording surface. Advanced models are designed to use a thin-film recording surface. Thin-film technology is the source for current progress in disk capacity and transfer rate. It was first introduced in small disks, partly due to its greater ability to withstand the more portable environment of the small computer. The hardness of the medium which provides this resiliency also reduces both the likelihood and consequences of head crashes.

Another magnetic recording technique is vertical, or perpendicular, recording. In this approach the miniature magnets which are formed in the recording media are oriented downward into the surface rather than longitudinally along the surface. This allows closer packing of the magnetized spots, not just because of spatial compression, but also because of improved magnetic interaction between adjacent spots. The adjacent spots repel each other in the longitudinal case but attract in the vertical case. This technique offers the potential for significantly extending recording density and the accompanying performance parameters.

Recording density is the product of the bit density along the recording track, in bits per inch (or bits per millimeter), and the number of tracks per inch (or tracks per millimeter) across the recording surface. For a given rotation rate of the disk, the bit density along the track determines the transfer rate. A comparison of these characteristics for various recording techniques is given in **Table 1**.

The point at which vertical recording becomes attractive to develop into commercial products depends in part upon the level of capability which can ultimately be achieved with thin-film technology. The density level achieved by vertical recording technology may represent a limit for magnetic recording. If so, one possible answer to the question of how further levels of performance can be obtained is optical recording.

Optical recording. Optical recording is a nonmagnetic disk technology that uses a laser beam to burn pits in the recording medium to represent the bits of information, and a lower-power laser to sense the presence or absence of pits for reading. This technology has the potential for higher ultimate recording density than magnetic recording. The medium is removable and relatively inexpensive. The removability is significant in light of the nonremovability of most current and projected high-capacity magnetic disks. The recording density increase is apparent when it is noted that 4-gigabyte capacity is achieved on a single disk, whereas current-model large-capacity (2.5-gigabyte) magnetic drives typically consist of a cabinet containing two disk assemblies, each assembly having 16 platters.

One of the first optical disk mass-storage devices has 4 gigabytes on a removable, nonerasable, 14-in. (350-mm) disk. The transfer rate of 1.5 megabytes per second buffered or 3.0 megabytes streaming is similar to that of conventional magnetic disks (3.0 for the IBM 3380). The average access time is slower than that of high-performance magnetic disks at 84.7 milliseconds, versus the 3380's 24 milliseconds, but track-to track access is a comparatively fast 1.0 millisecond. The corrected bit error rate is 1 in 10^{13}, which is compatible with magnetic disk standards.

In addition to the 14-in. (350-mm) disk for large-capacity systems, 12-in. (300-mm) optical disk systems in the 1-gigabyte capacity range have been produced for use with 16- or 32-bit microcomputer and minicomputer systems.

Optical technology has several disadvantages. First, the medium is not inherently erasable, although systems which can erase and rewrite are also in development. The primary problem in producing a commercial optical disk system has been getting the bit error rate down to an acceptable level, with sufficient recording density to be competitive with magnetic recording. To be competitive with magnetic tape, a bit error rate, after error detect and correct, of 1 in 10^{10} to 10^{11}

Table 1. Storage densities for various recording technologies

Technology	Bit density along track Bits/in.	Bits/mm	Track density Tracks/in.	Tracks/mm	Recording density 10^6 bits/in.^{2}	10^9 bits/mm^2
Magnetic recording						
Conventional (IBM 3380)	15,000	600	800	32	12	19
Thin-film*	25,000	1000	1,200	47	30	47
Vertical*	100,000	4000	1,200	47	120	190
Optical recording	15,000	600	15,000	600	225	350

*Figures are projections.

is needed, and to compete with magnetic disk, 1 in 10^{13} to 10^{14}. Through error detect and correct techniques, the 1 in 10^{13} level has been attained.

The bit error rate problem is far less critical for storage of documents and images, since bit dropout is seldom noticeable, in contrast with financial information, where it could be disastrous. This is the reason that optical disk recording was first used successfully in consumer and industrial systems for video-type image information, and for document storage and retrieval systems.

The nonerasability of the technology can be an advantage for some applications. Examples are data which must be kept for historical or audit-trail purposes, and applications where large amounts of data must be shipped among different locations.

When this technology matures, it will be an event of major significance, being a removable, large-capacity, random-access device using a recording technology with large potential for further growth. The potential for development of yet higher recording densities is perhaps the most significant factor, but in addition, having large capacity on a removable platter would allow some other kinds of system development. One possible system, referred to as a jukebox, would store on the order of 100 disks in an automatic retrieval and mounting device, so that a given disk could be fetched and accessed in around 5 seconds giving an on-line storage in the range of 500 gigabytes. Previous systems for very large on-line storage which have been delivered in significant quantity are the cartridge tape systems from IBM and CDC and automated tape libraries discussed below. The cartridge tape systems have capacities to 50 megabytes (IBM) and 8 megabytes (CDC) per cartridge; hence the optical system would provide a great improvement in the capacity available on the basic storage unit, and the automated tape libraries of course have the limitation of sequential data access.

Bubble memory devices. Bubble memories are chips rather than disks, but are different from semiconductor memories in that they are magnetic devices, in which the absence or presence of a magnetic domain is the basis for a binary 1 to 0. The performance characteristics of these devices makes them competitive as small-capacity secondary storage. A magnetic bubble is in reality a cylindrical magnetic domain with a polarization opposite to that of the magnetic film in which it is contained. These cylinders appear under a microscope as small circles (which give them their name) with diameters from 80 to 800 μin. (2 to 20 μm). The size of a bubble is determined by the material characteristics and thickness of the magnetic film.

Bubbles are moved or circulated by establishing a magnetic field through a separate conductor mounted adjacent to the bubble chip. A large portion of the bubble chip must be given over to circuitry for generating, detecting, and annihilating the bubbles. Magnetic-domain bubble devices typically operate in an endless serial loop fashion or in an organization with serial minor loops feeding major loop registers. Bubble memories are particularly well suited to applications such as portable recorders because of their physical advantages (low power requirements and light weight) and speed advantage over electromechanical devices such as cassettes and floppy disks. Like their electromechanical counterparts, bubble devices are nonvolatile; that is, they retain their contents when the power goes off.

The controller is central to any bubble memory system, which it serves as the interface between the bubble chip and the system bus. It generates all of the system timing and control functions and supervises the handshaking operations required to access and transfer data between the system bus and the bubble memory module. Usually a controller can operate more than one bubble chip module, in most cases up to eight modules. The function-driver integrated circuit produces the control currents required to generate and input or ouput tracks on the chip. The sense-amplifier integrated circuit converts the analog output signals produced by the bubble detector into a transmittable data stream that passes to the controller. The coil-driver integrated circuits excite the x and y coils of the bubble chip package with out-of-phase signals to produce the rotating field that moves the bubbles.

United States companies are producing 1-megabit and 4-megabit bubble memory chips. Under a cross-license and alternate source agreement, these companies have agreed to jointly adopt a low-height leaded package for complete component level interchangeability. Each company developed its peripheral chip set for the 4-megabit magnetic bubble module that will be compatible with the 1-megabit units.

For portable and other special applications, bubbles have definite advantages such as nonvolatility, low power, and high compactness. Performance capabilities relative to floppy disks are

100 kilobits per second for bubbles versus 200–250 kilobits per second for floppies, and 40 milliseconds average access time for bubbles versus 200–250 milliseconds for floppies. SEE MAGNETIC BUBBLE MEMORY.

General trends. The technologies which will provide the growth in performance in disk systems will also allow improved price-performance, so that the cost per byte on-line can be expected to continue to drop. Although this disscussion has concentrated on high-end disks in terms of performance parameters, small- and medium-range disks, including floppies, will benefit from the same technological and price-performance progression. Some of these technological developments in fact can appear first in the lower-end products, one such possibility being vertical recording in floppy diskettes.

In both hard disks and floppies, the higher recording densities permit progressively more compact packaging for microcomputers, but the constant change has aggravated the existing difficulties with lack of standardization, which is unfortunate for the potentially convenient interchange medium which the floppy diskette could provide. Although such possibilities as a 5-megabyte floppy diskette are impressive, the prospect for standards which would permit interchangeability are becoming less, with the proliferation of sizes and incompatible formats discussed above.

MAGNETIC TAPE UNITS

In magnetic tape units, the tape maintains physical contact with the fixed head while in motion, allowing high-density recording. The long access times to find user data on the tape are strictly due to the fact that all intervening data have to be searched until the desired data are found. This is not true of rotating disk memories or RAM word-addressable main memories. The primary use of tape storage is for seldom-used data files and as back-up storage for disk data files.

Half-inch tapes. Half-inch (12.5-mm) tape has been the industry standard since it was first used commercially in 1953. Half-inch magnetic tape drive transports are reel-to-reel recorders with extremely high tape speeds (up to 200 in. or 5 m per second), and fast start, stop (on the order of 1 millisecond), reverse, and rewind times.

Performance and data capacity of magnetic tape have improved by orders of magnitude, as shown in **Table 2**. Just prior to the 1970s came the single-capstan tape drive, which improved access times to a few milliseconds. These vacuum-column tape drives have such features as automatic hub engagement and disengagement, cartridge loading, and automatic thread operation. There are two primary recording techniques, namely, nonreturn-zero-inverted (NRZI) and phase-encoded (PE), used with packing densities of 800 and 1600 bytes per inch (31.5 and 63 bytes per millimeter). These typically use a 0.6-in. (15-mm) interrecord gap. In phase encoding, a logical "one" is defined as the transition from one magnetic polarity to another positioned at the center of the bit cell. "Zero" is defined as the transition in the opposite direction also at the center of the bit cell, whereas NRZI would involve only one polarity. The advantage of the phase-encoding scheme over NRZI is that there is always one or more transitions per bit cell, which gives phase encoding a self-clocking capability, alleviating the need for an external clock. The

Table 2. Standard recording densities for magnetic tape

Year	Number of tracks	Bit density along track bits/in.	bits/mm	Area density bits/in.²	bits/mm²
1953	7	100	4	1,400	2
1955	7	200	8	2,800	4
1959	7	556	22	7,784	12
1962	7	800	32	11,200	17
1963	9	800	32	14,400	22
1965	9	1600	63	28,800	45
1973	9	6250	246	112,500	174

disadvantage of phase encoding over NRZI is that at certain bit patterns the system must be able to record at twice the transition density of NRZI.

Computer-compatible magnetic tape units are available with tape drives of 6250 bytes per inch (246 bytes per millimeter). They have nine tracks, where eight bits are data and one bit is parity. Each track is recorded by a technique called group-coded record (GCR), which uses a 0.3-in. (7.5-mm) record gap. Every eighth byte in conjunction with the parity track is used for detection and correction of all single-bit errors. Thus, GCR offers inherently greater reliability because of its coding scheme and error-correction capability. It does, however, involve much more complex circuitry.

The on-line capacity is strictly a function of the number of tape drives that one controller can handle (eight is typical). A 2400-ft (730-m) nine-track magnetic tape at 6250 bytes per inch (246 bytes per millimeter) provides a capacity of approximately 10^9 bits, depending on record and block sizes.

Cassettes and cartridges. The most frequently used magnetic tape memory devices for microcomputer systems are cassette and cartridge tape units. Both provide very low-cast storage, although their access times are long and their overall throughput performance is not as great as that of floppy disks. Cassette and cartridge units both use ¼-in. (6-mm) magnetic tape.

The digital cassette transport was orginally an outgrowth of an audio cassette unit. Unfortunately, the very low-cost audio-designed transport did not meet the endurance needs of true digital computer applications. There are two basic design approaches to digital cassette transports: capstan drive and reel-to-reel drive. Capstan tape drives are better for maintaining long-term and short-term tape-speed accuracy, while reel-to-reel transports have better mechanical reliability.

During the 1960s the first true digital tape cartridge was developed. With the cassette, a capstan must penetrate the plastic case containing the tape in order to make contact. There is no such penetration system with the cartridge because the transport capstan simply drives an elastomer belt by pressing against the rim of the belt's drive wheel. This simplicity eliminates a major source of tape damage and oxide flaking.

Cassettes have undergone evolution as a digital medium, and capacity has increased to 10 megabytes, at a density of 5120 bits per inch (202 bits per millimeter). Transfer rates are 24 kilobits per second at 30 in. (0.75 m) per second, or 72 kilobits per second at 90 in. (2.25 m) per second. The ¼-in. (6-mm) streaming tape cartridge has a typical capacity range of 10 to 30 megabytes, with some available with over 50 megabytes. Transfer rates are 30 to 90 kilobits per second, at densities of from 6400 to 10,000 bits per inch (252 to 394 bits per millimeter).

Half-inch (12.5-mm) tape is also used for back-up for microcomputer hard disk systems. Configured to standard microcomputer packaging sizes, these give 50-megabyte capacity in 5¼-in. (133-mm) form, and 300 megabytes in 8-in. (200-mm) form.

MASS STORAGE TAPE SYSTEMS

With the gradual acceptance of virtual memory and sophisticated operating systems, a significant operational problem arose with computer systems, particularly the large-scale installations. The expense and attendant delays and errors of humans storing, mounting, and demounting tape reels at the command of the operating system began to become a problem. Cartridge storage facilities are designed to alleviate this problem.

Their common attributes are: capacity large enough to accommodate a very large data base on-line; access times between those of movable-head disks and tapes; and operability, without human intervention, under the strict control of the operating system. The cartridge storage facility is included within the virtual address range. All such configurations mechanically extract from a bin, mount on some sort of tape transport, and replace in a bin, following reading or writing, a reel or cartridge of magnetic tape.

Cartridge storage systems are hardware devices that need operating system and data-base software in order to produce a truly integrated, practical hardware-software system. Users require fast access to their files, and thus there is a definite need to queue up (stage) files from the cartridge storage device onto the disks. The data-base software must function efficiently to make this happen. In general, users base their storage device selection on the file sizes involved and the number of accesses per month. Magnetic tape units are used for very large files accessed seldom or infrequently. Mass-storage devices are for intermediate file sizes and access frequencies. Disk units are used for small files or those which are accessed often.

In practice, most users have been satisfied with tapes and disks, and have not chosen to install mass storage systems. During the 1970s, two basic kinds were delivered, although some others were built and installed in the earlier years. In different ways, these units combine the low cost of tape as a storage medium with the operating advantages of on-line access. One is a mechanical selection and mounting unit to load and unload tape reels onto and off standard magnetic tape units; another is a mechanical selection and accessing unit to operate with special honeycomb short-tape units. The first type (sometimes called automated tape libraries) eliminated manual tape-mounting operations. The main objective of the short-tape honeycomb cartridge system is to improve access time. The shorter tape (770 in. or 20 m, versus 2400 ft or 730 m) results in better access time. Operationally, the honeycomb cartridge tape system and the mechanical standard tape-mounting units are capable of handling 100 to 300 cartridge or tape loads per hour.

The first type of fully automated tape library uses standard magnetic tape (½ in. or 12.5 mm wide). Under computer control, this equipment automatically brings the tapes from storage, mounts them on tape drives, dismounts the tapes when the job is completed, and returns them to storage. Accessing up to 150 reels per hour, this unit can store up to 7000 standard tapes or 8000 thin-line reels in a lockable self-contained library that can service up to 32 tape drives and that can interface with up to four computers.

The honeycomb cartridge storage system uses a storage component called a data cartridge. Housed in honeycomb storage compartments, these 2 × 4 in. (50 × 100 mm) plastic cartridges can each hold up to 50,000,000 bytes of information on 770 in.(20 m) of magnetic tape approximately 3 in. (75 mm) wide. Whenever information from a cartridge is needed by the computer, a mechanism selects the desired cartridge and transports it to one of up to eight reading stations. There the data are read out and transferred to the staging disk drives. *See* COMPUTER; DATA-PROCESSING SYSTEMS; DIGITAL COMPUTER.

Bibliography. R. Brechtlein, Comparing disc technologies, *Datamation*, 24(1):130–150, January 1978; S. Chi, Advances in computer mass storage technology, *IEEE Comput.*, 19(5):60–74, May 1982; M. Elphick, Disk and tape memory systems, *Comput. Des.*, 22(1):85–126, January 1983; A. H. Eschenfelder, *Magnetic Bubble Technology*, 1980; E. R. Hnatek, *1982 Semiconductor Memories: An Update*, 1982; T. Moran, New developments in floppy disks, *Byte Mag.*, 8(3):68–82, March 1983; M. Plesset, Future developments in disc storage, *Data Process.*, 25(8):28–30, October 1983; R. M. White, Disk-storage technology, *Sci. Amer.*, 2432:(1)138–148, August 1980.

SEMICONDUCTOR MEMORIES
DAVID BURSKY

Devices for storing digital information that are fabricated by using integrated circuit technology. Semiconductor memories are widely used to store programs and data in almost every digital system. Initially developed as a replacement for magnetic core memories, which were used as the main computer storage memory, semiconductor memories started to appear in the early 1970s and have almost totally replaced core memories as the main computer memory elements.

Many different types of semiconductor memories are used in computer systems to perform various functions—bulk data storage, program storage, temporary storage, and cache (or intermediate) storage. Almost all of the memories are a form of random-access memory (RAM), where any storage location can be accessed in the same amount of time. However, there are many different types of RAMs, the most frequently used of which is the writable and readable memory that is simply referred to as a RAM.

Read/write RAMs. Although the RAM acronym indicates the random-access capability, it is a misnomer since almost all semiconductor memories except for a few specialty types can be randomly accessed. A more appropriate name for the memory would be a read/write RAM to indicate that data can be written into the memory as well as be read out of it.

Dynamic and static types. Even within this one class of memory, there are finer subdivisions. Basically there are two different types of read/write RAMs—dynamic and static. The RAM type refers to the structure of the actual storage circuit used to hold each data bit (the cell structure) within the memory chip. A dynamic memory uses a storage cell based on a transistor and capacitor combination, in which the digital information is represented by a charge stored on each of the capacitors in the memory array. The memory gets the name "dynamic" from the fact that the capacitors are imperfect and will lose their charge unless the charge is repeatedly replenished (refreshed) on a regular basis (every few milliseconds). If refreshed, the information will remain until intentionally changed or the power to the memory is shut off. Static memories, in contrast, do not use a charge-storage technique; instead, they use either four or six transistors to form a flip-flop for each cell in the array. Once data are loaded into the flip-flop storage elements, the flip-flop will indefinitely remain in that state until the information is intentionally changed or the power to the memory circuit is shut off.

In addition to static and dynamic RAMs, there is an attempt to combine both technologies, thus merging the high storage density of dynamic memory cells with the simplicity of use of static RAMs. Referred to as pseudostatic or pseudodynamic RAMs, these memories include circuits on the chip to automatically provide the refresh signals needed by the dynamic cells in the memory array. Since the signals do not have to be supplied by the external system, the memory appears to function like a static RAM.

Redundancy. As memory chips increase in storage capacity, manufacturing defects can often cause several storage cells to fail and thus render the chip useless. To counter that problem and thus improve production yield, many manufacturers have incorporated redundant storage cells that can be swapped into the memory array during unpackaged chip testing via the blowing of electrical fuses or the use of a laser to burn away microscopic fuses. Most static and dynamic RAMs now incorporate some degree of redundancy, and all memory types except the read-only memories can include a small number of redundant cells as a hedge against defects.

Capacity. In the early 1970s, dynamic memories with a capacity (density) of 1024 bits per chip were introduced. Improvements in semiconductor processing and circuit design have made practical an increase in density, first to 4096 bits on a chip, then to 16,384 bits, and in 1980 to 65,536 bits (often rounded off to 64 kbits). Dynamic RAMs with 262,144 bits (the 256k dynamic RAM) first appeared in 1982 and went into mass production in 1984. The first samples of 1-megabit dynamic RAMs (1,048,576 bits) were announced in 1984, and these memories went into limited production in 1985, thus yielding an increase in memory capacity of three orders of magnitude in about 15 years.

Until 1983, all dynamic RAMs were organized with word widths of 1 bit and depths of 1024, 4096, 16,384, and 65,536 words (often expressed as 1-k × 1, 4-k × 1, and so forth). However, 1983 saw new directions develop as dynamic RAMs with 4- and 8-bit-wide word widths were introduced at densities of 64 kbits. Application-specific memories that offer features such as special memory-access modes, multiple ports, and shift registers to improve memory performance in such systems as high-speed video displays also appeared. The diversification of architecture has continued with the announcement of 1-, 4-, and 8-bit-wide versions of 256-kbit and 1-megabit dynamic memories. Additionally, unique functions such as on-chip parity generation and checking for 8-k × 9 and 32-k × 9 chips were introduced in 1986.

Static memories require more complex structures for each cell, and thus cannot pack as many cells on a chip. They have typically lagged behind dynamic memories in density by a factor of four. For example, at the time the 1024-bit dynamic memory was introduced, static memories had densities of 256 bits per chip. In 1980, when the 64-kbit dynamic RAM was introduced, static densities were just reaching 16,384 bits on a chip. And, in 1983, as samples of the 256k dynamic RAM appeared, 64-kbit static RAMs were in limited production. The first 256-kbit static RAMs were announced in 1984, and went into limited production in 1985.

Additionally, static RAMs include special features to improve their versatility in various applications. One such feature is a reset capability that returns all bits to a "zero" state, while another is a "shadow" register used during system diagnostics to aid in troubleshooting.

Nonvolatile memories. There are many other forms of semiconductor memories in use—mask-programmable read-only memories (ROMs), fuse-programmable read-only memories (PROMs), ultraviolet-erasable programmable read-only memories (UV EPROMs), electrically alterable read-only memories (EAROMs) electrically erasable programmable read-only memories (EEPROMs), and nonvolatile static RAMs (NV RAMs). All of these memory types are also randomly accessible, but their main distinguishing feature is that once information has been loaded into the storage cells, the information stays there even if the power is shut off.

ROM. The first of these memory types, the ROM, is programmed by the memory manufacturer during the actual device fabrication. Here, though, there are two types of ROMs; one is called last-mask or contact-mask programmable, and the other is often called a ground-up design. In the last-mask type of ROM, the final mask used in the fabrication process determines the connections to the internal transistors. The connections, in turn, determine the data pattern that will be read out when the cell is accessed. The ground-up type of ROM is designed from the bottom up—all fabrication masks used in the multiple mask process are custom-generated.

Last-mask ROMs are theoretically less area-efficient (the final chip size is larger than for a ground-up design), and thus tend to cost slightly more since chip area is directly related to price. However, they offer a rapid turnaround time (the time it takes for a user to obtain finished and programmed devices from the manufacturer from the time the code pattern was provided to the manufacturer by the user), since all circuits can be premanufactured up to the next-to-last mask step. Typically, ground-up designs offer lower cost and slightly higher performance, since they are more area-efficient. However, ROMs require that the user make a commitment to a specific code pattern or place an order for a large number of devices to obtain the low unit cost.

ROMs can be had with capacities of up to 1 megabit, with almost all chips available with 8-bit word widths, which, at the largest size, results in a 128-k × 8 structure. The increased use of 16- and 32-bit microprocessors, however, has moved ROMs toward 16-bit-wide word organizations, and chips with such structures have been sampled at the 1-megabit level. Additionally, at that density the cost of manufacturing the chip and the manufacturing losses due to imperfections that destroy stored data bits require that some method to correct bad bits be used. Thus, ROMs with built-in error detection and correction circuits have been put into limited production. One design even goes so far as to provide 100% redundancy: for every bit there are two memory cells, each storing the same data. If one cell fails, the other cell takes over. However, this makes the size of the chip extremely large and is not a very economical or practical approach. SEE MICROPROCESSOR.

Fuse PROM. As an alternative to the mask-programmable memories, semiconductor manufacturers developed all the other programmable memory types to permit the users to program the memories themselves and order as few as they want, even a single device. The first of the user-programmable devices was the fuse PROM. Offered in standard sizes ranging from a few hundred bits to over 64,000 bits, the fuse-programmable memories are one-time programmable memories—once the information is programmed in, it cannot be altered. There are basically two types of fuse-programmable memories; one type uses microscopic fuse links that are blown open to define a logic one or zero for each cell in the memory array; the other type of fuse programming causes metal to short out base-emitter transistor junctions to program the ones or zeros into the memory.

Reprogrammable memories. The birth of the microprocessor in the early 1970s brought with it new memory types that offered a feature never before available—reusability. Information stored in the memory could be erased—in the case of the UV EPROM, by an ultraviolet light, and in the case of the EAROM, EEPROM, or NV RAM, by an electrical signal—and then the circuit could be reprogrammed with new information that could be retained indefinitely. All of these memory types are starting to approach the ideal memory element for the computer, an element that combines the flexibility of the RAM with the permanence of the ROM when power is removed. At the present time there are still some limiting factors in the various memory types that must be overcome before that ideal goal can be attained.

The ideal memory circuit should allow unlimited read and write operations without any unusual voltage levels or extra circuitry. At present, UV EPROMs require an external ultraviolet lamp to erase the stored information and a programming voltage of about 21 V (for old-generation UV EPROMs) and about 12.5 V for the newer versions. To operate in their read-only mode, the UV EPROMs just require a 5-V supply. The older EAROMs and EEPROMs (pre-1983) also required storage-control voltages of several times the read-mode supply voltage, and in many cases the EAROMs and EEPROMs also required external support logic to minimize the amount of control time that the host processor in a system had to devote to storing data into the memory. However, some of the newer EAROMs and EEPROMs have been able to place circuitry on the same chip to boost the standard 5-V supply voltage up to the level necessary to program or erase the cell, as well as provide the other necessary support functions. Coming closest to the ideal specification is the NV RAM, a memory that combines a static RAM with a nonvolatile memory array, so that for every stored bit there are two memory cells, one of which is volatile and the other nonvolatile. During normal system operation, the NV RAM uses the volatile memory array, but when it receives a special store signal, information held in the RAM area is transferred into the nonvolatile section. Thus the RAM section provides unlimited read and write operations, while the nonvolatile section provides back-up when power is removed.

However, the EAROM, EEPROM, and NV RAM suffer one common failing that keeps them from reaching the ideal—they wear out. The electrical process used to store information in the nonvolatile array causes a steady deterioration in the ability of the memory to retain data for a guaranteed time period. Currently available capabilities range from about 10,000 to over 1,000,000 write cycles, but many times that number are needed for general-purpose use.

To overcome the limited number of storage cycles possible with the true nonvolatile memory technologies, ultralow-power-consumption static RAMs (with a standby current of just 1 microampere or less) have been combined with some power control circuitry and a button-type long-life battery in a single package. When built into a system, this form of NV RAM operates with the characteristics of a static RAM when the system supplies power—fast access times and unlimited reads and writes. However, when the power supply line drops below a preset level, the control circuitry in the memory package detects the drop, disables the memory's ability to store new data, and then switches over to the built-in battery to keep the stored data alive until main power returns.

Semiconductor technology. The semiconductor technology used to fabricate all the different memory types spans the entire range of available commercial processes, as summarized in the **table**. The dynamic memory, originally introduced in a p-channel MOS process (PMOS),

Summary of memory types and technologies

Memory type	Maximum capacity[a] commercially available 1985–1986	Relative access speed[b]	Programmability	Technology
Dynamic RAM	1 Mbit	Fast/medium	Read/write, volatile	CMOS or NMOS
	1 Mbit	Fastest[c]	Read/write, volatile	CMOS or NMOS
Static RAM	256 kbit	Fast	Read/write, volatile	CMOS
	64 kbit	Fastest	Read/write, volatile	Bipolar, ECL
	4 kbit	Fast	Read/write, volatile	Bipolar, TTL
	16 kbit	Fast	Read/write, volatile	NMOS
	1 kbit	Fastest	Read/write, volatile	Gallium arsenide
ROM	1 Mbit	Fast/medium	Factory mask	CMOS or NMOS
PROM	4 kbit	Fastest	Fuse, one-time electrical	Bipolar ECL
	64 kbit	Fast	Fuse, one-time electrical	Bipolar TTL
	16 kbit	Medium	Fuse, one-time electrical	CMOS
	32 kbit	Fast	UV EPROM cell, one-time electrical	CMOS (floating gate)
UV EPROM	1 Mbit	Fast	Ultraviolet erasable, electrical programmability	CMOS or NMOS (floating gate)
	512 kbit	Fast	Ultraviolet erasable, electrical programmability	NMOS (floating gate)
EEPROM (and EAROM)	256 kbit	Fast	Electrically erasable	CMOS or NMOS (electron tunneling)
	64 kbit	Fast	Electrically erasable	MNOS (electron tunneling)
NV RAM	4 kbit	Fast	Read/write nonvolatile	NMOS (electron tunneling)
	64 kbit	Fast	Read/write nonvolatile[e]	CMOS (battery backup)

[a] 1 kbit = 1024 bits, 1 Mbit = 1,048,576 bits.
[b] Fastest ≤ 35 ns; 36 ns ≤ fast ≤ 150 ns; 151 ns ≤ medium ≤ 350 ns.
[c] Special static column or rapid serial-access mode.
[d] Limited life read/write capability.
[e] Unlimited read/write but limited nonvolatile storage capability.
[f] Built-in lithium battery allows unlimited storage and read/write operations.

has been upgraded through the use of higher performing n-channel MOS (NMOS) and, subsequently complementary MOS (CMOS) processes. The use of CMOS memory structures (the combination of both p- and n-channel devices to form the memory cells and supporting logic on the memory chip) permits a reduction of orders of magnitude in the standby power consumption, and often a reduction by a factor of two to five in the active power requirements of a memory chip, as compared to its NMOS equivalent. Typical dynamic RAMs provide access times that range from well under 100 nanoseconds per word for the fastest standard versions, while special operating modes such as page, serial nibble, and static column modes provide access to data at speeds as fast as 10 ns/bit. Speed selections with access times as slow as 300 ns are also available.

The NMOS static RAM has given way to CMOS at densities above 16 kbits, and in many cases even at densities below 16 kbits. Commercial devices with access times as fast as 15 ns have appeared in CMOS at capacities of 1024 bits. Prototype 256-kbit CMOS static RAMs have attained sub-50-ns access times. RAM organizations with word widths of 1, 4, and 8 bits are commonly available at most density levels. Slower versions of these memories, with access times stretching out to 400 ns, are also available.

For even faster access times, bipolar technologies such as emitter coupled logic (ECL) and forms of Schottky transistor-transistor logic (STTL) permit RAMs with access times of 3 to 5 ns to be fabricated. However, bipolar technologies consume the most power, and the speed is thus obtained at the expense of power—many of the bipolar RAMs consume two to three times the power of the NMOS memories. Another technology that has been applied to semiconductor memories is gallium arsenide. The nature of the material permits faster electron movement, and thus faster access times; several 1024-bit memories with access times of 1 to 2 ns have been realized.

A move toward CMOS technology for most other memory types has also taken place. UV EPROMs, ROMs, PROMS, and the various EAROMs, EEPROMs, and NV RAMs are available in NMOS and CMOS processes at various density levels. Access times for the various nonvolatile memories range from less than 100 ns in their read modes to about 10 ms when data are stored. Most of the ROMs and UV EPROMs are available only with 8-bit word widths, while PROMs are commonly offered in 4- and 8-bit-wide organizations. The various electrically alterable memories, however, offer a diverse choice of capacities and architectures that include devices with serial access modes to reduce the number of package pins. SEE COMPUTER STORAGE TECHNOLOGY; INTEGRATED CIRCUITS; LOGIC CIRCUITS.

Bibliography. C. Brown, Memories: More bits and more smarts, *Electr. Eng. Times*, no. 317, pp. 1, 16, February 18, 1985; D. Bursky, ISCCC: Digital circuits, *Electr. Des.*, 33(4):121–136, February 21, 1985; D. Bursky, Nonvolatile memories en route to higher density, speed and reliability, *Electr. Des.*, 32(17):123–144, August 23, 1984; B. C. Cole, Memories dominate ISCCC, *Electr. Week*, 58(6):51–60, February 11, 1985; T. Costlow, Fast static memories, *Electr. Des.*, 33(22):223–230, September 19, 1985; R. Sommers, Variety, versatility make nonvolatile memory difficult to forget, *Electr. Des.*, 33(13):78–96, June 6, 1985.

MAGNETIC BUBBLE MEMORY
J. EGIL JULIUSSEN

A memory storage technology which uses localized magnetized regions to store information. Magnetic bubble memory (MBM) is the integrated-circuit analogy to rotating magnetic memories such as disks and tapes.

Principles of operation. Magnetic bubble memories employ materials that are easily magnetized in one direction but are hard to magnetize in the orthogonal direction. The most commonly used materials are magnetic garnets which are deposited on a nonmagnetic substrate to form the basis of a bubble memory chip. A thin film of one of these materials, with the easy direction perpendicular to the surface, will allow only two natural directions of magnetization—up or down in the easy direction. When no external magnetic field is applied, the magnetic garnet film forms serpentine patterns of upward and downward magnetization. When a magnetic field is applied by sandwiching the film between two permanent magnets, cylindrical-shaped magnetic domains are formed in place of the serpentine structure. These cylinders are called magnetic bubbles and have a magnetization pointing in the opposite direction of the surrounding area. In effect, magnetic bubbles are magnetic islands in a magnetic sea of opposite magnetic polarity.

Storage locations. To make a memory of these magnetic bubbles, several functions must be performed. A bit of storage is represented as the presence or absence of a bubble at a given storage location. There are several methods of defining the storage locations, but the most common way is to use the chevron patterns shown in **Fig. 1**. These chevrons are made of a soft ferromagnetic material such as permalloy and are deposited on the surface of the magnetic garnet. There can be one bubble for each chevron.

Loop organization. The chevrons also serve as the path for bubble movement when the information is accessed. To organize the bubble memory bits, the chevron patterns are deposited to form loops along which the bubbles can travel. The simplest organization is one single, large loop. The drawback is that the bubbles must travel the entire length of the loop before the information can be retrieved, and this is time-consuming. Most bubble memory chips now use a more sophisticated architecture called the major/minor loop (**Fig. 2**). In these multiple storage loops, the length and the time taken to traverse a minor loop is much smaller than for one major, large loop. The information is retrieved by waiting until the desired bubbles are at the top of the minor loops. At that point one bubble from each minor loop is transferred to the major loop. This "bubble train" traverses the major loop, during which time the information can be read or new information can be substituted. When the bubble train has traveled once around the major loop, all the bubbles are transferred back into the minor loops. The commensurate lengths of the major loops and minor loops are such that the bubble train retains its original position in the minor loops.

Information retrieval. To move the bubbles along the loops, a rotating magnetic field must be generated. For each rotation of the magnetic field each bubble moves synchronously from one chevron to the next. In other words, the magnetic bubbles move within the material, but no physical motion takes place. This is the opposite of what takes place in other magnetic memories such as disks and tapes. Disks and tapes also store information as small magnetized regions. However, to retrieve this information, disks and tapes must physically move the magnetized re-

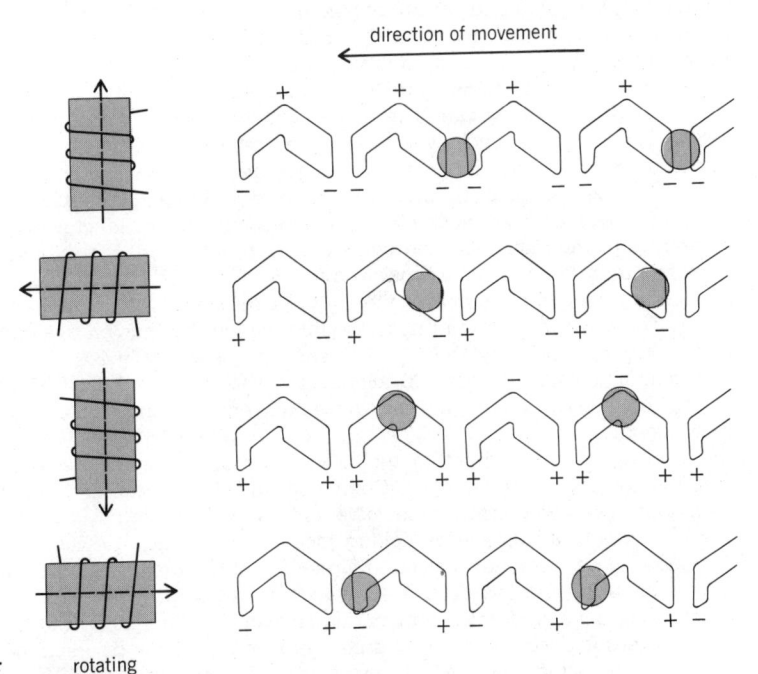

Fig. 1. Movement of magnetic bubbles under pattern of conductive chevrons.

rotating magnetic field

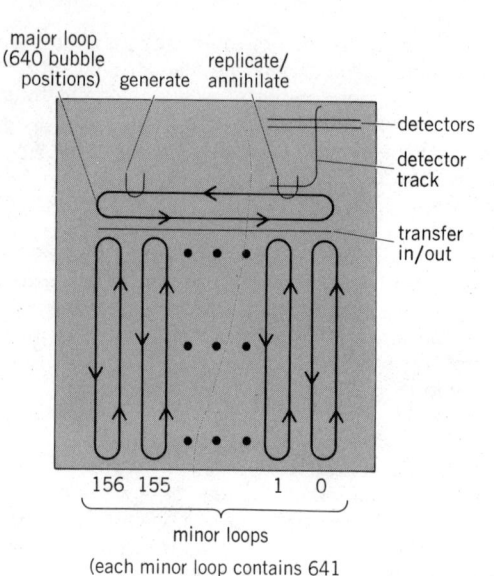

Fig. 2. Diagram of the major/minor loop architecture of a 100,000-bit magnetic bubble memory chip. With multiple storage loops, the time to traverse a minor loop is much reduced as compared with one major, large loop.

Labels on figure: major loop (640 bubble positions); generate; replicate/annihilate; detectors; detector track; transfer in/out; 156 155 ... 1 0; minor loops (each minor loop contains 641 bubble positions; 144 of the 157 minor loops are used)

gions past a read/write head. The "motion" of bubble memories is accomplished by using two orthogonal coils which are wound around the bubble memory chip.

Figure 3 shows the main components and operation of magnetic bubble memories, including the memory chip, the magnetic garnet material where bubbles are formed, the permalloy patterns which guide and control bubble movements, the two coils that power bubble movement, and the two permanent magnets that retain the information when power is removed giving the memory the property of nonvolatility. Various types of interfacing circuitry which are needed to make a complete bubble memory system are also shown.

Technology status. The fundamentals of bubble memories were discovered in the late 1960s. The bubble technology advanced very rapidly thereafter, and today 1,000,000 bits can be stored on a chip which is about 15 mm square. This chip, when enclosed inside two coils and two permanent magnets, is about a 1-in.-square (25-mm-square) package.

Bubble memory manufacturing is similar to semiconductor production. The materials are different, but the manufacturing steps are nearly identical. For this reason, major semiconductor manufacturers, as well as computer companies in the United States and other countries, have invested in the magnetic bubble memory technology.

The average time to retrieve the information depends on the length of the minor loops and speed of bubble memory shifting. The shift rate is typically 100 kHz and this is also the rate of information transfer, that is 100 kilobits per second. The 1,000,000-bit chips have minor loops lengths of about 2000 bits, and this gives an average information access time of approximately 10 milliseconds.

Compared to competing technologies, magnetic bubble memories have many desirable features and few disadvantages. Compared with both disks and floppy disks, magnetic bubble memories have lower access time, lower entry price, smaller physical size, and simpler interfacing, but have the disadvantage of lacking media removability. However, removable bubble memory cartridges have been introduced. Magnetic bubble memories also have the disadvantages of higher bit price and lower transfer rate compared with disks (other than floppy disks). On the other hand, compared with semiconductor memories, magnetic bubble memories have nonvolatility, lower bit price and more bits per chip, but have the disadvantages of higher access time, complex interfacing, and lower transfer rate. The advantages for bubble memories are strongest when a relatively small amount of secondary storage is needed—a few million bits or less. Appli-

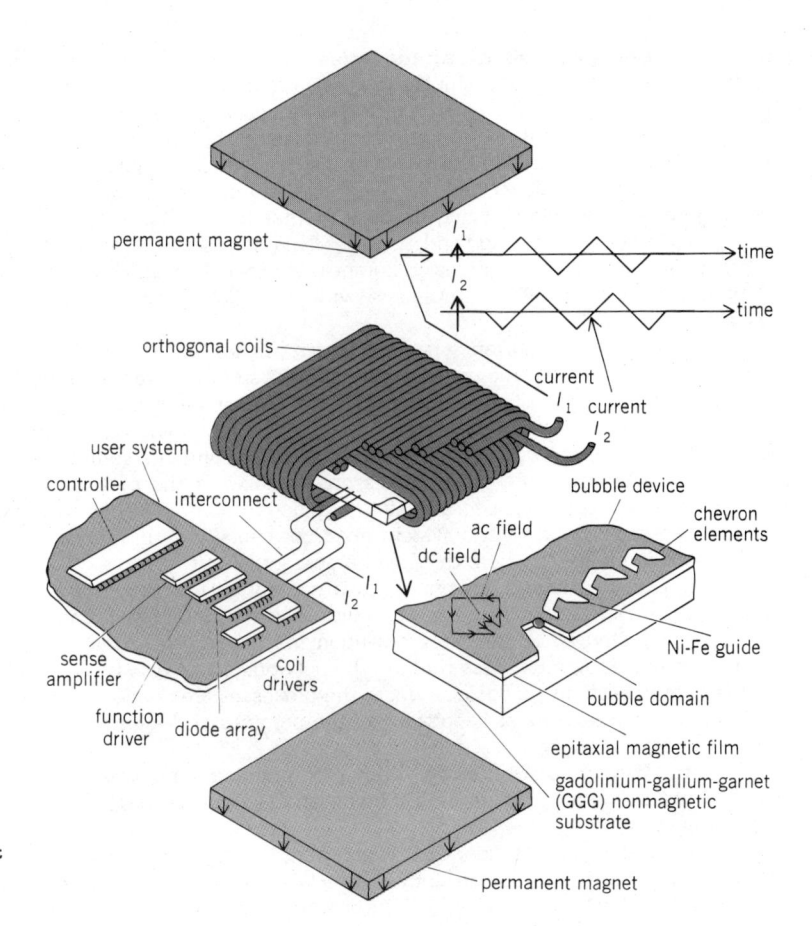

Fig. 3. Principal components and operation that are utilized in magnetic bubble memory.

cation examples are terminals, desk-top computers, computer-controlled machinery, test equipment, and similar microcomputer-based systems. *See* Computer storage technology; Integrated circuits.

Bibliography. H. Chang, *Magnetic Bubble Memory Technology*, 1978; A. H. Eschenfelder, *Magnetic Bubble Technology*, 1980; A. H. Eschenfelder, *Magnetic Bubble Theory*, 1981.

CONCURRENT PROCESSING
Brent T. Hailpern

The conceptually simultaneous execution of more than one sequential program on a computer or network of computers. The individual sequential programs are called processes. Two processes are considered concurrent only if they interact in some way. This interaction may range from cooperation (the exchange of information) to competition for scarce resources (such as the processor, the memory, or a printer). Concurrent processing is achieved on a single computer, that is, on a single processor, by interleaving the execution of the individual processes.

In comparison, distributed processing requires multiple processors for its implementation. According to this definition, all distributed programs are also concurrent programs, but the converse is not true.

Advantages and disadvantages. A common example of concurrent processing is a multiuser operating system, which allows more than one user process to be executed concurrently on the same processor. Many such systems do not allow the processes to communicate directly; they only coordinate the use of shared resources by the processes (for example, the static allocation of memory to the active processes or the dynamic allocation of processors to processes). This form of concurrency allows multiple users to share one processor, which is a necessity for timesharing systems, without having the user programs complicated by codes dealing with the sharing of resources, scheduling, and so forth. This modularity is an advantage of most concurrent systems over sequential systems: different parts of a problem can be relegated to semi-independent processes that will communicate with one another only when necessary. SEE MULTIACCESS COMPUTER.

This form of concurrency has disadvantages as well. The operating system causes an overhead in the use of the processor; an operating system that executes user processes sequentially would spend very little time in allocating the processor's resources or in switching between tasks.

Distributed systems present additional advantages and disadvantages in comparison with centralized concurrent systems. Distributed systems eliminate some of the contention for the processor, because there are more processors available in the system. Furthermore, a centralized system does not lend itself to graceful degradation as does a distributed system. The failure of one processor in a distributed system need not cause the entire system to fail, if the remaining processors can take up where the failed processor left off.

Though distributed systems reduce contention for processors, they create contention for the communication network. In a centralized system, interaction can take place through shared memory protected by some synchronization mechanism; in a distributed system all interaction and communication must pass through the network. There also is a cost for the higher availability of distributed systems, especially where the processes are cooperating closely. Each processor (or its operating system) must keep track of the progress of the other processors in order to recover in the event of a failure.

Specifying concurrency. Many programming languages provide the user with the ability to write concurrent programs. Different languages allow parallelism with different degrees of concurrency.

Languages such as Ada, CSP, Concurrent Pascal, Mesa, and Module provide for statement-level (or procedure-level) concurrency. These languages have either a construct that causes a new process to be initiated, executing some statement or procedure in parallel with the current process, or a construct that causes a set of statements or procedures to be executed in parallel. In either case, the user tells the system what portions of the code will be executed concurrently.

In contrast, some data flow languages provide for operator-level concurrency. In such languages, the program is specified without reference to concurrency; the compiler breaks the program down into its component operations, often as small as add or multiply. When the program executes, all operators can be executed in parallel; an operator can execute as soon as it has received values for all of its input operands. Upon termination it forwards its result to those operators requiring that result as input. SEE DATA FLOW SYSTEMS; PROGRAMMING LANGUAGES.

Communication and synchronization. Interprocess communication invokes two classes of concurrent systems: synchronous and asynchronous. In a synchronous system, all processors work in lockstep; that is, they all execute the same instruction at the same time (on different data). In asynchronous systems each process (and processor) works independently of the others. Asynchronous processes need only synchronize temporarily to exchange information or to request a service. Such synchronization and communication takes place in one of two ways: by reading and writing shared memory or by exchanging messages.

In shared memory systems, processes communicate by modifying shared variables. Such variables contain values, such as the number of free tape drives or the identity of the next process to control the processor. Though shared, these variables must be protected from simultaneous access by multiple processes. The processor hardware usually prevents simultaneous writing of the same memory location (thereby preventing meaningless data from being stored), but that is not enough. Higher-level synchronization is required to prevent interference between processes. Problems arise when one process reads a shared variable, intending to change it, but a second process changes the variable before the first process performs its change. When the first process finally makes its change, the second process's update is lost. It is necessary for a process to be able to gain exclusive access to a variable for more than a read or write. The portion of a program in which a process has exclusive control over shared data is called a critical section. There are many mechanisms for obtaining such protection; one example is the monitor. Monitors protect shared variables by allowing processes to access these variables only through special procedures; only one process may execute a monitor's procedure at a time, thus preventing the destructive interference.

Message-passing systems communicate by send-and receiving messages. Sending a message is more expensive (in terms of computer time and resources) than modifying a shared variable. A message must be built out of the data provided by the sending process, and then copied to the address space of the receiving process. This may entail multiple copies if the data must be passed through intermediate processes and networks. On the other hand, message systems have no shared variables to protect from concurrent interference. There are different types of message-passing systems that depend on whether the sending process must wait until the receiving process actually receives the message, and if so, whether it must wait for a reply.

Bibliography. G. R. Andrews, Synchronizing resources, *ACM Transactions on Programming Languages and Systems*, 3(4):405–430, October 1981; P. G. Ducksbury, *Parallel Array Processing*, 1986; K. Hwang and F. A. Briggs, *Computer Architecture and Parallel Processing*, 1984; R. H. Kuhn and D. A. Padua (eds.), *Tutorial on Parallel Processing*, IEEE Computer Society, 1981; G. J. Lipovski and M. Malek, *Parallel Computing: Theory and Comparisons*, 1987; P. D. Stotts, Jr., A comparative survey of concurrent programming languages, *ACM SIGPLAN Not.*, 17(9):76–87, September 1982.

MULTIPROCESSING
PETER C. PATTON

An organizational technique in which a number of processor units are employed in a single computer system to increase the performance of the system in its application environment above the performance of a single processor. In order to cooperate on a single application or class of applications, the processors share a common resource. Usually this resource is primary memory, and the multiprocessor is called a primary memory multiprocessor. A system in which each processor has a private (local) main memory and shares secondary (global) memory with the others is a secondary memory multiprocessor, sometimes called a multicomputer system because of the looser coupling between processors. The more common multiprocessor systems incorporate only processors of the same type and performance and thus are called homogeneous multiprocessors; however, heterogeneous multiprocessors are also employed. A special case is the attached processor, in which a second processor module is attached to a first processor in a closely coupled fashion so thatthe first can perform input/output and operating system functions, enabling the attached processor to concentrate on the application workload. SEE COMPUTER STORAGE TECHNOLOGY; OPERATING SYSTEM.

Classification. Multiprocessor systems may be classified into four types: single instruction stream, single data stream (SISD); single instruction stream, multiple data stream (SIMD); multiple instruction stream, single data stream (MISD); and multiple instruction stream, multiple data stream (MIMD). Systems in the MISD category are rarely built. The other three architectures may be distinguished simply by the differences in their respective instruction cycles:

In an SISD architecture there is a single instruction cycle; operands are fetched serially into a single processing unit before execution. Sequential processors fall into this category.

An SIMD architecture also has a single instruction cycle, but multiple sets of operands may be fetched to multiple processing units and may be operated upon simultaneously within a single instruction cycle. Multiple-functional-unit, array, vector, and pipeline processors are in this category. SEE SUPERCOMPUTER.

In an MIMD architecture, several instruction cycles may be active at any given time, each independently fetching instructions and operands into multiple processing units and operating on them in a concurrent fashion. This category includes multiple processor systems in which each processor has its own program control, rather than sharing a single control unit.

MIMD systems can be further classified into throughput-oriented systems, high-availability systems, and response-oriented systems. The goal of throughput-oriented multiprocessing is to obtain high throughput at minimal computing cost (subject to fail-soft equipment redundancy requirements) in a general-purpose computing environment by maximizing the number of independent computing jobs done in parallel. The techniques employed by multiprocessor operating systems to achieve this goal take advantage of an inherent processing versus input/output balance in the workload to produce balanced, uniform loading of system resources with scheduled response.

High-availability multiprocessing systems are generally interactive, often with never-fail real-time on-line performance requirements. Such application environments are usually centered on a common data base and are almost always input/output-limited rather than computer-limited. Tasks are not independent but are often interdependent at the data-base level. The operating system goal is to maximize the number of cooperating tasks done in parallel. Such systems may also process multiple independent jobs in a background mode. The additional hardware redundancy in a fault-tolerant system over a general-purpose multiprocessor can be considered a trade-off against software complexity and the time required for software check-pointing in a sequential mainframe system. SEE FAULT-TOLERANT SYSTEMS; REAL-TIME SYSTEMS.

The goal of response-oriented multiprocessing (or parallel processing) is to minimize system response time for computational demands. Applications for such systems are naturally computer-intensive, and many such applications can be decomposed into multiple tasks or processes to run concurrently on multiple processors. In the past, successful SIMD and MIMD parallel processors were often special-purpose machines dedicated to a single class of scientific or real-time signal processing applications. The interest in high-performance, low-cost computers able to handle combined numeric, symbolic, and signal processing tasks concurrently, for so-called fifth-generation applications, together with the availability of low-cost very large-scale integrated-circuit (VLSI) microprocessors has rekindled interest in response-oriented multiprocessing. SEE CONCURRENT PROCESSING; INTEGRATED CIRCUITS; MICROPROCESSOR.

Throughput-oriented multiprocessing. The performance of a classical shared-memory multiprocessor is limited by the so-called bandwidth of its shared memory (the total data transfer capacity of the memory bus). Access conflicts further reduce effective bandwidth and thus overall system performance. Studies on early multiprocessors showed interesting results on throughput loss as a function of effective memory bandwidth. For example, if a single processor had one unit of throughput, its dual processor had only 10% less throughput than two single processor systems, and a triple processor had 20% less throughput than three individual systems in a multicomputer rather than multiprocessor configuration. This was not a high penalty to pay for fail-soft function in an airline reservation system with 3000 remote agent terminals. Multiprocessors now exhibit similar performance characteristics up to six processors, that is, up to their effective memory bandwidth performance limit which has been enhanced by a higher degree of memory interleaving over earlier multiprocessor systems. Operating system software provides the key fail-soft capability in a throughput-oriented multiprocessor. The performance cost of software check-pointing is higher in sequential processors than in a multiprocessor. Since system protective tasks are redundant, the more processors the better, up to the effective bandwidth limits of the system's shared resources.

High-availability multiprocessing. Fault-tolerant multiprocessor systems were a natural development from throughput-oriented multiprocessor systems. While the trade-off that achieves fault tolerance is a hardware one—that is, more hardware units are used in order to achieve greater system availability—the technology employed is primarily a software one. Lower-level hardware redundancy is used in many such systems, but its successful deployment in applications is still a software issue. The basic requisite for a highly available system in most applications is that each major hardware and software component must at least be duplicated. The system requires two or more processors, two paths connecting the processors, and two paths from the processors to the data base. The system's disk controllers and communication controllers must be multiported, so that they may be connected to multiple processors. A high-availability database-oriented system requires five essential software ingredients: a network-communication subsystem, a data-communication subsystem, a data-base manager, a transaction manager, and an operating system. The network communication subsystem supports interprocess communication within a cluster of locally distributed processors. If the highly available system is also a node on a geographically distributed system, the communication subsystem must also support internode communication. SEE DATA-BASE MANAGEMENT SYSTEMS; DATA COMMUNICATIONS.

Response-oriented multiprocessing. The ideal performance characteristic for an N-processor system, on which a given problem could be partitioned into N similar tasks, would be a linear relationship between performance (the rate at which the system can solve a problem, in units of single-processor performance) versus the number of processors. M. Minsky was skeptical of this ideal, conjecturing that for large N the best hope was for $\log_2 N$ performance. In 1967 G. Amdahl suggested Amdahl's (second) law, stating that if a computer has two speeds of operation the slower mode will dominate performance even if the faster mode is infinitely fast. This leads to a $N/\log N$ performance in a multiprocessor performing a single application in multitask mode.

Minsky's conjecture now seems much too pessimistic, and parallel processing performance gains even greater than those predicted by Amdahl's law have become the goal. A sophisticated technique has been developed for the extraction of parallelism from FORTRAN DO-loops that can routinely exceed Amdahl's law for SIMD machines. While 100% efficiency is probably not attainable, many highly tailored applications based on careful manual extraction of parallelism have achieved efficiency ratings in the 80–90% range. SEE PROGRAMMING LANGUAGES.

Most computer engineers and architects see a high degree of multiprocessing or parallel processing as essential for achieving performance requirements for future computer systems for scientific computation, for fifth-generation or artificial intelligence (AI) applications, and for dedicated and embedded multiprocessors in control or automation systems. It is also widely accepted that a new parallel application and programming technology must be developed to make effective use of multiprocessors having hundreds or thousands of processors. The promise of high-performance systems made up of low-cost high-volume components (for example, microprocessor chips) rather than high-cost low-volume components draws computer architects and applications specialists toward the development of parallel processing technology. SEE ARTIFICIAL INTELLIGENCE; COMPUTER SYSTEMS ARCHITECTURE; DIGITAL COMPUTER; EMBEDDED SYSTEMS.

Bibliography. G. M. Amdahl, Validity of single processor approach to achieving large scale computing capabilities, *AFIPS Conf. Proc.*, 30:483–485, 1967; P. H. Enslow, Jr. (ed.), *Multiprocessors and Parallel Processing*, 1974; M. J. Flynn, Some computer organizations and their effectiveness, *IEEE CT*, 21(9): 948–960, 1972; M. T. Heath (ed.), *Hypercube Microprocessors*, 1986; M. A. Marsan et al., *Performance Evaluation of Multiprocessor Systems*, 1986; P. C. Patton, Multiprocessors: Architecture and applications, *IEEE Comput.*, June 1985.

DATA FLOW SYSTEMS
TILAK AGERWALA

An alternative to conventional programming languages and architectures, in which values rather than value containers are dealt with, and all processing is achieved by applying functions to values to produce new values. These systems can realize large amounts of parallelism (present in many applications) and effectively utilize very large-scale-integration (VLSI) technology.

Basic concepts. Data flow systems use an underlying execution model which differs substantially from the conventional one. The model deals with values, not names of value containers. There is no notion of assigning different values to an object which is held in a global, updatable memory location. A statement such as $X := B + C$ in a data flow language is only syntactically similar to an assignment statement. The meaning of $X := B + C$ in data flow is to compute the value $B + C$ and bind this value to the name X. Other operators can use this value by referring to the name X, and the statement has a precise mathematical meaning defining X. This definition remains constant within the scope in which the statement occurs. Languages with this property are sometimes referred to as single assignment languages. The second property of the model is that all processing is achieved by applying functions to values to produce new values. The inputs and results are clearly defined, and there are not side effects. Languages with this property are called applicative. Value-oriented, applicative languages do not impose any sequencing constraints in addition to the basic data dependencies present in the algorithm. Functions must wait for all input values to be computed, but the order in which the functions are evaluated does not affect the final results. There is no notion of a central controller which initiates one statement at a time sequentially. The model described above can be applied to languages and architectures.

Data dependence graphs. The computation specified by a program in a data flow language can be represented as a data dependence graph, in which each node is a function and each arc carries a value. Very efficient execution of a data flow program can be achieved on a stored program computer which has the properties of the data flow model. The machine language for such a computer is a dependence graph rather than the conventional sequence of instructions. There is no program counter in a data flow computer. Instead, a mechanism is provided to detect when an instruction is enabled, that is, when all required input values are present. Enabled instructions, together with input values and destination addresses (for the result), are sent to processing elements. Results are routed to destinations, which may enable other instructions. This mode of execution is called data-driven.

The **illustration** is an example of a machine language program for a data flow computer. Values are carried on tokens which flow on arcs of the graph. The graph in the illustration has

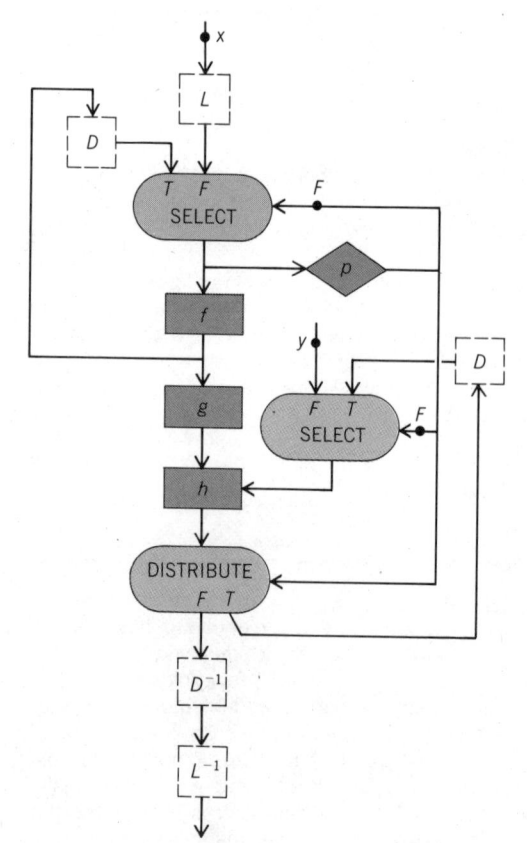

Machine language program for a data flow computer, represented as a data dependence graph.

four tokens initially. Tokens x and y carry input values; two control tokens have the value F. Iteration and conditional execution are achieved using the SELECT and DISTRIBUTE operators. SELECT routes a token to its output arc from either arc T or arc F, depending on the value of the control token on the horizontal input arc. DISTRIBUTE routes a token on its input arc to either the T or F output, depending on the value of the control token. All operators remove the input tokens used and produce a number of identical result tokens, one for each destination. In the illustration the initial output of the upper SELECT is a token with value x, since the control token has a value F. The input tokens x and F are removed, and two output tokens are produced, one for the function f and the other for the predicate p. It is a useful exercise to follow through the execution of the graph assuming that each arc is a first-in–first-out queue and can hold an unbounded number of tokens; and that L, L^{-1}, D, and D^{-1} are the identity operations.

Static and dynamic architectures. The execution model of a data flow computer as described above, though radically different from conventional processing, is the basis for most of the data flow machines now being investigated. Individual differences arise because of the amount of parallelism that can be realized, the mechanisms for detecting and scheduling enabled instructions, and the handling of data structures.

In static architectures, an instruction (like h in the illustration) is represented in memory by a packet which has an operation code, and space to hold two input values and one or more destination addresses. Hardware is provided with the memory to detect the arrival of both input operands. One restriction in static data flow computers is that no arc in the graph can carry more than one token during execution. Control signals are sent from destination nodes to source nodes to indicate the consumption of previous values. Nevertheless, static machines can realize several different forms of parallelism. For example, f and p can be evaluated simultaneously. Also, g and h can be executed in parallel since they form two stages in a pipeline. However, one form of parallelism cannot be realized. Assume that f and h are simple functions which compute very fast and that g is relatively slow. If the single-token-per-arc limitation is removed, then several tokens would accumulate at the input of g and the possibility of invoking multiple, simultaneous instantiations of g would arise. Dynamic data flow architectures can realize this form of parallelism.

Dynamic data flow architectures allow multiple tokens per arc. A token carries a value and a label. The label specifies a context, an iteration number, and a destination address. Each instruction knows its successors and sets the destination field of the result token appropriately. In addition, the L, D, D^{-1}, and L^{-1} operators (ignored so far in the illustration) modify the context and iteration number. The L operator creates a new context by stacking the previous context and iteration number, and also sets the new iteration number to 1. The D operator increments the iteration number. The D^{-1} operator resets the iteration number to 1, and the L^{-1} operator restores the old context and iteration number (stacked by L). Dynamic data flow computers use an associative memory to hold tokens which are waiting for their partners to be produced. This mechanism is used to bring together tokens with identical labels. When this event occurs, the destination instruction is fetched and, together with the input values, is sent to a processing element. On completion, result tokens are produced with appropriate values. With this mechanism, simultaneous evaluations of g are possible. Since h may not be associative, successive evaluations of h must proceed in the specified order. The token-labeling mechanism guarantees this, irrespective of the order in which the simultaneous evaluations of g are completed. The token-labeling concept can be extended to handle recursion and generalized procedure calls.

Data-driven and demand-driven execution. In data-driven execution, the sources of a node N produce the input values and execution of N is triggered when all input values are produced. With the second execution rule, called demand-driven, nothing happens until a result is demanded at a primary output of a graph. The corresponding node then demands its inputs. These demands flow opposite to the arcs in the graph until the primary inputs are reached. A node executes only if its result has been demanded and its own demands satisfied. An advantage of this approach is that the computations which occur are exactly those that are required. This rule is also called lazy evaluation.

Comparison of conventional systems. Conventional languages and architectures are characterized by the existence of a sequential controller and a global addressable memory which holds objects. Languages such as Fortran and PL/1 allow aliasing and side effects and impose sequencing constraints not present in the original algorithm. The compile step attempts to recover the parallelism obscured by the language and to generate a data dependence graph. Depending on the parallelism to be exposed, this can be a complex step. Code is then generated for a scalar processor, a vector processor, or a multiprocessor consisting of several uniprocessors sharing storage. Each alternative is examined below.

In uniprocessors, sequential decoding of instructions is necessary to place appropriate interlocks on storage and thereby guarantee the logical correctness of results. Techniques such as overlapping, pipelining, and out-of-sequence execution are used to design high-performance processors. However, because of the sequential decode, concurrency can be obtained only in a small window around the program counter. Furthermore, high-performance uniprocessors cannot effectively utilize VLSI technology.

The decoder limitation can be circumvented if a single instruction can initiate multiple operations on a data structure. This leads quite naturally to vector architectures. Portions of a program coded in instructions which have vector operands can be executed at very high speeds, limited only by hardware and memory bandwidth. However, not all applications with parallelism can be vectorized, and very sophisticated compiler analysis is needed to generate vector code automatically from sequential programs.

Conventional multiprocessing can utilize VLSI technology, but the key problem is the execution model with its global updatable memory. Since the processors execute asynchronously, the race conditions which can arise are prevented by embedding synchronization primitives in the code. Usually, the overhead for synchronization is large, and low-level parallelism cannot be realized. The code must be partitioned into relatively large blocks of computation with few synchronizing primitives. Moreover, if large amounts of parallelism are not obtained, the performance of the entire system can be critically dependent on processor-processor and processor-memory communications latency. The current state of development does not support compilation of sequential programs on a multiprocessor system. Also, multiprocessor code with embedded synchronization is extremely difficult to verify.

The complexity of the compile step for both vector and multiprocessor architectures can be reduced by extensions to sequential languages. However, this forces the programmer to consider parallelism explicitly, an added complexity.

Advantages and limitations. Data flow systems can overcome many of the disadvantages of conventional approaches. In principle, all the parallelism in the algorithm is exposed in the program and thus the programmer does not have to deal with parallelism explicitly. Since programs have mathematical properties, verification is simpler, and generation of the dependence graph from the program is a simple step. Systems of large numbers of flow-speed processors are possible, and the approach therefore exploits VLSI technology. If large amounts of parallelism are realized, then processor-memory and processor-processor communications latency is not as critical. Since there are constraints on the production and use of information, protection and security can be more naturally enforced.

Several important problems remain to be solved in data flow systems. The handling of complex data structures as values is inefficient, but there is no complete solution to this problem yet. Data flow computers tend to have long pipelines, and this causes degraded performance if the application does not have sufficient parallelism. Since the programmer does not have explicit control over memory, separate "garbage collection" mechanisms must be implemented. The space-time overheads of managing low levels of parallelism have not been quantified. Thus, though the parallelism is exposed to the hardware, it has not been demonstrated that it can be effectively realized. The machine state is large, and without the notion of a program counter, hardware debugging and maintenance can be complex. Data flow also shares problems with conventional multiprocessor approaches: program decomposition, scheduling of parallel activities, establishment of the potential of utilizing large numbers of slow processors over a variety of applications, and system issues such as storage hierarchy management and disk seek-time limitations.
SEE DIGITAL COMPUTER PROGRAMMING; PROGRAMMING LANGUAGES.
Bibliography. T. Agerwala and Arvind (eds.), Data flow systems, *Computer*, special issue, 15(2):10–69, February 1982; P. C. Treleaven et al., Data-driven and demand-driven computer architecture, *Comput. Surv.*, 14(1):93–143, March 1982.

FAULT-TOLERANT SYSTEMS
JOHN F. MEYER

Systems, predominantly computing and computer-based systems, which tolerate undesired changes in their internal structure or external environment. Such changes, generally referred to as faults, may occur at various times during the evolution of a system, beginning with its specification and proceeding through its utilization. Faults that occur during specification, design, implementation, or modification are called design faults; those occurring during utilization are referred to as operational faults. Design faults are due to mistakes made by humans or by automated design tools in the process of specifying, designing, implementing, or modifying a system. The source of an operational fault may be either internal or external to the system. Internal operational faults are due to physical component failures or human mistakes (when humans are integral parts of the system). External operational faults are due to physical phenomena (temperature, radiation, and so forth) or improper actions on the part of external systems and humans interacting with the system.

Fault prevention and fault tolerance. Both design faults and operational faults affect a system's ability to perform during use, typically resulting in reduced performance or failure. Faults are thus the primary concern in efforts to enhance system reliability (the probability of no system failures during a specified period of time) or, more generally, system performability (the probability distribution of system performance during a specified period of time). In order to satisfy a given reliability or performability requirement, faults can be attacked by two basic approaches: fault prevention and fault tolerance. Fault prevention is the more traditional approach; it comprises techniques which attempt to eliminate faults by avoiding their occurrence (for example, design methodologies, quality control methods, radiation shielding) or by finding and removing them prior to system utilization (for example, testing or verification methods). The use of fault tolerance techniques is based on the premise that a complex system, no matter how carefully designed and validated, is likely to contain residual design faults and to encounter unpreventable operational faults.

Faults and errors. To describe how systems tolerate faults, it is important to distinguish the concepts of fault and error. Relative to a description of desired system behavior at some specified level of abstraction, an error is a deviation from desired behavior caused by a fault. Since desired behavior may be described at different levels of abstraction (for example, the behavior of computer hardware may be described at the circuit level, the logic level, or the register-transfer level), a variety of errors can be associated with a given fault. Moreover, a fault can cause an error at one level without causing an error at another level. A fault is latent until it does cause an error, and it is possible for a fault to remain latent throughout the lifetime of a system without ever causing an error.

The distinction between fault and error is particularly important in the case of design faults. For example, a software design fault (commonly referred to as a bug) may remain latent for years before the software is finally executed in a manner that permits the bug to cause an execution error. The sense in which a system tolerates a fault is typically defined as some form of restriction on the errors caused by that fault. This term is usually used to refer to the prevention of errors at a level that represents the user's view of desired system behavior. Errors at this level are known as system failures and therefore a fault is tolerated if it does not cause a system failure. A system is fault-tolerant if all faults in a specified class of faults are tolerated.

Fault tolerance techniques. A variety of fault tolerance techniques are employed in the design of fault-tolerant systems, particularly fault-tolerant computing systems. Generally, fault tolerance techniques attempt to prevent lower-level errors (caused by faults) from propagating into system failures. By using various types of structural and informational redundancy, such techniques either mask a fault (no errors are propagated to the faulty subsystem's output) or detect a fault (via an error) and then effect a recovery process which, if successful, prevents system failure. In the case of a permanent internal fault, the recovery process usually includes some form of structural reconfiguration (for example, replacement of a faulty subsystem with a spare or use of an alternate program) which prevents the fault from causing further errors.

Typically, a fault-tolerant system design will incorporate a mix of fault tolerance techniques which complement the techniques used for fault prevention. The choice of these techniques and, more generally, the specific nature of the system's hardware and software architecture is highly dependent on both the types of faults anticipated and the reliability or performability requirements imposed by the system's application environment. *See* SOFTWARE ENGINEERING.

Bibliography. A. Avizienis, Fault-tolerant systems, *IEEE Transac. Comput.*, C-25(12):1304–1312, December 1976; T. Anderson and B. Randell (eds.), *Computing Systems Reliability*, 1979; T. Anderson and P. A. Lee, *Fault Tolerance: Principles and Practice*, 1981; D. P. Siewiorek and R. S. Swarz, *The Theory and Practice of Reliable System Design*, 1982.

EMBEDDED SYSTEMS
Roger Allan

Computer systems that cannot be programmed by the user because they are preprogrammed for a specific task and are buried within the equipment they serve. The term derives from the military, where computer systems are generally activated by the flip of a toggle switch or the push of a button. For example, an airplane pilot may wish to turn on the countermeasures equipment with the flip of a switch. There is no need for the pilot to be involved with the computer. The same holds true for a soldier who may direct a ground-to-ground missile against a target tank by the simple push of a button. In both cases, an embedded computer quickly goes to work.

The emergence of extremely small microcomputers on silicon chips about ¼ in. (6 mm) square made the concept of embedded systems for the military all the more desirable. As recently as 1960, it was difficult or impossible to embed a computer the size of a room into equipment which had to fit into, say, an airplane cockpit. The microcomputer changed all that.

The military establishment thus depends on microelectronics technology for the development of ever more sophisticated embedded systems. With very inexpensive microcomputer chips, not one but dozens of computers can be squeezed into a small piece of equipment the size of a lunch box, each preprogrammed to do a specific job. By doing only its own task, each microcomputer can devote its entire computational and analytical powers to that task, making possible extremely powerful military systems. *See Integrated circuits; Microcomputer; Microprocessor.*

VHSIC program. A manifestation of the military's interest in microelectronics technology to further progress in embedded systems is the Department of Defense's Very High Speed Integrated Circuit (VHSIC) program. The VHSIC program provides the military with integrated circuit chips sufficiently advanced to enable the United States to maintain a qualitative superiority in weapons and armaments over its adversaries.

The VHSIC program is spread over four phases, 0 through III. The first three phases were run concurrently. Phase 0 was a 1-year effort to analyze approaches to be employed in phases I and II for the development of very high-speed digital signal–processing integrated circuits, with speeds on the order of 10^{10} Hz and line definitions on the order of 1 micrometer or less. Line definition refers to the smallest dimensions of the various structures that make up the integrated circuit chip.

Phase I, started in 1980, and planned to run for 6 years, has been aimed at the development of a brassboard version of the VHSIC devices that could later be reduced to even smaller sizes on integrated circuit chips.

Phase II will provide a system demonstration of the subsystems constructed in phase I, as well as the capability for improved system performance with higher-performance design concepts. Phase III supplements phases I and II and provides new or alternate technology directions not covered in phases I and II.

Phase I employs integrated circuits with on-the-chip structural geometries of 1.25 μm. Devices made under this phase operate at a minimum clock frequency of 30 MHz and a minimum gate-frequency product of 10^{11} gate-Hz/cm^2. (The gate-frequency product is the number of logic gates—the most basic elements of a chip—times the clock frequency at which the integrated circuit on the chip operates. The cm^2 denotes the area of silicon on the chip required to implement this performance.)

The gate-Hz/cm^2 quantity, also known as throughput capacity, is a measure of the capability expected from a VHSIC device. By comparison, conventional, commercially available microprocessor chips have throughput capacities of 10^{10} gate-Hz/cm^2, or an order of magnitude slower than that expected from VHSIC integrated circuits in phase I. The military, on the other hand, is planning weapons systems with throughput capacities of 10^{13} gate-Hz/cm^2 or more. Such throughput rates mean that the smallest definable geometries of a VHSIC integrated circuit must be on the order of 1 μm or less, or total-system weights and power dissipation levels become too prohibitive.

All three branches of the armed services have major weapons programs designed with VHSIC chips, as can be seen from the **table**.

Ada programming language. In addition to the hardware digital-signal processors the military acquires from the VHSIC program, the Department of Defense needs software. The agency

ARCHITECTURE AND CIRCUITRY

Major defense areas and weapons systems served by the VHSIC program*

System area	Air Force	Army	Navy
Radar	Advanced medium-range air-to-air missile; advanced on-board signal processor; airborne warning and control system (AWACS); autonomous cruise-missile guidance; multifunction radar signal processor	Multimode fire-and-forget missile	Tactical air-to-air ground radar; surveillance radar
Imaging	Autonomous cruise-missile guidance	Target-acquisition/fire-control system; multimode fire-and-forget missile	Digital image processor
Antisubmarine warfare			Acoustic signal processor
Electronic warfare	Advanced defensive avionic system	High-mobility electronic-warfare weapons-targeting systems	Electronic systems module signal sorter
Command, Control and Communications (C³)	Signal processor chip set for Joint Tactical Information and Distribution System	Battlefield information distribution system	Antijam modern; NATO identification system

*From IBM Federal Systems Division, Manassas, Virginia.

adopted Ada as the single high-level software programming language for all three branches of the service to simplify procurements, the interchange of software programs among the services' branches, and training. SEE PROGRAMMING LANGUAGES.

Bibliography. R. Allan, Special issue on military electronics, *Electr. Des. Mag.*, 29(16):87–119, August 1981; W. H. Lee, VHSIC functions for signal processing, *1982 Southcon Professional Program*; L. W. Sumney, Special issue on war and peace, *IEEE Spectrum Mag.*, 19(10):93–94, October 1982.

OPTICAL COMPUTING
DAVID CASASENT

Some optical processors using multiple cells are special-purpose architectures. The parallel and high-speed features of optical systems can also be used to fabricate rather general-purpose optical computers (which can be used to perform general functions). Much research has been done on the optical realization of parallel processors for multiplication and addition. A parallel two-dimensional multiplication occurs when a two-dimensional spatially modulated light beam is passed through a two-dimensional transparency. Certain two-dimensional spatial light modulators can also produce an output that is the difference between two successive two-dimensional inputs or contains only the moving objects within a two-dimensional input scene. The addition of two two-dimensional data planes occurs if two spatially modulated beams are incident on a detector array simultaneously or sequentially. Various number representations have been used (such as residue arithmetic) to design efficient parallel optical and numerical computers. SEE COMPUTER SYSTEMS ARCHITECTURE; CONCURRENT PROCESSING; DIGITAL COMPUTER.

The most attractive class of general-purpose optical computers is presently optical linear algebra processors. These systems perform matrix-vector operations and similar linear algebra algorithms, often in a systolic form. The architecture for one rather general form of such a processor (see **illus.**) exemplifies the basic concepts. This system consists of a linear array of input point modulators (for example, laser diodes), each of which is imaged through a different spatial region

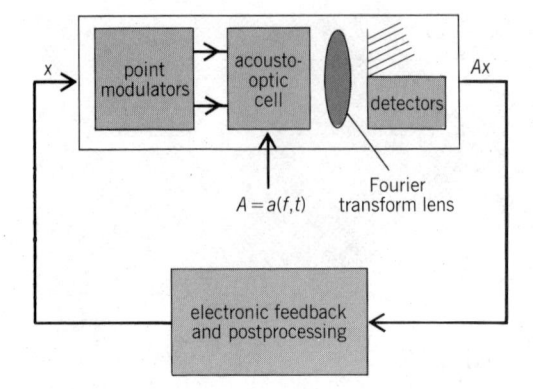

Optical linear algebra processor.

of an acoustooptic cell. The Fourier transform of the light distribution leaving the cell is formed on a linear output detector array. If the elements of N input vectors are fed simultaneously at time t to the acoustooptic cell, each vector on a different frequency f, then the transmittance of the cell will be N vectors (that is, a matrix A). If the input point modulators are fed in parallel with the elements of another vector x, then the product of the input vector and the N vectors in the cell is formed, and each vector inner product is produced (by the Fourier-transform lens) on a separate output detector. Thus, the system performs N vector inner products or a matrix-vector multiplication in parallel. With various frequency, time, and space encoding techniques, different electrical postprocessing, and various feedback configurations, all of the major linear algebra operations required in modern signal processing can be achieved on this one system. Use of multichannel acoustooptic cells and related architectures can increase the processing capacity of the system and allow optical processing of data to the accuracy possible on digital computers.

Bibliography. T. E. Bell, Optical computing: A field in flux, *IEEE Spectrum*, 23(8):34–37, August 1986; N. J. Berg and J. N. Lee (eds.), *Acousto-Optic Signal Processing: Theory and Practice*, 1983; D. Casasent, Coherent optical pattern recognition, *Opt. Eng.*, 24:26–32, January 1985; J. Hecht, Optical computers, *High Technology*, 7(2):44–49, February, 1987; J. Houston (ed.), Coming of age in optical computing (special issue) *Optics News*, April 1986; Special issue on digital optical computing, *Optical Engineering*, January 1986; Special issue on optical computing, *Proc. IEEE*, vol. 72, July 1984.

MICROCOMPUTER DEVELOPMENT SYSTEM
HARRY L. HELMS

A complete microcomputer system used to test and develop both the hardware and software of other microcomputer-based systems, from initial development through debugging of final prototypes.

A typical microcomputer development system (MDS) includes assembler facilities, a text editor, debugging facilities, and hardware emulation capabilities. Often a microcomputer development system will also include a test board for peripheral interfaces and other hardware, a floppy disk storage system, a video display terminal, a keyboard or keypad input device, and a provision for using a printing peripheral. A few microcomputer development systems include provisions for programmable read-only memory (PROM) devices.

The assembler permits instructions for the microcomputer to be written as mnemonics, which are then translated by the assembler into hexadecimal or binary machine language. The machine language program, known as an object file, is loaded into the microcomputer for execution. The program written in mnemonics is known as the source code, and is generated by the text editor. *See* DIGITAL COMPUTER PROGRAMMING.

A key component is the emulator, a combination of hardware and software which permits the MDS to emulate programs written for other microcomputer systems. Many emulators can execute source code programs for different microprocessors. A few emulators can also execute high-level languages such as BASIC, FORTRAN, and PASCAL. S*ee* P*rogramming languages.*

An MDS normally includes several software development and debugging tools. One common debugging facility is the trace function. This allows program execution to be halted at desired points so that central processing unit (CPU) registers or memory contents may be examined.

If true emulator and debugging facilities are not included in an MDS, a cross assembler will usually be provided. This is an assembler which accepts source code for one microprocessor type and compiles it by using a system for another microprocessor. However, it is not possible to run or debug programs by using a cross assembler.

Typical MDS random-access memory (RAM) capacity is 64K bytes or greater. A floppy disk–based mass storage system is now part of almost all available microcomputer development systems. S*ee* C*omputer storage technology;* S*emiconductor memories.*

Most microcomputer development systems support the development of just one microprocessor or family of microprocessors. However, microcomputer development systems have been introduced which can support several different microprocessors and high-level languages. S*ee* M*icrocomputer;* M*icroprocessor.*

INTEGRATED CIRCUITS

R*on* B*urghard,* Y*oussef* E*l-*M*ansy,* N*eil* B*erglund,*
B*ob* L. G*regory,* E*ugene* A. I*rene, and* P*aul* T. G*reiling*

B. L. Gregory and E. A. Irene coauthored the section Fabrication; P T. Greiling wrote the section Gallium Arsenide Circuits.

Miniature electronic circuits produced within and upon a single semiconductor crystal, usually silicon. Integrated circuits range in complexity from simple logic circuits and amplifiers, about $\frac{1}{20}$ in. (1.3 mm) square, to large-scale integrated circuits up to about $\frac{1}{3}$ in. (8 mm) square. They contain hundreds of thousands of transistors and other components which provide computer memory circuits and complex logic subsystems such as microcomputer central processor units.

Since the mid-1960s, integrated circuits have become the primary components of most electronic systems. Their low cost, high reliability, and speed have been essential in furthering the wide use of digital computers. Microcomputers have spread the use of computer technology to instruments, business machines, automobiles, and other equipment. Other common uses of large-scale integrated circuits are in pocket calculators and electronic watches. For analog signal processing, integrated subsystems such as FM stereo demodulators and switched-capacitor filters are made. S*ee* C*alculators:* D*igital computer;* M*icrocomputer.*

Integrated circuits consist of the combination of active electronic devices such as transistors and diodes with passive components such as resistors and capacitors, within and upon a single semiconductor crystal. The construction of these elements within the semiconductor is achieved through the introduction of electrically active impurities into well-defined regions of the semiconductor. The fabrication of integrated circuits thus involves such processes as vapor-phase deposition of semi-conductors and insulators, oxidation, solid-state diffusion, ion implantation, vacuum deposition, and sputtering.

Generally, integrated circuits are not straight-forward replacements of electronic circuits assembled from discrete components. They represent an extension of the technology by which silicon planar transistors are made. Because of this, transistors or modifications of transistor structures are the primary devices of integrated circuits. Methods of fabricating good-quality resistors and capacitors have been devised, but the third major type of passive component, inductors, must be simulated with complex circuitry or added to the integrated circuit as discrete components.

Simple logic circuits were the easiest to adapt to these design changes. The first of these, such as inverters and gates, were produced in the early 1960s primarily for miniaturization of missile guidance computers and other aerospace systems. Analog circuits, called linear integrated circuits, did not become commercially practical until several years later because of their heavy dependence on passive components such as resistors and capacitors. The first good-quality operational amplifiers for analog computers and instruments were produced in 1966. S*ee* A*nalog computer;* L*ogic circuits.*

TYPES OF CIRCUITS

Integrated circuits can be classified into two groups on the basis of the type of transistors which they employ: bipolar integrated circuits, in which the principal element is the bipolar junction transistor; and metal oxide semiconductor (MOS) integrated circuits, in which the principal element is the MOS transistor. Both depend upon the construction of a desired pattern of electrically active impurities within the semiconductor body, and upon the formation of an interconnection pattern of metal films on the surface of the semiconductor.

Bipolar circuits are generally used where highest logic speed is desired, and MOS for largest-scale integration or lowest power dissipation. Linear circuits are mostly bipolar, but MOS devices are used extensively in switched-capacitor filters.

Bipolar integrated circuits. A simple bipolar inverter circuit using a diffused resistor and an *npn* transistor is shown in **Fig. 1**. The input voltage V_{in} is applied to the base of the transistor. When V_{in} is zero or negative with respect to the emitter, no current flows. As a result, no voltage drop exists across the resistor, and the output voltage V_{out} will be the same as the externally applied biasing voltage, + 5 V in this example. When a positive input voltage is applied, the transistor becomes conducting. Current now flows through the transistor, hence through the resistor: as a result, the output voltage decreases. Thus, the change in input voltage appears inverted at the output.

The circuit symbol and the changes in input and output voltages during the switching process just described are illustrated in **Fig. 2**. The change in the output voltage occurs slightly later than the change in the input voltage. This time difference, called propagation delay, is an important characteristic of all integrated circuits. Much effort has been spent on reducing it, and values less than one-billionth of a second have been achieved.

Most simple digital circuits can be fabricated much as the inverter circuit described above. As an example, a photomicrograph of an early logic gate circuit is shown in **Fig. 3**. This circuit is one of the earliest digital integrated circuits, introduced commercially in 1961. For comparison, a 16-bit microcomputer digital integrated circuit introduced in 1983 is shown in **Fig. 4**. This circuit contains more than 3000 times as much circuitry, illustrating the tremendous increase in density that has occurred.

This tendency toward increased complexity is dictated by the economics of integrated circuit manufacturing. Because of the nature of this manufacturing process, all circuits on a slice are fabricated together. Consequently, the more circuitry accommodated on a slice, the cheaper the circuitry becomes. Because testing and packaging costs depend on the number of chips, it is desirable, in order to keep costs down, to crowd more circuitry onto a given chip rather than to increase the number of chips on a wafer.

Linear circuits. Integrated circuits based on amplifiers are called linear because amplifiers usually exhibit a linearly proportional response to input signal variations. However, the category

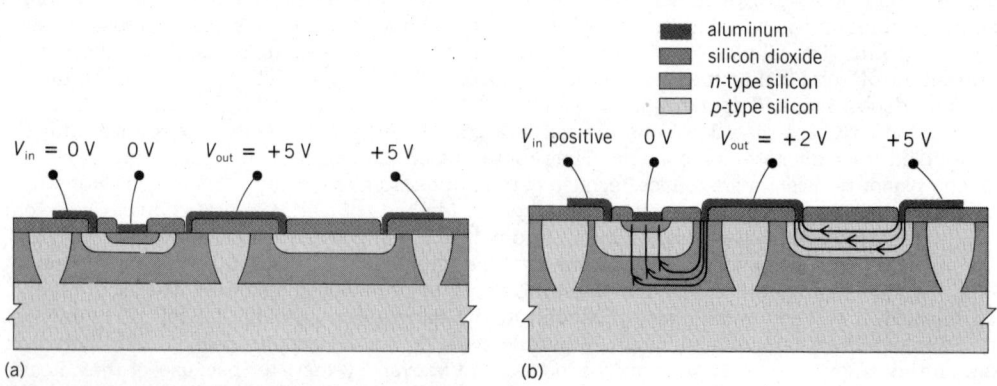

Fig. 1. Operation of bipolar inverter circuit. (a) Input voltage V_{in} is zero. (b) Positive input voltage applied; arrows indicate direction of current flow.

ARCHITECTURE AND CIRCUITRY   **89**

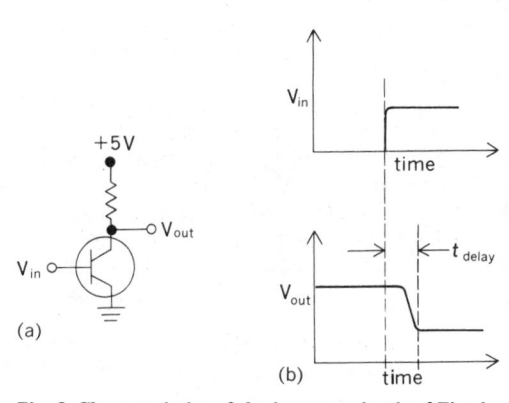

Fig. 2. Characteristics of the inverter circuit of Fig. 1. (a) Circuit symbol. (b) Switching waveforms.

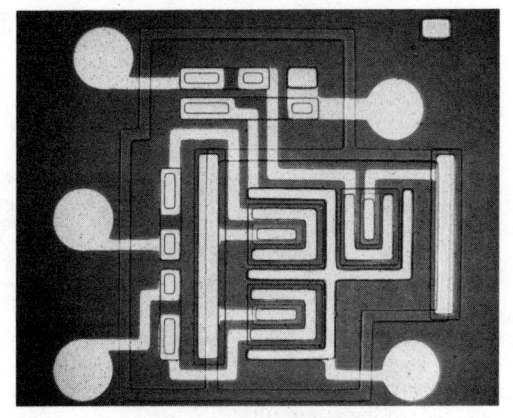

Fig. 3. Photomicrograph of early bipolar logic gate circuit. (*Fairchild Semiconductor*)

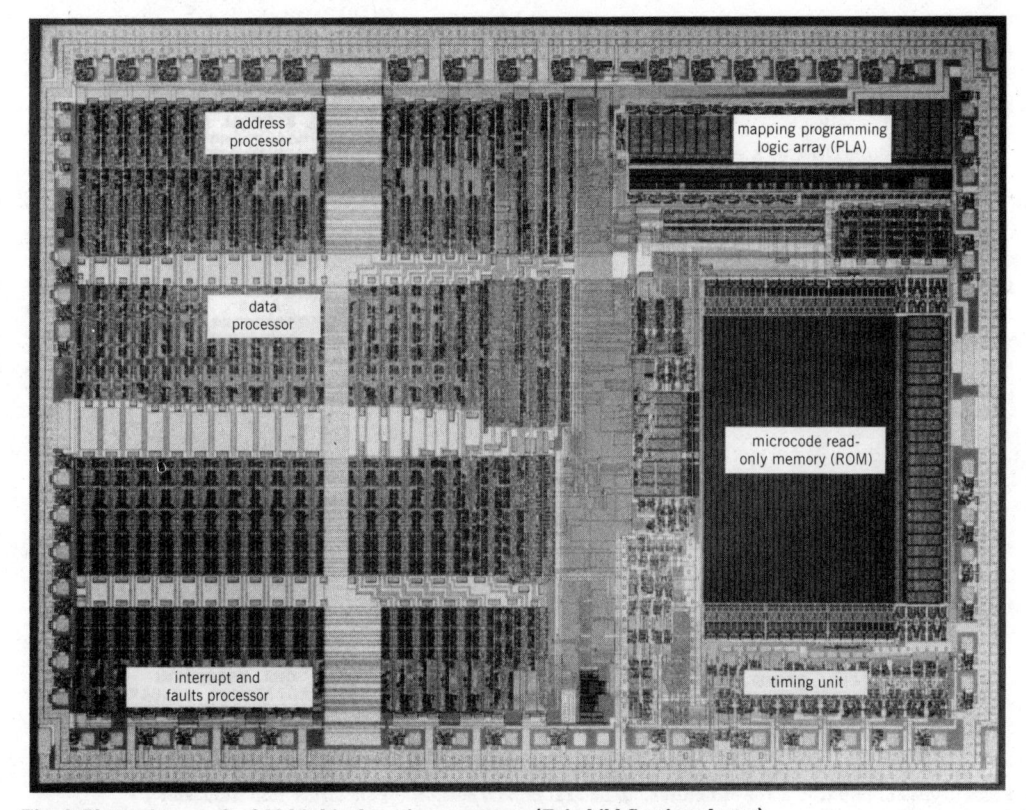

Fig. 4. Photomicrograph of 16-bit bipolar microprocessor. (*Fairchild Semiconductor*)

includes memory sense amplifiers, combinations of analog and digital processing functions, and other circuits with nonlinear characteristics. Some digital and analog combinations include analog-to-digital converters, timing controls, and modems (data communications modulator-demodulator units). SEE ANALOG-TO-DIGITAL CONVERTER; DATA COMMUNICATIONS.

A long-standing drawback in these circuits was the lack of inductors for tuning and filtering. That was overcome by the use of resistor-capacitor networks and additional circuitry. For low-frequency circuits the resistor in these networks is being replaced by the switched capacitor. At the higher frequencies, an oscillator-based circuit called the phase-locked loop provides a general-purpose replacement for inductors in applications such as radio transmission demodulation.

At first, the development of linear circuits was slow because of the difficulty of integrating passive components and also because of undesirable interactions between the semiconductor substrate and the operating components. Thus, much greater ingenuity was required to design and use the early linear circuits.

In addition, manufacturing economics favors digital circuits. A computer can be built by repetitious use of simple inverters and gates, while analog signal processing requires a variety of specialized linear circuits.

Semiconductor devices. In the continuing effort to increase the complexity and speed of digital circuits, and the performance characteristics and versatility of linear circuits, a significant role has been played by the discovery and development of new types of active and passive semiconductor devices which are suitable for use in integrated circuits. Among these devices is the *pnp* transistor which, when used in conjunction with the standard *npn* transistors described above, lends added flexibility to the design of integrated circuits.

Two types of *pnp* transistor structures, both compatible with standard integrated circuit technology, are shown in **Fig. 5**. Figure 5a shows the so-called lateral *pnp*, which is a *pnp* transistor formed between two closely spaced *p*-type diffuse regions. Since these can be formed using the same diffusion step, described below, by which the base of the *npn* transistor and the resistor are formed, this structure can be fabricated simultaneously with the rest of the circuit. The same is true of the substrate *pnp* shown n Fig. 5b, except here the *p*-type substrate is employed as the collector.

Other possibilities involve means of producing integrated circuits with resistors of high resistance values. In the standard resistor process, described below, high resistances require long resistors, which in turn require large chips to accommodate them. An alternate approach is to use the *n* region between the diffused *p* region and the substrate as the resistor. This semiconductor region has a significantly higher resistance than that formed by the *p*-type diffusion. However, due to the reverse bias between the *n* region and the two *p* regions enclosing it from top and bottom, such resistors have highly nonlinear current-voltage characteristics. An alternate scheme involves the use of a very thin film of high-resistivity metal deposited by evaporation or sputtering on top of the insulating silicon dioxide layer. Such films can display resistivities as much as a hundred times higher than that of the diffused *p* region, and since their deposition is performed after the entire semiconductor structure is complete, they can be used in conjunction with any type of integrated circuit.

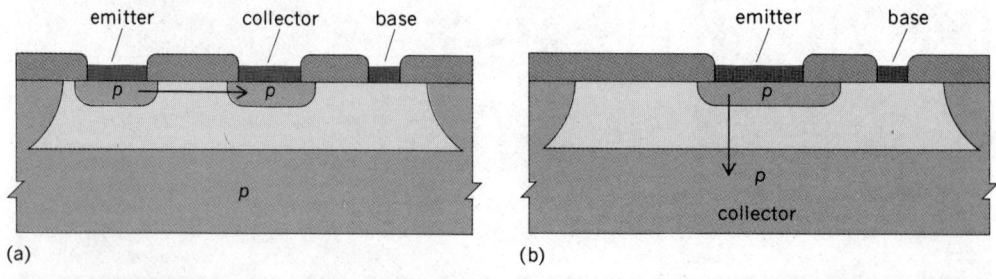

Fig. 5. Types of *pnp* transistor structures. (*a*) Lateral *pnp* transistor. (*b*) Substrate *pnp* transistor. Arrows indicate direction of useful transistor action.

Several alternatives to *pn*-junction isolation are in use. These involve etching around the transistor regions, so that oxide or air isolates the components. Called dielectric isolation, the technique was initially used in military circuits to stop radiation-induced currents from flowing through and destroying the circuits. It is now used commercially to reduce circuit capacitance, thus speeding up operation, and to reduce the silicon area required for each transistor. It is not yet widely used, however, because it complicates the basic process.

MOS integrated circuits. The other major class of integrated circuits is called MOS because its principal device is a metal oxide semiconductor field-effect transistor (MOSFET). It is more suitable for very large-scale integration (VLSI) than bipolar circuits because MOS transistors are self-isolating and can have an average size of less than a millionth of a square inch (5×10^{-5} mm^2). This has made it practical to use over 1,000,000 transistors per circuit. Because of this high density capability, MOS transistors are used for high density random-access memories (RAMs; **Fig. 6**), read-only memories (ROMs), and microprocessors. SEE COMPUTER STORAGE TECHNOLOGY; MICROPROCESSOR; SEMICONDUCTOR MEMORIES.

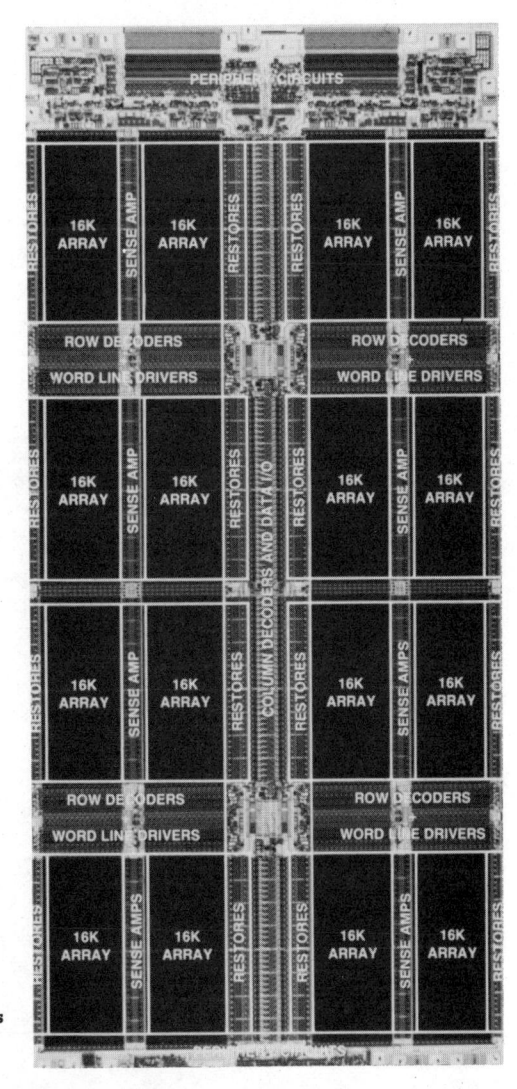

Fig. 6. Photomicrograph of MOS LSI circuit used as 262,144-bit random-access memory (RAM). (*Intel Corp.*)

Several major types of MOS device fabrication technologies have been developed since the mid-1960s. They are: (1) metal-gate p-channel MOS (PMOS), which uses aluminum for electrodes and interconnections; (2) silicon-gate p-channel MOS, employing polycrystalline silicon for gate electrodes and the first interconnection layer; (3) n-channel MOS (NMOS), which is usually silicon gate; and (4) complementary MOS (CMOS), which employs both p-channel and n-channel devices. In 1984 the silicon gate NMOS and CMOS were the dominant technologies, with CMOS using silicon gates becoming the most attractive for new designs.

Both conceptually and structurally the MOS transistor is a much simpler device than the bipolar transistor. In fact, its principle of operation has been known since the late 1930s, and the

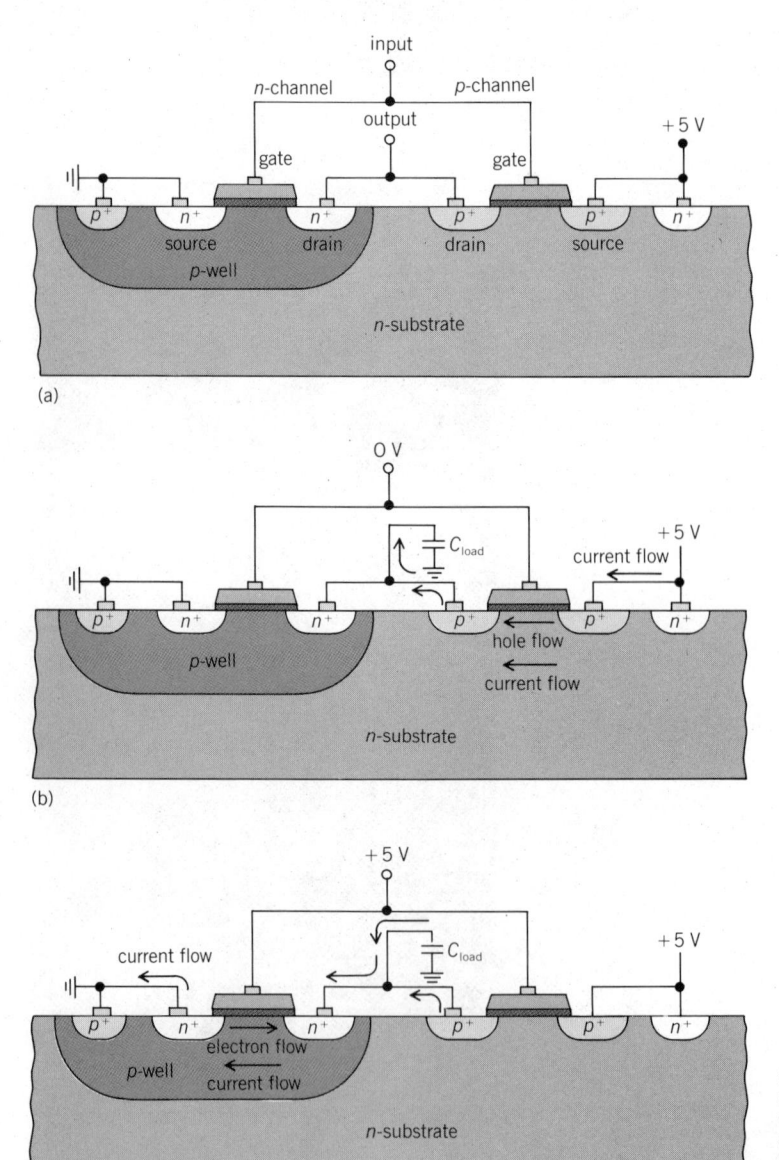

Fig. 7. Simple CMOS inverter circuit. (a) Schematic cross section. (b) Current flow when input is "low" at 0 V. (c) Current flow when input is "high" at 5 V.

research effort that led to the discovery of the bipolar transistor was originally aimed at developing the MOS transistor. What kept this simple device from commercial utilization until 1964 is the fact that it depends on the properties of the semiconductor surface for its operation, while the bipolar transistor depends principally on the bulk properties of the semiconductor crystal. Hence MOS transistors became practical only when understanding and control of the properties of the oxidized silicon surface had been perfected to a very great degree.

CMOS. A simple CMOS inverter circuit is shown in **Fig. 7** and a circuit schematic in **Fig. 8**. The gates of the n-channel and p-channel transistors are connected together as are the drains. The common gate connection is the input node while the common drain connection is the output node. A capacitor is added to the output node to model the loading expected from the subsequent stages on typical circuits.

When the input node is in the "low state", at 0 V, the n-channel gate to source voltage is 0 V while the p-channel gate to source voltage is -5 V. The n-channel transistor requires a positive gate-to-source voltage, which is greater than the transistor threshold voltage (typically 0.5–1 V), before it will start conducting current between the drain and source. Thus, with a 0-V gate-to-source voltage it will be off and no current will flow through the drain and source regions. The p-channel transistor, however, requires a negative voltage between the gate and source which is less than its threshold voltage (typically -0.5 to -1.5 V). The -5-V gate-to-source potential is clearly less than the threshold voltage, and the p-channel will be turned on, conducting current from the source to the drain, and thereby charging up the loading capacitor. Once the capacitor is charged to the "high state" at 5 V, the transistor will no longer conduct because there will no longer be a potential difference between the source and drain regions.

When the input is now put to the "high state" at 5 V, just the opposite occurs. The n-channel transistor will be turned on while the p-channel will be off. This will allow the load capacitor to discharge through the n-channel transistor resulting in the output voltage dropping from a "high state" at 5 V to a "low state" at 0 V. Again, once there is no potential difference between the drain and source (capacitor discharged to 0 V), the current flow will stop, and the circuit will be stable.

This simple circuit illustrates a very important feature of CMOS circuits. Once the loading capacitor has been either charged to 5 V or discharged back to 0 V, there is no current flow, and the standby power is very low. This is the reason for the high popularity of CMOS for battery-based systems. None of the other MOS technologies offers this feature without complex circuit techniques, and even then will typically not match the low standby power of CMOS. The bipolar circuits discussed above require even more power than these other MOS technologies. The price for CMOS's lower power are the additional fabrication steps required (10–20% more) when compared to NMOS.

Sampled-data devices. In addition to the digital logic applications discussed above with the simple inverter circuit, MOS devices also offer unique features for some analog circuit applications. These include signal-processing applications that are based on sampled-data techniques.

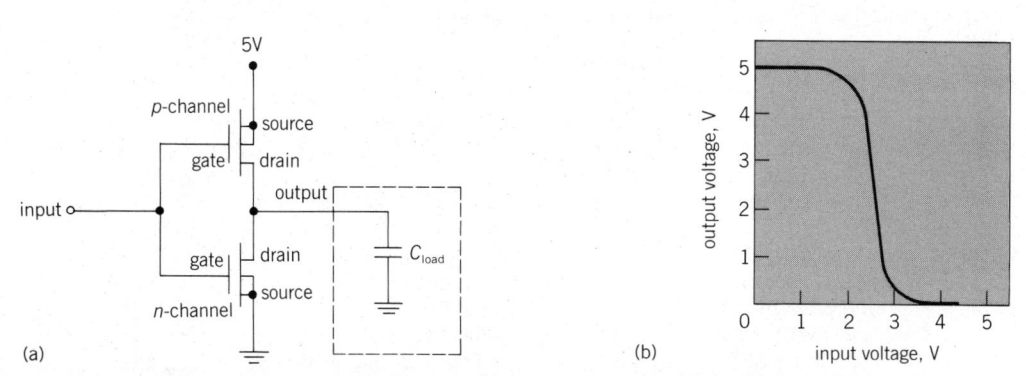

Fig. 8. Characteristics of the CMOS inverter circuit of Fig. 7. (a) Circuit diagram. (b) Transfer characteristics.

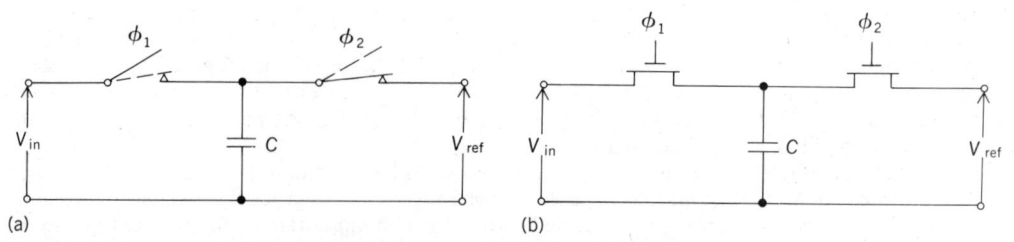

Fig. 9. Switched-capacitor circuit. (a) Schematic of an *RC* section. (b) Implementation of the switches with MOS transistors with clocks applied to their gates.

Two classes of devices, namely, charge-coupled devices (CCD) and switched-capacitor networks, play the major role in these applications.

In CCDs the stored charge at the semiconductor surface can also be made to propagate along the surface via potential wells created by a series of these MOS structures. The storage cell in the RAM circuit of Fig. 6 can be viewed as using a single CCD element for each bit.

The capacitance C from the MOS structure can be integrated with MOS transistors, which are used as switches, to form a switched-capacitor circuit (**Fig. 9**). One of the switches ϕ_1 is closed when the other switch ϕ_2 is open, and vice versa. The circuit is equivalent to a resistor with a value of $R = T/C$, where T is the sampling interval. The advantage of the technique is the high quality and the high value of resistors that can be put on an integrated circuit. These resistors combined with capacitors and operational amplifers (all made with MOS technology) can be used to make active filters. Since many stages of these filters can be integrated into one chip, precise filters are now possible with integrated circuit technology. These filters are having a tremendous impact on low-frequency filters (frequencies less than 100 kHz) and will be used extensively in telecommunication equipment.

INTEGRATED OPTICAL DEVICES

Semiconductors have long been used as light sensors. Advances in large-scale integration (LSI) have enabled large arrays of sensors, such as solid-state television cameras, to be made commercially. MOS LSI is now preferred for sensor arrays because it permits large amounts of control logic to be fabricated in the same circuit as the sensors.

In MOS optical arrays, the sensors are MOS devices or CCD elements. The sensor portion of the circuit views the scene through a transparent window. Light variations in the scene viewed cause variations in charge, producing signals transferable in shift-register fashion to processing stages such as amplifiers. These arrays have numerous applications, from measuring and sorting objects on production lines to optical character readers, which automatically translate written information to digital computer input codes. *See Character recognition.*

MICROCOMPUTERS

The LSI development having the most profound effect on electronic equipment economics and design in general is the microcomputer. The complexity and capability of these circuits, introduced in 1971, have expanded greatly. Initially these integrated circuits were applied to dedicated functions with the tailoring of that function being done with the ROM circuits on the chip. However, there are now many different types of microprocessor circuits ranging from the simple microcontroller types of functions to very complex computers on a chip such as the 16-bit microprocessor shown in **Fig. 10**.

This rapid development has been a result of both the technology which allows more circuits to be placed on a chip and circuit innovation. The technology increased the number of transistors on a chip from a few thousand in 1971 to over 400,000 in 1984. The circuit innovations include both digital techniques and the combination of analog and digital processing functions on the same chip. Both analog-to-digital and digital-to-analog data conversion circuits have been combined with the digital processor into one integrated circuit.

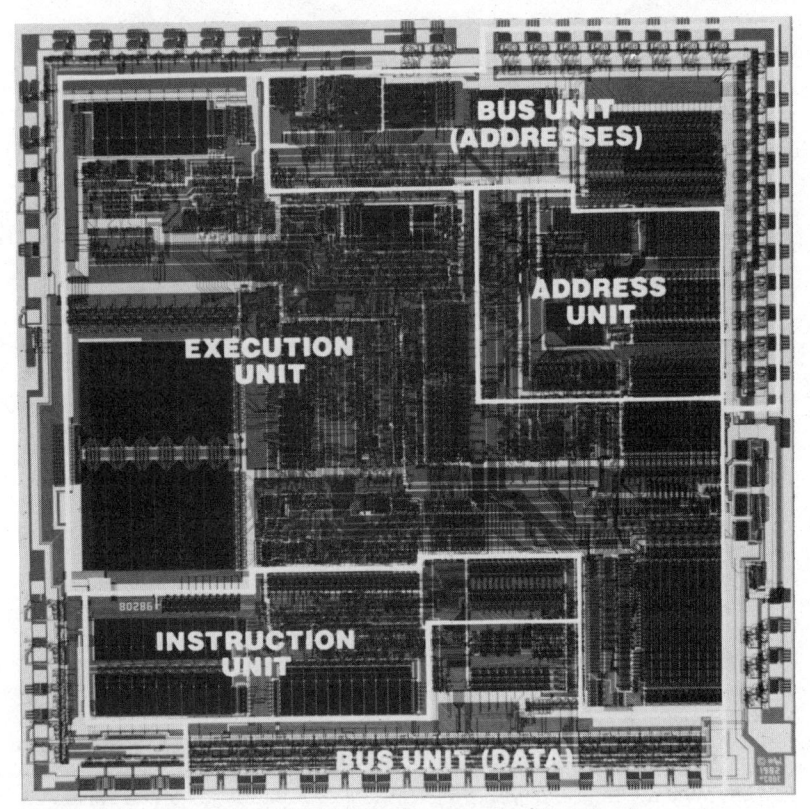

Fig. 10. Photomicrograph of 16-bit MOS microprocessor. (*Intel Corp.*)

As the technology enables the development of more complex circuits, the problem becomes not one of how to build these complex circuits but of what to build. The application of these circuits is rapidly becoming limited by the effort in programming them, rather than by their inherent capability. The emphasis in the future will be to apply circuit design features to reduce the rapidly increasing complexity of programming.

Although these LSI circuits are being used in calculators, automobiles, instruments, appliance controls and many other applications, realization of their potential is just beginning. As the power of the computer is captured in the relatively inexpensive integrated circuit, the role of integrated circuits will continue to expand rapidly.

FABRICATION

Integrated-circuit fabrication begins with a thin, polished slice of high-purity, single-crystal semiconductor (usually silicon) and employs a combination of physical and chemical processes to create the integrated-circuit structures described above. Junctions are formed in the silicon slice by the processes of thermal diffusion or high-energy ion implantation. Electrical isolation between devices on the integrated circuit is achieved with insulating layers grown by thermal oxidation or deposited by chemical deposition. Conductor layers to provide the necessary electrical connections on the integrated circuit are obtained by a variety of deposition techniques. Precision lithographic processes are used throughout the fabrication sequence to define the geometric features required.

Requirements. The integrated-circuit fabrication process is quite sensitive to both particulate and impurity contamination. Airborne particulates must be minimized during the fabrication sequence, since even small (1-micrometer) particles on the wafer surface can cause defects. A particulate-free fabrication ambient is normally achieved by the use of vertical laminar-flow clean rooms or benches (**Fig. 11**). Lint-free garments are worn to minimize operator-borne particulates. To minimize impurity contamination effects, the chemicals, solvents, and metals which are used must be of the highest possible purity (electronic grade). Yellow light is necessary in the clean room because of the ultraviolet-sensitive photolithographic processes employed.

The precision and cleanliness requirements of integrated-circuit processing necessitate high discipline throughout the process sequence. This is achieved by extensive operator training, in-process tests and inspection with continual feedback, and a high degree of equipment calibration and control. The physical environment and operator attitude in an integrated-circuit fabrication facility are important factors for successful operation.

Processes. The basic relationship between the major processes in integrated-circuit fabrication is shown schematically in **Fig. 12**. Film formation is normally followed by impurity doping or lithography. Lithography is generally followed by etching, which in turn is followed by impurity doping or film formation. Impurity doping is normally followed by film formation or lithography. A complete integrated-circuit process sequence requires many cycles through the flow diagram in Fig. 12. For example, metal gate CMOS requires seven cycles through lithography. The complete flow time for a CMOS process is approximately 2 to 6 weeks, depending on process complexity.

Film formation. Film formation employs thermal oxidation to produce silicon dioxide (SiO_2) films, chemical vapor deposition to produce silicon, silicon dioxide, or silicon nitride (Si_3N_4) films, or vacuum evaporation/sputtering to produce metal films.

The atoms on the surface of a silicon single crystal from which integrated circuits are manufactured are chemically bound only in the direction of the bulk of the crystal, and not in the other or free direction. The resultant so-called silicon dangling bonds are very reactive and may bond to oxygen or nitrogen or other impurities from the atmosphere, so that a large variety of reactions can occur. Each of these reactions will result in different electrical properties for the silicon surface, a serious problem in designing a manufacturing process in which extremely large numbers of identically operating and reliable devices are produced on silicon chips. The solution to this dilemma is to tie up the dangling bonds with a chemically stable and electrically insulating film that will not interfere with the electrical characteristics of the silicon surface. A material with these properties that can be easily prepared in thin-film form on silicon is silicon dioxide.

Fig. 11. Vertical laminar-flow clean room for integrated-circuit fabrication.

ARCHITECTURE AND CIRCUITRY 97

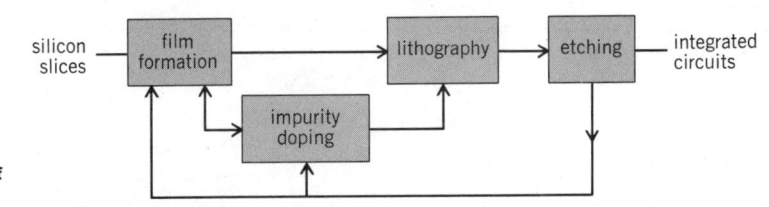

Fig. 12. Integrated-circuit fabrication sequence form. Fabrication normally proceeds in the direction of the arrows.

The silicon dioxide film is made by the reaction of a carefully cleaned and polished single-crystal silicon surface with an oxidant gas, usually oxygen or steam, at temperatures ranging from 1500 to 2200°F (800 to 1200°C) in a quartz-walled furnace tube (**Fig. 13**a). The reaction occurs rapidly and exothermically on the silicon surface. As the oxide film grows, the rate of oxidation decreases, because the oxidant must transport to the silicon surface through the growing film. For large film thicknesses and at high oxidation temperatures, this transport controls the film growth kinetics, while for thin films the surface reaction is dominant.

Fig. 13. Modern integrated-circuit fabrication equipment. (*a*) Diffusion furnace. (*b*) Atmospheric-pressure chemical vapor deposition (CVD). (*c*) Low-pressure CVD. (*d*) Vacuum evaporator. (*e*) Ion implanter. (*f*) Contact mask aligner. (*g*) Direct step-on-water machine. (*h*) Plasma etcher.

Chemical vapor deposition (CVD) is a gas-phase process where a film deposit is obtained by combining the appropriate gases in a reactant chamber at elevated temperatures. A typical CVD reaction (silox process) is given below. Figure 13b shows a cold-walled, atmospheric-pressure

$$SiH_4 + O_2 \xrightarrow[\text{(750–930°F)}]{\text{(400–500°C)}} SiO_2 \downarrow + 2H_2 \uparrow$$
$$\text{(Deposits as film)}$$

CVD system where the silicon slice is heated by rf energy. Figure 13c shows a low-pressure CVD system where the slices and process gases are heated in a partially evacuated furnace tube. This low-pressure process produces very uniform film thicknesses.

Evaporation or sputtering of metal coatings is performed in a vacuum, with metal transport being produced either by heat (evaporation) or bombarding ions (sputtering). The vacuum evaporator in Fig. 13d uses fixturing with planetary motion during evaporation. This achieves uniform metal thickness over surface topology on the silicon slice.

Impurity doping. The unique electronic properties of semiconductors are produced by substituting selected impurities at silicon lattice positions in the silicon crystal, a process called doping. The distortions in the chemical bonding due to the presence of impurities at lattice positions cause some of the bonding electrons in the crystal to have a higher energy than in a perfect crystal lattice and therefore be available for electronic conduction. Similarly, holes, which are the absence of bonding electrons, are produced by other kinds of impurities. Both electrons and holes can carry electric current. In order to construct complex integrated circuits, the impurities must be placed in adjacent regions in the semiconductor surface. The two predominant methods of doping semiconductor surfaces are thermal diffusion in high-temperature furnaces (Fig. 13a) and ion implantation.

In the diffusional doping process, the regions of the silicon surface to be doped are exposed to a concentration of the dopant while maintaining a high temperature. Boron and phosphorus are dopants which can be introduced by thermal diffusion at temperatures from 1500 to 2200°F (800 to 1200°C). At these temperatures the silicon lattice contains a significant number of vacant lattice sites, that is, crystal lattice sites with missing silicon atoms. The impurity atoms can migrate from vacant site to vacant site. The driving force for this diffusion process is the concentration gradient of impurity atoms. Near the silicon surface there exists a large concentration of dopant, while in the silicon only a small number of impurities exist. There is a tendency for these concentrations to be equalized, thereby eliminating the gradient. When the impurity has diffused to the proper depth and is in the appropriate concentration in the silicon, the process is stopped. Other regions that are not to receive dopant are masked by using impenetrable films known as diffusion masks.

As device requirements become more stringent, very sharp diffusion profiles are needed so that the device size can be reduced. The solid-state diffusion process does not afford sufficient control for the most advanced device processes. For this purpose, the use of the direct implantation of impurity ions (electrically charged atoms) into the silicon lattice has been developed.

Ion implantation is also used when greater precision of dopant concentration is required or when a reduced temperature cycle is advantageous. Ion implantation makes use of intense, uniform beams of high-energy ions (typically 10–500 keV) of the desired dopant. These beams are formed in specialized accelerators such as Van de Graaff generators under high vacuum conditions (Fig. 13e). The beams can be focused, accelerated, and purified by using mass spectrometry techniques such as electrostatic plates and magnetic fields. The desired beam is them made to impinge on the silicon substrate which has appropriate masking so that the dopant beam impinges on the proper area of the silicon surface. The energy is sufficient for the ions in the beam to penetrate the silicon surface, leaving a distribution of dopant. The position of the peak of the distribution can be altered by altering the beam energy. The amount of dopant can be altered by the beam current and time of exposure. Damage is caused by the collisions of the ions in the beam with the atoms in the silicon lattice, but much of the damage can be removed by thermal annealing at temperatures of about 1500°F (800°C). Remarkably sharp dopant profiles of precise concentration can be achieved by using this technique.

Lithography. Lithography is necessary to define the small geometries required in integrated circuits. In lithography the silicon slice is coated uniformly with a thin film of photosensitive material called resist. If the lithography is to be performed optically, the integrated-circuit pattern to be transferred to the resist is first created on a glass plate or "mask." This pattern can then be transferred to the resist by a number of optical techniques. These techniques range from direct contact printing using a collimated source of ultra-violet light (Fig. 13f), to optical projection of a single integrated-circuit pattern with associated reduction (for example, 10:1, 1:1) and a precise x-y motion of the silicon slice (direct step-on-wafer; Fig. 13g). Electron-beam direct patterning can be performed, without a mask, by using a controllable electron beam and an electron-sensitive resist. Lithography has also been achieved with x-rays, by their projection through a special mask in close proximity to the slice. Direct step-on-wafer photolithography, the most advanced of the optical lithographic techniques, is capable of defining 1 μm (4×10^{-5} in.) geometries. Electron-beam and x-ray lithography have demonstrated the capability to define features substantially smaller than 1 μm.

Etching. Etching is necessary to transfer the resist pattern achieved through lithography to the underlying surface. Traditionally, integrated-circuit fabrication has employed wet chemical processes to etch lines and features. These techniques utilize the chemical reactivity with an etchant of the material to be etched. The difference between the etch rate of the masking material and that of the substrate is related to this chemistry. The chemical etching of crystalline materials can be either isotropic or anisotropic. In isotropic etching the etchant attacks the crystal equally in all directions without regard to the different densities of atoms and structural features in the different directions in a crystal. Amorphous materials etch isotropically. Anisotropic etching takes advantage of different reactivities of the different crystal planes due to bonding and density differences. Usually anisotropic etches are milder etches that take full advantage of chemical differences. Anisotropic etching enables the construction of intricate patterns in silicon surfaces and therefore permits the practice of constructing devices in etched regions or on unetched mesa areas.

As with diffusion, wet chemical etching is limited in terms of size of the lines or features to be formed (no less than 3–4 μm or 1.2–1.6×10^{-4} in.) and, more important, the aspect ratio of the features, that is, their height-to-width ratios. Dense packing and small device size require high-aspect-ratio etching. Dry plasma etching, reactive ion etching, and ion milling are advanced techniques being developed to overcome the limits of chemical etching. In plasma etching (Fig. 13h), the most advanced of these techniques, the vertical etch rate can be adjusted to be much greater than the lateral etch rate. This enables the etching of fine lines and features without loss of definition, even in films approaching 1 μm in thickness.

For plasma etching, a plasma is formed above a masked surface to be etched by adding large amounts of energy to a gas at low pressures. This is commonly accomplished by electrical discharges in gases at about 10^{-3} atm (10^{-2} Pa). A plasma contains ions, free radicals, and neutral species, all with high kinetic energies. By adjusting the electrical potential of the substrate to be etched, the charged species in the plasma can be directed to impinge on the substrate and thereby impact the nonmasked regions. The force of the high-energy impact can knock out substrate atoms. This plasma etching process can be made more effective with the use of gases in the plasma that are reactive with the material to be etched. In particular, the reactants should form volatile products that can be carried away by the vacuum system. Such gases usually contain halogens (fluorine, chlorine, and bromine). Reactive ion etching combines the energetic etching effects of the plasma with the reactivity of the gases and the formation of energetic reactive species in the plasma.

Bipolar process flow. The principal steps involved in the fabrication of the simple bipolar inverter circuit of Fig. 1 are shown schematically in **Fig. 14**. An inverter requires only a transistor and resistor, shown in cross section. Complete digital integrated circuits generally contain tens to hundreds of inverters and gates interconnected as counters, arithmetic units, and other building blocks. As indicated by Fig. 14g, hundreds of such circuits may be fabricated on a single slice of silicon crystal. This feature of planar technology—simultaneous production of many circuits—is responsible for the economic advantages and wide use of integrated circuits.

The starting material is a slice of single-crystal silicon, more or less circular, up to 6 in. (150 mm) in diameter, and a fraction of an inch (a few millimeters) thick. Typically, this material is doped with p-type impurities (Fig. 14a). A film of semiconductor, less than 0.001 in. (25 μm) thick, is then grown upon this substrate in a vapor-phase reaction of a silicon-containing compound. The conditions of this reaction are such that the film maintains the single-crystal nature

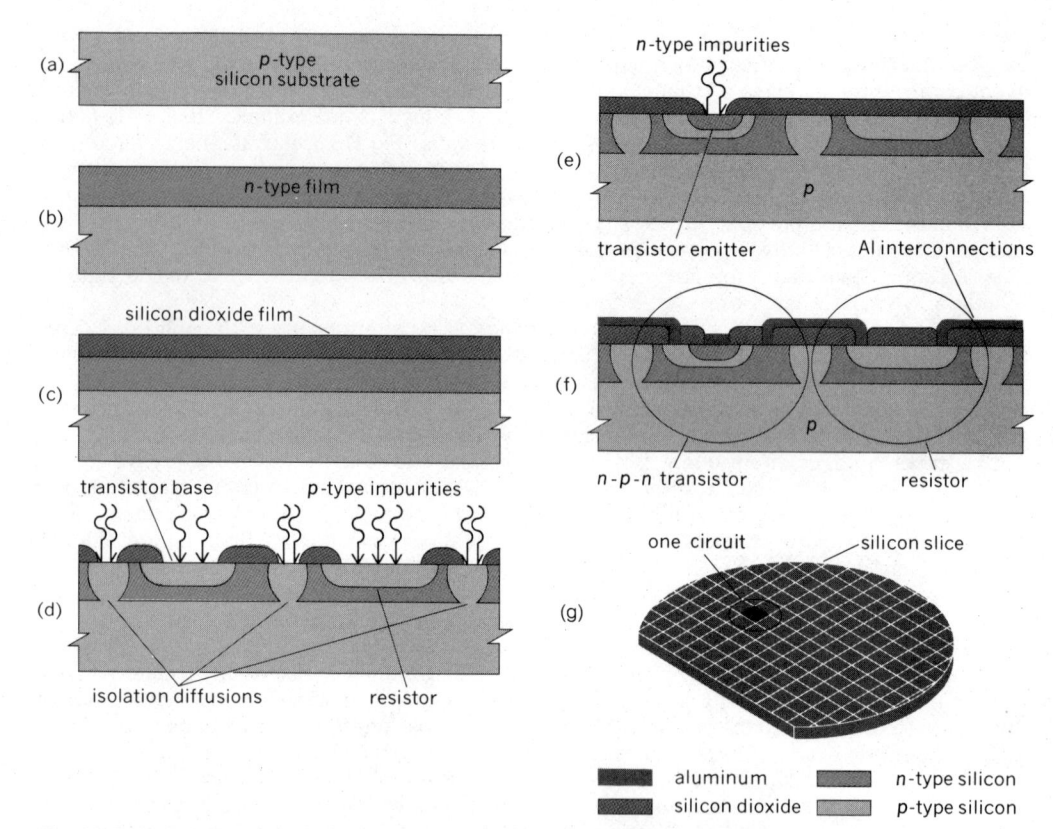

Fig. 14. Steps in fabrication of bipolar inverter circuit. (*a*) Initial *p*-type substrate. (*b*) Growth of *n*-type film. (*c*) Growth of oxide film. (*d*) Opening of windows in oxide layer and formation of isolation regions, transistor base, and resistor. (*e*) Regrowth and formation of windows in oxide layer, and formation of transistor emitter. (*f*) Opening of contacts and deposit of metal. (*g*) Numerous circuits incorporated on a silicon slice.

of the substrate. Such films are called epitaxial (Greek for "arranged upon"). By incorporating *n*-type impurities into the gas from which the film is grown, the resulting epitaxial film is made *n*-type (Fig. 14*b*).

Next, the silicon slice is placed into an oxygen atmosphere at high temperatures (2200°F or 1200°C). The silicon and oxygen react, forming a cohesive silicon dioxide film upon the surface of the slice that is relatively impervious to the electrically active impurities. (Fig. 14*c*).

To form the particular semiconductor regions required in the fabrication of electronic devices, however, *p*- and *n*-type impurities must be introduced into certain regions of the semiconductor. In the planar technology, this is done by opening windows in the protective oxide layer by photoengraving techniques, and then exposing the slice to a gas containing the appropriate doping impurity. In the case of an integrated circuit, the isolation regions—*p*-type regions which, together with the *p*-type substrate, surround the separate pockets of the *n*-type film—are formed first by the diffusion of a *p*-type impurity. This is followed by a shorter exposure to *p*-type impurities during which the base region of the transistors and the resistors are formed (Fig. 14*d*).

Next, the slice is again covered with oxide, smaller windows are cut over the transistor base regions, and *n*-type impurities are permitted to diffuse in these regions to form the emitters of the transistors (Fig. 14*e*). As the lateral and vertical dimensions of these devices become smaller, control of the number and position of these impurities becomes more important. This has resulted in the increased use of ion implantation to introduce these impurities into the silicon.

Openings are cut in the oxide layer at all places where contact to the silicon is desired. Then a metal, aluminum for example, is deposited over the entire slice by vacuum evaporation or sputtering, and finally the undesired aluminum is removed by photoengraving, leaving behind aluminum stripes which interconnect the transistor and the resistor (Fig. 14f).

The preparation of the thousands of inverter circuits on the silicon slice is now complete. The slice is cut apart, much as a pane of glass is cut, and the individual circuits are tested and packaged.

Both the transistor and the resistor are formed within a separate pocket of n-type semiconductor surrounded on all sides by p-type regions. When the inverter circuit is operated, a reverse bias develops between the n-type pocket and its surroundings. The depletion region separating the n- and p-type regions has a very high resistance; consequently, the individual transistors and

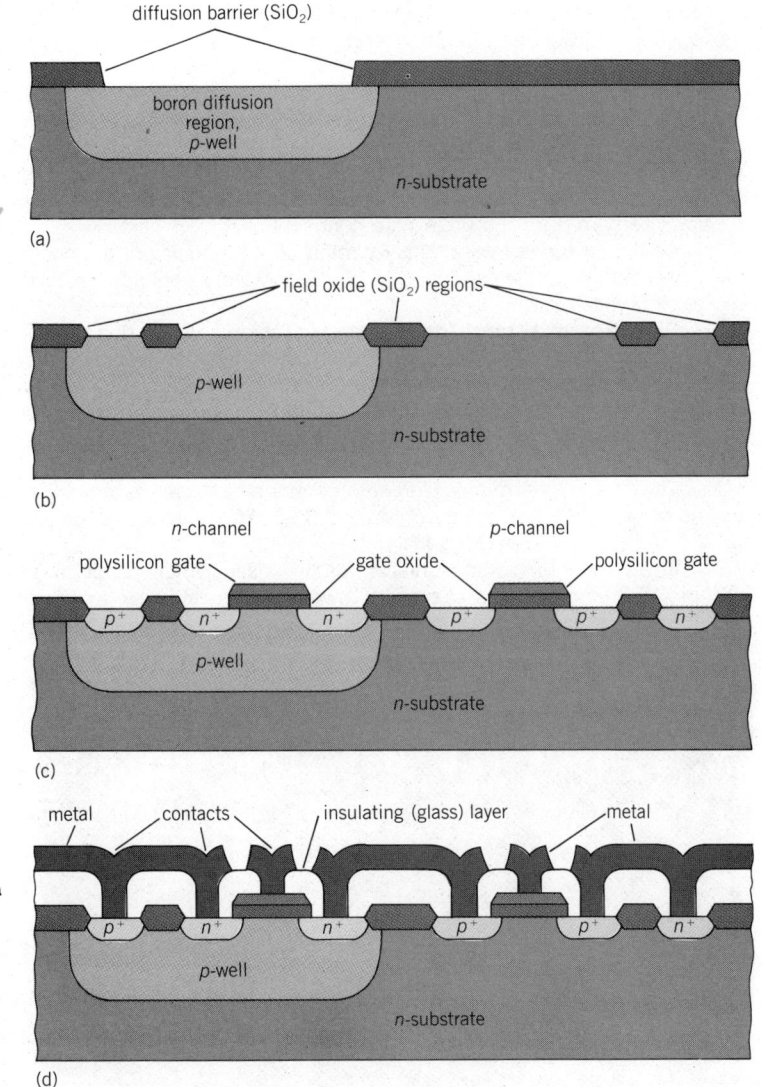

Fig. 15. Steps in fabrication of CMOS inverter circuit. (a) Introduction of p well. (b) Growth of field oxides. (c) Addition of gate oxides, polysilicon gates, and junctions. (d) Deposit of insulating layer, opening of contacts, and deposit of metal.

resistors are electrically isolated from each other, even though both of them have been formed within the same semiconductor crystal.

CMOS process flow. The principal steps in fabricating the simple CMOS inverter circuit of Fig. 7 are illustrated in **Fig. 15**. Again, as in the bipolar case, the process starts with the highly polished single slice of silicon crystal. For CMOS the first step is typically to put in the p-well regions for the n-channel devices, if the original silicon wafer is n-type (Fig. 15a). It is also possible to start with a p-type wafer in which n-well regions are introduced for the p-channel transistors. This discussion will be confined to the p-well case.

After the wells have been introduced, thick oxide layers (0.5–1 μm or 2–4 $\times$ 10^{-5} in. thick) are grown in specific regions to isolate the transistor junctions from each other (Fig. 15b). Next the transistor gate oxides (typically 0.02–0.1 μm or 1–4 $\times$ 10^{-6} in. thick) are grown. Prior to the silicon gate deposition, implants may be used to control the threshold voltages of the transistors. Polysilicon is then deposited for the gate regions and doped with impurities to reduce the resistance. The gate regions are then defined by using photoresist and lithography, and the polysilicon and thin gate oxide is removed where it is not wanted. The transistors are now ready for the introduction of impurities for the source and drain junctions. With CMOS, separate masking steps are required to introduce the phosphorus or arsenic for the n-channel source and drain junctions and the boron for the p-channel source and drain junctions (Fig. 15c).

An insulating layer (typically a glass) to isolate the polysilicon gate conductor from the aluminum metallization is now deposited. Openings in the glass layer are made for the metal to make contact to the polysilicon lines and junctions. The metal is then deposited and the regions to be removed are etched away after using photoresist and lithography techniques (Fig. 15d). Finally a scratch protection passivation layer is deposited over the metal with openings made at the bond pad areas for the bond wire connections.

As in the bipolar case, the isolation of the transistors is accomplished by reverse-biased junctions. The substrate is always at the highest chip voltage while the p-well is always at the lowest chip voltage.

Changes in technology. Integrated-circuit fabrication technology changes rapidly due to the steadily decreasing feature size of the individual circuit elements, the improvements in yields allowing large chip sizes and the advances in equipment required for the finer features and increasing wafer sizes. Because of these rapid changes a fabrication facility will remain state of the art in capability for no more than 3–5 years without making major equipment and process changes.

The sizes of the circuit elements continue to decrease as improvements in the lithography and etching techniques are incorporated (**Fig. 16**). This reduction in feature sizes has a direct impact on the chip sizes (**Fig. 17**).

In addition to making smaller feature sizes which result in smaller chips for the same circuitry, the tendency has also been toward a rapid increase in circuit density. The outcome is that the chip sizes actually increase as more circuits are added than what would be gained by

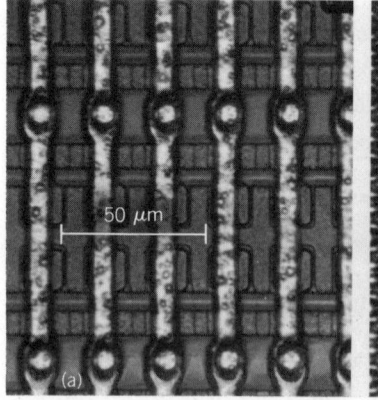

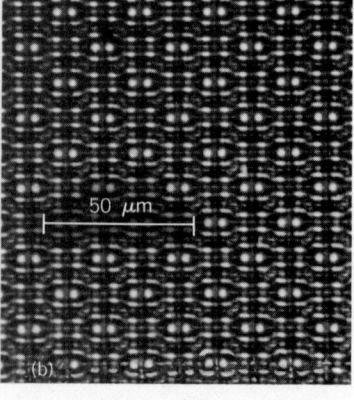

Fig. 16. Increased density from advanced technology as seen in cell areas of (a) 4096-bit random-access memory (1974) and (b) 262,144-bit random-access memory (1984). (*Intel Corp.*)

ARCHITECTURE AND CIRCUITRY 103

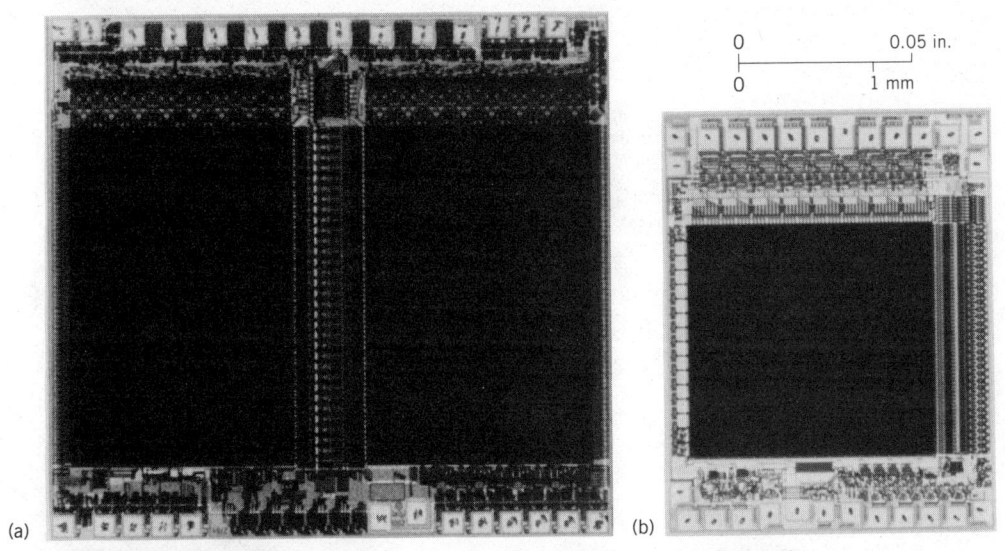

Fig. 17. Photographs of 65,536-bit electrically programmable read-only memory (EPROM) circuits. (a) 1981 manufacturing technology; chip area of 24,025 square mils (15.5 mm^2). (b) 1984 manufacturing technology; chip area of 11,500 square mils (7.4 mm^2). (*Intel Corp.*)

the smaller feature sizes (**Fig. 18**). This has allowed the density of memory circuits to quadruple every 3 years instead of 4–5 years.

One of the major reasons that it has been economical to increase the chip size is that the size of the silicon wafer used during processing continues to increase (**Fig. 19**). Where in 1970 2-in. (50-mm) wafers were common, by 1980 4-in. (100-mm) wafers were the choice for new manu-

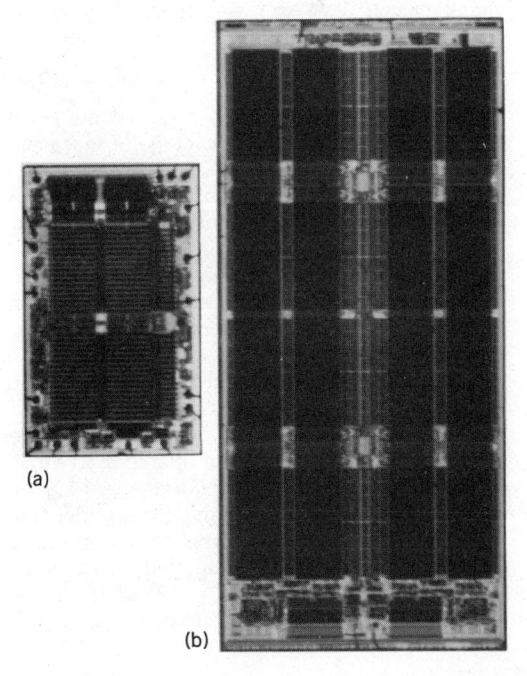

Fig. 18. Increase in die (chip) size from (a) 4096-bit random-access memory (1974) to (b) 262,144-bit random-access memory (1984). (*Intel Corp.*)

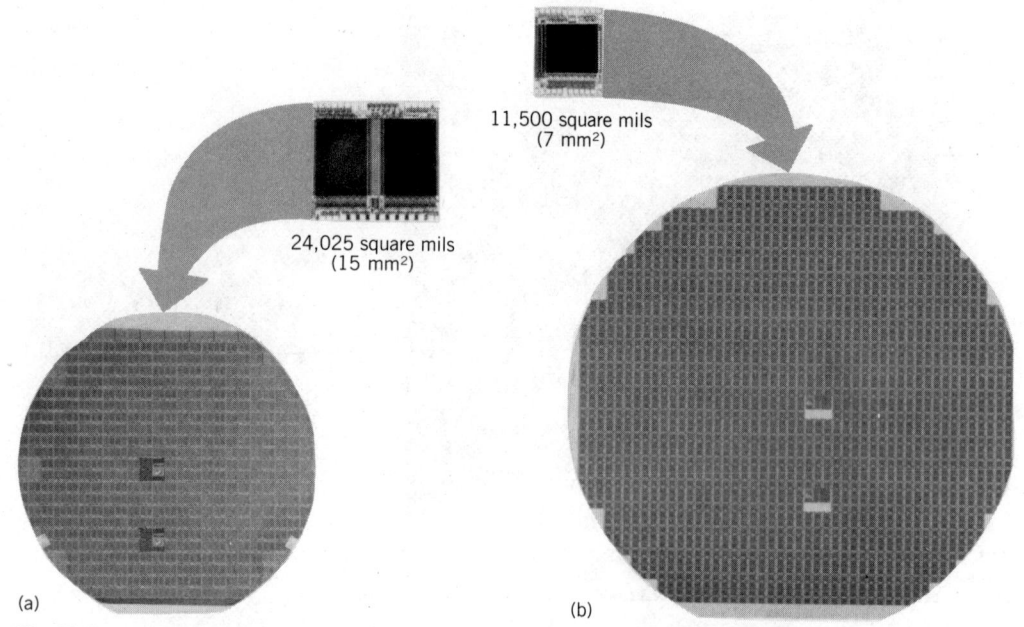

Fig. 19. Increased die per wafer available when decreasing the chip area plus increasing the wafer area. (*a*) 4-in. (100-mm) wafer. (*b*) 6-in. (150-mm) wafer. (*Intel Corp.*)

facturing lines. During the mid-1980s, the 6-in. (150-mm) wafer was the direction of new manufacturing lines. The larger wafer plus the smaller feature sizes of the newer technologies continue to decrease the cost of integrated circuits. This tendency is showing signs of slowing down, however, due to the fact that new manufacturing equipment results in a fixed cost per square inch of silicon. Two examples are the step-and-repeat photolithography and ion implanters which have slower throughput for the large wafers.

GALLIUM ARSENIDE CIRCUITS

Integrated circuits based on gallium arsenide (GaAs) have come into increasing use since the late 1970s. The major advantage of these circuits is their fast switching speed.

Galium arsenide FET. The gallium arsenide field-effect transistor (GaAs FET) is a majority carrier device in which the cross-sectional area of the conducting path of the carriers is varied by the potential applied to the gate (**Fig. 20**). Unlike the MOSFET, the gate of the GaAs FET is a Schottky barrier composed of metal and gallium arsenide. Because of the difference in work functions of the two materials, a junction is formed. The depletion region associated with the junction is a function of the difference in voltage of the gate and the conducting channel, and the doping density of the channel. Be applying a negative voltage to the gate, the electrons under the gate in the channel are repelled, extending the depletion region across the conducting channel. The variation in the height of the conducting portion of the channel caused by the change in the extent of the depletion region alters the resistance between the drain and source. Thus the negative voltage on the gate modulates the current flowing between the drain and the source, as shown by the linear region of operation in Fig. 20*c*. As the height of the conducting channel is decreased by the gate voltage or as the drain voltage is increased, the velocity of charge carriers (electrons for *n*-type gallium arsenide) under the gate increases (similar to water in a hose when its path is constricted by passing through the nozzle). The velocity of the carriers continues to increase with increasing drain voltage, as does the current, until their saturated velocity is obtained (about 10^7 cm/s or 3×10^5 ft/s for gallium arsenide). At that point the device is in the saturated region of operation; that is, the current is independent of the drain voltage.

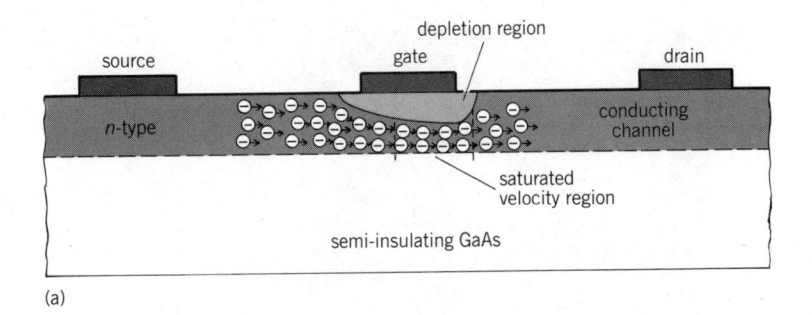

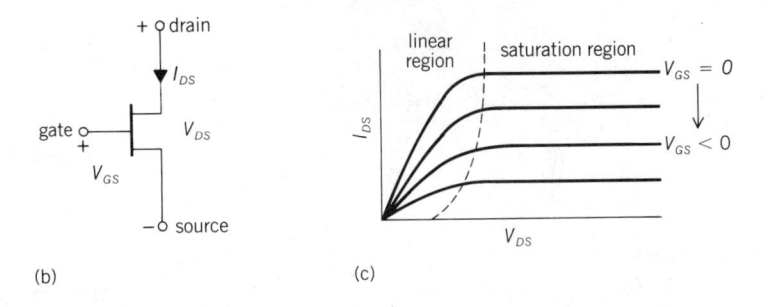

Fig. 20. Gallium arsenide FET. (a) Cross section. (b) Circuit symbol. (c) Current-voltage characteristics. I_{DS} = drain source current. V_{DS} = drain source voltage. V_{GS} = gate source voltage.

The high-frequency operation of a device is limited by the transit time of the carriers under the gate. The time during which the velocity of electrons (output signal) is modulated by the voltage on the gate (input signal) must be short compared to any change of the input voltage. Because electrons in gallium arsenide have a high saturated velocity, GaAs FETs operate at very high frequencies. The high-frequency performance is also improved by decreasing the gate length (the length of the path of the electrons under the gate) by using special lithographic techniques to define the gate during processing. Gallium arsenide FETs with gate lengths as short as 0.1 μm (4×10^6 in.) have been fabricated resulting in a potential frequency of operation of approximately 100 GHz.

Fast switching speed. As noted above, the major advantage of gallium arsenide integrated circuits over silicon integrated circuits is the faster switching speed of the logic gate. The reason for the improvement of the switching speed of GaAs FETs with short gate lengths (less than 1 μm or 4×10^{-5} in.) over silicon FETs of comparable size has been the subject of controversy. In essence, the speed or gain-bandwidth product of a FET is determined by the velocity with which the electrons pass under the gate. The saturated drift velocity of electrons in gallium arsenide is twice that of electrons in silicon; therefore the switching speed of gallium arsenide might be expected to be only twice as fast.

However, this simplified model neglects several important aspects of the problem. One way to determine the switching speed of a logic circuit is to calculate the total capacitance that must be charged or discharged as the logic level is switched, and the current drive available. The larger the current drive and the smaller the capacitance, the faster the switching speed. Since gallium arsenide integrated circuits are fabricated on semi-insulating substrates, the parasitic capacitance to ground is much smaller than for silicon integrated circuits. The only comparable small-capacitance silicon technology is CMOS/SOS (silicon on sapphire). Also, because of the higher mobility, the transconductance of a GaAs FET is much higher than for a silicon FET, and the associated parasitic resistances are lower. Thus, there is more current change for a given amount of input voltage. Finally, the mobility of gallium arsenide is six to eight times that of silicon, and even though the saturated velocities of gallium arsenide and silicon are within a factor of two, the electrical field necessary for the carriers to reach velocity saturation in gallium arsenide (about 4 kV/cm) is much less than in silicon (about 40 kV/cm). Therefore, when operating at the low

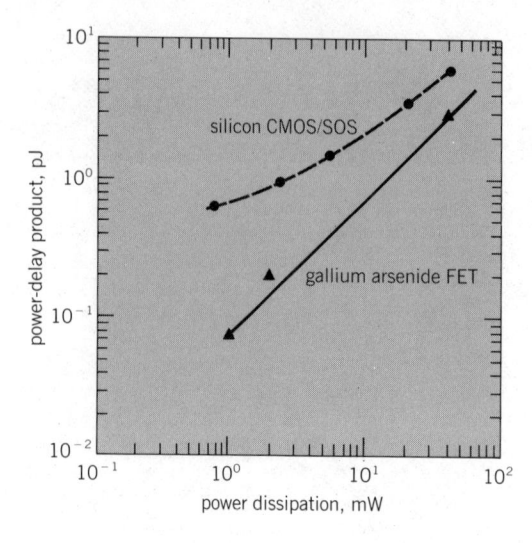

Fig. 21. Comparison of gallium arsenide and silicon inverter performance.

voltages typical of GaAs FETs, the speed ratio of similar gallium arsenide and silicon FETs is approximately proportional to their low-field mobilities. At higher voltages, the speed ratio decreases because the carrier velocity (current) continues to increase in silicon whereas the carriers are saturated in gallium arsenide; however, this increase in speed is at the expense of increased power dissipation. This effect explains the experimental results plotted in **Fig. 21**, where the power-delay products of silicon and gallium arsenide inverters with 1-μm-gate-length (4 × 10^{-5} in.) FETs are plotted as functions of power dissipation.

Device technologies. There are several device choices for high-speed gallium arsenide integrated circuits, each with certain advantages and disadvantages.

Depletion-mode FET (DFET). This is the most mature of the device technologies (**Fig. 22**). The DFET has the largest current drive capacity per unit device width for an all-GaAs FET device. This contributes to its high speed and high power dissipation. The pinchoff voltage of the DFET is determined by the channel doping and thickness under the Schottky barrier gate. This voltage can be made quite large (about −2.5 V) in order to improve the noise immunity of logic gates in which they are used.

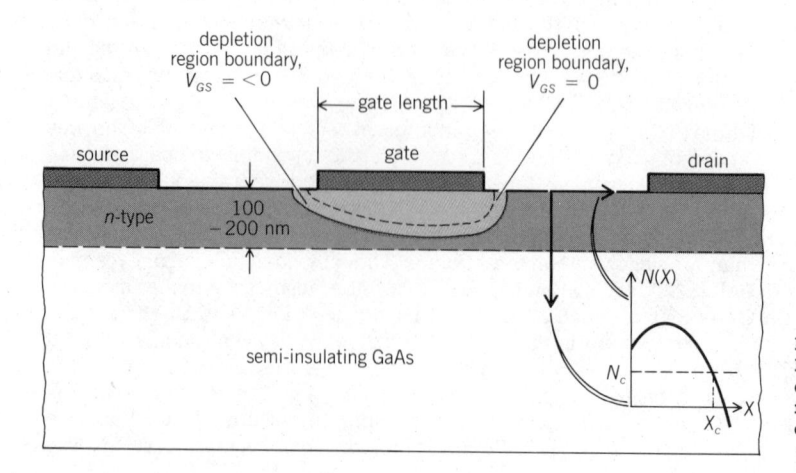

Fig. 22. Depletion-mode FET (DFET). Graph shows doping density $N(X)$ as function of depth X. N_c = compensation density; X_c = channel thickness.

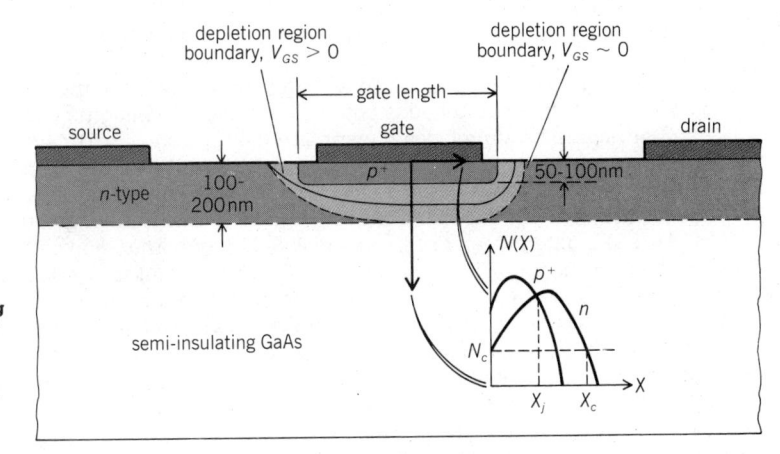

Fig. 23. Enhancement-mode junction FET (E-JFET). Graph shows doping density $N(X)$ as function of depth X in both n and p^+ regions. N_c = compensation density; X_c = channel thickness; X_j = junction depth.

Enhancement-mode FET (ENFET). This low-current, low-power device is realized by increasing the pinchoff voltage to zero or above. The logic swing for the ENFET is limited to the difference between the pinchoff voltage (approximately 0 V) and the forward turn-on voltage of the Schottky barrier gate (approximately + 0.5 V), thus providing a significantly lower noise immunity for logic gates using ENFETs. The realization of medium-scale integration (MSI) and LSI chips in which the noise margins are small requires stringent process controls to fabricate devices across the wafer with very small variations in pinchoff voltage.

Enhancement mode junction FET (E-JFET). In this device the Schottky barrier of the ENFET is replaced with an implanted p region that forms a pn junction for the gate (**Fig. 23**). The E-JFET has all the advantages of the ENFET with respect to low power plus the additional advantage of a slightly larger logic swing due to the larger turn-on voltage of the pn junction. The ultimate speed of the E-JFET will be less than an ENFET of similar dimesions because the added side wall gate capacitance of the pn-junction gate is a significant fraction of the total gate capacitance at submicrometer gate lengths.

Logic gate configurations. Three different logic gate configurations (**Fig. 24**) are presently the most popular approaches to high-speed gallium arsenide logic circuits. The buffered-FET logic (BFL) gate is the fastest gate for reasonable fanouts but dissipates the most power (approximately 5–10 mW/per gate). The Schottky diode FET logic (SDFL) gate dissipates about one-fifth the power of the BFL; however, it is slower by about a factor of two. Finally, direct-coupled FET logic (DCFL) gates using enhancement-mode FETs have the lowest power consump-

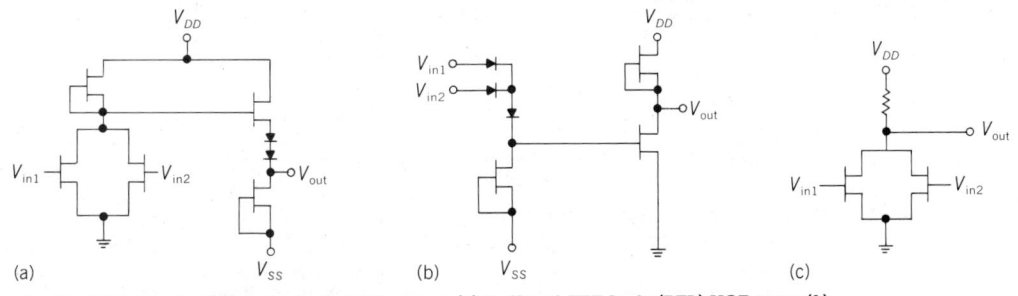

Fig. 24. High-speed gallium arsenide logic gates. (a) Buffered FET logic (BFL) NOR gate. (b) Schottky diode FET logic (SDFL) NOR gate. (c) Direct-coupled FET logic (DCFL) NOR gate. V_{in} = input voltage, V_{out} = output voltage, V_{DD} = drain supply voltage, V_{SS} = source supply voltage.

tion (about 50 μW/per gate) at gate delays two to four times those of BFL for complex logic circuits.

The BFL gate using DFETs requires level shifting to make the input and output logic levels compatible. This extra circuitry adds both delay to the switching time of the gate and extra power consumption; however, it provides buffering to the next stage and therefore has very good fanout (fanout is the number of identical logic gates it must drive) and on-off chip drive capabilities. Because of the high power dissipation and the large device count per gate, BFL will not be suitable for circuits with the complexity of large scale integration (greater than 1000 gates).

The SDFL gate incorporates very small Schottky barrier diodes (1×2 μm or 4×10^{-5} by 8×10^{-5} in.) to perform the input logical-OR function and to provide level shifting. The invert function is performed by the DFETs in the second stage. Because of the lower power dissipation and small diodes, packing densities of more than 1000 gates/mm^2 (645,000 gates/in.^{2}) are achievable. Large fan-in does not require any significant chip area because of the small diodes; however, SDFL gates are very fanout-sensitive, and for fanouts of greater than 3 either buffers or much wider DFETs must be incorporated to maintain the speed. Because of the medium power dissipation and high packing density, SDFL is suitable for large-scale integration applications but not for circuits with the complexity of very large-scale integration (more than 10,000 gates).

DCFL incorporating ENFETs is inherently much simpler than BFL or SDFL since there is no need for level shifting. The very low power consumption and circuit simplicity lead to high packing density (more than 5000 gates/mm^2 or 3.2×10^6 gates/in.^{2}) at only slightly slower speeds.

Gallium arsenide logic gate applications and issues			
Gallium arsenide technology	Target applications	Feasibility issues	Competing silicon technology
Buffered FET logic (BFL)	SSI (small-scale integration)-MSI (medium-scale integration) superfast logic-prescalers, multiplexers, demultiplexers, fast cache memory	Most producible, uses large logic swings with good noise margin; tolerant of FET threshold variations; least area efficient.	Emitter-coupled logic (ECL) and submicrometer MOS
Schottky diode FET logic (SDFL)	High-speed LSI (large scale integration), for example, 8×8 multiplier; arithmetic-logic unit (ALU), gate arrays	Replaces FETs with diodes for logic function; usually smaller noise margin than BFL, but still fairly tolerant of threshold variations; circuit design is complicated by fanout sensitivity	Bipolar LSI; 1-μm MOS LSI
Direct-coupled FET logic (DCFL)	Low power or VLSI (very large scale integration) applications, memory, gate arrays	Uses enhancement FETs; low-noise margin; requires excellent threshold control	1-μm MOS VLSI

The **table** lists the projected applications for each of the three logic gates, along with the competing silicon technology.

Bibliography. N. G. Enspruch et al. (eds.), *VLSI Electronics, Microstructure Science*, vols. 1–12, 1981–1985; D. J. Elliott, *Integrated Circuit Fabrication Technology*, 1982; P. R. Gray and R. G. Meyer, *Analysis and Design of Analog Integrated Circuits*, 2d ed., 1984; P. T. Greiling, The future impact of GaAs digital ICs, *IEEE Journal on Selected Areas in Communications*, 1985; R. S. Muller and T. I. Kamins, *Device Electronics for Integrated Circuits*, 1986; E. H. Nicollian and J. R. Brews, *MOS (Metal Oxide Semiconductor) Physics and Technology*, 1982; W. F. Ruska, *Microelectronic Processes: An Introduction to the Manufacture of Integrated Circuits*, 1987; S. M. Sze (ed.), *VLSI Technology*, 2d ed., 1988.

LOGIC CIRCUITS
R. R. SHIVELY AND W. V. ROBINSON

The basic building blocks used to realize consumer and industrial products that incorporate digital electronics. Such products include digital computers, video games, voice synthesizers, pocket calculators, and robot controls. SEE CALCULATORS; DIGITAL COMPUTER; ROBOTICS; VOICE RESPONSE.

The change that has enabled widespread economical use of digital logic once found only in very expensive, room-sized computers has been a dramatic evolution in device technology. Logic circuits which comprise several basic electronic devices (typically transistors, resistors, and diodes) were once designed with each device as a separate physical entity. Now, very large-scale integration of devices offers up to several hundred thousand equivalent basic devices on one small piece of silicon, typically rectangular with maximum dimensions of a few tenths of an inch (1 in. = 25 mm) per side. SEE INTEGRATED CIRCUITS.

This dramatic reduction in size has been accompanied by a number of effects. The cost and power consumption per logic device have been greatly reduced. The modestly priced digital watch that can run for over a year on a tiny battery exemplifies these effects.

Logic circuit operation. Logic circuits process information encoded as voltage or current levels. The adjective "digital" derives from the fact that symbols are encoded as one of a limited set of specific values. While it would be feasible to encode information using many distinct voltage levels (for example, each of 10 voltage levels might correspond to a distinct decimal digit value), there are several reasons for using binary or two-valued signals to represent information: the complexity of the sending and receiving circuit is reduced to a simple on-off switch type of operation corresponding to the two-valued signals; the speed of operation is far greater since it is not necessary to wait until a changing signal has had time to converge to a final value before interpreting its binary value; and the on-off operation makes the circuitry very tolerant of both changing characteristics of devices due to aging or temperature-humidity environment and electromagnetically induced noise added to the voltage levels.

Since signals are interpreted to be one of only two values (denoted as 0 and 1), a group of four such signals must be used to represent a decimal digit, as an example. A very commonly used convention in computers and terminals is to use a group of eight binary signals to represent alphabetic, numeric, and in general any keyboard-derived symbol. The eight signals enable encoding any of 256 character or symbol values.

More generally, the binary digits, or bits, are used in a number system with digit weights that change by multiples of 2 rather than multiples of 10 as in the decimal system. In this system, successive digits or bits have weights of 1, 2, 4, 8, . . . , in contrast to the decimal system where successive digits have weights of 1, 10, 100, ... SEE NUMBER SYSTEMS.

Types of logic functions. All logic circuits may be described in terms of three fundamental elements, shown graphically in **Fig. 1**. The NOT element has one input and one output; as the name suggests, the output generated is the opposite of the input in binary. In other words, a 0 input value causes a 1 to appear at the output; a 1 input results in a 0 output. Two NOT elements in series, one output driving the input to the other, simply reproduce a copy of the input signal.

The AND element has an arbitrary number of inputs and a single output. (Electrical characteristics of devices used or physical packaging of devices result in some practical limit to the number of inputs allowed.) As the name suggests, the output becomes 1 if, and only if, all of the inputs are 1; otherwise the output is 0. The AND together with the NOT circuit therefore enables searching for a particular combination of binary signals. If, for example, a signal is needed that goes to 1 only when signals A, B, and C are 1, 0, and 1, respectively, then the circuit indicated in **Fig. 2** will generate the desired output.

The third element is the OR function. As with the AND, an arbitrary number of inputs may exist and one output is generated. The OR output is 1 if one or more inputs are 1.

The operations of AND and OR have some analogies to the arithmetic operations of multiplication and addition, respectively. The collection of mathematical rules and properties of these operations is called Boolean algebra.

While the NOT, AND, and OR functions have been designed as individual circuits in many circuit families, by far the most common functions realized as individual circuits are the NAND and

110 COMPUTER SCIENCE SOURCE BOOK

Logic Symbol   **Truth Table**

Elementary Elements:

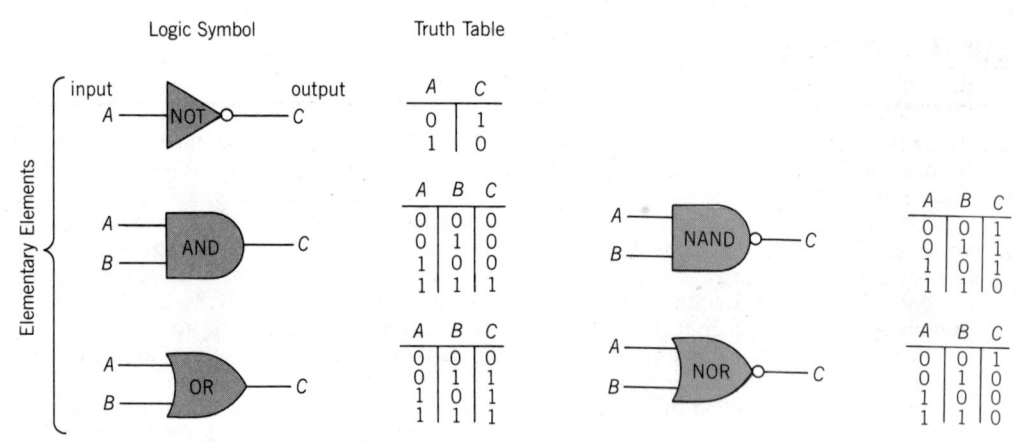

NOT gate: input A → NOT → output C

A	C
0	1
1	0

AND gate: A, B → AND → C

A	B	C
0	0	0
0	1	0
1	0	0
1	1	1

OR gate: A, B → OR → C

A	B	C
0	0	0
0	1	1
1	0	1
1	1	1

NAND gate: A, B → NAND → C

A	B	C
0	0	1
0	1	1
1	0	1
1	1	0

NOR gate: A, B → NOR → C

A	B	C
0	0	1
0	1	0
1	0	0
1	1	0

Fig. 1. Logic elements.

NOR circuits of **Fig. 1**. A NAND may be described as equivalent to an AND element driving a NOT element. Similarly, a NOR is equivalent to an OR element driving a NOT element. (The reason for this strong bias favoring inverting outputs is that the transistor, and the vacuum tube which preceded it, are by nature inverters or NOT-type circuit devices when used as signal amplifiers.) An interesting property of the NAND or NOR circuits is that all logic functions may be accessed using either type of circuit. A NOT element, for example, is realized as a one-input NAND. An AND element is realized as NAND followed by a NOT element. An OR element is realized by applying a NOT to each input individually and then applying the resulting outputs to the NAND as inputs.

Combinational and sequential logic. As the names of the logic elements described suggest, logic circuits respond to combinations of input signals. In an arithmetic adder, for example, a network of logic elements is interconnected to generate the sum digit as an output by monitoring combinations of input digits; the network generates a 1 for each output only in response to those combinations in the addition table that call for it.

Logic networks which are interconnected so that the current set of output signals is responsive only to the current set of input signals are appropriately termed combinational logic.

An important further capability for processing information is memory, or the ability to store information. In digital systems, the memory function has been provided for by a variety of technologies, including magnetic cores, stored charge, magnetic bubbles, and magnetic tape. The logic circuits themselves must provide a memory function if information is to be manipulated at the speeds the logic is capable of. The logic elements defined above may be interconnected to provide this memory by the use of feedback. SEE COMPUTER STORAGE TECHNOLOGY.

The circuit indicated in **Fig. 3** illustrates a basic and perhaps the most commonly used form of memory circuit. Normally both inputs A and B to the cross-coupled NAND gates are at the voltage corresponding to logic 1; if a 0 is applied to signal A, outputs C and D assume the values 0 and 1, respectively, based on the definition of NAND operation; the outputs retain these values after input A is returned to the quiescent value of 1. Conversely, if B is set to 0 while A is 1, then the outputs C and D become 1 and 0, respectively, and again retain these values after B is returned to a value of 1. In the jargon of logic circuit design, this circuit is variously called a flip-

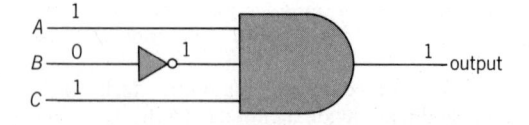

Fig. 2. Logic circuit whose output is 1 only when input signals A, B, and C are 1, 0, and 1, respectively.

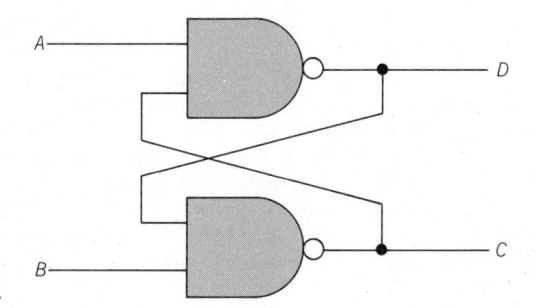

Fig. 3. Memory element.

flop, toggle, or trigger. Like the light switch on the wall, the circuit retains one of two stable states after the force initiating change to that state is removed. This circuit is therefore well matched to the storage of binary or two-valued signals. Logic circuit networks that include feedback paths to retain information are termed sequential logic networks, since outputs are in part dependent on the prior input signals applied and in particular on the sequence in which the signals were applied.

Logic circuit embodiment. Several alternatives exist for the digital designer to create a digital system.

Ready-made catalog-order devices can be combined as building blocks. In this case, manufacturers have attempted to provide a repertoire of logic networks that will find common usage and generality. Some examples of the types of circuits found in digital circuit manuals or catalogs are: arrays of individual logic gates (typically four to six) with outputs and inputs available as external connections to the device; arrays of memory elements (flip-flops) used to hold a collection of binary signals or digits; arithmetic adders capable of adding four corresponding binary digits from each of two binary numbers and of being cascaded to produce an adder for any multiple of four digits; and multipliers capable of forming the product of two 16-bit numbers in a single step (that is, a combinational multiplier).

The significance of these examples is that the number of gates or logic elements realized on individual devices ranges from a few to several thousand. Clearly a design that can use the devices with larger gate counts is likely to be more compact and more economical.

A second and increasingly common realization of logic gates is custom-designed devices. Two factors which make this practical are computer-aided-design (CAD) tools and libraries of subnetworks that can be used as building blocks. Custom design of a logic network implies the generation of highly complicated artwork patterns, called masks, for use in photographic-development-like steps used to produce the integrated circuit networks. The availability of a library of subnetworks for which this artwork has already been generated reduces the additional artwork required to interconnection patterns among these library elements to set up the desired logic network. *See* COMPUTER-AIDED DESIGN AND MANUFACTURING.

A third option is gate-array devices. In this case, the device vendor manufactures devices comprising a two-dimensional array of logic cells. Each cell is equivalent to one or a few logic gates. The final layers of metallization that determine the exact function of each cell and interconnect the cells to form a specific network are deferred until the customer orders such a device. This procedure uses the advantage of mass production for the majority of processing steps necessary to manufacture a device, including most of the necessary artwork. Since the interconnecting metallization layers are a relatively small and simple part of the total device fabrication, the customization cost and time can be reduced significantly by this method relative to a totally custom fabrication. The sacrifice in this approach is that the packing density of the two-dimensional array will tend to be less than a custom-designed layout, since routing channels must allow for reasonably general interconnection patterns.

A fourth option in realizing logic functions is programmable logic arrays, or PLAs. The manufactured part has the potential for realizing any of a large number of different sets of logic functions; the particular functions produced are determined by actually blowing microscopic fuses built into the device, in effect removing unwanted connections. In one device, each of 16 device-input signals is an input to each of 48 AND gates; the 48 AND outputs are input signals to 8 OR gates that generate the device outputs. Selective removal of inputs to the AND gates, and between the AND and OR gates, enables implementation of a wide variety of functions.

A fifth embodiment of logic network functions involves the use of table look-up. A logic network has several binary input signals and one or more binary outputs. The transformation of input signal combinations to output signal values need not be realized by AND-OR-type logic elements at all; instead, the collection of input signals can be grouped arbitrarily as address digits to a memory device. In response to any particular combination of inputs the memory device location that is addressed becomes the output. For example, a logic network function involving 10 binary inputs and 8 binary output signals could be realized with a single memory device that holds 1024 memory cells, with 8 bits stored in each cell. (Ten bits addresses $2^{10} = 1024$ locations.)

The form of memory device used for table look-up is usually read-only, that is, memory contents are defined as part of the manufacturing process by means of the last layer of metallization, or one of a number of other means is used to fix the memory cell contents so that it is not necessary to reload the memory after each turn-off of power.

Typically, this approach may lead to slower operation than the use of logic circuits, but in some cases can lead to very significant economies.

The last form of logic network embodiment that will be discussed is the microcomputer. A microcomputer is a single device that includes a read-only memory to hold a program, a processor capable of reading and executing that program, and a small read-write memory for scratch working space. Just as a memory device provides an efficient realization of a combinational network, the equivalent of a highly complex sequential network can be had with a microcomputer, as evidenced by electronic games. Two important advantages of this approach are that little or no custom-device fabrication is required, and the programmability permits utilization of complicated and modifiable equivalent networks. SEE MICROCOMPUTER; MICROPROCESSOR.

As with table look-up, the principal disadvantage of this approach is that the speed of operation may be slower than if an actual network of high-speed logic circuits were used.

Technology. There are basically two logic circuit families in widespread use: bipolar and metal-oxide-semiconductor (MOS).

The basic MOS device is formed by using a silicon substrate which has been doped in such a way as to greatly increase the hole/electron relative density, forming a p-type substrate. In addition to the substrate, two diffused n-type regions are formed. A layer of metal, insulated from the substrate by a deposit of oxide, is situated between the two n regions. This metal connection is known as the gate, and the two n regions are called the source and drain; since the device is symmetrical in every respect, source and drain are functionally interchangeable. When a sufficient voltage exists between the metal gate and the substrate, electrons are conducted between the drain and source connections, essentially shorting the two together. Otherwise, a high resistance exists between the two. Thus, the gate input is analogous to the control lever of a switch. In like manner, an n-type doping of the substrate, along with a p-type source and drain, may be used to implement the switch. This will result in hole migration between source and drain when the gate is turned on.

The simplest MOS logic structure is the transmission gate (also known as pass transistor and steering logic); only one transistor is used to implement the function, where source and gate leads represent the two input variables, and the drain becomes the output value. The transistor is turned on when the gate voltage is above the threshold voltage that assures sufficient current flow through the channel; in other words, it acts as a short between source and drain. This is analogous to a mechanical switch in the "on" position. When the gate is below the threshold potential the switch is opened, thus performing an AND-like function on the inputs.

The NAND logic function is also easily derived with MOS circuits. **Figure 4** shows a sample NAND circuit in which the transistors A, B, and C are configured in series and must therefore all be in the "on" state for a conduction path from output Z to ground to be established. If A, B and C are all above threshold, output Z is shorted to ground or is forced to logical zero. On the other hand, if any of A, B, or C are off, an open circuit essentially exists between Z and ground. In this case, output node Z exhibits much less resistance to the power source ($R \ll R_a + R_b + R_c$) and therefore will be at the voltage potential of the power source.

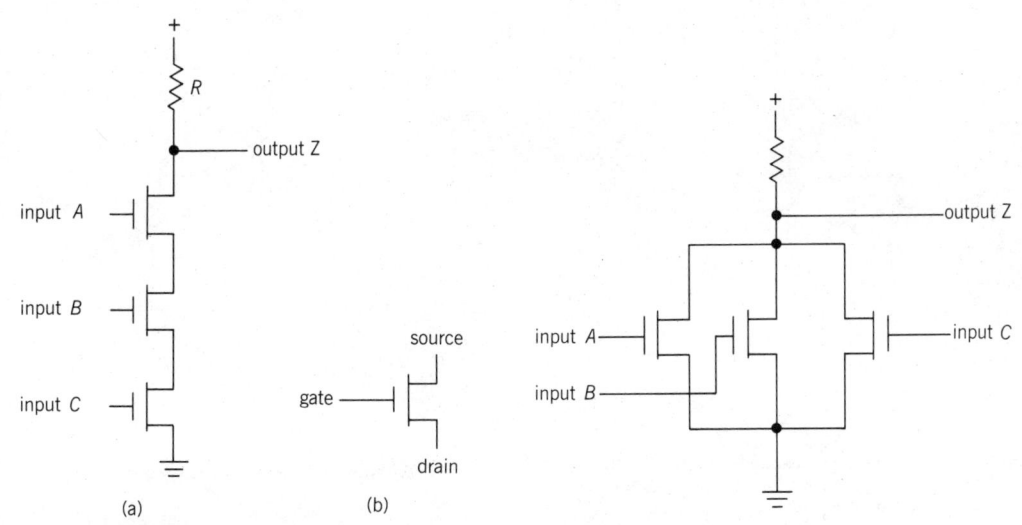

Fig. 4. MOS NAND gate. (a) Circuit configuration. (b) MOS transistor (*n* or *p*), the basic circuit device.

Fig. 5. MOS NOR gate.

This NAND circuit can be reconfigured into the NOR circuit of **Fig. 5**. Here, the transistors *A*, *B*, and *C* are in parallel instead of in series, and it is easily seen that when any of the inputs are turned on the output will be grounded. Otherwise, *Z* will be pulled up to the power supply voltage.

Another useful MOS logic structure is the AND-OR-INVERT, which performs the logic functions exactly as stated in the name. The A-O-I is shown in **Fig. 6** to be a combination of the NAND and NOR configurations. Output *Z* is low only if the function (*A*1 AND *A*2) OR (*B*1 AND *B*2) is high.

As described earlier, either an *n*-channel substrate (NMOS) or a *p*-channel substrate (PMOS) may be used to implement the logic structures. Additionally, both types may be used concurrently in the logic circuit to fabricate a more sophisticated device. **Figure 7** shows an inverter built with both NMOS and PMOS devices. When the input is low, the NMOS transistor

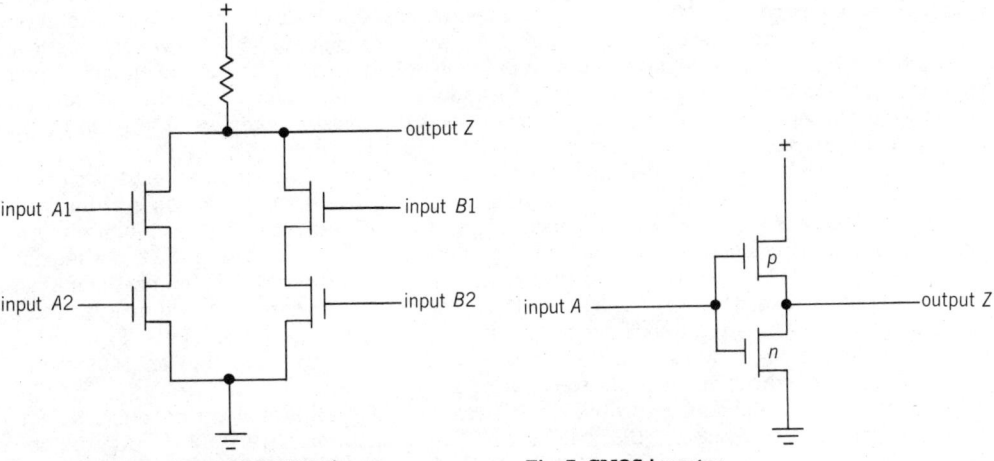

Fig. 6. MOS A-O-I (AND- OR-INVERT) gate.

Fig. 7. CMOS inverter.

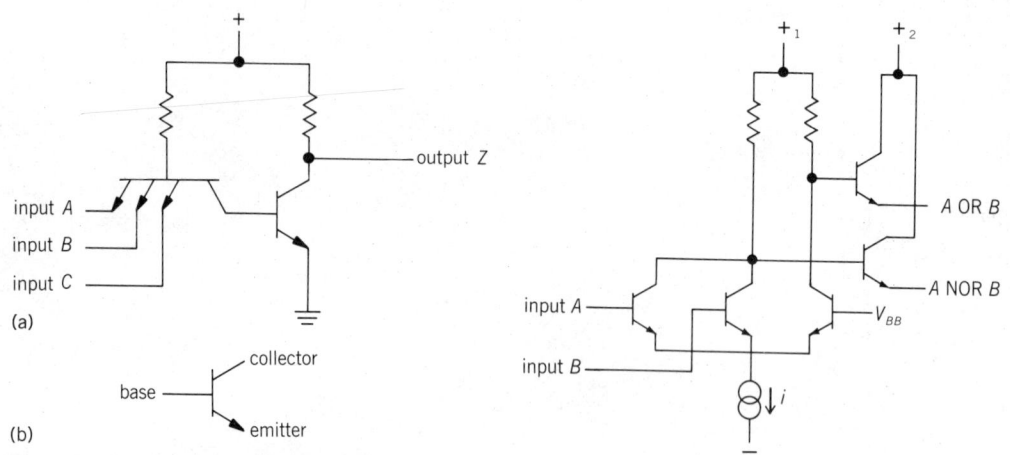

Fig. 8. TTL (transistor-transistor-logic) NAND gate. (a) Circuit configuration. (b) Bipolar junction transistor (*npn*), the basic circuit device.

Fig. 9. ECL (emitter-coupled-logic) OR/NOR gate.

is cut off and the PMOS transistor conducts, shorting the output to the power source. On the other hand, when the input is high, the PMOS gate is shut off and the NMOS gate shorts the output to ground, thus performing the inverter function. The advantage of such a complementary configuration, known as CMOS, is primarily one of power dissipation. Owing to the fact that only one complementary transistor conducts at any time (other than the short overlap during switching), there is always a very high resistance from the power source to ground, and therefore very little current flows through the pair. The primary disadvantage of CMOS over the common MOS circuit is the increased fabrication complexity due to the n and p substrates occupying the same chip, and the secondary disadvantage is the increased area needed to build the CMOS structure because of the use of complementary pairs.

The charge carriers in an MOS transistor are either free electrons or holes. For this reason, MOS is known as a unipolar device. In contrast, devices which utilize both free electrons and hole migration are made. These are known as bipolar devices, such as the junction transistor. Although general comparisons are hard to make, these devices typically exhibit much less input resistance and demand a more sophisticated fabrication technique than do MOS devices, but offer the advantage of accentuated high-frequency response. In terms of logic realization, the bipolar family encompasses many common circuit types. Perhaps the best-known and most widely used implementation of logic switches is the bipolar transistor-transistor logic, or TTL. Shown schematically in **Fig. 8**, the basic TTL NAND gate is formed by a multiemitter transistor (turned on only if every input is high) followed by an output transistor that acts as a pullup/buffer. Thus, the first transistor performs an AND operation on the inputs and the second transistor completes the NAND by performing an inversion.

TTL transistors are operated in the saturation mode; in other words, the transistors are driven hard to either the cutoff or the saturation limits. This overdriving introduces a time delay that does not exist if the transistors are operated in the nonsaturated mode. Such nonsaturating logic, while inherently faster, is more susceptible to noise since it is biased in the linear region.

Current-mode logic, or CML, is a popular form of nonsaturation logic and most often takes the configuration of emitter-coupled logic, or ECL. The basic ECL gate is shown in **Fig. 9** to be composed of current-steering transistors that perform an OR operation on the inputs. Typically, the gate output is amplified by an emitter-follower transistor, and both the true and complement signals can be made available with no added delay as outputs.

Bibliography. A. E. Almaini, *Electronic Logic Systems*, 1986; M. Mandl, *Introduction to Digital Logic Techniques and Systems*, 1983; J. Millman, *Microelectronics*, 1979; N. M. Morris, *Logic Circuits*, 3d ed., 1984; H. Taub, *Digital Circuits and Microprocessors*, 1982; C. A. Wiatrowski and C. H. House, *Logic Circuits and Microcomputer Systems*, 1980.

MICROPROCESSOR
SAMUEL C. LEE

A central processor unit (CPU) on a single integrated circuit (IC) chip. The physical size of a typical microprocessor wafer is around 0.2 in. × 0.2 in. (5 mm × 5 mm), but may vary from one microprocessor to another. **Figure 1** is a magnified view of a typical microprocessor. Based on its word size (bits), the commercially available microprocessors can be classified as 4-bit, 8-bit, 16-bit, 32-bit, or bit-sliced. The physical size and the number of pins of a microprocessor chip are proportional to its word size. The longer the word size, the bigger the chip, and the greater the number of pins required. The first and shortest word-size microprocessor was the Intel 4004, manufactured by Intel Corporation in 1970. Since then, the microprocessor has grown continually bigger and more powerful.

Architecture and instruction set. Each microprocessor has its own architecture, which encompasses the general layout of its major components, the principal features of these components, and the manner in which they are interconnected. However, the major components of all microprocessors are the same: (1) the clock; (2) control unit, comprising the program counter (PC), instruction register (IR), processor status word (PSW), and stack pointer (SP); (3) control memory; (4) bus control; (5) working register; (6) arithmetic/logic unit (ALU); (7) internal memory or stack. Their general layout is shown in **Fig. 2**. They are also called the hardware of a microprocessor. Besides the hardware, a microprocessor has its instruction set or software. According to the type of operations that the instructions perform, an instruction set can be subdivided into group operations for arithmetic, data transfer, branching, logic, and input/output (I/O). A set of logically related instructions stored in memory is referred to as a program. The microprocessor

Fig. 1. Typical microprocessor (Intel 8085). (*Intel Corp.*)

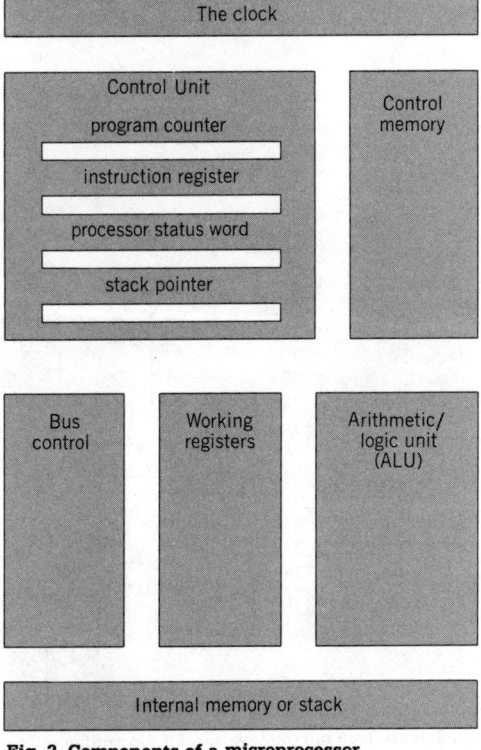

Fig. 2. Components of a microprocessor.

"reads" each instruction from memory in a logically determinate sequence, and uses it to initiate processing actions.

Fundamentals of operations. Even though the architectures and instruction sets of different microprocessors are different, their fundamentals of operation are the same. For example, the pin configuration and the block diagram of the architecture of Intel 8085, one of the commonly used microprocessors, are shown in **Fig. 3**. The 8085 contains a register array with both dedicated and general-purpose registers: (1) a 16-bit program counter; (2) 16-bit stack pointer; (3) six 8-bit general-purpose registers arranged in pairs: BC, DE, HL; (4) temporary register pair: WZ; (5) serial I/O register pair; (6) interrupt control register.

The 16-bit program counter fetches instructions from any one of 2^{16} or 65,536 possible memory locations. When the RESET IN pin of 8085 is made logic 0, the program counter is reset to zero; when the RESET IN pin is returned to logic 1, the control unit transfers the contents of the PC to the address latch, providing the address of the first instruction to be executed. Thus, program execution in the 8085 begins with the instruction in memory location zero.

8085 instructions are 1 to 3 bytes in length. The first byte always contains the operation code (OP) code). During the instruction fetch, the first byte is transferred from the memory by way of the external data bus through the data bus buffer latch into the instruction register. The PC is automatically incremented so that it contains the address of the next instruction if the instruction contains only 1 byte, or the address of the next byte of the present instruction if the instruction consists of 2 or 3 bytes.

In the case of a multibyte instruction, the timing and control section provides additional operations to read in the additional bytes. The timing and control section uses the instruction decoder output and external control signals to generate signals for the state and cycle timing and for the control of external devices. After all the bytes of an instruction have been fetched into the microprocessor, the instruction is executed. Execution may require transfer of data between the microprocessor and memory or an I/O device. For these transfers, the memory or I/O device address placed in the address latch comes from the instruction which was fetched or from one of the register pairs used as a data pointer: HL, BC, or DE.

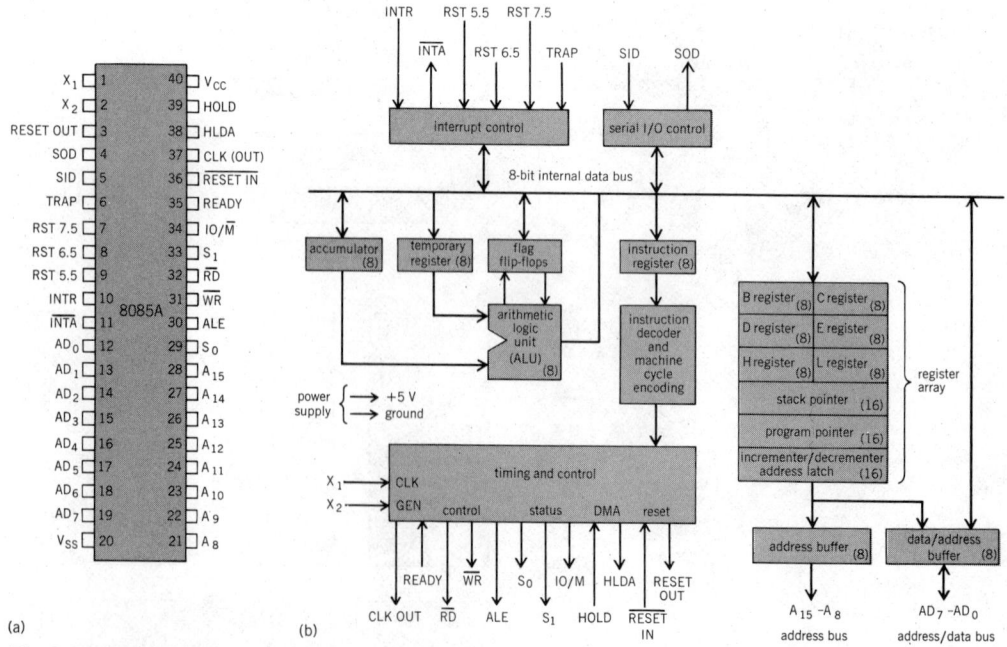

Fig. 3. Intel 8085 microprocessor. (a) Pin configuration. (b) Block diagram. (*Intel Corp.*)

The six general-purpose registers in the register array can be used as single 8-bit registers or as 16-bit register pairs. The temporary register pair, WZ, is not program-addressable and is only used by the control unit for the internal execution of instructions. For example, to address an external register for a data transfer, WZ is used to hold temporarily the address of an instruction read into the microprocessor until the address is transferred to the address and address/data latch.

The 16-bit stack pointer, SP, always points to the top of the stack allocated in external memory. The stack, as previously indicated, primarily supports interrupt and subroutine programming.

The 8085's arithmetic/logic unit performs arithmetic and logic operations on data. The operands for these operations are stored in two registers associated with the ALU: the 8-bit accumulator and the 8-bit temporary register. The accumulator is loaded from the internal bus and can transfer data to the internal bus. Thus, it serves as both a destination and source register for data. The temporary register stores one of the operands during a binary operation. For example, if the contents of register B are to be added to the contents of the accumulator and the result left in the accumulator, the temporary register holds a copy of the contents of register B while the arithmetic operation is taking place.

Associated with the ALU is the 5-bit flag register, F, which indicates conditions associated with the results of arithmetic or logic operations. The flags indicate zero, a carry-out of the high-order bit, the sign (most significant bit), parity, and auxiliary carry (carry-out of the fourth bit). S*EE* D*IGITAL COMPUTER PROGRAMMING.*

Bit-sliced microprocessors. Bit-sliced microprocessors achieve a high performance level which the single-chip microprocessors are unable to provide. The major logic of a central processor is partitioned into a set of large-scale-integration (LSI) devices as opposed to being placed on a single chip. The chip set is used as the basic building block to construct a microprogrammed central processor which can be configured in various ways. Unlike the single-chip microprocessor, several identical processor elements can be wired in parallel to achieve a desirable word length. The microprogrammed architecture allows the addition of new instructions without modifying the hardware wiring, and consequently provides a flexibility that is very desirable.

Digital system design. The main difference between the microprocessor digital system design and the hard-wired logic digital system design is that the former uses the microprocessor to replace hard-wired logic by storing program sequences in the read-only memory (ROM) rather than implementing these sequences with gates, flip-flops, counters, and so on. After the design is completed, any modifications or changes may be made by simply changing the program in the ROM. The microprocessor digital system design is now widely used because of the following advantages:

1. Manufacturing costs of industrial products can be significantly reduced.

2. Products can get to the market faster, providing a company with the opportunity to increase product sales and market share.

3. Product capability is enhanced, allowing manufacturers to provide customers with better products, which can frequently command a higher price in the marketplace.

4. Development costs and time are reduced.

5. Product reliability is increased, while both service and warranty costs are reduced. S*EE* S*EMICONDUCTOR MEMORIES.*

Applications. Typical application areas include: industrial sequence controllers; machine tool controllers; point-of-sale terminals; intelligent terminals; instrument processors; traffic light controllers; weather data collection systems; and process controllers. S*EE* D*IGITAL COMPUTER;* I*NTEGRATED CIRCUITS;* M*ICROCOMPUTER.*

Bibliography. D. L. Cannon and G. Luecke, *Understanding Microprocessors*, 2d ed., 1984; S. Evanczuk, *Microprocessor Systems: Software, Hardware, and Architecture*, 1984; C. M. Gilmore, *Introduction to Microprocessors*, 1982; J. D. Greenfield (ed.), *Microprocessor Handbook*, 1985; D. V. Hall, *Microprocessors and Interfacing: Programming and Hardware*, 1986; F. J. Hall, F. J. Hill, and G. R. Peterson, *Digital Logic and Microprocessors*, 1984.

3
DATA CONVERSION AND OUTPUT

Analog-to-digital converter	120
Digital-to-analog converter	123
Digital counter	125
Character recognition	128
Electronic display	134
Computer graphics	143

ANALOG-TO-DIGITAL CONVERTER
DANIEL H. SHEINGOLD

A device for converting the information contained in the value or magnitude of some characteristics of an input signal, compared to a standard or reference, to information in the form of discrete states of a signal, usually with numerical values assigned to the various combinations of discrete states of the signal.

Analog-to-digital (A/D) converters are used to transform analog information, such as audio signals or measurements of physical variables (for example, temperature, force, or shaft rotation) into a form suitable for digital handling, which might involve any of these operations: (1) processing by a computer or by logic circuits, including arithmetical operations, comparison, sorting, ordering, and code conversion, (2) storage until ready for further handling, (3) display in numerical or graphical form, and (4) transmission.

If a wide-range analog signal can be converted, with adequate frequency, to an appropriate number of two-level digits, or bits, the digital representation of the signal can be transmitted through a noisy medium without relative degradation of the fine structure of the original signal. SEE COMPUTER GRAPHICS; DATA COMMUNICATIONS; DIGITAL COMPUTER.

Concepts and structure. Conversion involves quantizing and encoding. Quantizing means partitioning the analog signal range into a number of discrete quanta and determining to which quantum the input signal belongs. Encoding means assigning a unique digital code to each quantum and determining the code that corresponds to the input signal. The most common system is binary, in which there are 2^n quanta (where n is some whole number), numbered consecutively; the code is a set of n physical two-valued levels or bits (1 or 0) corresponding to the binary number associated with the signal quantum. SEE BIT.

Figure 1 shows a typical three-bit binary representation of a range of input signals, partitioned into eight quanta. For example, a signal in the vicinity of 3/8 full scale (between 5/16 and 7/16 will be coded 011 (binary 3). SEE NUMBER SYSTEMS.

Conceptually, the conversion can be made to take place in any kind of medium: electrical, mechanical, fluid, optical, and so on (for example, shaft-rotation-to-optical); but by far the most commonly employed form of A/D converters comprises those devices that convert electrical voltages or currents to coded sets of binary electrical levels (for example, +5 V or 0 V) is simultaneous (parallel) or pulse-train (serial) form, as shown in **Fig. 2**. The serial output is not always made available.

The converter depicted in Fig. 2 converts the analog input to a five-digit "word." If the coding is binary, the first digit (most significant bit, abbreviated MSB) has a weight of 1/2 full scale, the second 1/4 full scale, and so on, down to the nth digit (least-significant bit, abbreviated LSB), which has a weight of 2^{-n} of full scale (1/32 in this example). Thus, for the output word shown, the analog input must be given approximately by the equation shown. The number of

$$\frac{16}{32} + \frac{0}{32} + \frac{4}{32} + \frac{2}{32} + \frac{0}{32} = \frac{22}{32} = \frac{11}{16} \text{ FS (full scale)}$$

bits, n, characterizes the resolution of a converter. The **table** translates bits into other conventional measures of resolution in a binary system.

Figure 2 also shows a commonly used configuration of connections to an A/D converter: the analog signal and reference inputs; the parallel and serial digital outputs; the leads from the power supply, which provides the required energy for operation; and two control leads—a start-

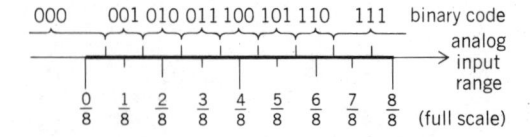

Fig. 1. A three-bit binary representation of a range of input signals.

DATA CONVERSION AND OUTPUT

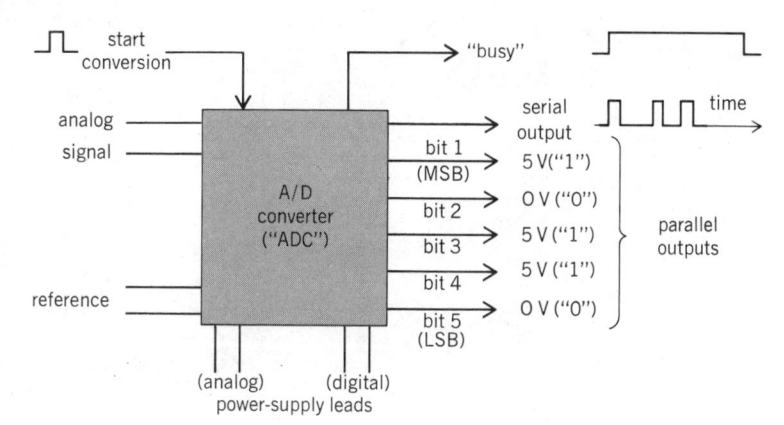

Fig. 2. Basic diagram of an analog-to-digital converter, showing parallel and serial (return-to-zero) output formats for code 10110.

conversion input and a status-indicating output (busy) that indicates when a conversion is in progress. The reference voltage or current is often developed within the converter.

Second in importance to the binary code and its many variations is the binary-coded decimal (BCD), which is used rather widely, especially when the encoded material is to be displayed in numerical form. In BCD, each digit of a radix-10 number is represented by a four-digit binary subgroup. For example, the BCD code for 379 is 0011 0111 1001. The output of the A/D converter used in digital panel meters is usually BCD.

Techniques. There are many techniques used for A/D conversion, ranging from simple voltage-level comparators to sophisticated closed-loop systems, depending on the input level, output format, control features, and the desired speed, resolution, and accuracy. The two most popular techniques are dual-slope conversion and successive-approximations conversion.

Binary resolution equivalents*

Bit	2^{-n}	$1/2^n$ (fraction)	dB (decibels)	$1/2^n$ (decimal)	%	Parts per million
FS†	2^0	1	0	1.0	100	1,000,000
MSB‡	2^{-1}	1/2	−6	0.5	50	500,000
2	2^{-2}	1/4	−12	0.25	25	250,000
3	2^{-3}	1/8	−18.1	0.125	12.5	125,000
4	2^{-4}	1/16	−24.1	0.0625	6.2	62,500
5	2^{-5}	1/32	−30.1	0.03125	3.1	31,250
6	2^{-6}	1/64	−36.1	0.015625	1.6	15,625
7	2^{-7}	1/128	−42.1	0.007812	0.8	7,812
8	2^{-8}	1/256	−48.2	0.003906	0.4	3,906
9	2^{-9}	1/512	−54.2	0.001953	0.2	1,953
10	2^{-10}	1/1024	−60.2	0.0009766	0.1	977
11	2^{-11}	1/2048	−66.2	0.00048828	0.05	488
12	2^{-12}	1/4096	−72.2	0.00024414	0.024	244
13	2^{-13}	1/8192	−78.3	0.00012207	0.012	122
14	2^{-14}	1/16,384	−84.3	0.000061035	0.06	61
15	2^{-15}	1/32,768	−90.3	0.0000305176	0.003	31
16	2^{-16}	1/65,536	−96.3	0.0000152588	0.0015	15
17	2^{-17}	1/131,072	−102.3	0.00000762939	0.0008	7.6
18	2^{-18}	1/262,144	−108.4	0.000003814697	0.0004	3.8
19	2^{-19}	1/524,288	−114.4	0.000001907349	0.0002	1.9
20	2^{-20}	1/1,048,576	−120.4	0.0000009536743	0.0001	0.95

*From D. H. Sheingold (ed.), *Analog-Digital Conversion Handbook*, Analog Devices, Inc., 1972.
†Full scale.
‡Most significant bit.

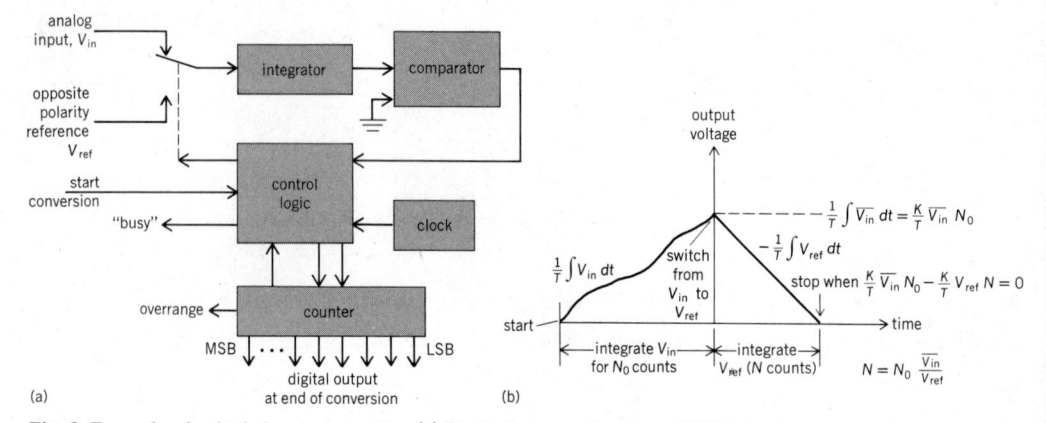

Fig. 3. Example of a dual-slope conversion. (*a*) Block diagram of converter. (*b*) Integrator output. Here, k is a constant, and T is the *RC* (resistor-capacitor) time constant of the integrator.

Dual slope. Dual-slope converters have high resolution and low noise sensitivity; they operate at relatively low speeds—usually a few conversions per second. They are primarily used for direct dc measurements requiring digital readout; the technique is the basis of the most widely used approach to the design of digital panel meters.

Figure 3*a* is a simplified block diagram of a dual-slope converter. The input is integrated for a period of time determined by a clock-pulse generator and counter (Fig. 3*b*). The final value of the signal integral becomes the initial condition for integration of the reference in the opposite sense, while the clock output is counted. When the net integral is zero, the count stops. Since the integral "up" of the input over a fixed time (N_0 counts) is equal to the integral "down" of the fixed reference, the ratio of the number of counts of the variable period to that of the fixed period is equal to the ratio of the average value of the signal to the reference.

Successive approximations. Successive-approximations conversion is a high-speed technique used principally in data-acquisition and computer-interface systems. **Figure 4***a* is a

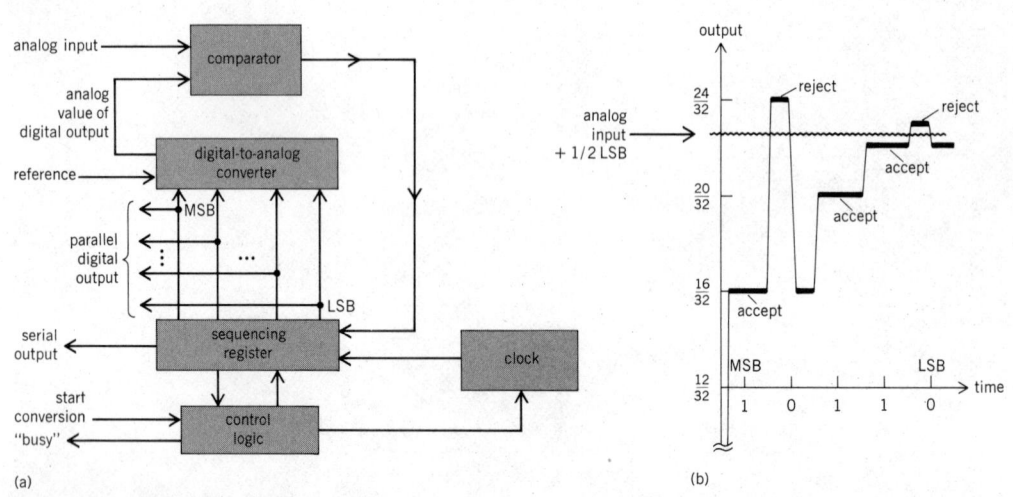

Fig. 4. Successive-approximations conversion. (*a*) Block diagram of converter. (*b*) Digital-to-analog converter output for the example in Fig. 2.

simplified block diagram of a successive-approximations converter. In a manner analogous to the operation of an apothecary's scale with a set of binary weights, the input is "weighed" against a set of successively smaller fractions of the reference, produced by a digital-to-analog (D/A) converter that reflects the number in the output register. *See* D*igital-to-analog converter*.

First, the MSB is tried (1/2 full scale). If the signal is less than the MSB, the MSB code is returned to zero; if the signal is equal to or greater than the MSB, the MSB code is latched in the output register (Fig. 4b). The second bit is tried (1/4 full scale). If the signal is less than 1/4 or 3/4, depending on the previous choice, bit 2 is set to zero; if the signal is equal to or greater than 1/4 or 3/4, bit 2 is retained in the output register. The third bit is tried (1/8 full scale). If the signal is less than 1/8, 3/8, 5/8, or 7/8, depending on previous choices, bit 2 is set to zero; otherwise, it is accepted. The trial continues until the contribution of the least-significant bit has been weighed and either accepted or rejected. The conversion is then complete. The digital code latched in the output register is the digital equivalent of the analog input signal.

Physical electronics. The earliest A/D converters were large rack-panel chassis-type modules using vacuum tubes, requiring about 1.4 ft^3 (1/25 m^3) of space and many watts of power. Since then, they have become smaller in size and cost, evolving through circuit-board, encapsulated-module, and hybrid construction, with improved speed and resolution. Single-chip 12-bit A/D converters with the ability to interface with microprocessors are now available in small integrated-circuit packages. Integrated-circuit A/D converters, with 6-bit and better resolution and conversion rates to beyond 50 MHz, are also commercially available. *See* M*icroprocessor*.

Bibliography. Analog Devices Inc. staff (ed.), *Analog-Digital Conversion Handbook*, 3d ed., 1986; G. B. Clayton, *Data Converters*, 1982; B. Loriferne, *Analog-Digital and Digital-Analog Conversion*, 1982; I. D. Seitzer, *Electronic Analog to Digital Converters*, 1983; T. Young, *Digital Processing of Analog Signals*, 1985.

DIGITAL-TO-ANALOG CONVERTER
Daniel H. Sheingold

A device for converting information in the form of combinations of discrete states or a signal, often representing binary number values, to information in the form of the value or magnitude of some characteristics of a signal, in relation to a standard or reference. Most often, it is a device which has electrical inputs representing a parallel binary number, and an output in the form of voltage or current.

Figure 1 shows the structure of a typical digital-to-analog converter. The essential elements, found even in the simplest devices, are enclosed within the dashed rectangle. The digital inputs, labeled u_i, $i = 1, 2, \ldots, n$, are equal to 1 or 0. The output voltage E_o is given by Eq. (1), where V_{REF} is an analog reference voltage and K is a constant. Thus, for a 5-bit binary converter with latched input code 10110, the output is given by Eq. (2).

$$E_o = KV_{REF} (u_1 2^{-1} + u_2 2^{-2} + u_3 2^{-3} + \cdots + u_n 2^{-n}) \tag{1}$$

$$E_o = \left(\frac{16}{32} + \frac{0}{32} + \frac{4}{32} + \frac{2}{32} + \frac{0}{32}\right) KV_{REF} = \frac{11}{16} KV_{REF} \tag{2}$$

Bit 1 is the "most significant bit" (MSB), with a weight of 1/2; bit n is the "least significant bit" (LSB), with a weight of 2^{-n}. The number of bits n characterizes the resolution. *See* A*nalog-to-digital converter*; N*umber systems*.

Uses. Digital-to-analog (D/A) converters (sometimes called DACs) are used to present the results of digital computation, storage, or transmission, typically for graphical display or for the control of devices that operate with continuously varying quantities. D/A converter circuits are also used in the design of analog-to-digital converters that employ feedback techniques, such as successive-approximation and counter-comparator types. In such applications, the D/A converter may not necessarily appear as a separately identifiable entity.

Circuitry. The fundamental circuit of most D/A converters involves a voltage or current reference; a resistive "ladder network" that derives weighted currents or voltages, usually as

124 COMPUTER SCIENCE SOURCE BOOK

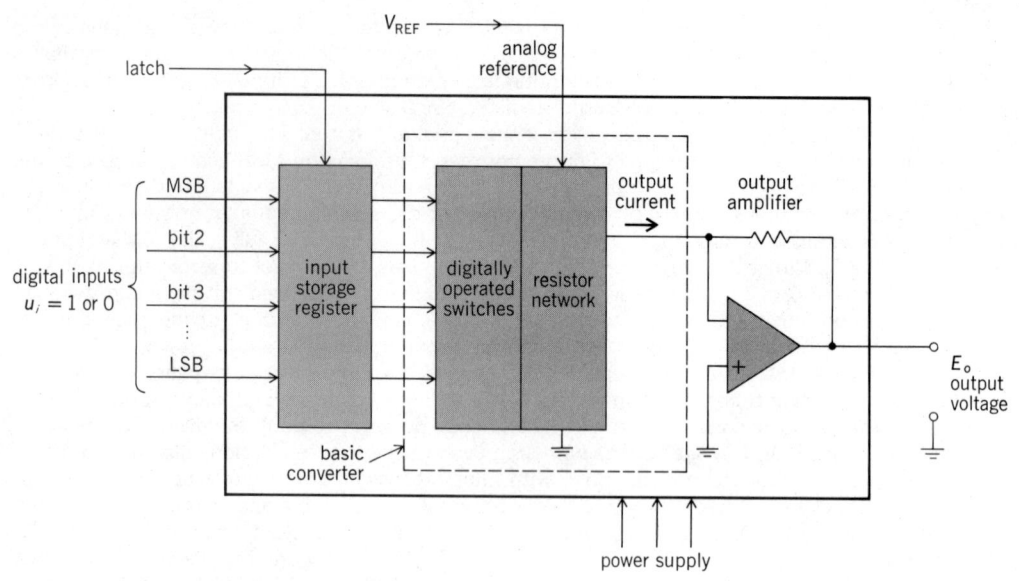

Fig. 1. Structure of a typical digital-to-analog converter.

discrete fractions of the reference; and a set of switches, operated by the digital input, that determines which currents or voltages will be summed to constitute the output.

An elementary three-bit D/A converter is shown in **Fig. 2**. Binary-weighted currents developed in R_1, R_2, R_3 by V_{REF} are switched either directly to ground or to the output summing bus (which is held at zero volts by the operational-amplifier circuit). The sum of the currents develops an output voltage of polarity opposite to that of the reference across the feedback resistor R_f. The **table** shows the binary relationship between the input code and the output, both as a voltage and as a fraction of the reference.

The output of the D/A converter is proportional to the product of the digital input value and the reference. In many applications, the reference is fixed, and the output bears a fixed

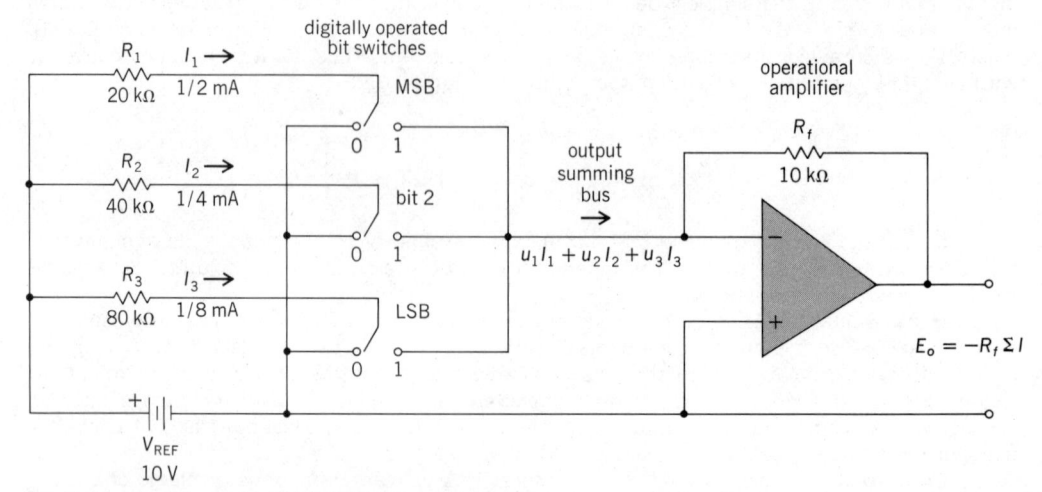

Fig. 2. Circuit of elementary 3-bit digital-to-analog converter.

Input and output of converter in Fig. 2				
Digital input code			Analog output	
u_1	u_2	u_3	$-E_o$, volts	$\dfrac{E_o}{V_{REF}}$
0	0	0	0	0
0	0	1	1.25	1/8
0	1	0	2.5	2/8
0	1	1	3.75	3/8
1	0	0	5.0	4/8
1	0	1	6.25	5/8
1	1	0	7.5	6/8
1	1	1	8.75	7/8

proportion to the digital input. In other applications, the reference, as well as the digital input, can vary; a D/A converter that is used in these applications is thus called a multiplying DAC. It is principally used for imparting a digitally controlled scale factor, or "gain," to an analog input signal applied at the reference terminal. *See* ANALOG COMPUTER.

Construction. Except for the highest resolutions (beyond 16 bits), commercially available D/A converters are generally manufactured in the form of dual in-line-packaged integrated circuits, using bipolar, MOS, and hybrid technologies. A single chip may include just the resistor network and switches, or may also include a reference circuit, output amplifier, and one or more sets of registers (with control logic suitable for direct microprocessor interfacing). *See* INTEGRATED CIRCUITS.

Bibliography. Analog Devices Inc. staff (ed.), *Analog-Digital Conversion Handbook*, 1986; G. B. Clayton, *Data Converters*, 1982; B. Loriferne, *Analog-Digital and Digital-Analogy Conversion*, 1982; I. D. Seitzer, *Electronic Analog to Digital Converters*, 1983.

DIGITAL COUNTER
MICHAEL E. WRIGHT

An instrument which, in its simplest form, provides an output that corresponds to the number of pulses applied to its input.

Types. Counters may be categorized into two types: the Moore machine or the Mealy machine. The simpler counter type, the Moore machine, has a single count input (also called the clock input or pulse input), while the Mealy machine has additional inputs that alter the count sequence. Digital counters take many forms: geared mechanisms (tape counters and odometers are examples), relays (old pinball machines and old telephone switching systems), vacuum tubes (old test equipment), and solid-state semiconductor circuits (most modern electronic counters). This article will stress solid-state electronic counters.

Most digital counters operate in the binary number system, since binary is easily implemented with electronic circuitry. Binary allows any integer (whole number) to be represented as a series of binary digits, or bits, where each bit is either a 0 or 1 (off or on, low or high, and so forth). *See* NUMBER SYSTEMS.

Figure 1 shows a four-bit binary counter that can count from 0 to 15; the sixteenth count input causes the counter to return to the 0 output state and generate a carry pulse. This action of the counter to return to the 0 state with a carry output on every sixteenth pulse makes the four-bit binary counter a modulo 16 counter. The four binary-digit outputs Q_D, Q_C, Q_B, and Q_A are said to have an 8-4-2-1 "weighting" because, if Q_D through Q_A are all ones, then the binary counter output is $1111_2 = 1 \times 2^3 + 1 \times 2^2 + 1 \times 2^1 + 1 \times 2^0 = 8 + 4 + 2 + 1 = 15_{10}$, where the subscripts indicate the base of the number system. In **Fig. 1**a, the counter state-flow diagram is

COMPUTER SCIENCE SOURCE BOOK

(a)

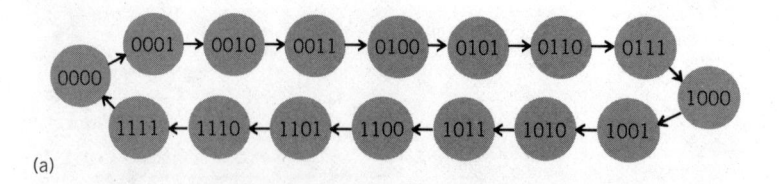

number of count pulses	binary output	octal (base 8)	decimal (base 10)	hexadecimal (base 16)
0	0000	0	0	0
1	0001	1	1	1
2	0010	2	2	2
3	0011	3	3	3
4	0100	4	4	4
5	0101	5	5	5
6	0110	6	6	6
7	0111	7	7	7
8	1000	10	8	8
9	1001	11	9	9
10	1010	12	10	A
11	1011	13	11	B
12	1100	14	12	C
13	1101	15	13	D
14	1110	16	14	E
15	1111	17	15	F
16	0000	0	0	0

(b)

(c)

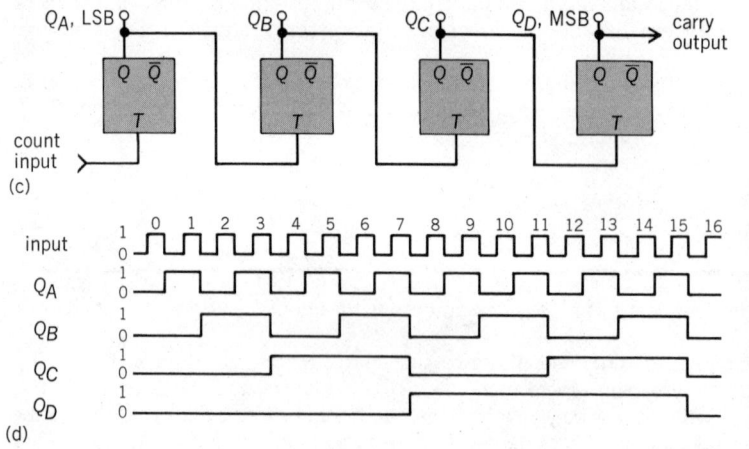

(d)

Fig. 1. Four-bit binary counter using trigger flip-flops; this is a Moore machine. (*a*) State-flow diagram. (*b*) Table of the counter output in various number systems. (*c*) Circuit block diagram. LSB = least significant bit; MSB = most significant bit. (*d*) Output waveforms.

shown. The word "state" refers to the number, the datum, in the counter; this datum is stored in four flip-flop devices, each of which is a memory bit that stores the current value of one binary digit. Each possible state is represented by the numerical output of that state inside a circle. Upon receiving a count pulse, the counter must change state by following an arrow from the present state to the next state. In Fig. 1*b*, a table is given showing the counter output after a given number of input pulses, assuming that the counter always starts from the 0 state. The counter output is listed in binary, octal, decimal, and hexadecimal. Figure 1*c* shows a block diagram of the counter built with T flip-flops, and Fig. 1*d* shows the counter waveforms through time, with a periodic count input. The T flip-flop is a device that has either a 0 or a 1 on its Q output at all times. When the count input T moves from the 1 state to the 0 state, the flip-flop output must change state, from a 0 to a 1 or a 1 to a 0. The carry output produces a 1-to-0 transition on every sixteenth count input, producing a divide-by-16 function.

The four bits of the counter of Fig. 1 can be grouped together and used to represent a single hexadecimal digit; in Fig. 1b, each counter output state represents one hexadecimal digit. A two-digit hexadecimal counter requires two sets of four-bit binary counters, the carry output from the first set of counters driving the count input of the second set of counters.

A decimal counter built from four binary counters is shown in **Fig. 2**. Let four bits of data from the binary counter represent one decimal digit. The counter will work in the same way as the counter of Fig. 1, except that all the flip-flops are reset to the 0 state when the counter moves from the $1001_2 = 9$ state, instead of advancing to the $1010_2 = 10$ state. Besides the AND gate that is now used to detect the 1001 state of the counter and enable the resets, the circuit block diagram shows a new type of flip-flop. The "SR" flip-flop acts like a T flip-flop with an additional input that forces the Q output to a 1 state when the S (set) input is high and the T input has had a 1-to-0 transition applied. An R (reset) input acts as the S input does, except that the Q output goes to 0. This example decimal counter has an 8-4-2-1 weighted output that is known as binary coded decimal (B.C.D.). A seven-segment display is easily interfaced to the binary-coded-decimal counter using a binary-coded-decimal-to-seven-segment decoder/driver circuit that is widely available.

Applications. Digital counters are found in much modern electronic equipment, especially equipment that is digitally controlled or has digital numeric displays. A frequency counter, as a test instrument or a channel frequency display on a radio tuner, consists simply of a string of decade counters that count the pulses of an input signal for a known period of time, and display that count on a seven-segment display. A digital voltmeter operates by using nearly the same idea, except that the counter counts a known frequency for a period of time proportional to the input voltage. SEE ANALOG-TO-DIGITAL CONVERTER.

A digital watch contains numerous counter/dividers in its large-scale integration (LSI) chip, usually implemented with complementary metal oxide semiconductor (CMOS) technology. A typical watch generates a 32,768-Hz crystal oscillator signal that is divided by 2^{15} (15 T flip-flop binary counters) to produce a 1-Hz signal that is counted as seconds by using two decimal counters that reset and produce a carry at every sixtieth count. That carry output is counted as a minutes display, generating another modulo 60 carry pulse for the hours display. The hours counters produce a carry at every twenty-fourth count to run the days counter and display; that counter generates a carry pulse every 28 to 31 days, depending on the month. SEE INTEGRATED CIRCUITS.

Digital computers may contain counters in the form of programmable interval timers that count an integral number of clock pulses of known period, and then generate an output at the end of the count to signal that the time period has expired. Most of the counters in a microprocessor consist of arithmetic logic units (ALU) that add one many-bit number to another, storing

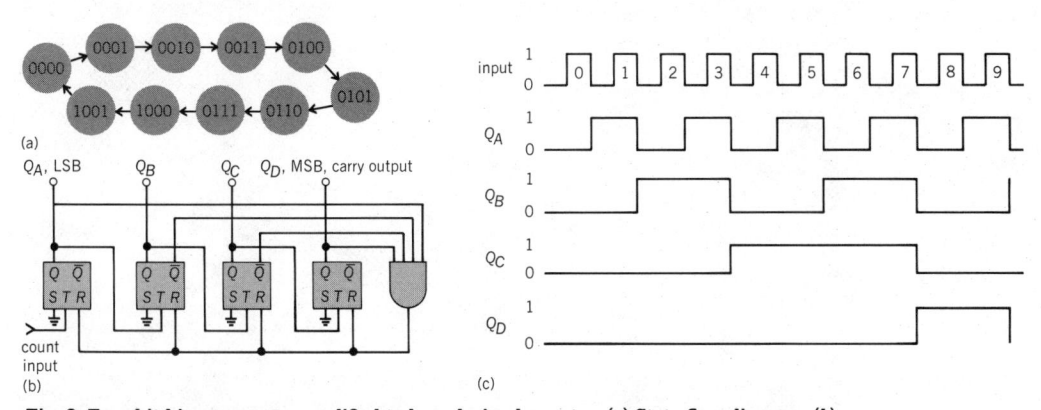

Fig. 2. Four-bit binary counter modified to be a decimal counter. (a) State-flow diagram. (b) Circuit block diagram. LSB = least significant bit; MSB = most significant bit. (c) Output waveforms.

the results in a memory location. The program and data counters are examples of this kind of counter. *See* DIGITAL COMPUTER; MICROPROCESSOR.

Counter specifications. Counters have progressed from relays to light-wavelength-geometry very large-scale-integrated circuits. There are several technologies for building individual digital counters. Single counters are available as integrated circuit chips in emitter-coupled logic (ECL), transistor-transistor logic (TTL), and CMOS. The three technologies are listed in the order of decreasing speed and decreasing power dissipation. ECL will operate to 600 MHz, TTL to 100 MHz (Schottky-clamped), and CMOS to 5 MHz. Standard, high-volume production n-channel metal oxide semiconductor (NMOS) LSI can implement a 1-bit binary counter in a 100 × 100 μm^2 (39 × 3.9 mil^2) area that will operate to 10 MHz. A gallium arsenide metal-semiconductor field-effect transistor (MESFET) master-slave *JK* flip-flop has been produced that operates at 610 MHz in a 390 × 390 μm^2 (15 × 15 mil^2) surface area while consuming the power of an NMOS.

CHARACTER RECOGNITION
LAVEEN N. KANAL

The technology of using machines to automatically identify human-readable symbols, most often alphanumeric characters, and then to express their identities in machine-readable codes. This operation of transforming numbers and letters into a form directly suitable for electronic data processing is an important method of introducing information into computing systems. *See* DATA-PROCESSING SYSTEMS.

Character recognition machines, sometimes called character readers, print readers, scanners, or reading machines, automatically convert printed alphanumeric characters or symbols into a machine-readable code at high speeds. The output of the character recognition machine may be temporarily stored on magnetic disks or magnetic tape. Alternatively, the recognition system may be operated on line with the data processor (**Fig. 1**). The first commercial application of character recognition was in the banking industry, which adopted magnetic ink character recognition (MICR). In most applications, the printed or typed characters are sensed optically; this process is called optical character recognition (OCR).

Optical mark reading (OMR) refers to the simpler technology of optically sensing marks. The information being read is encoded as a series of marks such as lines or filled-in boxes on a

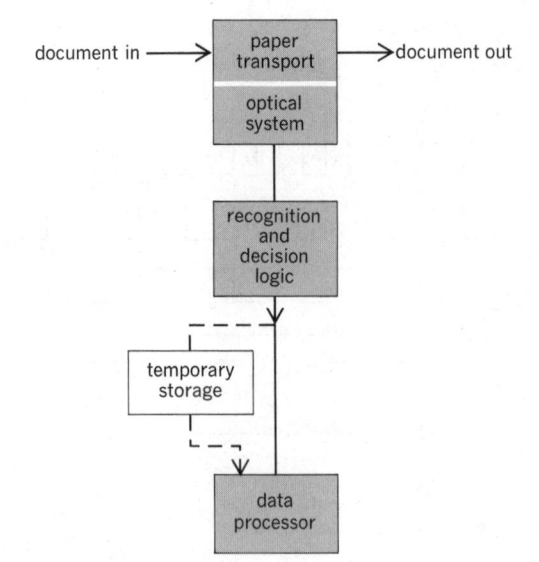

Fig. 1. Diagram of optical character recognition system.

test answer sheet, or as some special pattern such as the Universal Product Code (UPC). The UPC uses a predetermined and reproducible standard pattern which corresponds to each number in a 10-digit code. A relatively simple optical scanner detects the pattern and then decodes the number.

There are various manual alternatives to automatic character recognition equipment for data entry. These include keypunch, key tape, and key disk systems, in which the data are entered through a keyboard and are recorded on punched cards, magnetic tape, or rotating magnetic disks, respectively. Keyboard terminals are another approach to on-line data entry. Manual keystroking is a tedious and costly operation, and it is therefore advantageous to use automatic character recognition equipment whenever the form of the information to be entered is consistent with the capabilities of the character recognition system. Limited-vocabulary isolated-word voice recognition equipment is now available for data entry. However, voice input is also a slow process and would not be competitive with OCR in situations where the data already exist in printed or typed form.

PATTERN RECOGNITION

The technology of automatically recognizing complex patterns is being developed in the context of numerous military and civilian applications such as: the analysis of aerial and satellite images obtained with visible, infrared, radar, and multispectral sensors, for the detection and classification of military objects, terrain types, weather patterns, and land use patterns; identification of individuals or medical conditions using fingerprint, palmprint, blood cell, tissue cell, chromosome, and x-ray images; processing of voice, sonar, electrocardiogram, electroencephalogram, seismic, and other waveforms to detect and classify "signatures" of different events or conditions: automatic detection of flaws in sheet glass, bottles, textiles, paper, printed circuit boards, and integrated circuit masks; recognition of alphanumeric characters or reading for the blind, and analysis, clustering, and classification of survey and experimental data obtained in diverse disciplines.

OPTICAL CHARACTER RECOGNITION

Of all the above application areas, OCR is the single most important commercial application of pattern recognition technology.

Functional systems. The technologies used in OCR systems include optical, electronic, mechanical, and computer techniques. In general an OCR system has the following functional systems: input; transport; scanner; preprocessor; feature extraction and classification logic; and output.

Transport. The problems of feeding, transporting, and handling paper, especially at high speeds, have caused much difficulty in some applications of OCR, for example, in postal address reading for mail sorting. Turnaround documents, such as credit card slips, have tight contraints on size and quality of paper and so are much easier to transport at high speeds than mail in which size, thickness, and paper quality have only recently become subject to some constraints. Page readers may have to handle only a couple of documents per second, but each page may contain up to 2000 characters. And in some applications, for example, the reading of sales tags with a hand-held "wand," motion of the paper is completely avoided.

Scanning. The scanner converts reflected or transmitted light into an electric signal which is then digitized by an analog-to-digital (A/D) converter. Although simpler to design, transmitted light scanning requires the additional step of making a (film) transparency of every image to be read, and hence is less suitable than reflected light scanning for high-volume applications unless the documents already exist in microfilm form or are routinely microfilmed for ease of storage. SEE ANALOG-TO-DIGITAL CONVERTER.

One categorization of optical scanners is whether they employ a flying-spot or a flying-aperture principle. In the first case a spot of light sequentially illuminates successive portions of the material to be read, and all the reflected or transmitted light is collected by a detector. An example is the cathode-ray-tube (CRT) flying-spot scanner, where the CRT beam may be moved to sequentially strike the phosphor on the tube face, and the glow of the spot on the phosphor screen illuminates the corresponding spot on the document. In flying-aperture devices the entire document is flooded with light, but light is collected sequentially spot by spot from the illuminated image. An example is Vidicon scanners in which a document is flooded with light from an ordinary light source, and the reflected or transmitted light impinges upon the photoconductive target of the Vidicon. The image on the surface causes a variation in the local charge concentration, which is converted into a video signal by sequentially scanning the photoconductive surface with an electron beam.

Mechanical scanners, television cameras, CRT flying-spot scanners, solid-state linear and two-dimensional array scanners, and electrooptical scanners which use a laser as the source of illumination are the main scanning techniques which have been employed in commercial OCR systems.

Mechanical motion of the document is usually used to scan successive lines of print. Earlier OCR systems also used a rotating or oscillating mirror or a prism to scan across each line of print, and to collect the signal from a single vertical column in a character or form an entire character using a photocell array.

In solid-state scanners, instead of mechanically or electronically scanning a single beam across the region of interest, the region is sampled in small, discrete, adjacent areas by electronically switching between elements in the array. Flying-spot devices use linear or two-dimensional light-emitting-diode (LED) arrays. Flying-aperture devices use arrays of photodiodes or phototransistors.

The most commonly used scan pattern is a raster scan in which the flying spot or flying aperture sequentially scans the character area by using a sawtooth pattern. A line-following pattern has been used in some hand-print readers. Because of microprocessors, completely programmable scanners are economically feasible, making it easier to rescan rejected characters, scan blank areas at low resolution for increased throughput, and perform various preprocessing functions.

Preprocessing. Preprocessing refers to line finding, character location and isolation, normalization and centering, and related processing functions that may be needed prior to feature extraction and classification. The nature and degree of preprocessing needed depend on whether the material being read consists of stylized fonts, typescript, typeset text, or hand-printed characters.

Stylized font characters such as the ISO-A or OCR-A (**Fig. 2**) and ISO-B or OCR-B (**Fig. 3**) character sets have well-defined and closely controlled formats and line spacing. Documents using stylized font characters usually also have special symbols to guide the scanner to each field of data; special ink invisible to the optical scanner is used to print material not to be read by the OCR. Contrasted with these well-defined formats which are easy to handle automatically, are the format control problems created when reading general typeset material involving text interspersed with illustrations, tables, and so forth. In such situations, current commercial OCRs require human direction of the scanner to the appropriate data field.

Procedures available for line-finding include adaptive line-following algorithms which compensate for baseline drift in the lines of print. For situations where characters are not uniformly well spaced or in which easily detectable boundaries do not occur where expected, character

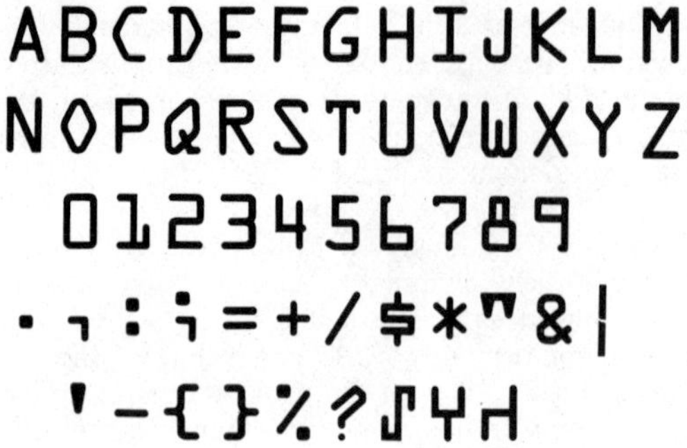

```
ABCDEFGHIJKLM
NOPQRSTUVWXYZ
0123456789
• ┐ : ; = + / $ * " & |
' - { } % ? ♪ Ч ┐
```

Fig. 2. Character set (ISO-A) approved by the American Standards Association for use in optical character recognition applications.

DATA CONVERSION AND OUTPUT   131

```
1234567890
ABCDEFGHIJKLM
NOPQRSTUVWXYZ
abcdefghijklm
nopqrstuvwxyz
*+-=/.,:;"'_
?!()<>[]%#&@^
¤£$|\ ¥■ ──
```

Fig. 3. ISO-B character set for international usage.

segmentation may involve a scanning aperture smaller than that used for subsequent classification. Various heuristic procedures are used to separate touching characters, eliminate noise such as isolated dots, and smooth out gaps or breaks in line segments.

The extent of rotation and skew correction, character segmentation, size normalization, centering, and noise elimination achievable on individual characters prior to classification determines how sophisticated the feature extraction and algorithms must be for a given application. Many commercial OCRs use simple template matching classification logic, which gives adequate performance only if variations of the above type have been essentially eliminated.

Feature extraction and classification. When simple template matching is inadequate, recognition is achieved by extracting distinctive features and using them in a decision logic to classify the characters. Decision logics are designed by using statistics of features obtained from sets of learning samples representative of the applications for which the OCR is intended.

Most high-speed commercial OCRs use special hardware for preprocessing, feature extraction, and classification, although there exists at least one high-performance, high-speed postal address reader which uses general multiprocessors and software recognition. Optical correlation, resistor summing networks, and parallel digital logic circuits represent some of the ways in which character and feature templates and weighted masks have been implemented in hardware. Centering of the character being scanned within a recognition "window," referred to as registration, may be done by shifting the digitized character through a discrete number of successive positions in a one- or two-dimensional shift register. Approaches to segmenting a line of print into individual characters include comparing successive vertical scans to give an explicit segmentation of the entire line or alternatively looking for peaks in the output of the classifier to implicitly segment each character.

Element design. The design of different elements of an OCR, that is, the transducer, the preprocessing, features, and classification logic, is determined by the type of characters and quality of material that is to be read. Some aspects which affect the design, such as line and character spacing, character-size and stroke-width variability, number of character classes, and differentiability of most similar characters, are a function of the character fonts that are used. Independent of the character fonts are other aspects, such as the reflectance of the paper, quality of the printing, and format of the document. Various standards by the American National(ANSI) contain specifications and recommendations for the paper, print quality, format rules, and measuring techniques for various classes of OCR applications.

OCR APPLICATIONS

The classes of OCR applications range from highly controlled stylized fonts to unconstrained multifont typewritten, printed, and handwritten characters encountered by postal address readers. Important elements in rating the performance of an OCR are the error rate, the throughput, the number of fonts capable of being recognized, and the cost, size, and reliability of the machine. The error rate has two components: the undetected substitution rate and the reject rate, that is, the proportion of characters not classified into any character class.

Stylized font characters. Stylized characters are designed to make automatic recognition easier. Two widely used special fonts are the ISO-A (Fig. 2), which was the first character set standardized by the International Standards Organization, and ISO-B (Fig. 3), originally promoted in Europe as being more natural looking. ANSI has also proposed a standard for hand-printed characters (**Fig. 4**). Stylized fonts are used extensively on turnaround documents such as

0 1 2 3 4 5 6 7 8 9 A B C D E F G H I J
K L M N O P Q R S T U V W X Y Z + − . ,
¢ † " # $ % ξ ´ ( ) * / : ; < = > ? @ \
^ _ [ ] ¡ Ä Ë Ï Ö Ü Á É Í Ó Ú À È Ì Ò Ù
Â Ê Î Ô Û Å Ø Ç Ñ β £ ¥ ⌐ ⌙

Fig. 4. Proposed standard character set for hand-printed OCR applications.

utility bills and gasoline credit card slips (**Fig. 5**). A common example of stylized font character recognition is the magnetic ink character recognition (MICR) system which is used on bank checks. This special font, adopted as a standard by the American Banking Association, is called E-13B (**Fig. 6**). Error rates for single-font stylized character readers can be about 1 substitution in 200,000 characters and 1 reject in 20,000. Single-stylized-font OCR wands, that is, hand-held readers, are being used more and more in inventory and point-of-sale applications. User-programmable hand-held wands in which a microprocessor can be programmed through the wand by reading special codes in the stylized character set have been introduced.

Postal address readers. At the opposite end of the scale from stylized font characters is the variability of character fonts used in postal address readers. Postal address readers sort mail in a number of large cities in the United States, and additional OCR and bar code readers are to be installed. Together with the introduction of a nine-digit business zip code and special incentives for large-volume business mailers, this equipment improves service for large-volume mailers.

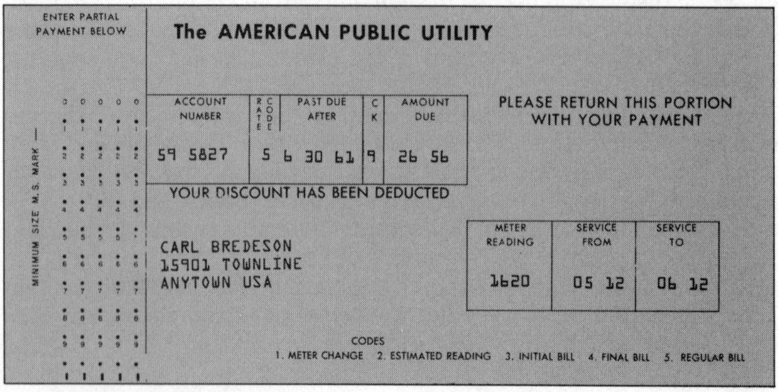

Fig. 5. Typical document for optical character recognition systems use.

DATA CONVERSION AND OUTPUT **133**

Fig. 6. E-13B font in magnetic ink on the bottom of a typical bank check to permit electronic processing.

High-volume business mailers already participate in a special "red tag" program in which batches of mail suitable for automatic reading and sorting are sorted and tagged before being sent to the post office for automatic mail sorting.

In the machine reading of outgoing mail one can make use of relationships between the city, state, and zip code on the last line of the address. Thus better recognition and missort rates can be expected on outgoing mail than on incoming mail. Performance figures on the postal address reader SARI show that the state of the art of postal address reading is well advanced. On a sample of 1,250,487 live mail pieces, a true throughput of 32,078 letters per hour was obtained with a recognition rate of 97% and a missort rate of 0.01% on outgoing mail, and a recognition rate of 93% and missort rate of 0.46% on incoming mail. On incoming mail the missort rate figure includes missorting of street numbers. The volume of mail is such that even when a substantial percentage is rejected by the OCR and diverted to subsequent manual sorting, automatic sorting of the rest can still be cost-effective.

The reading of hand-printed zip codes has been successfully accomplished in Japan by requiring that the numerals be carefully written in boxes preprinted on a standard location on the envelope. Such constraints avoid the problem of segmenting the characters and help humans adapt to the characteristics suitable for machine readability of hand-printed numerals. Preprinted boxes on envelopes are likely to be adopted by many postal services. To encourage experimentation and comparative evaluation of approaches to automatic reading of handwritten zip codes, the U.S. Postal Service has prepared two data bases. The first, CONSCRIPT, consists of multilevel digitized data tapes of the video scan from five-digit postal zip codes and six-digit numeric codes from constrained handwritten OCR forms. The second, ZIPSCRIPT, consists of multilevel digitized tapes of zip codes selected from samples or envelopes collected at dead-letter mail offices.

Typewritten and typeset characters. Many data-entry and word-processing applications are aided by the automatic reading of material typed in one of the various popular typewriter fonts. Performance figures similar to those quoted for stylized font characters may be obtained with certain typewriter fonts, that is, modified Courier, when typed on a specially aligned typewriter using carbon film ribbon, high-quality paper, and well-specified format conventions. In general, with standard typefaces, error rates are likely to be one or two orders of magnitude higher, depending on the typeface and print quality.

The large number of styles and the segmentation of variable-width characters make the automatic reading of typeset text much more difficult than typewritten material. There are more classes of characters in each font, many symbols, and combinations of characters called ligatures, for example, fi, ffi, and fl. OCR performance on variable-pitch typeset material is much lower than on typewritten and stylized OCR fonts; 1 in 100 characters may be incorrectly classified.

A major application for automatic reading of typeset text is computerized information retrieval. One application of mixed-font OCR is a commercially available reading machine for the blind. By coupling the reader to a speech synthesizer, the OCR's output is voiced at an adjustable rate between 100 and 300 words per minute. The human listener soon learns to make sense of the output even when a high fraction of the characters is incorrectly recognized.

Hand-printed characters. A number of manufacturers offer OCRs for constrained hand-printed numerics, and a few offer readers for constrained alphanumeric hand-printed characters. State payroll tax forms, driver's license applications, magazine subscription renewal forms, and other short forms with boxes and directions on how to print the characters give evidence of the business use of constrained hand-printed OCR. The recogniton performance depends, among other things, on the number of writers, the number of different character classes, and the training of the writers.

The problem of recognizing unconstrained handprinted characters is a challenging one and is similar to the problem of classifying reasonably good-quality machine-printed characters from an unlimited number of fonts all mixed together. The variability of characters printed by the same individual is large, with an even larger variability encountered between different individuals. Performance figures of the order of 95–98% correct recognition for alphanumerics and 99.5% correct recognition for numerals only, have been found for an "untrained but motivated population." Providing feedback and display of rejected and misclassified characters to the writers can result in a much lower error rate. A commercially available OCR for reading unconstrained numerals handwritten on bank checks is in operation.

Cursive writing. On-line recognition of cursive writing by using features of the stylus motion appears to lead to the future possibility of devices for signature verification, and is being studied by a number of investigators. Non-real-time approaches to automatic recognition of cursive alphanumeric script have not gone beyond the laboratory investigation phase.

Different alphabets. In principle, OCR can be performed on characters of any alphabet belonging to any language. Work has been reported on OCR for Cyrillic, Devanagri (Hindi), Arabic, Chinese, and Katakana alphabets. One OCR recognizes Russian capital letters, digits, punctuation marks, and arithmetic and other symbols—53 characters in all. Chinese or Japanese character recognition is a very special problem in which the number of possible categories is very large—tens of thousands. But the variability in each character is very small, for the font as known in English does not exist. Thus a particular Chinese character in a newspaper or a book does not vary much from sample to sample. Moreover, the problems of character separation in Chinese or Japanese are easier to resolve than in English since a character usually has a definite size and constant pitch.

PROSPECTS

The increasing use of microprocessor technology is aimed at developing low-cost, decentralized OCR devices which can handle a wide variety of fonts and formats. Combinations of word-processing and OCR equipment, and OCR and facsimile store and forward communications are likely to lead to many new applications for OCR. S*EE* D*IGITAL COMPUTER;* M*ICROPROCESSOR;* W*ORD PROCESSING.*

Bibliography. V. Capellini and R. Marconi (eds.), *Advances in Image Processing and Pattern Recognition*, 1986; L. N. Kanal and A. Rosenfield (eds.), *Progress in Pattern Recognition 2*, vol. 1, 1985; G. Nagy, Engineering considerations in optical character recognition, *Proc. COMPCON*, San Francisco, IEEE Cat. 8OCH1491-OC, pp. 402–406, February 1980; C. Y. Suen, Automatic recognition of hand-printed characters: The state of the art, *Proc. IEEE*, 68:469–487, April 1980; S. Watanabe, *Pattern Recognition: Human and Mechanical*, 1985; T. Y. Young and K. S. Fu, *Pattern Recognition and Image Processing*, 1986.

ELECTRONIC DISPLAY
L*AWRENCE* E. T*ANNAS*, J*R.*

An electronic component used to convert electrical signals into visual imagery in real time suitable for direct interpretation by a human operator. It serves as the visual interface between human and machine. The visual imagery is processed, composed, and optimized for easy interpretation and minimum reading error. The electronic display is dynamic in that it presents information within a fraction of a second from the time received and continuously holds that information, using refresh or memory techniques, until new information is received. The image is created by electronically making a pattern from a visual contrast in brightness on the display surface without the aid of mechanical or moving parts.

The use of electronic displays for presentation of graphs, symbols, alphanumerics, and video pictures has doubled every several years. The biggest growth rate has been for utilitarian and industrial users. Electronic displays have largely replaced traditional mechanical and hardcopy (paper) means for presenting information. This change is due to the increased use of computers, microprocessors, low-cost large-scale integration (LSI) electronics, and digital mass memories. The success of the hand-held calculator was directly attributable to the availability of low-cost LSI electronics and low-cost electronic numeric displays. *See* CALCULATORS; COMPUTER GRAPHICS; COMPUTER STORAGE TECHNOLOGY; INTEGRATED CIRCUITS; MICROPROCESSOR.

Electronic transducers and four-digit (or more) flat-panel displays have been used to replace the galvanometer movement, thermometer scale, barometer movement, and other forms of scientific instrumentation. Large signs, arrival and departure announcements, and scoreboards also use electronic means to portray changing messages and data. One of the major electronic displays applications is in home color television.

The computer terminal using a cathode-ray tube (CRT) is one of the most important industrial applications of electronic displays. The standard computer terminal displays 25 lines of 80 characters, for a total of 2000 characters, which correspond to one-half of a typed page. The computer terminal with a microprocessor, minicomputer, and mass memory serve to replace the office paper, typewriter, and file cabinet. *See* WORD PROCESSING.

Cathode-ray tube. The primary applications of the cathode-ray tube are in home entertainment television, scientific and electrical engineering oscilloscopes, radar display, and alphanumeric and graphic electronic displays.

The basic elements of the cathode-ray tube are shown in **Fig. 1**. The viewing screen is coated with a phosphor which emits light when struck with a beam of high-energy electrons. The electrons are emitted from the cathode at the rear of the tube in a beam that is focused electrostatically (or magnetically) to a dot or spot on the phosphor screen and positioned in horizontal and vertical coordinates by magnetic (or electrostatic) forces. The cathode grids and electron-focusing lenses are incorporated into a subassembly called the gun. The beam is accelerated toward the phosphor by a high voltage (20 kV or more) at the anode grid conductor.

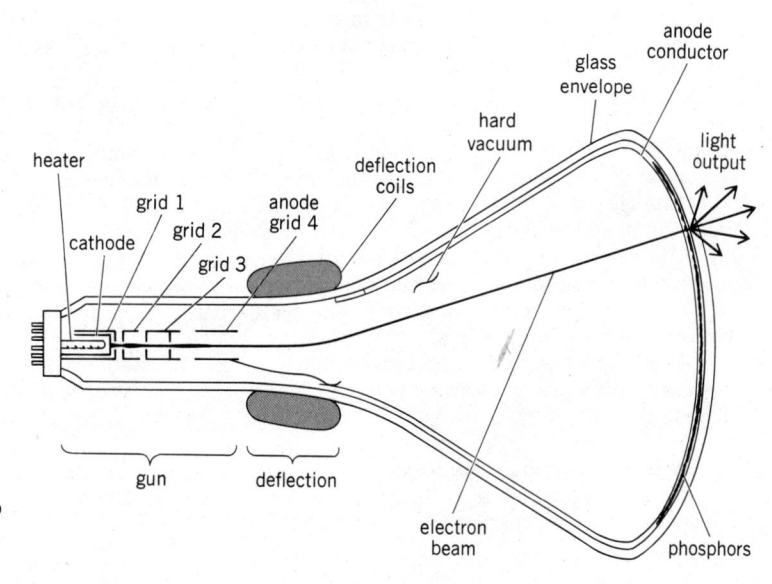

Fig. 1. Cathode-ray tube using electrostatic and magnetic deflection.

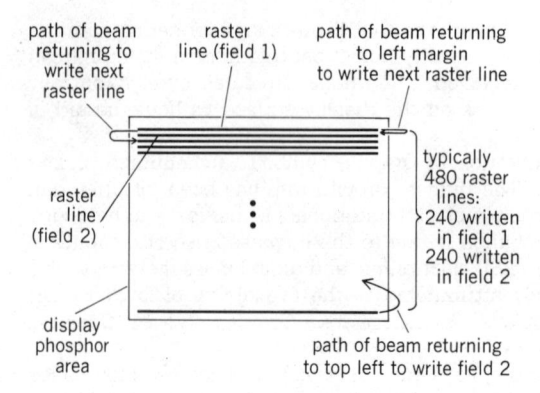

Fig. 2. Cathode-ray-tube raster for television, using interlace.

The cathode-ray-tube raster is shown in **Fig. 2**. Imagery is created on the screen as the raster is traced out. The video signal is applied, after amplification, directly to grid 2 of the gun, and controls the amplitude of the electron beam and thus the luminous output at the display surface. The deflection coils steer the beam to trace out the raster. The horizontal-scan deflection signal causes the beam to trace out the horizontal lines and then fly back for the next line. The vertical-scan deflection signal causes the beam to be stepped down the raster and then retraced to the top left corner at the beginning of each frame. Two fields are interlaced, with the raster lines of one traced between those of the other. The purpose of the interlace is to minimize flicker in the picture.

Flat-panel displays. Because of the depth dimension of the cathode-ray tube, there has been a concentrated effort to develop flat-panel displays. A primary motivating factor has been to achieve a flat television receiver which could be hung on a wall. The electrical phenomena most extensively developed for flat-panel displays are gas discharge (plasma), electroluminescence, light-emitting diode, cathodoluminescence, and liquid crystallinity. The cost of flat-panel displays is higher than cathode-ray tubes on a per-character basis for higher information content displays such as the 200-character computer terminal. The flat-panel technologies are utilized extensively in portable displays and numeric displays using several hundred characters and less.

Flat-panel displays are typically matrix-addressed. A row is enabled to accept display information in parallel via the column lines. The electronics commutate through the rows, serving the same purpose as the vertical deflection amplifier of the cathode-ray tube. The column data are shifted into the column drivers, and at the proper time applied to the column lines.

The flat-panel matrix addressing electrodes are shown in **Fig. 3**. The thickness is approximately 0.5 in. (13 mm). The row and column lines are spaced at 60 lines per inch (24 lines per centimeter). The intersection of each row line with each column line defines a pixel. A pixel or pel is a picture element, and denotes the smallest addressable element in an electronic display.

The flat-panel technologies are summarized in **Table 1**; each approach has unique advantages. The more important considerations include luminous efficiency, addressability, duty factor, gray scale, color, and cost. The capabilities in each area have evolved to the point of cost-effective applications to commercial and military products. For the vectorgraph and video display categories, liquid-crystal, electroluminescent, and gas-discharge or plasma displays have emerged as the most cost-effective approaches.

Display categories. Electronic displays can be categorized into four classifications, as shown in **Table 2**. Each classification is defined by natural technical boundaries and cost considerations. The categorization is useful in visualizing the extent to which electronic displays are used.

Special-purpose displays. The categorization of Table 2 emphasizes direct-view-type electronic displays which are of primary interest to industry. There are other special-purpose displays used in very sophisticated applications.

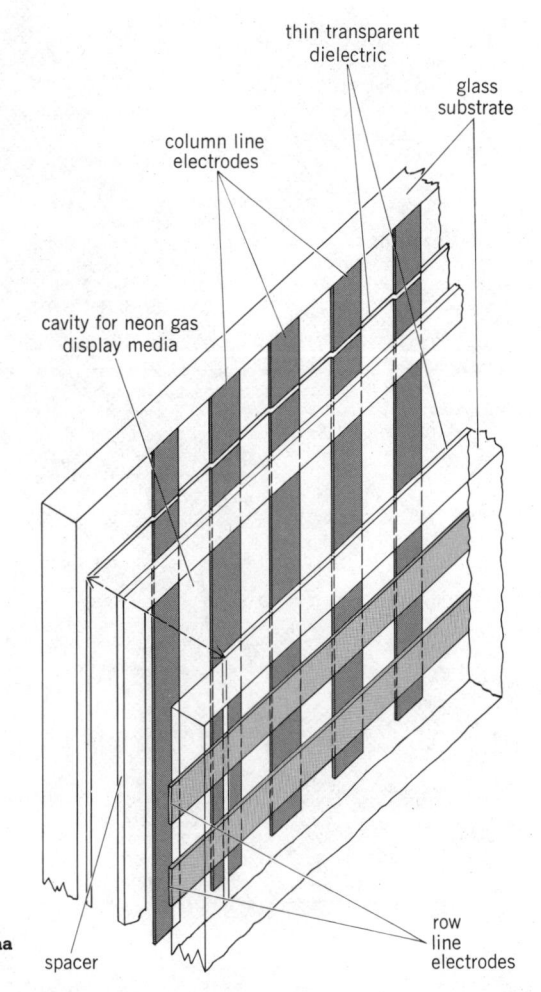

Fig. 3. Diagram of an exploded section of a plasma flat-panel display.

Projection display. In the projection display an image is generated on a high-brightness cathode-ray tube or similar electronic image generator, and then optically projected onto a larger screen. To illuminate screens larger than approximately 3 × 4 ft (1 × 1.3 m) and in color, multiple cathode-ray tubes or light valves are used. The light valve is any direct view display optimized for reflecting or transmitting the image, with an independent collimated light source for projection purposes. Light valves create images to control the reflection of light to be projected onto the screen. This permits powerful light sources such as xenon lamps to be used independent of the image-generating technique. Oil-film light valves and liquid-crystal light valves are examples of devices used in large command and control and theater-size electronic display presentations.

Three-dimensional imagery. True three-dimensional imagery can be created electronically by several techniques. One technique requires goggles using PLZT (lead zirconate titanate modified with lanthanum) electrooptical ceramic eyepieces over each eye. The eyepieces are electronically controllable shutters, with the ability to be reversibly switched from open to closed in microseconds. Two images from two television cameras placed to obtain the desired stereoscopic effects are electronically interlaced and displayed on one cathode-ray tube monitor. Each image is sequentially displayed from each camera at tv video rates. The goggles are synchronized to be

Table 1. Flat-panel technologies

Technology	Phenomena
Emissive displays	
Gas discharge	Cathode glow from conducting gaseous discharge
Plasma panel	Alternating-current capacitively coupled gas discharge
Light-emitting diode	Electron injection in a forward-biased *pn* semiconductor junction
Vacuum fluorescence	Electron bombardment of phosphor in hard vacuum under control of a grid
Electroluminescence	Electron conduction in polycrystalline phosphors due to high electric field
Flat cathode-ray tube	Electron bombardment of phosphor in hard vacuum under control of a grid or cathode
Nonemissive displays	
Liquid crystallinity	Electrostatic rotation of organic compounds which exhibit liquid crystallinity
Electrochromism	Charging and discharging chemical systems (battery) which exhibit a color change in accordance with Faraday's law
Colloidal suspensions	Electrostatic transport or rotation of light-absorbing particles in a colloidal suspension
Electroactive solids	Ferroelectric and ferromagnetic materials with a significant electrooptic effect
Electromechanical	Mechanical motion of elements causing a contrast change

opened and closed so that only the right eye sees the image from the right camera and the left eye sees the image from the left camera. The viewer sees true three-dimensional perspective while looking at the cathode-ray tube monitor through the goggles.

Helmet-mounted and heads-up displays. Helmet-mounted displays (sometimes called visually coupled displays) and heads-up displays are used in aircraft. In both of these displays the image is projected, usually from a cathode-ray tube onto a combining glass, and collimated to be in focus at infinity. The combining glass screen is designed to reflect the display imagery to the viewer, usually at selected wavelengths of light, while being sufficiently transmissive for the viewer to see the scene beyond. The primary application for the heads-up display is to present critical aircraft performance, such as speed and altitude, on a combining glass at the windscreen for pilot monitoring while permitting the pilot to look out the window for other aircraft or the runway. The primary application for the helmet-mounted display is to present, on a combining glass within the visor of the helmet of a helicopter gunner, primary information for directing firepower. The angular direction of the helmet is sensed and used to control weapons to point in the same direction in which the gunner is looking.

Color. Color can be created on a cathode-ray tube equipped with a shadow mask duplicating quite closely all colors that occur in nature. This is done in the cathode-ray tube by using three different electron guns and three phosphors in a triad of red, green, and blue on the screen at each pixel. The shadow mask is a metal screen with a hole for each pixel. It is located in the

DATA CONVERSION AND OUTPUT **139**

Table 2. Electronic display spectrum of applications

Classification	Characteristics	Applications	Electronic technologies
Pseudoanalog	Dedicated arrangement of discrete pixels used to present analog or qualitative information	Meterlike presentations, go/no-go messages, legends and alerts, analoglike (watch) dial	Gas discharge, light-emitting diodes, liquid crystal, incandescent lamps
Alphanumeric	Dedicated alphanumeric pixel font of normally less than 480 characters; most common is 4- and 8-character numeric displays	Digital watches, calculators, digital multimeters, message terminals, games	Liquid crystal, light-emitting diodes, vacuum fluorescent, gas discharge, incandescent lamps
Vectorgraphic	Large orthogonal uniform array of pixels which are addressable at medium to high speeds; normally, monochromatic with no gray scale; may have memory; normally, over 480 characters and simple graphics	Computer terminals, TWX terminals, arrivals and departures, scheduling terminals, weather radar, air-traffic control, games	Cathode-ray tube, plasma panels, gas discharge, vacuum fluorescent, electroluminescence, other technologies in advanced development
Video	Large orthogonal array of pixels which are addressed at video rates (30 frames per second); monochromatic with gray scale or full color; standardized raster scan addressing interface, arrays of pixels approximately 512 rows by 512 columns	Entertainment television, graphic arts, earth resources, video repeater, medical electronics, aircraft flight instruments, computer terminals, command and control, games	Cathode-ray tube, other technologies in advanced development

path of the beam between the deflection area and phosphor screen. Electron beams from each of three guns are constrained by each shadow mask hole to hit each respective phosphor dot. The gun, shadow-mask holes, and phosphor dots are aligned during manufacturing so that the three beams converge to pass through the single hole (or slit) in the shadow mask and then diverge as the beams emerge with sufficient separation to impact the three different phosphor dots. If all three guns are on simultaneously, the eye, upon close inspection, sees a red, a green, and a blue dot of light at each pixel. However, at a normal viewing distance, the three dots merge together in the retina of the eye, and from the laws of additive color, the pixel appears white.

Penetration phosphors are also used to create color on cathode-ray tube displays to eliminate the need for the shadow mask and extra guns. However, the color is limited and the brightness is low. Normally, two phosphors are placed on the screen in two layers or in microspheres of two layers. The gun and cathode-ray-tube anode are operated in two energy states to produce either a high-energy or a low-energy electron beam switchable in time. The high-energy beam penetrates the first phosphor layer and is stopped at the second layer. It then excites the second layer to produce its characteristic color. The low-energy beam is stopped by the first phosphor layer and excites it to produce its characteristic color. The two phosphor colors most often used are red and green. Intermediate-energy beams make it possible to fractionally excite both layers to get color combinations of red and green such as yellow and orange. Practical considerations limit this color approach to these four. Full color would require at least three primary colors such as red, green, and blue. Three layers of phosphors are limited in brightness due to practical considerations and have not been commercially available.

Monochromatic color is readily produced by flat-panel display technologies. Gas discharge is normally orange, owing to the neon gas. Other monochromatic colors are feasible. Light-emitting diode (LED) luminance is normally red, yellow, or green. A red or green state has been achieved which is switchable in a single diode by current control. Blue light-emitting diodes have been made in research devices. Electroluminescence is normally yellow or green, owing to the manganese or copper activator, respectively. Other monochromatic colors have been demonstrated in research devices. A wide range of color effects has been demonstrated in research devices with passive flat-panel displays such as liquid-crystal, electrophoretic, and electrochromic technologies. In flat-panel as in CRT displays, full color is produced by using a triad of red, green, and blue for each pixel.

Full color is very important for entertainment television displays. Most industrial electronic displays do not need or use full color. The most efficient monochrome from each display technology is normally used; for example, red for light-emitting diode, orange for gas discharge, and orange-yellow for electroluminescence. Limited color displays are sometimes used in industrial applications such as aircraft weather radar and artificial horizons, computer-aided multilayer circuit design, earth resources studies, air-route traffic control, and medical electronic displays. In all of these applications, the display instrument is usually a cathode-ray tube using the shadow-mask color technique.

Display technique. The essence of electronic displays is based upon the ability to turn on and off individual picture elements (pixels: **Fig. 4**). The pixel is the smallest controllable element of the display. A typical high-information-content display will have a quarter million pixels in an orthogonal array, each under individual control by the electronics. The pixel resolution is normally just at or below the resolving power of the eye. Thus, a good-quality picture can be created from a pattern of activated pixels.

The pixel concept for electronic displays has evolved from the modern flat-panel display technologies and digital electronics. It has been extended to the analog-raster-scan cathode-ray tube in the following way: The electron beam from the gun is deflected magnetically (or electrostatically), so as to sweep across the phosphor and thereby cause a line to luminesce on the face of the cathode-ray tube. In digitally modulated cathode-ray tubes, the cathode is modulated by a sine wave as the beam is swept across the face of the cathode-ray tube. Here, instead of a continuous line, a string of dots results. Each dot corresponds to a pixel. Each pixel is on when the beam density is high, and off when the beam is off. The beam is turned off between pixels. The pixels are refreshed from 30 to 60 times per second on a cathode-ray tube.

Pixels are created in all the rows of the entire cathode-ray-tube raster in what is called a CRT-digital raster. This approach is commonly used in industrial applications and computer terminals, since it is easily interfaced with digital electronics. Home entertainment television uses an analog-raster-scan approach, as do nearly all video systems.

There are some applications in which a nonraster approach is used to create alphanumeric characters and vectors on cathode-ray tubes. The electron beam is deflected under control of the deflection amplifiers to stroke out each line of the image. When characters and vectors are generated this way, they are like Lissajous figures, as opposed to (digital or analog) raster characters and vectors. The Lissajous characters and vectors are best suited to large (25-in. or 62.5-cm di-

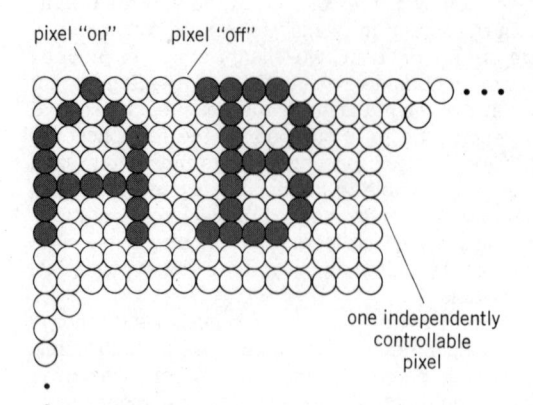

Fig. 4. Pixel array used for creating electronic display images.

agonal) cathode-ray tubes and where there are numerous vectors, straight lines, and curves. Vectors and curves drawn with the raster technique have stair steps. Lissajous vectors and curves are always smooth and continuous. Lissajous techniques are yielding to the digital raster in newer designs as the cost of digital electronics improves.

Font. With flat-panel displays and cathode-ray-tube digital-raster displays, alphanumeric character fonts are created by turning on the appropriate pixels in an array. One standard size is a 5×7 array with two pixels between characters and two pixels between rows, (Fig. 4). All the letters and numbers can be created on this common array format. Several other combinations of pixels may be used to create the letter A. The viewer soon becomes accustomed to the minor variation. Readers do not read pixels but read letters and words, and therefore the exact detail of the character pixel pattern is of a secondary consideration. In general, the more pixels available in the basic array, the more esthetically pleasing is the character, at the cost of additional electronics to control the extra pixels. The viewing distance is normally far enough so that the pixels blur together.

A very efficient and elegant array has evolved for portraying numeric characters only, called the seven-bar font (**Fig. 5**). Each bar is a pixel by definition. This font was initially considered crude when compared to the Leroy font and other more esthetic printer fonts. It is now universally accepted. A similar 14 bar font is sometimes used for alphanumeric characters.

Display electronic addressing. The numeric or alphanumeric display electronic drive may be performed in a single LSI metal oxide semiconductor (MOS) chip mounted in a single dual in-line package (DIP) suitable for direct assembly on a printed circuit board. All the timing, logic, memory, resistors, and drivers are contained in a single chip. A four- or seven-bit character code is serially fed into the chip for display (**Fig. 6**).

A computer terminal (**Fig. 7**) will incorporate a microprocessor unit and a cathode-ray-tube controller to perform master control and cathode-ray-tube housekeeping tasks. A line of video data is loaded into the shift register for serial drive of the video amplifier at the time a raster line starts. The shift register is loaded during flyback time from the character generator. The character generator is a decoder transforming the alphanumeric information in coded form such as ASCII (American National Standard Code for Information Interchange) into pixel signals for each raster line. The ASCII code is stored in the display refresh memory. The entire cathode-ray-tube frame is stored in this memory, and is continuously displayed until changed under control of the microprocessor unit. New information can come from the mass memory, the keyboard, or other subsystems on the data bus and address bus, all under control of the microprocessor unit.

The cathode-ray-tube controller performs all the housekeeping tasks for proper cathode-ray-tube operation. These include the vertical- and horizontal-raster synchronization signals, the cursor control, blinking, blanking, interlace, paging, and scrolling. The cathode-ray-tube controller is a single LSI MOS chip, as are most of the other blocks shown in Fig. 7.

Developing applications. The market needs for electronic displays have accelerated the advancement of the technology in three areas: personal computers, automotive panels, and portable television.

Personal computers. These devices have evolved extremely rapidly with the development of better processors, larger memories, and more powerful software. There has been significant marketing pressure to make them more portable and smaller so as to use less desk space.

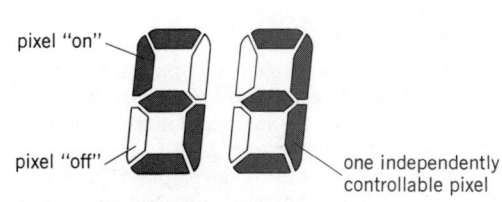

Fig. 5. Seven-bar numeric font.

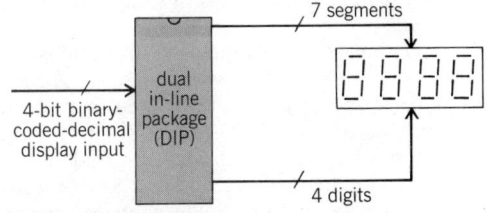

Fig. 6. Block diagram of LSI MOS electronic drive for numeric display.

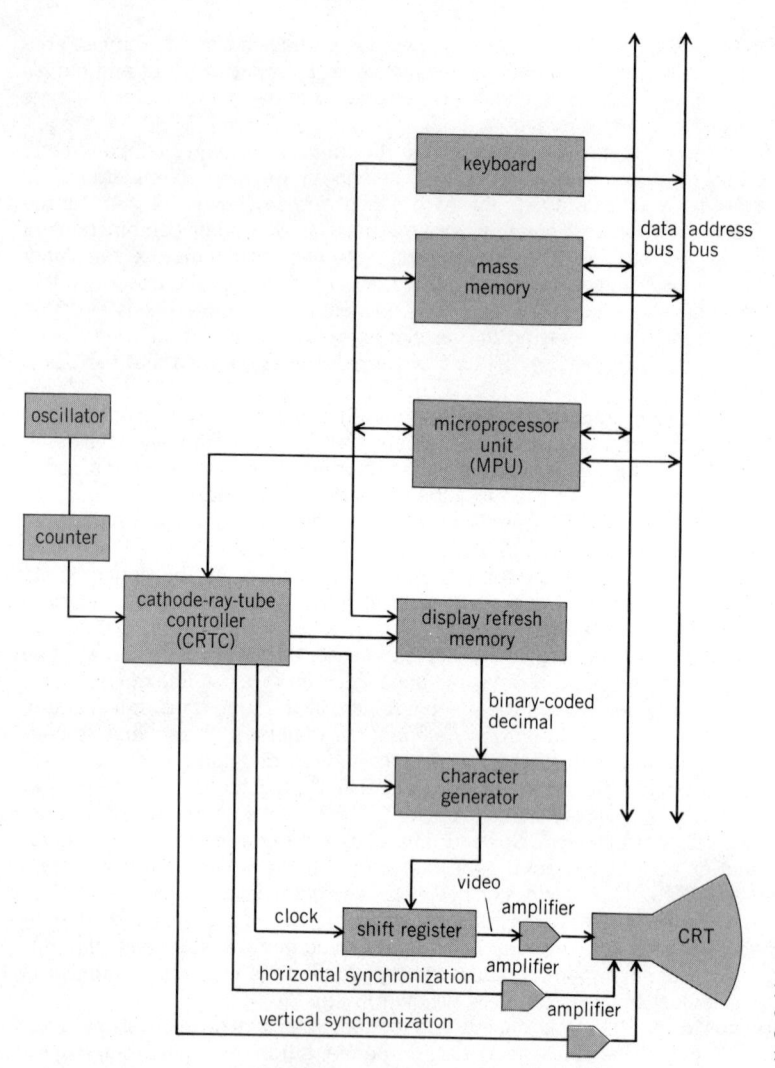

Fig. 7. Block diagram of LSI electronics for a smart computer terminal cathode-ray-tube display.

There are four categories of personal computers dictated by size and power requirements which in turn are dictated mostly by the available display technologies. These four categories are: lap computers, portable computers, transportable computers, and desktop computers.

The lap computer, as the name implies, is small in size with limited functionality, operates with its own internal power, and uses a liquid-crystal display of approximately 320 alphanumeric characters.

The portable computer is, in its most simple definition, a fully functional computer with a handle and an internal power source. This segment of the family of personal computers is limited because of the display performance or cost. Liquid-crystal technology is used because it meets the cost, power, and 2000-character size requirement. However, the liquid-crystal technology performance is compromised when expanded upward to the larger character sets. The lack of adequate performance in conventional liquid-crystal techniques accelerated the development of active matrix addressing techniques such as cadmium selenide (CdSe) semiconductor polycrystalline thin-film transistors and amorphous silicon. These techniques improve the performance of the liquid-crystal display but at a cost penalty. Electroluminescent and electrophoretic displays are strong contenders for this application. The cathode-ray-tube and gas-discharge displays are too heavy and consume too much power to be used in portable computers.

The transportable computer differs from the portable computer primarily with regard to the power source. The power source for a portable computer consists of internally packaged batteries. The transportable computer relies on an external power source; it either uses a battery pack or is plugged into the house power. The biggest user of power is the display. The initial display technology was a scaled-down cathade-ray tube with compromises in performance. The flat-panel displays are most appropriate, since they are truly portable in briefcase size, without compromised performance. The most promising technology is the electroluminescent display with its excellent ergonomics and low power, and the gas discharge and plasma panels are next in contention. The gas discharge technologies are most limited by their weight and power efficiency.

The desktop computers use cathode-ray-tube displays almost exclusively. The use of flat-panel technologies could greatly improve the size and performance of the displays, however, cost is a major consideration. Flat-panel approaches using electroluminescent and gas-discharge displays are two to three times more expensive than cathode-ray tubes. This cost difference results from the extra supporting electronics for row and column drivers needed for matrix-addressed flat-panel displays. Finally, the element of a color display is a desired feature in desktop computers. The cost of a cathode-ray-tube color display is not much more than a black-and-white flat-panel display. SEE MICROCOMPUTER.

Automotive panels. Automobiles require several displays: the integrated performance cluster including speed, engine status, and so forth; digital indicators including time, temperature, and so forth; and a high-resolution navigation display including map, position indication, and so forth. The sheer number of assemblies has presented serious difficulties for the display industry.

Portable television. As with the portable transistor radio, cost and performance are the dominant factors determining the utilization of portable television. The most significant component which affects cost and performance is the display, and the most difficult performance goals to be achieved within cost limitations are low power, weight, and volume, and sunlight readability. Two approaches are a black-and-white flat cathode-ray tube and a color liquid-crystal display, both approaching a 4-in.-diagonal (100-mm) size. The cathode-ray tube is viewed from the back side of the faceplate, which greatly enhances its power efficiency and sunlight readability. The liquid-crystal display uses the twisted nematic mode of operation and amorphous silicon electronics for addressing the matrix of color triads for each pixel, and complementary-metal-oxide-semiconductor (CMOS) drivers for the row and column lines. The colors are created by strips of red, green, and blue filters for each row of pixels which are illuminated by a uniform rear area light source covering the entire display.

COMPUTER GRAPHICS
JOHN E. WARD

The process of pictorial communication between humans and computers. The traditional (and still most widely used) means of inputting problems to computers and receiving answers has been the alphanumeric form—the letters, numbers, punctuation marks, and other symbols which can be handled by such input/output devices as punched-card and tape or disk peripherals, teletypewriters, and line printers. While any problem and its solution can be reduced to the alphanumeric form by suitable coding conventions, it is often an unnatural and time-consuming way for the human to think and work. An analogous situation would be the publication of a technical textbook without illustrations, with diagrams replaced by word descriptions, graphs by tables of numbers, and so forth. Anyone who has tried to visualize an odd-shaped plot of land from the usual word form of deed description "starting at bound mark, 321 feet northerly, thence 195 feet southeasterly, 82 feet easterly, . . ." can appreciate the difficulty of quickly comprehending a computer result presented in this way.

Output devices such as televisionlike cathode-ray-tube (CRT) displays and automatic mechanical plotting boards which operate under computer control permit the computer to draw almost any conceivable form of pictorial output. When a computer is equipped with such devices and suitable controlling programs, the user (the person desiring computations to be performed) can request in preparing a program and input data that the results of the calculations be output graphically, that is, as charts, drawings, or appropriate pictorial representation. Use of graphical output devices is showing a rapid increase, particularly in engineering applications. However, graphical output alone is only half the story—graphical input is also used in many situations. These will be discussed in turn.

Graphical output. Graphical output devices are of two types: cursive writing and raster scan. In cursive writing, the CRT electron beam or the plotting pen is moved so as to trace out the lines and points making up the displayed output in sequential fashion, much as one draws with pencil and paper. Primarily line-type copy is produced. In a raster-scan output device, the beam or pen sweeps the entire display surface in a regular, repetitive pattern (as in television), and passes every location at a specific time. Drawing is therefore accomplished by energizing the beam or pen at appropriate times in the pattern cycle, and every point in the display area can be written in a single scan. Cursive writing formerly predominated in both graphic displays and hard-copy plotters, largely because of the much higher data requirements of raster scanning, where output data are required for every point, indicating whether it is to be visible or not. Beginning in the 1980s, however, advances in low-cost, solid-state circuits and memories have provided ready and inexpensive means of driving raster-scan displays. SEE INTEGRATED CIRCUITS; SEMICONDUCTOR MEMORIES.

Cursive output. The simplest forms of cursive computer-controlled plotting boards or CRT displays are the point-plotting types. In these devices the computer specifies numerically the x and y coordinates of a point on the drawing surface or viewing screen, which causes an ink dot or spot of light to be made at the appropriate location. In the case of a CRT, it is usual to covert the numerical values to analog voltages by means of digital-to-analog converters, and then to use these voltages to drive the deflection system of the CRT (**Fig. 1**). It is common to divide each deflection axis into 1024 (10 binary digits) distinct addresses, which provides over a million possible dot locations. The speed of plotting depends upon the distance that the electron beam must move between dots, and varies from 1 microsecond for adjacent addresses to perhaps 30 microseconds for full-screen deflection between dots. Screen sizes are usually about 10 to 15 in. (25 to 38 cm) square, limited primarily by CRT cost and technology. SEE DIGITAL-TO-ANALOG CONVERTER.

Mechanical plotting boards, which must physically move the pen and the writing surface relative to each other, bear considerable resemblance to numerically controlled machine tools. Mechanical plotting is of course much slower than moving an electron beam in the CRT. Slowness of plotting, coupled with the fact that a picture element once drawn cannot be erased, makes plotting boards unattractive for interactive graphics. However, the resolution of plotting can be increased by simply making the writing surface bigger (up to 6 × 8 ft or 1.8 to 2.4 m in some models), permitting much more detailed drawings than can be displayed on a CRT. Also, plotters with multiple styli to write in color are available. For more information on the use of plotting boards SEE ENGINEERING DRAWING.

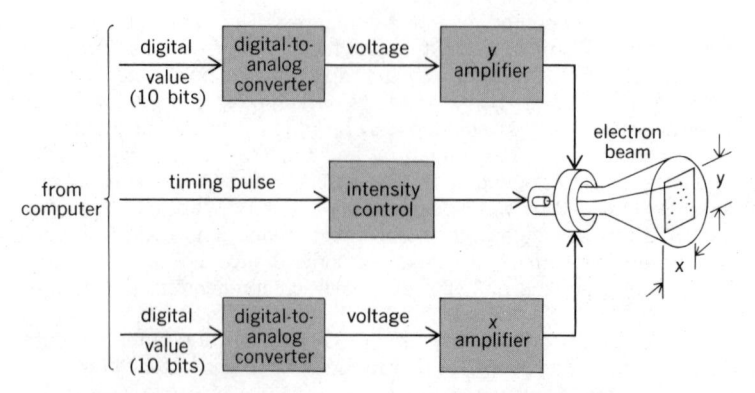

Fig. 1. Point-plotting CRT output display.

The point-plotting mode of operation described above, while seemingly rudimentary, provides a complete drawing capability. Closely spaced dots plotted in a row merge into continuous appearing lines, letters and numbers can be formed from arrays of dots similar to those used in football scoreboards, and so forth. The main disadvantage of point-plotting devices is that large amounts of data are required to produce a picture (20 or more binary digits for each point) which places a burden on the computer, and the plotting speed is limited. This latter factor is most important in CRT displays, where the entire picture must be "refreshed" (continuously rewritten) 30 or more times per second in order to provide a flicker-free presentation. For example, if the CRT is refreshed 30 times per second and the plotting time is 5–30 µs per point, pictures containing only up to a few thousand points can be displayed.

Most cursive display systems now include additional hardware to provide high-speed symbol and line (vector) drawing capabilities (**Fig. 2**). The point mode operates as described previously, but the other two modes produce an entire picture element with a single command from the computer, and at a much higher plotting rate than if it were drawn with individual points. Line generators operate with specification either of both end points or of the length of line to be plotted relative to current beam position. In either case all of the intermediate points on the line are automatically filled in by the line generator of the display system, by rapid point plotting (incremental digital technique) or by continuously sweeping the beam (analog technique).

Of the two techniques the analog technique is considerably faster, permitting a line to be drawn clear across the screen in as little as 30 µs. Symbol generators take many forms, the more common being based on arrays of dots, stroke techniques, or incremental tracing of the symbol shapes. The key feature of any of these is a local fixed memory which contains the detailed information about the shape of each symbol. Thus, the only input the symbol generator needs is the symbol code (6 to 8 binary digits) to tell it which symbol to plot. Current symbol generators permit as many as 4000 symbols to be displayed at a refresh rate of 30 frames per second. The capacity of a point-plotting display at the same refresh rate would be only 50–100 symbols, since 10–20 points are needed per symbol.

Some display systems have been designed with additional display functions to improve performance in special situations. Examples are generators for drawing circles or other common geometric curves with one command, hardware for scaling or rotating three-dimensional representations without requiring recomputation of the display data, and automatic insertion of perspective into three-dimensional representations.

Raster-scan output. Raster-scan output has long been used in alphanumeric CRT displays, in which it is relatively easy to arrange a character generator to synthesize small symbols in synchronism with the scan. Simple, low-resolution graphics based on combinations of special symbols has also become feasible; this technique is used in teletext and videotext. High-resolution, synchronous graphics generation in scan format is, however, so much more difficult that new techniques had to be developed. A frame memory, or bit map, is one such technique (**Fig. 3**).

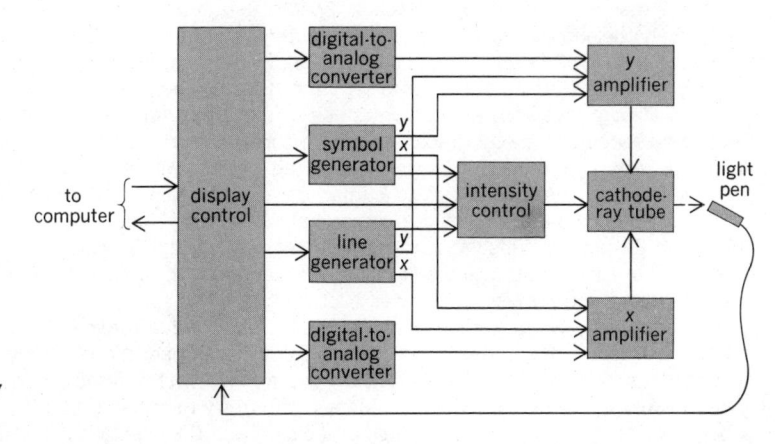

Fig. 2. General display system organization.

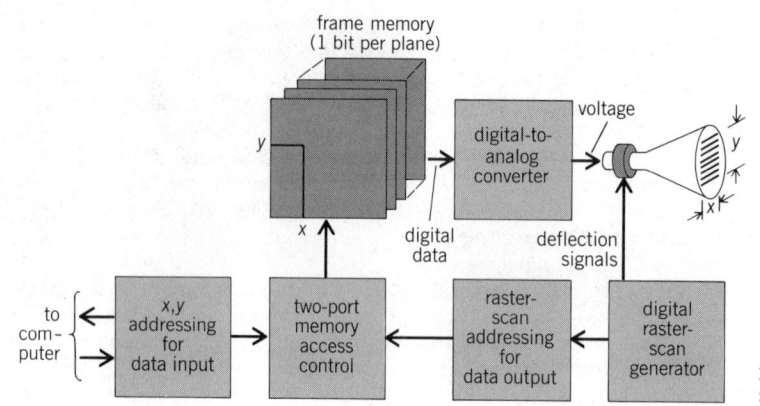

Fig. 3. Frame-memory raster-scan display.

The CRT intensity is controlled by reading out and decoding a sequence of words that the computer has stored in the memory, one word per x,y location. The number of bits per word in the memory depends on the number of intensity levels (colors) desired. SEE VIDEOTEXT AND TELETEXT.

The memory is of two-port design, in which the scan-synchronous addressing for display readout has priority. Access time is sufficient, however, for the computer to write new display information into the memory. Display resolutions of up to 2000 by 2000 points are possible at frame rates of up to 60 per second (completely flicker-free), exceeding cursive display capabilities. No symbol or line generation elements are shown. These tasks are now accomplished in computer software, since they no longer have to be done in real time to drive the display, and can include area fill-in, shading, and hidden-line elimination for realistic display of solid objects. With the proper software, the more advanced raster-scan display systems can produce pictorial output approaching photographic quality (monochrome or color), but not necessarily at a fast enough new-frame rate to simulate real-time motion. There, cursive displays still have an advantage. Raster-scan displays, however, can be used to produce movie films, one frame at a time, and such computer animation is widely used.

In a different fashion, plotting technology has also advanced from a single, cursive writing stylus to linear arrays of individual styli (some spaced as finely as 200 to the inch or 8 to the millimeter) which draw complete pictures or text pages in one straight-line sweep across the display area. As in raster-scan CRTs, writing data must be supplied for every point in the display area, but no styli movement data are required.

Graphical input. Before discussing graphical input, it is necessary to distinguish between the two major ways of using a computer: batch operation and on-line operation. In batch operation the user has no direct access to the computer and is usually not present during the time when the job is running in the computer. A computing job must be completely prepared ahead of time, with detailed specification of input data and program, desired output, and alternate courses of action in case of certain error conditions. If an error occurs, the user must then review what results are received, make corrections in the input, and resubmit the job. This process may have to be repeated several times before all errors are corrected and a satisfactory run is achieved. Although graphical output as described in the preceding section is quite feasible, the forms of graphical input which require close human-computer interaction are not usually feasible.

In on-line operation, on the other hand, the user has direct input/output access to the computer through a console or terminal of some sort during the time a job is running in the computer. In this situation a result or partial result may be immediately presented to the user for decision as to correctness or the need for further input to correct errors or extend the solution, and the computer waits to receive further information before proceeding with the job. Turnaround time is reduced from the hours or days typical of batch operation to a few seconds, providing the intimate human-computer relationship needed for two-way (interactive) graphical communication. It is obvious, however, that having a large computer which can perform millions of operations per second wait idly while the user makes a decision and takes action is an inefficient use of valuable computer resources. Thus, on-line operation was at first restricted to experimental research facilities and special situations, such as air-traffic control and military systems, where rapid, joint human-computer decision making is essential. However, two developments in computer technology have acted to greatly increase adoption of on-line interaction: small, inexpensive computers, which can be used economically in a dedicated (one-user) mode of operation; and time-sharing techniques for large computers, which permit a computer to economically service a number (perhaps 10–100) of on-line users by switching instantly to work for another user when a particular job reaches a point where human decision is required. Both of these developments have sparked the growing interest in interactive computer graphics. S*EE* M*ICROCOMPUTER;* M*ULTIACCESS COMPUTER.*

In noninteractive graphical input, specialized off-line equipment such as curve tracers and coordinate digitizers (human-guided or automatic) permit a sketch or drawing to be converted to the alphanumeric form on punched cards, punched tape, or magnetic tapes and disks. Such data can be used as input in batch computing but will be subject to the slow error-correction process.

The second, or interactive, form of graphical input requires on-line access to the computer. In this case, hand-held input devices, such as writing styli used with electronic tablets and light pens used with on-line CRT displays, permit the human to sketch a problem description, say, a bridge truss to be analyzed, in an on-line interactive mode in which the computer acts as a drafting assistant with unusual powers. For example, since the computer can analyze each element of a sketch as it is entered and apply precoded rules and constraints such as "all lines shall be either exactly vertical or exactly horizontal," it can instantly convert a rough freehand motion of the light pen into an accurate picture element. The computer can also establish connectivity between various picture elements so that the shape of the displayed object, say, a rectangle, can be altered by simply indicating with the light pen that one of the sides should be moved. Since the computer knows which lines are connected together, it can automatically adjust the lengths of the adjoining sides as any one side is moved.

There are two key concepts in this process. One is that the computer be continuously informed of the poisition of the hand-held input device as it is moved over the display screen or writing surface, and the other is that a displayed picture element may be identified to the computer for action such as moving it or erasing it by simply pointing to it with the input device. The action to be taken at any particular time is made known to the computer by additional manual input actions such as pushing one of a number of button switches on a panel, or pointing with the input device to one of a number of alternate commands (called light buttons or a pick list) displayed on the viewing screen along with the picture (usually along the bottom or one edge of the screen).

Interactive input/output arrangements. Devices used in interactive computer graphics include light pens, electronic tablets, the mouse, the touch screen, CRT recorders, and direct-view storage tube (DVST) displays.

Light pens. The light pen, used for graphical input in conjunction with on-line CRT displays, consists of a photodetector mounted in a pen-shaped holder. When the pen is held over a displayed picture element, the pen senses the light created while the electron beam is writing that particular element and sends a signal to the computer (**Fig. 4**). Since the computer knows which element it is writing at any given time, the time of receipt of the signal from the pen immediately identifies to the computer which element in the picture the pen is pointing at, providing a convenient and natural method for the human user to "discuss" a picture with the computer. Because the light pen is a passive device which can only respond to displayed information, it provides no information to the computer when held over a blank part of the screen. Thus, in order to draw with a light pen, it is necessary to perform a process known as pen tracking. One way to do this is to continuously display a tracking cross, a cross-shaped pattern made up of dots, which is slightly larger than the field of view of the pen. As each dot is plotted, the pen reports whether or not it "saw" it, and by comparing the number of dots seen on each arm of the cross, the computer can keep the cross continuously aligned with the pen as the pen is moved over the viewing screen. The pen-tracking process is fairly effective for input drawing, but suffers from lack of precision and the use of a substantial amount of computing time to perform.

Electronic tablets. The effort to find a better input means than the light pen produced a number of new devices, one of which is the electronic tablet. A number of different electronic detection principles are used in making tablets, but the end result is the same: The circuitry

Fig. 4. On-line interactive graphics console.

produces a pair of digital x and y coordinate values corresponding continuously to the position of a writing stylus upon the surface of the tablet. The advantage of the tablet is that no computer time is required for operation as in pen tracking (except to sample the input from the tablet). Also, the tablet can be placed on the table in front of the display screen, producing a more natural writing position for the user. Another advantage of tablets is that in most of them the stylus is capacitively coupled to the tablet surface, permitting the curves or drawings which already exist in paper form to be placed on the tablet surface and traced as input.

To provide interaction between the tablet and the display, it is usual to display a cursor (a dot or tracking symbol) corresponding to the current position of the stylus on the writing surface. The user then uses the stylus to steer this cursor around the screen to point to displayed objects, draw additional picture elements, and so forth. Other devices such as joy sticks, track balls, and slewing buttons are also used to steer cursors on the screen in many displays. These are all of relatively low cost and provide satisfactory pointing capability; however, the two-axis form of control that is characteristic of these devices is too awkward to permit drawing.

Mouse. The mouse was developed in the 1960s, but only in the 1980s did it become popular in connection with graphical input for small personal computers. It is a small box about the size of a pack of cigarettes, with wheels mounted at right angles. As the mouse is held in the hand and moved over the surface of a table or drawing in a fixed orientation, it generates x and y signals similar to those from a tablet, and controls a cursor.

Touch screen. Another interaction device from the 1960s that gained new popularity in the 1980s is the touch screen, which permits pointing at displayed objects with the finger. This has advantages for information screens in public places because there is no external device or wiring. Various implementations include arrays of sonic- or light-beam sensors interruptible by the finger, and crossed-wire matrices or transparent resistive sheets that sense and measure the

DATA CONVERSION AND OUTPUT 149

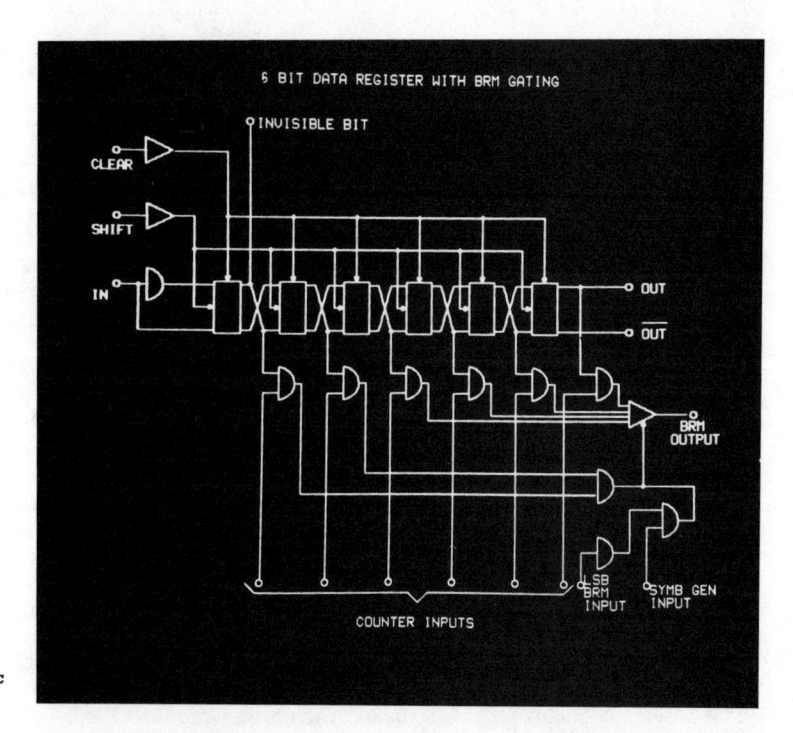

Fig. 5. Display of electronic circuit.

Fig. 6. Example of computer-produced map.

point of finger contact. The precision of pointing is generally not as high as in the devices above, but is satisfactory for many purposes.

CRT recorders. CRT recorders operate like CRT displays, but are desgined to record graphic images on film rather than display them for human viewing. This permits use of small, high-resolution CRTs with pu to 4000 dot addresses in each axis. Essentially, CRT recorders act like high-speed plotting boards capable of producing 2–10 pictures per second. One interesting use of CRT recorders is to produce animated movies.

DVST displays. Direct-view storage tube (DVST) displays have come to the fore as a means of avoiding the refresh requirements fo standard CRT displays, particularly in low-cost remote display terminals driven over low bandwidth telephone-line connections. The DVST is analogous to the "Etch-a-Sketch" toy, maintaing any picture element once written until the entire screen is electronically erased.

Applications. Graphic output from computers operated in batch mode has received wide acceptance in a variety of scientific and business applications (**Figs. 5** and **6**). Computer-produced graphs and charts are sufficiently readable to permit direct use in reports, eliminating laborious and costly manual plotting and drafting. In applications such as highway layout and piping layouts in ships and refineries, direct pictorial output is of great value. Interactive graphics is not yet used as widely because of its dependence on the availability of on-line computing facilities, but has already been applied in such diverse fields as integrated circuit design, dress-pattern layout (with automatic scaling of patterns for different sizes), aircraft design, and study of molecular structures. A whole field, called computer-adied design, depends on interactive computer graphics for the intimate, pictorial person-computer communications required. SEE COMPUTER-AIDED DESIGN AND MANUFACTURING; DIGITAL COMPUTER.

Bibliography. L. Ameraal, *Programming Principles in Computer Graphics*, 1986; I. O. Angell, *Advanced Graphics with the IBM Personal Computer*, 1985; S. Harrington, *Computer Graphics*, 2d ed., 1987; D. Hearn and M. P. Baker, *Computer Graphics*, 1986; T. L. Kunii, *Advanced Computer Graphics*, 1986; D. F. Rogers, *Procedural Elements for Computer Graphics*, 1985.

4
COMPUTATION: THEORY AND MATHEMATICS

Algorithm	152
Automata theory	153
Boolean algebra	156
Number systems	158
Bit	164
Data reduction	165
Numerical analysis	165
Matrix theory	170
Linear programming	173
Nonlinear programming	175
Graph theory	177

ALGORITHM
EARL C. JOSEPH

A precise formulation of a method for doing something. In computers, an algorithm is usually a collection of procedural steps or instructions organized and designed so that computer processing results in the solution of a specific problem.

Algorithms play an important role in computers. Donald Knuth has suggested that science may be defined as knowledge which is understood well enough to be taught to a computer. In this view, the concept of an algorithm or computer program furnishes an extremely useful test for the depth of knowledge about any particular subject, and the process of going from an art to a science involves learning how to construct an algorithm.

Algorithms are employed to accomplish specific tasks using data and instructions when applying computers. The task may be well definable in either mathematical or nonmathematical terms; it may be either logical or heuristic, and either simple or complex; and it may be either computational or data-processable, or involve sensing and control. In any case, the task must be definable. Then an algorithm can be devised and specified for a computer to perform the required task.

Properties. Algorithms are further characterized by several properties. Either the data set over which the algorithm will operate or the process of how the computer is to get access to the data must be specifiable. The process required to be performed can be defined with a finite set of operations or actions together with a unique starting point. The sequence of steps, the tree, the list, or the network describing the process is mappable. This, however, does not imply that the path through these steps is known, since in some cases the data or prior process steps will dictate the actual path. That is, for classical computers it must be possible to "program" the algorithm. The algorithm process must terminate, either with the task completed or with some kind of indication that the task (problem) is unsolvable.

Algorithms define the method of operation for performing a task. However, for each task to be performed, there usually are many different mappable methods for the computer to execute it—but they are not of equal desirability. From the above definitions and characterizations it follows that any computer program that does its intended task is also an algorithm. But to be practical an algorithm must perform its task within the time and memory capacity constraints of the system.

Hardware implementation. The so-called silicon revolution has spawned the emergence and growth of smart machines. These devices have embedded microcomputerlike logic which gives them some degree of adaptability to their environment and functionality well beyond that of their dumb forerunners. In such a role, and others, the microcomputer logic becomes an algorithm, the hardware embodiment of a task process. SEE EMBEDDED SYSTEMS; MICROPROCESSOR.

As each generation of computers has emerged, a growing amount of software (programs and algorithms) has been cast in hardware, resulting in so-called hard software. Most computers in the pre-first generation (the late 1940s) did not have sequenceable and combinational primitive instructions, such as multiply and divide, wired in. In the first generation of computers (the early 1950s) these primitives were wired into the hardware. The second computer generation (the 1960s) saw the hardware implementation of computational algorithms, such as hardware algorithms for indexing, floating point, and trigonometric and square root functions. With the third computer generation (the 1970s) came hard software language/control algorithms, such as executive control, I/O (input/output), HLL (High Level Language), microprocessor, and system hardware algorithms. Fourth-generation computers (the 1980s) have hard software application algorithms, such as hardware in the form of peopleware primitives, profession (for example, management) algorithms, accounting primitives (for example, payroll), and MIS and courseware primitives. General-system hardware algorithms, are being developed, and institutional, inference, artificial intelligence, and robotic hardware algorithms are expected in the 1990s.

Most future algorithms for hard software will either (1) be incorporated as part of the hardware architecture of computers or "calculator" devices; (2) be cast as an optional adjunct for attachment to a computer system, memory, calculator, or information appliance to make it smarter; or (3) become a stand-alone, special-purpose machine—for example, a "payroll machine" or an "electronic file cabinet." Smart people/information appliances could well become the major interface to computers, data bases, information bases, and knowledge-based systems driven by hardware algorithms. SEE DIGITAL COMPUTER; DIGITAL COMPUTER PROGRAMMING.

AUTOMATA THEORY
JERZY W. GRZYMALA-BUSSE

A theory concerned with models (automata) used to simulate objects and processes such as computers, digital circuits, nervous systems, cellular growth, and reproduction. Automata theory helps engineers design and analyze digital circuits which are parts of computers, telephone systems, or control systems. It uses ideas and methods of discrete mathematics to determine the limits of computational power for models of existing and future computers. Among many known applications of finite automata are lexical analyzers and hardware controllers.

The concept now known as the automaton was first examined by A. M. Turing in 1936 for the study of limits of human ability to solve mathematical problems in formal ways. His automaton has become known as a Turing machine. The Turing machine is too powerful for simulation of many systems. Therefore, some more appropriate models were introduced, such as the finite-state machine. There exist some intermediate automata between Turing machines and finite-state machines, such as linear bounded automata and push-down automata.

Turing machines and intermediate automata. The Turing machine is a suitable model for the computational power of a computer. Its usefulness follows from the thesis of A. Church which may be reformulated as: The computational power of the Turing machine represents a limit for any realizable computer.

A Turing machine has two main parts: a finite-state machine with a head, and a tape (**Fig. 1**). The tape is infinite in both directions and is divided into squares. The head sees at any

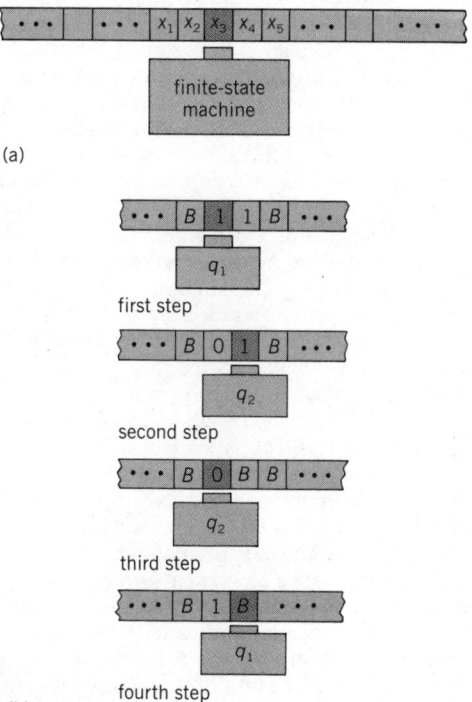

Fig. 1. Turing machine. (a) General idea. (b) An example of a computation.

moment of time one square of the tape and is able to read the content of the square as well as to write on the square. The finite-state machine is in one of its states. Each square of the tape holds exactly one of the symbols, also called input symbols or machine characters. It is assumed that one of the input symbols is a special one, the blank, denoted by B.

At any moment of time, the machine, being in one of its states and looking at one of the input symbols in some square, may act or halt. The action means that, in the next moment of time, the machine erases the old input symbol and writes a new input symbol on the same square (it may be the same symbol as before, or a new symbol; if the old one was not B and the new one is B, the machine is said to erase the old symbol), changes the state to a new one (again, it is possible that the new state will be equal to the old one), and finally moves the head one square to the left, or one square to the right, or stays on the same square as before.

For some pairs of states and input symbols the action is not specified in the description of a Turing machine; thus the machine halts. In this case, symbols remaining on the tape form the output, corresponding to the original input, or more precisely, to the input string (or sequence) of input symbols. A sequence of actions, followed by a halt, is called a computation. A Turing machine accepts some input string if it halts on it. The set of all accepted strings over all the input symbols is called a language accepted by the Turing machine. Such languages are called recursively enumerable sets.

For example, a Turing machine with three input symbols, 0, 1, and B, and three states, q_1, q_2, and q_3, is given by the table below. R, L, and S mean move the head one step to the right, to

	0	1	B
q_1	1 q_3 S	0 q_2 R	
q_2	1 q_1 R	B q_2 L	
q_3			

the left, or stay on the same square, respectively. The entry 1 q_3 S in row q_1 and column 0 of the table means that if the Turing machine reads 0 in the state q_1, then, in the next moment of time, it will print 1 on the same square, the next stage will be q_3, and the head will stay on the same square. The blank entry in row q_1 and column B means that if the machine reads blank B in the state q_1, it will halt. It is assumed that the Turing machine always starts the computation in its initial state q_1. An example of a computation for input string 11 is given in Fig. 1b. The output is 1. This Turing machine will convert the input string 1010 into the output string 0101.

Another automaton is a nondeterministic Turing machine. It differs from an ordinary, deterministic Turing machine in that for a given state and input symbol, the machine has a finite number of choices for the next move. Each choice means a new input symbol, a new state, and a new direction to move its head. The computational power of a nondeterministic Turing machine is the same as a deterministic one, suitably constructed.

A linear bounded automaton is a nondeterministic Turing machine which is restricted to the portion of the tape containing the input. The restriction of the Turing machine to a portion of the tape which is bounded by some linear function of the length of input results in the same computational power as the restriction of the Turing machine to the portion of the tape containing just the input—hence the name.

The capability of the linear bounded automaton is smaller than that of a Turing machine. The languages accepted by linear bounded automata are called context-sensitive. The class of all context-sensitive languages is a proper subclass of the class of recursively enumerable sets.

A computational device with yet smaller capability than that of a linear bounded automaton is a push-down automaton. It consists of a finite-state machine that reads an input symbol from a tape and controls a stack. The stack is a list in which insertions and deletions are possible, both operations taking place at one end, called the top. The intuitive model of a stack is a pile of books on a floor or dishes on a shelf. Symbols from some alphabet are inserted to the top of the stack by a "push" operation. The topmost element may be deleted from the stack by a "pop" operation. The device is nondeterministic, so it has a number of choices for each next move. Two types of moves are possible. In the first type, a choice depends on the input symbol, the top element of the stack, and the state of the finite-state machine. The choice consists of selecting a next state of the finite-state machine, removing the top element, leaving the stack without the top element, or replacing the top element by a sequence of symbols. After performing a choice, the input head reads the next input symbol. The other type is similar to the first one, but now the input symbol is not used and the head is not moved, so the automaton controls the stack without reading input symbols. *See Abstract data types.*

A push-down automaton accepts the set of all input strings for which there exists a sequence of moves causing it to empty its stack. Any such set is called a context-free language. The class of context-free languages is a proper subclass of the class of context-sensitive languages.

Finite-state machines. A finite-state automaton, or a finite-state machine, or a finite automaton, is a computational device having a fixed upper bound on the amount of memory it uses. It should be clear that the amount of memory for Turing machines, linear bounded automata, or push-down automata is unlimited. One approach to finite automata is through the concept of an acceptor. The finite automaton examines an input string (that is, a sequence of input symbols, located on the tape) in one pass from left to right. It has a finite number of states, among which one is specified as initial. The assumption is that the finite automaton starts scanning of input standing in its initial state. Some of the states are called accepting states. The finite automaton has a transition function (or next-state function) which maps each state and input symbol into the next state. In each step the finite automaton computes the next state and reads the next input symbol. If after reading the entire input string the last state is accepting, the string is accepted; otherwise it is rejected. The language of the finite automaton (called also a regular language or regular event) is the set of all strings over the set of input symbols that are accepted. The class of regular languages is a proper subclass of the class of context-free languages.

For example, consider the finite acceptor presented in **Fig. 2**. It has two input symbols, 0 and 1, and four states, q_0, q_1, q_2, and q_3, where q_0 is initial and q_2 is accepting (in the example there is just one accepting state). Actions are denoted by arrows. For example, if, in the initial state, the acceptor reads input symbol 0 on the tape, the next state is q_3. The regular language of this acceptor is the set consisting of the following strings: 11, 101, 1001, 10001, ...

Another approach to the definition of the finite automaton is presented below. A finite automaton is a quintuple $(S, \Sigma, \Omega, M, N)$, where S is a finite nonempty set (state set), Σ is a finite nonempty set (input set), Ω is a finite nonempty set (output set), M is a function (next-state function, transition function) of $S \times \Sigma$ into S, and N is a function (output function) into Ω in the case of Mealy automaton or S into Ω in the case of Moore automaton.

A special case of the Moore automaton corresponds to the first approach to the definition of a finite automaton. Namely, it is necessary to select one state and call it initial, to set Ω equal to the set $\{0,1\}$, and to define N by: $N(s) = 1$ if and only if s is accepting. The difference between the two approaches is not fundamental.

Degenerated finite automata, defined as those with just one state, are called combinational automata or combinational networks.

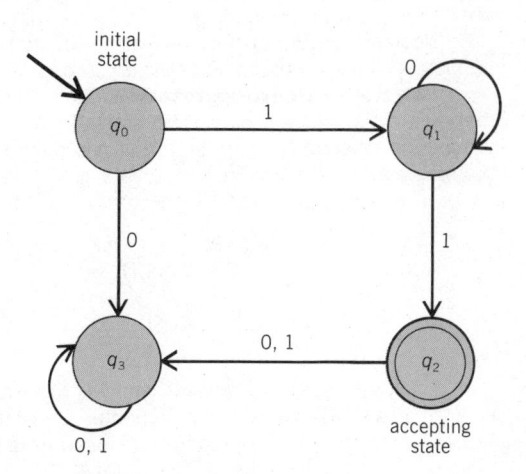

Fig. 2. Finite acceptor.

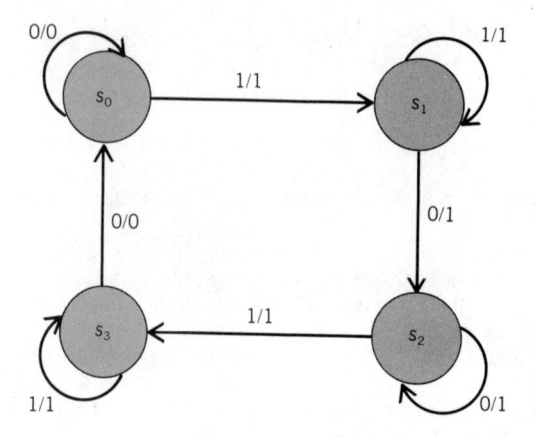

Fig. 3. Finite automaton.

An example consists of the ball-point pen with a button. Possible input symbols are: 0 (releasing the button of the pen) and 1 (pushing the button of the pen). Possible output symbols are also 0, which means that the pen cannot be used to write, and 1, which means that it can. As follows from the analysis of the pen, a finite automaton which models it has four states s_0, s_1, s_2, and s_3. Actions of a finite automaton, modeling a pen, are shown in **Fig. 3** as arrows labeled by fractions. A numerator of the fraction describes an input symbol, a denominator an output symbol. For example, an arc from s_0 to s_0, denoted by 0/0, should be interpreted as: if the state is s_0, and the input symbol is 0, then the next state is again s_0, and the output symbol is also 0.

Bibliography. Z. Bavel, *Introduction to the Theory of Automata*, 1983; J. L. Gersting, *Mathematical Structures for Computer Science*, 1982; J. Hartmanis and R. E. Stearns, *Algebraic Structure Theory of Sequential Machines*, 1966; J. E. Hopcroft and J. D. Ullman, *Introduction to Automata Theory, Languages, and Computation*, 1979; Z. Kohavi, *Switching and Finite Automata Theory*, 2d ed., 1978; R. McNaughton, *Elementary Computability, Formal Languages and Automata*, 1982.

BOOLEAN ALGEBRA
Garrett Birkhoff

A branch of mathematics that was first developed systematically, because of its applications to logic, by the English mathematician George Boole, around 1850. Closely related are its applications to sets and probability.

Boolean algebra also underlies the theory of relations. A modern engineering application is to computer circuit design. *See Digital computer.*

Set-theoretic interpretation. Most basic is the use of boolean algebra to describe combinations of the subsets of a given set I of elements; its basic operations are those of taking the intersection or common part $S \cap T$ of two such subsets S and T, their union or sum $S \cup T$, and the complement S' of any one such subset S. These operations satisfy many laws, including those shown in Eqs. (1), (2), and (3).

$$S \cap S = S \quad S \cap T = T \cap S$$
$$S \cap (T \cap U) = (S \cap T) \cap U \quad (1)$$

$$S \cup S = S \quad S \cup T = T \cup S$$
$$S \cup (T \cup U) = (S \cup T) \cup U \quad (2)$$

$$S \cap (T \cup U) = (S \cap T) \cup (S \cap U)$$
$$S \cup (T \cap U) = (S \cup T) \cap (S \cup U) \quad (3)$$

If O denotes the empty set, and I is the set of all elements being considered, then the laws set forth in Eq. (4) are also fundamental. Since these laws are fundamental, all other algebraic laws of subset combination can be deduced from them.

$$O \cap S = O \quad O \cup S = S \quad I \cap S = S$$
$$I \cup S = I \quad S \cap S' = O \quad S \cup S' = I \quad (4)$$

In applying boolean algebra to logic, Boole observed that combinations of properties under the common logical connectives *and*, *or*, and *not* also satisfy the laws specified above. These laws also hold for propositions or assertions, when combined by the same logical connectives. SEE LOGIC CIRCUITS.

Boole stressed the analogies between boolean algebra and ordinary algebra. If $S \cap T$ is regarded as playing the role of st in ordinary algebra, $S \cup T$ that of $s + t$, O of 0, I of 1, and S' as corresponding to $1 - s$, the laws listed above illustrate many such analogies. However, as first clearly shown by Marshall Stone, the proper analogy is somewhat different. Specifically, the proper boolean analog of $s + t$ is $(S' \cap T) \cup (S \cap T')$, so that the ordinary analog of $S \cup T$ is $s + t - st$. Using Stone's analogy, boolean algebra refers to boolean rings in which $s^2 = s$, a condition implying $s + s = 0$.

Boolean algebra arises in other connections, as in the algebra of (binary) relations. Such relations $\rho, \sigma, \ldots$ refer to appropriate sets of elements $I, J, \ldots$. Any such ρ can be defined by describing the set of pairs (x,t), with x in I and y in J, that stand in the given relation—a fact symbolized $x \rho y$, just as its negation is written $x \rho' y$. Because of this set-theoretic interpretation, boolean algebra obviously applies, with $x(\rho \cap \sigma)y$ meaning $x \rho y$ and $x \sigma y$, and $x(\rho \cup \sigma)y$ meaning $x \rho y$ or $x \sigma y$.

Abstract relationships. Before 1930, work on boolean algebra dealt mainly with its postulate theory, and with the generalizations obtained by abandoning one or more postulates, such as $(p')' = p$ (brouwerian logic). Since $a \cup b = (a' \cap b')'$, clearly one need consider $a \cap b$ and a' as undefined operations. In 1913 H. M. Sheffer showed one operation only $(a|b = a' \cap b')$ need be taken as undefined. In 1941 M. H. A. Newman developed a remarkable generalization which included boolean algebras and boolean rings. This generalization is based on the laws shown in Eqs. (5) and (6). From these assumptions, the idempotent, commutative, and associative laws (1) and (2) can be deduced.

$$a(b + c) = ab + ac \quad (5) \qquad a1 = 1 \quad a + 0 = 0 + a = a \quad aa' = 0 \quad (6)$$
$$(a + b)c = ac + bc \qquad\qquad a + a' = 1$$

Such studies lead naturally to the concept of an abstract boolean algebra, adefined as a collection of symbols combined by operations satisfying the identities listed in formulas (1) to (4). Ordinarily, the phrase boolean algebra refers to such an abstract boolean algebra, and this convention is adopted here.

The class of finite (abstract) boolean algebras is easily described. Each such algebra has, for some nonnegative integer n, exactly 2^n elements and is algebraically equivalent (isomorphic) to the algebra of all subsets of the set of numbers $1, \ldots, n$, under the operations of intersection, union, and complement. Furthermore, if m symbols $a_1, \ldots, a_m$ are combined symbolically through abstract operations $\cap, \cup,$ and $'$ assumed to satisfy the identities of Eqs. (1) to (4), one gets a finite boolean algebra with 2^{2^m} elements—the free boolean algebra with m generators.

Infinite relationships. The theory of infinite boolean algebras is much deeper; it indirectly involves the whole theory of sets. One important result is Stone's representation theorem. Let a field of sets be defined as any family of subsets of a given set I, which contains with any two sets S and T their intersection $S \cap T$, union $S \cup T$, and complements S', T'. Considered abstractly, any such field of sets obviously defines a boolean algebra. Stone's theorem asserts that, conversely, any finite or infinite abstract boolean algebra is isomorphic to a suitable field of sets. His proof is based on the concepts of ideal and prime ideal, concepts which have been intensively studied for their own sake. Because ideal theory in boolean algebra may be subsumed under the ideal theory of rings (via the correspondence between boolean algebras and boolean rings mentioned earlier), it will not be discussed here. A special property of boolean rings (algebras) is the fact that, in this case, any prime ideal is maximal.

The study of infinite boolean algebras leads naturally to the consideration of such infinite distributive laws as those in Eqs. (7a) and (7b).

$$x \cap (\bigcup_B y_\beta) = \bigcup_B (x \cap y_\beta) \quad (7a) \qquad \bigcap_{C}[\bigcup_{A\gamma} u_{\gamma,\alpha}] = \bigcup_F [\bigcap_C u_{\gamma,\phi(\gamma)}]$$
$$x \cup (\bigcap_B y_\beta) = \bigcap_B (x \cup y_\beta) \qquad\qquad \bigcup_C[\bigcap_{A\gamma} u_{\gamma,\alpha}] = \bigcap_F [\bigcup_C u_{\gamma,\phi(\gamma)}] \quad (7b)$$

For finite sets B of indices $\beta = 1, \ldots, n$, if $\cap_B y\beta$ means $y_1 \cup \cdots \cup y_n$, and so on, the laws (7) and (7') follow by induction from (1) to (3). Also, if the symbols x, y_β, and so on, in (7) and (7') refer to subsets of a given space I, and if $\cup_B y_\beta$ and $\cap_B y_\beta$ refer to the union and intersection of all y_β in B, respectively, then (7) and (7') are statements of general laws of formal logic. However, they fail in most infinite boolean algebras. This is shown by the following result of Alfred Tarski: If a boolean algebra A satisfies the generalized distributive laws (7) and (7'), then it is isomorphic with the algebra of all subsets of a suitable space I. A related result is the theorem of L. Loomis (1947) which states: Every σ-complete boolean algebra is isomorphic with a σ-field of sets under countable intersection, countable union, and complement.

In general, such completely distributive boolean algebras of subsets may be characterized by the properties of being complete and atomic. These properties may be defined roughly as the properties that (a) there exists a smallest element $\cup_B y_\beta$ containing any given set B of elements y_β, and (b) any element $y > 0$ contains an atom (or point) $p > 0$, such that $p > x > 0$ has no solution (from Euclid, "A point is that which has no parts"). Condition (b) is also implied by the "descending chain condition" of ideal theory.

Other forms. Nonatomic and incomplete boolean algebras arise naturally in set theory. Thus, the algebra of measurable sets in the line or plane, ignoring sets of measure zero, is nonatomic but complete. The field of Borel sets of space is complete as regards countable families B of subsets S_β, but not for uncountable B. Analogous results hold for wide classes of other measure spaces and topological spaces, respectively. In any zero-dimensional compact space, the sets which are both open and closed (which "disconnect" the space) form a boolean algebra; a fundamental result of Stone shows that the most general boolean algebra can be obtained in this way.

Many other interesting facts about boolean algebra are known. For instance, there is an obvious duality between the properties of $\cap$ and $\cup$ in the preceding discussion. However, so many such facts have natural generalizations to the wider context of lattice theory that the modern tendency is to consider boolean algebra as it relates to such generalizations. For instance, the algebras of n-valued logic, intuitionist (brouwerian) logic, and quantum logic are not boolean algebras, but lattices of other types. The same is true of the closed sets in most topological spaces.
Bibliography. G. Birkhoff, *Lattice Theory*, 3d ed., Amer. Math. Soc. Colloq. Publ., vol. 25, 1967; G. Birkhoff and S. MacLane, *Survey of Modern Algebra*, 4th ed., 1977; G. Boole, *An Investigation of the Laws of Thought*, 1854; B. Buchberger et al. (eds.), *Computer Algebra*, 1983; S. D. Comer (ed.), *Universal Algebra and Lattice Theory*, 1985; H. Levitz and K. Levitz, *Logic and Boolean Algebra*, 1979; R. Sikorski, *Boolean Algebras*, 3d ed., 1969.

NUMBER SYSTEMS
DERRICK H. LEHMER

Integral numbers may be represented as linear combinations of powers of any convenient and arbitrarily chosen base. The choice of the base is not always made on a rational basis, the number systems have been based on 5, 6, 10, and 60. More recently, systems based on 2 and 8 have proved quite useful in computer applications. The duodecimal number system, in which numbers are represented as linear combinations of powers of 12, has certain advantages because 12 has the factors 1, 2, 3, 4, 6, and 12.

Decimal system. Every positive integer is uniquely a polynomial in 10 with coefficients, called digits, taken from 0, 1, . . . , 9. The fact that

$$205714 = 4 + 1 \cdot 10 + 7 \cdot 10^2 + 5 \cdot 10^3 + 0 \cdot 10^4 + 2 \cdot 10^5$$

is nearly always lost in present-day teaching, and in the hurried application of ordinary arithmetic. In fact, numbers are likely to be thought of as merely an orderly arrangement of decimal digits.

The decimal method of representing numbers comes from India and Arabia and is only a few centuries old in Europe. The base, 10, is due to the biological fact that humans have that many articulate fingers and thumbs. The positional significance, including the meaning and usefulness of zero, is of oriental origin.

The operations of addition and multiplication consist of the corresponding operations with polynomials, together with rules that serve to keep the results inside the system so that they can be used in future operations. In the case of addition of two numbers, use is made of either the familiar "carry" rule or the addition table, while for multiplication, use is made of the multiplication table to help represent the product of two digits as a two-digit number. These apparently nonalgebraic operations are so dominant that the basic polynomial structure of the numbers is obscured. Thus, the multiplication of polynomials is done by a more intelligent method than that used for numbers. For example, the multiplication of 2057 by 3416 can be carried out as follows:

$$\begin{array}{r} 2\ 0\ 5\ 7 \\ 3\ 4\ 1\ 6 \\ \hline 6,1\ 7,3\ 3,4\ 2 \\ 8,5\ 3,3\ 7 \\ \hline 7\ 0\ 2\ 6\ 7\ 1\ 2 \end{array}$$

Commas separate those pairs of digits that arise from sums of products of pairs of digits taken one each from the original numbers, and having equal significance. Thus, 53, the fourth most significant contribution, is given by

$$53 = 2 \cdot 6 + 0 \cdot 1 + 4 \cdot 5 + 3 \cdot 7$$

This process can be carried out either from right to left or from left to right, and in the latter case, may be terminated when half done if the least significant half on the product is not needed.

In connection with the design and use of automatic computers, in which numbers of a limited size only may be added and multiplied at one time, precautions against overflow in addition, and approximation by rounding in multiplication further complicate the execution of ordinary arithmetic. This creates a system that, strictly speaking, fails to satisfy the axioms of arithmetic. This causes serious difficulties in some problems involving millions of additions and multiplications.

Subtraction introduces negative numbers that may be handled by introducing a special digit called a sign digit with its own rules of combination, or by introducing complementation in which the digits of a number are subtracted from 9, except for the last nonzero digit which is subtracted from 10. Thus to subtract 20570 from 34162, 20570 may be complemented, and 34162 added to it to obtain the desired difference, 13592:

$$\begin{array}{r} \ldots 99979430 \\ \ldots 00034162 \\ \hline \ldots 00013592 \end{array}$$

Numbers that begin with a run of nines are considered negative in this system. Of course care must be taken to guard against overflow in which a very large positive number might be confused with a very small negative one.

Division is a process that can be carried out only rarely with absolute exactness in the decimal system, the process usually being nonterminating. This introduces the notion of infinite decimal expansions and the more or less theoretical operations with such numbers. In practice, truncation and rounding are used as in $\frac{2}{3} = .66667$, with consequent errors and departure from the axioms of arithmetic. In this case a quantity like ab/c is not unique but may depend upon the order in which the indicated operations are performed. For complicated and extensive problems involving only the four rational operations of arithmetic, an adequate analysis of the errors involved may be very costly indeed.

Automatic calculation in this simulated real number system may be facilitated by the use of a normalizing coding device called "floating arithmetic." In this system a positive real number is expressed as a truncated decimal between .1 and 1 times the appropriate power of 10. Thus the number π on a 10-digit decimal machine could be coded 3141592751. In interpreting this "word," the machine separates the last two digits, 51, and subtracts 50 to get the exponent (possibly negative) of the power of 10 by which the mantissa .31415927 would have to be multiplied to obtain π correct to eight decimals. Rules for multiplying and adding in this system are easily formulated. They involve inspection, comparison, and manipulation of the exponents, followed by appropriate shifting right or left of the mantissas, and finally a normalization and reassembly of the answer as a "floating word." The system has the advantage of greater control over numbers of widely varying orders of magnitude. The disadvantages include slower operation, often by a factor of 5 or more, and occasional unpredictable loss of information.

Besides the operation of complementation, there are other nonarithmetic operations with decimal numbers, for example, comparison. Two numbers may be compared for size by a simple inspection of their corresponding digits, beginning from the left and stopping at the first case of inequality. This simple but important property is worth mentioning because comparison is almost impossible in certain other systems. An unusual use of decimal digits is the so-called middle-of-the-square method of generating random numbers. By this method the next 10-digit random number is obtained from the preceding one by squaring the latter and selecting from the square the central 10 digits.

There are many interesting properties of the digits of integer numbers. The simpler ones depend on the theory of congruences. The most familiar fact of this sort is the statement that a number is even if, and only if, its last digit is even. A similar statement is true with respect to divisibility by 5. If a number is diminished by the sum of its digits, the result is a multiple of 9. This fact is the basis for the scheme for checking arithmetic by "casting out nines," at one time known to every school boy. Elevens may be cast out in like manner if the digits are added with alternating signs. Thus, $34162 - (2 - 6 + 1 - 4 + 3) = 34166$, is a multiple of 11. Similarly, grouping the digits by threes, $44535599 - (599 - 535 + 44) = 44535491$ is a multiple of $1001 = 7 \cdot 11 \cdot 13$. This fact is sometimes used to check desk calculator computations by casting out 100s. It is also used to decide quickly whether a given number is divisible by 7, 11, or 13. The number 44535599 is not divisible by 7, 11, or 13 since $599 - 535 + 44 = 108$ is not.

Squares of integers have digital properties. For example, the final digit of a square is either 0, 1, 4, 5, 6, or 9, never 2, 3, 7, or 8. There are only 22 combinations of two digits in which a square can end, and so on. Such facts are sometimes used in finding the factors of a given number by expressing is as a difference of two squares. The rapid recognition of nonsquares is also helpful in many other diophantine problems.

The representation of real numbers requires infinite, that is, unending, decimals. If the digits of such a decimal ultimately become periodic, the decimal is the ratio P/Q of two integers, and conversely. The length of the period is a complicated function of Q, depending on the prime factors of numbers of the form $10^n - 1$. If, and only if, Q is of the form $2^a 5^b$, the decimal expansion of P/Q terminates. In such cases P/Q has in reality two expansions. Thus $7/5 = 1.4000 \ldots = 1.3999 \ldots$.

The great majority of decimals do not become periodic, or in other words, almost all real numbers are irrational. The class of irrational algebraic numbers, such as the square root of 2, that are roots of polynomials with integer coefficients, is almost completely obscured by other real numbers in their decimal representation. There are only a few statements that can be made about the digits of such numbers other than the obvious one of nonperiodicity. For example, if k consecutive zeros occur, then they cannot occur "too soon" for an infinity of k. On the other hand, almost all real numbers have perfectly normal decimal expansions in the sense that each digit occurs, on the average, one-tenth of the time, each ordered pair one-hundredth of the time, and so on. Whether π, e, or $\sqrt{2}$ are normal is not known. The totality of all known examples of normal numbers is countable.

Almost everything that has been said so far about the decimal system applies with equal force and very little modification to a general system based on an integer $b > 1$ instead of 10. The fact that people "know" all the powers of 10 but not the powers of 7 or 12 is purely psychological and based on tradition. Beyond the fact that 10 is even, there is little to recommend it as a base. The Babylonians used 60, a large but useful base that is still in vogue for measurement of time and angles. The mathematician J. d'Alembert and many others after him urged the adoption of $b = 12$ with its six divisors. The advent of electronic computers has made a good case for $b = 8$ or some other power of 2. Probably base 8 is used by humans more than any base except 10. For $b > 10$, new characters are needed to represent the extra digits. Although there is no agreement

COMPUTATION: THEORY AND MATHEMATICS   **161**

as to which characters to adopt, the modern tendency is to use roman letters because they are easily available on the typewriter. The adoption of a second system brings up the question of translating or converting numbers from one system to the other. Methods for doing this are explained in following sections on binary and octal systems.

Binary system. In the binary system every positive integer is the sum of distinct powers of 2 in just one way. Thus $434 = 2^8 + 2^7 + 2^5 + 2^4 + 2^1$, and this expressed by writing 110110010. The digits corresponding to 2^0, 2^2, 2^3, and 2^6 are zero, since these powers do not occur in 434. The first dozen integers are written as follows:

1	1	4	100	7	111	10	1010
2	10	5	101	8	1000	11	1011
3	11	6	110	9	1001	12	1100

The great advantage of the binary system lies in the fact that there are only two kinds of binary digits, or "bits," namely 0 and 1. This not only gives a simplified arithmetic but provides a language in which to treat two-valued functions or bistable systems. Among its disadvantages is the fact that the binary system requires nearly three times as many digits to represent a given number as does the familiar decimal system.

Digital computers invariably use the binary system. Computers code the decimal digits into binary form, while the purely binary machines use full binary arithmetic.

The physical representation of binary numbers, or information, is possible in many forms. A row of lights, some on and some off, may be interpreted as a binary number. A set of condensers, some charged and some not, a set of high and low voltages, or a set of magnets with fluxes in one direction or another are electronic examples of media for the processing and retention of data in the binary system. The fact that there are only two states to recognize accounts for the great reliability of such computing systems.

The conversion of decimal, or base 10, integers into the binary system can be done in two ways. First, one may substract from the given integer the highest power of 2 not exceeding this number and record a 1 in the binary position corresponding to this power of 2. The remainder of this subtraction, if not zero, now replaces the original number and the process is repeated until a zero remainder is obtained.

Alternatively, one may divide the given number by 2 and record the remainder, 0 or 1, as the final binary digit. The quotient in this division now replaces the given number and the process is repeated and continued until a quotient of zero is reached. The two methods are illustrated in the case of converting 434 to the binary system:

```
       434                    434
      -256                    217        0
       178    1               108       10
      -128                     54       010
        50   11                27       0010
       -32                     13       10010
        18   1101               6       110010
       -16                      3       0110010
         2   11011              1       10110010
        -2                      0       110110010
         0   110110010
```

Both processes have obvious inverses for going from the binary system to the decimal system. In the first case, the indicated powers of 2 are simply added together, and in the second case, a sequence of doubling operations is used, followed by the addition of 0 or 1 as specified by the given binary number. For numbers between 0 and 1 similar procedures are available. Either the subtraction of powers of 2 (negative powers) can be continued or the given number can be doubled, followed by subtraction of whichever of the numbers 0 or 1 will make the remainder lie between 0 and 1, and the operation continued with the remainder as before. The reader may wish to test his understanding by verifying that 43.4294 has the following binary representation:

101011.01101101111011010 . . .

Arithmetic in the binary system is remarkably simple. For addition, only $1 + 1 = 10$ is needed, while the multiplication table reduces to $1 \cdot 1 = 1$. Examples of addition and multiplication are

110101	(53)	1101	(13)
11001	(25)	1011	(11)
1001110	(78)	1101	
		1101	
		1101	
		10001111	(14)

Such simple operations are readily performed electronically with extreme rapidity and reliability.

The binary system is useful not only to represent numbers but also to record and process information. In fact the unit of information is a binary digit. For example, given a set S of objects and a property P, it is possible to record which obects have the property P, and which do not, by assigning a binary position to each object of S and recording there a 1 or 0 according as the property P is, or is not, possessed by the corresponding object. Thus if the objects are the first odd numbers and P is the property of primality, the binary number

$$N = .01110110110100110010 \ldots$$

is equivalent to the list of odd primes

$$3, 5, 7, 11, 13, 17, 19, 23, 29, 31, 37, \ldots$$

A binary computer, with its ability to extract and examine a given binary digit, can use this compact method of storing information. The operation $N + N$ replaces N, which shifts the digits one place to the left and produces overflow if, and only if, the corresponding number is a prime, can be used in general to select the successive members of S having a property P. Other combinatorial processes involving several coded binary numbers can be used to advantage with a binary computer. For example, one can make a search for those objects of S that have a set of specified properties $P_1, P_2, \ldots$.

The binary system is implicit in a number of different arithmetical operations and games. The so-called Russian peasant method of multiplying by doubling and halving is a case in point. To multiply 323 by 146, form two columns of figures (in the decimal system)

146	~~323~~
73	646
36	~~1292~~
18	~~2584~~
9	5168
4	~~10336~~
2	~~20672~~
1	41344
	47158

Each term of the first column is the integer part of half the preceding term. Each term of the second column opposite an even number in the first column is struck out. The sum of the remaining numbers give the desired product 47158. The method works because, in forming the first column, one is, in effect, converting 146 to the binary system.

Another operation in which binary representation is effective is that of raising a given base B to a high integer power. Suppose that

$$n = b_k b_{k-1} \ldots b_2 b_1 b_0$$

is the binary representation of the integer n. To compute B^n most efficiently, form recursively the numbers w_l, defined by

$$w_0 = B^{bk} = B$$
$$w_1 = B^{bk-1}(w_0)^2$$
$$\cdots\cdots\cdots\cdots$$
$$w_i = B^{bk-i}(w_{i-1})^2$$

Then $w_k = B^n$. In fact

$$w_k = B^{b_0}(w_{k-1})^2 = B^{b_0 + 2[b_1 + 2(b_2 + \cdots)]}$$

so that the exponent is

$$b_0 + 2b_1 + 2^2 b_2 + \cdots + 2^k b_k = n$$

Octal system. To write a number in the octal system, once it has been expressed in the binary system, one merely groups the binary digits by threes, beginning at the binary point and working to the left and right. Thus the decimal number 43.4294 gives

(101)(011).(011)(011)(011)(110)(110)(10.)

or simply 53.333664, where the last digit should perhaps be 5. On the other hand, decimal to octal conversion can be accomplished directly by either of the two methods that correspond in an obvious way to those given for decimal to binary conversion. Thus, by subtracting appropriate multiples of powers of 8, beginning with the largest possible power,

$$5280 = 1 \cdot 8^4 + 2 \cdot 8^3 + 2 \cdot 8^2 + 4 \cdot 8$$

so that in the octal system there are 12240 feet in a mile. Alternatively, one may divide 5280 by 8, getting 0 as remainder and 660 as quotient. Dividing 660 by 8, 4 and 82 are obtained. Dividing 82 by 8 gives 2 and 10. Dividing 10 by 8 gives 2 and 1. This gives the digits in reverse order.

Octal to decimal conversion may be effected by the use of a convenient table of powers of 8, a sample of which follows:

n	8^n	n	8^n
0	1	-1	.125000
1	8	-2	.015625
2	64	-3	.001953
3	512	-4	.000244
4	4096	-5	.000031
5	32768	-6	.000004

The octal system with its eight digits 0, 1, . . . , 7 affords a convenient way of condensing the lengthier display of the binary system. Arithmetic in the octal system resembles the familiar decimal arithmetic. The addition and multiplication tables are as shown:

Addition

	0	1	2	3	4	5	6	7
0	0	1	2	3	4	5	6	7
1	1	2	3	4	5	6	7	10
2	2	3	4	5	6	7	10	11
3	3	4	5	6	7	10	11	12
4	4	5	6	7	10	11	12	13
5	5	6	7	10	11	12	13	14
6	6	7	10	11	12	13	14	15
7	7	10	11	12	13	14	15	16

Multiplication

	0	1	2	3	4	5	6	7
0	0	0	0	0	0	0	0	0
1	0	1	2	3	4	5	6	7
2	0	2	4	6	10	12	14	16
3	0	3	6	11	14	17	22	25
4	0	4	10	14	20	24	30	34
5	0	5	12	17	24	31	36	43
6	0	6	14	22	30	36	44	52
7	0	7	16	25	34	43	52	61

Examples of addition and multiplication in the octal system are

```
   4375          5734
   3704            16
  -----        ------
  10301         43450
                5734
               ------
              123010
```

Octal arithmetic can be checked by "casting out sevens" (instead of nines) by adding the digits. Thus for the addition problem above,

$$4375 \equiv 4 + 3 + 7 + 5 = 23$$
$$\equiv 2 + 3 = 5 \qquad (\mathrm{mod}\ 7)$$
$$3704 \equiv 3 + 7 + 0 + 4 = 16$$
$$\equiv 1 + 6 \equiv 0 \qquad (\mathrm{mod}\ 7)$$
$$10301 \equiv 1 + 3 + 1 = 5 \qquad (\mathrm{mod}\ 7)$$

Checking by casting out nines involves taking the octal digits with alternating signs. Thus,

$$4375 \equiv 5 - 7 + 3 - 4 = -3 \equiv 6 \quad (\mathrm{mod}\ 9)$$
$$3704 \equiv 4 - 0 + 7 - 3 = 8 \quad (\mathrm{mod}\ 9)$$
$$10301 \equiv 1 + 3 + 1 = 5 \equiv 6 + 8 \quad (\mathrm{mod}\ 9)$$

The octal system requires only 10% more digits than the decimal system to represent the same amount of information. Some computing systems use base 16, in which case binary information is handled in sets of four bits. This system is more compact than the decimal system, 100 hexodecimals being equivalent to 120 decimals, but it requires a multiplication table with nearly three times as many entries.

Computing systems of binary type have subroutines for the conversion of any kind of decimal information into binary information during input, and vice versa during output, so that a facility in octal arithmetic is needed only rarely during checking and testing of a new problem.
SEE DIGITAL COMPUTER; NUMERICAL ANALYSIS.

Bibliography. R. H. Bruck, *Survey of Binary Systems*, 3d ed., 1971; T. Dantzig, *Number, the Language of Science*, 4th ed., 1967; C. Reid, *From Zero to Infinity*, 2d ed., 1960; H. Schmid, *Decimal Computation*, 1974, reprint 1983; E. Sondheimer and A. Rogerson, *Numbers and Infinity: An Historical Account of Mathematical Concepts*, 1981.

BIT
HELMUT E. THIESS

In the pure binary numeration system, either of the digits 0 or 1. The term may be thought of as a contraction of binary digit. SEE NUMBER SYSTEMS.

In a binary notation, bits are used as two different characters. For example, in the American National Standard Code for Information Interchange (ASCII), a seven-bit coded character set, the seven bits 1000111 represent the letter G.

Bit is widely used as a synonym for binary element, a constituent element of data that takes either of two values or states (on-off, yes-no, zero-one, and so forth). The brains of animals and registers, memories, and other storage devices of digital computers and electronic calculators store bits (binary elements) as the smallest unit of information.

During a meeting in the late winter of 1943/1944 in Princeton, New Jersey, convened by John von Neumann and Norbert Wiener, engineers, physiologists, and mathematicians found that it was convenient to measure information in terms of numbers of yeses and noes and to call this unit of information a bit. Strictly speaking, the bit of von Neumann, Wiener, and their associates is the binary element and not the binary digit.

A byte is a string of bits (binary elements) operated on or treated as a unit and usually shorter than a word. An eight-bit byte comprises eight bits. In precise usage, n-bit bytes are called quartet, quintet, . . ., octet, and so forth. Byte is derived from bite.

A word is a string of bits (binary elements) that consists of two or more bytes. The terms halfword, fullword, and doubleword are also used.

A computer word is a word stored in one computer location, usually 16, 32, 36, 48, or 64 bits in length, depending on the design of the computer.

In microcomputers or in particular applications, a nybble is a strong of bits (binary elements) operated on as a unit, larger than a bit, and smaller than a byte. Nybble is derived from nibble. SEE DIGITAL COMPUTER.

In information theory, bit is a synonym for the new, preferred term shannon, a unit of measure of information equal to the decision content of a set of two mutually exclusive events. For example, the decision content of a character set of eight characters equals three shannons (the logarithm of 8 to base 2). A shannon also is called an information content binary unit. A hartley is the information content decimal unit. These unit names were adopted by the International Organization for Standardization (ISO) in 1975, honoring C. E. Shannon and R. C. L. Hartley.

DATA REDUCTION
Raymond J. Nelson

The transformation of information, usually empirically or experimentally derived, into corrected, ordered, and simplified form.

The term data reduction generally refers to operations on either numerical or alphabetical information digitally represented, or to operations which yield digital information from empirical observations or instrument readings. In the latter case data reduction also implies conversion from analog to digital form by human reading and digital symbolization or by mechanical means. See Analog-to-digital converter; Digital computer.

Data reduction is used to prepare data in a form suitable for scientific computation, statistical analysis, and control of industrial processes and operations, and for data processing in business applications. Examples are the preparation of data obtained from test runs in missile development, wind tunnel experiments, industrial product sampling, or from readings of sensing instruments in process control.

In applications where the raw data are already digital, data reduction may consist simply of such operations as editing, scaling, coding, sorting, collating, and tabular summarization.

More typically, the data reduction process is applied to readings or measurements involving random errors. These are the indeterminate errors inherent in the process of assigning values to observational quantities. In such cases, before data may be coded and summarized as outlined above, the most probable value of a quantity must be determined. Provided the errors are normally distributed, the most probable (or central) value of a set of measurements is given by the arithmetic mean or, in the more general case, by the weighted mean.

Data reduction may also involve operations of smoothing and interpolation, because the results of observations and measurements are always given as a discrete set of numbers, while the phenomenon being studied may be continuous in nature.

In a smoothing problem a function is empirically given (for example, positions of a body as a function of time) as a collection of points (t_1, x_1), (t_2, x_2), . . ., (t_n, x_n) where the values of the variables, perhaps both independent and dependent, are inaccurate. A common procedure is to fit an nth-order (commonly second-order) parabola by least squares to the data points, thus obtaining a representation that will satisfy as nearly as possible all of the given pairs, but perhaps none exactly.

In interpolation a function is known in tabular form. The problem is to determine values between the tabulated points.

Any of the above-mentioned procedures may be carried out on a digital computer or built into a process control system or procedure.

NUMERICAL ANALYSIS
Carl de Boor

The development and analysis of computational methods (and ultimately of program packages) for the minimization and the approximation of functions, and for the approximate solution of equations, such as linear or nonlinear (systems of) equations and differential or integral equations. Originally part of every mathematician's work, the subject is now often taught in computer science departments because of the tremendous impact which computers have had on its development. Research focuses mainly on the numerical solution of (nonlinear) partial differential equations and the minimization of functions.

Numerical analysis is needed because answers provided by mathematical analysis are usually symbolic and not numeric; they are often given implicitly only, as the solution of some equation, or they are given by some limit process. A further complication is provided by the rounding error which usually contaminates every step in a calculation (because of the fixed finite number of digits carried).

Even in the absence of rounding error, few numerical answers can be obtained exactly. Among these are (1) the value of a piecewise rational function at a point and (2) the solution of a (solvable) linear system of equations, both of which can be produced in a finite number of arithmetic steps. Approximate answers to all other problems are obtained by solving the first few in a sequence of such finitely solvable problems. A typical example is provided by Newton's method: A solution c to a nonlinear equation $f(c) = 0$ is found as the limit $c = \lim_{n \to \infty} x_n$, with x_{n+1} a solution to the linear equation $f(x_n) + f'(x_n)(x_{n+1} - x_n) = 0$, that is, $x_{n+1} = x_n - f(x_n)/f'(x_n)$, $n = 0, 1, 2, \ldots$. Of course, only the first few terms in this sequence $x_0, x_1, x_2, \ldots$ can ever be calculated, and thus one must face the question of when to break off such a solution process and how to gauge the accuracy of the current approximation. The difficulty in the mathematical treatment of these questions is exemplified by the fact that the limit of a sequence is completely independent of its first few terms.

In the presence of rounding error, an otherwise satisfactory computational process may become useless, because of the amplification of rounding errors. A computational process is called stable to the extent that its results are not spoiled by rounding errors. The extended calculations involving millions of arithmetic steps now possible on computers have made the stability of a computational process a prime consideration.

Interpolation and approximation. Polynomial interpolation provides a polynomial p of degree n or less which uniquely matches given function values $f(x_0), \ldots, f(x_n)$ at corresponding distinct points $x_0, \ldots, x_n$. The interpolating polynomial p is used in place of f, for example in evaluation, integration, differentiation, and zero finding. Accuracy of the interpolating polynomial depends strongly on the placement of the interpolation points, and usually degrades drastically as one moves away from the interval containing these points (that is, in case of extrapolation).

When many interpolation points (more then 5 or 10) are to be used, it is often much more efficient to use instead a piecewise polynomial interpolant or spline. Suppose the interpolation points above are ordered, $x_0 < x_1 < \cdots < x_n$. Then the cubic spline interpolant to the above data, for example, consists of cubic polynomial pieces, with the ith piece defining the interpolant on the interval $[x_{i-1}, x_i]$ and so matched with its neighboring piece or pieces that the resulting function not only matches the given function values (hence is continuous) but also has a continuous first and second derivative.

Interpolation is but one way to determine an approximant. In full generality, approximation involves several choices: (1) a set P of possible approximants, (2) a criterion for selecting from P a particular approximant, and (3) a way to measure the approximation error, that is, the difference between the function f to be approximated and the approximant p, in order to judge the quality of approximation. Much studied examples for P are the polynomials of degree n or less, piecewise polynomials of a given degree with prescribed breakpoints, and rational functions of given numerator and denominator degrees. The distance between f and p is usually measured by a norm, such as the L_2 norm $(\int |f(x) - p(x)|^2 dx)^{1/2}$ or the uniform norm $\sup_x |f(x) - p(x)|$. Once choices 1 and 3 are made, one often settles 2 by asking for a best approximation to f from P, that is, for an element of P whose distance from f is a small as possible. Questions of existence, uniqueness, characterization, and numerical construction of such best approximants have been studied extensively for various choices of P and the distance measure. If P is linear, that is, if P consists of all linear combinations

$$\sum_{i=1}^{n} a_i p_i$$

of certain fixed functions $p_1, \ldots, p_n$, then determination of a best approximation in the L_2 norm is particularly easy, since it involves nothing more than the solution of n simultaneous linear equations.

Solution of linear systems. Solving a linear system of equations is probably the most frequently confronted computational task. It is handled either by a direct method, that is, a method which obtains the exact answer in a finite number of steps, or by an iterative method, or by a judicious combination of both. Analysis of the effectiveness of possible methods has led to a workable basis for selecting the one which best fits a partcular situation.

Direct methods. Cramer's rule is a well-known direct method for solving a system of n linear equations in n unknowns, but it is much less efficient than the method of choice, elimination. In this procedure the first unknown is eliminated from each equation but the first by subtracting from that equation an appropriate multiple of the first equation. The resulting system of $n - 1$ equations in the remaining $n - 1$ unknowns is similarly reduced, and the process is repeated until one equation in one unknown remains. The solution for the entire system is then found by back-substitution, that is, by solving for that one unknown in that last equation, then returning to the next-to-last equation which at the next-to-last step of the elimination involved the final unknown (now known) and one other, and solving for that second-to-last unknown, and so on.

This process may break down for two reasons: (1) when it comes time to eliminate the kth unknown, its coefficient in the kth equation may be zero, and hence the equation cannot be used to eliminate the kth unknown from equations $k + 1, \ldots, n$; and (2) the process may be very unstable. Both difficulties can be overcome by pivoting, in which one elects, at the beginning of the kth step, a suitable equation from among equations $k, \ldots, n$, interchanges it with the kth equation, and then proceeds as before. In this way the first difficulty may be avoided provided that the system has one and only one solution. Further, with an appropriate pivoting strategy, the second difficulty may be avoided provided that the linear system is stable. Explicitly, it can be shown that, with the appropriate pivoting strategy, the solution computed in the presence of rounding errors is the exact solution of a linear system whose coefficients usually differ by not much more than roundoff from the given ones. The computed solution is therefore close to the exact solution provided that such small changes in the given system do not change its solution by much. A rough but common measure of the stability of a linear system is the condition of its coefficient matrix. This number is computed as the product of the norm of the matrix and of its inverse. The reciprocal of the condition therefore provides an indication of how close the matrix is to being noninvertible or singular.

Iterative methods. The direct methods described above require a number of operations which increases with the cube of the number of unknowns. Some types of problems arise wherein the matrix of coefficients is sparse, but the unknowns may number several thousand; for these, direct methods are prohibitive in computer time required. One frequent source of such problems is the finite difference treatment of partial differential equations (discussed below). A significant literature of iterative methods exploiting the special properties of such equations is available. For certain restricted classes of difference equations, the error in an initial iterate can be guaranteed to be reduced by a fixed factor, using a number of computations that is proportional to $n \log n$, where n is the number of unknowns. Since direct methods require work proportional to n^3, it is not surprising that as n becomes large, iterative methods are studied rather closely as practical alternatives.

The most straightforward iterative procedure is the method of substitution, sometimes called the method of simultaneous displacements. If the equations for $i = 1, \ldots, n$ are shown in Eq. (1), then the rth iterate is computed from the $r - 1$st by solving the trivial equations for $x_i^{(r)}$ shown in Eq. (2) for $i = 1, \ldots, n$, where the elements $x_i^{(0)}$ are chosen arbitrarily.

$$\sum_{j=1}^{n} a_{ij} x_j = b_i \qquad (1) \qquad \sum_{j \neq i} a_{ij} x_j^{(r-1)} + a_{ii} x_i^{(r)} = b_i \qquad (2)$$

If for $i = 1, \ldots, n$, the inequality

$$\sum_{j \neq i} |a_{ij}| \leq |a_{ii}|$$

holds for some i, and the matrix is irreducible, then $x_i^{(r)} \underset{r}{\to} x_i$ is the solution. For a matrix to be irreducible, the underlying simultaneous system must not have any subset of unknowns which can be solved for independently of the others. For practical problems for which convergence occurs, analysis shows the expected number of iterations required to guarantee a fixed error reduction to be proportional to the number of unknowns. Thus the total work is proportional to n^2.

The foregoing procedure may be improved several ways. The Gauss-Seidel method, sometimes called the method of successive displacements, represents the same idea but uses the latest available values. Equation (3) is solved for $i = 1, \ldots, n$. The Gauss-Seidel method converges

$$\sum_{j<i} a_{ij}x_j^{(r)} a_{ii}x_i^{(r)} + \sum_{j>i} a_{ij}x_j^{(r-1)} = b_i \tag{3}$$

for the conditions given above for the substitution method and is readily shown to converge more rapidly.

Further improvements in this idea lead to the method of successive overrelaxation. This can be thought of as calculating the correction associated with the Gauss-Seidel method and overcorrecting by a factor ω. Equation (4) is first solved for y. Then $x_i^{(r)} = x_i^{(r-1)} + \omega(y - x_i^{(r-1)})$

$$\sum_{j<i} a_{ij}x_j^{(r)} + a_{ii}y + \sum_{j>i} a_{ij}x_j^{(r-1)} = b_i \tag{4}$$

Clearly, choosing $\omega = 1$ yields the Gauss-Seidel method. For problems of interest arising from elliptic difference equations, there exists an optimum ω which guarantees a fixed error reduction in a number of iterations proportional to $n^{1/2}$, and thus in total work proportional to $n^{3/2}$.

A number of other iterative techniques for systems with sparse matrices have been studied. Primarily they depend upon approximating the given matrix with one such that the resulting equations can be solved directly with an amount of work proportional to n. For a quite large class of finite difference equations of interest, the computing work to guarantee a fixed error reduction is proportional to $n^{5/4}$. The work requirement proportional only to $n \log n$ quoted earlier applies to a moderately restricted subset.

Overdetermined linear systems. Often an overdetermined linear system has to be solved. This happens, for example, if one wishes to fit the model

$$p(x) = \sum_{j=1}^{n} a_j p_j$$

to observations $(x_i, y_i)_{i=1}^m$ with $n < m$. Here one would like to determine the coefficient vector $\mathbf{a} = (a_1, \ldots, a_n)^T$ so that $p(x_i) = y_i$, $i = 1, \ldots, m$. In matrix notation, one wants $A\mathbf{a} = \mathbf{y}$, with A the m-by-n matrix $[p_j(x_i)]$. If $n < m$, one cannot expect a solution, and it is then quite common to determine $\mathbf{a}$ instead by least squares, that is, so as to minimize the "distance" $(\mathbf{y} - A\mathbf{a})^T(\mathbf{y} - A\mathbf{a})$ between the vectors $\mathbf{y}$ and $A\mathbf{a}$. This leads to the so-called normal equations $A^T A\mathbf{a} = A^T \mathbf{y}$ for the coefficient vector $\mathbf{a}$. But unless the "basis functions" $p_1, \ldots, p_n$ are chosen very carefully, the condition of the matrix $A^T A$ may be very bad, making the elimination process above overly sensitive to rounding errors. It is much better to make use of an orthogonal decomposition for A.

Assume first that A has full rank (which is the same thing as assuming that the only linear combination P of the functions $P_1, \ldots, p_n$ which vanishes at all the points $x_1, \ldots, x_m$ is the trivial one, the one with all coefficients zero). Then A has a QR decomposition, that is, $A = QR$, with Q an orthogonal matrix (that is, $Q^T = Q^{-1}$), and R an m-by-n matrix whose first n rows contain an invertible upper triangular matrix R_1, while its remaining m-n rows are identically zero. Then $(\mathbf{y} - A\mathbf{a})^T \cdot (\mathbf{y} - A\mathbf{a}) = (Q^T\mathbf{y} - R\mathbf{a})^T(Q^T\mathbf{y} - R\mathbf{a})$ and, since the last m-n entries of $R\mathbf{a}$ are zero, this is minimized when the first n entries of $R\mathbf{a}$ agree with those of $Q^T\mathbf{y}$, that is, $R_1\mathbf{a} = [(Q^T\mathbf{y})(i)]_1^n$. Since R_1 is upper triangular, this system is easily solved by back-substitution, as outlined above. The QR decomposition for A can be obtained stably with the aid of Householder transformations, that is, matrices of the simple form $H = I - (2/\mathbf{u}^T)\mathbf{u}\mathbf{u}^T$, which are easily seen to be orthogonal and even self-inverse, that is, $H^{-1} = H$. In the first step of the process, A is premultiplied by a Householder matrix H_1 with $\mathbf{u}$ so chosen that the first column of H_1A has zeros in rows $2, \ldots, m$. In the next step, one premultiplies H_1A by H_2 with $\mathbf{u}$ so chosen that H_2H_1A retains its zeros in column 1 and has also zeroes in column 2 in rows $3, \ldots, m$. After $n - 1$ such steps, the matrix $R := H_{n-1} \ldots H_1A$ is reached with zeros below its main diagonal, and so $A = QR$ with $Q := H_1 \ldots H_{n-1}$.

The situation is somewhat more complicated when A fails to have full rank or when its rank cannot be easily determined. In that case, one may want to make use of a singular value decomposition for A, which means that one writes A as the product USV, where both U and V are orthogonal matrices and $S = (s_{ij})$ is an m-by-n matrix that may be loosely termed "diagonal," that is, $s_{ij} = 0$ for $i \neq j$. Calculation of such a decomposition is more expensive than that of a QR decomposition, but the singular value decomposition provides much more information about A.

For example, the diagonal elements of S, the so-called singular values of A, give precise information about how close A is to a matrix of given rank, and hence make it possible to gauge the effect of errors in the entries of A on the rank of A. SEE MATRIX THEORY.

Differential equations. Classical methods yield practical results only for a moderately restricted class of ordinary differential equations, a somewhat more restricted class of systems of ordinary differential equations, and a very small number of partial differential equations. The power of numerical methods is enormous here, for in quite broad classes of practical problems relatively straightforward procedures are guaranteed to yield numerical results, whose quality is predictable.

Ordinary differential equations. The simplest system is the initial value problem in a single unknown, $y' = f(x,y)$, and $y(a) = \eta$, where y' means dy/dx, and f is continuous in x and satisfies a Lipschitz condition in y; that is, there exists a constant K such that for all x and y of interest, $|f(x,y) - f(x,z)| \leq K|y - z|$. The problem is well posed and has a unique solution.

The Euler method is as follows: $y_0 = \eta$, Eq. (5) holds, and $i = 0, 1, 2, \ldots, (b - a)/h$.

$$y_{i+1} = y_i + hf(x_i, y_i) \tag{5}$$

Here h is a small positive constant, and $x_i = a + ih$. Analysis shows that as $h \to 0$, there exists a constant C such that $|y_k - y(x_k)| \leq Ch$, where $y(x_k)$ is the value of the unique solution at x_k, and $a \leq x_k \leq b$. This almost trivial formulation of a numerical procedure thus guarantees an approximation to the exact solution to the problem that is arbitrarily good if h is sufficiently small, and it is easy to implement. A trivial extension of this idea is given by the method of Heun, Eq. (6).

$$y_{i+1} = y_i + 1/2h[(f(x_i,y_i) + f(x_i + h, y_i + hf(x_i,y_i))] \tag{6}$$

The method of Heun similarly is guaranteed to approximate the desired solution arbitrarily well since there exists another constant C_1 such that the $\{y_i\}$ satisfy relation (7). This is clearly

$$|y_k - y(x_k)| \leq C_1 h^2 \tag{7}$$

asymptotically better than the method of Euler. It is readily found to be practically superior for most problems. Further improvement of this type is offered by the classical Runge-Kutta method, Eq. (8), where $\phi(x,y,h) = \frac{1}{6}[k_1 + 2k_2 + 2k_3 + k_4]$, and $k_1 = f(x,y)$, $k_2 = f(x + h/2, y + hk_1/2)$,

$$y_{i+1} = y_i + h\phi(x_i,y_i,h) \tag{8}$$

$k_3 = f(x + h/2, y + hk_2/2)$, and $k_4 = f(x + h, y + hk_3)$. For this method there exists a constant C_2 such that $|y_k - y(x_k)| \leq C_2 h^4$.

The foregoing methods are called single-step since only y_i is involved in the computation of y_{i+1}. The single-step methods yielding the better results typically require several evaluations of the function f per step. By contrast, multistep methods typically achieve high exponents on h in the error bounds without more than one evaluation of f per step. Multistep methods require use of $y_{i-\alpha}$ or $f(x_{i-\alpha},y_{i-\alpha})$ or both for $\alpha = 0, 1, \ldots, j$ to compute y_{i+1}. Typical is the Adams-Bashforth method for $j = 5$, Eq. (9).

$$y_{i+1} = y_i + \frac{h}{1440}[4277\,f(x_i,y_i) - 7923\,f(x_{i-1},y_{i-1}) + 9982\,f(x_{i-2},y_{i-2})$$
$$- 7298\,f(x_{i-3},y_{i-3}) + 2277\,f(x_{i-4},y_{i-4}) - 475\,f(x_{i-5},y_{i-5})] \tag{9}$$

Analysis shows the solution of this Adams-Bashforth procedure to satisfy relation (10) for

$$|y_k - y(x_k)| \leq C_3 h^6 \tag{10}$$

some constant C_3. A large number of valuable multistep methods have been studied. If f is nontrivial to evaluate, the multistep methods are less work to compute than the single-step methods for comparable accuracy. The chief difficulty of multistep methods is that they require j starting values and, therefore, cannot be used from the outset in a computation.

Partial differential equations. Methods used for partial differential equations differ significantly, depending on the type of equation. Typically, parabolic equations are considered for which the prototype is the heat flow equation, Eq. (11), with $u(x,0)$ given on $x\epsilon[0,1]$, say, and $u(0,t)$

and $u(1,t)$ given for $t > 0$. A typical finite difference scheme is shown in Eq. (12), where $i - 1$,

$$\frac{\partial^2 u}{\partial x^2} = \frac{\partial u}{\partial t} \qquad (11) \qquad (w_{i,n})_{x\bar{x}} = \frac{w_{i,n+1} - w_{i,n}}{k} \qquad (12)$$

..., $1/h - 1$, $w_{0,n} = u(0,t_n)$, and $w_{1/h,n} = u(1,t_n)$, with $(w_i)_x = (w_{i+1} - w_i)/h$, $(w_i)_{\bar{x}} = (w_{i-1})_x$, and $w_{i,n}$ is the function defined at $x_i = ih$, $t_n = nk$. Analysis shows that as $h,k \to 0$, the solution $w_{i,n}$ satisfies $|w_{i,n} - u(x_i,t_n)| < C(h^2 + k)$ for some constant C if $k/h^2 \leq \frac{1}{2}$, but for k/h^2 somewhat larger than $\frac{1}{2}$, $w_{i,n}$ bears no relation at all to $u(x_i,t_n)$.

The restriction $k/h^2 \leq \frac{1}{2}$ can be removed by using the implicit difference equation, Eq. (13), but now simultaneous equations must be solved for $w_{i,n+1}$ each step. The inequality,

$$(w_{i,n+1})_{x\bar{x}} = \frac{w_{i,n+1} - w_{i,n}}{k} \qquad (13)$$

$|w_{i,n} - u(x_i,t_n)| < C(h^2 + k)$, still holds for some constant C. An improved implicit formulation is the Crank-Nicolson equation, Eq. (14).

$$\frac{1}{2}(w_{i,n} + w_{i,n+1})_{x\bar{x}} = \frac{w_{i,n+1} - w_{i,n}}{k} \qquad (14)$$

As $h,k \to 0$, solutions satisfy relation (15) for some constant C; again h/k is unrestricted.

$$|w_{i,n} - u(x_i,t_n)| < C(h^2 + k^2) \qquad (15)$$

Such techniques can readily extend to several space variables and to much more general equations. The work estimates given above for iterative solution of simultaneous equations, such as Eq. (14), apply for two-space variables.

Work using variational techniques to approximate the solution of parabolic and elliptic equations has been most fruitful for broad classes of nonlinear problems. The technique reduces partial differential equations to systems of ordinary differential equations. Analysis shows that solutions obtained approximate the desired solution, as within a constant multiple of the best that can be achieved within the subspace of the basis functions used. Practical utilization suggests this to be the direction for most likely future developments in the treatment of partial differential systems.

Bibliography. A. W. Al-Khafaji and J. R. Tooley, *Numerical Analysis with Computer Applications*, 1986; J. C. Butcher, *The Numerical Analysis of Ordinary Differential Equations*, 1987; M. K. Jain, S. R. K. Lyengar, and R. K. Jain, *Numerical Methods for Scientific and Engineering Computation*, 1985; M. J. Maron, *Numerical Analysis: A Practical Approach*, 2d ed., 1986; S. Yakowitz and F. Sziderovszky, *An Introduction to Numerical Computations*, 1986.

MATRIX THEORY
Ross A. Beaumont

A matrix is a rectangular array of numbers, or other elements, of form (1). The array A is an m by

$$A = \begin{pmatrix} a_{11} & a_{12} & \cdots & a_{1n} \\ a_{21} & a_{12} & \cdots & a_{2n} \\ \cdots & \cdots & \cdots & \cdots \\ a_{m1} & a_{m2} & \cdots & a_{mn} \end{pmatrix} \qquad (1)$$

n matrix with m rows and n columns, and the size of A is said to be m by n. The rows of a matrix are always numbered from the top down and the columns from left to right. The position of each element in the array is given by its subscripts; that is, a_{ij} is the element in the ith row and jth column. Since every element of A is represented by a_{ij} as i takes on the values $1, 2, \ldots, m$ and j the values $1, 2, \ldots, n$, a_{ij} is called the typical element of A, and the compact notation $A = (a_{ij})$ is used when the size of A is given.

Matrices have application as computational devices in such widely diversified fields as economics, psychology, statistics, engineering, physics, and mathematics. In mathematics, mat-

COMPUTATION: THEORY AND MATHEMATICS

rices are useful tools in the study of linear systems of algebraic equations, linear differential equations, linear mappings and transformations, and bilinear and quadratic forms.

For example, in the linear system of equations

$$-3x + 2y - 6z = 10$$
$$7x - y + 3z = 0$$
$$x + y - 5z = 1$$

the letters x, y, and z are merely symbols which stand for possible numerical solutions, and the only significant features of this system are the numbers which appear in the equations and their relative positions. Therefore, these equations are completely described by the 3 by 4 matrix which is labeled (2).

$$\begin{pmatrix} -3 & 2 & -6 & 10 \\ 7 & -1 & 3 & 0 \\ 1 & 1 & -5 & 1 \end{pmatrix} \quad (2)$$

Similarly the properties of the linear substitution which describes a rotation of axes of a cartesian coordinate system, are completely determined by the square 2 by 2 matrix

$$\begin{pmatrix} \cos\theta & -\sin\theta \\ \sin\theta & \cos\theta \end{pmatrix}$$

If $m = n$ in (1), A is called a square matrix of order n. If $m = 1$, A is a row matrix, and if $n = 1$, A is a column matrix. The elements a_{ij} of A, for which $i = j$, are the principal diagonal elements. A diagonal matrix is a matrix such that $a_{ij} = 0$ if $i \neq j$, and a scalar matrix is a square diagonal matrix with equal diagonal elements. An identity matrix is a scalar matrix in which the common diagonal element is the number 1. An n by n identity matrix is denoted by I_n.

Matrices can be regarded as generalized numbers, and their utility in applications depends on the possibility of combining them in certain definite ways. The matrix operations of addition, subtraction, and multiplication are defined in terms of these same operations for the elements, and they satisfy some, but not all, of the rules of ordinary algebra. In discussing these matrix operations it is assumed that the elements of the matrices are numbers.

Two matrices $A = (a_{ij})$ and $B = (b_{ij})$ are equal if they have the same size m by n and $a_{ij} = b_{ij}$ for all i, j. Matrices $A = (a_{ij})$ and $B = (b_{ij})$ of the same size m by n are added by adding correspondingly placed elements; that is, $A + B = C = (c_{ij})$ is an m by n matrix where $c_{ij} = a_{ij} + b_{ij}$ for all i, j. It follows that matrix addition is associative and commutative, that is, $(A + B) + C = A + (B + C)$ and $A + B = B + A$, as is the case for numbers. The m by n matrix with 0 in every position is denoted by 0, and is called a null matrix. Then $A + 0 = 0 + A = A$. The matrix $-A = (-a_{ij})$ is the negative of the matrix $A = (a_{ij})$, and $A + (-A) = 0$. Subtraction of m by n matrices is defined by $B - A = B + (-A) = (b_{ij} - a_{ij})$.

A matrix $B = (b_{ij})$ is conformable with respect to a matrix $A = (a_{ij})$ if B has size n by q and A has size m by n; that is, B has the same number of rows as A has columns. The matrix product AB is defined only when B is conformable with respect to A. The product $C = AB$ is an m by q matrix and the element in the i, j position of C is obtained by multiplying the n elements in the ith row of A into the n elements in the jth column of B, term by term, and adding these products. Thus if

$$A = \begin{pmatrix} 2 & 0 & -1 \\ 4 & 1 & 1/2 \end{pmatrix} \quad \text{and} \quad B = \begin{pmatrix} 5 \\ 1 \\ -2 \end{pmatrix} \quad \text{then} \quad AB = \begin{pmatrix} 12 \\ 20 \end{pmatrix}$$

If A and B are square matrices of the same size, then both AB and BA are defined. Matrix multiplication is associative. If A is m by n, B is n by q and C is q by r, then $(AB)C$ and $A(BC)$ are equal m by r matrices. Also, when the matrices A, B, and C have the proper sizes for the operations to be defined, $A(B + C) = AB + AC$ and $(A + B)C = AC + BC$. If A is m by n, then for identity matrices of the proper sizes, $AI_n = I_mA = A$. Unlike the case for numbers, it may happen for matrices that $AB \neq BA$ and $AB = 0$ with $A \neq 0$ and $B \neq 0$.

The product of a matrix A and a number a is called a scalar product and is obtained by multiplying every element a_{ij} of A by a. Thus:

$$1/2 \begin{pmatrix} 4 & -3 & 1/3 \\ 0 & 2 & 1 \end{pmatrix} = \begin{pmatrix} 2 & -3/2 & 1/6 \\ 0 & 1 & 1/2 \end{pmatrix}$$

The transpose of an m by n matrix A is the n by m matrix B which has as its ith row the ith column of A and as its jth column the jth row of A for all i, j. If the transpose of a matrix A is denoted by A', and B is conformable with respect to A, then $(AB)' = B'A'$. A matrix A is symmetric if $A = A'$. A symmetric matrix is necessarily square.

A square n by n matrix is nonsingular if the determinant of A is not zero. Otherwise A is singular. A nonsingular matrix A has a unique inverse, that is, a matrix A^{-1} such that $AA^{-1} = A^{-1}A = I_n$. The inverse of a nonsingular matrix is easily described but is difficult to compute for matrices of large size. Many important applications require the calculation of the inverse, and numerical methods are used to approximate the elements of the inverse.

Two m by n matrices A and B are equivalent if there exist nonsingular matrices P and Q such that $B = PAQ$.

The matrices A and B are equivalent if, and only if, B can be obtained from A by a sequence of elementary transformations which consists of the following operations: interchanging two rows (or columns) of A; multiplying the elements of a row (or column) of A by a fixed number and adding to the corresponding elements of another row (or column) of A; multiplying the elements of a row (or column) of A by a nonzero number. A matrix A can be carried into a matrix with r ones on the principal diagonal and zeros elsewhere by a sequence of elementary transformations. The number r is called the rank of A, and the process of reducing A to this diagonal form is called the reduction of A to canonical form. The rank of A can be defined intrinsically as the largest order r of a nonvanishing minor of A. For example, matrix (2) has a rank 3 since the three-rowed minor

$$\begin{vmatrix} -3 & 2 & -6 \\ 7 & -1 & 3 \\ 1 & 1 & -5 \end{vmatrix} = 22 \neq 0$$

and the canonical form of this matrix is

$$\begin{pmatrix} 1 & 0 & 0 & 0 \\ 0 & 1 & 0 & 0 \\ 0 & 0 & 1 & 0 \end{pmatrix}$$

Two square n by n matrices A and B are similar if there exists a nonsingular matrix P such that $B = PAP^{-1}$. A linear transformation, or substitution, labeled (3), can be written $y = Ax$,

$$\begin{aligned} y_1 &= a_{11}x_1 + a_{12}x_2 + \cdots + a_{1n}x_n \\ y_2 &= a_{21}x_1 + a_{22}x_2 + \cdots + a_{2n}x_n \\ &\cdots\cdots\cdots\cdots\cdots\cdots\cdots \\ y_n &= a_{n1}x_1 + a_{n2}x_2 + \cdots + a_{nn}x_n \end{aligned} \quad (3)$$

where y and x are n by 1 column matrices and $A = (a_{ij})$ is the matrix of the transformation. If new variables $z = P$ and $w = Px$, where P is nonsingular, are substituted, $P^{-1}z = AP^{-1}w$ or $z = PAP^{-1}w$ is obtained. Thus the given linear transformation in terms of the new variables has a matrix which is similar to A. The theory of a single linear transformation is given by finding canonical forms for the matrix of the transformation under similarity.

If $A = (a_{ij})$ is an n by n square matrix and x is a variable, the matrix

$$Ix - A = \begin{pmatrix} x - a_{11} & a_{12} & \cdots & a_{1n} \\ a_{21} & x - a_{22} & \cdots & a_{2n} \\ \cdots & \cdots & \cdots & \cdots \\ a_{n1} & a_{n2} & \cdots & x - a_{nn} \end{pmatrix}$$

is called the characteristic matrix of A. The determinant $|Ix - A|$ of $Ix - A$ is a polynomial in x of degree n, and the equation $|Ix - A| = 0$ is called the characteristic equation of A. The roots of the characteristic equation are the characteristic values, or eigenvalues, of A. Many applications in mathematics and physics require information about the characteristic values of a matrix.

A quadratic form in n variables $x_1, x_2, \ldots, x_n$ is a polynomial of degree 2 which can be written as the matrix product xAx', where $x = (x_1, x_2, \ldots, x_n)$ is a row matrix and A is an n by n symmetric matrix. If a change of variable $x = yP$ is made, the result is $xAx' = yPAP'y'$. If P is nonsingular, the new matrix PAP' is said to be congruent to A. The simplification of a quadratic form consists of simplifying a symmetric matrix A by a congruence transformation. A matrix A can be reduced to various diagonal forms by congruence transformations, the particular form depending on the number system (that is, rational, real, or complex numbers) which contains the elements of A and the elements of the transforming matrix P. When A has been reduced to diagonal form, the corresponding quadratic form is a sum of squares of the new variables $y_1, y_2, \ldots, y_n$.

A square matrix A with complex number elements is hermitian if $A = \overline{A'}$, where $\overline{A}$ is the matrix obtained from A by replacing each element of A by its complex conjugate. The reduction of a hermitian matrix to diagonal form by a matrix transformation of the form $P A \overline{P}'$ is called a conjunctive reduction.

A nonsingular matrix P with real number elements is called orthogonal if $P' = P^{-1}$. The congruence transformation which replaces a square matrix A with real number elements by PAP', where P is an orthogonal matrix, is called an orthogonal transformation. If A is a real symmetric matrix, then A can be reduced by an orthogonal transformation to a diagonal matrix which has the n characteristic values of A on the diagonal. The characteristic values of a hermitian matrix and a real symmetric matrix are real numbers.

A nonsingular matrix P with complex number elements is called unitary if $\overline{P}' = P^{-1}$. The similarity transformation PAP^{-1} where P is unitary is a unitary transformation. The diagonal form obtained for a hermitian matrix A by a unitary transformation has the characteristic values of A on the diagonal.

Bibliography. F. A. Graybill, *Matrices with Applications in Statistics*, 2d ed., 1983; A. Jennings, *Matrix Computation for Engineers and Scientists*, 1980; A. W. Joshi, *Matrices and Tensors in Physics*, 2d ed., 1984; P. Lancaster and M. Tismenetsky, *The Theory of Matrices*, 1985; G. Stephenson, *An Introduction to Matrices, Sets and Groups for Science Students*, 1986.

LINEAR PROGRAMMING
Alan J. Hoffman

A mathematical subject whose central theme is finding the point where a linear function defined on a convex polyhedron assumes its maximum or minimum value. Although contributions to this question existed earlier, the subject was essentially created in 1947, when G. B. Dantzig defined its scope and proposed the first, and still most widely used, method for the practical solution of linear programming problems. The largest class of applications of linear programming occurs in business planning and industrial engineering. Its basic concepts are so fundamental, however, that linear programming has been used in almost all parts of science and social science where mathematics has made any penetration. Furthermore, even in cases where the domain is not a polyhedron, or the function to be maximized or minimized is not linear, the methods used are frequently adaptions of linear programming. *See* Nonlinear programming.

General theory. A typical linear programming problem is to maximize expression (1), where $x_1, \ldots, x_n$ satisfy the conditions shown by notation (2). The a_{ij}, c_j, and b_1 are constants;

$$c_1 x_1 + \cdots + c_n x_n \quad (1)$$

$$\begin{aligned} x_j &\geq 0 \\ a_{11} x_1 + \cdots + a_{1n} x_n &\leq b_1 \\ &\cdots \\ a_{m1} x_1 + \cdots + a_{mn} x_n &\leq b_m \end{aligned} \quad (2)$$

$x_1, \ldots, x_n$ are variables.

Sometimes the problem may be to minimize rather than to maximize; sometimes some of the variables may not be required to be nonnegative; sometimes some of the inequalities $a_{i1} x_1 + \cdots + a_{in} x_n \leq b_i$ may be reversed, or be equalities.

The linear inequalities, which the variables satisfy, correspond algebraically to the fact that the variable point $x = (x_1, \ldots, x_n)$ lies in a convex polyhedron. Hence, the principal mathematical bases for linear programming are the theory of linear equalities, a part of algebra, and the theory of convex polyhedra, a part of geometry. The most important theoretical foundations are as follows.

If the function $c_1x_1 + \cdots + c_nx_n$ does not become arbitrarily large for points $x = (x_1, \ldots, x_n)$ on the convex polyhedron, a maximum is attained at a vertex of the polyhedron.

If there is a maximum in the stated problem, then there is a minimum in the dual problem of minimizing $b_1y_1 + \cdots + b_my_m$, where notation (3) applies. Further, the maximum and mini-

$$\begin{aligned} y_i &\geq 0 \\ a_{11}y_1 + \cdots + a_{m1}y_m &\geq c_1 \\ \cdots \cdots \cdots \cdots \cdots \cdots \cdots \\ a_{1n}y_1 + \cdots + a_{mn}y_m &\geq c_n \end{aligned} \quad (3)$$

mum are the same number. This duality theorem is essentially equivalent to the minimax theorem. Both the duality theorem and the minimax theorem are algebraic paraphrases of the geometric fact that if a point is not contained in a convex polyhedron then a hyperplane can be found which separates the point from the polyhedron. The duality theorem is also closely related to the concept of Lagrange multipliers.

In an important class of linear programming problems, there is imposed an additional requirement that some or all of the variables must be whole numbers. If the numbers $b_1, \ldots, b_n$ are whole numbers, and if every square submatrix of (a_{ij}) has determinant 0, 1, or -1, then the integrality requirement will be automatically satisfied. In any case, the faces of the convex hull of the integral points inside a polyhedron can be found by a finite process in which, at each stage, a new inequality is determined by taking a non-negative linear combination of previous inequalities and replacing each coefficient by the largest integer not exceeding it.

Methods of calculation. The most popular method for solving linear programs, that is, the finding of the $x = (x_1, \ldots, x_n)$ which maximizes $c_1x_1 + \cdots + c_nx_n$, is the simplex method, developed by Dantzig in 1947. The method is geometrically a process of moving from vertex to neighboring vertex on the convex polyhedron, each move attaining a higher value of $c_1x_1 + \cdots + c_nx_n$, until the vertex yielding the greatest value is reached. Algebraically, the calculations are similar to elimination processes for solving systems of algebraic equations. The computer programs used try to take advantage of the fact that almost all the matrices (a_{ij}) arising in practice have very few nonzero entries.

The popularity of the simplex method rests on the empirical fact that the number of moves from vertex to vertex is a small multiple (about 2–4) of the number of inequalities in most of the thousands of problems handled, although it has never been proved mathematically that this behavior is characteristic of "average" problems.

There have also been developed methods of calculation specifically tailored for special classes of problems. One such class (network flows) is exemplified by the transportation problem described below. Another important class is where most of the columns of (a_{ij}) are not known explicitly in advance, but consist of all columns which satisfy some particular set of rules. The idea used here (known in different contexts as the column-generation or the decomposition principle) is that the new vertex prescribed by the simplex method can be found if a solution is achieved for the problem of maximizing a linear function defined on the set of columns satisfying the particular rules.

The technology of solving integer linear programming problems is not stabilized. Methods vary from testing integral points near the optimum fractional point to systematic methods for generating relevant faces of the convex hull of the integral points satisfying the given inequalities.

Applications. Let a_{ij} denote the number of units of nutrient j present in one unit of food i. Let c_j be the minimum amount of nutrient j needed for satisfactory health, b_i be the unit price of food i. Let the variables y_i denote respectively the number of units of food i to be bought. Then the dual problem is the so-called diet problem, to maintain adequate nutrition at least cost. It has been used in planning feeding programs for several varieties of livestock and poultry. With a different interpretation of the symbols, the same format describes the problem of combining raw materials in a chemical process to produce required end products as cheaply as possible.

In another situation, let c_{ij} be the cost of shipping one unit of a given product from warehouse i to customer j for all m warehouses i and all n customers j pertaining to a business. Let a_i be the amount available at warehouse i, and b_j the amount required by customer j. The transportation problem is to ship the required amounts to the customers at least cost. Thus, if x_{ij} is the amount to be shipped from i to j, then minimize notation (4), where $x_{i1} + \cdots + x_{in} \leq a_i$ ($i = 1, \ldots, m$) and $x_{1j} + \cdots + x_{mj} = b_j$ ($j = 1, \ldots, n$).

$$c_{11}x_{11} + \cdots + c_{mn}x_{mn} \tag{4}$$

The foregoing are representative of the business applications of linear programming, several hundred of which have now been reported. The best-known applications outside business have been to economic theory and to combinatorial analysis. In both instances, the duality theorem has been used to illuminate and generalize previous results.

Bibliography. V. Chvatal, *Linear Programming*, 1983; S. I. Gass, *Linear Programming*, 5th ed., 1985; J. P. Ignizio, *Linear Programming in Single and Multiple Objective Systems*, 1982; K. Murty, *Linear Programming*, 1983; N. Wu and R. Coppins, *Linear Programming and Extensions*, 1981.

NONLINEAR PROGRAMMING
RICHARD A. TAPIA

An area of applied mathematics concerned with finding the values of the variables which give the smallest or largest value of a specified function in the class of all variables satisfying prescribed conditions. The function which is to be optimized is called the objective function, and the functions defining the prescribed conditions are referred to as the constraint functions or constraints. This general problem is called the nonlinear programming problem. The study of the theoretical and computational aspects of the nonlinear programming problem is called nonlinear programming, mathematical programming, or optimization theory. When there are no constraints, the nonlinear programming problem is said to be unconstrained; otherwise the problem is said to be constrained. If the objective function and the constraint functions are linear, the nonlinear programming problem is said to be a linear programming problem. When the objective function is quadratic and the constraints are linear, the nonlinear programming program is said to be a quadratic programming problem. *See* LINEAR PROGRAMMING.

General theory. The general nonlinear programming problem can be stated as notation (1), where $x = (x_1, \ldots, x_n)$ are the variables of the problem, f is the objective function, g_i are the

$$\begin{align} &\text{minimize } f(x) \\ &\text{subject to } g_i(x) \geq 0, \quad i = 1, \ldots, m \\ &\qquad\qquad\quad h_j(x) = 0, \quad j = 1, \ldots, p \end{align} \tag{1}$$

inequality constraints, and h_j are the equality constraints. By changing f to $-f$, a maximization problem is transformed to a minimization problem. Moreover, an inequality constraint in the form $g_i(x) \geq 0$ is equivalent to $-g_i(x) \leq 0$. Consequently the format of problem (1) can handle both types of inequality constraints and both minimization and maximization problems.

The basic theory deals with conditions which a solution of the nonlinear programming problem (1) must satisfy. In the case when the objective function and the constraint functions are differentiable, the most important necessary conditions are the Karush-Kuhn-Tucker conditions. Consider the lagrangian function (2) whose added variables $u = (u_1, \ldots, u_m)$ and $w =$

$$L(x,u,w) = f(x) - \sum_{i=1}^{m} u_i g_i(x) + \sum_{j=1}^{p} w_j h_j(x) \tag{2}$$

$(w_1, \ldots, w_p)$ are called Lagrange multipliers. The Karush-Kuhn-Tucker theory says that if x solves problem (1), then there exists u and w so that the triple (x,u,w) satisfies system (3) of equations and

$$\nabla f(x) - \sum_{i=1}^{m} u_i \nabla g_i(x) + \sum_{j=1}^{p} w_j \nabla h_j(x) = 0 \tag{3}$$

$$\begin{align} g_i(x) &\geq 0, \quad i = 1, \ldots, m \\ h_j(x) &= 0, \quad j = 1, \ldots, p \\ u_i g_i(x) &= 0, \quad i = 1, \ldots, m \\ u_i &\geq 0, \quad i = 1, \ldots, m \end{align}$$

inequalities. The notation $\nabla f(x)$ is used to denote the gradient of f at x or the vector of partial derivatives at x with respect to the n independent variables. In order for this theory to be valid, an additional assumption called the constraint qualification must be made. Numerous constraint qualifications have been formulated; a useful but somewhat restrictive constraint qualification requires the gradients of the constraints which are actively involved in the solution to form a linearly independent set.

While the Karush-Kuhn-Tucker conditions (3) are only necessary conditions—meaning that, in general they are not sufficient to ensure that x will solve problem (1)—in the case that f and the g_i are convex and the h_j are affine, these necessary conditions are also sufficient conditions. The Lagrange multipliers are also called dual variables. In many problems in business, economics, and engineering, the dual variables have a useful interpretation in terms of sensitivity of the objective function to a particular constraint.

The branch of nonlinear programming which does not require the functions in problem (1) to be differentiable is called nondifferentiable programming or nondifferentiable optimization. Although this area has not received as much attention as the differentiable case, it has become the subject of considerable research activity and has increased in importance.

Scope of application. Many of the quantitative problems in business, economics, and engineering design can be expressed as nonlinear programming problems. General computational methods have been designed and implemented on large digital computers. Many problems which were considered large in 1970 are now considered small and can be solved efficiently. While considerable progress has been made in both the design and algorithms and computer technology, there are still many practical large nonlinear programs which cannot be solved. Research has been aimed at taking advantage of the structure of the particular problem in question. One important example of structure is sparseness. Sparseness would occur if the nonlinear programming problem had many variables, but the objective function and each constraint function involved only relatively few variables.

Computational methods. Computational methods for the unconstrained optimization problem are well understood. For the unconstrained optimization problem, the Karush-Kuhn-Tucker conditions specialize to $\nabla f(x) = 0$. The preferred class of algorithms for this problem is the class of quasi-Newton methods which approximate the solution by the iterates given by Eq. (4), where B_k is an $n \times n$ matrix and the superscript -1 denotes the process of matrix inversion.

$$x^{k+1} = x^k - \alpha^k B_k^{-1} \nabla f(x_k) \qquad (4)$$

The scalar α_k in Eq. (4) is chosen to approximately solve the one-dimensional optimization problem in α: minimize $f[x^k - \alpha B_k^{-1} \nabla f(x^k)]$. The special case of the quasi-Newton method, Eq. (4), which arises by choosing B_k equal to the identity matrix is the gradient method, while the special case which arises by choosing $B_k = \nabla^2 f(x^k)$ (the hessian matrix of f at x^k, that is, the matrix of second-order partial derivatives of f at x^k) is Newton's method. The gradient method is so slow that it should generally not be used, and Newton's method requires so much work per iteration that it is of questionable value. The class of quasi-Newton methods called secant methods requires that $B_{k+1}^{-1} y = s$ in Eq. (4), where $s = x^{k+1} - x^k$ and $y = \nabla f(x^{k+1}) - \nabla f(x^k)$. This class of methods seems to be the best currently available, and the preferred formula for B_{k+1}^{-1} is the Broyden-Fletcher-Goldfarb-Shanno (BFGS) secant update formula, Eq. (5), where the superscript T denotes

$$B_{k+1}^{-1} = \frac{B_k^{-1} - [sy^T B_k^{-1} + (B_k^{-1} y - s)s^T]}{\left(\frac{s^T y + ss^T(y^T B_k^{-1} y)}{(s^T y)^2} \right)} \qquad (5)$$

matrix transposition.

The BFGS secant method is substantially faster than the gradient method, but not as fast as Newton's method. It requires more work than the gradient method, and less than Newton's method per iteration. Overall it is the preferred algorithm. The choice of α_k in Eq. (4) is important and the subject of current research.

There is lack of agreement of computational methods for attacking the constrained optimization problem. However, a reasonable approach to extending the successful secant methods from unconstrained optimization to constrained optimization appears to be the method of successive quadratic programming. Specifically the solution x is approximated by the iterates x^k which satisfy Eq. (6), where Δx solves the quadratic programming problem of notations (7). The BFGS secant update for the matrix B_k is given by Eq. (8), where $s = x^{k+1} - x^k$ and $y =$

$$x^{k+1} = x^k + \alpha_k \Delta x \qquad (6)$$

$$\text{minimize } q(\Delta x) = \nabla f(x^k)^T \Delta x + {}^1\!/_2 \Delta x^T B_k \Delta x$$
$$\text{subject to } \nabla g_i(x^k) \Delta x + g_i(x^k) \geq 0, \quad i = 1,\ldots,m \qquad (7)$$
$$\nabla h_j(x^k) \Delta x + h_j(x^k) = 0, \quad j = 1,\ldots,p$$

$$B_{k+1} = \frac{B_k + yy^T}{s^T y} - \frac{B_k s s^T B_k}{s^T B_k s} \qquad (8)$$

$\nabla_x L(x^{k+1}, u^{k+1}, w^{k+1}) - \nabla_x L(x^k, u^{k+1}, w^{k+1})$, with the multipliers u^{k+1}, and w^{k+1} obtained from the solution of the quadratic programming problem (7). The notation $\nabla_x L$ denotes the vector of partial derivatives of L taken with respect to the x variables. The choice of the scalar α_k in Eq. (6) is the subject of current research. It is known that in the case of unconstrained optimization and constrained optimization of the choice $\alpha_k = 1$ for large k is optimal.

There is considerable activity in the general area of algorithms for constrained optimization problems, and the development of effective and efficient algorithms for this general problem can be expected. However, there is still a considerable amount of work to be done in this area.

Bibliography. M. Avriel, *Nonlinear Programming*, 1976; J. E. Dennis and J. J. Moré, Quasi-Newton methods, motivation and theory, *SIAM Rev.*, 19:46–89, 1977; R. Hartley, *Linear and Nonlinear Programming*, 1986; D. G. Kuenberger, *Linear and Nonlinear Programming*, 1984; G. P. McCormick, *Nonlinear Programming*, 1983; O. Mangasarian (ed.), *Nonlinear Programming 4*, 1981.

GRAPH THEORY
JONATHAN L. GROSS

A branch of mathematics that belongs partly to combinatorial analysis and partly to topology. Its applications occur (sometimes under other names) in electrical network theory, operations research, organic chemistry, theoretical physics, and statistical mechanics, and in sociological and behavioral research. Both in pure mathematical inquiry and in applications, a graph is customarily depicted as a topological configuration of points and lines, but usually is studied with combinatorial methods.

Origin of graph theory. Graph theory and topology are said to have started simultaneously in 1736 when L. Euler settled the celebrated Königsberg bridge problem. In Königsberg, there were two islands linked to each other and to the banks of the Pregel River by seven bridges. **Figure 1** illustrates both this setting and its topological abstraction as a graph. The points *a*, *b*, *c*, *d* correspond to land areas, and the connecting lines to bridges. The problem is to start at one of the land areas and to cross all seven bridges without ever recrossing a bridge. Euler proved that there is no solution, and he established a rule that applies to any connected graph: such a traversal is possible if and only if at most two points are odd, that is, each is the terminus for an odd number of lines. Euler also proved that the number of odd points in a graph is always an even number. Thus, a complete traversal without recrossing any lines is possible if the number of odd points is zero or two. If zero, the complete traversal ends at the starting point.

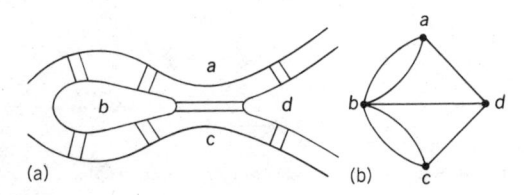

Fig. 1. Königsberg bridge problem. (*a*) The seven bridges of Königsberg. (*b*) Corresponding graph.

In geometry a graph might arise as the set of vertices and edges of a convex, three-dimensional polyhedron, such as a pyramid or a prism. Euler derived an important property of all such polyhedra. Let V, E, and F be the numbers of vertices, edges, and faces of such a polyhedron. Euler proved that $V - E + F = 2$, which is now called the Euler equation. For instance, a cube has $V = 8$, $E = 12$, and $F = 6$, so that $8 - 12 + 6 = 2$. Euler's observations have been extended to a theorem about imbeddings of graphs in surfaces and to the Euler-Poincaré characteristic for cell complexes in combinatorial topology.

Definitions. A graph consists of a set of points, a set of lines, and in incidence relation that designates the end points of each line. In many applications no line starts and ends at the same point. (Such a line would be called a loop.) Also, no two lines have the same pair of end points. A graph whose lines satisfy these conditions is called simplicial. The valence of a point is the number of lines incident on it, calculated so that a loop is twice incident on its only end point. Two graphs are isomorphic if there is one-to-one correspondence from the point set and line set of one onto the point set and line set, respectively, of the other that preserves the incidence relation. The point correspondence $a \to a'$, $b \to b'$, $c \to c'$, $d \to d'$ indicates an ismorphism between the two graphs of **Fig. 2**.

An automorphism of a graph is an isomorphism of a graph with itself. For instance, a plane rotation of 120° would yield an automorphism of either of the two graphs in **Fig. 3**. A plane reflection through a vertical axis would also yield an automorphism of either of them. The set of all automorphisms of a graph G forms the automorphism group of G. R. Frucht proved in 1938 that every finite group is the automorphism group of some graph. Two graphs are homeomorphic (**Fig. 4**) if, after smoothing over all points of valence 2, the resulting graphs are isomorphic.

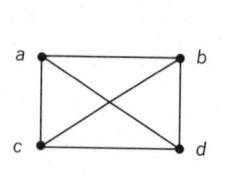

Fig. 2. Two isomorphic graphs.

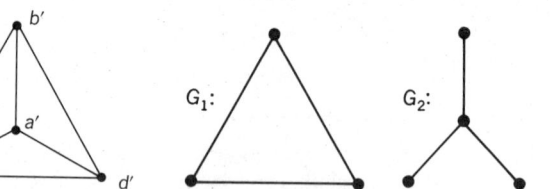

Fig. 3. Two graphs for which either a 120° rotation or a vertical reflection is an automorphism.

Map coloring problems. Drawing a graph on a surface decomposes the surface into regions. One colors the regions so that no two adjacent regions have the same color, rather like a political map of the world. It is a remarkable fact that for a given surface, there is a single number of colors that will always be enough no matter how many regions occur in a decomposition of the surface. The smallest such number is called the chromatic number of that surface. It is easy to draw a plane map, as in **Fig. 5**, that requires four colors. In 1976 K. Appel and W. Haken settled

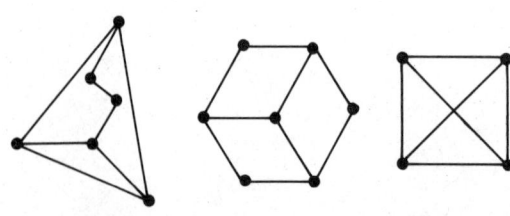

Fig. 4. Homeomorphic but nonisomorphic graphs.

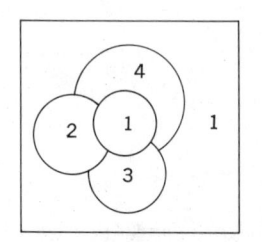

Fig. 5. Plane map requiring four colors.

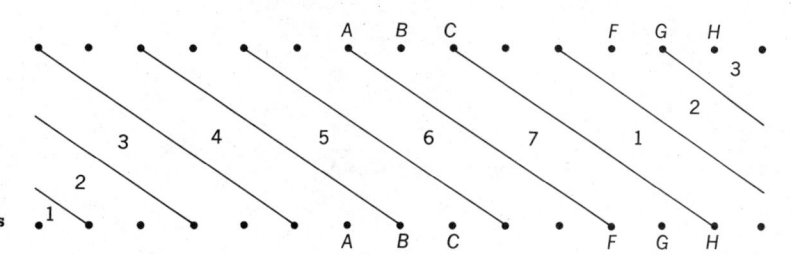

Fig. 6. Map on a torus (doughnut) that requires seven colors. To form the torus, paste opposite sides of the rectangle together.

a problem dating back to about 1850, by showing that four colors are always enough for plane maps.

Some maps on more complicated surfaces require more than four colors. For instance, **Fig. 6** illustrates a map on a torus (the surface of a doughnut) that needs seven. To obtain the toroidal map from the rectangular drawing, first match the top to the bottom to get a cylindrical tube. Then match the left end of the cylinder to the right end to complete the torus. Whereas, before this matching, region 7 meets only regions 1 and 6, after the matching it also meets region 2 along *FG*, region 3 along *GH*, region 4 along *AB*, and region 5 along *BC*. In fact, after the matching, each of the seven regions borders every other region. It follows that seven colors are necessary. No map on the torus needs more than seven colors, as P. J. Heawood proved in 1890. G. Ringel and J. W. T. Youngs completed a calculation in 1968 of the chromatic numbers of all the surfaces except the plane or sphere.

Planarity. A graph is planar if it can be drawn in the plane so that none of its lines cross each other. Neither of the two graphs in **Fig. 7** can be drawn in the plane. K. Kuratowski proved

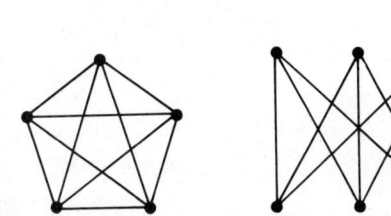

Fig. 7. Prototypes of all nonplanar graphs.

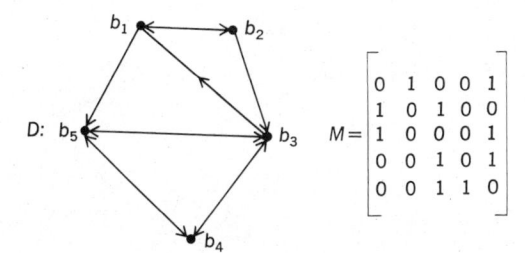

Fig. 8. A digraph and its adjacency matrix.

in 1930 that a graph is planar if and only if it contains no subgraph homeomorphic to either of two two graphs. Testing all the subgraphs might be a very tedious process, even on a fast computer. In 1974 J. Hopcroft and R. Tarjan obtained an extremely fast alternative planarity test. The time it takes a computer to perform the Hopcroft-Tarjan test is linearly proportional to the time it takes to read its point set into the computer.

There are methods to decide for any graph and any surface whether the graph can be drawn on the surface without edge crossings. The time to execute such methods is unfeasibly large for most graphs and most surfaces except the plane or the sphere. Ringel has constructed many important special drawings on higher-genus surfaces.

Variations. In a directed graph, or digraph, each line *ab* is directed from one end point *a* to the other end point *b*. There is at most one line from *a* to *b*. The adjacency matrix $M = (m_{ij})$ of a digraph *D* with points $b_1, b_2, \ldots, b_n$ has the entry $m_{ij} = 1$ if the line $b_i b_j$ occurs in *D*; otherwise $m_{ij} = 0$ (**Fig. 8**).

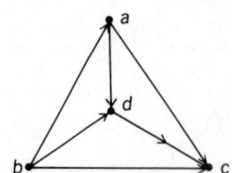

Fig. 9. A tournament.

An oriented graph is obtained from an ordinary graph by assigning a unique direction to every line. If there is one line between ever pair of points and no loops, an ordinary graph is called complete. An oriented complete graph is called a tournament (**Fig. 9**).

Bibliography. Y. Alavi et al., (eds.), *Graph Theory with Applications to Algorithms and Computer Science*, 1985; B. Bollobas, *Graph Theory and Combinatorics*, 1984; G. Chartrand, *Introductory Graph Theory*, 1985; A. Gibbons, *Algorithmic Graph Theory*, 1985; M. Gondran and M. Minoux, *Graphs and Algorithms*, 1984; J. L. Gross and T. W. Tucker, *Topological Graph Theory*, 1987; R. J. Wilson, *Introduction to Graph Theory*, 3d ed., 1985.

5

PROGRAMMING AND SOFTWARE

Digital computer programming	182
Operating system	186
Programming languages	187
Abstract data types	211
Software engineering	215

DIGITAL COMPUTER PROGRAMMING
FRED J. GRUENBERGER

The art of writing instructions to control the operation of a stored-program digital computer. More generally, programming refers to the analysis and planning of a problem solution, in which the phase of instruction writing is referred to as coding.

Binary operation. The programming process will be described in terms of the most common form of digital computer. This machine operates internally entirely in binary (base 2) arithmetic and logic, and is arranged so that information is stored and accessed in units termed words. A typical word size is 32 binary digits, or bits, although word sizes range in current practice from 8 to 60 bits.

Notation. The binary, word-oriented machines (now the dominant type) call for a notation that is either pure binary, or octal (base 8) or hexadecimal (base 16), the latter two being simply conveniences for programmers while they work. The discussion here is in terms of decimal, to simplify understanding of computer principles and to avoid lengthy digression to number systems other than decimal, such as binary, but it must be kept in mind that the basic nature of the machines is binary.

Number operations. The purpose of a computer is to manipulate information that is stored within the machine in the form of binary numbers. These numbers can be treated as symbols and can represent alphabetic information or anything else the programmer wishes to manipulate. In the simplest case they are numbers and are to be treated arithmetically. Each word contains one number and its associated algebraic sign. The instructions which dictate the operations to be performed on such numbers (data) are also numbers and are also stored one per word in the same physical medium as the data. The stored programming concept presumes that there is no physical difference between these two types of numbers and that the instruction numbers may also be manipulated, in the proper context, as data.

Addresses. Each word in storage is assigned an address in order to refer to it, in a manner analogous to postal addresses. The addressing scheme is part of the hardware of the machine, and is wired in permanently. Word addresses range from zero to the storage size of the machine, typically from 00000 through 32,767. Any word may be loaded with any desired information. Some of this information is the data of the problem being processed; the rest is the instructions to be executed. The machine is designed basically to execute instructions in the order in which they are stored, advancing sequentially through the instruction words as addresses that increase by one.

Instruction format. Each instruction contains two basic parts: (1) a coded number that dictates what operation is to be performed, for example, ADD, MULTIPLY, and STORE; and (2) the address of the word (data) on which to perform that operation. Thus, suppose the data stored in words 12345, 12346, and 12347 are to be added together. The work is performed in a storage device called the accumulator, which is the same size as one storage word. Three operation codes are involved; namely, LOAD ACCUMULATOR, ADD, and STORE ACCUMULATOR, for which the corresponding operation codes might be 100, 123, and 234. The instructions must also reside in storage, say at addresses (called locations for instructions) 01017, 01018, 01019, and 01020. Then, the program shown in **Fig. 1** applies.

All the data and instruction numbers are in storage before execution begins. The logical sequence is controlled by a counting device called the instruction counter, which is set, for this program, to 01017. Line 1, when executed, causes the contents of the first data word to be moved

Location	Operation	Address	Line no.
01017	100	12345	1
01018	123	12346	2
01019	123	12347	3
01020	234	12348	4

Fig. 1. A straight-line program. Line numbers are for reference with comments made in the text.

to the accumulator, destroying the information previously stored there. During this operation the instruction counter advances by one, thus completing one cycle of operation, and the process repeats. Line 2 calls for the information in word 12346 to be added to the contents of the accumulator, and line 3 does the same for the information stored at 12347. Each of these operations involves moving stored information; all such moves follow the pattern that read-in (for example, to the accumulator) is destructive, but read-out (for example, from a referenced storage word) is nondestructive. Thus, after the additions, the data words are still in storage in their original form. Line 4 is the logical inverse of line 1; the information now in the accumulator is moved to word 12348 (and still remains in the accumulator).

Each computer type has a wired-in set of operation codes. Inexpensive machines may offer as few as 16; large machines have several hundred.

Programming. The program of Fig. 1 is a straight-line program; that is, its instructions are executed strictly in sequence as stored. The stored-program computer gains its power from two additional concepts. The first concept is derived naturally in that the words of information referenced by an instruction can be other instruction words; thus, a computer can manipulate its own instructions and alter them dynamically, particularly in their address portions, during the execution of a program. The second concept concerns the ability to branch, based on the condition of the accumulator at any given moment. Basically, the machine can interrogate the accumulator and, on the basis of its contents being negative, zero, or positive, call for operating on the instruction counter so that the next executed instruction is not at the location that is one more than the last excuted location, but is any other desired location. This branch of control may also be called for arbitrarily, that is, not based on the condition of the accumulator. For the available branch instructions the address portion is then the location of the next instruction rather than that of a data word. The operation codes are of the form BRANCH, BRANCH ON MINUS, BRANCH ON ZERO, BRANCH ON NONZERO, and so forth.

The program of Fig. 1 would serve to form the sum of three words of information, but would form a poor pattern if there were 10,000 words to be added. In the latter situation there would be 10,001 instruction words, all but two of which would be monotonously similar, differing only in the regular progression of 10,000 addresses. The capabilities of the computer allow for the larger task to be looped; that is, a few instructions can be used over and over.

Flow-charting. The logic of any problem situation can be expressed graphically in a flow chart. For the problem of summing the contents of 10,000 words, the flow chart of **Fig. 2** applies. Instructions are written to add the contents of one word (call its address x) to the word SUM. Prior to executing these instructions, it is arranged to set the contents of SUM to zero, and the value of address x to that of the first of the 10,000 words of data. After the contents of any word of data are added to SUM, a check is made to determine whether the word just added was the last word of data. If so, the repetitive task has been completed. If not, the address x is incremented by one, and the process continues. Programmed loops thus follow the pattern of initialization, performance of one case, a test for the last case, modification from case to case, and branch back to the performance block.

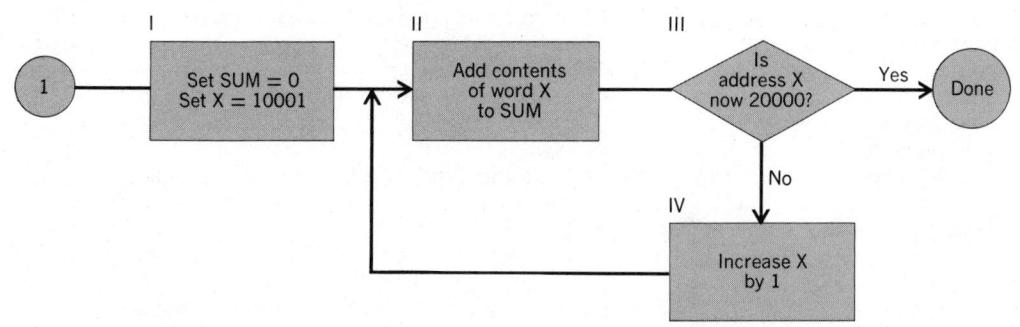

Fig. 2. Flow chart for the program of Fig. 3.

Data and constants:

Address	Value
10001–20000	data words
20001	SUM
20002	000 00000
20003	000 10001
20004	123 20000
20005	000 00001

Instructions:

Location	Operation	Address	Line no.
01000	100	20002	1
01001	234	20001	2
01002	100	20003	3
01003	235	01005	4
01004	100	20001	5
01005	123	(00000)	6
01006	234	20001	7
01007	100	01005	8
01008	122	20004	9
01009	002	01014	10
01010	100	01005	11
01011	123	20005	12
01012	234	01005	13
01013	001	01004	14
01014	Continue with the problem		

Fig. 3. A programmed loop. Line numbers are for reference with comments made in the text.

The program of **Fig. 3** implements, in the same hypothetical machine code, the loop shown. Following is a list of the operation codes used:

    100 Load accumulator
    234 Store accumulator
    235 Store the address portion of the accumulator
    123 Add to the accumulator
    122 Subtract from the accumulator
    002 Branch if accumulator is zero
    001 Branch unconditionally

The distinct stages of the loop are marked off. The performance block is at locations 01004–01006. Line 5 calls for the word designated for the SUM to be loaded into the accumulator. The contents of one word, x, is added to it. The address of x is shown as zero, but will never be executed as such. The result of the addition is stored back at SUM (word 20001).

The contents of word 20001 must be set to zero; this is done by lines 1 and 2. Lines 3 and 4 ensure that x is preset to 10001. Lines 8–10 examine the instruction containing x (that is, all of the word at 01005) and effect an exit from the loop when the value of x is 20000. If the exit conditions are not met (as they will not be for 9999 traverses of the loop), the branch to 01014 indicated on line 10 is not taken and the modification steps of lines 11–13 are executed, whose function is to increase the value of x by one. The four sections ruled off in Fig. 2 correspond directly to the boxes of the flow chart for Fig. 3; line 14 performs the unconditional branch back to block II.

Programming languages. Programming for a digital computer could be done as illustrated in Fig. 3, but is far more awkward in binary and, moreover, becomes increasingly difficult as programs get longer. For these and other reasons, programmers prefer to work in languages that are at a higher level than the machine language shown. The use of mnemonic operation codes (BZE for BRANCH ON ZERO, in place of the number 002) and the replacement of all absolute machine addresses by symbols greatly speed up the work of the programmer at the modest cost of an extra computer run whose sole function is the translation back to the language used in Fig. 3. The translating program is called an assembler, and the language used is assembly language. Generally, assembly language follows the format of the machine language and is one-for-one with it; that is, for every instruction written in assembly language, one machine language instruction will be produced.

Most programming is done in the language of compilers, for example, FORTRAN or COBOL. Compiler language permits a format that fits the problems rather than the machine, and is many-to-one. For example, a statement (instruction) in FORTRAN can be written Y=B**2−4.0*A*C to correspond to the algebraic expression $b^2 - 4ac$ (an asterisk being used for multiplication, and two adjacent asterisks denoting the raising to powers). As with assemblers, a separate machine run is needed to translate from the compiler language to the language of the machine; the translating program is called a compiler. The better compilers achieve a measure of machine independence in that programs in compiler language can be compiled into different machine languages without alteration.

The looping technique illustrated in Fig. 3 is one of the two basic building blocks of the programmer. The other is the closed subroutine. Both techniques have the purpose of allowing a small number of instructions to be executed many times. The typical example of the closed subroutine is the short program for the calculation of square root. Such a program might consist of 30 instructions and be needed at eight different places within a large program. The set of 30 instructions could be inserted eight times into the main program, but this would waste the programmer's time and storage space in the machine. The 30 instructions can be stored once, and simple arrangements can be made in the main program to cause their linkage and return at each of the eight points at which the square-root operation is needed.

The concept of the subroutine leads to systematic libraries of tested subroutines that build up for each machine type. Further extensions of this idea lead to whole packaged programs furnished by the manufacturers, to proprietary programs that are offered for sale, and to higher languages designed for specific problem areas.

The **table** describes the most frequently used high-level programming languages.

Frequently used high-level programming languages

Language	Description	How implemented	Features
FORTRAN	Language for scientific and engineering work	Compiled	The oldest high-level language; very widely used
COBOL	Language for business data processing	Compiled	Widely used in business
BASIC	Simplified language aimed at beginners; universally available on microcomputers	Interpreted	Easily learned, but limited in its scope
Pascal	Language for scientific and engineering work	Compiled	Encourages the constructs of structured programming; very popular in the academic community
LISP	Specialized language for list processing	Compiled	Leading language for work in artificial intelligence

While the cost of nearly everything else in computing (central processors, storage devices, and input/output devices) continues to fall over the years, the cost of software (that is, computer programs) has risen. This is due in part to the greater complexity of the problems being attacked, and in part to the complexity of a computer system, which is the entity made up of the computer itself plus large control programs called operating systems. Attention has recently turned to methods and techniques, such as structured programming, for improving this situation. SEE DIGITAL COMPUTER; PROGRAMMING LANGUAGES; SOFTWARE ENGINEERING.

Bibliography. H. Abelson and G. Sussman, *Structure and Interpretation of Computer Programs*, 1984; R. Backhouse, *Program Construction and Verification*, 1986; D. W. Barron and J. Bishop, *Advanced Programming: A Practical Course*, 1986; J. N. Fernandez and R. Ashley, *Introduction to Computer Programming*, 1984; C. W. Gear, *Computer Organization and Programming*, 4th ed., 1985; D. A. Sordillo, *Programming for Non-Programmers*, 1986.

OPERATING SYSTEM
Harry L. Helms

A set of programs to control and coordinate the operation of hardware and software in a computer system. Operating systems typically consist of two sets of programs. Control programs direct the execution of user application programs and support programs. They also supervise the location, storage, and retrieval of data (including input and output to various peripherals) and allocate the resources of the computer system to the different tasks entered into the system. Processing programs include applications programs; utility programs; system diagnostics; and language translators, such as compilers and interpreters.

There are five general types of operating systems:

1. Real-time. Processing functions are executed within narrow time limits, as in updating a data bank or reading and evaluating input from a sensor or transducer. See Real-time systems.

2. Serial or batch. Tasks or jobs are run one at a time according to a schedule determined by the operating system.

3. Multiprogramming. Two or more jobs may be run concurrently in the same system.

4. Time sharing. Multiple users have simultaneous access to the system. A user is not aware that others have access to the system; the impression is that of exclusive use of the system. See Multiaccess computer.

5. Multiprocessing. Two or more processing units are coupled together to execute a single job. See Multiprocessing.

Control programs. The control program has an executive function and a system resource allocation and management function. The executive function arranges the computer system environment necessary to run a job. One task of the executive function is to schedule the jobs. Jobs may be scheduled sequentially, but many operating systems permit scheduling on the basis of assigned priorities. The executive function directs communications between the computer system and human operator, and communications between the processor and various input and output peripherals.

The system resource allocation and management function is sometimes referred to as the supervisor. A key task of the supervisor is to allocate, monitor, and control the computer system's main memory space. The supervisor controls and synchronizes the tasks necessary to execute the instructions in a program as well. The supervisor also manages data within the system. For example, it allocates space on disks for data storage. It is responsible for constructing and developing data structures, and it maintains directories of data files within the system.

Modern supervisors are increasingly sensitive to the problem of data security, particularly unauthorized access to data files. The most common security device is the password, a code which must be correctly entered into a computer system before a user can have access to a computer system's data files. The supervisor may also record all users of a system along with the data files accessed and the amount of time each user spent using the system. See Computer security.

Processing programs. Processing programs include applications developed for use with a computer system, and translators which convert high-level languages such as COBOL, FORTRAN, and BASIC into the assembly language used by the processor. See Digital computer programming; Programming languages.

Several software development and diagnostic support aids are also part of the processing programs. A common feature is the presence of several debugging aids to assist in the proper development and use of applications programs. Commonly, these aids will indicate why a program failed to execute properly. These aids give an output to the user, known as a diagnostic. Most systems also include several utilities, which permit the user to accomplish such tasks as transferring data from one storage medium to another or duplicating storage disks.

Time-sharing applications. Much effort in recent years has been directed toward the development of operating systems for time sharing and multiprogramming tasks. Many commercial companies have been organized which sell access time to a large computer system on a time-sharing basis. The customers have a terminal at their place of business and are linked to the computer by telephone lines. Customers are billed according to the amount of time they use the computer. Such systems require a supervisor which restricts access to customers and adequately protects against unauthorized or fraudulent use. Large commercial users of computers need multiprogramming capability, which allows jobs to be run according to priority. Some multiprogramming systems permit programs to be run during off-peak hours. This allows a computer system to be utilized around the clock, giving more efficient use of computing resources.

Microcomputer systems. The growth of microcomputers has resulted in the development of operating systems specifically designed for them. Perhaps the most widely used is CP/M (control program for microprocessors), an operating system developed by Digital Research Corporation. CP/M is used with 8-bit microprocessor microcomputers. Another system is Unix, developed by Bell Labs for use with the C programming language. Unix has been adopted for several 16-bit microprocessor microcomputers.

Work has been done on the development of multiprocessing operating systems for microcomputers. In these systems, for example, a 16-bit microprocessor could be used for such tasks as actual computation and an 8-bit microprocessor could be used for such tasks as input and output. The essential task of these operating systems is to coordinate the activities of the two microprocessors. This task is often complicated by the fact that various microprocessors operate at different speeds. However, interest in multiprocessing operating systems for microcomputers can be expected to spread since multiple microprocessors can perform certain tasks more effectively than single microprocessors. SEE DIGITAL COMPUTER; MICROCOMPUTER; MICROPROCESSOR.

Bibliography. H. Katzan, Jr., *Operating Systems*, 2d ed., 1986; M. Milekovic, *Operating Systems Concept and Design*, 1987; A. S. Tannenbaum, *Operating Systems: Design and Implementation*, 1987.

PROGRAMMING LANGUAGES
J. D. GANNON AND M. D. WEISER

Notations with which people can communicate algorithms to computers and to one another. To accomplish this, programmers specify a sequence of operations to be applied to data objects. SEE ALGORITHM.

Computers process a rather low-level machine language, which has simple instructions (load, add, and so forth) and data (for example, words or partial words including those containing instructions). Example (1) shows machine code that assigns the absolute value of B−C to A.

Location	Machine code	Meaning	
040003	100020040001	load B into register A1	
040004	250320040002	subtract C from register A1	
040005	741020040007	GOTO 040007 if A1 positive	(1)
040006	110020000000	negate A1	
040007	010020040000	store contents of A1 into A	

Writing in machine code places a tremendous burden on the programmers. They must write in an unusual number base (for example, eight), and transfer data from memory to registers in order to perform operations. They must know the machine's operation codes for the operations. [These appear in the first two digits of the machine code in example (1). Thus, load is 10; branch is 74; store is 01.] Finally, they must know the addresses of the operands (both registers and data words) and instructions (to be able to skip some operations with branches). In example (1) the last five digits give the address of one operand. Thus A is at 40000, B at 40001, C at 40002, and the target of the branch instruction at location 40005 is the instruction at 40007.

The introduction of assembler languages eased communication between programmers and machines by permitting symbolic rather than numeric or positional references for operation codes (opcodes) and addresses. Additional data and instructions could therefore be added to a program without changes to existing instructions. Thus, in example (2), which shows assembler code that

Opcode	Operands	Comments
L	A1, B	
AN	A1, C	·A1 := B − C
BP	A1, NEXT	
N	A1	·A1 := −A1
S	NEXT A1, A	· A := |B − C|

(2)

assigns the absolute value of B − C to A, instructions could be added between the branch positive, BP, and its destination.

Unfortunately, assembler language does not go very far in improving programmers' ability to communicate algorithms. A programmer must still be concerned with expressing algorithms in a form suitable to particular machines. For instance, if an expression requires more registers than are available, the programmer must create temporary variables to hold partial results of expressions. High-level languages allow programmers to communicate more easily with one another by providing structures that hide the architecture of the machine. Expressions in high-level languages can be written almost as they are in algebra so that the programmer need not worry about which register contains a particular computation or which registers are available. Higher-level control structures like the IF statement make it easier to see the overall structure of a program than do low-level branch instructions. High-level language code for assigning the absolute value of B − C to A is shown in example (3).

$$\begin{array}{l} A := B - C; \\ \text{IF } A < 0 \\ \quad \text{THEN} \\ \qquad A := -A \end{array}$$

(3)

See Digital computer programming; Digital computers.

STRUCTURE OF PROGRAMMING LANGUAGES

The components of a program and their relationships are shown in **Fig. 1**. The basic executable unit of a programming language is a program. Programs contain declarations of data and procedures, and a sequence of statements to be executed.

Objects, variables, and identifiers. Programming languages manipulate objects or values like integers or files. Objects are referred to by their names, called identifiers. Constant objects, such as the number 2 (one of whose names is the literal "2"), do not change. Variable objects may contain either other objects or the names of other objects. The same identifier may denote different objects at different places in the program or at different times during execution. Also, a single object may have several names, or aliases. Variable and constant identifiers are introduced by data declarations. Declarations (4) introduce the constant KilometersPerMile (whose value is

CONST
KilometersPerMile = 0.6;

VAR
Miles, Hours, MilesPerHour;

(4)

0.6) and the variables Miles, Hours, and MilesPerHour. Notice that in this example the object 0.6 has two names.

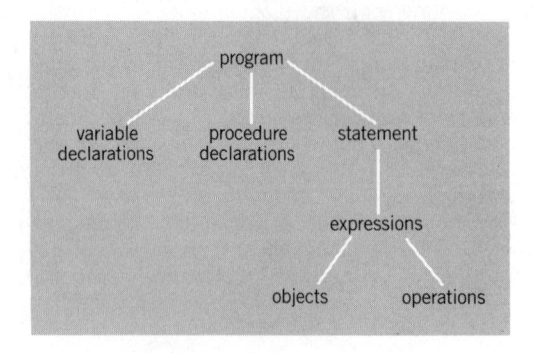

Fig. 1. Components of a high-level language.

Expressions. Expressions combine objects and operators to yield new objects. They may be written in one of several forms. Infix operators appear between their operands, as in expression (5); prefix operators precede their operands, as in expression (6); and postfix operators follow their operands, as in expression (7). Most languages adopt infix notation for binary operators and prefix

$$B * B - 4 * A * C \quad (5) \qquad (-(* B\ B)(* (* 4\ A)\ C)) \quad (6) \qquad ((B\ B\ *)((4\ A\ *)\ C\ *)-) \quad (7)$$

notation for unary operators. LISP uses only prefix operators, FORTH only postfix operators.

Two ideas govern the order in which infix operators are applied to their operands in expressions: precedence and associativity. Operators of higher precedence are evaluated before those of lower precedence. A typical operator precedence hierarchy is shown in (8). Operators with equal

$$\begin{array}{ll} \text{Highest precedence} & *(\text{multiply})/(\text{divide}) \\ & +(\text{add}) - (\text{subtract}) \\ & < \ <= \ = \ <> \ > \ >= \\ & (\text{relationals}) \\ & \text{NOT} \\ \downarrow & \text{AND} \\ \text{Lowest precedence} & \text{OR} \end{array} \quad (8)$$

precedence are usually left associative, that is, they are evaluated from left to right.

Not all languages using infix notation have the same operator precedence or associativity. PASCAL has fewer levels in its precedence hierarchy: NOT has the highest precedence, AND has the same precedence as *, and OR has the same precedence as +. APL has no precedence among its operators, which are right associative. Thus $5 - 4 + 3$ has the value -2 in APL.

Statements. Important types of statements include assignment statements, compound statements, conditional statements, repetitive statements, and GOTO statements.

Assignment statements. Assignment statements assign values to variables. In an assignment of form (9), the value in the object denoted by B is assigned to the object denoted by

$$A := B \qquad (9)$$

A. The order of evaluation of the two sides of an assignment statement differs among languages—some insist on left-to-right evaluation, while others leave the order of evaluation undefined. Some languages permit the same value to be assigned to several variables in a single statement; for example, the value of C can be assigned to both A and B by using statements (10). Other lan-

$$A, B := C \quad \{\text{PL}/1\} \qquad\qquad A := B := C \quad \{\text{ALGOL 60}\} \qquad (10)$$

guages, like C (which uses the symbol = for assignment), treat assignment just like any other operator in an expression. Thus statement (11) assigns $C + 2$ to B and $C + 5$ to A.

$$A = (B = C + 2) + 3 \qquad (11)$$

Compound statements. A compound statement (12) groups a sequence of statements

$$\text{BEGIN stmt1; stmt2; ... stmtn END} \qquad (12)$$

into a single statement. Execution of statements within a sequence of statements is in the order in which the statements appear in the sequence.

Conditional statements. The IF statement (13) allows a programmer to indicate that a

$$\text{IF expression THEN statement} \qquad (13)$$

statement is to be executed if a stated condition is true. If the expression is true, the statement following the THEN is executed followed by the statement after the IF statement. If the expression is false, the statement is skipped. Many languages permit execution of one of two alternate statements with the form of IF statement (14). If the expression is true, statement 1 is executed; oth-

$$\text{IF expression THEN statement1 ELSE statement2} \qquad (14)$$

erwise statement 2 is executed. In either case, execution continues with the statement after IF.

Repetitive statements. One of the advantages offered by computers is performing the same operations repetitively. Two statements in programming languages support this kind of execution: FOR and WHILE. The FOR statement (15) is generally used when a programmer knows how many times a statement is to be executed. The statement is executed a number of times given by (16), where expression1 and expression2 are the first and second expressions in statement (15). For example, statement (17) will write "hello" three times (2 − 0 + 1 = 3). If the first expression is greater than the second, the statement is not executed. While the statement is executed, the variable identifier (control variable) takes on successive values from the list (18).

$$\text{FOR variable-identifier} := \text{expression TO expression DO statement} \tag{15}$$

$$\text{expression2} - \text{expression1} + 1 \tag{16}$$

$$\begin{aligned}&\text{FOR i} := 0 \text{ to } 2 \text{ DO} \\ &\quad \text{write ("hello")}\end{aligned} \tag{17}$$

$$<\text{expression1, expression1} + 1, \ldots, \text{expression2}> \tag{18}$$

Usually the control variable may not be assigned to within the loop, and its value is usually considered to be undefined at the end of execution of the FOR statement. The two expressions are evaluated once at the start of execution of the FOR statement rather than each time the statement is executed. Thus, changing the values of the variables in these expressions has no effect on the number of times the statement is executed, as is illustrated in example (19). The statement is

$$\begin{aligned}&\text{First} := 1; \\ &\text{Last} := 5; \\ &\text{FOR Index} := \text{First TO Last DO} \\ &\quad \text{BEGIN} \\ &\qquad \text{First} := \text{First} + 1; \\ &\qquad \text{Last} := \text{Last} - 1; \\ &\qquad \text{write (Index, First, Last)} \\ &\quad \text{END}\end{aligned} \tag{19}$$

executed five times, even though the values of First and Last are changed during execution. The results printed by this statement are shown in (20).

Index	First	Last	
1	2	4	
2	3	3	
3	4	2	(20)
4	5	1	
5	6	0	

The WHILE statement (21) is used when continued execution depends on a condition that

$$\text{WHILE expression DO statement} \tag{21}$$

is true for an unknown number of repetitions. The statement is executed as long as the expression is true. When the expression becomes false, execution continues with the statement after the WHILE. The code fragment (22) can be used to approximate the square root of N by successive approximation.

$$\begin{aligned}&\text{WHILE abs } (X - N/X) > 0.1 \text{ DO} \\ &\quad X := 0.5 * (X + N/X)\end{aligned} \tag{22}$$

While the two approximations of the square root, X and N/X, differ by more than 0.1 (that is, the absolute value of their difference is greater than 0.1), new approximations are computed. After some unknown number of iterations, the difference between the two approximations is small enough and execution of the WHILE statement ceases.

GOTO statements. The lowest-level control statement in most languages is the GOTO statement (23). This statement provides for the direct transfer of control to a statement labeled with the identifier that is the argument of the GOTO statement.

$$\text{GOTO identifier} \tag{23}$$

Any of the previous conditional or repetitive statements can be simulated with GOTO statements. For example, the previous WHILE statement would appear as (24).

$$\begin{aligned}&\text{Test:} &&\text{IF abs }(X - N/X) < 0.1 \text{ THEN GOTO Done};\\ & &&X := 0.5 * (X + N/X); \\ & &&\text{GOTO Test}; \\ &\text{Done:} &&\ldots\end{aligned} \tag{24}$$

Many programming languages have eliminated the GOTO statement because it widens the gap between the textual structure and execution-time behavior of a program's source text. Control can transfer to a label from almost any GOTO statement in a program, and GOTO statements can be either forward or backward jumps. In addition, GOTO statements can affect storage allocation in many languages.

Procedures. As problems grow more complex, they must be divided into subproblems that can be solved independently. This approach to problem solving is supported by procedure declations, which group sequences of statements together and associate identifiers with the statements. A procedure identifier abstracts the details of the computation carried out by the statements of the procedure by encapsulating them. Procedures also help reduce the size of a program by permitting similar code to be written only once.

Procedure declarations, whose form is shown in (25), look just like programs, except they

$$\begin{aligned}&\text{PROCEDURE ProcedureName;}\\ &\{\text{data declarations}\}\\ &\{\text{procedure declarations}\}\\ &\text{BEGIN }\{\text{ProcedureName}\}\\ &\quad\{\text{Sequence of statements}\}\\ &\text{END }\{\text{ProcedureName}\}\end{aligned} \tag{25}$$

start with the word PROCEDURE instead of "program." In some languages each procedure has its own local data and procedure declarations. Since execution begins with the first statement of a program, the sequence of statements of a procedure can be executed only if they are explicitly invoked by a procedure-call statement containing the name of the procedure.

When the name of a procedure appears in a sequence of statements the procedure is called; that is, execution of the current sequence is suspended and the statement sequence associated with the procedure name in its declaration is executed. When execution of this sequence is completed, execution resumes in the previous sequence right after the procedure statement.

The designers of ALGOL 60 defined the effect of a procedure statement in terms of textual substitution. Their definition has come to be known as the copy rule. Essentially, the copy rule states that each procedure statement can be replaced by a compound statement containing the text of the procedure.

A procedure declaration is called recursive if it contains a procedure-call statement that invokes the procedure being defined. The WHILE statement that approximates the square root of N could be replaced by program fragment (26). If the approximation was not close enough, a new

$$\begin{aligned}&\text{PROCEDURE Approximate;}\\ &\text{BEGIN }\{\text{Approximate}\}\\ &\quad\text{IF abs}(X - N/X) > 0.1 \\ &\quad\quad\text{THEN}\\ &\quad\quad\quad\text{BEGIN}\\ &\quad\quad\quad\quad X := 0.5 * (X + N/X);\\ &\quad\quad\quad\quad\text{Approximate}\\ &\quad\quad\quad\text{END}\\ &\text{END; }\{\text{Approximate}\}\\ &\text{BEGIN}\\ &\quad\ldots;\\ &\quad\text{Approximate};\\ &\quad\ldots\\ &\text{END}\end{aligned} \tag{26}$$

estimate would be assigned to X, execution of the current sequence of statements would be suspended, and control would be transferred to the first statement of a new copy of Approximate. When the approximation is close, the current copy of the procedure terminates and control is returned to the statement following the last procedure invocation. Since there are no more statements in this copy of the procedure, it also returns to a previous copy, which returns to a previous copy, and so forth. Eventually control returns to the statement after the first call of Approximate (indicated by ellipses). As this example demonstrates, recursion is not always the most efficient technique to use in problem solving. However, it can be a valuable tool in divide-and-conquer approaches to problem solving. With the exception of FORTRAN and COBOL, most programming languages support this feature.

DATA TYPES

Data types are sets of values and the operations that can be performed on them. Data types offer programmers two principal advantages: abstraction and authentication. Data types hide representational details from programmers so they do not have to be concerned whether characters are represented by ASCII or EBCDIC codes, or whether they are left-aligned and blank-filled or right-aligned and zero-filled in machine words. The concept of data type also provides useful redundancy. The appearance of a variable as an operand in an expression implies a particular type for the variable (for example, A + B implies that A and B are either integer or real) that may be checked against the type of its current value.

Scalar types. Scalars are indivisible units of data; they are treated as single complete entities. Most languages contain several scalar types. The most common are integer, real, boolean, and character.

Integer. Integer constants are positive and negative whole numbers and zero. Since machines have finite word lengths, only a subset of the integers are provided, as in (27), where

$$\{-\text{MAXINT}, \ldots, -2, -1, 0, 1, 2, \ldots, \text{MAXINT}\} \tag{27}$$

MAXINT is a constant identifier corresponding to the largest integer value that can be represented on a particular machine. The usual arithmetic and relational operators are defined for integer values.

Boolean. The boolean type consists of the constant values false and true, and the operators NOT, AND, OR. NOT is a unary prefix operator, taking a boolean argument and returning a boolean result. AND and OR are binary infix operators that each take two boolean values and produce a single boolean result. *See Boolean algebra.*

Character. The character constants are the uppercase and lowercase alphabetic characters, digits, and other punctuation symbols. Character constants are usually indicated by enclosing them in single quotation marks (for example, 'a', '7', or '?'). To represent the character constant, which is itself a single quote, a special notation is used (for example, doubling the internal quote '''' or using a special escape character '\' in the C language). Almost all languages allow character comparison; however, the result of comparisons may differ across languages. In some languages, expression (28) is true, while in others it is false. However, languages generally define the relational operators on character values so that expressions (29) are valid.

$$'a' < 'A' \tag{28}$$

$$\begin{array}{c} 'A' < 'B' < 'C' \ldots < 'Y' < 'Z' \\ 'a' < 'b' < 'c' \ldots < 'y' < 'z' \\ '0' < '1' < '2' \ldots < '8' < '9' \end{array} \tag{29}$$

Real. Real numbers may be represented either as decimal fractions (for example, 1234.56) or in scientific notation (for example, 1.23456E3). The operators are the same as for type integer. Care must be exercised in the use of the equality and inequality operators, = and <>, on real values because the finite-word length restrictions on real machines can lead to problems of round-off and truncation so that, for example, expression (30) can occur.

$$1.0 <> (1.0/3.0 * 3.0) \tag{30}$$

Enumerated types. New types can be defined by listing (enumerating) the constants of the type. The only operators that may be applied to operands with enumerated types are the relational operators. The enumerated type (31) defines a new type whose constants are the iden-

$$\text{(Jan, Feb, Mar, Apr, May, June, July, Aug, Sept, Oct, Nov, Dec)} \tag{31}$$

tifiers Jan, Feb, and so forth. The order of appearance of the identifiers in the type declaration defines their relative values (that is, the constant identifier with the smallest value appears first). Thus, relational operators can be applied to those objects, as in expression (32).

$$\text{Jan} < \text{July} \tag{32}$$

Constant identifiers declared in an enumerated type often replace mappings of integers to concepts in programs. For example, programmers who declare the enumerated type (31) and use its constants in their programs would not have to remember if 1 or 0 was used to represent January.

References. While variables usually hold values of objects, they may also hold the name of some object. Variables that can hold such values are called references or pointers. Reference constants are object names and a special value "nil" (which points to no variable). The operations defined for reference values are equality and dereferencing. Dereferencing is a unary operation that maps a pointer to the object it references. Dereferencing an object containing a reference (for example, by appending $^\wedge$ to the object as in $X^\wedge$) yields the object referenced. An example of dereferencing is statement (33), in which X contains a reference to Y and Y contains the value 2.

$$\text{write } (X^\wedge, Y) \ \{\text{prints 2} \quad 2\} \tag{33}$$

The result of dereferencing nil is undefined.

Languages also have operations that create reference values. For example, statement (34)

$$X := \text{NEW (integer)} \tag{34}$$

creates an object of type integer (with no initial value) and makes X point at the object.

Since reference variables hold object names, an assignment between two reference variables X and Y results in X and Y pointing at the same object (**Fig. 2**). Thus $X = Y$ and $X^\wedge = Y^\wedge$. If X and Y are both dereferenced before the assignment (**Fig. 3**), the objects, $X^\wedge$ and $Y^\wedge$, will contain the same values, but could still be distinct objects. Thus $X <> Y$, but $X^\wedge = Y^\wedge$.

Aggregate types. Collections of related values can be represented by aggregate types. Aggregate types can be characterized by the types of the objects that are their elements and the manner in which the elements are accessed. Elements of a collection can have homogeneous or heterogeneous types, and can be selected by their position in a collection or by a name associated with them.

Arrays. An array is a mapping from a domain specified by a sequence of values to a range whose members are the values of the elements of the array. In statement (35), the array A is

$$\text{VAR A: ARRAY } [-3 .. 5] \tag{35}$$

declared to have the domain $\{-3, -2, \ldots, 4, 5\}$.

In ALGOL, PL/1, PASCAL, and ADA, all the elements of an array must have the same type, but this restriction does not apply in SNOBOL, LISP, and APL.

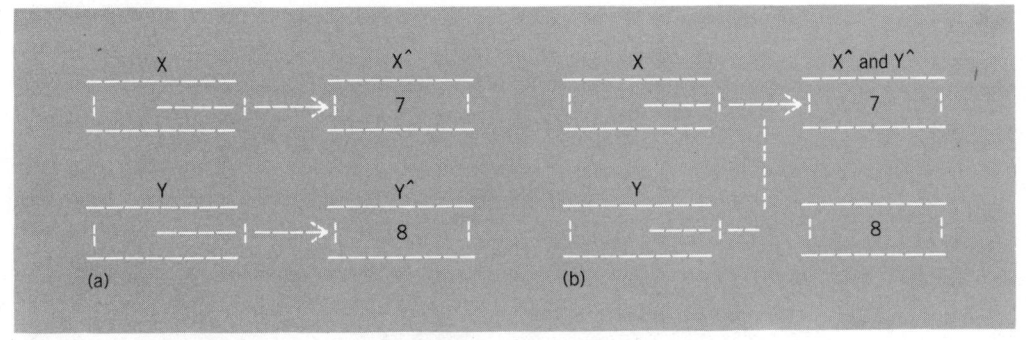

Fig. 2. Effect of the assignment Y: = X. (*a*) Before Y: = X. (*b*) After Y: = X.

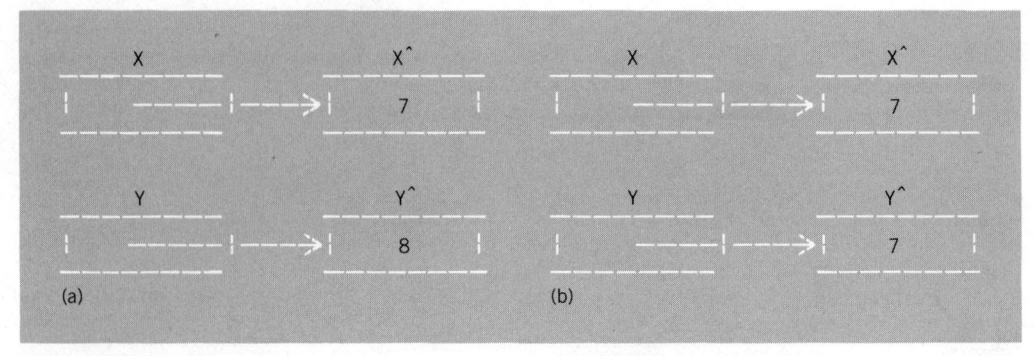

Fig. 3. Effect of the assignment $Y^\wedge := X^\wedge$. (a) Before $Y^\wedge := X^\wedge$. (b) After $Y^\wedge := X^\wedge$.

Very few operations are defined for array objects. The access operation is called subscription and is usually indicated by enclosing an expression indicating the position of the desired element in brackets or parentheses. Thus, if A is an array, expression (36) selects its $I + J$th element. Arrays often have multiple dimensions, each of which has its own range of values as subscripts. A chess board could be represented as an 8×8 array, as in statement (37).

$$A(I + J) \text{ or } A[I + J] \qquad (36) \qquad \qquad \text{VAR B: ARRAY } [1 \mathrel{..} 8, 1 \mathrel{..} 8] \qquad (37)$$

The diagonal elements of the board B are given by (38). Some languages (for example,

$$B[1, 1] \; B[2, 2] \; B[3, 3] \; B[4, 4] \; B[5, 5] \; B[6, 6] \; B[7, 7] \; B[8, 8] \qquad (38)$$

ALGOL 68 and ADA) permit parts of arrays to be referenced by using trimming or slicing operations. Thus, expression (39) selects the first two rows of the board.

$$B[1:2, 1:8] \qquad (39)$$

Most languages permit an array object to be assigned to an array variable; the values of the object are copied to the corresponding locations in the variables. PL/1 permits the assignment of a single value to every element in an array. The assignment (40) is equivalent to (41). APL and ADA have array literals; the assignment (42) is equivalent to (43).

$$A := 0 \qquad (40) \qquad \qquad A[1] := 0; \; A[2] := 0; \ldots \qquad (41)$$

$$\text{Odds} := (1, 3, 5, 7, 9) \qquad (42) \qquad \text{Odds}[1] := 1; \; \text{Odds}[2] := 3; \ldots; \; \text{Odds}[5] := 9 \qquad (43)$$

APL has the richest collection of array operators, having extended many of its operators which take scalar operands to work on array operands as well.

Records. Records have components of different types (called fields), which are explicitly accessed by identifiers (called selectors). For instance, in PL/1, X. Name is a qualified name that selects record component Name from record X. If X is a record object of the type given in (44),

```
         RECORD
           Name: ARRAY[1 .. 20];
           Address: RECORD
                      StNumber;
                      StName: ARRAY[1 .. 10];
                      City: ARRAY[1 .. 10];                (44)
                      State: ARRAY[1 .. 2];
                      ZipCode
                    END;
           Age;
           Salary
         END
```

the names of the components are: X. Name, X. Address, X. Address. StNumber, X. Address. StName, X. Address. City, X. Address. State, X. Address. ZipCode, X. Age, and X. Salary. Some components of the record are scalar variables, some are arrays, and one (X. Address) is a record. The term record comes from COBOL and business data processing.

BINDING ATTRIBUTES TO VARIABLES

Both constant and variable objects have values and attributes. Among the most important attributes of an object are its type, scope, and extent.

Scope. In most programming languages, the same identifier can name distinct objects in different parts of a program. The scope of an identifier is that part of a program in which the identifier has the same meaning. Generally that section of program is called a scope unit and corresponds to a procedure or compound statement. The set of objects that can be referenced in a scope unit is called the environment.

Identifiers are either declared locally (that is, in the immediately enclosing scope unit) or nonlocally (that is, in some other scope unit). Locally declared identifiers are like bound variables in formulas—their meaning does not change no matter where the procedure or compound statement containing their declaration is placed in a program, and is not available outside the scope unit. Nonlocally declared identifiers are like free variables—their meaning can depend on the placement of the text in which they are referenced or the execution sequence of the program.

In the program (45), the scope units are the program P and the procedures Q and R. The identifier I names distinct locally declared variables in P and R, and J names another variable in Q. The scope of each local identifier is marked to the right of the program.

With the exception of the reference to I in Q, all identifier references are to locally declared variables.

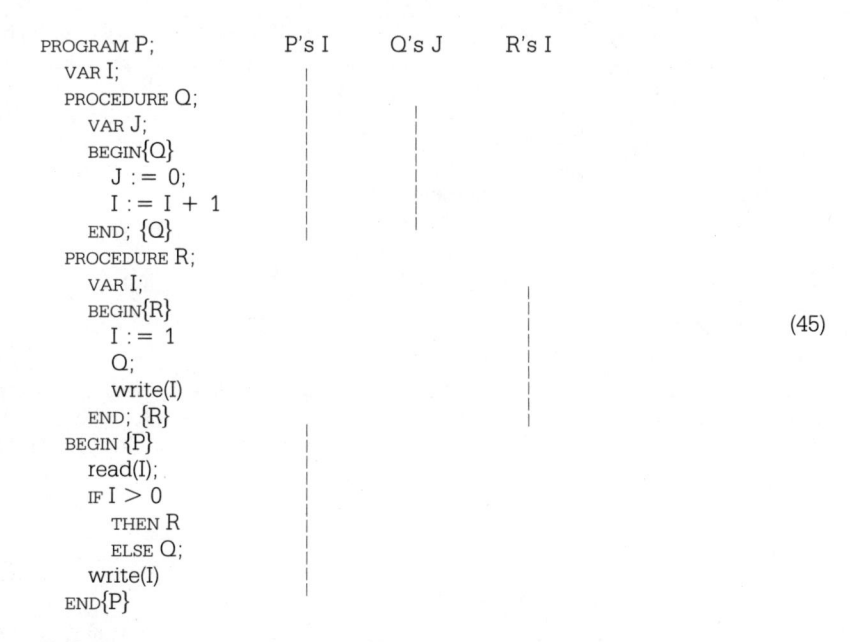

```
PROGRAM P;              P's I      Q's J      R's I
   VAR I;
   PROCEDURE Q;
      VAR J;
      BEGIN{Q}
         J := 0;
         I := I + 1
      END; {Q}
   PROCEDURE R;
      VAR I;
      BEGIN{R}
         I := 1
         Q;
         write(I)
      END; {R}
   BEGIN {P}
      read(I);
      IF I > 0
         THEN R
         ELSE Q;
      write(I)
   END{P}
```
(45)

There are three ways to resolve references to nonlocal variables:

1. Consider the use of nonlocal variables to be illegal. This scope rule is associated with both older languages like FORTRAN and modern languages like EUCLID.

2. Bind the reference to a declaration for the identifier occurring in the innermost lexically enclosing scope (for example, I is declared in P and P encloses Q). This method is called a static

scope rule because it is based on the program text which does not change during execution. Among the languages using this scope rule are ALGOL, PL/1, PASCAL, C, and ADA.

3. Bind the reference to a declaration in the procedure which has been most recently called, but has not yet completed execution. [In example (45), if the value read into I were greater than 0, the reference to I in Q would be bound to the declaration for I in R. Otherwise the reference would be bound to the declaration of I in P.] This association method is called a dynamic scope rule because nonlocal references can be bound to different variables depending on the sequence of statements executed. SNOBOL, LISP, and APL have dynamic scope rules.

Data type. Data types may be associated with objects statically via declarations or dynamically via assignment statements. In statically typed languages, the type associated with an object remains the same throughout the scope of the object. Declaration (46) binds the type INTE-

$$\begin{array}{l} \text{VAR} \\ \quad \text{I: INTEGER;} \\ \quad \text{Ch: CHARACTER;} \end{array} \qquad (46)$$

GER to I and CHARACTER to Ch. In dynamically typed languages, the type of an object is usually determined by the type of its value. Assigning a new value to a variable can change the type of the variable. Thus, in example (47), X initially has type integer and subsequently has type character.

$$\begin{array}{l} X := 5; \\ \text{write } (X - 3); \quad \{\text{print: 2}\} \\ X := \text{'h'}; \\ \text{write } (X) \quad \{\text{print: h}\} \end{array} \qquad (47)$$

ALGOL, PL/1, PASCAL, C, and ADA are statically typed languages; SNOBOL, LISP, and APL are dynamically typed.

In statically typed languages the type of a variable may not be known when it is declared, or the variable may need to be bound to objects of several different types during the course of the program. Type unions permit variables to be bound to objects with different types. Two kinds of type unions exist: free and discriminated. In a free union, the programmer is permitted to treat a variable as being of any of the types in the union. In a discriminated union, another field, called the tag field, identifies the type of the object. Unions are often represented as records in which enumerated types are used to select alternatives. In example (48), a record type is defined that

$$\begin{array}{l} \text{RECORD} \\ \quad \text{CASE (Int, Chr) OF} \\ \quad\quad \text{Int: (Ival: INTEGER);} \\ \quad\quad \text{Chr: (Cval: CHARACTER)} \\ \text{END} \end{array} \qquad (48)$$

contains a single field whose name is either Ival or Cval. The number of the constant identifiers in the CASE portion of the record determines the number of alternate fields.

In example (49), X is treated as though its type were a free union of the types INTEGER and CHARACTER.

$$\begin{array}{l} \text{IF } Y = 0 \\ \quad \text{THEN X. Ival} := 12 \\ \quad \text{ELSE X. Cval} := \text{'c'}; \\ \text{X. Ival} := \text{X. Ival} + 1 \end{array} \qquad (49)$$

All the assignment statements in example (49) are legal. However, the final assignment adds one to the numeric representation for the character 'c' if the statement following the ELSE is executed.

The free union in example (49) could be converted to a discriminated union by adding a field named Tag whose value is either Int or Chr, depending on the value contained in the second field, as in (50).

RECORD
   Tag: (Int, Chr);
   CASE (Int, Chr) OF   (50)
      Int: (Ival: INTEGER);
      Chr: (Cval: CHARACTER)
END

Extent. The extent or lifetime of a variable is the period of program execution during which the storage is allocated. Static storage is created at the beginning of the program execution and not deallocated until program termination. Local storage for variables is created on entry to the block or procedure containing the variable's declaration and destroyed on exit. Dynamic storage is created and destroyed by execution of special statements in the programming language.

Consider procedure (51). In a language like FORTRAN, the same storage location can be

PROCEDURE P;
   VAR X;
   BEGIN   (51)
      {sequence of statements}
   END

used for X no matter how many times P is invoked. The value of X is preserved between calls to P. However, in languages like ALGOL, PL/1, PASCAL, C, and ADA, local storage for X is allocated on each entry to the procedure and freed on each exit, so that the value of X is lost between executions of P. Local storage allocation permits two procedures to share storage locations if the procedures do not call one another. In example (52), the arrays A and B can share the same storage locations.

PROGRAM Prog;
   PROCEDURE P;
      VAR A: ARRAY [1 .. 100];
      BEGIN {P}
         {sequence of statements not containing
            a call of Q}
      END; {P}
   PROCEDURE Q;
      VAR B: ARRAY[1 .. 75];   (52)
      BEGIN {Q}
         {sequence of statements not
            containing a call of P}
      END; {Q}
   BEGIN
      P;
      Q
   END

Storage can be created dynamically through the execution of a statement like (53). Such

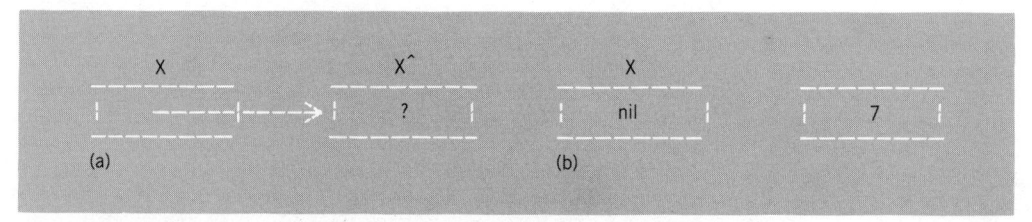

Fig. 4. Execution sequence resulting in garbage. (a) After new (X). (b) After X: = nil.

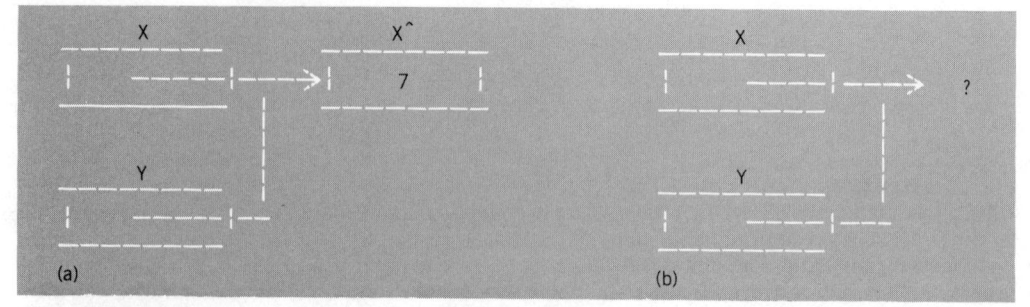

Fig. 5. Execution sequence which results in dangling reference. (*a*) After Y: = X. (*b*) After dispose (X).

storage is independent of the structure of the source code of the program and remains allocated until a corresponding statement (54) is executed.

$$\text{Ptr} := \text{new ( )} \quad (53) \quad\quad\quad \text{dispose(Ptr)} \quad (54)$$

Care must be taken that all dynamically allocated storage can be referenced through a pointer or the storage becomes garbage. The sequence of statements (55) results in the execution

$$X := \text{new (INTEGER)}; \ X^\wedge := 7; \ X := \text{nil} \quad (55)$$

sequence shown in **Fig. 4**, in which the storage formerly referenced by X becomes garbage because there is no way to reference it. Dangling references are created when storage referenced by several pointers is freed. In the sequence of statements (56), Y contains a dangling reference

$$\text{new(X)}; \ X^\wedge := 7; \ Y := X; \ \text{dispose(X)} \quad (56)$$

to the storage formerly referenced by X. X may also contain a dangling reference if its contents are not set to nil by dispose, as in **Fig. 5**.

PARAMETERS

Parameters communicate information between the calling environment and the environment of the called procedure. Although this can be accomplished by referencing nonlocal variables, communicating with parameters permits a procedure to work on different variables each time it is called. Formal parameters are identifiers that are locally declared in a procedure definition; actual parameters are expressions in a procedure call statement. In the program fragment (57), which shows two versions of a procedure named Max, X and Y are formal parameters and

```
PROCEDURE Max (X, Y);      PROCEDURE Max;
  BEGIN {Max}                BEGIN {Max}
    IF X > Y                   IF X > Y
    THEN                       THEN
      write (X)                  write (X)
    ELSE                       ELSE
      write (Y)                  write (Y)
  END; {Max}                 END; {Max}
BEGIN                      BEGIN
  . . .                      . . .
  Max(A, B);                 X := A;                          (57)
  Max(A + 2, B - 3);         Y := B;
  . . .                      Max;
END                          X := A + 2;
                             Y := B - 3;
                             Max;
                             . . .
                           END
Parameter version          Nonlocal version
```

A, B, A + 2, and B − 3 are actual parameters. The nonlocal version of Max is slightly longer than the parameter version because the calling environment must initialize the nonlocal references before Max is called. This requires the calling environment to know the implementation details of Max, thereby losing some of the advantages of abstraction which were gained by making Max a procedure.

The correspondence between the formal and actual parameters is positional—the first actual parameter is bound to the first formal parameter, and so forth. Several different kinds of parameter binding occur in programming languages: reference, value, result, and name. The key issues in binding are when the binding takes place (usually when the procedure is called, but possibly each time a formal parameter is referenced in the procedure body), and what is bound (the value or address of the actual, or perhaps a procedure that computes the address of the actual).

Reference binding. When an actual parameter is bound by reference to a formal parameter, an alias is set up between the name of the actual parameter and the name of the formal parameter. The word alias is used because both names identify the same object. The object identified by the actual is evaluated at the point of call. Each time a value is assigned to a formal reference parameter, the value of the corresponding actual parameter is also altered. Thus reference parameters can be used to supply input values to procedures and to return values computed by the procedure.

Value binding. Many arguments to procedures are used as inputs only; no value is returned through these parameters. Input parameters are bound by value to formal parameters. In value binding, the value of the actual parameter at the point of call is assigned to a new object which is bound to the formal parameter, but no alias is established between the formal and the actual parameters. Thus, any assignment to a formal value parameter changes the value of the formal but not that of the actual parameter.

Result binding. A procedure called to compute an output can use result binding to assign the value to a result parameter. At the point of call, the actual parameter is bound by reference to its corresponding formal parameter. However, during execution of a procedure, assignments to a result parameter alter a local copy of the variable, but not the actual parameter. When the procedure completes execution, the result is transmitted by assigning the value of the formal parameter to the actual parameter.

Name binding. In name binding, actual parameters are passed unevaluated to formal parameters and are evaluated only when necessary. Actually, a procedure that computes the object represented by the actual parameter (called a thunk) is bound to the formal parameter. Each time the formal parameter is referenced, its corresponding thunk is called to deliver the actual object. This method of parameter transmission occurs only in ALGOL 60.

Examples of different bindings. Program (58) illustrates the differences in parameter binding mechanisms.

```
PROGRAM Bindings;
  VAR
    A: ARRAY[1 .. 2];
    I;
  PROCEDURE P (X, Y);
    BEGIN {P}
      Y := I + 1;
      X := Y + 3;
      A[1] := A[1] + 20
    END; {P}
  BEGIN
    A[1] := 1;
    A[2] := 1;
    I := 1;
    P(A[I], I);
    write (I, A[1], A[2])
  END
```
(58)

The results printed for the different binding mechanisms are summarized in table (59).

$$\begin{array}{lcccc} \text{Bindings} & \text{I} & \text{A[1]} & \text{A[2]} & \\ \text{Value} & 1 & 21 & 1 & \\ \text{Reference} & 2 & 25 & 1 & \\ \text{Result} & 2 & 5 & 1 & \\ \text{Name} & 2 & 21 & 5 & \end{array} \quad (59)$$

In value binding, only the assignment to A[1] causes a change in the variables in the calling environment. X is aliased to A[1] and Y is aliased to I in reference binding. Thus the change to Y is reflected in I, and the changes to both X and A[1] affect the value of the latter. While the result mechanism yields the same bindings as the reference mechanism, the values of the result parameters (Y = 2 and X = 5) are not assigned to the actuals until P finishes execution. Thus the result of adding 20 to the value of A[1] is lost. As long as no local identifiers of P have the same name as any of the actual name parameters, name binding can be simulated by rewriting P's text with the text of the actuals replacing that of the formals, as in (60).

$$\begin{aligned} &\text{I} := \text{I} + 1; \\ &\text{A[I]} := \text{Y} + 3; \\ &\text{A[1]} := \text{A[1]} + 20 \end{aligned} \quad (60)$$

Since I is incremented from 1 to 2 by the first assignment statement, A[2] rather than A[1] is altered by the second assignment.

FUNCTIONS

Function declarations are similar to procedure declarations. But unlike a procedure, which communicates its results by assigning values to its parameters, a function communicates a distinguished value known as the result of the function. This result of the function is often indicated by assigning a value to the name of the function. The declaration of the function Max2 is given by (61).

$$\begin{aligned} &\text{FUNCTION Max2 (X, Y);} \\ &\quad \{<\text{Max2} := \text{if } X > Y \text{ then } X \text{ else } Y>\} \\ &\quad \text{BEGIN } \{\text{Max2}\} \\ &\quad \text{IF } X > Y \\ &\quad\quad \text{THEN} \\ &\quad\quad\quad \text{Max2} := X \\ &\quad\quad \text{ELSE} \\ &\quad\quad\quad \text{Max2} := Y \\ &\quad \text{END; } \{\text{Max2}\} \end{aligned} \quad (61)$$

Function calls look like procedure calls; the name of the function is followed by a list of actual parameters. However, there is an important difference between function and procedure calls. Since functions deliver values, function calls are expressions which may appear either within larger expressions or alone wherever an expression could appear in a program. Procedure calls, which do not deliver values, are statements.

To find the maximum of three values, Max3 could be declared, as in (62). The expression

$$\begin{aligned} &\text{FUNCTION Max3 (X, Y, Z);} \\ &\quad \{<\text{Max3}> := <\text{the largest value in [X, Y, Z]}>\} \\ &\quad \text{BEGIN } \{\text{Max3}\} \\ &\quad\quad \text{Max3} := \text{Max2(X, Max2(Y, Z))} \\ &\quad \text{END; } \{\text{Max3}\} \end{aligned} \quad (62)$$

in the assignment statement would be evaluated by first calling Max(Y, Z) to obtain the maximum of Y and Z, and then calling Max2 again with X and the result of the earlier call.

Side effects. When a statement in a procedure or function alters the value of a nonlocal variable or reference or name parameter, the procedure is said to have a side effect. It may not be quite accurate to call such assignments in procedures side effects, because procedures must include such statements in order to communicate their results. Therefore, they are really main effects of procedures. Side effects in functions are less desirable because they make the results of expression evaluation unpredictable. While languages specify the order in which operators are applied, they do not always define the order in which operands are fetched in expressions. For example, if Identity returned the value of its actual parameter, but increased the value of its reference parameter and the nonlocal variable N1, as in (63), then expression (64) might have any of the values in (65).

$$\begin{aligned}&\text{FUNCTION Identity (Parm);}\\&\text{BEGIN \{Identity\}}\\&\quad \text{Identity} := \text{Parm};\\&\quad \text{Parm} := \text{Parm} + 1;\\&\quad \text{N1} := \text{N1} + 3\\&\text{END; \{Identity\}}\end{aligned} \tag{63}$$

$$\text{N1} + \text{Identity(In)} + \text{In} \tag{64}$$

N1 + In + In + 1	{if the operands are fetched left to right T1 := N1; T2 := Identity(In); T3 := In; Result := T1 + T2 + T3}
N1 + 3 + In + In	{if the operands are fetched right to left T1 := In; T2 := Identity(In); T3 := N1; Result := T3 + T2 + T1}
N1 + In + In	{if both operands are fetched before the call T1 := N1; T2 := In; T3 := Identity(In); Result := T1 + T3 + T2}
N1 + 3 + In + In + 1	{if both operands are fetched after the call T1 := Identity(In); T2 := N1; T3 := In; Result := T2 + T1 + T3}

(65)

Thus, it is good programming practice to avoid side effects in functions and to use procedures instead when side effects are desired.

Procedure and function parameters. When procedures and functions are passed as parameters, they are bound like name parameters. Actual procedure parameters are passed unevaluated to procedures and evaluated each time they appear in procedure call statements.

Procedure parameters may contain references to nonlocal identifiers that must be bound to variables. Deep binding associates a procedure parameter's nonlocal identifiers with variables in the environment in which the procedure was created. Shallow binding associates these identifiers with variables in the environment when the procedure is invoked.

In example (66), P contains a nonlocal reference to A, and Q is a function that returns a procedure that is subsequently invoked in R.

```
PROGRAM Main;
  VAR A, B;
  PROCEDURE P;
    BEGIN {P}
      A := A + 10;
      write(A)
    END; {P}
  FUNCTION Q(Proc);
    VAR A;
    BEGIN {Q}
      A := 2;
      Q := Proc
    END; {Q}
  PROCEDURE R(Proc);
    VAR A;
    BEGIN {R}
      A := 3;
      Proc; {really invokes P}
      write(A)
    END; {R}
  BEGIN {Main}
    A := 1;
    B := Q(P);
    B ( );
    write(A)
  END {Main}
```
(66)

In ALGOL-like languages, nonlocal references are associated with the variables in the environment in which the procedure is declared. This deep binding associates the references to A in P with the A declared in Main. Thus the output of the program is: 11 3 11.

In LISP, either deep or shallow binding can be specified by applying one of the functions FUNCTION and QUOTE to the value returned by Q, as in (67).

```
FUNCTION Q(Proc);        FUNCTION Q(Proc);
  VAR A;                   VAR A;
  BEGIN {Q}                BEGIN {Q}
    A := 2;                  A := 2;
    Q := FUNCTION            Q := QUOTE
         (Proc)                   (Proc)
  END; {Q}                 END; {Q}
    Deep binding          Shallow binding
```
(67)

The use of FUNCTION in Q binds P's A to the variable declared in Q, the most recently declared version of A since LISP has a dynamic scope rule. The program output is: 12   3   1.

The use of QUOTE in Q delays the binding of P's A until P is invoked as Proc in R. At this time, P's A is bound to the most recent declaration of A, which occurs in R. Thus the program output is: 13   13   1.

While the ability to pass procedure and function parameters may seem too exotic to include in a programming language, it does facilitate construction of generic software. The alternative to passing a function parameter to a procedure is to embed the function's source in the procedure. The procedure can only operate with one specific function, not with any function passed to it.

APPLICATIVE AND OBJECT-ORIENTED LANGUAGES

Most programming languages are imperative languages, because their programs largely consist of a series of commands to assign values to objects. Examples of imperative languages are ALGOL, PL/1, FORTRAN, ADA, COBOL, and PASCAL. Two other types of languages exist: applicative and object-oriented. No commonly used language is purely imperative, applicative, or object-oriented, so every language has some characteristics of each type of language.

Applicative languages. A purely applicative language would be one in which there are no statements, only expressions without side effects. The name applicative refers to the repeated application of functions to the results of other functions to specify an algorithm. LISP, APL, and VAL are three languages in which programs are largely applicative.

LISP has a well-defined applicative subset known as pure LISP. Programs in LISP consist of a sequence of expressions known as S-expressions. If functions with side effects are excluded from these expressions, then the language becomes pure LISP. Pure LISP excludes such functions as SET, which assigns a value to a variable, and DEF (or DEFUN), which declares that a variable is a procedure with a certain body.

A program to find the absolute value of B − C would be written in pure LISP as in (68).

$$(\text{COND } ((> (-B\ C)\ 0)\ (-B\ C))$$
$$(t\ (-C\ B)))\qquad(68)$$

COND is a function that takes a list of ordered pairs of expressions and returns the value of the second member of a pair whose first member evaluates true. The expression pairs are given by (69). LISP uses prefix notation for operators, so the first member of the first pair is given by (70). The first member of the second pair, "t," or true, ensures that COND always delivers some result.

$$((> (-B\ C)\ 0)\ (-B\ C))\text{ and }(t\ (-C\ B))\quad(69)\qquad\qquad B - C > 0 \qquad(70)$$

The main advantage of applicative over imperative programming is mathematical elegance. An applicative description of an algorithm has the form of a mathematical function definition, and so all the accumulated power of mathematical analysis can be used to understand it. This is especially useful in proving programs correct.

Object-oriented languages. Programs written in object-oriented languages consist of sequences of commands directed at objects. An object receiving a command invokes an internal procedure to respond to the command. Assignment statements are replaced by commands to objects requesting that they change their values.

SMALLTALK, ACTORS, and LISP are three languages that encourage object-oriented programming. As with applicative languages, there is an object-oriented subset of LISP, called FLAVORS. Since the only way to do something in an object-oriented language is to direct a command at an object, object-oriented programming means passing messages to objects. For instance, the way to add two integers in SMALLTALK is to pass a message to the first integer requesting that it add itself to the second integer.

A program to compute the absolute value of B − C might be written in object-oriented form as in (71). This program is read: send a message to the integer object asking it to make a

$$\begin{array}{l}(\text{send INTEGER "new" "A"}) \\ (\text{send A "assign" B}) \\ (\text{send A "−" C}) \\ (\text{send A "absolute"})\end{array}\qquad(71)$$

new integer A, send A an assign message with message body B, send A a subtract message with message body C, finally send A a message asking it to take the absolute value of itself.

One advantage of object-oriented programming is the encapsulation of responses to commands within each object. When adding two numbers the programmer need not be concerned with whether the numbers are integer or real. The number receiving the "add-yourself-to" message is responsible for knowing how to add itself to any reasonable other number, and for saying if it cannot. This is achieved in imperative languages such as ADA by using encapsulated data types.

A second advantage of object-oriented programming is the power of mixing types of objects. If the programmer defined a type of object which could respond to messages to add itself to things, and another type of object which could respond to messages to print itself, then by mixing types a new kind of object would be created which could do both. In LISP FLAVORS the "vanilla flavor" is the set of messages to which all objects respond; more complex objects are created by mixing other flavors in with vanilla.

DEFINING NEW DATA TYPES

Procedure and function declarations define new operations that operate on existing objects. Type declarations add new objects and operations to a programming language. Designing programs with user-defined types allows solutions to be stated in problem-oriented rather than machine-oriented terms. ALGOL 68- and PASCAL-type declarations allow programmers to define the representation of new objects of the data types, and ALGOL 68 permits the definition of operations. For example, declaration (72) defines a new type named Rational.

    TYPE Rational = RECORD
              Numerator,
                 Denominator: (72)
                 INTEGER
       END

Once this definition is made, PASCAL programmers can declare variables and parameters with type Rational, but cannot add rational numbers without manipulating implementation directly (73). Dealing with the fields of the representation negates many advantages of abstraction.

    VAR Op1, Op2, Result: Rational;
    BEGIN
       . . .
       {Result: = Op1 − Op2}
       Result. Denominator : =   (73)
         Op1. Denominator * Op2. Denominator;
       Result. Numerator : =
         Op1. Numerator * Op2. Denominator
         + Op1. Denominator * Op2. Numerator
    END

Procedures and functions can be defined in PASCAL and operators in ALGOL 68 to encapsulate these sequences of operations, hiding the details of how functions are computed. However, these definitions are independent of the type definitions, that is, programmers can still directly manipulate the representation of objects. SIMULA 67 introduced the class concept to bind the definition of the representation and operations together, but still did not prohibit programmers from accessing the representation directly. By limiting access to objects with user-defined types to procedures defining operations, programmers can deal with data abstractly (that is, without caring how the data are represented). This enables programmers to change the representation of objects (for example, to improve the efficiency of their programs by changing the representation of rationals from a pair of integers to a single real) without changing any part of the program except the type definition and the procedures and functions implementing the operations. CLU, EUCLID, and ADA all have data abstraction functions that limit access to objects' representations. In example (74), written in ADA, the type Rational and the addition operator for rational numbers

    PACKAGE Rat IS
    TYPE Rational IS PRIVATE;
    FUNCTION "+" (Op1, Op2: Rational)
       RETURN Rational;
      . . .
    PRIVATE
    TYPE Rational IS RECORD
       Numerator, Denominator: INTEGER;
       END RECORD;   (74)
    END; —Package Rat
    PACKAGE BODY Rat IS
      . . .
       FUNCTION "+" (Op1, Op2: Rational)
         RETURN Rational IS
        . . .
       END "+";
    END Rat;

is made available through a package specification. However, the appearance of the word PRIVATE in the definition of Rational prevents programmers from accessing the fields of the record used to represent a rational number.

PARTICULAR LANGUAGES

The more widely used languages include FORTRAN, ALGOL, COBOL, BASIC, PL/1, APL, SNOBOL, LISP, PASCAL, C, and ADA.

FORTRAN. FORTRAN was designed in the mid-1950s by a group at IBM headed by John Backus for efficient scientific applications. To achieve this goal, the data and control components of the language are very simple, providing programmers with low-level hardware operations.

FORTRAN control structures are particularly primitive; neither compound statements nor unbound repetitive statements are part of the language. Two conditional statements (arithmetic and logical IF's) and a bounded iteration statement (DO) provide the only relief from GOTO's and labels. An arithmetic IF, statement (75), provides a three-way branch depending on whether its expression is negative, zero, or positive. A logical IF, statement (76), permits execution of a single

IF (expression) MinusLabel, ZeroLabel, Plus Label   (75)   IF (expression) statement   (76)

statement, which cannot be a DO or an IF, if its expression is true. The absence of nested statements causes heavy use of GOTO's and labels, as shown in example (77).

```
       IF (X GE 0) GOTO 1     IF X > = 0
          GOTO 2                 THEN
       1  A = B - C              A := B - C                          (77)
          GOTO 3                 ELSE
       2  A = C - B              A := C - B
       3  CONTINUE
          FORTRAN version     ALGOL version
```

A revision of the FORTRAN language, FORTRAN-77, adopted many of ALGOL's control constructs.

Scaler data types include logical, integer, real, double-precision real, and complex. Arrays with homogeneous elements provide the only aggregate types. Types are associated with variables statically through declarations.

Procedures may not be nested in FORTRAN, so references are either global or local. The global variables are partitioned into named common blocks, which must be mentioned in a procedure if the procedure contains nonlocal references. Storage for both global and local variables is statically allocated before program execution, so local variables retain values between invocations of the procedures in which they are declared.

FORTRAN has both procedures and functions, but neither can be recursive. Parameter transmission is by reference, and procedures can be transmitted. Functions may only return scalar results.

ALGOL 60. ALGOL was designed by an international committee in the late 1950s and early 1960s as a language for scientific computation. The elegance of ALGOL's structure has made it the basis for several subsequent language design efforts, most notably ALGOL 68 and PASCAL, and its control structures have even been adopted by PL/1 and later versions of FORTRAN. ALGOL was also the first language whose syntax was defined with a formal grammar (called Backus-Naur Form or BNF after two of the principal designers of ALGOL). The concise definition of the language has made it an object of study in the computer science community for many years.

ALGOL control statements are very much like statements (12)–(15). However, all repetitive statements are variants of the FOR statement, and compound statements are units of scope that may contain declarations of their own local variables.

ALGOL has integer, real, and boolean scalar types; aggregate types are restricted to arrays with homogeneous elements. ALGOL has static rules for both scope- and data-type association. Unless they are declared as OWN, variables in ALGOL programs are locally allocated, coming into existence in the block or procedure in which they are declared and being deleted when that program unit finishes execution. The lack of user-defined data types and dynamic storage allocation limits the applications of ALGOL.

Procedures and functions can be recursive and accept parameters which have the standard data types as well as labels and procedures. Parameter binding can be either by name (the default) or by value.

COBOL. COBOL was designed in 1959 and 1960 as a language to support business applications on computers. As was the case with FORTRAN, efficiency was a primary concern. Because of its intended application area, COBOL has relatively poor features for specifying computations (such as expressions, functions, and parameters), but strong features for data description and input/output.

Two of the most noticeable features of COBOL programs are the English-like syntax and the division of programs into four parts. Either English-language syntax or algebraic notation can be used in expressions, as in (78).

$$\text{ADD B, C, GIVING A} \qquad (78)$$
$$\text{COMPUTE A = B + C}$$

The identification division provides documentation, the procedure division describes algorithms, the data division contains descriptions of the files and working storage used in the procedure division, and the environment division collects machine-dependent information.

Statements in procedure divisions are grouped into labeled paragraphs. COBOL contains the usual IF and GOTO statements, but has unusual repetitive and procedure statements. The tasks of these last two statements are accomplished by the PERFORM statement (79) that executes a

$$\text{PERFORM label 1 THRU label N} \qquad (79)$$

sequence of paragraphs before control is returned to the statement following the PERFORM. Bounded and unbounded repetition are also specified using PERFORMS, as in (80).

$$\text{PERFORM label 1 THRU label N expression TIMES} \qquad (80)$$
$$\text{PERFORM label 1 THRU label N UNTIL condition}$$

Numbers and character strings are the basic data types of COBOL. Data structuring is provided with arrays and records. Level numbers on declarations describe the hierarchical relationship of the data (with the exception of some special level numbers). Types are specified by picture clauses that specify how many characters are needed to represent the values to be assigned to the variables.

Procedures with parameters and local data are optional COBOL features. No functions are provided and procedures may not be recursive. Unless a version of COBOL contains these optional features, all variables in the data division are global and statically allocated. Like FORTRAN, the values of all variables (even those declared in local data divisions) are retained between calls.

BASIC. T. E. Kurtz and J. G. Kemeny developed BASIC at Darmouth College in the early 1960s. The goal of their design was to provide nonscience majors with a simple, interactive language.

BASIC supports real and string data as well as one- or two-dimensional arrays of one of these primitive types. Dimension statements permit string lengths and array subscripts to be specified. Variable names are restricted to single letters, followed by an optional digit if the variable is numeric or $ if the variable is a string. Thus, types are statically associated with variables.

Statements in BASIC programs are numbered, and control passes through them sequentially unless altered by a GOTO or conditional branch statement, such as statement (81). Repeated execution can be specified by a FOR statement.

$$\text{IF expression THEN statement-number} \qquad (81)$$

There are no procedure declarations in BASIC; any sequence of statements can be considered to be a procedure. Procedure calls are indicated by the appearance of a GOSUB statement (82)

$$\text{GOSUB statement-number} \qquad (82)$$

that transfers control to the indicated statement number. The procedure is executed until a RETURN statement is encountered. The lack of procedure declarations means that the notions of parameters and scope rules are foreign to BASIC.

PL/1. PL/1 was designed by a committee organized by the IBM Corporation in the mid-1960s. The language was designed to meet the needs of a broad range of applications: scientific, business applications, and systems. PL/1 combines and extends many of the features of FORTRAN (parameter binding and formated input/output), ALGOL (scope rules, variable extents, recursive procedures, and control structures), and COBOL (record structures and picture data types). By providing redundant features from different languages, the designers have made the language difficult to learn and encouraged users to stay in one of the FORTRAN, COBOL, or ALGOL subsets of PL/1. The control structures of PL/1 are like those of ALGOL, except that repetitive statements are introduced by DO instead of FOR.

Numeric types in PL/1 permit the programmer to specify four attributes: mode (real or complex), scale (fixed or floating point), base (decimal or binary), and precision (the number of digits). Since most programmers do not want to provide such detail in declarations (and it may hinder transportability to machines with different word lengths), PL/1 compilers provide many defaults. (There are actually more attributes describing the variable's lifetime and initial value.) PL/1 also provides bit and character strings with lengths that are either fixed or varying up to a maximum, as well as a reference type called POINTER. Both arrays and COBOL records called structures are provided.

PL/1 has static scope rules and type association. The extent of a variable may be either static (ALGOL's own), automatic (ALGOL's local), based, or controlled. The last two extent attributes provide dynamic storage allocation using the predefined procedures ALLOCATE and FREE. The based attribute can be used to provide free unions because pointer variables may reference data of any type. Example (83) illustrates this facility. The declaration of based variables does not cause

$$\begin{aligned}&\text{DECLARE Int FIXED BASED;}\\&\text{DECLARE Chr CHARACTER(4) BASED;}\\&\text{DECLARE P POINTER;}\\&\text{ALLOCATE Int SET P;}\\&\text{P->Int = 64;}\\&\text{PUT LIST(P->Chr);}\end{aligned}$$
(83)

storage to be reserved, but rather defines a template. The ALLOCATE statement reserves enough storage for an integer object and binds a reference to the object to P. The assignment statement dereferences P and treats the resulting object as an integer in order to assign the value 64 to the object. The PUT (or write) statement dereferences P and treats the resulting object as a character. Controlled storage must also be explicitly allocated and freed by the programmer, but unlike based storage only the last object allocated may be referenced. Thus, the language provides programmer-defined stack operations.

PL/1 may have recursive procedures and functions. Parameter transmission is by reference as in FORTRAN, but labels, procedures, and functions can also be transmitted as in ALGOL. PL/1 also provides primitives for parallel execution of procedures and for handling interrupts.

APL. APL was designed by Kenneth Iverson during the mid-1950s to the mid-1960s. It is an interactive language whose operators accept and produce arrays with homogeneous elements of type number or character. The only control construct is a GOTO statement, but this is inconsequential since many APL programs have a strong applicative flavor. Although they often consist of an imperative sequence of assignments, APL programs generally operate on array objects to produce new array objects. Thus repetitive constructs are not needed as frequently as they are in ALGOL-like languages.

There is really no such thing as an APL program because functions are defined independently and invoked either interactively by the programmer or by another function. A function definition for IN, which finds the positions at which one word appears in another, is shown in (84).

$$\begin{aligned}&\nabla\quad Z \leftarrow A \text{ IN } B;\ J\\&[1]\quad J \leftarrow (\Lambda[1] = B)/\iota\rho B\\&[2]\quad J \leftarrow (J \le 1 + (\rho B) - \rho A)/J\\&[3]\quad Z \leftarrow (B[J^\circ + {}^-1 + \iota\rho A]^\wedge = A)/J\\&\nabla\end{aligned}$$
(84)

IN would require at least one loop if it were written in an ALGOL-like language.

APL functions consist of sequentially numbered statements, which may have control transferred to them via GOTO statements. A and B are formal parameters (only two are allowed but they can be arrays), J is a local variable, and Z is a special identifier that is assigned the result of any function. Parameters are passed by value and nonlocal references are resolved dynamically. Types are associated with variables and storage is allocated for variables dynamically. For example, if IN is invoked with the sequence of commands (85), then X and Y are dynamically allocated and assigned values of type vector of characters.

$$X \leftarrow \text{'THE'}$$
$$Y \leftarrow \text{'THE MEN THEN WENT HOME'} \quad (85)$$
$$X \text{ IN } Y$$

The assignment statements in function (84) have the following effects. A[1] = B returns a vector whose length is the same as B's length, and whose values are either 1 where A[1] = B[k] for $1 < = k < =$ Length (B) or 0 otherwise. The rho operator (ρ) gives the length of B, and the iota operator (ι) generates a vector of length B whose values are 1, 2, . . . , ρB. The first vector is used to compress the second by selecting those values from the second vector for which the corresponding value in the first vector is one. Thus J is assigned a vector with values (1 9 17). The second statement checks that a word with the same length as A could really start at these positions (without running past the end of the vector). The final statement subscripts B with a matrix of positions of words that could match A to obtain a matrix of characters, as in (86). The rows of this matrix are compared to the vector A, yielding a matrix (87) containing 1's where the

$$B \begin{vmatrix} 1 & 2 & 3 \\ 9 & 10 & 11 \\ 17 & 18 & 19 \end{vmatrix} = \begin{vmatrix} \text{THE} \\ \text{THE} \\ \text{T H} \end{vmatrix} \quad (86) \qquad \begin{vmatrix} 1 & 1 & 1 \\ 1 & 1 & 1 \\ 1 & 0 & 0 \end{vmatrix} \quad (87)$$

values of the corresponding elements are equal and 0's otherwise. The elements of the rows are "anded" to form a vector of 0's and 1's (1 1 0) that is used to compress J.

SNOBOL. During the 1960s, SNOBOL was developed by Ralph Griswold at Bell Laboratories as a string processing language. It went through several forms, only one of which is still in use: SNOBOL 4. SNOBOL has no real control constructs. Instead, every statement either "succeeds" or "fails" and may optionally GOTO a new statement depending on success or failure. SNOBOL statements provide extremely powerful operators for string manipulation. For instance, SNOBOL statement (88) will assign the value a to X and the value b to Y. The operators used here

$$\text{"This is a, this is b" "a" . X ARB "b" . Y} \quad (88)$$

are the blank before a which means pattern match; the "." which means assign, and "arb" which matches an arbitrary string.

Data types are dynamically declared and converted in SNOBOL, so that the same variable can at one instance contain an integer and the next instant contain a procedure. User-defined types permit the use of records. An interesting aggregate type is the "table," which is an array addressed by content. Variables are dynamically scoped.

SNOBOL has both procedures and functions, which may be recursive. Parameter transmission is by value, and procedures can be transmitted. Functions may return any type, including type NAME which can be used as the target of an assignment statement.

SNOBOL is used for string processing applications, such as editors, compilers, and data bases. It executes rather slowly, so once a program has been coded and debugged in SNOBOL it is often recorded in a more efficient language, such as PASCAL.

LISP. LISP was invented by John McCarthy while at MIT in the late 1950s. It is a very widely used language in the artificial intelligence community, which has never agreed on what version of LISP should be standard. The two most widely used forms are INTERLISP and MACLISP. SEE ARTIFICIAL INTELLIGENCE.

The basic type in LISP is the list, usually denoted by a sequence of items in parentheses. LISP programs also take the form of lists, thus LISP programs can manipulate themselves or other LISP codes. The only syntax in LISP is the matching of parentheses, thus LISP is easy to extend by adding additional functions.

Procedures and functions are recursive in LISP, and parameters are transmitted by value. The power of LISP comes from the representation of everything by lists, which leads to very powerful environments of tools and extensions to LISP. LISP is a good language to write experimental programs, since its flexibility is useful for dealing with the unexpected. However, it executes slowly and uses a lot of memory.

PASCAL. PASCAL was developed by Niklaus Wirth in 1969 to obtain a language which would be suitable to teach programming as a systematic activity with constructs that could be implemented reliably and efficiently. The control structures of PASCAL are similar to statements (12)–(15) and (21). However, a CASE statement (whose design had been proposed in a language called ALGOLX designed by Wirth and C. A. R. Hoare) was added as an additional selection statement. This statement permits execution of one alternative among several statements based on the value of a selection expression. The alternative selections are labeled and selection is performed by name rather than by position to minimize the chance for errors resulting from rearranged or omitted statements. Statement (89) is a sample CASE statement. If this expression has

$$\begin{array}{l}\text{CASE expression OF}\\ \quad\text{Reader: statement1;}\\ \quad\text{Disk, Tape: statement2;}\\ \quad\text{Printer: statement3}\\ \text{END}\end{array} \quad (89)$$

the value Disk, statement2 is executed and control skips to the statement following the CASE statement.

PASCAL scalar types include integer, real, character, and boolean. PL/1's POINTER type is improved by adding information about the type of data referenced. Thus the PASCAL types "reference to type1" and "reference to type2" are not compatible, so assignments cannot take place between variables of one of these types and values of the other. Pascal extends ALGOL 60's data-structuring facilities by adding sets, records, files, and user-defined types. Type unions can be obtained through use of variant records.

Like ALGOL, PASCAL has a mandatory declaration of variables, static scope rules, and static association of types with variables. Except for those accessed through other reference variables, variables are locally allocated on procedure entry and deleted on procedure exit. Variables accessed via reference variables are dynamically allocated and freed by using NEW and DISPOSE, respectively.

Both procedures and functions can be recursive in PASCAL. Variables of any type can be bound by value (the default) or by reference to formal parameters. Procedures and functions can also be passed as parameters. Functions are limited to returning scalar or reference values as their results.

C language. C was designed and implemented in 1972 by Dennis Ritchie to implement the Unix operating system. Similar to PASCAL in many ways, C has enumerated types, records (called structures), the case statement, and reference variables. The main difference between programming in C and other languages is the extensive use of reference variables, which are defined to be equivalent to arrays. For instance, program (90) declares an integer array named

$$\begin{array}{l}\text{int array [10], *pointer = array;}\\ \text{array (3) = 1;}\\ \text{*(pointer + 3) = 0;}\end{array} \quad (90)$$

array and a pointer to array named pointer. The first assignment statement sets the fourth element of the array to 1, and the second assignment sets it to zero. The dereferencing operator in C is represented by *. Reference variables allow the programmer to specify algorithms which are particularly efficient to execute on the underlying machine, at the expense of writing code which is difficult to read.

C is usually used within the Unix operating system which is entirely written in C. Unix extends C to have storage allocation, multitasking and interrupt handling, and very flexible input/output facilities. *See* OPERATING SYSTEM.

ADA. ADA was designed by a group from Cii-Honeywell Bull headed by Jean Ichbiah in the mid-1970s. This group won a competition sponsored by the Department of Defense to design a new language to support development of embedded systems. ADA was designed using PASCAL as a base, to meet the reliability and efficiency requirements imposed by these applications.

Design decisions to include static scope rules and static association of types and variables were made in the name of reliability. ADA's most important contribution is to extend PASCAL's user-defined type to include packages; these permit users to define new operations and encapsulate the representations of their new types. While reliability required that types be statically associated with variables in ADA, efficiency required that controlled escapes from these associations be possible by specifying a target type for an expression. In example (91), a ten-element

      TYPE Seq IS ARRAY (Integer RANGE <>) OF Integer;
      SUBTYPE Decile IS Seq(1 . . 10);
      A: Decile;   (91)
      B: ARRAY (1 . . 100) OF Integer;
      A := Decile(B(11 . . 20));

slice [similar to expression (39)] of B is assigned to A. Decile coerces the expression B(11 . . 20) to the same type as A, making the assignment possible.

    Like PL/1, ADA contains an exception-handling code so that code designed to handle exceptional situations can be separated from that for normal processing. For example, if a compound statement contained division operations and none of the divisors should be zero, the ADA structure (92) might be used. If a division by zero occurs in the body of the compound statement,

      BEGIN
        . . . statements containing
           divisions
      EXCEPTION
        WHEN Numeric__Error =>
        . . . statements to inform user of   (92)
           error situation
        WHEN OTHERS =>
        . . . all other errors besides
           numeric errors
      END;

control is transferred to the statements in the exception handler labeled Numeric__Error. After these statements are executed, control returns to the caller. All other errors raised in the compound statement are handled by the OTHERS exception handler. If no exception handlers are specified, exceptions are propagated to the caller. Exceptions can also be declared and raised by users

      TASK BODY Buffer IS
        . . . local declarations
      BEGIN
        LOOP
          SELECT
            WHEN QLength < Max =>
            ACCEPT Put(N: IN
              Integer) DO
                . . . statement list
            END;
              . . . statement list   (93)
          OR
            WHEN QLength > 0 =>
            ACCEPT Get(Result: OUT
              Integer) DO
                . . . statement list
            END;
              . . . statement list
          END SELECT;
        END LOOP;
      END Buffer;

to handle the exceptional conditions of their applications (for example, stack overflow or singular matrix).

Efficiency considerations make it possible for programmers to describe interfaces to programs written in other languages and to access machine-level components (for example, instructions and particular memory locations).

Because many embedded systems are real-time applications, ADA provides tasks that can be concurrently executed, but communicate in very controlled ways. The ADA fragment (93) shows a task named Buffer with two entry points, Put and Get, defined by ACCEPT statements. Other concurrently executing tasks call Buffer through one of its two entry points, for example, Buffer Put(12). Each time the SELECT statement is executed, all the expressions guarding the operations (that is, those expressions after the WHEN's) are evaluated. From those entries whose expressions evaluate to true, one is arbitrarily chosen for execution. The task whose call was chosen and the Buffer task rendezvous until the statements between ACCEPT and END are executed. Then each task is free to proceed with its own execution.

Bibliography. C. Ghezzi and M. Jazayeri, *Programming Language Concepts*, 2d ed., 1987; E. Horowitz, *Fundamentals of Programming Languages*, 2d ed., 1983; H. Ledgard and M. Marcotty, *The Programming Language Landscape*, 1981; E. I. Organick, A. I. Forsythe, and R. P. Plummer, *Programming Language Structures*, 1978; T. W. Pratt, *Programming Languages: Design and Implementation*, 2d ed., 1984; G. Silverman and D. B. Turkiew, *Computers and Computer Languages*, 1988.

ABSTRACT DATA TYPES
ROGER KING

Mathematical models which may be used to capture the essentials of a problem domain in order to translate it into a computer program.

Motivation. It is generally understood that people join a line by standing at the end of the line and are serviced from its front. Stepping into the middle of a line violates the rules of line etiquette, as does servicing someone from the middle of the line.

To describe a particular line of people, it suffices to keep track of the first and last person as the line moves. Then, it will always be far behind whom a new person must stand and who must be served next. Such a description of a line is an example of an abstract data type (ADT). It is a model for representing some sort of structure, with rules for making changes to that structure. The rules may be expressed as operators that perform specific functions.

In the field of computer programming, lines are usually called queues. For a person to enter a queue would be to perform an insertion; to leave the front of a queue would be a deletion. When the rules of line etiquette are broken, that is, an individual enters into or is serviced from the middle, the queue becomes a list. A list is a queue where insertions and deletions may be made at any point.

There are many examples of abstract data types, but this formalism is rarely useful in everyday life. However, an ADT queue would be quite helpful in representing a customer line as a computer program. The queue could be used to express certain business operations in terms of a well-understood model for representing information. This would allow the programmer to simplify the problem to that of implementing the queue in a computer language and then using the queue to represent a business function. Techniques for implementing queues are readily available.

Abstract data types allow the use of previously discovered programming techniques. Another benefit of ADTs is that they allow a programmer to encapsulate the rules for altering a model within a set of procedures, and ignore these details when using the given ADT. In other words, the programmer concerned with modeling a business function could forget exactly how an insertion or deletion is made when procedures that perform these functions are used. *See DIGITAL COMPUTER PROGRAMMING.*

ADTs and data structures. An ADT is indeed abstract, in that it must be translated into a programming language. This is done by using program data structures, which are formed from the primitive abstract data types supported directly by the given language. The programmer must also implement operators (for example, insert and delete in the queue example) that follow the rules for manipulating the ADT. In essence, then, ADTs are conceptualizations built of simple data structures and augmented with high-level operators. When an ADT is used as the model of information in a specific application, an instance of the ADT is said to be defined. SEE PROGRAMMING LANGUAGES.

For example, an instance of a queue used to model a business function could be implemented as a sequential set of text strings in main memory. This implementation is illustrated in **Fig. 1**. Each text string contains the name of a person in line. The rules for manipulating the queue could be implemented by keeping track (in two variables) of the location of the first and last position in the queue. In Fig. 1a, the queue is shown with four values entered, and markers for the front and end of the queue. If insertions and deletions cause the first position in the queue to migrate to the end of the allocated queue space, the queue will wrap around on itself. When the last position in the queue is used, the next new value will be inserted in the first position. In Fig. 1b, values 1 and 2 have been removed from the front, and value 3 is now first. The queue has wrapped around, and value $n + 1$, the last value, is situated where value 1 used to be.

Classification of data types. Abstract data types may be grouped according to the ways they arrange information. Typical abstract data types are discussed below; with each one, particular classes of problems that are best solved using the given ADT are discussed. First, linearly organized data types represent information as a one-dimensional series of elements. Second, nonlinear modeling techniques arrange this information so that one element may be logically followed by more than one other element. (This corresponds to a customer line where there is more than one person directly behind any specific person.) Third, an unordered data type assumes no specific order of the elements of the type. (This corresponds to customers waiting in a chaotic group.) The first three data types are examples of models used to represent information in the fast-access, main memory of a computer. Other data types are oriented toward mass storage devices like magnetic tapes and disks.

Before more interesting ADTs may be considered, however, it is necessary to discuss the primitive ADTs that are typically used to form more complicated data types.

Primitive ADTs. There are a number of simple abstract types that are typically implemented directly in a high-level programming language. These include integers and real numbers (with appropriate arithmetic operators), booleans (with appropriate logical operators), text strings (often a programming language provides no special operators for manipulating strings), and pointers. An instance of a pointer data type has as its value a logical address of the instance of another ADT. The ADT pointer is usually implemented as an integer containing the main memory address of some data item. The primitive ADTs generally serve as implementations of the elements of a more sophisticated data type. For example, in the queue example, the data type text string was suggested as a model of the underlying implementation.

Queues, lists, and stacks. Queues, lists, and stacks are one-dimensional; what varies are the operators used to manipulate each ADT. A queue needs only two operators: one to insert and one to delete. To use a list, it is also necessary to have operators that may delete any element within the list or insert an element anywhere in the list. This may be done by an operator that steps through the list, locating the elements to insert or delete one by one, or by an operator that

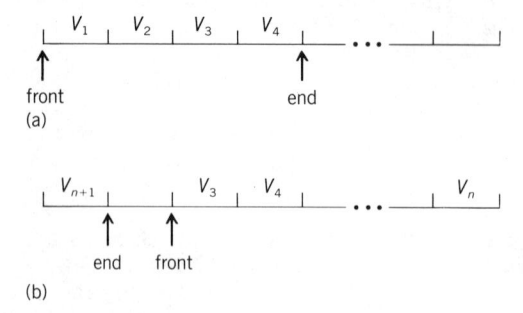

Fig. 1. A queue (a) with four values entered, and markers for the front and end of the queue, and (b) with values 1 and 2 removed from the front, and the queue wrapped around so that value $n + 1$, the last value, is situated where value 1 used to be.

locates an element to insert or delete in the list according to some means of identification. A list is a useful ADT for keeping track of sorted information in a situation where insertions and deletions in the middle are common. As an example, a personal telephone directory could be viewed as a list.

A list is clearly a queue with somewhat more generalized data operations. Varying the accessing methods of an ADT usually implies a change in the underlying data structure as well; for example, in a list it is necessary to be able to make insertions and deletions in the middle, not just at the ends. Thus, a list could be represented as a data structure which consists of a set of variables arranged in pairs. These variables would be instances of two different primitive ADTs of the programming language. In each pair, one variable, of type text string, would describe the value of an element (for example, in the telephone directory, a person's name and phone number) and the other, of type pointer, would indicate the next element pair in the queue (**Fig. 2**).

A stack is essentially a queue in which insertions and deletions are both made at the front. Thus, the last element inserted is the first deleted. An insertion is commonly called a push and a deletion is called a pop. Stacks are used when modeling tasks that must be interrupted and then completed. An uncompleted task is pushed onto the stack when it is interrupted, and popped off when it is resumed. Several tasks may be pushed on top of each other; they are popped in reverse order.

Trees and graphs. A tree is an ADT where each element may be logically followed by two or more other elements. These are called its children. Each element in a tree may, as always, be of some other abstract data type and is called a node. The element that points to a node is called its parent. A tree may typically be accessed at any node; thus a tree in which each node has at most one child is a list.

A search of, an addition to, or a deletion from a tree is usually based upon an assigned order within the tree. For example, suppose that the tree consists of a number of nodes, each of which may point to two others. (This structure is called binary tree.) Besides the two pointers, each node would contain a value or set of values. The tree may be ordered such that the left child of any node has a value less than the parent that points to it, and the right child has a larger one (**Fig. 3**). Trees are often used to model complex decision spaces; each node represents a process with some number of possible outcomes.

A graph (**Fig. 4**) is in essence a generalized tree: each node may have more than one parent. In some graphs, there is no parent/child dominance; a path between two nodes (called a link) may be traversed in either direction. Further, in many graphs there may be any number of links emanating from a given node. Graphs are often used to model communication and transpor-

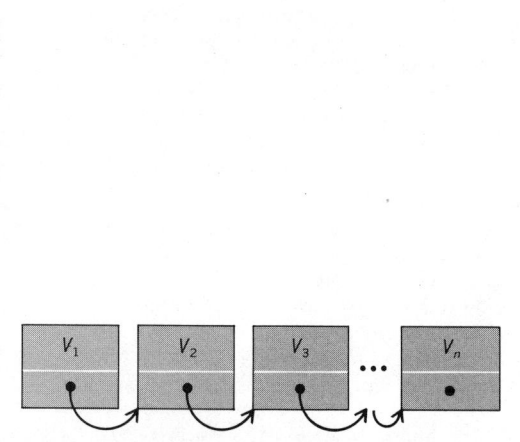

Fig. 2. Implementation of a list; arrows are used to indicate pointer variables.

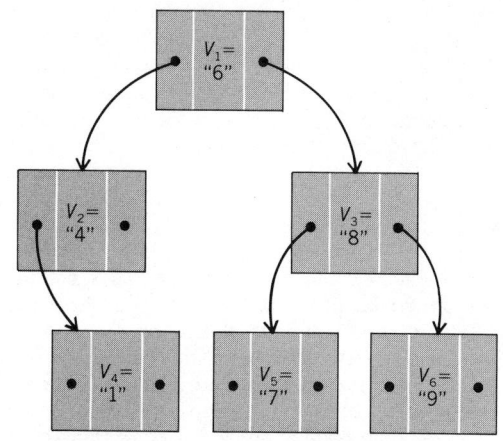

Fig. 3. Implementation of a sorted binary tree. The values V_1, V_2, and so forth are keys that are used to order the tree.

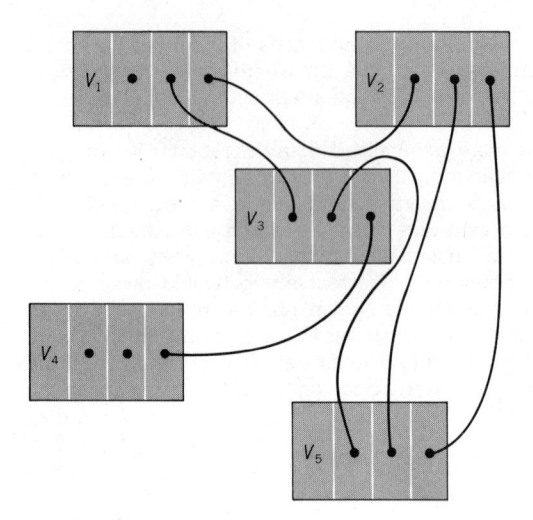

Fig. 4. ADT graph.

tation networks. For example, a graph could represent the American road network, with each node representing a city and each link representing a road. Common operations on a graph are to add a link of a specified weight between two nodes or to find the shortest path between two nodes.

Sets. A set is a data structure that models some group of related concepts. Just as with mathematical sets, the elements of the ADT set are not ordered. For example, an ADT set called colors may consist of the various colors of the rainbow. The set may be represented within a program as the set of character strings: red, yellow, and so forth.

Set operators usually perform insertions and deletions, form set unions and intersections, compare two sets for equality, test to see if an element is in a set, and so forth. Sets are commonly used to solve algebraic problems. For example, a compiler typically contains a module called a lexical analyzer which breaks the input program into identifiable pieces. One of the primary tasks of a lexical analyzer is to judge the legality of each character. For example, when the analyzer encounters a "[" or an "a" it might check to see if the character is an element of a set that contains all the legal characters of the language.

Files and data bases. A file is collection of identically formatted records, each containing some number of fields. Each field value is an atomic value, consisting of an integer, character string, real number, and so forth. Unlike the previously mentioned abstract data types, files typically model data stored on an external medium (magnetic disk, tape, and so forth).

Files are accessed either sequentially or randomly, meaning either that one is forced to step sequentially through the file until the desired record is located (for example, a tape file) or that a given record may be located with one logical search operation (for example, a disk). Operators on sequential files usually locate the first record in the file and then step to the next sequential record. Random files also provide operators for locating a record or set of records, given some value or set of values for one or more of the fields. (There is a clear parallel between queues and lists as main memory models and sequential and random files as mass storage models.)

Files are the backbone of external storage structures. They are used whenever main memory is insufficient in size to contain all the information required to solve a programming problem. Often, a file is constructed to consist of a series of records where each one will be transformed into an element in another data structure as the file is read into main memory. Thus, a number of records in a file may be read in and placed in a queue for processing, and when the queue is empty another group of records is read in.

A data base is an extension of the ADT file. The difference between a data base and a file is that a data base is a complex system containing many files and rules for interrelating the data on various files. For example, a typical data base operator is MERGE, which takes two files that share a common field format and forms one file containing the elements of both, sorting them in some manner. *See Data-base management systems*.

Relation to algorithms. Abstract data types have been discussed as conceptualizations of typical program data structures. Algorithms are techniques for solving programming problems which use the data structures and programs that implement ADTs. A sound knowledge of ADTs and a familiarity with common implementation techniques provide the background necessary to simplify the derivation of many algorithms. *See Algorithm*.

SOFTWARE ENGINEERING
Ware Myers

The process of engineering software, that is, not only the programs that run on a computer, but also the requirements of definition, functional specification, design description, program implementation, and test methods that lead to this code. Engineering implies the systematic application of scientific and technological knowledge through the medium of sound engineering principles to reach a practical goal. This goal becomes practical through the process of trading off performance, reliability, cost, and other characteristics of the resulting product in the light of the funds and time available for development. In short, software engineering is based on fundamental engineering principles and guided by economic considerations.

MOTIVATION

In the early years of computer development, as computer generations succeeded one another, the hardware performance-price ratio kept climbing at an average rate of about 25% a year; it was still advancing rapidly in the early 1980s. Programming productivity, on the other hand, while hard to measure, gained at a much slower rate—something like 7–9% per year. The continuing hardware improvement created a series of computer systems on which it was economically feasible to run ever larger programs, but the slower rate of improvement in programming led to progressively larger programming organizations requiring more levels of management. Some software systems approached a million instructions and absorbed 5000 worker-years of development time. By the mid-1960s the fact that program development almost defied effective management control was becoming evident.

Programs of this era were not only extremely large, but frequently lacked clarity as well. They were typically all in one piece, that is, not modularized. The sequence of program execution from one instruction to the next in line would jump instead to an instruction that was pages away in the program listing. A reader could track one or two of these jumps or branches, but scores of them made the program logic hard to grasp.

Since the product being developed was something of a mystery, it was nearly impossible for managers to find out enough about it to supervise the work of the programmers, to coordinate them with other groups, or to estimate how much time such poorly defined tasks would take or how many programmers were needed. It was under these circumstances that the NATO Software Engineering Conference (1968) pointed out the direction in which solutions to the "software crisis" should be sought.

Several aspects of software engineering may be distinguished. From one vantage point it appears as a process taking place over time, a process that is divided into perhaps a half dozen principal stages. Each stage can be examined more closely, and the various methods employed can be identified. Finally, from a broader point of view, the software development process must be managed.

DEVELOPMENT STAGES

A programmer tends to program, that is, to write a series of instructions in a programming language, and to give less thought to other stages of what is really, considered as a whole, a design process. On the other hand, in terms of software engineering, the problem-solving steps that have been learned in the other branches of engineering may be applied also here.

In general, these steps include formulating the problem, searching for and developing solutions, evaluating the solutions in terms of the goals, and refining and verifying the solution selected. In each branch of engineering these general steps have been adapted to the needs of the branch. In software engineering there is now considerable agreement on the six stages shown in **Fig. 1**. As work proceeds through this series of stages, the findings of later stages flow back to influence earlier stages.

Requirements definition. In the first stage, requirements definition, the basic question is what exactly the user expects the software to do. This problem-oriented definition provides the guide to later development stages and a checklist upon which the using and the development organizations can achieve agreement on what must be done. It provides a base against which the resulting software can eventually be compared for acceptance by the user.

If the using organization is unfamiliar with what computing systems can do and the development organization is inexperienced in the user's application area, defining the requirements becomes a learning process for both. Even if both organizations have some experience, the definition of requirements will still involve learning. In addition, this learning continues into later stages as the problem becomes better understood. Consequently the requirements definition must be revised periodically to match what has been learned.

Functional specification. At the functional specification stage, the user requirements are converted into a specification of the functions to be performed by the proposed system. While the requirements definition may have set values for some performance objectives that were closely related to the problem circumstances, the functional specification carries the goal-setting process further. Under constraints set by the current capabilities of computer technology and the user's resources, the specification sets target numbers for performance, reliability, compatability, and other product objectives.

This specification should serve at least three purposes. It should fulfill the needs expressed by the requirements definition and at the same time characterize the system to be built. It should lead into the design stage, and it can do this more effectively if the specification mirrors the structure of the problem. Finally, its clear expression of the functions and objectives should establish the criteria against which the completed system will be functionally tested.

Design. Software design is the process of going from what a system is to do to how it is to do it. In this stage the designer transforms the functional specification into a form from which the programmer can more easily code the problem represented by the specification into a list of programming instructions. While small, simple problems can sometimes be coded directly by a programmer, experience shows that most real problems cannot be coded directly and that an intervening design step is needed.

Design includes the task of partitioning (or decomposing) the entire problem area into subsystems, routines, subroutines, modules, and so forth, which individually become easier to

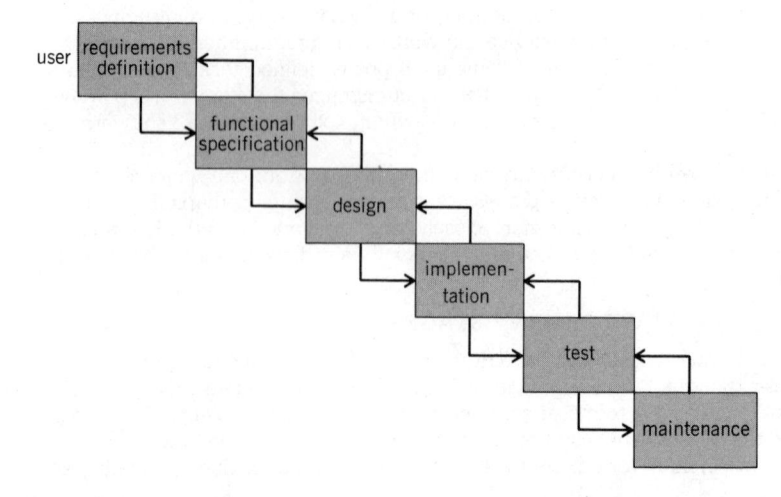

Fig. 1. Engineering development life cycle.

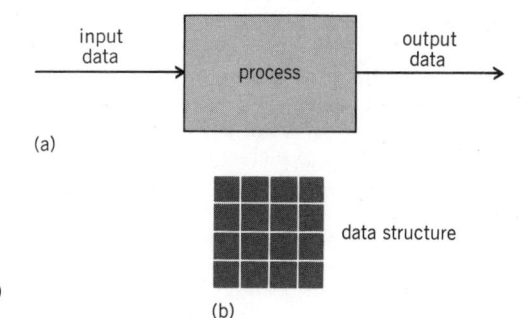

Fig. 2. Data considered from two points of view: (a) their processing and (b) their structure.

understand than the whole. Together these elements may be thought of as a hierarchy, like an organization chart, or alternatively, a flow diagram, like a strip road map. In either case, a key task of the design process is determining the manner in which these elements relate to one another—their interconnections. Developing the best possible arrangement—best in terms of the constraints imposed by the product specified and development resources—makes design an engineering activity.

The nature of design is suggested by **Fig. 2**. Input data go in, and undergo some processing; and output data come out (Fig. 2a). The data have some kind of structure, suggested by Fig. 2b. During the process of detailed design, this diagram is expanded by using a variety of methods described later.

Implementation. In its essentials the implementation stage transforms the output documents of the design stage into program instructions. These instructions are converted by a software support program called a compiler or an interpreter into machine code, that is, the binary digits that constitute the internal language of a computer.

In practice, however, if the program is of more than trivial size, the probability of making errors in programming is high. One of the most effective ways of finding these errors is the program review, conducted before the program is compiled. In a formal review the full weight of the organization is put behind the effort. The errors found are formally recorded and analyzed to provide corrective feedback to the entire programming organization. Unfortunately the reliance on the formal organization may discourage the willing cooperation of the psychologically less secure programmers.

To overcome this drawback, the structured walk-through was conceived. The programmer arranges the meeting and invites his or her peers. Management is not included, and no formal record of the errors found is filed. The term walk-through is derived from the practice of assigning sample values to the data and walking these numbers through the program steps one by one. This less threatening atmosphere is believed to make it easier for a programmer to cooperate in finding errors and later correcting them. The point of view of the structured walk-through is that programming is known to be difficult and the peer group is there to help.

Errors can occur in the earlier stages, too. In fact, studies of the development process indicate that errors tend to be more frequent in the early stages than in the later ones, and more expensive to correct in later stages than in earlier ones. Thus it is important to review the results at each stage and to eliminate errors as early as possible.

Testing. After the program is compiled, it is tested, that is, a set of values is assigned to the inputs, the program is run, and the program outputs are compared to the correct outputs. Since the test is being done by computer, a large number of input sets may be run. Moreover, the task of comparing the test output with the known correct output can also be performed by computer. When this match fails, the circumstances are reported back to the programmer to find and correct the errors.

While the above outlined testing task is simple in concept, it becomes difficult in execution. The reasons are that each input may have a large number of values, combinations of these numbers become larger still, and the number of different paths through a processing network of more than trivial size is enormous. Even at computer speeds, the test of all combinations and paths might run up into years of test time. So it becomes the task of test personnel to devise test procedures that exercise the program adequately in a reasonable time and at affordable cost.

Maintenance. The term maintenance, adopted from hardware terminology, has a different meaning in software. Software maintenance takes place in response to finding a previously unknown error, or to a change in the environment in which the system functions, or to an opportunity to improve performance. The "repair" does not return the software to its original state, as hardware repair does. It advances the system to a new and sometimes poorly understood state. One result is often the introduction of further errors, leading to the need for further maintenance as soon as they are discovered, and so on.

Software has been considered, perhaps unwisely, to be easily changeable. It followed, then, that it could be adapted to new circumstances simply by changing it, unlike hardware, which has to be redesigned and manufactured as a new model. Experience has demonstrated, however, that unstructured software is rather difficult to change successfully. As a result of the ensuing errors and complications, such software tends to deteriorate over time as changes are implemented.

METHODS

The stages of the life cycle provide a framework for spreading a number of activities over the time dimension, and consequently limiting the number which must be dealt with at any one time. Still, in each stage of a large system under development there remains too much complexity to deal with all at once. Psychological research has revealed that the human mind can only cope with about five to nine entities at a time. Above this limit people lose track of some of the factors and make errors.

Although the physical computer is a very complex machine, the software interfaces not only to this complex machine, but also to the great complexity of all the rest of the natural and human-made world, at least potentially. The development of large software systems is probably the most complex analytical task that the human race has ever encountered.

Thus one of the tasks of software engineering is to acquire from computer scientists or to develop for itself methods for partitioning a problem area into pieces small enough to be dealt with by the limited human brain. Concomitant with this task is that of finding satisfactory ways to represent this process of analysis and synthesis, both to bolster the capability of the analyst and to communicate the results of the work to others.

Structured design. At the beginning of the design stage, the designer knows that there are inputs and outputs, joined by a process, as diagrammed in Fig. 2. The methods of design are used to break out further detail. One way is by means of the flow of data, as shown in **Fig. 3**. The transformation of the data, symbolized by the circles, may be further refined in a series of steps into a greater number of individually simpler operations. Another way is to show the flow or movement of program control from one process or decision point to another, as the flow chart does (**Fig. 4**).

Thus, the problem, as defined by the requirements and specification, is decomposed into smaller pieces and these, in turn, into still smaller pieces until a minimal size, called the software module, is reached.

If the decomposition process begins at the top and works downward, it is called top-down design. If it begins with other machines with which the program is to interface, it sorts out first

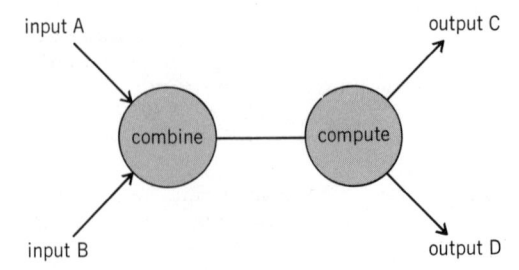

Fig. 3. Data flow diagram. Data inputs are transformed by the operations specified in each circle.

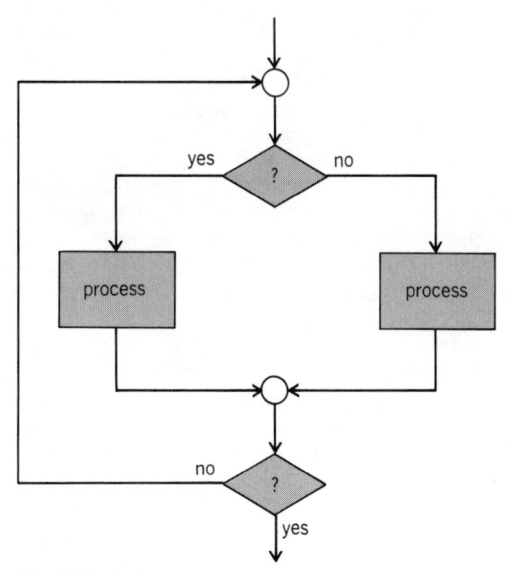

Fig. 4. Flow chart.

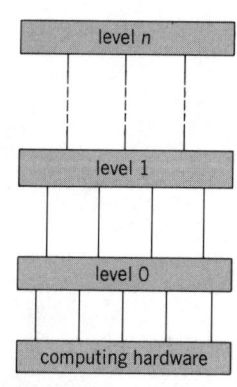

Fig. 5. Levels of abstraction. Building on the hardware, each level retreats further from detail.

the functions needed to manage these interfaces, then builds a structure up from there, and is called bottom-up design. The several levels of program modules form a hierarchy.

This hierarchy may be thought of as a series of levels of abstraction (**Fig. 5**). Each level is composed of a number of modules (**Fig. 6**). The levels-of-abstraction concept is comparable to the working levels of an organization chart. Modules on the bottom level handle details, such as physical files of data. Modules on higher levels deal with broader matters. Only such information is abstracted from a lower-level module as is necessary for a higher-level module to perform its duties. The rest is "hidden," easing the comprehension task of programmers of higher-level mod-

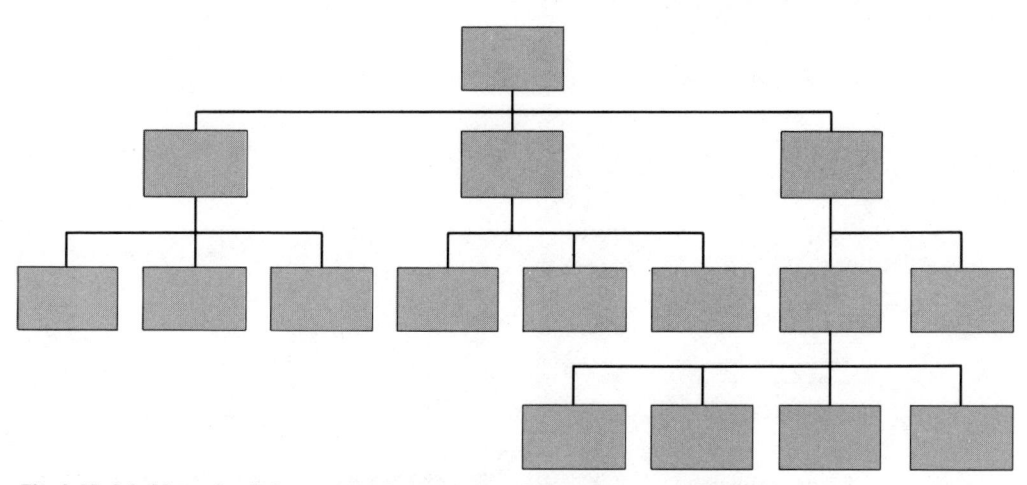

Fig. 6. Module hierarchy. Software modules are arranged in a structure, with defined relationships between the modules.

ules. Similarly, all the programmer of a lower-level module need know about higher-level modules is that they may call this lower-level module in some prescribed form.

Levels and modules compose a structure. However, the fact of "structure" is not inherent in either the problem or the ultimate program. At the beginning, the problem looks like a "big buzzing confusion." At the other end of the development process, the program is a large linear list which may be complicated by branch or jump instructions that can move the sequence of execution up or down the list at any time, sometimes pages away (**Fig. 7**). It may have no more perceptible structure than a long string tangled by a kitten. Modularization has not been an obvious approach, and in fact most programs before the 1970s were not modularized.

The business of design is to introduce order. The purpose of modularization is to reduce the number of entities with which the designer and later the programmer have to work at a given time. Also, a program with structure is easier to maintain and modify.

In a modular program there are two sets of entities. One set consists of the function or functions that the module is to perform internally. The other comprises the interrelationships it is to have with other modules. Complexity is reduced if the module is "cohesive," that is, performs only one function or a few closely related functions. Complexity is also reduced if the "coupling" between modules is limited and clearly defined. Under these circumstances a designer has only a few functions and a few relationships to keep in mind at one time.

Software engineers have conceived these and other ways of helping themselves think through the complexities of software design. In contrast to the earlier methods, modern practices emphasize structure, both in methodology and the result, and have come to be called structured design.

Design data representation. One achievement of other branches of engineering has been to draw systems so as to convey the intent of the designer to the manufacturer and others.

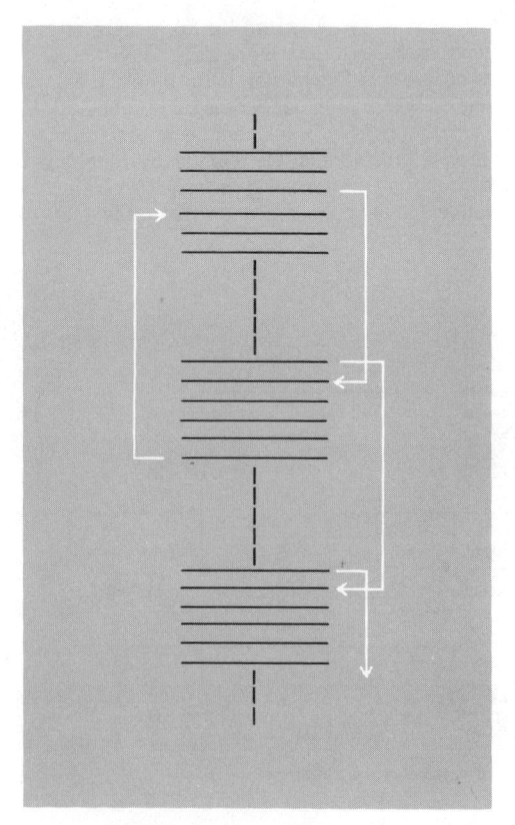

Fig. 7. Part of a sequential list of instructions containing branches or jumps that move the sequence of execution up or down the list.

Software designers, too, need methods of documenting their design data for its many users. The prime use is to convey the design to the programmers. However, the design data representation also serves as a source for test engineers, software maintenance programmers, and documentation specialists.

Software design took over the flow chart (Fig. 4) from other branches of engineering and still uses it widely. However, it has drawbacks. For one thing flow charts are not naturally structured. Hence several other forms of design data representation have been developed and gained adherents, and new methods are still being developed.

In a broad sense these representation techniques can be divided into three classes: diagrammatic, decision tables, and pseudocode. The diagrammatic techniques, of which the flow chart is one, represent module functions and relationships in some kind of visual form. Some examples are data flow diagrams, structure charts, HIPO (hierarchy plus input-process-output) charts, Nassi-Shneiderman charts, SDAT (structured design analysis technique), and data-structure charts (Warnier-Orr and Jackson method).

The decision table is a tabular method of sorting out the logic of a problem (**Fig. 8**). It has the advantage over the diagram methods of considerably compressing the amount of space needed for analysis.

Pseudocode is a combination of logical structures, the flow of control, and a language (**Fig. 9**). The logical structures are such constructs as:

Do first operation *then* second operation
If condition *then* action *else* other action
While condition *do* action

Mathematically, all logical operations can be reduced to just these three. However, other logical operations exist, and it is often shorter and more convenient to make use of them.

The flow of control proceeds from one line of pseudocode to the next. Digressions to distant parts of the list of operations are not inherent in this method.

The language is normally English, or the user's natural language. Hence pseudocode is not a high-level programming language, since such languages are, by definition, compilable. (A compiler is a computer program that recognizes only the words permitted by the high-level programming language with which it works; it is not set up to recognize all the words of a natural language.) On the other hand, if the logical constructs available in a particular programming language are used in a pseudocode analysis and the blanks in the logical operations are filled in with terms belonging to that language (and, hence, recognizable by its compiler), then one has, in effect, moved to the implementation stage and programmed the design.

Through the use of pseudocode it is possible to start with a very broad version of the initial problem, since there is no limit to the concepts that may be employed. As the problem is gradually

CONDITIONS				
newcomer to field	Y	N		
want more information on topic			Y	N
ACTIONS				
read this article carefully	X			
scan article quickly		X		
read referenced encyclopedia article			X	
no action				X

Fig. 8. Decision table. The user lists conditions at the top which have binary answers, yes or no. At the bottom are the actions that result from each state of the conditions.

```
Begin software engineering study
    If newcomer to this field then
        Read this article carefully
    Else
        Scan article quickly
    Endif
    If want more information on a topic then
        Read referenced encyclopedia article
    Endif
    If want pursue field further then
        Consult one of bibliography items
        Do until your interest is satisfied
            Read bibliography items
            If item is irrevelant then
                Proceed to next item
            Endif
        Enddo
    Endif
    If you have understood this pseudocode then
        Congratulations! you have the idea of
            pseudocode as a design technique
    Endif
End software engineering study
```

Fig. 9. Example of pseudocode, a software design data representation technique.

worked through, the pseudocode is refined in a stepwise manner to solve in more detail smaller pieces of the big problem. Ultimately a level of refinement is reached at which the conversion to programming language is deemed to be feasible without problems.

Structured programming. Contemporary programming languages incorporate the basic control structures (logic operations) in their instruction sets. In consequence, the final refinement of the design stage is simply converted to the corresponding logic structure of the language and is then compilable. However, the earlier programming languages, such as Fortran, were not based on these structures, and as a result the control structures from the design stage have no direct counterparts in the programming language. To overcome this deficiency, versions of these languages have been developed which do contain the control structures. However, these versions have to be first processed by a preprocessor (a computer operation) into the standard language, which is then compiled in the normal manner. SEE PROGRAMMING LANGUAGES.

In a structured program there is ideally one entry point to the module and one exit point. Branch or Go-To instructions are used to signify its structure and enhance its readability. In general, each module of the design turns into only a page or two of code listing, short enough to be readily comprehensible by persons other than the programmer. Understandability is further enhanced by preceding the actual code with a module description in natural language. The pseudocode design may also be included. Particular lines are further explained by comments. Such a program is said to be machine-documented. In this form it is more readily updated and accessible to later users.

SOFTWARE MANAGEMENT

The methods of software engineering find application in business, industry, and government. The problems are often very large. The resulting projects employ many people and substantial resources over long time periods. Personnel, money, and time are the factors with which management works, so that software development becomes subject to the methods of management: planning, organizing, scheduling, directing, monitoring, controlling, and so on. But because software engineering is relatively new, experienced managers lack working experience in it, and software engineers have not had time to grow into management. Even when some of them do, the pace of oncoming technology may outmode them.

If management could confine itself to management and engineers to engineering, the problems would be fewer and less severe. In software, however, there is reason to believe that management decisions, that is, decisions properly within the management sphere, can influence design matters, and vice versa.

It is well established, for example, that large software projects consume more development resources per unit of accomplishment than smaller projects, largely because of the increased burden of training, coordination, and communication. Mealy's "law" states: There is an incremental person who, when added to a project, consumes more energy (resources) than he or she makes available. Thus, beyond a certain point, adding resources (people) slows progress, in addition to increasing the cost.

One solution to this problem is to break large projects into small components. But management cannot make independent small projects simply by ordering them. If the small projects are all aspects of one large problem area, then there are relationships between them. In that case, coordinating relationships between projects takes just as much time as coordinating the same relationships within one large project; the technical relationships are there in both cases.

Of course, a large system can be partitioned into subsystems and eventually modules and the work divided, but this task—maximizing cohesiveness and minimizing coupling—is highly technical. The extent to which a system can be decomposed into independent systems is an engineering question, not a matter of managerial prerogative.

To take another example, the assignment of personnel is a common management responsibility. At the beginning of a project a manager might wish to assign to it right away the number of people that the project is planned to average over its lifetime, to get it off to a good start. Unfortunately, only a few highly skilled people can be usefully employed in the first design steps. More than these few just get in the way. One experienced software manager recommends sending the extra ones off to pertinent training programs. As the few sort out the problems and begin to structure the design, they create new elements to which more talent can be applied. This process repeats itself, and the staff gradually expands. It appears that the proper timing of additional personnel is largely dependent on the rate of technical progress. Again, management has the authority, but should be guided in its exercise by technical considerations.

According to Frederick P. Brooks, Jr., adding worker-power to a software project that is running behind schedule only slows it down further. In other words, under the circumstances that Brooks described, the managerial prerogatives of setting schedules and monitoring them appear to be hollow rights. There seem to be factors at work, technical in nature, more powerful than adding more people can offset.

EFFECTIVENESS

The very success of computer systems led to the software predicament: software became too costly, too error-prone, too complex, too hard to maintain, too people-heavy. In fact, these problems threaten to delay the spread of computers into new fields.

It is now clear that the methods of software engineering, while not easy to apply, do help overcome the software predicament. Formal studies of the before-and-after type show improvements in the 25–75% range in cost, error reduction, and productivity. Executives with before-and-after experience have reached similar conclusions.

SOFTWARE PORTABILITY

Portability refers to the ease with a program can be moved from one computer environment to another. If there were just one programming language, translated to just one type of computer by one compiler, then all application programs would be portable. However, with the many different types of computers and application domains and the hundreds of programming languages and compilers available, a particular program is generally not transportable between different types of computers, domains, or languages.

It follows, then, that a large number of programmers are needed, and this number would have to increase as rapidly as the number of different installations. The discrepancy between the rate at which hardware can be manufactured (very fast) and the rate at which programmers can be found and trained (very slow) is called the software crisis. One way to ameliorate this crisis is to improve the portability of software. Portability could be enhanced if the computer community were willing to settle on a limited number of languages, standardize them, and adhere to the standards. In practice, most implementations of languages have deviated to some degree from the language standard, thus restricting portability. In the past some manufacturers may have tacitly accepted incompatability as a means to lock up a captive market, but this attitude seems to be declining as the software crisis becomes more evident.

Another approach is to accept at least some variety in computers and languages as a given, and develop exchange methods. Several companies translate a number of languages into a common intermediate code, variously called *p*-code or *q*-code, and then translate that into the native assembly language of each of many processors.

SOFTWARE PIRACY

Piracy refers to the process of copying commercial software without the permission of the originator. It is the dark side of portability—without portability piracy could not exist. Piracy is found among amateurs, who copy programs for friends without direct pecuniary gain, and professionals, who copy programs in quantity for sale at low prices to amateurs.

The amateurs seem to have need for more software, little money, and the feeling that just a few copies among friends will not make any difference. However, surveys reveal that thousands of amateurs are pirating software for their friends. All together they do make a difference; in fact, some suppliers have abandoned the amateur marketplace. In any case others' work is being appropriated by amateurs without recompense.

The professional pirates have a need to make money. They are not likely to be deterred by the fact that moralists consider copying to be unethical; it would have to be illegal to have an effect on them. There are three approaches in law to protecting intellectual effort: patents, copyrights, and trade secrets.

Algorithms—and thus commercial software—are unpatentable. Source programs can be copyrighted, but object code cannot, because it is not intended to be read by a human being, thus making it legal (perhaps) to copy the 0 and 1 code of a read-only memory.

Several courts have ruled in different ways on this question and it remains unclear. As for the trade secrets approach, a for-sale program can be kept secret only to the extent that it can be coded to prevent copying. Code protection is being used, leading to an escalating contest between the code writers and the code breakers. Some feel that Congress should take up the Supreme Court's invitation, repeated several times, to draft a law suited to the peculiarities of software. Others hope that the courts will eventually sort out the inconsistencies. *See* DIGITAL COMPUTER; DIGITAL COMPUTER PROGRAMMING.

Bibliography. F. P. Brooks, Jr., *The Mythical Man-Month: Essays on Software Engineering*, 1975; P. Freeman and A. I. Wasserman, *Tutorial: Software Design Techniques*, 4th ed., 1983; R. W. Jensen and C. C. Tonies, *Software Engineering*, 1979; C. Jones, *Programming Productivity*, 1985; K. LaBudde, *Structured Programming Concepts*, 1987; O. Lecarme and M. Pellissier-Gart, *Software Portability*, 1986; R. H. Stern and J. L. Squires, Can we stop software theft?, *IEEE Micro*, 2(1) 12–25, February 1982; R. C. Tausworthe, *Standardized Development of Computer Software*, 1977; E. Yourdon and L. L. Constantine, *Structured Design: Fundamentals of a Discipline of Computer Program and System Design*, 1979.

6
COMPUTER COMMUNICATIONS AND NETWORKS

Multiaccess computer	**226**
Data communications	**228**
Packet switching	**233**
Local-area networks	**235**
Wide-area networks	**238**
Teleprocessing	**240**
Videotext and teletext	**241**
Electronic mail	**243**

MULTIACCESS COMPUTER
PHILIP H. ENSLOW, Jr.

A computer system in which computational and data resources are made available simultaneously to a number of users. Users access the system through terminal devices, normally on an interactive or conversational basis. A multiaccess computer system may consist of only a single central processor connected directly to a number of terminals (that is, a star configuration), or it may consist of a number of processing systems which are distributed and interconnected with each other as well as with the user terminals.

The primary purpose of multiaccess computer systems is to share resources. The resources being shared may be simply the data-processing capabilities of the central processor, or they may be the programs and the data bases they utilize. The earliest examples of the first mode of sharing are the general-purpose, time-sharing, computational services. Examples of the latter mode are airlines reservation systems in which it is essential that all ticket agents have immediate access to current information. Both of these classes of systems are still popular, with the proportion and importance of distributed application systems continuing to increase in areas such as corporate management and operations. SEE DATA-BASE MANAGEMENT SYSTEMS.

There are a number of economic factors supporting the growth of multiaccess systems. Primary among these are improvements in hardware performance and economics, with the latter being the principal factor. Digital-computer hardware continues to exhibit rapidly decreasing costs while its operational capabilities increase. At the same time most of the other cost factors involved with corporate operations such as labor, travel, and communications are increasing, and the cost of time delays in operations such as inventory management and confirming orders, as well as the cost of investment funding, is becoming significant.

System components. The major hardware components of a multiaccess computer system are terminals or data entry/display devices, communication lines to interconnect the terminals to the central processors, a central processor, and on-line mass storage.

Terminals may be quite simple, providing only the capabilities for entering or displaying data. Also utilized in multiaccess systems are terminals having an appreciable amount of "local intelligence" to support simple operations like editing of the displayed text without requiring the involvement of the central processor. Some terminals provide even more extensive support, such as the local storage of small amounts of text. It is also possible to assemble clusters of terminals to share local logic and storage.

The interconnecting communication lines can be provided by utilizing the common-user telephone system or by obtaining leased, private lines from the telephone company or a specialized carrier. Another important source of data circuits is a value-added network specializing in providing data transmission services. SEE DATA COMMUNICATIONS.

The communications interface for the processor may be provided by an integral hardware component or by a separate device known as a communications controller or front-end (communications) processor. The detailed operations involved in the control of a single communications line are not very great; however, servicing a large number of such lines may present an appreciable load to the central processor; therefore, separate hardware for communications interfacing is almost essential in a multiaccess computer system.

A central processor suitable for use in a multiaccess system must include the capability to support a large central memory as well as the communications interface mentioned above and the on-line mass storage discussed below.

The desirable characteristics of a mass storage device are: the ability to quickly locate any desired data; the ability to transfer data at a very high speed; the provision of economical storage for a large quantity of data; and a high degree of reliability.

The most common form of mass storage is rotating magnetic disks. Originally, magnetic drums were utilized for this purpose; however, the price, performance, and capacity of disks have resulted in their replacing drums. SEE COMPUTER STORAGE TECHNOLOGY.

System operating requirements. A multiaccess system must include the following functional capabilities: (1) multiline communications capabilities that will support simultaneous conversations with a reasonably large number of remote terminals; (2) concurrent execution of a number of programs with the ability to quickly switch from executing the program of one user to executing that of another; (3) ability to quickly locate and make available data stored on the mass storage devices while at the same time protecting such data from unauthorized access.

The ability of a system to support a number of simultaneous sessions with remote users is an extension of the capability commonly known as multiprogramming. In order to provide such service, certain hardware and software features should be available in the central processor. Primary among these is the ability to quickly switch from executing one program to another while protecting all programs from interference with one another. These capabilities are normally provided by including a large central memory in the processor, by providing hardware features that support rapid program switching, and by providing high-speed transfers between the central memory and the mass storage unit on which the programs and the data they utilize are stored.

Memory sharing is essential to the efficient operation of a multiaccess system. It permits a number of programs to be simultaneously resident in the central memory so that switching execution between programs involves only changing the contents of the control registers. The programs that are resident in central memory are protected from interfering with one another by a number of techniques. In earlier multiprogramming systems, this was accomplished by assigning contiguous memory space to each program and then checking every access to memory to ensure that a program was accessing only locations in its assigned space. The drawback to this type of memory allocation is that the entire program had to be loaded into memory whenever any portion of it was to be executed. A popular memory management technique is the utilization of paging. The program is broken into a number of fixed-size increments called pages. Similarly, central memory is divided into segments of the same size called page frames. (Typical sizes for pages and page frames are 512 to 4096 bytes.) Under the concept known as demand paging, only those pages that are currently required by the program are loaded into central memory. Page frames may be assigned to a given program in a random checkerboard fashion. Hardware capabilities are provided to automatically manage the assignment of page frames as well as to make them appear to the program as one continuous address space. At the same time, the hardware provides memory access protection.

Software capabilities. The control software component of most interest to an interactive user is the command interpreter. It is only one portion of a larger control program known as the operating system; however, in multiaccess systems it differs greatly from the command interpreter in a system providing batch multiprogramming service on a noninteractive, non-terminal-oriented bases. This routine interacts directly with users, accepting requests for service and translating them into the internal form required by the remainder of the operating system, as well as controlling all interaction with the system.

The operating system must also have the capability for controlling multiprogramming; that is, the concurrent execution of a number of user programs quickly switching from one to another during their execution as well as controlling memory sharing. The capability to page the memory as outlined above can be utilized to provide users with the impression that each has available a memory space much larger than is actually assigned. Such a system is said to provide a virtual memory environment. Similarly, the ability of the operating system to quickly change context from one executing program to another will result in users' receiving the impression that each has an individual processor. This is especially true when considering the large difference between the response and thinking time of a human compared to the computer's processing time. For the interactive users, such a capability results in the impression of having a private virtual machine.

The mass storage device mentioned above as hardware required for a multiaccess system must be supported by an efficient file management system. The latter is responsible for maintaining current information as to the physical location of the data stored on the mass storage device as well as providing a capability for quickly locating those data and controlling their transfer to the central memory for utilization. In addition, the file management system must provide protection of data from unauthorized access. SEE DATA-PROCESSING SYSTEMS; DIGITAL COMPUTER.

Bibliography. D. W. Davies et al., *Computer Networks and Their Protocols*, 1979; F. Halsall, *Introduction to Data Communications and Computer Networks*, 1986; W. Stallings, *Data and Computer Communications*, 1985; A. S. Tanenbaum, *Computer Networks: Toward Distributed Processing Systems*, 1981.

DATA COMMUNICATIONS
Mark M. Rochkind

The function of electronically conveying digitally encoded information from a source to a destination where the source and destination may be displaced in space (distance) and time. Encoded information can represent alphabetic, numeric, and graphic forms. Such information may originate as keystrokes at a terminal, as images on a page, as motion of a hand-held stylus, as a signal from some electrical or mechanical measurement device, or as output from a computer. The data communications function includes management and control of connections as well as the actual transfer of information.

Digitally encoded information typically takes the form of a series of 1's and 0's called bits (contraction for binary digit). Groups of eight bits are often referred to as bytes. Standard codes (such as ASCII and EBCDIC) have been adopted to establish a correspondence between bytes (patterns of eight bits) and alphabetic, numeric, and commonly used graphic and control characters. These codes are used for the interchange of information among equipments made by different manufacturers. *See Bit.*

Data communications usually do not refer to the conveyance of voice and video, although these too may be digitally encoded and then conveyed in digital form just as data are conveyed. The increased use of computers in the design and implementation of communications systems and the efficiencies realized from the handling of digitally encoded information have markedly broadened the range of data communications, and tend to mask old distinctions between data communications and other forms of information transfer.

Data communications has evolved from a function serving simple terminal-to-terminal communications (telegraphy) to one dominated by communications with and among computers. Terminal-to-computer communications remains a sizable component of traffic, but the migration of intelligence into terminal systems (an aspect of distributed processing) is causing terminals to take on more of the communications characteristics of computers. Networks of terminals and computers are serving the needs of business, education, government, industry, medicine, recreation, and other forms of human endeavor. These systems, both publicly and privately owned and operated, manage and direct the movement of data between stations (terminals, computers, and other sources of digitally encoded information) and across networks. Where two stations are geographically separated, data communications manages the transfer of information as a displacement in space. Where there is value in delaying the transfer of information, data communications manages the transfer also as a displacement in time (**Fig. 1**). Access to and the movement of information have become activities of great social and commercial importance. *See Multiaccess Computer.*

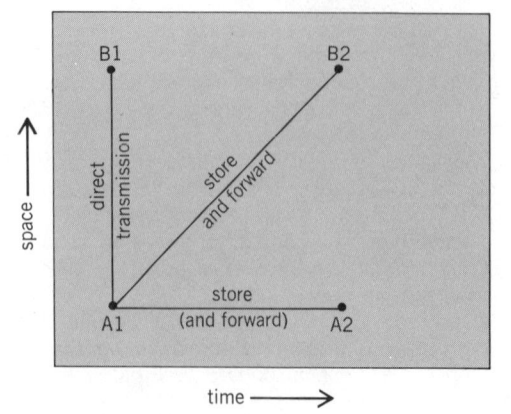

Fig. 1. Data communciations involving displacements in both space (distance) and time. Points A1 and B1 are separated by distance; the movement of data from A1 to B1 involves a displacement in space. Points A1 and B2 are separated by both distance and time; transfers between A1 and B2 require data to be stored by the data communications system before delivery. Points A1 and A2 are displaced in time but not in distance; for this case, data are transmitted, stored, and then returned to the originating station.

Types of applications. Data communications applications fall into three principal categories: transaction-oriented, message-oriented, and batch-oriented (**Fig. 2**). Transaction-oriented applications (Fig. 2a) involve the transfer of small amounts of data in the range of tens to hundreds of bytes and frequently require minimal delay in the transfer process. Transaction-oriented applications are typically bidirectional or conversational. Information is exchanged between source and destination stations. Examples are inquiry-response, information retrieval, and time-sharing, where people at terminals are communicating with large computers. For these applications, data communications serves stations displaced in space. Travel agents inquiring about seat availability, insurance agents inquiring about policy status, researchers accessing data banks, assembly-line process control, 24-hour bank tellers, merchants performing credit checks, computers monitoring life support systems, and retailers updating inventory status are examples of transaction-oriented applications.

Message-oriented applications (Fig. 2b) involve data transfers in the range of hundreds to a few thousand bytes or characters and are usually unidirectional, information flows from source to destination. Message applications frequently take advantage of time displacement (store and forward) as well as space displacement, and they exhibit data transfer options which go beyond the simple movement of information between two points. Examples of message-oriented applications are the transmittal of administrative messages within a corporate entity, the distribution of press releases, and price list updates being sent to field offices. Data entry uses, such as sales order processing, where information is collected from many sources for delivery to one or several destinations at some later time represent a large component of activity. Single messages carrying multiple addresses, addresses in the form of mnemonics (easily remembered names), requirements to journal (store) messages and to confirm the delivery of messages are examples of functions being served by data communications systems. Messages may be originated at terminals or in computers.

Batch-oriented applications (Fig. 2c) involve the transfer of thousands or even millions of bytes of data and are usually point-to-point (place-to-place) and computer-to-computer. Moving work from one computer to another (remote job entry), distributing the results of some centralized data-processing function, facsimile transmission, and updating distributed copies of data bases from some central site are examples of batch-oriented applications.

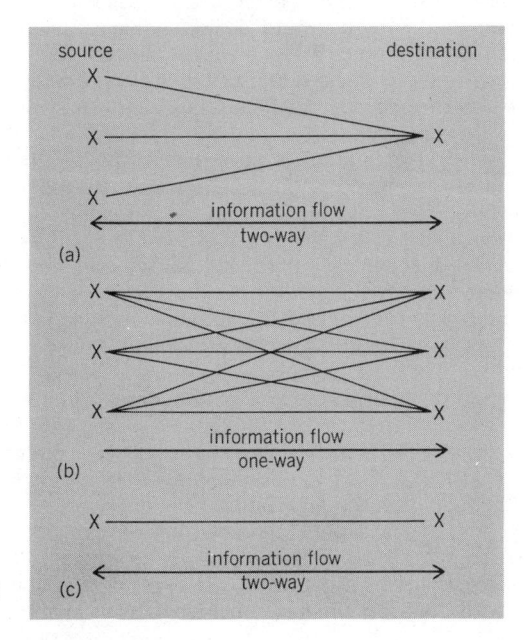

Fig. 2. Three principal categories of data communications. (*a*) Transaction-oriented. (*b*) Message-oriented. (*c*) Batch-oriented.

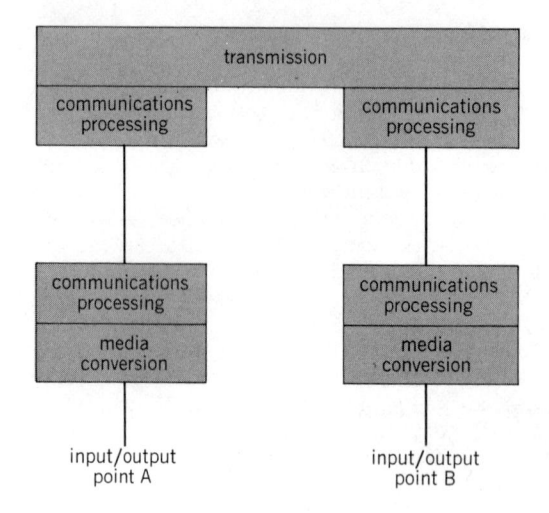

Fig. 3. Relationship of three functional components of data communications: media conversion, communications processing, and transmission.

Transaction, message, and batch-oriented applications exhibit different needs in terms of total bytes transferred, delay, and special features. Consequently, they impose different demands upon the functional components of data communications: media conversion, communications processing, and transmission (**Fig. 3**).

Media conversion. Media conversion achieves the conversion of some input, such as a keyboard keystroke, graphic material, a signal representing some measurement, and information recorded on magnetic media such as tape or disk, into a digitally encoded signal which may be transmitted. Likewise, it achieves the conversion of a digitally encoded signal into similar forms of useful output. Typical media conversion devices such as card reader/punches, paper tape reader/punches, magnetic tape systems, and printers remain in use. However, the proliferation of data communications applications where people at terminals converse with computers has caused media conversion to be most often associated with the interactive terminal. Input is typically supported by a keyboard device, while output takes the form of a hard-copy printer or screen display. The latter may be a cathode-ray-tube device (television monitor), a plasma panel, or a light-emitting diode (LED) or liquid-crystal array. Point-of-sale stations are interactive terminals which include both keyboard entry and laser- or magnetic-actuated pattern recognition devices for inputs.

The migration of intelligence into terminals in the form of storage and processing has enabled the use of all kinds of sensory devices as inputs and outputs. Optical character recognition, spoken-word recognition, tactile panels, light pens, facsimile devices, and x-y encoders all serve as input devices. Multicolor graphic displays, voice synthesizers, microfiche generators, and robots (mechanical servos) represent other important forms of output. Storage in the forms of floppy disks and magnetic bubble arrays are supplementing the more conventional cassette tape, and highly compact forms of storage such as video (optical memory) disks can be expected to be used as well. SEE CHARACTER RECOGNITION; COMPUTER GRAPHICS; COMPUTER STORAGE TECHNOLOGY; ELECTRONIC DISPLAY; SPEECH RECOGNITION; VOICE RESPONSE.

Communications processing. Communications processing provides the management and control in data communications systems. In the data terminal or media conversion system, it must at least manage the protocol (rules) used for intelligibly exchanging information with other stations including the administration of techniques designed to detect errors in transmission. Depending on the application, it may be necessary to perform code conversion and to multiplex or concentrate inputs from several terminals into a single output stream. It may also be desirable to augment variable data input via keyboard with fixed or automatically generated data such as date, time, operator identity, or location. The communications-processing function organizes encoded data into units suitable for transmission. Simple protocols demand that data be organized

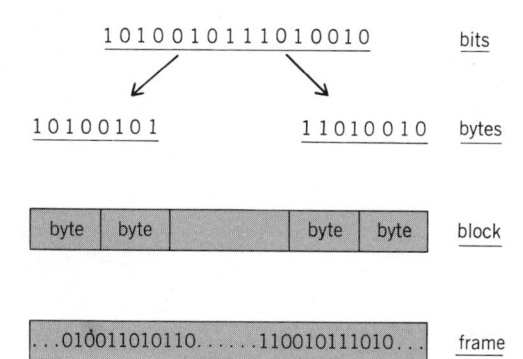

COMPUTER COMMUNICATIONS AND NETWORKS

```
                    1 0 1 0 0 1 0 1 1 1 0 1 0 0 1 0       bits
                        ↙                   ↘
                  1 0 1 0 0 1 0 1       1 1 0 1 0 0 1 0   bytes


                          | byte | byte |    | byte | byte |   block


Fig. 4. Organization of data into units suitable for   |...010011010110......110010111010...|   frame
transmission.
```

into single bytes. More complex and efficient protocols require the organization of bytes into blocks (hundreds of bytes) or bits into frames (**Fig. 4**). Blocks and frames typically begin with recognizable patterns of bytes and bits respectively. Still more sophisticated protocols include the organization and management of logical units of information ranging in size from 50 to about 1000 bytes called packets or messages.

For point-to-point transaction- or batch-oriented data communications applications involving only space displacement, little more is required of communications processing. For network applications, communications processing uses storage and processing to assure the proper addressing and formatting of packets and messages. To support time displacement, communications processing enables information to be stored for later retrieval, scheduled for later delivery, and delivered with return confirmation.

Transmission. Transmission accomplishes the physical transfer of data. It includes the provision of transmission channels, the signal conversions necessary to use such channels, and any required switching among channels.

Terminals and computers may be connected to transmission facilities via standardized interfaces. Where dedicated wire paths of up to a few miles can be established, so-called limited distance or baseband data sets (modems) enable the digital transmission of data at rates up to tens of thousands of bits per second (bps). At shorter distances, transmissions at more than 1,000,000 bits per second can be supported. Dedicated paths using optical fibers can support transmissions at rates of tens of millions of bits per second. Approaches such as infrared transmission enable open-air channels to be supported. Radio and satellite transmission are used as well.

Use of telephone network. Since it is generally impractical to install privately owned cables beyond single buildings or campus environments and because transmission distances of more than a few miles are commonly of interest, the conventional approach is to use the telephone network for transmission facilities. Where such facilities are analog (such as channels which support voice signals), modems are required to convert the digitally encoded information produced at the terminal or computer into modulated analog form, and vice versa. Where digital facilities are available at a user's location, no analog-digital conversion is necessary, but a device to assure synchronization of timing signals and to perform other control functions must be used. SEE ANALOG-TO-DIGITAL CONVERTER; DIGITAL-TO-ANALOG CONVERTER.

Channels may be provided on a dedicated (private line) or switched (dial) basis. Dedicated channels may be used for multipoint connections which serve several terminals (**Fig. 5**). For such multipoint configurations, a polling scheme is used to assure that the channel is used by only one terminal at a time. Dedicated channels are commonly available to support rates up to 56,000 bits per second. Special arrangements can result in channels to support rates of 230,400 and 1,544,000 bits per second. Dial channels typically support up to 4800 bits per second; higher rates may be supported under special circumstances.

Asynchronous and synchronous transmission. Asynchronous and synchronous modes of transmission are used. In asynchronous transmission, bytes of data are transmitted

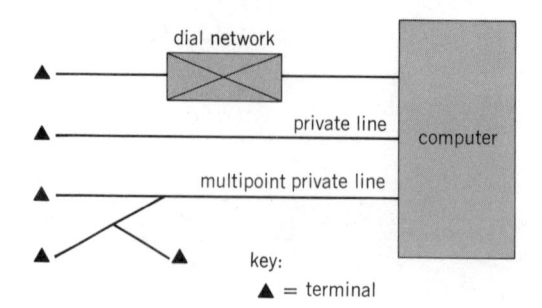

Fig. 5. Connection arrangements for terminals and computers.

independently of one another. Each byte begins with a start bit and ends with at least one stop bit. The time between bytes of data transmitted is variable. Asynchronous transmission is used at low speeds to support simple protocols used by low-cost terminals. Typical speeds are 75, 110, 134.5, 150, 300, 600, and 1200 bits per second full duplex (inboth directions simultaneously). Synchronous transmission is more efficient than asynchronous transmission and is used to support more complex and efficient protocols. There are no start or stop bits. Data bits [for bit-synchronous protocols like X.25, derived by CLITT, an international standards body] or bytes [for byte-synchronous protocols like BSC (Binary Synchronous Communications) X3.28, defined by ANSI, an American standards body] follow one another in a precisely timed and correlated way. Typical speeds for dedicated channels are 2400, 4800, 9600, 19,200, and 56,000 bits per second full duplex. Typical dial speeds are 2400 and 4800 bits per second.

Switching. To support applications where communications among multiple stations is required, data communications systems offer switching beyond that available in the dial switching capabilities of the telephone network. Circuit switching, packet switching, and message switching are the common forms (**Fig. 6**). Circuit (line) switching (Fig. 6a) results in the establishment

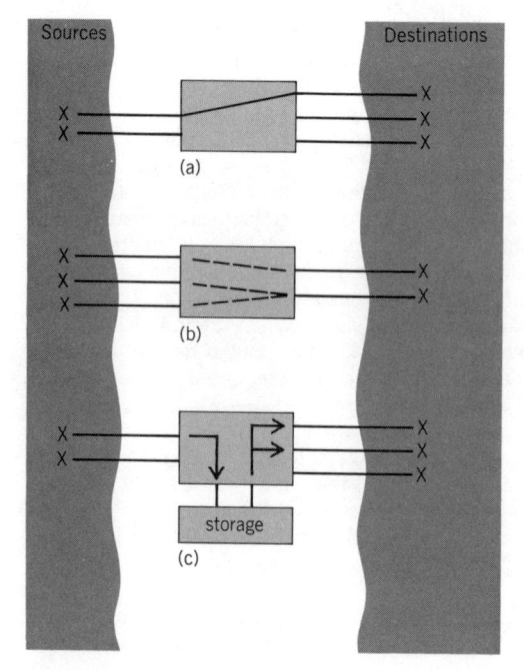

Fig. 6. Switching in data communications system. (*a*) Circuit switch. (*b*) Packet switch. (*c*) Message switch.

of point-to-point channels, single-circuit paths where there is a direct connection between the incoming and outgoing lines to the switch, for the duration of a desired transmission. It is most suitable for batch-oriented applications.

Packet switching (Fig. 6b) permits a single access channel to be used for multiple concurrent transmissions. Data to be transmitted to different destinations are formed into packets to which addresses are assigned. These packets with variable addresses are output onto a transmission channel to be switched by a packet switch to their intended destinations. Likewise, packets received on a single transmission channel may have originated at different sources. In packet switching, packets are typically received, instantaneously stored, and then retransmitted over an appropriate outgoing line. There is no direct connection between the incoming and outgoing lines as in circuit switching. It is the role of a protocol handler to multiplex (mix or intersperse) packets into a single stream of data to be transmitted and to demultiplex (sort or separate) received packets into independent streams of data. Packet switching is most suitable for short transaction-oriented transmissions where multiple concurrent transmissions must be supported between a serving computer and remote terminals.

Message switching (Fig. 6c) is most suitable for message-oriented applications. A message switch performs communications processing as well as switching in managing the storage and distribution of messages. Whereas packets are most often created for the benefit of conveying information, including messages, messages are logical entities which represent the full informational content of a transaction and thus may be manipulated in more complex ways than packets. In message switching, a message is typically received, stored, and then retransmitted over an appropriate outgoing line at an appropriate time. As in packet switching, there is no direct connection between the incoming and outgoing lines. SEE VIDEOTEXT AND TELETEXT.

Bibliography. T. C. Bartee, *Data Communications, Networks and Systems*, 1985; F. Halsall, *Introduction to Data Communications and Computer Networks*, 1986; G. Held and R. Sarch, *Data Communciations: A Comprehensive Approach*, 1984; J. D. Lenk, *Handbook of Data Communications*, 1984; K. Sherman, *Data Communications: A Users Guide*, 2d ed., 1985.

PACKET SWITCHING
PRAMODE K. VERMA

A software-controlled means of directing digitally encoded information in a communication network from a source to a destination. Switching and transmission are the two basic functions that effect communication on demand from one point to another in a communication network, an interconnection of nodes by transmission facilities (see **illus**.). Each node functions as a switch in addition to having potentially other nodal functions such as storage or processing.

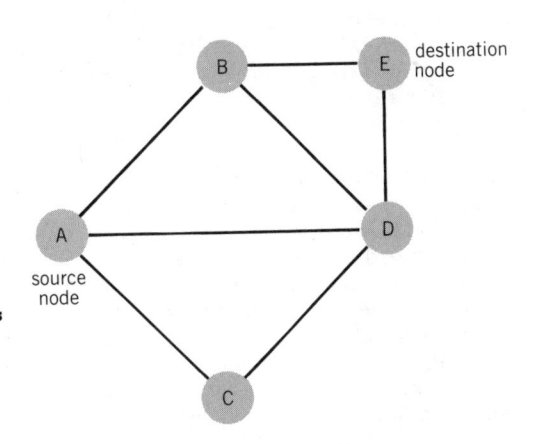

Communication network with five switching nodes interconnected by transmission facilities. Information arriving at the originating or source node can be switched to the destination node through a variety of possible end-to-end paths, for example, ABE, ADE, ABDE, ACDE.

Switching techniques. Switched (or demand) communication can be classified under two main categories: circuit-switched communication and store-and-forward communication. Store-and-forward communication, in turn, has two principal categories: message-switched communication (message switching) and packet-switched communication (packet switching).

In circuit switching, an end-to-end path of a fixed bandwidth (or speed) is set up for the entire duration of a communication or call. The bandwidth in circuit switching may remain unused if no information is being transmitted during a call. In store-and-forward switching, the message, either as a whole or in parts, transits through the nodes of the network one node at a time. As the name implies, the entire message, or a part of it, is stored at each node and then forwarded to the next.

In message switching, the switched message retains its integrity as a whole message at each node during its passage through the network from the source node to the destination node. For very long messages, this requires large buffers (or storage capacity) at each node. Also, in situations where one or more intermediate nodes are involved, the constraint of receiving the very last bit of the entire message before forwarding its first bit to the next node may result in unacceptable delays. Packet switching can be viewed as a technique which breaks a large message into fixed-size, small packets and then switches these packets through the network as if they were individual messages. This approach reduces the need for large nodal buffers and "pipelines" the resources of the network so that a number of nodes can be active at the same time in switching a long message, reducing significantly the transit delay of the original message through the network. One important characteristic of packet switching is that network resources are consumed only when data are actually sent.

Being a class of store-and-forward switching, packet switching can readily accommodate source and destination end points that are operating at different speeds within the limits imposed by the network. The underlying link-layer protocol (discussed below) in packet switching can also incorporate error detection and correction capability based on error detection by cyclic redundancy coding (CRC) and correction by retransmission of the packet in error.

Packet switching requires the use of one technique to break a message successively into smaller packets—usually 128 octets long—and another technique to reassemble the packets at the destination node, in sequence, to recreate the original message. Different packets coming from a single message could take different paths between the source and the destination nodes, although this procedure is not currently used in commercial implementations.

Packet format. The International Organization for Standardization (ISO) has formulated a conceptual model, known as the open system interconnection (OSI) model, for exchange of information between dissimilar entities. The link-layer and the network-layer protocols represent the second and the third layers in this hierarchy. Briefly, the link-layer protocol is responsible for ensuring the integrity of data across a single link. The network-layer protocol is responsible for delivering statistically multiplexed data transparently across a network.

During their passage through the network, the user data are contained within a packet which is itself contained within (link-layer) frames which are transmitted from one node to the next. The link-layer and network-layer protocols ensure that packets in error are retransmitted with their original packet numbers so that the integrity of the message is maintained as well as the integrity of the packet reassembly process.

Packet networks. The practicality and efficiency of a geographically large network using packet switching was first demonstrated in the early 1970s by ARPANET, developed by the Advanced Research Project Agency of the U.S. Department of Defense. A number of subsequent public packet networks have been developed, including Telenet and Accunet in the United States, Datapac in Canada, Transpac in France, and DDX in Japan.

All public packet networks require that terminals and computers connecting to the network use a standard access protocol such as X.25, standardized by the CCITT (International Telegraph and Telephone Consultative Committee), which is an arm of the International Telecommunication Union, an agency of the United Nations. Interconnection of one public packet network to others is carried out by using X.75, another CCITT standardized protocol.

Packet networks can provide three services: switched virtual circuits, known as virtual calls; permanent virtual circuits; and datagrams. A virtual circuit is a bidirectional, transparent, flow-controlled path between a pair of logical or physical ports. (A transparent path or connection implies that all bit patterns, including all data and control characters, will be transferred across that path without any mutilation.) A switched virtual circuit is a temporary association, while a permanent virtual circuit is a permanent association between two communicating end points (also called data terminal equipments, or DTEs) of a packet network. A datagram is a self-contained user data unit containing sufficient information to be routed to the destination DTE (independently of all other data units) without the need for a call to be established. The datagram service is not presently available on any public packet network. The standard X.25 protocol does not support datagram service.

Charges for the use of public packet networks are usually based on the number of packets (or octets) switched and, in some cases, connect time or user requests for special capabilities. This is in contrast to circuit switching where users are charged for usage of the network by connect time only.

Applications. Data communication (or computer communication) is the primary application for packet networks. Computer communication traffic characteristics are fundamentally different from those of voice traffic. Data communication at speeds from several hundred bits to 56–64 kilobits per second is quite common. Data traffic is usually bursty, lasting from several milliseconds in an inquiry response application to several minutes or hours in an application involving the transmission of long files with millions of bits. The holding time for data traffic is also widely different from one application to another. These characteristics of data communication make packet switching an ideal choice for most applications. SEE DATA COMMUNICATIONS.

The possibility of voice communication using packet switching has been explored. Packet switching can allow better use of transmission resources because unused bandwidth can be allocated to other users while a speaker is listening, saving on overall transmission resources. However, several technical factors concerning speech communication by packet switching still await economic solutions. These obstacles, coupled with the large investment in the circuit-switched public network for voice (the telephone network), make it unlikely that packet switching will find wide application for voice communication in the near future.

Bibliography. P. Baran, Some perspectives on networks past, present, and future, *Inform. Process.*, 77:459–464, 1977; P. E. Green, Jr. (ed.), *Computer Network Architectures and Protocols*, 1983; L. Kleinrock, On communications and networks, *IEEE Transac. Comput.*, C-25:1326–1335, 1979; R. D. Rosner, *Packet Switching*, 1982; J. V. St. Amand, *A Guide to Packet-Switched Value-Added Networks*, 1986; Special Issue on Packet Communication Networks, *Proc. IEEE*, vol. 66, no. 11, November 1978; Special Issue on Packet Radio Networks, *Proc. IEEE*, vol. 75, no. 1, January 1987.

LOCAL-AREA NETWORKS
NORMAN F. SCHNEIDEWIND

A system consisting of a set of nodes that are interconnected by a set of links. The nodes and links cover a relatively small geographic area, ranging from a few feet to a mile. The nodes may be terminals, microcomputers, minicomputers, mainframes, printers, hard disks, or work stations. The links may be coaxial cable, twisted-pair wires, or fiber-optic cable. SEE DATA-PROCESSING SYSTEMS; DIGITAL COMPUTER; MICROCOMPUTER.

Purposes. There are many reasons for developing and using local-area networks (LANs), including message communication, resource sharing, improved productivity, file transfer, application performance improvement, and combinations of these functions.

Message communication. With a local-area network it is possible to provide an electronic mail capability because the nodes are connected, thus allowing for the transfer of a message from one node to another. SEE ELECTRONIC MAIL.

Resource sharing. As microcomputers proliferate, it becomes increasingly expensive for management to provide every worker with a fully equipped machine, including disks, printers, modems, and software. A more economical alternative is to provide only a minimal work station capability for hundreds of workers and to provide a few expensive devices which can be shared by many users. In some cases, certain users have repositories of software and files which many users wish to access. Accessibility is improved significantly if users can access these resources electronically by file transfer from a server node (for example, a relatively expensive microcomputer which contains a hard disk and printer) to their work station or by using the server as a remote computer.

Improved productivity. Lagging productivity of office workers and professional people is of great concern to industry. One of the first steps taken to alleviate this problem was the widespread use of personal computers in the office. This movement represented only a limited attack on the problem. Although each worker had access to his or her own data, two important ingredients were missing: ability to communicate electronically with other workers and access to corporate data. Without going through an expensive mainframe, data accessibility was not available laterally from worker to worker or vertically from worker to management, and vice versa. If there is one aspect that characterizes the modern work force, it is multichannel communication. A local-area network facilitates this communication through its internodal message paths and, when equipped with the necessary hardware and software, provides communication with corporate mainframe computers.

File transfer. A frequent need of computer users is to transfer a file that is stored on one local computer to another local computer. The file may consist of a program, data, or both. There can be many reasons for doing a file transfer, including the following:

1. The program or data is needed at a particular local computer in order to execute a program.

2. The file resides on a server node and the user wants to transfer it to his or her work station. Typically, the copy at the server node is read-only in nature so that important information cannot be altered by unauthorized users; the system manager controls access and updating action. However, a copy can be transferred to the user's work station where the data can be both read and written, and the copy treated as a private file.

3. The user receives a request to transfer a file to another user.

Application performance improvement. Access to more and better software packages and hardware via a network should result in improvement of the functional performance of the user's applications. This is a principal motivation for networking. The advantage of greater accessibility to resources must be weighed against the following possible disadvantages: slower response time caused by the use of communication facilities; increased complexity of operations engendered by being a member of a local-area network; and temporary lock-out from file access to server nodes caused by concurrent multiple-user activity.

Multiple applications. Seldom is a local-area network built for a single application (for example, electronic mail) or reason, but more likely for a number of the reasons given above. Since local-area networks are built from general-purpose computers, it is possible to provide for a variety of applications in a single local-area network. Thus a user can integrate the applications of, perhaps, data-base management, electronic mail, and word processing. S*ee* D*ata*-*base management systems;* W*ord processing.*

Architectures. The three characteristics, not mutually exclusive, that differentiate local-area network architectures are control, topology, and communication technology.

Control. Control refers primarily to the techniques used for allowing access to the communications medium and resolving contention. There are three major control techniques: carrier sense, mutliple access with collision detection (CSMA/CD); token passing; and centralized switching.

In CSMA/CD systems, nodes are connected to a bus and have multiple, or concurrent, access to the communication medium (for example, coaxial cable). Nodes listen for existing transmissions to determine whether it is safe to transmit; hence, the terminology "carrier sense," or sensing the carrier. Unfortunately, this terminology is a misnomer in those local-area networks which do not use modulated transmission. If no transmission is detected, a node will transmit. Due to signal propagation delay, a node cannot be certain that no other node is transmitting. Therefore, overlapping transmissions, or collisions, can occur. Nodes are designed to detect a collision. When a nodes does so, it transmits a jam signal so that all transmitting nodes can recognize it and abort their transmission. Affected nodes probabilistically reschedule their next attempt to transmit. This technique is inexpensive and has good performance at low to medium loads; performance is significantly degraded at high loads. Due to repeated collisions, a node may be delayed in transmitting for an indefinite amount of time. (If collisions persist beyond a system-specified limit, an error is reported.) Thus there is no upper limit on response time, and performance must be described probabilisitically.

Token passing is a control technique that guarantees an upper limit on response time (that is, deterministic performance), but is more complex and expensive than CSMA/CD. This technique is used on rings and buses and uses a control message called the token for granting permission to a node to transmit. In a ring local-area network, for example, the token is rotated in the ring until a node that has data to transmit captures it. Since the node which acquires the token must release it after transmitting and the token returns to the transmitting node, every node is guaranteed to have access to the communication medium within a calculable time. Generally, this method has poorer performance than CSMA/CD at light loads (more overhead) and better performance at high loads (no collisions).

Centralized switching is used primarily in private automatic branch exchange (PABX) systems, which were first used for voice communication, and are challenging other types of local-area networks for market supremacy by emphasizing the integration of voice and data in one network. This technique is used in star configurations where all data are sent from the origin, through a switch, and out to the destination. Its performance is usually worse than the other two techniques but has the significant advantage that the telephones in every office and the switching equipment in many of them can be naturally extended for use in data communication.

Topology. Topology refers to the way in which nodes are connected. There are three major arrangements: bus, ring, and star. The mutual interdependence of the control technique and the topology of a local-area network may be demonstrated as follows:

1. When nodes are connected to a bus, they can all access the bus simultaneously; therefore, there must be an arbitration technique like CSMA/CD to referee access. An alternative is to use token passing on a bus, but this requires a complex control mechanism.

2. When nodes are connected in a ring, there is the opportunity to regulate their access to the communication medium by circulating a token in the ring which must be captured by a node in order for it to acquire the right to transmit.

3. The star topology is natural for centralized switching because every node is connected to the hub of the network; this central node performs switching and routing.

Communication technology. There are two major communication technologies: baseband and broadband. Baseband is unmodulated transmission; it transmits at the original frequency of the digital data. It is used with CSMA/CD, coaxial cable, or twisted-pair wire transmission, and a ring topology. A fiber-optic bus is also a possibility, but it is more natural to use it on a ring, as fiber-optic transmission is unidirectional. Since transmission on a bus spreads in both directions simultaneously from the source, it is difficult to control multiple reflections in a bus-type fiber-optic cable. Since baseband is unmodulated transmission and does not transmit in different frequency bands, it is usually limited to a single service (for example, data).

Broadband transmission is modulated and is based on community antenna television (CATV) technology. It is used with CSMA/CD, coaxial transmission, and bus topology. Systems can be single-cable or dual-cable. In the former, transmissions are directed to a frequency translator called the headend which converts all transmitted frequencies to higher received frequencies. The headend retransmits at the higher frequency to the receiving node. This method is necessary to distinguish transmission and reception on a single cable. It is unnecessary on a dual-cable system because one cable is used for transmitting and the other for receiving. The dual-cable system has twice the capacity of a single-cable system but it is more expensive. A feature of any broadband system is its multiservice capability. This is the result of its multichannel communication characteristic, wherein different frequency bands can be used for different services (for example, data, voice, and television).

The PABX uses a different communication technology. Pulse-code modulation is used to quantize the analog voice signal into a binary bit stream for efficient digital transmission. This method is also compatible with integrating voice with data, since the data are already in digital form and can be merged with the digitized voice information. *See Data communication.*

Bibliography. D. G. Baker, *Local Area Networks with Fiber Optic Applications*, 1986; K. C. Gee, *Introduction to Local Area Computer Networks*, 1984; A. Hopper and D. Wheeler, *Local Area Networks*, 1986; A. J. Mayne, *Linked Local Area Networks*, 2d ed., 1986; C. Ungaro, *The Local Network Handbook*, 1986.

WIDE-AREA NETWORKS
NORMAN F. SCHNEIDEWIND

Systems consisting of sets of nodes that are interconnected by sets of links. The nodes and links cover a relatively large geographic area, usually on the order of hundreds of miles. This very general definition provides a framework for describing any one of a large number of network configurations, each of which may differ in application, hardware, software and other features. For example, the nodes may be used for switching and routing messages in a communications network; the nodes in another network may be host computers which do application processing. The links in one network may be land-line cables; in another network, they may be satellite channels. In contemporary networks, it is common to find a variety of nodes and links; each type is allocated to tasks which it can do effectively. SEE DIGITAL COMPUTER.

Purposes. There are many reasons for developing and using wide-area networks (WANs), including message communication, resource sharing, remote computing, file transfer, integrated networking, application performance improvement, and combinations of some or all of these functions.

Message communication. With computer-based communication, it is possible to provide very flexible and high-speed mail systems. Messages can be sent, received, examined, forwarded, answered, stored, recalled, and deleted. Message examination may be performed by using a variety of criteria, including sender, subject, date, old, new, answered, unanswered, and key words. Sophisticated distribution lists can be composed. Users may subscribe to bulletin board services which allow them to automatically receive messages about specified subjects. SEE ELECTRONIC MAIL.

Resource sharing. A major advantage of networks is that a variety of hardware, operating systems, and software packages can be made available to a large community of users at reasonable cost. Economical operation is achieved because resources are shared by the users, who pay for services on a pro rata basis. SEE DIGITAL COMPUTER PROGRAMMING; OPERATING SYSTEM.

Remote computing. In many situations the computer hardware and software needed to do a job are not available on the user's premises. It may be possible for the user to access resources through a computer network. A key idea in networking is to make computing independent of distance. That is, except for possible differences in performance (for example, response time), it should be as convenient for a user to access a computer which is 3000 mi (4800 km) away as to access a personal computer in the user's office. Related to this idea is the objective of eliminating distance as a constraint to computing and opening up many more opportunities to satisfy computing needs than are provided by locally available resources. SEE MULTIACCESS COMPUTER.

File transfer. A frequent need of computer users is to transfer a file which is stored on one computer to another computer. The file may consist of a program, data, or both. The transfer may be from a remote computer to the user's local computer, or vice versa. There can be many reasons for doing a file transfer, including the following: (1) the program or data are needed at a particular computer in order to execute a program; (2) the user wants faster or more economical access (reduced communication line charges) to the file from his or her local computer; (3) the file may be a public-domain file which the user wants to transfer into his or her account; (4) the file may consist of operating-system software which can be used on a particular computer more effectively because of that computer's greater storage capacity or speed; or (5) the user receives a request to transfer a file to another user.

Integrated networking. Networks are frequently developed or extended to tie together a conglomerate of networks whose purpose is to provide resource sharing and communication across a variety of diverse networks. This is an extremely important activity in networking—integrating wide-area networks and local-area networks (LANs) which were built with different technologies; connecting networks to allow flow of data between nations; and extending the geographic span of networks to provide greater user accessibility. SEE LOCAL AREA NETWORKS.

Application performance improvement. A user who has access to more and better software packages and hardware via a network ought to be able to improve the functional performance of his or her applications. This is the motivation for much of networking. The advantage of greater accessibility to resources must be weighed against possibly slower response time and lower reliability caused by the use of communication facilities.

Multiple applications. Seldom is a network built for a single application (for example, electronic mail). Since networks are built from general-purpose computers, it is possible to provide for a variety of applications in a single network and to extend this concept further by internetting (that is, tieing multiple networks together). Thus the user can integrate the applications of, for example, data-base management, scientific computing, electronic mail, and word processing. S*EE* D*ATA-BASE MANAGEMENT SYSTEMS;* W*ORD PROCESSING.*

Architectures. Modern networks are designed according to standards which have been developed by international standards organizations. Standards were developed to facilitate compatibility between networks and to allow for a mix of vendor equipments in a network. The most common standard is the International Standards Organization (ISO) layered model. A layer is a partition of a network which has responsibility for a major function (for example, switching and routing). The layered concept provides the following advantages: (1) manufacturers can design their networks to implement the specifications of specific layers, thereby achieving compatibility with the standard; (2) the complicated architecture is partitioned into understandable and maintainable pieces; and (3) a hierarchical design approach is implemented, whereby a given layer N uses its functions and the services of the layer below it, $N-1$, to provide a service for the layer above it, $N+1$, analogous to the way in which human activities are organized.

ISO model. The ISO seven-layer model was developed to achieve compatibility among diverse networks developed by various vendors and nations. The model specifies what is to be accomplished by each layer; it does not specify how it is to be accomplished. Each layer specifies requirements for protocols, which are sets of rules and procedures for the exchange of information in a network. The primary functions of each layer are as follows:

1. Physical layer: Physical transmission of data between two nodes.
2. Data link layer: Reliable transmission of data between two nodes.
3. Network layer: Switching and routing across all switching nodes in the network.
4. Transport layer: End-to-end control of communication between processes, where a process is a program in execution.
5. Session layer: Opens, closes, coordinates, and monitors sessions between communicating processes. (A session consists of the activities which take place when a user processes a transaction in a computer network.)
6. Presentation layer: Formats user input data for presentation to the system and formats system data for presentation to the user.
7. Application layer: Processes user application functions.

Types of services. There are two major services offered by networks which are related to network architecture: datagram and virtual circuit.

Datagram service provides best-effort type of message delivery and is used in noninteractive applications (for example electronic mail and transaction processing where no interaction with the user is necessary). Loosely speaking, this type of service may be considered one-way transmission. Each datagram (a type of message) is transmitted independently of other datagrams. There is no relationship between datagrams; hence, there is no need to sequence them. In addition, since this is a fast, low-cost service, extensive error checking is not performed on the received data. Only the physical, data link, and network layers are needed to implement datagram service.

In contrast, virtual circuit service is for interactive processing, where sequenced, error-checked message delivery is essential for correct transmission and response of interactive commands (for example, text editing). In addition to the layers used in datagram service, virtual circuit service requires the functions of the transport layer to sequence, acknowledge, and error-check the datagrams so that the user's interactive session is executed correctly. Some networks (for example, the Defense Data Network of the Department of Defense) provide both a datagram service and a virtual circuit service, where datagram service can be used either alone or to support virtual circuit service. S*EE* D*ATA COMMUNICATIONS.*

Bibliography. D. W. Davies et al., *Computer Networks and Their Protocols*, 1979; F. Halsall, *Introduction to Data Communications and Computer Networks*, 1986; P. E. Green, Jr., *Computer Network Architectures and Protocols*, 1982; K. Sherman, *Data Communications: A User's Guide*, 2d ed., 1985; W. Stallings, *Data and Computer Communications*, 1985; A. S. Tanenbaum, *Computer Networks*, 1981; E. A. Yakubaitis, *Network Architectures for Distributed Computing*, 1983.

TELEPROCESSING
NORMAN F. SCHNEIDEWIND

A form of information handling in which a data-processing system utilizes communication facilities. The chief example of this mode of computing is computer time-sharing, which requires communication support facilities, both hardware and software. Communications support facilities will be considered in terms of the logical communications support required by the user, and the hardware or software which are required to implement communications support functions.

Logical communications support. It is important to consider any computer or communications requirement first in terms of the logical process which the user wants to perform independent of the actual physical (that is, hardware and software) means of implementation. Logical process refers to functions, operations, the sequence of operations, and characteristics of the data to be manipulated by the operations. For example, the user may require an information retrieval function consisting of systematic inquiry-response operations in which each inquiry triggers a response which may consist of one line of data presented on a terminal screen. This scenario immediately suggests a logical half-duplex operation: data can flow in both directions between terminal and computer but in only one direction at a time. This will be the case even if the hardware and software used to implement the support function are capable of full duplex operation, transmitting data in both directions simultaneously. By understanding the logic of their requirements, users are able to specify a functional requirement which will constrain the implementation to essential capabilities, thus making the installation cost-effective.

One of the major user considerations in specifying time-sharing communications support is the choice between asynchronous and synchronous communication. The contrast between the two types of communication has both logical and physical aspects. From the logical standpoint, asynchronous communication is characterized by sporadic transmissions of data from terminal to computer—independent bursts in time and content, as in inquiries made for a particular purpose. This mode can be compared to synchronous communication in which data transmissions are neither time- nor content-independent, as during file transfers between a microcomputer and a mainframe machine. This consideration has major implications concerning the nature of the hardware-software solution, as discussed below. SEE DATA COMMUNICATIONS.

Hardware. The major pieces of communications hardware which are required to support timesharing are a terminal, a modem and communication facility, and a communication controller at the mainframe computer site.

Terminal. The terminal may have line or full-screen editing capability. Line editing refers to an editing or data manipulation capability which is limited to adding or changing only one line of text with each terminal entry action, usually the carriage return. Line editing is also associated with the use of typed commands for editing lines of text. In contrast, a full-screen editing capability provides cursor-controlled editing over an entire screen of text or an entire file by scrolling to position various pages of text on the screen. By moving the cursor to various positions on the screen, numerous changes can be made prior to an entry action resulting from an Enter or Return key depression. Because of the relatively low data transmission rate and the sporadic data entry pattern, line editing terminals are typically asynchronous, whereas the block transmission format of a full-screen editing terminal demands high-speed, clock-controlled transmission as in synchronous communication. Because of the low cost of asynchronous-communication line editing, so-called dumb terminals are ubiquitous. They are designed for dial-up communication on telephone channel facilities and usually support the ASCII data code. The pervasiveness of this type of communication generates the demand for other hardware components: modems and communication facilities and controllers.

Modem and communication facility. A modem is required to convert the digital signals of the terminal to the analog signals of the telephone network and back again to the digital signals of the computer. Important modem characteristics involve choices between asynchronous or synchronous communication; half-duplex or full-duplex operation; the use of an acoustic coupler or a direct connect; and dial-up, leased line, or limited distance communication. An acoustic coupler is a type of modem which converts two frequency tones (one for binary one and one for binary zero) to the analog signal used on a telephone line, and vice versa. A direct connect, on the other hand, is a pair of wires which directly connects a terminal to a computer without going through the telephone network. In a dial-up communication service, users dial a computer service through their modems, whereas in leased-line communication a line is leased from the telephone company for guaranteed access to the computer. A limited-distance modem is used within a building for improving the signal quality when there is a long distance between the terminal and computer. This modem is not used for external communication (outside a building) on the telephone network.

The great majority of requirements are satisfied by an asynchronous, half-duplex, direct-connect, dial-up modem. Exceptions to this will occur when (1) the mainframe computer hardware requires a synchronous full-duplex protocol, (2) the terminal must be portable (requiring an acoustic coupler), (3) a leased line is used because guaranteed access is required, or (4) a limited-distance modem is installed, with telephone cable but without telephone company service, to improve communication quality. If, as in the typical case, a full-screen edit terminal is hardwired to the mainframe computer with coaxial cable, no modem is required.

Communication controller. In the planning of teleprocessing requirements, the characteristics of equipment in the mainframe computer room with which the terminal communicates are frequently overlooked. This may be a controller, front-end processor, or mainframe. The terminal and modem must be compatible with the protocol used by the mainframe or its subordinate unit, such as the controller. For example, IBM protocols are often half-duplex; ARPANET protocols are full-duplex. Communications capabilities acquired by the user must be compatible with the way that data are handled by the remote computer. Since there is a great variety of protocols, it is desirable to have communications parameters (for example, half-duplex) established and changed by menu-driven communications software, which operates in concert with the modem. However, even with this flexibility, there are some fundamental physical parameters, such as control signal frequencies, bandwidth, and modulation technique, which software cannot control. Therefore, to guarantee compatibility it is necessary that a modem conform to modem standards that were developed by the Bell System.

Software. As indicated above, an important addition to teleprocessing communications support is software for providing communications parameter management, menu-selectable commands for invoking a variety of communication protocols, and some constraints on terminal-to-mainframe file transfer. Usually these capabilities are furnished by a microcomputer which takes the place of the terminal with disk storage, an asynchronous communication adapter board installed in the microcomputer, asynchronous communications software operating in the microcomputer and compatible with its operating system, and a modem which is compatible with both the communications software and adapter. *See Microcomputer.*

Once the communication program is loaded into memory, under control of the operating system, communication parameter files may be created, modified, or invoked. After a communication file has been created, it can be invoked by entering its name at the proper place in the menu, with the result that the mainframe computer is automatically dialed, connection is established, and the modem is set to the correct communication parameters. The creation of a series of communication parameter files allows various time-sharing computer services to be contacted without any need for physical adjustments, such as changing modem switch settings. Most communication software packages provide linkages to various information retrieval services. In addition, a limited file-transfer capability is usually provided. As data are scrolled to the screen by the mainframe computer, it can be recorded in a microcomputer disk file or listed on its printer. Conversely, data from a microcomputer disk file can be recorded in a file of a mainframe computer if that file has been opened by that computer's editor and the editor is set to the insert mode, allowing the file to receive new data. *See Digital computer; Multiaccess computer; Operating system.*

Bibliography. F. Halsall, *Introduction to Data Communications and Computer Networks*, 1986; J. E. McNamara, *Technical Aspects of Data Communication*, 2d ed., 1982; W. Stallings, *Data and Computer Communications*, 1985; A. Tanenbaum, *Computer Networks*, 1981.

VIDEOTEXT AND TELETEXT
Ronald P. Uhlig

Computer communications services that take advantage of standard television receivers and use them as display terminals to retrieve information from data bases. A "black box" is placed between the television set and the signal carrier. The signal carrier may be a telephone network, a data communications network, a television cable, or a broadcast signal. The black box receives data from the signal carrier. It formats that data into a signal suitable for display on the television set. The user interacts with the black box to determine what information is actually displayed on the screen of the television set.

Both videotext and teletext use the same display technology. The difference between them is that videotext is a two-way, or interactive, service, which allows the user to interact with the service in selecting information to be displayed, while teletext is a broadcast service. In the teletext service, preprogrammed sequences of frames of data are broadcast cyclically. The user interacts with the black box to "grab" the frames of relevant information. The textual and graphic information in teletext is inserted into the "blanking period" in television signals. While select frames of information can be viewed in the teletext service, the user cannot interact with the data base.

In videotext, the black box is actually a limited computer terminal which uses the television screen for display. Both videotext and teletext provide the user with a numeric keypad for interacting with the black box. Some videotext terminals also provide, as an option, a full alphanumeric keyboard for interacting with videotext services.

In both videotext and teletext the user will normally make selections from a series of menus to select the desired information. In videotext the user may then continue to interact with the service selected.

Display alternatives. Alphamosaic, alphageometric, and alphaphotographic are three different display technologies that may be used with videotext and teletext services.

Alphamosaic, the first to be introduced, is the kind of display technology used in many video games. The screen is divided into a series of rectangular mosaic elements. The picture to be displayed is transmitted as a series of rasters, line by line, similar to the way that a basic television signal is transmitted. Both alphanumeric characters and pictures are built up from these elements, a line at a time.

Alphageometric technology is more closely related to conventional computer graphics. The alphageometric format is the basis for the Canadian Telidon technology, which has heavily influenced the American Telephone and Telegraph videotext standard for North America. This technology stores and transmits commands to draw graphic objects on the display screen. For example, the command to draw an arc will consist of a series of instructions giving the location of the center of the circle, the radius of the circle, the starting point of the arc (in degrees), and the end point of the arc. Each object to be drawn on the screen is transmitted as a series of commands. SEE COMPUTER GRAPHICS.

The alphageometric display technology gives higher-resolution images and requires lower bandwidths for data transmission than alphamosaic. However, the black box which acts as a computer terminal is more complex. It translates graphics commands into the actual display on the television screen. The alphageometric display black box does more processing than the alphamosaic black box.

Alphaphotographic display technology provides the highest resolution of the three alternatives, making it possible to incorporate full-color photographs into the data. The display quality is similar to a normal, good-quality television frame. Conceptually, there is little difference between alphaphotographic and alphamosaic technologies. However, in alphaphotographic the size of the displayed mosaic element is reduced to the minimum displayable picture element on the television tube. In practice, alphamosaic videotext systems are designed to operate at much lower bandwidths, while alphaphotographic systems require relatively high bandwidths to the videotext terminal.

The data which make up frames of information are different for each of the three display technologies. Some work has been done to allow conversion from one format to another, but one cannot generally retrieve information stored in one format and display it on a terminal equipped for a different format.

Services. A variety of information has been made available on videotext and teletext, with varying degrees of acceptance. A few examples follow.

Data-base retrieval forms a major class of videotext and teletext services. Examples include restaurant guides, hotel information, stock market information, and travel information. These are suitable for both the broadcast mode of teletext and the interactive mode of videotext.

Typically, a user might start with a menu listing categories for hotels or restaurants. Upon selecting one of the categories, the user is given a screen with more information, such as a list of four-star hotels or a list of Chinese restaurants. The user can continue a tree-structured search until the desired information is obtained.

Another major class of services is interactive, and therefore is suitable only for videotext. Examples include calculation services, electronic mail, teleshopping, and financial services. Calculation services prompt the user for inputs to a program which does the calculation and displays the result. Electronic mail generally requires a full keyboard to input the text of a message to be sent from one user to another. Teleshopping displays items a user might want to purchase, and accepts orders, like a catalog store, when the user chooses to purchase an item. A variety of financial services, such as transferring funds from one account to another, are possible. SEE ELECTRONIC MAIL.

Because of its inherent one-way broadcast nature, teletext service can be offered only on a subscription basis. However, videotext services can be charged on the basis of individual requests. This offers a real potential for stimulation of the information marketplace. SEE CONSUMER ELECTRONICS; DATA-BASE MANAGEMENT SYSTEMS; DATA COMMUNICATIONS; ELECTRONIC MAIL; MULTIACCESS COMPUTER; TELEVISION RECEIVER.

Bibliography. A. Alber, *Videotex/Teletext: Principle and Practices*, 1985; P. Hurly et al., *The Videotex and Teletext Handbook*, 1985; J. Tydeman et al., *Teletext and Videotext in the United States: Market Potential, Technology, and Public Policy Issues*, 1982; *Videotex '84 U.S.A. Proceedings*, On-Line Publications Ltd., 1984.

ELECTRONIC MAIL
Victor P. Boyd

Any of various systems that transmit some form of electronic (usually digital) representation of a page or message from one location to another. The two locations may be as close as two adjacent terminals or as far as halfway around the world. Some forms of transmission capability have existed for a long time, but the term electronic mail appeared with the computer and integrated-circuit technology explosion. The emergence of inexpensive, high-speed scanners (which convert hard copy to an electronic representation) and error-free compression (a method of reducing the transmission time required) may be the primary catalysts that created the term electronic mail. The widespread usage of this term, however, probably results from the ability of large numbers of users to create electronic messages at readily available computer terminals. SEE INTEGRATED CIRCUITS.

Because the term electronic mail is so commonly used in the field of communications, it has acquired a variety of meanings and interpretations, with regard to both the role of the originator and that of the recipient. The term has even been used to describe a communication that is received as a synthesized vocal output (voice), although this rare usage will probably not persist because, in general, electronic mail is applied to a communication that can be viewed by the recipient. The most used and meaningful definitions are discussed below.

Small computers. As late as 1970, home and small-business computers were experimental novelties; they were used mostly as stand-alones without being interconnected. Communication between such computers was either nonexistent or nearly impossible. As more people and companies became users, due primarily to decreasing costs and increasing capability, they began to see the advantages and economics of exchanging information through the electronic format in which the data existed. Software developers and common carriers were quick to make available what was needed to accomplish this interconnect capability. Most small computers are now able to communicate with one another and thus become electronic mail terminals. SEE COMPUTER; MICROCOMPUTER.

The small-business-computer industry uses the term electronic mail to des͏͏be the ability to receive on one terminal a textual message that originated on another term   ͏e output is normally a pictorial display on a computer monitor, which can be printed if ͏   ͏eiving terminal is so equipped.

Facsimile. Although the facsimile was invented in 1843 by Alexander Bain, the major practical use of a facsimile-type machine was by the wire news services to transmit pictures.

These were called by various names, including wirephoto. These machines were slow compared to current technology, but were engineering marvels in the 1930s. It was not until the mid-1960s that a more general commercial facsimile machine became available.

The major problem in utilizing these machines then was that they were relatively expensive and could only be used to communicate with identical machines, which greatly reduced their value. Also, they were slow, usually taking 6 min to transmit a single page, which led to high operational line costs. In 1980 the Consulting Committee for International Telephone and Telegraph (CCITT), an international telecommunications organization, agreed to a standard for facsimile machines which could transmit a page in less than 1 min. These were called Group 3 machines. The popularity of this form of electronic mail is due to the high quality of the output copy. SEE FACSIMILE.

The term electronic mail is used in conjunction with compatible facsimile equipment for sending and receiving of memoranda, documents, sketches, tables, and so forth. This use of the term is primarily by the equipment manufacturers, in reference to the capability of the facsimile equipment to perform that function. The output of the high-resolution machines is a close reproduction of the original.

Telegraphy. Some services which have been available for a long time, such as telegrams, Telex, and TWX, have been referred to as the first electronic mail services. They have been undergoing a major modernization and image "facelifting," with computer-controlled switching and advanced designed terminal equipment, which may justify using a modern name such as electronic mail. The output is a text-only message.

The best known of this type of electronic mail, the telegram, has been available for over 100 years. A spinoff service which can fall within this definition is the Mailgram (of Western Union), which combines a textual input with high-speed electronic transmission to over 140 locations, where a hard copy is generated, enveloped, and placed into the regular daily delivery system of the U.S. Postal Service.

Office automation systems. The modern office automation systems industry uses the term electronic mail in conjunction with the ability of their equipment to transfer correspondence. The correspondence is generated on one terminal, stored in a central file, and retrieved by another compatible terminal with access to that central file. The output of these systems is, once again, text-only, but differs from that described above in that the format usually resembles a standard typewritten correspondence page.

Such systems are growing in acceptance. They usually have a communications capability that permits all or selected terminals and printers in the system to have access to messages stored in the central processor. However, their use will remain restricted to an individual company, and not interconnected with other companies, for security reasons. SEE WORD PROCESSING.

Specially designed services. Finally, the term electronic mail is applied to specially designed services that transfer a message page from one geographic location to another by electronic communication methods. This use of the term is usually without restriction as to the type of originating equipment, but the output is normally hard copy and most often hand-delivered to the addressee in an envelope, which makes it more like traditional mail. The major drawback in any such mail service is, of course, the ability of the originator to be able to complete the delivery of the message to the recipient. An example of this problem is that if the originator uses a computer to generate the message the recipient must have a compatible computer to accept the message. To overcome this problem and still make use of today's available high-speed transmission capability and maintain lower prices, the originator often makes use of the U.S. Postal Service's daily delivery of hard-copy mail.

Bibliography. S. Connell and L. A. Galbraith, *Electronic Mail: A Revolution in Business Communications*, 1982; T. B. Cross and M. B. Raizman, *Networking: An Electronic Mail Handbook*, 1985; Eastern Management Group, *Report on Electronic Mail*, January 1984; P. L. Probst, The subminute digital facsimile explosion, *Telecommunications*, pp. 53–54, September 1982; A. Simpson (ed.), *The Office of the Future*, no. 2: *Planning for Electronic Mail*, Gower Publishing, Great Britain, 1982; P. Vervest, *Electronic Mail and Message Handling*, 1985.

7

ARTIFICIAL INTELLIGENCE

Artificial intelligence	246
Expert systems	250
Intelligent machine	254
Natural language processing	258
Computer vision	262
Speech recognition	267
Voice response	276

ARTIFICIAL INTELLIGENCE
Allen Newell

The subfield of computer science concerned with understanding the nature of intelligent action and constructing computer systems capable of such action. It embodies the dual motives of furthering basic scientific understanding and making computers more sophisticated in the service of humanity.

Many activities involve intelligent action—problem solving, perception, learning, symbolic activity, creativity, language, and so forth—and therein lie an immense diversity of phenomena. Scientific concern for these phenomena is shared by many fields, for example, psychology, linguistics, and philosophy of mind, in addition to artificial intelligence. This implies no contradiction, the phenomena being rich enough to support many starting points and diverse perspectives. The starting point for artificial intelligence is the capability of the computer to manipulate symbolic expressions that can represent all manner of things, including the programs of action of the computer itself.

The approach of artificial intelligence is largely experimental, although it contains some general principles and small patches of mathematical theory. The unit of experimental investigation is the computer program. New programs are created to explore and test new ideas about how intelligent action might be attained. Artificial intelligence lives in a world of throw-away programs; once a program has yielded its bit of scientific evidence, it is often of little further interest.

Foundations. The foundations of artificial intelligence are divided into representation, problem-solving methods, architecture, and knowledge. The four together are necessary ingredients of any intelligent agent.

Representation. To work on a task, a computer must have an internal representation in its memory, for example, the symbolic description of a room for a moving robot, or a set of algebraic expressions for a program integrating mathematical functions. The representation also includes all the basic programs for testing and measuring the structure, plus all the programs for transforming the structure into another one in ways appropriate to the task.

Many representations may be used. The task may pass through a sequence of representations with successive processing, or through alternative representations to find a good one. The representation used for a task can make an immense amount of difference, turning a problem from impossible to trivial.

Problem-solving methods. Given the representation of a task, a method must be adopted that has some chance of accomplishing the task. Artificial intelligence has gradually built up a stock of relevant problem-solving methods (the so-called weak methods) that apply extremely generally: generate-and-test (a sequence of candidates is generated, each being tested for solutionhood); heuristic search (sequences of operations are tried to construct a path from an initial situation to the desired one); hill climbing (a measure of progress is used to guide each step); means-ends analysis (the difference between the desired situation and the present one is used to select the next step); operator subgoaling (the inability to take the desired next step leads to a subgoal of making the step feasible); planning by abstraction (the task is simplified, solved, and the solution used as a guide); and matching (the present situation is represented as a schema to be mapped into the desired situation by putting the two in correspondence). An important feature of all the weak methods is that they involve search. One of the most important generalizations to arise in artificial intelligence is the ubiquity of search. It appears to underlie all intelligent action.

Architecture. A general intelligent agent has multiple means for representing tasks and dealing with them. Also required is an operating frame within which to select and carry out these activities. Often called the executive or control structure, it is best viewed as a total architecture (as in computer architecture), that is, a machine that provides data structures, operations on those data structures, memory for holding data structures, accessing operations for retrieving data structures from memory, a programming language for expressing integrated patterns of conditional operations, and an interpreter for carrying out programs. Any digital computer provides an architecture, as does any programming language. Architectures are not all equivalent, and the scientific question is what architecture is appropriate for a general intelligent agent.

In artificial intelligence, this question has taken the form of determining what language is good for programming artificial intelligence systems. Although the question is seemingly about research tools, in reality its investigation has been a search for the properties that make intelligence possible. The main development has been the list-processing languages, which embody a general homogeneous and flexible notion of symbols and symbolic structure. LISP, one of the early list-processing languages, has evolved until it functions as the common language for artificial intelligence programs. Work on high-level artificial intelligence languages has added to the architecture four notions that previously had existed only separately: (1) the goal, a data structure to be an associative focus for knowledge relevant to obtaining the desired situation; (2) a uniform data base to hold all knowledge, avoiding ad hoc encodings for each type of data; (3) pattern-directed invocation, or finding what method or process to use by matching rather than having to know its name; and (4) the incorporation of search into the fabric of the programming language, so that search can be used anywhere. *See Programming languages.*

Knowledge. The basic paradigm of intelligent action is that of search through a space of partial solutions (called the problem space) for a goal situation. The search is combinatorial, each step offering several possibilities, leading to a cascading of possibilities in a branching tree. What keeps the search under control is knowledge, which tells how to choose or narrow the options at each step. Thus the fourth fundamental ingredient is how to represent knowledge in the memory of the system so it can be brought to bear on the search when relevant.

A general intelligent system will have immense amounts of knowledge. This implies a major problem, that of discovering the relevant knowledge as the solution attempt progresses. This is the second problem of search that inevitably attends an intelligent system. Unlike the combinatorial explosion characteristic of the problem space search, this one involves a fixed, though large, data base, whose structure can be carefully tailored by the architecture to make the search efficient. This problem of encoding and access constitutes the final ingredient of an intelligent system.

Examples. Three examples will provide some flavor of research in artificial intelligence.

Games. Games form a classical arena for artificial intelligence. They provide easily defined, isolated worlds which still permit the indefinite play of reason.

All the ingredients of an artificial intelligence program can be seen in game programs. A chess program must have a representation of the current chess position. Besides the bits that describe the position, there must be procedures for analyzing the position and for making the moves to create new legal positions. All these capabilities constitute the representation. Their efficiency is important; some special computing hardware has even been designed to make them faster.

The basic method used for chess is to generate the moves and test their worth. The test is a form of heuristic search that explores the consequences of a candidate move many potential moves into the future. This search is combinatorial and much too big to accomplish without the aid of knowedge. The main technique for bringing knowledge to bear is the evaluation function, which can be applied to a position to estimate directly its chance of being on a winning path. Many features of the position are calculated, each representing a bit of chess knowledge (for instance, queens are better than pawns). Such value functions are heuristic, only approximating a correct analysis. Evaluation turns the search into hill climbing. Not all the knowledge stems from the evaluation functions; many subtleties of the search allow great improvement.

The Northwestern chess program searches about 10^6 positions per move in tournament play (about 2.5 min per move). It has played in many official tournaments against human competition and has an official U.S. Chess Federation rating of a low expert. At fast play (5 min per game) it has beaten several grand masters. The program's large search compared with that of humans (estimated at a few hundred positions at most) illustrates that exploiting the speed and reliability of computers can produce a distinctive style of problem solving.

A program for another game, backgammon, illustrates further the role of knowledge. In 1979 a program developed at Carnegie-Mellon University played an exhibition match with the world backgammon champion Luigi Villa, winning 7 points to 1. Since backgammon involves chance as well as skill, the program in fact is not the superior player, but it is definitely formidable.

The interest in the feat from an artificial intelligence point of view is twofold. First is the calibration against human talent under real conditions. Second is the mechanisms that enabled such play; these are the basic scientific contribution. In backgammon, the number of moves from a single position is so large that search is almost totally ineffective. Instead, the evaluation function must contain an immense amount of knowledge of the game. The success of the program rests in part on using separate evaluation functions during different regions of play and, moreover, adjusting the transitions between these different views so that they are smooth and continuous. Analysis reveals a general principle: discontinuous jumps in value (in crossing a boundary of two evaluation regions) inevitably lead to serious errors. The discovery of this principle, its testing by being embodied in a program, and its tentative support by the program's success form a typical example of scientific activity and progress in artificial intelligence.

Perception. Perception is the formation, from a sensory signal, of an internal representation suitable for intelligent processing. Though there are many types of sensory signals, computer perception has focused on vision and speech. Perception might seem to be distinct from intelligence, since it involves incident time-varying continuous energy distributions prior to interpretation in symbolic terms. However, all the same ingredients occur: representation, search, architecture, and knowledge. Thus, perception by computers is a part of artificial intelligence.

Speech perception starts with the acoustic wave of a human utterance and proceeds to an internal representation of what the speech is about. A sequence of representations is used: the digitization of the acoustic wave into an array of intensities; the formation of a small set of parametric quantities that vary continuously with time (such as the intensities and frequencies of the formants, bands of resonant energy characteristic of speech); a sequence of phones (members of a finite alphabet of labels for characteristic sounds, analogous to letters); a sequence of words; a parsed sequence of words reflecting grammatical structure; and finally a semantic data structure representing the final meaning.

Speech perception is difficult, because the encoding of the intended utterance by the speaker is extremely convoluted, the acoustic wave at any point being influenced in complex ways by substantial context on either side. Added to this are multiple sources of noise and variability (for example, speakers differ and vary over time). To unravel this requires search, generating hypotheses about the identity of some element in the representation (for example, a phone or a word) and then testing how well it fits with the other hypothesized elements. Several possibilities can be hypothesized at each point (and at each level of representation), the whole becoming combinatorial. Thus, knowledge about the encoding and noise at each level must be brought to bear to control the search: knowledge of speech articulation, phonological regularities, lexical restrictions, grammar, the task, and so forth.

There are speech recognition programs that recognize continuous speech with high accuracy (a few percent utterance error) from several speakers with vocabularies of about 1000 words in environments that are not too noisy, within restricted grammatical and task contexts. These higher-level restrictions are extremely important. Recent work indicates that humans are several magnitudes better than current computer systems in extracting the phonetic codes directly from the speech signal, without use of higher-level knowledge. Discovering how that happens is an active area of research. SEE SPEECH RECOGNITION.

Expert systems. Extensive experience enables humans to exhibit expert performance in many tasks, even though no firm scientific or calculational base exists and the knowledge does not exist in any explicit form. So-called expert artificial intelligence systems attempt to exhibit equivalent performance by acquiring and incorporating the same knowledge that the human expert has. Many attempts to apply artificial intelligence to socially significant tasks take the form of expert programs. Even though the emphasis is on knowledge, all the standard ingredients are present: representation of the task, methods of manipulating the representation, an architecture to make processing easy, as well as the knowledge.

An example is MYCIN, developed at Stanford University, which makes judgments on the diagnosis of bacterial infection in patients and proposes courses of therapy with antibiotics. MYCIN operates as a consultant by interacting with a physician who knows the history of the patient. The knowledge of the program is encoded in a large number of if-then rules, for example, "If the site of the culture is blood, and the identity of the organisms may be pseudomonas, and the patient has ecthyma gangrenosum skin lesions, then there is strongly suggestive evidence (.8) that the identity of the organism is pseudomonas." There are several hundred such rules, which jointly encode what expert physicians know about the signs, symptoms, and causes of disease and the effects of drugs. The program uses these rules to search for a diagnosis, letting them guide what specific knowledge it must seek from the physician about the patient.

Obtaining and codifying such hitherto implicit expert knowledge is a critical aspect of developing artificial intelligence expert programs. That entire bodies of knowledge could be embodied as sets of active if-then rules, even though they did not yet form a coherent scientific theory, has been an important discovery.

A number of expert systems (including MYCIN) have shown performance at levels of quality equivalent to average practicing professionals (for example, average practicing physicians) on the restricted domains over which they operate, as shown by careful tests. Incorporation into ongoing practice, which has not yet generally occurred, depends on many other aspects besides the intrinsic intellectual quality (for example, ease of interacting, system costs). From a scientific viewpoint, the lessons in understanding the nature of knowledge and its organization are already apparent. These expert systems illustrate that there is no hard separation between pure and applied artificial intelligence; finding what is required for intelligent action in a complex applied area makes a significant contribution to basic knowledge. *See* Expert systems.

Scope and implications. Research in artificial intelligence spreads out to explore the full range of intellectual tasks. The three areas above—games, speech, and medical diagnosis—are only a sample. Significant work has been done on puzzles and reasoning tasks, induction and concept identification, symbolic mathematics, theorem-proving in formal logic, natural language understanding, vision, robotics, chemistry, engineering analysis, and computer-program synthesis and verification, to name only the most prominent. As in any developing science, there occurs both a recurrence of the basic ideas (about representation, search, architecture, and knowledge) and the discovery of new mechanisms; both extend existing ideas and reveal limits.

Artificial intelligence has close ties with several surrounding fields. As part of computer science, it plays the role of expanding the intellectual sophistication of the tasks to which computers can be applied. Various subfields, once viewed as part of artificial intelligence, have become autonomous fields, most notably symbolic mathematics and program verification. The work on vision and speech shares its concern with signal processing with the field of pattern recognition in electrical engineering.

The relation of artificial intelligence to the study of cognitive and linguistic processes in humans is especially important. Human experimental psychology and linguistics underwent a transformation in the late 1950s, coincident with the birth of artificial intelligence, to an essentially symbolic and information-processing viewpoint. The sources were much broader than artificial intelligence, especially in linguistics, but the history of these three fields has been intertwined ever since. The relations with linguistics have been marked with controversy, but the relations with cognitive psychology (as human experimental psychology has come to be called) have been mostly symbiotic. The psychological theories of problem solving, long-term memory structure, and the organization of knowledge are essentially the theories from artificial intelligence. In fact, a new interdiscipline, cognitive science, has emerged to encompass artificial intelligence, cognitive psychology, linguistics, philosophy of mind, and cognitive anthropology.

Fascination with accomplishing mental activities by mechanical means has a long history; it became channeled into cybernetics, which had its advent in the 1940s. Cybernetics focused on the role of feedback mechanisms and on the analysis of purpose they made possible in mechanical terms. Artificial intelligence did not really begin until the emergence of the digital computer. This added to the notions of cybernetics the notions of symbolic systems and programmability; it shifted concern from the construction of simple adaptive circuits to experimentation with programs, which is still the hallmark of artificial intelligence. Many of the pioneers of digital computers and operational mathematics played some part in the prehistory of artificial intelligence: Claude Shannon, John von Neumann, Norbert Wiener, and above all Alan Turing. However, the start of the field is usually located in the last half of the 1950s, when a large amount of important work was done, associated with the names of John McCarthy, Marvin Minsky, Oliver Selfridge, Herbert Simon, and Allen Newell.

The major centers for artificial intelligence research are in the United States (primarily at Stanford, the Massachusetts Institute of Technology, and Carnegie-Mellon), but research exists in all major countries. The success in expert systems, even though only a few applications are yet in routine use, has precipitated substantial commercial activity, including the formation of many

small venture firms. Noteworthy in this regard has been the coordinated effort by the Japanese government and industry to develop a fifth-generation computer, which is to be a supercomputer designed for artificial intelligence applications. The specific design objectives for this system are extremely ambitious along multiple dimensions of computer architecture and technology, as well as artificial intelligence. However, in the light of Japan's success in capturing major industrial markets, this effort has been taken seriously by other industrial nations, such as Britain and the United States, and an increase in activity in artificial intelligence around the world has occurred.
SEE AUTOMATA THEORY; DIGITAL COMPUTER; DIGITAL COMPUTER PROGRAMMING; INTELLIGENT MACHINE; ROBOTICS.

Bibliography. E. A. Feigenbaum and P. McCorduck, *The Fifth Generation: Artificial Intelligence and Japan's Challenge to the World*, 1983; N. Nilsson, *Principles of Artificial Intelligence*, 1980; A. Newell and H. A. Simon, *Human Problem Solving*, 1972; E. Rich, *Artificial Intelligence*, 2d ed., 1987; E. Shortliffe, *Computer Based Medical Consultations: MYCIN*, 1976; P. Winston, *Artificial Intelligence*, 2d ed., 1983.

EXPERT SYSTEMS
FREDERICK HAYES-ROTH

Methods and techniques for constructing human-machine systems with specialized problem-solving expertise. The pursuit of this area of artificial intelligence research has emphasized the knowledge that underlies human expertise and has simultaneously decreased the apparent significance of domain-independent problem-solving theory. In fact, a new set of principles, tools, and techniques have emerged that form the basis of knowledge engineering.

Expertise consists of knowledge about a particular domain, understanding of domain problems, and skill at solving some of these problems. Knowledge in any specialty is of two types, public and private. Public knowledge includes the published definitions, facts, and theories which are contained in textbooks and references in the domain of study. But expertise usually requires more than just public knowledge. Human experts generally possess private knowledge which has not found its way into the published literature. This private knowledge consists largely of rules of thumb or heuristics. Heuristics enable the human expert to make educated guesses when necessary, to recognize promising approaches to problems, and to deal effectively with erroneous or incomplete data. The elucidation and reproduction of such knowledge are the central problems of expert systems.

Importance of expert knowledge. Researchers in this field suggest several reasons for their emphasis on knowledge-based methods rather than formal representations and associated analytic methods. First, most of the difficult and interesting problems do not have tractable algorithmic solutions. This is reflected in the fact that many important tasks, such as planning, legal reasoning, medical diagnosis, geological exploration, and military situation analysis, originate in complex social or physical contexts, and generally resist precise description and rigorous analysis. Also, contemporary methods of symbolic and mathematical reasoning have limited applicability to the expert system area; that is, they do not provide the means for representing knowledge, describing problems at multiple levels of abstraction, allocating problem-solving resources, controlling cooperative processes, and integrating diverse sources of knowledge in inference. These functions depend primarily on the capacity to manipulate problem descriptions and apply relevant pieces of knowledge selectively. Current mathematics offers little help in these tasks.

The second reason for emphasizing knowledge is pragmatic: human experts achieve outstanding performance because they are knowledgeable. If computer programs embody and use this knowledge, they too attain high levels of performance. This has been proved repeatedly in the short history of expert systems. Systems have attained expert levels in several tasks: mineral prospecting, computer configuration, chemical structure elucidation, symbolic mathematics, chess, medical diagnosis and therapy, and electronics analysis.

The third motivation for focusing on knowledge is the recognition of its intrinsic value. Knowledge is a scarce resource whose refinement and reproduction creates wealth. Traditionally, the transmission of knowledge from human expert to trainee has required education and internship periods ranging from 3 to 20 years. By extracting knowledge from humans and transferring it to computable forms, the costs of knowledge reproduction and exploitation can be greatly reduced. At the same time, the process of knowledge refinement can be accelerated by making the previously private knowledge available for public test and evaluation.

In short, expert performance depends critically on expert knowledge. Because knowledge provides the key ingredient for solving important tasks, it reflects many features characteristic of a rare element: it justifies possibly expensive mining operations; it requires efficient and effective technologies for fashioning it into products; and a means of reproducing it synthetically would be "a dream come true."

Distinguishing characteristics. Expert systems differ in important ways from both conventional data processing systems and systems developed by workers in other branches of artificial intelligence. In contrast to traditional data-processing systems, artificial intelligence applications exhibit several distinguishing features, including symbolic representations, symbolic inference, and heuristic search. In fact, each of these characteristics corresponds to a well-studied core topic within artificial intelligence. Often a simple artificial intelligence task may yield to one of the formal approaches developed for these core problems. Expert systems differ from the broad class of artificial intelligence tasks in several regards. First, they perform difficult tasks at expert levels of performance. Second, they emphasize domain-specific problem-solving strategies over the more general, "weak" methods of artificial intelligence. Third, they employ self-knowledge to reason about their own inference processes and provide explanations of justifications for the conclusions they reach. As a result of these distinctions, expert systems represent an area of artificial intelligence research with specialized paradigms, tools, and system-development strategies.

Accomplishments. There have been a number of notable accomplishments by expert systems: PROSPECTOR discovered a molybdenum deposit whose ultimate value will probably exceed $100 million: R1 configures customer requests for computer systems; DENDRAL supports hundreds of international users daily in chemical structure elucidation; CADUCEUS embodies more knowledge of internal medicine than any human (approximately 80% more) and can correctly diagnose complex test cases that baffle experts; PUFF integrated knowledge of pulmonary function disease with a previously developed domain-independent expert system for diagnostic consultations and now provides expert analyses at a California medical center.

Types of systems. Most of the knowledge-engineering applications fall into a few distinct types, summarized in the **table**.

Interpretation systems infer situation descriptions from observables. This category includes surveillance, speech understanding, image analysis, chemical structure elucidation, signal inter-

Generic categories of knowledge engineering applications

Category	Problem addressed
Interpretation	Inferring situation descriptions from sensor data
Prediction	Inferring likely consequences of given situations
Diagnosis	Inferring system malfunctions from observables
Design	Configuring objects under constraints
Planning	Designing actions
Monitoring	Comparing observations to plan vulnerabilities
Debugging	Prescribing remedies for malfunctions
Repair	Executing a plan to administer a prescribed remedy
Instruction	Diagnosing, debugging, and repairing students' knowledge weaknesses
Control	Interpreting, predicting, repairing, and monitoring system behaviors

pretation, and many kinds of intelligence analysis. An interpretation system explains observed data by assigning symbolic meanings to them which describe the situation or system state accounting for the data. *See Character recognition; Speech recognition.*

Prediction systems present the likely consequences of a given situation. This category includes weather forecasting, demographic predictions, traffic predictions, crop estimations, and military forecasting. A prediction system typically employs a parameterized dynamic model with parameter values fitted to the given situation. Consequences which can be inferred from the model form the basis of the predictions.

Diagnosis systems predict system malfunctions from observables. This category includes medical, electronic, mechanical, and software diagnosis. Diagnosis systems typically related observed behavioral irregularities with underlying causes by using one of two techniques. One method essentially uses a table of associations between behaviors and diagnoses, and the other method combines knowledge of system design with knowledge of potential flaws in design, implementation, or components to generate candidate malfunctions consistent with observations.

Design systems develop configurations of objects that satisfy the constraints of the design problem. Such problems include circuit layout, building design, and budgeting. Design systems construct descriptions of objects in various relationships with one another and verify that these configurations conform to stated constraints. In addition, many design systems attempt to minimize an objective function that measures costs and other undesirable properties of potential designs. This view of the design problem can subsume goal-seeking behavior as well, with the objective function incorporating measures of goal attainment. *See Computer-aided design and manufacturing.*

Planning systems design actions. These systems specialize in problems with the design of objects that perform functions. They include automatic programming, robot, project, route, communication, experiment, and military planning problems. Planning systems employ models of agent behavior to infer the effects of the planned agent activities. *See Robotics.*

Monitoring systems compare observations of system behavior to features that seem crucial to successful plan outcomes. These crucial features, or vulnerabilities, correspond to potential flaws in the plan. Generally, monitoring systems identify vulnerabilities in two ways. One type of vulnerability corresponds to an assumed condition whose violation would nullify the plan's rationale. Another kind of vulnerability arises when some potential effect of the plan violates a planning constraint. These correspond to malfunctions in predicted states. Many computer-aided monitoring systems exist for nuclear power plant, air traffic, disease, regulatory, and fiscal management tasks, although no fielded expert systems yet address these problems.

Debugging systems prescribe remedies for malfunctions. These systems rely on planning, design, and prediction capabilities to create specifications or recommendations for correcting a diagnosed problem. Computer-aided debugging systems exist for computer programming in the form of intelligent knowledge base and text editors, but none of them qualify as expert systems.

Repair systems develop and execute plans to administer a remedy for some diagnosed problem. Such systems incorporate debugging, planning, and execution capabilities. Computer-aided systems occur in the domains of automotive, network, avionic, and computer maintenance, as well as others, but expert systems are just entering this field.

Instruction systems incorporate diagnosis and debugging subsystems which specifically address student behavior. These systems typically begin by constructing a hypothetical description of the student's knowledge. Then they diagnose weaknesses in the student's knowledge and identify an appropriate remedy. Finally, they plan a tutorial interaction intended to convey the remedial knowledge to the student.

An expert control system adaptively governs the overall behavior of a system. To do this, the control system must repeatedly interpret the current situation, predict the future, diagnose the causes of anticipated problems, formulate a remedial plan, and monitor its execution to ensure success. Problems addressed by control systems include air traffic control, business management, battle management, mission control, and others.

Systems components. The **illustration** shows an idealized representation of an expert system. No existing expert system contains all the components shown, but one or more components occur in every system. The ideal expert system contains: a language processor for problem-oriented communications between the user and the expert system; a blackboard for recording

ARTIFICIAL INTELLIGENCE

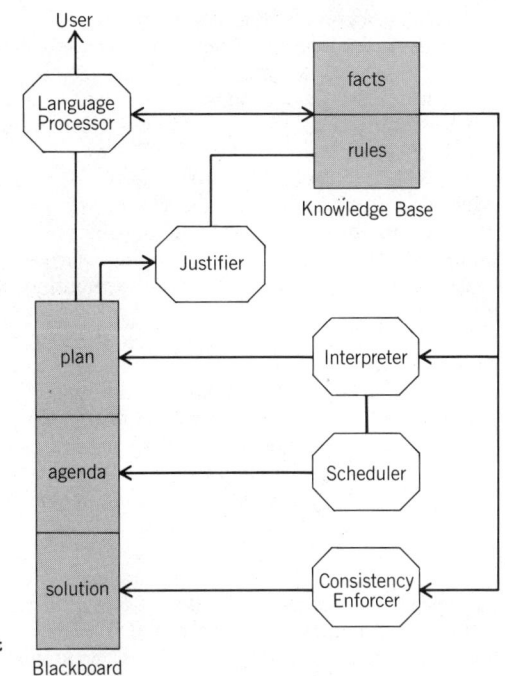

Anatomy of an ideal expert system.

intermediate results; a knowledge base comprising facts plus heuristic planning and problem-solving rules; an interpreter that applies these rules; a scheduler to control the order of rule processing; a consistency enforcer that adjusts previous conclusions when new data or knowledge alter their bases of support; and a justifier that rationalizes and explains the system's behavior.

The user interacts with the expert system in problem-oriented languages, usually some restricted variant of English, and in some cases through means of a graphics or structure editor. The language processor mediates information exchanges between the expert system and the human user. Typically, the language processor dissects, or parses, and interprets user questions, commands, and volunteered information. Conversely, the language processor formats information generated by the system, including answers to questions, explanations and justifications for its behavior, and requests for data. Existing expert systems generally employ natural language parsers written in INTERLISP to interpret user inputs, and use less sophisticated techniques exploiting "canned text" to generate messages to the user. *See Programming languages.*

The blackboard is a global data base that records intermediate hypotheses and decisions which the expert system manipulates. Every expert system uses some type of intermediate decision representation, but only a few explicitly employ a blackboard for the various types of ideal expert system decisions. The illustration shows three types of decisions recorded on the blackboard: plan, agenda, and solution elements. Plan elements describe the overall or general attack the system will use to solve the current problem, including current plans, goals, problem states, and contexts. For example, a plan may recommend processing all low-level sensor data first; formulating a small number of most promising hypotheses; refining and elaborating each of these hypotheses until the best one emerges; and, finally, focusing exclusively on that candidate until the complete solution is found. This kind of plan has been incorporated in several expert systems. The agenda elements record the potential actions awaiting execution. These generally correspond to knowledge-base rules which seem relevant to some decision placed on the blackboard previously. The solution elements represent the candidate hypotheses and decisions that the system has generated thus far, along with the dependencies, called links, that relate decisions to one another.

The scheduler maintains control of the agenda and determines which pending action should be executed next. Schedulers may utilize considerable abstract knowledge, such as "do the most profitable thing next" and "avoid redundant effort." To apply such knowledge, the scheduler needs to prioritize each agenda item according to its relationship to the plan and to other solution elements. To do this, the scheduler generally needs to estimate the effects of applying the potential rule.

The interpreter executes the chosen agenda item by applying the corresponding knowledge-base rule. Generally, the interpreter validates the relevance conditions of the rule, binds variables in these conditions to particular solution blackboard elements, and then makes rule-prescribed changes to the blackboard. Interpreters of this sort are generally written in LISP because of its facilities for manipulating and evaluating programs. However, other languages are also suitable.

The consistency enforcer attempts to maintain a consistent representation of the emerging solution. This may take the form of likelihood revisions when the solution elements represent changing hypothetical diagnoses and when some new data are introduced. Alternatively, the enforcer might implement truth maintenance procedures when the solution elements represent changing logical deductions and their truth-value relationships. Most expert systems use some kind of numerical adjustment scheme to determine the degree of belief in each potential decision. This scheme attempts to ensure that plausible conclusions are reached and inconsistent ones avoided.

The justifier explains the actions of the system to the user. In general, it answers questions about why some conclusion was reached or why some alternative was rejected. To do this, the justifier uses a few general types of question-answering plans. These typically require the justifier to trace backward along blackboard solution elements from the questioned conclusion to the intermediate hypotheses or data that support it. Each step backward corresponds to the inference of one knowledge-base rule. The justifier collects these intermediate inferences and translates them to English for presentation to the user. To answer "why not" questions, the system uses a heuristic variant of this technique. Supposedly, it can identify a possible chain of rules that would reach the questioned conclusion but which did not apply because the relevance condition of some rule failed. The justifier explains the system's decision to reject a possible conclusion by claiming that such failed conditions impede all reasoning chains that can support the conclusion.

Finally, the knowledge base records rules, facts, and information about the current problem that may be useful in formulating a solution. While the rules of the knowledge base have procedural interpretations, the facts play only a passive role. SEE ARTIFICIAL INTELLIGENCE; DATA-PROCESSING SYSTEMS.

Bibliography. P. Harmon and D. King, *Expert Systems: Artificial Intelligence in Business*, 1985; P. Klahr and D. A. Waterman, *Expert Systems: Techniques, Tools, Applications*, 1986; R. I. Levine, D. E. Drang, and B. Edelson, *A Comprehensive Guide to AI and Expert Systems*, 1986; W. J. Van Melle, *System Aids in Constructing Consultation Programs*, 1981; R. Webster and L. Miner, Expert systems: Programming problem-solving, *Technology*, 2(1):62–73, 1982.

INTELLIGENT MACHINE
JOHN F. JARVIS

Any machine that can accomplish its specific task in the presence of uncertainty and variability in its environment. The machine's ability to monitor its environment allowing it to adjust its actions based on what it has sensed, is a prerequisite for intelligence. The term intelligent machine is an anthropomorphism in that intelligence is defined by the criterion that the actions would appear intelligent if a person were to do it. A precise, unambiguous, and commonly held definition of intelligence does not exist.

Examples of intelligent machines include industrial robots equipped with sensors, computers equipped with speech recognition and voice synthesis, self-guided vehicles relying on vision rather than on marked roadways, and so-called smart weapons, which are capable of target identification. These varied systems include three major subsystems: sensors, actuators, and control.

The class of computer programs known as expert systems is included with intelligent machines, even though the sensory input and output functions are simply character-oriented communications. The complexity of control and the mimicking of human deductive and logic skills makes expert systems central in the realm of intelligent machines. *See* EXPERT SYSTEMS; ROBOTICS; SPEECH RECOGNITION; VOICE RESPONSE.

Intelligent control. Since the physical embodiment of the machine or the particular task performed by the machine does not mark it as intelligent, the appearance of intelligence must come from the nature of the control or decision-making process that the machine performs. Given the centrality of control to any form of intelligent machine, intelligent control is the essence of an intelligent machine. The control function accepts several kinds of data, including the specification for the task to be performed and the current state of the task from the sensors. The control function then computes the signals needed to accomplish the task. When the task is completed, this also must be recognized and the controller must signal the supervisor that it is ready for the next assignment (**Fig. 1**).

Automatic, feedback, or regulatory systems such as thermostats, automobile cruise controls, and photoelectric door openers are not considered intelligent machines. Several important concepts separate these simple feedback and control systems from intelligent control. While examples could be derived from any of the classes of intelligent machines, robots will be used here to illustrate five concepts that are typical of intelligent control. (1) An intelligent control system typically deals with many sources of information about its state and the state of its environment. A robot may contain a vision system and tactile sensors in addition to the internal position sensors that allow calculation of its spatial location. Given multiple sources of information, the intelligent control function evaluates them as needed based on the nature of the functions that must be performed at any instant. (2) An intelligent control system can accommodate incomplete or inconsistent information. For example, a robot expecting to pick up a single object from a conveyor belt may be confronted with two overlapping objects or no objects. (3) Intelligent control is characterized by the use of heuristic methods in addition to algorithmic control methods. A heuristic is a rule of thumb, a particular solution or strategy to be used for solving a problem that can be used for only very limited ranges of the input parameters. A possible heuristic for solving a particular robot-implemented insertion task would be to move the part incrementally along an outward spiral path, retrying the insertion, if the original attempt should fail. This heuristic could be repeated many times until an area large compared to positional uncertainties was covered. Clearly, such a heuristic is applicable only to a very small fraction of robot tasks. (4) An intelligent machine has a built-in knowledge base that it can use to deal with infrequent or unplanned events. An intelligent robot would have mechanisms, both sensors and heuristics, ensuring its own and its operator's

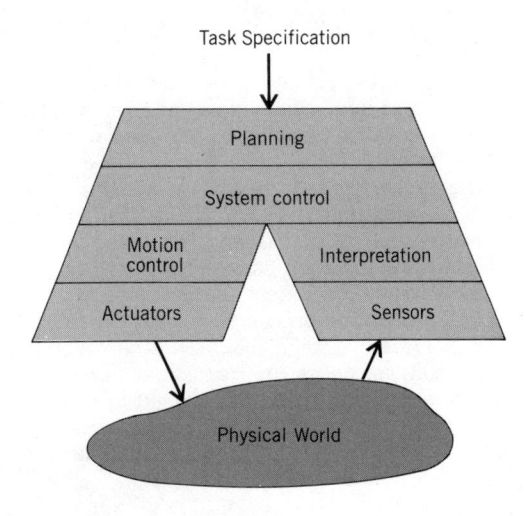

Fig. 1. Flow of information and data in a typical intelligent machine.

safety. (5) An algorithmic control approach assumes that all relevant data for making decisions is available. The heuristic approach is predicted on the knowledge that all relevant data cannot be made available, even in principle, and that the control system will have to resolve ambiguous cases.

Intelligent robots. To clarify these very general concepts and to illustrate them with more detail, a sensor-equipped robot performing an electronics assembly task will be described. The task is to pick a part from an egg-carton-like pallet, inserting it into a test fixture, and, if it tests acceptably, to insert it into the appropriate place on the printed wiring board being assembled. A human worker, especially one with some experience in production line assembly, could be instructed in this task in a few minutes and would also know, without further instruction, what actions to take for the many exceptional conditions that can arise in this type of activity. Outlining the steps that must be taken to program a robot to accomplish the same task will illustrate the amount of prior knowledge possessed by a person and the general level of complexity of programming in an environment where all relevant data and actions must be stated completely and unambiguously. The robot program will be given in verbal outline form rather than coded in a particular robot programming language. The numbers are used both for specifying branches in the flow of control and for referencing in the discussions that follow.

1. Wait for a printed wiring board to enter the assembly station.
2. Take an image of the parts presentation pallet: an egg-carton arrangement that separates and loosely orients the parts.
3. Locate a part in the image.
4. If the pallet is empty, move it to the stacking area and signal the conveyor to move a fresh pallet into position. Resume at step 2.
5. If a part is present, pick up the part and position it in the visual inspection station. Take an image of the bottom of the part. Determine the location and orientation of the pin field.
6. If an incorrect pin field is seen, deposit the part in the reject bin and resume at step 2.
7. If the pin field is correct, orient the robot hand based on the observed orientation of the part and insert the part into the electrical test station.
8. Signal the electrical test to begin.
9. If the test fails, remove the part from the test fixture and deposit it in the reject bin. Then resume at step 2.
10. If the electrical test was passed, regrasp the part to ensure it is accurately held by the robot. Remove it from the test fixture and move it to a point just above the insertion location on the printed wiring board.
11. Insert the part in the printed wiring board by moving it vertically downward while monitoring the force. When the vertical force reaches a specified value, stop the robot's vertical motion.
12. Check the vertical position of the robot hand when it stopped moving. If it is at a height indicating that the part was inserted, release the part, retract the robot hand, and resume at step 1.
13. If the part was not inserted correctly, move the robot hand in the plane of the printed wiring board by a small increment along a prescribed path and resume at step 11.

Several comments can be made about a robot that is following the above program and the program itself. Such a robot would appear to be intelligent given the definition in the beginning of the article. There is variability in the robot's environment, and it is using a variety of sensory data to guide its actions. However, the program is incomplete. There are many things that can go wrong that have not been accounted for: If a hole in the printed wiring board for the part is missing, the insertion cannot be successfully accomplished. In this case, program steps 11, 12, and 13 form an apparent infinite loop. Many other similar problems lurk in this program. The program also presupposes significant capabilities and data in the robot and related vision system. The vision system and robot must be calibrated; that is, a procedure must be periodically executed that calculates the transformations between the robot and vision system coordinates. The vision system must be programmed to recognize first what the part looks like in the context of the pallet (step 3) and second what a correct pin field looks like (step 5). The precise locations of all points of reference for the robot must be determined. The search strategy to be followed if the part is not inserted correctly (step 13) must be carefully defined. The calibration and teaching programs required to accomplish these steps may be as complex as the primary task.

Execution of the assembly program and all of the implied subsidiary functions defines the control capability of the robot. The threshold of intelligent control is reached when the system can deal with many of the infrequent and exceptional conditions without requiring outside intervention or assistance. A second part of intelligent control is the development of the detailed programs given a high-level statement of the task requirements. This is the planning function (Fig. 1). Systems of this level of complexity are primarily found in robotics research laboratories. The automatic planning of complex robot control programs given high-level task descriptions is an area of research.

Control hierarchy. The control function in an intelligent machine is generally implemented as a hierarchy of processes. The upper levels are responsible for global decision-making processes and for the planning phases of the task. The lower levels implement critical time-dependent subtasks. In **Fig. 2** the interconnection of a group of processors forming a vision-controlled robot is diagrammed. The manipulator arm is itself controlled by a two-level hierarchy. The lower level consists of a processor that performs the servo function for each joint of the arm. The robot controller converts world coordinates supplied by the system controller into the values for each joint required to place the robot hand in the desired location. The robot controller also divides complete movement specifications into a series of short steps that result in coordinated motion and controlled velocity of the robot. *See* SERVOMECHANISM.

The control program outlined in the robot example would be executed on the system-level control processor. In addition to the vision, manipulator, and safety subsystems, the system-level controller would also be the interface with the robot operator and the factory communications system. The partitioning of subtasks onto autonomous communicating processors is a natural and economic way to obtain increased system performance by using multiple microprocessors. *See* MICROPROCESSOR.

Computer vision. A computer vision system interprets the contents of a large array (256 × 256 is common) of intensity values that is the computer representation of a frame of a television

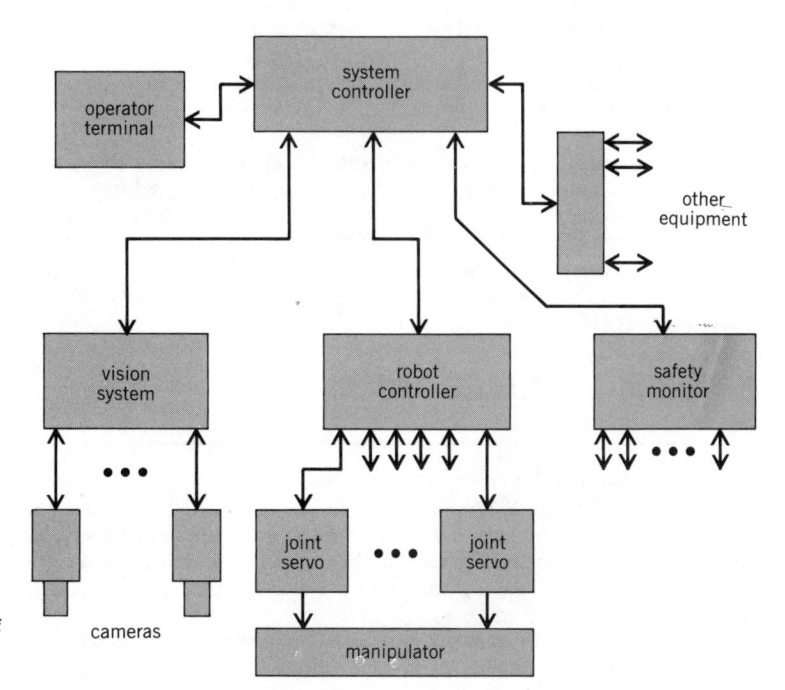

Fig. 2. Interconnection of processors forming a sensor-based robot.

image. Interpret in this context means to find, recognize, or inspect a prespecified object or group of objects. The first processing step is to isolate or segment the image of the object from the background image. The most common technique in use is to create a high-contrast image, typically by backlighting the object of interest, which allows a simple threshold to be used for the segmentation. Objects in the image are found at those locations where the intensity value is less than some prespecified constant. Lower-contrast images, such as a part in a pallet, require segmentation techniques that rely on rapid changes in brightness (edges) or differences in intensity between two images, or techniques that look for specific visual features by using any of a large number of matched filter techniques. The amount of computation required to segment a low-contrast image is significantly greater than that required by thresholding. Once an object image is segmented from the background, a set of parameters known as features is calculated. The set of features, which may include the object area, perimeter, number of holes and any other enumerable parameter, is compared to a model of the object either to ascertain its identity or to compare it to some inspection criteria. The specific set of features needed for a specific visual recognition problem depends on the exact appearances of the objects in complex ways with the result that the feature set is normally determined empirically. Similarly, orientation and location quantities are also computed for the segmented image. Generally, an image represents a two-dimensional projection of a three-dimensional object. Correction to the perceived shape and location may have to be made based on its location relative to the viewing camera. No matter what complexity of techniques are used in its construction, a computer vision system is invariably implemented with a dedicated processor.

Expert systems. The control schemes outlined above are algorithmic even if the resulting system behavior appears intelligent. The explicit programming methods described do not lend themselves to situations where several alternative actions could be rationally considered. In the explicit programming of a complex task, there is very little opportunity to use default actions for many infrequent conditions. The method of expert systems is expected to provide a paradigm for a better way of robot task planning and execution. Expert systems consist of a knowledge base and an inference procedure for obtaining a result consistent with the contents of the knowledge base, given an arbitrary set of input conditions. The knowledge base is represented by a collection of condition-action statements (rules). The primary difficulties are in obtaining an adequate collection of rules for the task and in defining an appropriate strategy for resolving inconsistencies or ambiguities when applying rules to a given problem. A specific robot task would be programmed by adding a set of rules, describing the particular operation to be formed, to an existing, and probably much larger, set of rules that defined the default and exception-handling behavior of the robot. SEE EXPERT SYSTEMS.

Interconnection of machines. Another trend expected in the area of intelligent machines is their interconnection into cooperating groups to address larger tasks. Standardization of information exchange protocols and languages describing various fields of work are prerequisites to any extensive development of interconnected, cooperating systems.

Slow, steady improvements may be expected in intelligent machine capabilities. Progress will follow in microprocessors with the availability of other functions implemented as very large-scale integrated (VLSI) circuits. SEE INTEGRATED CIRCUITS.

NATURAL LANGUAGE PROCESSING
BONNIE WEBBER

Computer analysis and generation of natural language text. The goal is to enable natural languages, such as English, French, or Japanese, to serve either as the medium through which users interact with computer systems such as data-base management systems and expert systems (natural language interaction), or as the object that a system processes into some more useful form such as in automatic text translation or text summarization (natural language text processing). SEE DATA-BASE MANAGEMENT SYSTEMS.

In the computer analysis of natural language, the initial task is to translate from a natural language utterance, usually in context, into a formal specification that the system can process further. Further processing depends on the particular application. In natural language interaction, it may involve reasoning, factual data retrieval, and generation of an appropriate tabular, graphic, or natural language response. In text processing, analysis may be followed by generation of an appropriate translation or a summary of the original text, or the formal specification may be stored as the basis for more accurate document retrieval later. Given its wide scope, natural language processing requires techniques for dealing with many aspects of language, in particular, syntax, semantics, discourse contest, and pragmatics. (Analysis and generation of spoken natural language, not discussed in this article, also involve techniques for dealing with acoustic phonetics, phonology, stress, and intonation.) SEE SPEECH RECOGNITION; VOICE RESPONSE.

Parsing. The aspect of natural language processing that has perhaps received the most attention is syntactic processing, or parsing. Most current techniques for parsing an input string of words involve (1) a description of the allowable sentences of the language (the grammar); (2) an inventory of the words of the language with their inflectional, syntactic, and possibly semantic properties (the lexicon); and (3) a processor which operates on the grammar, the lexicon, and the input string (the parser). This processor (1) simply accepts the input string, if grammatically well formed, or rejects it (a recognizer); (2) associates the string, if well formed, with its structure (or structures, if ambiguous) according to the grammar (an analyzer); or (3) associates the string with some other representation, for example, a semantic characterization (a transducer). Syntactic processing is important because certain aspects of meaning can be determined only from the underlying structure and not simply from the linear string of words.

One of the oldest parsing techniques, called augmented transition networks (ATNs), grew out of a system for parsing context-free (CF) languages, called recursive transition networks (RTNs). A recursive transition network parser consists of a set of named graphs or networks, each consisting of a set of nodes or states connected by a possibly ordered set of directed labeled arcs. The labels correspond to (1) words or classes of words that can be recognized or "consumed" on the arc; (2) the empty symbol, indicating an arc that can be taken without consuming any input; or (3) the name of a network, which indicates that the next segment of the input string must be recognizable by that network. Each network has a start state and one or more end states. If the parser can move through a network from start to end by consuming a segment of the input string, that segment is said to be recognizable by that network. SEE GRAPH THEORY.

An augmented transition network adds to the basic recursive transition network framework the ability to set and test variables or registers, thereby giving it the power to recognize a wider class of languages than a recursive transition network. An augmented transition network is appearing because its grammar is relatively easy to specify. Its weaknesses lie in the simple, uniform control structure provided by the basic augmented transition network (that is, unguided backtracking) and in its power, felt to be more than is needed for recognizing a natural language.

Current trends are to construct parsers and grammars which appear to follow more closely human parsing strategies and which have less power. In particular, researchers have begun to give almost context-free descriptions of natural languages, thereby allowing them to use slightly extended versions of efficient context-free parsing techniques. Such descriptions include generalized phrase structure grammar (GPSG), immediate dominance/linear precedence (ID/LP) grammar, and tree adjoining grammar (TAG).

Semantic analysis. A second phase of natural language processing, semantic analysis, involves extracting context-independent aspects of a sentence's meaning. These include the semantic roles played by the various entities mentioned in the sentence. For example, in the sentence "John unlocked the toolbox," "John" serves as the agent of the unlocking and "the toolbox," serves as the object; in "This key will unlock the toolbox," "this key" serves as the instrument. Context-independent aspects of sentence meaning also include quantificational information such as cardinality, iteration, and dependency. For example, in the sentence "In every car, the mechanic checked to see that the engine was working," the checking is iterated over each car; the identity of the engine depends on the identity of the car, while that of the mechanic does not; and the cardinality of engines per car is one. Thus there are as many engines as cars, but possibly only one mechanic. The representational formalism used by the system for semantic analysis (for example, first-order predicate calculus, case grammar, conceptual frames, procedures, and so forth) is usually chosen for its ability to convey those aspects of semantics that the system requires for later processing. For example, if temporal position (past/present/future) is not significant, it will not be captured in the formalism.

Most semantic analysis is done by applying pattern-action rules either during parsing or afterward. The pattern part of a rule consists of clauses, each of which specifies the presence of a particular lexical item, usually the head of some syntactic substructure (for example, the main verb of a clause or sentence or the head noun of a noun phrase); or a particular syntactic substructure (for example, a relative clause, to be interpreted as a restriction on the class described by the rest of the noun phrase). A pattern clause may also specify a test on another part of the current substructure. The action part of a rule usually calls for building a piece of semantic representation, often requiring the semantic analysis of some other part of the syntactic substructure. For example, there may be a pattern-action rule associated with "unlock" as the main verb of a clause. A test in the pattern may require that the subject of the clause be interpretable as an animate agent. The rule's action may call for the inclusion of a conceptual frame for the concept "unlock" as part of the semantic representation of the sentence. The rule's action may further specify that the agent role of the frame be filled by the semantic interpretation of the subject of the clause, and that the object role be filled by the semantic interpretation of the direct object. In some systems, a rule can have optional pattern clauses and actions: thus, the rule pattern for "unlock" might optionally specify a "with" prepositional phrase whose noun phrase object can be interpreted as a tool. If so, the rule action might additionally call for instantiating the instrument role in the frame with the semantic interpretation of the prepositional phrase object.

Contextual analysis. Given that most natural languages allow people to take advantage of discourse context, their mutual beliefs about the world, and their shared spatio-temporal context to leave things unsaid or say them with minimal effort, the purpose of a third phase of natural language processing, contextual analysis, is to elaborate the semantic representation of what has been made explicit in the utterance with what is implicit from context. Two major linguistic devices that contextual analysis must deal with are ellipsis and anaphora.

Ellipsis. Ellipsis involves leaving something unsaid. To handle ellipses computationally, techniques are required for recognizing that something is indeed missing and for recovering the ellipsed material. When the utterance is a sentence fragment and not a complete sentence, it is fairly easy to recognize that something is missing. An example appears in the following sequence:

User: What is the length of the JFK?
System: ⟨some number of feet⟩
User: The draft?

On the other hand, since parsers are usually designed for well-formed input, either the system's grammar must be revised to accept sentence fragments or a special error-recovery routine must take over after the parser fails. When an utterance is syntactically well formed, it may still be elliptic in that some needed conceptual material is missing, as in the following example:

User: What maintenances were performed on plane 3 in May 1971?
System: ⟨list of maintenances⟩
User: What maintenances were performed on plane 48?

In the user's second question, the time period of interest is missing, and the question should not be answered until it is recovered. (It is clearly May 1971.)

The primary technique for recovering ellipsed material is a simple one, based on semantic features. For sentence fragment ellipses, the previous discourse is searched for the most recent utterance containing a constitutent with the same features as the fragment. The utterance minus that constituent is taken as the ellipsed material. For conceptual ellipses in a syntactically well-formed sentence, the previous discourse is searched for the most recent utterance with a constituent having the required semantic features. That constituent is taken to be the ellipsed material. In each case, a new well-formed sentence is then constructed and processed as if the ellipsis had never occurred. For instance, in the first example, both "length" and "draft" are properties of ships. Thus, given the fragmentary utterance "The draft?," What is ____ of the JFK?" is found as the ellipsed material. The question "What is the draft of the JFK?" is then interpreted and answered normally. This technique works often, but does not constitute a general solution. A more powerful solution has been developed based on recognizing a user's goals in producing an utterance, but has been found conputationally efficient only in very narrow task-oriented domains. This will be discussed below.

Anaphora. Anaphoric expressions are very simple words or phrases which cospecify something previously evoked by the discourse or are strongly associated with something so evoked. Instances of anaphora include definite pronouns such as "he," "she," "it," "they," and definite noun phrases such as "the mechanic" and "the cars." The problem is that anaphora can be interpreted only in context, and the semantic interpretation of a sentence is not complete until all anaphoric expressions are resolved and the cospecified entities identified.

Early computational approaches to anaphora resembled those for dealing with ellipses: entities described in previous sentences were searched for the most recently mentioned one with appropriate semantic features. Now recency has been replaced by the notion of focus as a basis for anaphora resolution. Immediate focus reflects the particular thing the speaker is talking about; global focus involves things associated with it or in which it participates, and gives a sense of what may be talked about next. Techniques have been developed for tracking immediate focus, projecting ahead from the current utterance what may be focused on in the next one. This is useful for resolving anaphora, in that it predicts what entities are likely to be respecified anaphorically.

Pragmatics. A fourth phase of natural language processing, pragmatics, takes into account the speaker's goal in uttering a particular thought in a particular way—what the utterance is being used to do. In an interaction, this will influence what constitutes an appropriate response. For example, an utterance which has the form of a yes/no question or an assertion may have the goal of eliciting information (for example: "Do you know how to delete a control-Z?," "I can't get the set file protection command to work."). Because it is inappropriate (and possibly at times dangerous) to take a user's utterances literally or to assume that the user will take those of the system literally, computational techniques must be devised for relating the syntactic shape and semantic content of an utterance to its pragmatic function.

Plan recognition. One important approach to this problem has been to view language understanding as plan recognition. The actions (either communicative or physical) that constitute the plan may be motivated in one of two ways: goals in the world that the person wants to accomplish, for which he or she needs to elicit or offer aid or information; or aspects of an already ongoing interaction that need attention—for example, confusion over the speaker's foregoing utterance may lead the listener to seek clarification.

A user seeking particular information from the system illustrates clearly a plan-recognition approach to language understanding. The user's utterance—a well-formed sentence or an ellipsed fragment—is taken as a request for information that the user believes he or she needs in order to accomplish some goal, a goal which is not as yet presumed to be known to the system. Just as a medical diagnosis system uses rules which link findings back to those diseases which commonly manifest them, the plan-recognition system uses rules which link utterances back to those domain goals which need the intended information in order to be achieved. For example, consider the utterance "The train to Windsor?" made to a system serving as train information clerk. The system interprets this as a request: the user wants to know some property of that train in order to fulfill his or her goal. The system then tries to figure out what that goal is, in order to figure out what information the user might be requesting. There are only two possible goals considered: meeting a train and boarding one. The description "train to X" does not match that of incoming train, so the user's goal is taken to be boarding the Windsor train. To board a train, one needs to know its departure time and track. Since the system does not have evidence of the user's knowing either of these properties, it responds with both: "It leaves at 3:15, from track 7." Currently, it is only by limiting the domain, and hence the range of possible goals the system needs to consider, that such a plan-based approach to pragmatics and natural language processing becomes feasible.

Cooperative principle. Because pragmatics acknowledges language use, it also acknowledges expectations that speakers and listeners have about the form and content of utterances, based on normal conventions of use. This has been well described by the philosopher Paul Grice, who noted that speakers acknowledge a "cooperative principle" of conversation (by either upholding it or purposely flouting it), which he further specified in terms of conversational maxims of quantity, quality, manner, and relation. For example, the quantity maxim states: "Make your contribution as informative as is required (for the current purposes of the exchange). Do not make it more informative than is required."

The cooperative principle and its maxims are important to natural language processing because, if a system does not behave in accord with normal conventions of use, the user is likely to be confused or misled by the system's behavior. Conversely, if the system does not interpret the user's behavior in terms of normal conventions of use, the system is unlikely to understand the user correctly, if at all. In particular, the cooperative principle and its maxims reveal a method of implicit communication which Grice termed implicature. An implicature is basically an aspect of an utterance's interpretation which makes no contribution to its truth value (that is, semantics) but constrains its appropriateness in discourse. For example, consider the following discourse:

Q: Is there a gas station on the next block?
R: Yes.

The simple "yes" answer implicates to Q that, as far as R knows, the gas station is able to provide its normal services and hence fulfill Q's probable goal. Q reasons that if R knew that the gas station was closed and hence could not fill Q's needs, R would have said so: that is, R would have said "Yes, but it's closed." Thus a system must be as aware of implicatures (both the user's and its own) as it is aware of what is communicated explicitly.

Overall organization. As for fitting the pieces together, there is no single way that natural language analysis is done. Some systems have a single processor for syntactic, semantic, contextual, and pragmatic analysis, with no distinction made as to the source of that knowledge. Some systems keep the knowledge sources separate but apply them simultaneously, extracting whatever can be derived at the moment and using whatever information is available. Other systems are very modular, separating the knowledge sources and specifying when they should be applied. Efficiency, extensibility, and transportability are some of the important issues to be considered when evaluating a system for natural language analysis.

Natural language generation. The bulk of early research in natural language processing was formerly directed at natural language analysis. Now researchers have taken up seriously the task of natural language generation. Generation is not just the reverse of analysis because the status of user and system are fundamentally different. Systems can be developed which tolerate users' mechanical errors (for example, spelling, typing, and grammatical mistakes), treating them as insignificant variations. Users, on the other hand, may not be able to figure out which aspects of the system's natural language behavior reflect simple nonfluencies (for example, those due to limited lexical or grammatical options) and which embody significant aspects of communication. Moreover, the system's sense of language must be more highly developed for generation, lest it confuse or mislead the user by what it communicates or how. Work on explanation is also a significant aspect of natural language generation. SEE ARTIFICIAL INTELLIGENCE.

Bibliography. B. G. Bara and G. Guida, *Computational Models of Natural Language Processing*, 1984; R. E. Cullingford, *Natural Language Processing: A Knowledge Engineering Approach*, 1985; B. Grosz et al. (eds.), *Readings in Natural Language Processing*, 1986; *Proceedings of the Association for Computational Linguistics*; *Proceedings of the International Conference on Computational Linguistics*; H. Tennant, *Natural Language Processing*, 1981; T. Winograd, *Language as a Cognitive Process*, 1982.

COMPUTER VISION
R. C. GONZALEZ

The use of digital computer techniques for extracting, characterizing, and interpreting information in visual images of a three-dimensional world; it is also known as machine vision. Visual sensing technology is receiving increased attention as a means to endow machines with the capability of exhibiting in a greater degree of "intelligence" in dealing with their environment. Thus, a robot or other machine that can "see" and "feel" should be easier to train in the performance of complex tasks while requiring less stringent control mechanisms than preprogrammed machines. A sensory, trainable system is also adaptable to a much larger variety of tasks, thus achieving a degree of universality that ultimately translates into lower production and maintenance costs.

The computer vision process may be divided into five principal areas: sensing, segmentation, description, recognition, and interpretation. These categories are suggested to a large extent by the way in which computer vision systems are generally implemented. It is not implied that human vision and reasoning can be neatly subdivided, nor that these processes are carried out independently of each other. For instance, it is logical to assume that recognition and interpretation are highly interrelated functions in a human. These relationships, however, are not yet understood to the point where they can be modeled analytically. Thus, the subdivision of functions discussed below may be viewed as a practical (albeit limited) approach for implementing computer vision systems, given the level of understanding and the analytical tools presently available.

Visual sensing. Visual information is converted to electrical signals by the use of visual sensors. The most commonly used visual sensors are vidicon cameras and solid-state diode arrays. Vidicons are the usual vacuum-tube cameras used as television imaging devices. An input video signal is digitized and transferred to a computer an an image of a size ranging typically from 64 × 64 to 512 × 512 discrete image elements, depending on the resolution requirements of a given application.

Solid-state devices are available as linear and area arrays. If the scene to be imaged is in continuous, uniform motion (as in belt conveyors), a linear array can be used to scan a line across the conveyor, and the motion of an object in the direction perpendicular to scan produces the desired two-dimensional image. In a one-dimensional array each element is read every N time intervals, where N is the number of image elements in the line, whereas in a two-dimensional array each element is read every N^2 time intervals; therefore, the two-dimensional array maintains a higher output data rate while allowing a long integration time for noise reduction. Linear arrays with resolution exceeding 2048 elements are available.

In order for a vision system to be able to interact with its environment, a geometric relationship between the real world and the images in the picture seen by the system must be established. This relationship is a transformation of measurements from a three-dimensional coordinate system to the image coordinate system, or vice versa. Essential to the derivation of the object-image relationship is a precise mathematical description for the camera (that is, a camera model). The use of two or more cameras and their mathematical models allows extraction of three-dimensional information, such as depth.

Illumination of a scene is an important factor affecting the complexity of vision algorithms. Arbitrary lighting of the environment often results in low-contrast images, specular reflections, shadows, and extraneous details. When control of the illumination is possible, the lighting system should illuminate the scene so that the complexity of the resulting image is minimized, while the information required for analysis is enhanced. For instance, the so-called structured lighting approach used in some industrial vision systems projects points, stripes, or grids onto the scene. The way in which these features are distorted by the presence of an object simplifies the computer interpretation of the scene. Two examples of this approach are shown in **Fig. 1**.

Segmentation. Segmentation is the process that breaks up a sensed scene into its constituent parts or objects. Hundreds of segmentation algorithms have been proposed since about 1970. This is still an active area of research because of its importance as the first processing step in any practical computer vision application. Although image segmentation has proved to be a difficult task in unconstrained situations such as automatic target detection, the problems encountered in industrial applications can be considerably simplified by special lighting techniques such as those discussed above.

Segmentation algorithms are generally based on one of two basic principles: discontinuity and similarity. The principal approach in the first category is edge detection. The principal approaches in the second category are thresholding and region growing. Most edge-detection techniques for industrial applications are based on the use of spatial convolution masks in order to reduce processing time. The idea is to move a mask over the entire image area, one image element location at a time and, at each location, to compute a measure proportional to discontinuity (for example, the gradient) in the image area directly under the mask. Thresholding is by far the most widely used approach for segmentation in industrial applications of computer vision.

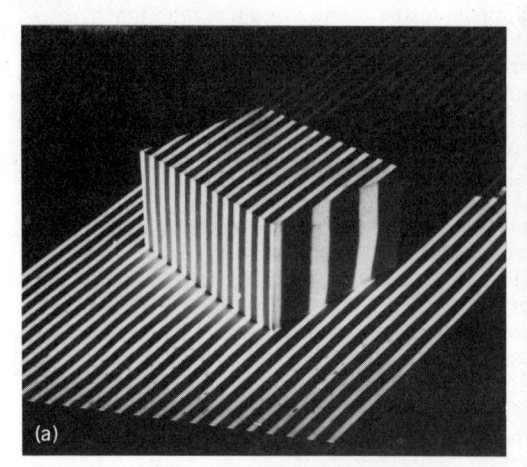

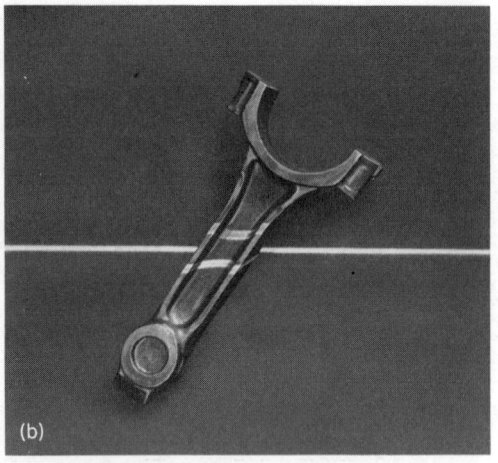

Fig. 1. Two examples of scene illumination by structured lighting. (*a*) Illumination of a block by a series of parallel strips of light (*from W. Myers, Industry begins to use visual pattern recognition, Computer, 13(5):21–31, 1980.*) (*b*) Illumination of a workpiece by two strips of light which coincide at a background surface (*from F. Rocher and E. Keissling, Methods for analyzing three-dimensional scenes, Proceedings of the 1975 International Conference on Artificial Intelligence, American Association for Artificial Intelligence, pp. 669–673*).

There are two reasons. First, thresholding techniques (in their simpler forms) are fast, and in addition, they are quite straightforward to implement in hardware. Second, the lighting environment is usually a controllable factor in industrial application; this results in images that often readily lend themselves to a thresholding approach for object extraction. Region-growing techniques are applicable in situations where objects cannot be differentiated from each other or the background by thresholding or edge detection. Although region growing has been used extensively in scene analysis, it has not found wide applicability in industrial applications because this method is usually impractical from a computational or hardware implementation point of view, and many of the problems which would require region growing for segmentation can usually be handled by special lighting or other enhancement techniques. A considerable amount of work has dealt with techniques that attempt to incorporate contextual information in the segmentation process. This includes the use of relaxation, plan-guided analysis and the use of semantic information.

Description. The description problem in computer vision is one of extracting features from an object for the purpose of recognition. Ideally, these features should be independent of object location and orientation and should contain enough discriminatory information to uniquely identify between objects. Descriptors for computer vision are based primarily on shape and amplitude (for example, intensity) information. Shape descriptors attempt to capture invariant geometrical properties of an object. Approaches for shape analysis and description are generally either global-oriented (region-oriented) or boundary-oriented. Global techniques include principal-axes analysis, texture, two- and three-dimensional moment invariants, geometrical descriptors such as p^2/A (where p is the length of the perimeter and A is the area) and the extrema of a region, topological properties, and decomposition into primary convex subsets. Boundary-oriented techniques include Fourier descriptors, chain codes, graph representations, of which strings and trees are special cases, and shape numbers. Boundary feature extraction is often preceded by linking procedures which fit straight-line segments or polynomials to the edge points resulting from segmentation. An example of object description by extraction of its boundary and principal directional axes is shown in **Fig. 2**.

Recognition. Recognition is basically a labeling process; that is, the function of recognition algorithms is to identify each segmented object in a scene and to assign a label (for example,

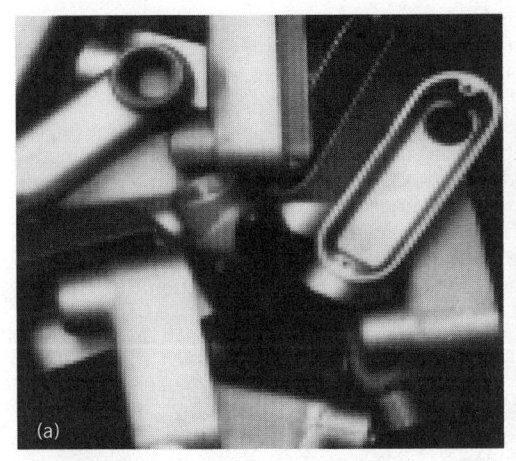

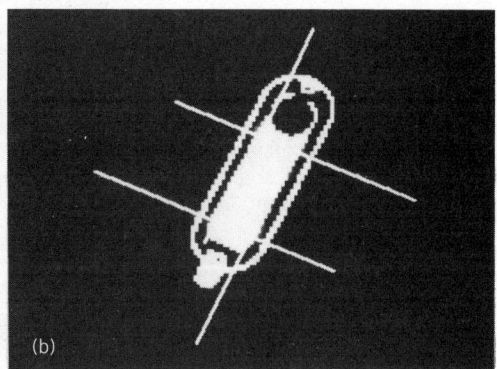

Fig. 2. Description of an object by extraction of its boundary and principal directional axes. (a) Bin of workpieces. (b) Description of one of the segmented objects. (*From J. Birk, R. Kelley, and H. Martins, An orienting robot for feeding workpieces stored in bins, IEEE Trans. SMC, SMC-11:151–160, 1981*)

wrench, seal, or bolt) to that object. Recognition approaches presently in use may be subdivided into two principal categories: decision-theoretic and structural. Decision-theoretic techniques are based on the use of decision (discriminant) functions. Given M object classes, $\omega_1, \omega_2, \ldots, \omega_M$, the basic problem in decision-theoretic pattern recognition is to identify M decision functions, $d_1(x), d_2(x), \ldots, d_M(x)$, with the property that, for any pattern x^* from class ω_i, $d_i(x^*) > d_j(x^*)$, for $j = 1, 2, \ldots, M, j \neq i$. The objective is to find M decision functions such that this condition holds for all classes with minimum error in classification. *See Decision theory*.

Decision-theoretic methods deal with patterns on a quantitative basis and largely ignore structural interrelationships among pattern primitives. Structural methods of pattern recognition attempt to describe fundamental relationships among pattern primitives via discrete mathematical modes. Here, the most widely used method is syntactic pattern recognition in which concepts and results from formal language theory provide the basic mechanisms for handling structural descriptions. The existence of a recognizable and finitely describable structure is essential in the success of the syntactic approach. Basically, a formal grammar is developed to generate elements of a language that defines a pattern class, and an automaton (or equivalently, a parsing algorithm) is developed to recognize precisely that same language. Such a language may consist of strings of primitives and relational operators (for example, directed line segments along the boundary of a polygonal representation of a workpiece) or of higher-order data structures, such as trees, graphs, and webs.

One of the most significant recent extensions of syntactic techniques has been the inclusion of semantic evaluations simultaneously with syntactic analysis by means of attributed grammars. In this approach, a pattern primitive is defined by two components: a token or symbol from a finite alphabet, and an associated list of attributes consisting of logical, numerical, or vector values. The syntactic rules provide the basic structural description, while the semantic rules assign meaning to that description.

Interpretation and models. In this discussion, interpretation is viewed as the process which endows a vision system with a higher level of conception about its environment. Sensed information, tasks to be performed, and types of parts to be handled are all essential items in establishing the level of competence and adaptability of a vision system. Given the limited state of development in "truly intelligent" vision systems, careful definition of a constrained set of operating conditions is essential. This is usually accomplished via models.

The structure and complexity of a model depends on the stage of visual processing in which it is used. Computer vision techniques may be divided into three basic levels of processing: low-, medium-, and high-level vision. Although this division is somewhat arbitrary, it does provide a convenient method for categorizing the various processes that are inherent components of a computer vision system.

Low-level vision techniques attempt to extract "primitive" information from a scene. Examples of the use of models in low-level vision procedures range from modeling the characteristics of incident and reflected light properties of a body, to the detection of edge segments in a scene by modeling an edge as an abrupt change in intensity amenable to detection by gradient operators. Medium-level vision refers to procedures which use the results from low-level vision to produce structures that somehow carry more meaning than the elements extracted by the low-level vision process. Medium-level vision processes include edge linking, segmentation, description,

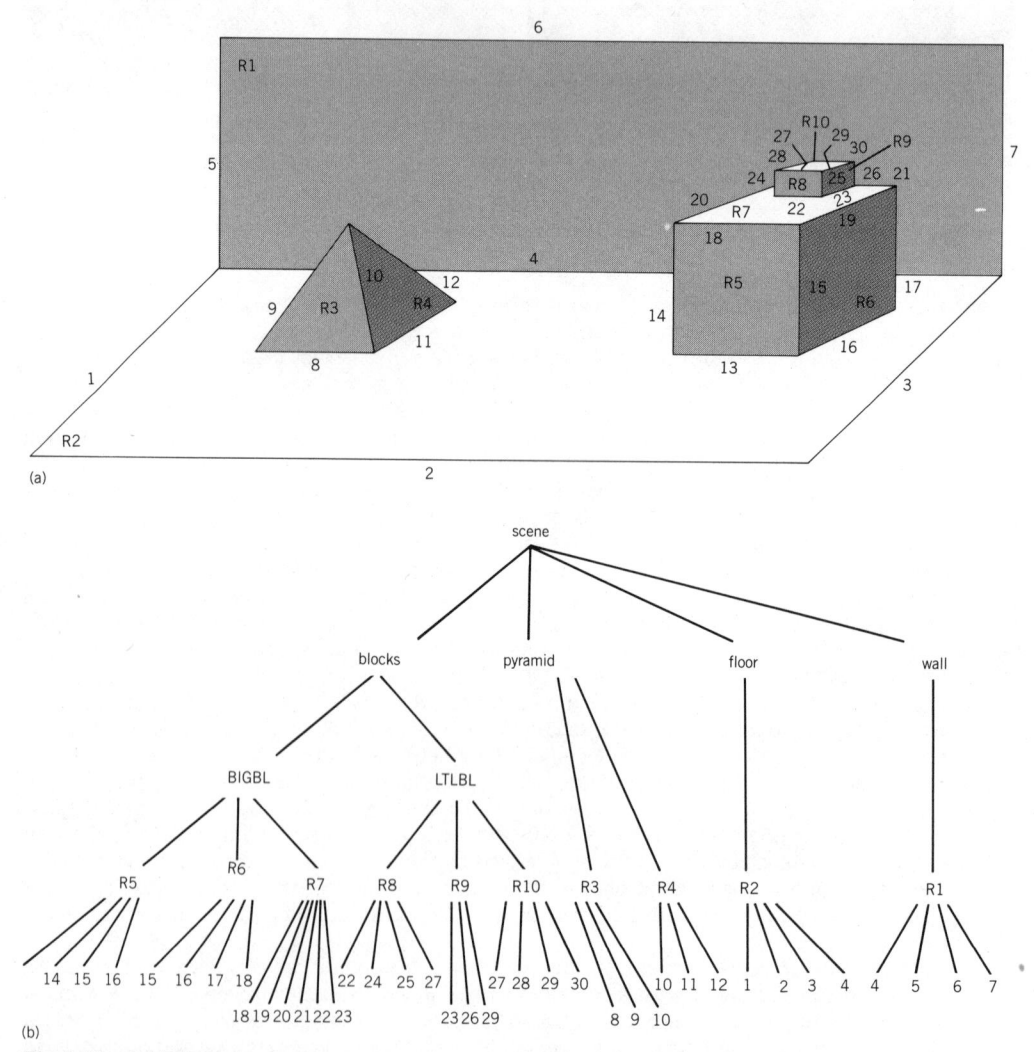

Fig. 3. Hierarchical representation of a scene. (*a*) Scene with blocks, pyramid, floor, and wall. (*b*) Hierarchical representation. (*After M. G. Thomason and R. C. Gonzalez, Database Representation in Hierarchical Scene Analysis, in L. Kanal and A. Rosenfeld, eds., Progress in Pattern Recognition, Elsevier-North Holland, 1982*)

and recognition of individual objects. High-level computer vision may be viewed as the process that attempts to emulate cognition. At this level of processing, the present knowledge and understanding of a suitable model is considerably more vague and speculative. While models for low- and medium-level vision tend to be rather specific in nature, a model for high-level vision encompasses a considerably broader spectrum of processing functions, ranging from the actual formation of a digital scene through interpretation of interrelationships between objects in a scene. **Figure 3** illustrates modeling of a scene by decomposing it into successively simpler elements. The simplest element considered in this case is an edge. Thus, regions are composed of edges, objects are composed of regions, and the scene is composed of objects. *See* ARTIFICIAL INTELLIGENCE; CHARACTER RECOGNITION; COMPUTER GRAPHICS; ROBOTICS.

Bibliography. H. G. Barrow and J. M. Tenebaum, Computational vision, *Proc. IEEE*, 69:572–595, 1981; G. G. Dodd and L. Rossol (eds.), *Computer Vision and Sensor-Based Robots*, 1979; K. S. Fu, C. S. G. Lee, and R. C. Gonzalez, *Robotics: Control, Sensing, Vision, and Intelligence*, 1987; R. C. Gonzalez and R. Safabakhsh, Computer vision techniques for industrial applications and robot control, *Computer*, 15(12):17–32, 1982; A Rosenfeld (ed.), *Techniques for Three D Machine Perception: Machine Intelligence and Pattern Recognition*, vol. 3, 1985.

SPEECH RECOGNITION
Wayne A. Lea

The process of analyzing an acoustic speech signal to identify the linguistic message that was intended, so that a machine can correctly respond to spoken commands. Procedures must be incorporated for distinguishing linguistic contrasts from irrelevant acoustic changes that are due to variabilities among speakers and environmental conditions.

Motivation. Speaking commands to a computer is the ultimate in natural human-to-machine communications. Natural, spontaneous interactions are possible, with little or no user training, permitting direct access by the physically handicapped or those who cannot type well. The user can communicate in the dark or blinding light, around obstacles, and while walking about in an area, without direct contact with a computer console or need for large data-input devices. Telephones and radios can become low-cost computer input terminals, and there is interest in voice control of toys, appliances, wristwatch calculators, and other consumer products.

Speech allows rapid data entry and frees the user's hands and eyes for other tasks. Experiments show that complex tasks can be accomplished in half the time if speech is allowed as one mode of interaction. Even when one of the communicators is replaced by a restricted machine that can recognize only single words or phrases, preceded and followed by pauses, the speed and accuracy of complex data entry are still better for speech than for keyboard or graphical pen.

Speech recognizers have been advocated, sold, and used for various hands-busy applications such as: quality control and inspection; package sorting for automatic conveyor systems; control of machine tools; entry of topographical data in mapmaking facilities; and cockpit controls. Voice-actuated wheelchairs, hospital room environmental controls, and recognizer-resynthesizer translators for pathological speech are of public interest. Telephone banking, voice authorization of credit card transactions, and catalog ordering are other applications, which introduce difficulties related to telephone bandwidth, noise, and distortions.

Difficulty. Fluent conversation with a machine is difficult to achieve because of intrinsic variabilities and complexities of speech, as well as limitations in current practical capabilities. Recognition difficulty increases with vocabulary size, confusability of words, reduced frequency bandwidth, noise, frequency distortions, the population of speakers that must be understood, and the form of speech to be processed. To limit the problem, speech recognizers have been primarily confined to small vocabularies of words with large differences in sound structure, and isolated words, with pauses before and after each word. As illustrated in **Fig. 1**, word boundaries are then relatively easy to find, as transitions into and out of silences. Contextual influences of surrounding words on the pronunciation of each word are minimized by pausing. In contrast, the continuous flow of natural speech can make it difficult to tell when one word ends and the next word begins. Coarticulatory degenerations from ideal dictionary pronunciations (for example, "dija" for "did

268 COMPUTER SCIENCE SOURCE BOOK

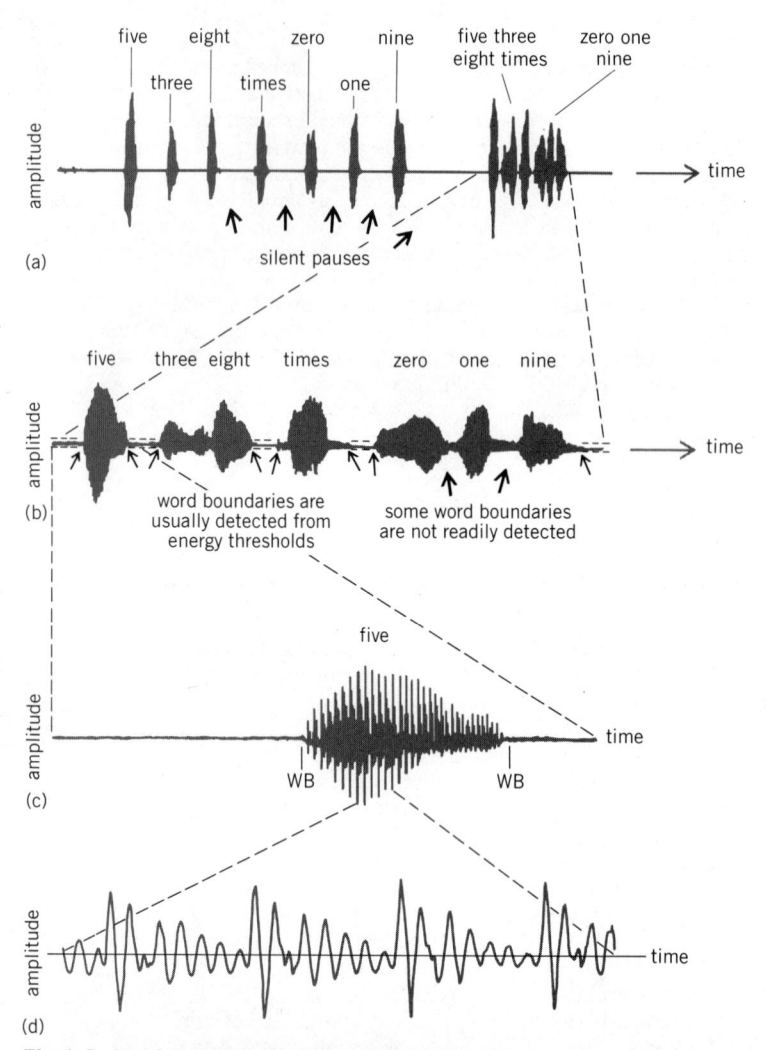

Fig. 1. Series of progressively more detailed views of an acoustic waveform, showing how a recognizer can detect utterance boundaries and identify words and messages. (*a*) Words isolated from each other by silent pauses, followed by a continuously spoken version of a calculator command. (*b*) Waveform of the continuous-speech portion of *a*, showing how some, but not all, word boundaries can be detected from energy thresholds. (*c*) Further expansion of the time scale of part of the waveform of *b*, so that the constantly changing sound structure within the word "five" is evident, and word boundaries (**WB**) are illustrated. (*d*) Local resonant structure of the diphthongal transition from /a/ to /1/ in the "five" of diagram *c*.

you," or "lisum" for "list some") can be avoided with strict constraints (formats) on allowable word sequences, and can be practically eliminated by pausing between words, but at some loss in naturalness and speed of data entry.

  Isolated word recognizers are thus the easiest to develop, followed in turn by recognizers of digit strings and strictly formatted word sequences. Sometimes the identification of every spoken word is not necessary, and detecting key words in context is enough to determine the topic of a conversation. Such a word-spotting system usually deals only with the important words, which are stressed and well articulated, easing the recognition, despite arbitrary contexts. Full understanding of the total sentence meaning and intended machine response involves cooperative use of many "knowledge sources" like acoustics, phonetics, prosodics, restricted syntax, semantics, and task-dictated discourse constraints. The term speech-understanding system is frequently used to describe such a sentence-understanding device. An even more ambitious system goal would involve accurately identifying all the words in any possible utterance, yielding what is variously called a phonetic typewriter, an automatic transcription facility, a speech-to-text machine, or a task-independent continuous-speech recognizer.

Accuracy. The difficulty of recognition is closely correlated with required recognition accuracy, defined as the percentage of all received utterances that are correctly identified (that is, for which the machine response is as intended). Substitutions of the wrong response are usually considered more serious than machine rejections of the utterance as being too similar to other possible utterances to be reliably categorized. Studies are needed regarding necessary accuracy in various practical situations, although most field tests suggest that 4% error rates are not acceptable to serious users. Error rates alone are not necessarily the best total measures of the effectiveness of recognizers. Usually it is the total cost of interactions (errorful or not) that determines the merit of a vocal (or manual) input facility, and users need to examine the distribution of errors among various vocabulary items, and the likelihoods of falsely rejecting an acceptable vocabulary word or falsely accepting an extraneous noise or background conversation, and so forth, along with the total consequences of each such error.

One of the most important areas in speech recognition technology is the human factors aspect, concerned with determining what specific tasks warrant voice input, what accuracies are needed, and how to balance the trade-offs between versatility and cost, criticality of errors and technical feasibility, and exploitation of task constraints versus flexible enhancement for use on new tasks.

Operation of speech recognizers. Speech recognition requires the transformation of the continuous-speech signal into discrete representations which may be assigned proper meanings, and which, when comprehended, may be used to effect responsive behavior. Only some of the information in the speech signal is related to selecting the correct machine response, so that a critical task is to extract all, and only, those parts that convey the message. Recognizers primarily differ on how they reduce the data to message-distinguishing features, and how they classify utterances from that reduced data.

Figure 2 illustrates one general structure for how a machine acquires knowledge of expected pronunciations and compares input data with those expectations. Since most devices must be trained to the specific pronunciation of each talker, a precompiling stage involves the user speaking sample pronunciations for each allowable utterance (word, phrase, or sentence), while identifying each with its typewritten form or a vocabulary item number. Later, when an unknown utterance is spoken, it is compared with all the lexicon of expected pronunciations to find which training sample it most closely resembles. For complex utterances, other linguistic and situational information can be used to help guide and confirm hypothesized word sequences. Figures 1, 3, 4, and 5 detail some of the processes needed in the system components diagrammed in Fig. 2.

Word boundary detection. Figure 1 illustrates the initial process of detecting word boundaries, for word sequences with or without deliberate pauses between words. Silent pauses (Fig. 1a) permit easy detection of word onsets at transitions from no signal to high energy (above some threshold amount), and word offsets as energy dips below the threshold. In continuous speech, pauses normally occur only at boundaries between sentences or clauses, or at thoughtful hesitations just before important words. Even the rapidly spoken calculator command shown in Figure 1b shows more prominent energy dips, and very brief pauses, between words than is usual in conversationally flowing speech. Word boundary confusions can occur, however, when short silences (usually less than 100 ms in duration) during stop consonants (/p, t, k/) may look like intended pauses. Thus, a word such as "transportation" could appear to divide into three "words": "transp," "ort," and "ation." Recognizers looking for pauses between words must thus measure the duration of the pause, to distinguish short consonantal silences from longer deliberate pauses.

Feature extraction. Once a word or other utterance unit has been delimited, its identity can be determined from the details of its pronunciation. Figures 1c and d show that the sound structure in a word is constantly changing, with frequent alternations (and transitions) between

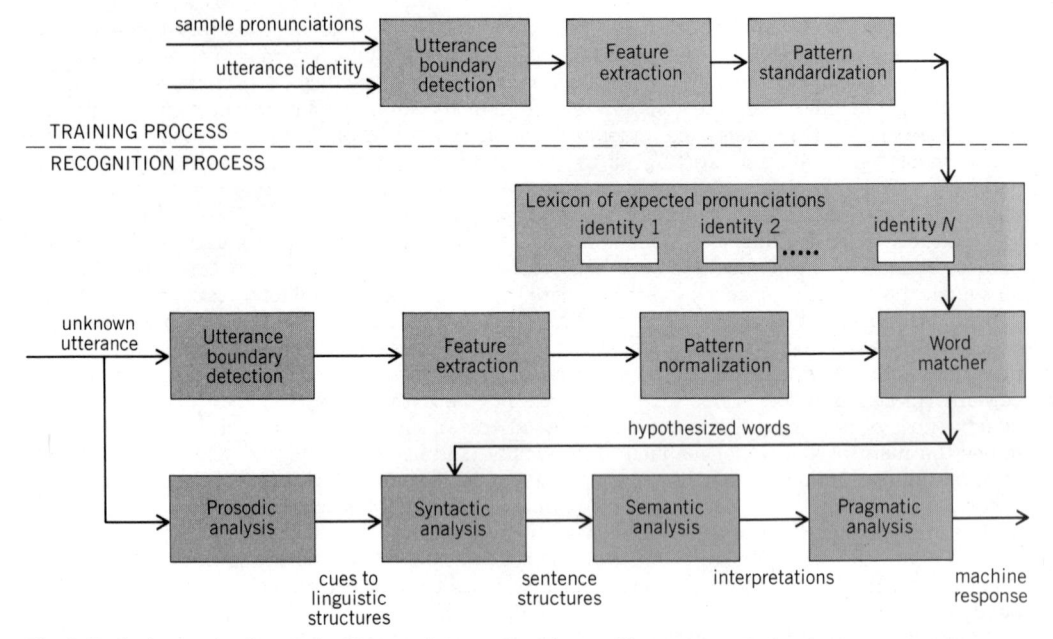

Fig. 2. Typical structure for a trainable speech recognizer that could recognize words, phrases, or sentences.

vowellike damped resonant structures and weak or noiselike consonantal sounds such as /p, t, k, f, s/. Not all aspects of the pronunciation of a word will be consistent from time to time, from one talker to another, or from one context to another. Hence, important information-carrying features are usually sought in the acoustic data to detect contrasts of linguistic significance and to detect segments such as vowels and consonants.

Figure 3 shows a few typical acoustic parameters used in recognizers. From the acoustic waveform, one can extract local peak values, such as at 1 in Fig. 3a, as an amplitude measure. Also, the sum of the squares of all waveform values over a time window can provide a measure of the energy in that window of speech data. The number of times the signal passes through a value of zero (zero crossings) can be used as a cue to vowellike smooth waveforms (with few crossings per unit time) versus noiselike fricative segments (with many crossings per unit time). The time between the prominent peaks at onsets of pitch cycles can be used to determine the pitch period T_0, or its inverse, the rate of vibration of the vocal cords, called fundamental frequency or F_0. Resonant frequencies are evident from the number of peaks per pitch period. For example, the third pitch period in Fig. 3a shows seven local peaks, indicating a ringing resonance of about seven times the fundamental frequency. This resonance is the first formant or vocal tract resonance of the /a/-like vowel, and is one of the best cues to the vowel identity.

Figure 3b shows the superimposed results of two methods for analyzing the frequency content of the short sample of speech in Fig. 3a. The computer can achieve rapid determination of the total jagged Fourier frequency spectrum, with its peaks at harmonics of the fundamental frequency, using a fast Fourier transform (FFT). However, to extract the exact positions of major spectral peaks at the formants of the speech, an advanced method called linear predictive coding (LPC) can yield the smoothed-linear predictive coding spectrum shown passing through the middles of the vertical jumps of the FFT spectrum. The peaks in such a spectrum then indicate the basic resonant frequencies of the speaker's vocal tract, and can be tracked versus time, as in Fig. 3c, to indicate the nature of the vowel being articulated. Another common spectral analyzer is a filter bank, with narrow bandpass filters spaced across the frequency spectrum, to monitor the amount of energy in each frequency range versus time.

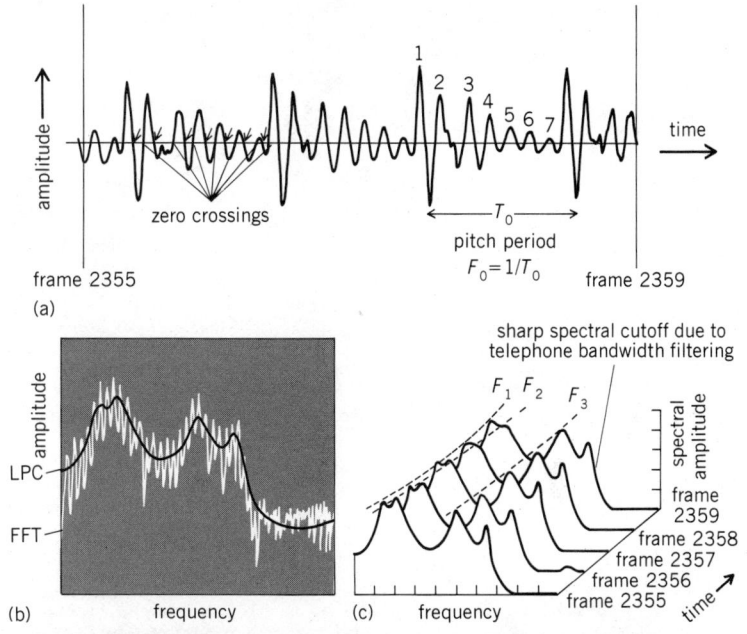

Fig. 3. Typical acoustic parameters used in speech recognizers. (a) Time waveform of Fig. 1c, showing parameters that can be extracted. (b) Frequency spectrum of the waveform of a, with the detailed frequency spectrum derived from a fast Fourier transform (FFT) being smoothed by linear predictive coding (LPC) to yield a smooth spectrum from which formats can be found as the spectral peaks. (c) Smoothed LPC spectra for five successive short time segments (frames, each 6.4 ms long), with formants F_1, F_2, and F_3 tracked as the spectral peaks.

Pattern standardization and normalization. Figure 4 shows why a recognizer needs pattern standardization and pattern normalization components. The word "five" spoken on two successive occasions in Fig. 4a has different amplitudes (A1 and A2). A recognizer must neglect (normalize for) such amplitude variations that have nothing to do with intended linguistic contrasts. Also, as a comparison of Fig. 4b and c illustrates, the timing of speech events may not be the same for two repetitions of the same utterance. With identical time scales, the /w/ in 4b lines up with the timing of the /ʌ/ in c. A recognizer must realign the data, so that the proper portions of an unknown utterance are aligned with corresponding portions of the templates. This normally requires nonuniform time normalization, as suggested by the different phonemic durations in Fig. 4. Dynamic programming is a method for trying all reasonable alignments, and picking the one that yields the closest match to each template. Another possible pattern normalization might be speaker normalization, such as moving one speaker's formants in a pattern such as Fig. 3c up or down the frequency axis to match those of a "standard" speaker, for whom the machine has been trained. Channel normalization is another need; if training data were collected under broadband conditions, but unknown utterances come over the band-limited telephone, the sharp cutoff due to telephone filtering may have to be introduced into the training data before spectral comparisons. During training, the speaker's data for amplitudes, timing, and spectral content can be set to standard values, or calibrated, so that unknowns can later be warped (normalized) to match those standard values.

Word matching. From such feature extraction, standardization, and normalization processes, an array of feature values versus time can be obtained. During training, this array can be stored as a template of expected pronunciation; during recognition, a new array can be compared with all stored arrays, to see which word is closest to it. This involves a distance measure that

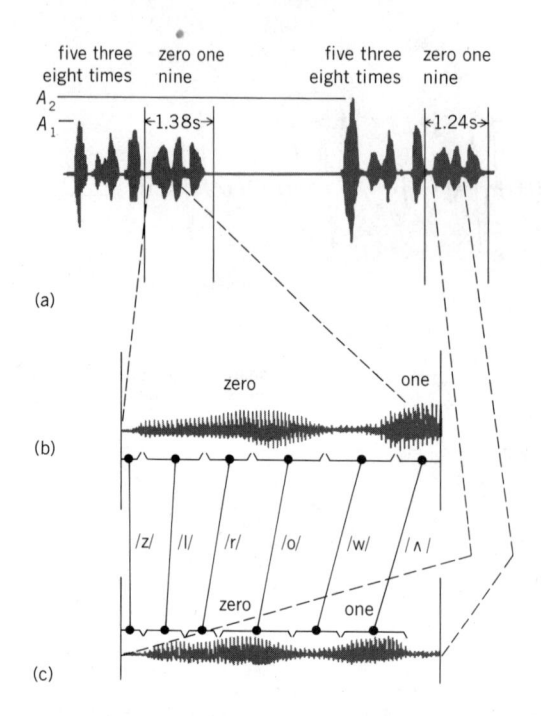

Fig. 4. Two successive utterances of the same phrase, showing need for amplitude and time normalization processes in speech recognizers. (a) Utterances in succession, showing differences in amplitudes A_1 and A_2. (b,c) Expansion of portions of the utterances, showing how rate of speaking can cause misalignment of data, so that time normalization is needed.

weights all the features and time slices in some manner, and accumulates a total difference in structure from one array to another.

Ambiguities in possible wording result from errors and uncertainties in detecting the expected sound structure of an utterance. Some "robust" segments like vowels and strong consonants may be evident, but a variety of words could usually correspond with a detected sound structure. To prevent catastrophic errors in word identifications, recognizers will often give a complete list of possible words, in decreasing order of agreement with the data (that is, increasing distance from the input pattern). For each time period of the unknown utterance, the word matcher of Fig. 2 then hypothesizes many words that are to varying degrees close to the sound structure of the incoming speech in that region. As shown in **Fig. 5**, the first word might look like "five," based on the correspondence between the detected vowel AY and the expected vowel AY, and the matching of initial and final consonants "f" and "v" also. The first word is also similar to "nine" and "times" in a small vocabulary of calculator terms. Later in the utterance, words such as "zero," "seven," "clear," and "one" might compete as candidates for the same region of speech. One reason for such potential confusions is that a practical recognizer may mislabel segments, fail to detect certain segments, or insert segments that are not actually in the utterance. Figure 5 shows only the more robust detected segments, such as vowels and some consonants, around which the remainder of the sound structure must be carefully (but less reliably) matched.

Higher-level linguistic components. A challenge for speech recognizers is how to keep down the combinatorial explosion of alternative word sequences to consider. That is the primary purpose for higher-level linguistic components such as prosodics, syntax, semantics, and pragmatics. Prosodic information such as intonation can help distinguish questions from commands, and can divide utterances into phrases and rule out word sequences with incorrect syllabic prominences or stress patterns. A syntactic rule may be written into the computer to disallow consideration of ungrammatical sequences like two operators in a row, so that "plus divide," "multiply clear plus," and so forth, are ruled out from hypothesized word sequences. A collection of such word-sequence constraints forms a grammar. Most practical recognizers use a simple grammar

ARTIFICIAL INTELLIGENCE 273

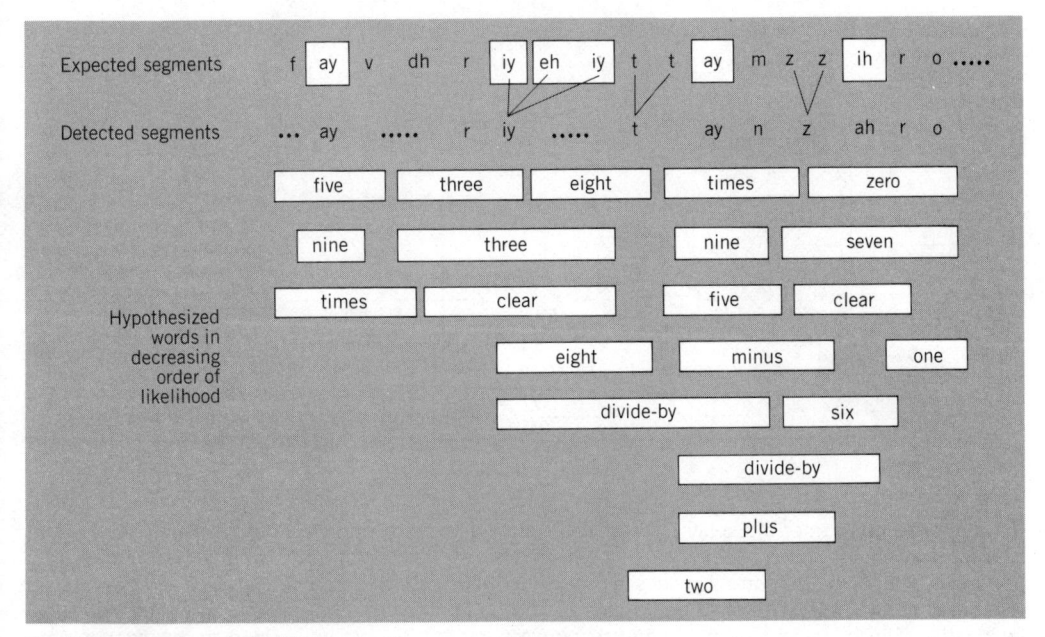

Fig. 5. Process of word matching.

type called a finite-state grammar that determines the allowable next words based on the immediately preceding word. A semantic constraint might disallow meaningless but grammatical sequences such as "zero divide by zero." A pragmatic constraint might eliminate unlikely or impractical sequences such as the useless initial "zero" in "zero one nine" of Fig. 1. In a chessplaying task, to take another example, syntactic rules limit word sequences to those for acceptable statements of movements of pieces, such as "pawn to queen four"; semantic rules then would rule out illegal or meaningless moves; pragmatic rules would discount the likelihood of ridiculous or counterproductive moves, such as moves that were just made in the immediately previous step. Some sophisticated recognizers have included all these sources of knowledge to help correctly identify an utterance. Isolated word recognizers usually use finite-state grammars, if any higher-level linguistics is used at all.

It is also possible to restructure the recognizer components shown in successive steps in Fig. 2. One promising structure avoids the propagation of errors through successive stages of a recognizer by having all the components intercommunicate directly through a "blackboard" or central control component that, for example, might allow syntax or semantics to affect feature-extraction or word-matching processes, or vice versa.

Practical implementations. Figure 6 illustrates the variety of available hardware and software implementations of speech recognizers. A primary distinguishing specification of speech recognizers is the type of speech handled, whether it be "isolated words" separated by pauses, or "connected word sequences" (digits, or other words from some small vocabulary, spoken in rapid succession but with strict syntactic formats), or "continuous speech" within entire natural sentences. Another important distinction is whether the recognizer must be trained to the speaker's voice ("dependent") or can work with essentially any voice without prior training ("independent"). The solid blocks in Fig. 6 indicate many attempts at achieving the type of recognizer represented by the coordinates of that position, while open boxes suggest that few attempts were made at that particular type of capability.

Types of recognizer. Each type of recognizer begins from a foundation of research systems (typically implemented on general-purpose computers). In the 1970s, expensive full commercial systems were first offered that stood alone and provided a recognizer box, a microphone or

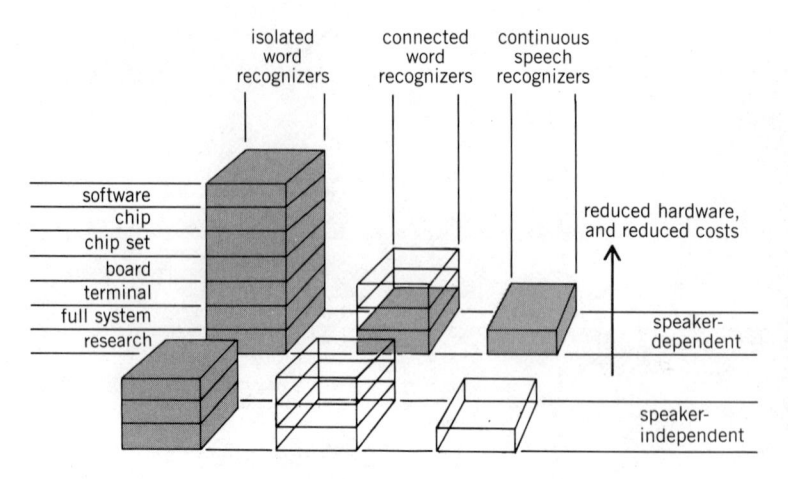

Fig. 6. Types of hardware and software configurations for speech recognition under various application conditions. Shaded boxes represent many attempts at that type of recognizer, while open boxes indicate only a few attempts at that type of device.

headset, an alphanumeric display to show recognizer decisions, and facilities for using recognition results to affect machinery responses. However, with the expanding availability of computers to perform the display and control processes, the late 1970s saw the emergence of "voice terminals" that were compatible with (and could look to the computer just like) manual interfaces such as keyboards. These voice terminals were recognition circuit boards embedded in a box that provided necessary power and interfacing to other equipment.

The 1980s began with the popularity of a simpler recognition device, a single circuit board, with the special recognition algorithms implemented on microprocessors, read-only memories, random-access memories, and related analog or hybrid hardware. A few manufacturers have offered integrated-circuit chip sets, or single chips, that can be incorporated into users' boards or systems as the simplest form of recognition hardware. SEE INTEGRATED CIRCUITS; MICROPROCESSOR; SEMICONDUCTOR MEMORIES.

The widespread trend toward flexible software has penetrated the speech recognition industry, so that in the mid-1980s some companies began offering licensable software for speech recognition, rather than providing specific special-purpose hardware. SEE MICROCOMPUTER.

The focus in the speech recognition industry has been on the easiest problem of speaker-dependent isolated-word recognition, but clear trends are toward limited forms of connected speech and speaker independence in commercial devices, especially for telecommunications applications. Research on the challenges of continuously spoken sentences forms an integral part of the international effort toward intelligent fifth-generation computers. SEE ARTIFICIAL INTELLIGENCE; DIGITAL COMPUTER.

Circuit-board implementation. Figure 7a schematically illustrates a typical circuit-board implementation of a popular method of word (or word-sequence) recognition using linear predictive coding for spectral data representation, and dynamic programming for time alignment and word matching. The microphone or telephone handset signal is amplified, digitized through a general-purpose 12-bit analog-to-digital converter chip, and subjected to an acoustic analysis procedure on either a special-purpose linear predictive coding chip or a general-purpose digital signal processor chip. Linear prediction is a method of separating the speech signal into an "excitation" component due to the human vocal cords (or a vocal-tract noise source) and a vocal-tract transfer function or filter that shapes the excitation to the form of multiple-resonance structure produced by the varying-cross-section human vocal tract. The smooth frequency spectra of Fig. 3 illustrate the prominent peaks that correspond to the acoustic resonances of the vocal tract. A linear predictive analysis involves determining the necessary coefficients (usually 10–15 in number) for specifying an inverse filter that separates such smooth resonance structure from the harmonically rich pulses produced by the vocal cords (or the noisy spectrum of a frication noise source in the vocal tract). SEE ANALOG-TO-DIGITAL CONVERTER.

A matrix of such linear predictive coding coefficients versus time thus represents the artic-

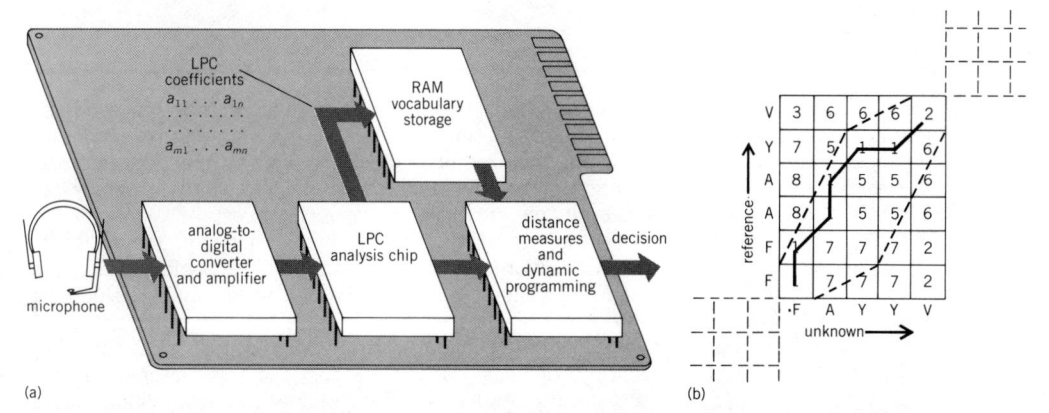

Fig. 7. Practical speech recognizer based on linear predictive coding (LPC) analysis and dynamic programming. (a) Major components of a circuit-board speech recognizer using LPC analysis. (b) Matrix of speech sound differences between reference words and word portions of unknown inputs. Alternative alignments are allowed within the parallelogram, and the path with least accumulated distance (heavy line) is chosen for best alignment of reference and input words.

ulatory structure of a word. Word matching can be based on comparing such coefficients with those found throughout each word of the vocabulary with which the recognizer is trained. In a practical speech recognizer, a distance measure is developed to determine how different two sets of linear predictive coding coefficients are, and such distances are calculated for every analysis frame of the input word compared to every analysis frame of training samples. As Fig. 7b illustrates, the analysis frames of the input can be distributed along one (horizontal) axis, while those of a candidate reference word from the training data can be aligned along the other (vertical) axis, and the distances between the respective frames of the input and reference words can be entered into the corresponding intersection cells in the matrix. To decide if the reference word occurred, the distances along the best possible (lowest-accumulated-distance) alignment of input and reference data are accumulated. If that distance is less than the distance for any other reference word inserted in place of the illustrated reference word, then that reference word is accepted as the identity of the input.

Since words spoken at different times may vary in duration and detailed timing, nonuniform alignment may be necessary. Dynamic programming is a method for picking that path through all the successive distance increments that produces the lowest accumulated distance. As shown by the heavy line in Fig. 7b, a couple of frames of "f"-like sound of the reference word may be identified with a single "f"-like frame of the input, or two input frames of "y"-like sound may be associated with one such frame in the reference. Dynamic programming restricts alignments to local paths of specific shape, such as horizontal steps, vertical steps, or diagonal steps, but not negative-slope steps, and so forth. Indeed, it usually is found computationally efficient and realistic to restrict alignment paths to lie within a parallelogram such as the illustrated one of slopes between ½ and 2.

As indicated by the matrices of broken lines extending each way from the basic single-word matrix, it is possible to apply dynamic programming to word sequences, looking for beginning and end points of each word, and matching with reference words by best paths between such end points. The same procedure can be applied with larger (or smaller) units, in successive steps, to yield "multiple-level" dynamic programming, which is used in some commercial recognition devices. *See* V*oice response*.

Bibliography. J. L. Flanagan, Synthesis and recognition of speech: Teaching computers to listen, *Bell Lab. Rec.*, pp. 146–151, May–June 1981; W. A. Lea, *Computer Recognition of Speech*, 1986; W. A. Lea, *Trends in Speech Recognition*, 1980, reprint 1986; L. Rabiner and R. Shafer, *Digital Processing of Speech Signals*, 1979; S. E. Levinson and M. Y. Liberman, Speech recognition by computers, *Sci. Amer.*, 244(4):64–76, April 1981.

VOICE RESPONSE
Wayne A. Lea

The process of generating an acoustic speech signal that communicates an intended message so that a machine can respond to a request for information by talking to the human user. Communication of speech from the machine to the human requires abilities to convert machine information into a desired word sequence, with the pronunciations of all desired words carefully sequenced and inflected to produce the natural flow of continuous speech waves.

Talking machines permit natural interactions that can be valuable for announcing warnings, reporting machine status, or otherwise informing the computer user, especially when the user cannot view displays, due to concurrent visual tasks, visual handicap, or remote telephone links. The many advantages of voice interactions with machines and the expanding uses of computers in offices, factories, schools, and homes have encouraged the development, sales, and use of voice response systems as voice warning devices, cockpit advisory systems, automated telephone-directory assistance systems, time-of-day services, bank-by-phone facilities, talking clocks and appliances, toys that speak, and automatic readers of printed texts for the blind. Low-cost synthesizers on circuit boards or in microminiaturized integrated circuit chips are rapidly giving machines the ability to speak.

Reproduction of stored speech. For simple tasks involving small vocabularies, machine production of speech is not difficult to achieve. Human speech can be stored and reproduced later on demand, using techniques similar to those in familiar devices like audio tape recorders, phonograph records, and other analog or digital magnetic media. Simple machine control of the position of the pickup device on an audio recorder can determine the sequence of words or phrases. The earliest commercial voice response devices were simple machine-accessed analog recordings on tape loops and magnetic drums.

Word concatenation systems. It is only a small conceptual step from such recorders to the simplest form of modern voice response system, called a word concatenation system (**Fig. 1**). Acting like automated tape recorders, word concatenation systems can retrieve previously spoken versions of words or phrases and carefully concatenate them without pauses to approximate normally spoken word sequences.

The processes involved in word concatenation begin off-line, when a trained speaker (for example, a radio announcer) in a quiet booth speaks words or phrases from a selected vocabulary,

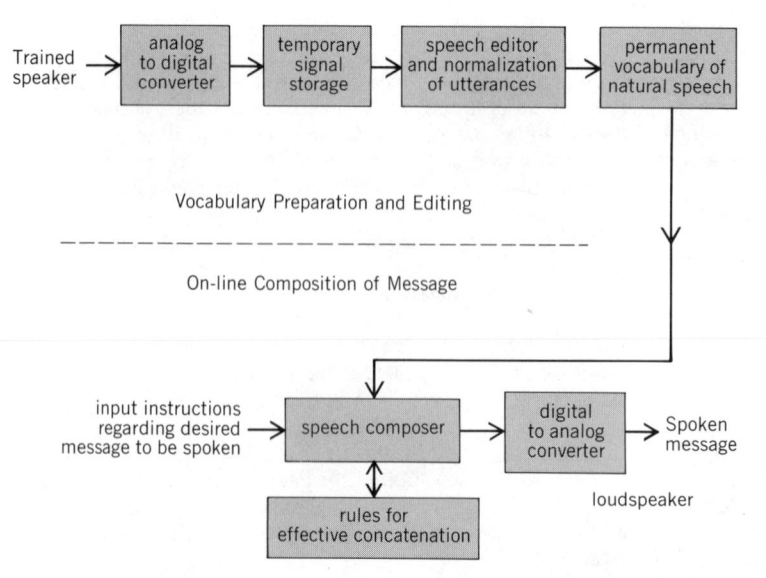

Fig. 1. Voice response system which is based upon concatenation of words spoken by a human.

and this high-quality speech is digitized and placed in a temporary signal store. The speech is edited (automatically or with human help) to adjust sound levels, to locate the beginning and ending of each word, to assess the naturalness and clarity of the pronunciation, and to check the inflection of the voice. If necessary, words may be spoken again until good examples are obtained. Some systems store two versions of certain words: one with flat intonation for nonfinal positions in word sequences, and another with the characteristic falling intonation of terminal parts of declarations and commands. The result is a pronunciation dictionary, or permanent store of human utterances of desired words or phrases, as illustrated on the left in **Fig. 2**. It is not uncommon for some vocabulary items to be long phrases like "voice response system" or "at the tone the time will be," spoken as a unit.

Voice response from the machine is accomplished later by input instructions dictating to the "synthesis program" or utterance composer that (for the example shown at the top of Fig. 2) the first word to be spoken will be some vocabulary item I_{68}, then comes item I_{82}, then I_5, then I_9, and then I_{47}. The composer produces $I_{68}I_{82}I_5I_9I_{47}$, heard as "The voice response system concatenates human speech," as a juxtaposing of the stored signals for each of the vocabulary items. Such juxtaposing will usually be guided by internal rules that select nonterminal versus terminal versions of words, like I_{46} versus I_{47} in Fig. 2. Rules may also correct for anomalies or bad transitions at junctures between words. The concatenated word sequence then is converted into a continuous signal that drives a loudspeaker. Figure 2 shows another utterance being generated in the same fashion, but with a different word sequence.

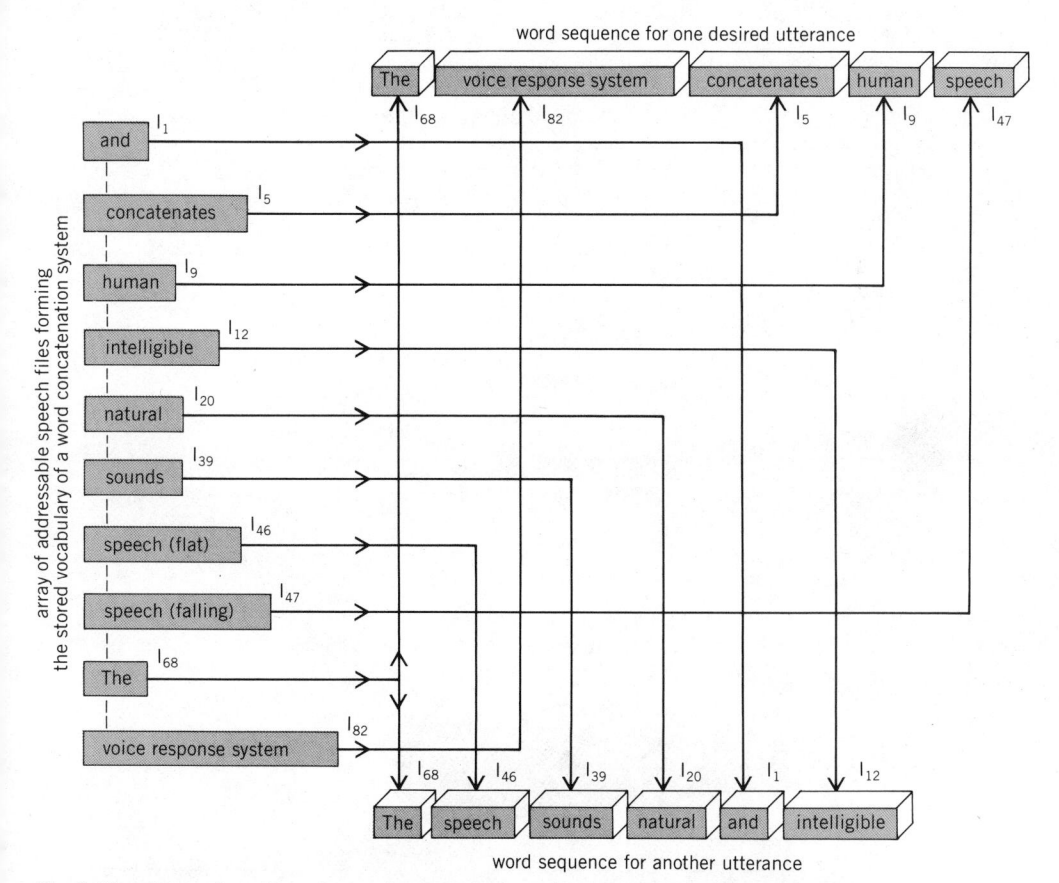

Fig. 2. Waveforms of words or phrases from the dictionary are connected end to end to achieve connected voice output from a word concatenation system.

There are problems with such a simple head-to-tail composition of word sequences. The speech may sound choppy, with unnatural intonations and timing, and with noticeable breaks at word boundaries. Also, the storage of a high-quality digitized waveform may require as much as 64,000 bits per second of speech, so that large computer disk packs can store perhaps at most 1200 seconds of speech, and microcomputer memories might be able to store only hundreds, or perhaps only a few tens, of words. Low-cost concatenation systems are thus restricted to small vocabularies. SEE COMPUTER STORAGE TECHNOLOGY.

Parameterized voice response systems. A spectrum of alternative solutions to the storage problem for voice response is illustrated in **Fig. 3**. There is a general tradeoff between storage requirements and the complexity of coding and decoding of the speech. Storage requirements can be reduced substantially by first extracting informative parameters from the original human speech and later reconstructing speech from such stored parameters. Parameterized voice response systems typically use signal-processing methods like delta modulation, adaptive differential pulse-code modulation, spectral filtering through a bank of band-pass filters (channel encoding), linear predictive coding (LPC), or tracking of important speech features like natural resonant frequencies (formants) of the speaker's vocal tract and fundamental frequency (pitch) of the voice. Such parameterized approaches assume that not all the information in the original signal is important to conveying the message. Informative parameters totaling about 16,000 bits/s to as low as 600 bits/s can be stored as simplified instructions for controlling reconstitution of the waveform.

Figure 4 illustrates a parameterized voice response system based on extensive evidence that the resonant peaks (formants) of the voice are important cues to the identities of vowels and other vowellike sounds. Words or phrases spoken by a human are analyzed in off-line mode to extract time variations of the frequencies (F_1, F_2, F_3) and amplitudes (A_1, A_2, A_3) of the formants, as well as the variations of the rate of vibration (fundamental frequency F_0, or pitch) and amplitude A_0 of the vocal cords versus time. The system notices "unvoiced" periods when the vocal cords are not vibrating, so that the signal is an aperiodic noise of amplitude A_N. All these parameters may require less than 1000 bits/s for vocabulary storage.

Later, upon input of a command specifying the desired message, the formant synthesizer reconstructs the overall acoustic character of the speech by using the stored parameters to control signal generation processes in the random number generator (for unvoiced speech), the pitch pulse or glottal wave generator (for controlling fundamental frequency), and the bank of resonating

Increasing Storage Requirements

64,000 bits/s	600 to 16,000 bits/s	200 bits/s	60 bits/s
word concatenation systems	parameterized voice response systems	phonemic synthesizers	text-to-speech synthesizers

Increasing Complexity of Synthesis Equipment

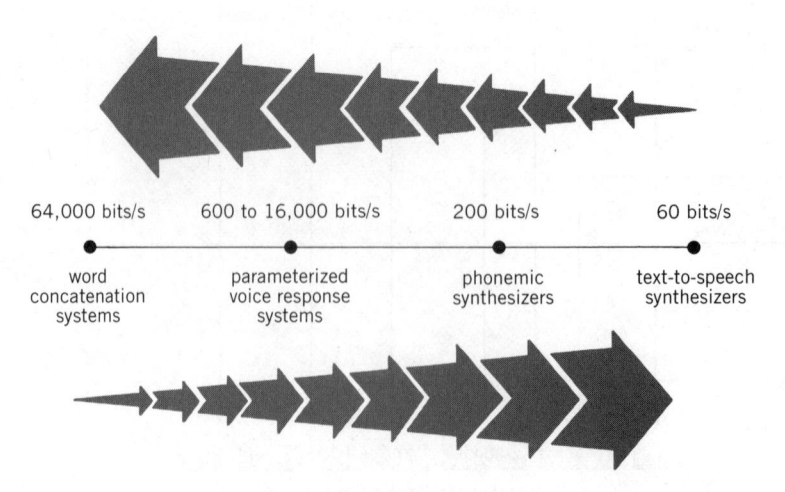

Fig. 3. Spectrum of alternative types of voice response systems.

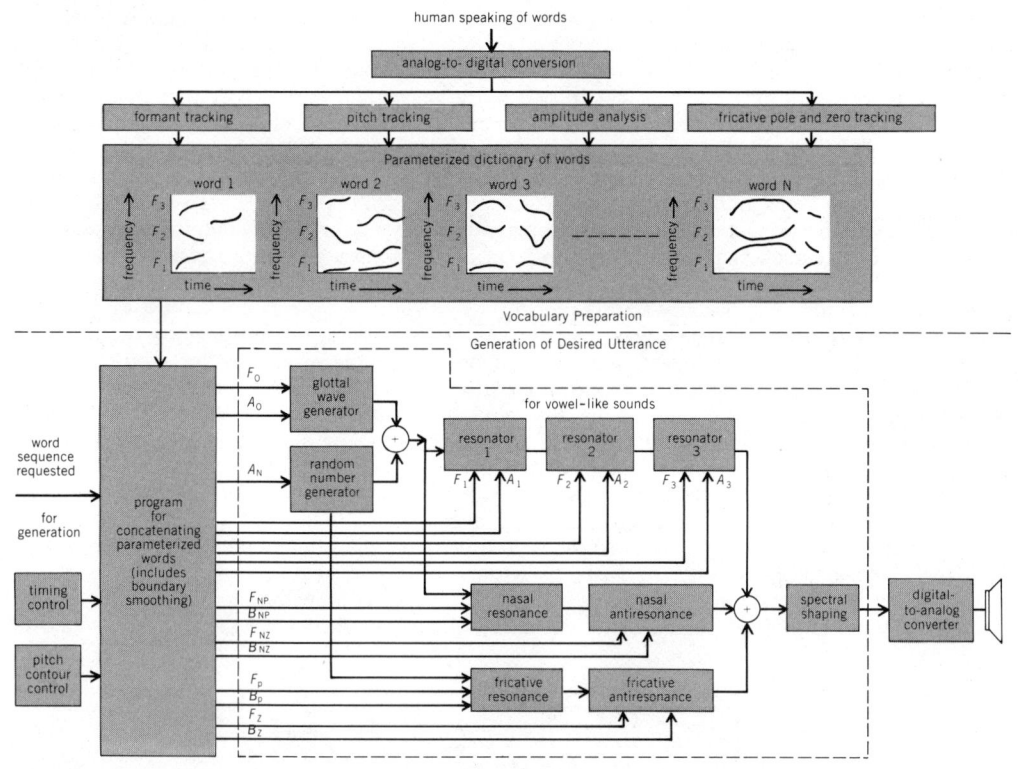

Fig. 4. Parameterized voice response system based on formant analysis and resynthesis. F_1, F_2, and F_3 are formants.

digital filters (controlled by formant amplitudes and frequencies). For fricative sounds, the formant resonances are replaced by broad spectral peaks (of frequency F_P and bandwidth B_P) and antiresonances (frequency F_Z and bandwidth B_Z). A separate path for the nasal tract also has its own resonances (frequency F_{NP} and bandwidth B_{NP}) and antiresonances (frequency F_{NZ} and bandwidth B_{NZ}). The combination of these processes produces a signal resembling the resonating or noiselike character of each portion of the original speech.

One advantage of the parameterized voice response system is the possibility of altering the parameters to have them differ from the original speech. For example, formant trajectories, or prosodic characteristics like pitch, durations of certain parameter configurations, and intensity of the speech, can be computer-controlled to achieve smooth transitions at word boundaries. Words spoken with flat pitch contours can be analyzed and resynthesized with the terminal intonation fall of a command or the terminal rise of a yes-no question. Such parameterized synthetic speech can thus be valuable in testing the perceptual consequences of various acoustic parameter patterns.

Phonemic synthesizers. Another type of speech generation system listed in Fig. 3 is a phonemic synthesizer. Human speech is not the direct basis for stored representation of words or phrases in this type of system. Rather, each word is abstractly represented as a sequence of expected vowels and consonants (phonemes, or phones if more detailed articulatory contrasts are included). Speech is composed or synthesized by juxtaposing the expected phonemic sequence for each word with the sequences for preceding and following words. Each phonemic unit is used as a set of instructions for the form of acoustic data to be produced at the appropriate times during the utterance. For example, the phonemic sequence /faɪr/ could dictate that a formant synthesizer will first produce a period of weak unvoiced noise like an /f/, followed by an /a/-like vowel period of voiced, resonant sound, with formant frequencies placed appropriately for the phoneme /a/, followed by an /ɪ/-like vowel period of voiced, resonant sound, with formant frequencies of an /ɪ/, followed by an /r/-like resonant period. Transitions into and out of each expected target configuration of formant data will be necessary, and must be derived either by computer rules or by human judgment. Similarly, the durations and intensities of each phoneme must be specified, as must the pitch of the voice during each voiced period. Such a synthesizer system thus requires extensive rule-governed modeling of the steady-state sound structures of phonemes, and predictions of the forms of transitions. Also, prosodic features must be specified by rules. Commercially available phonemic synthesizers have typically not provided comprehensive sets of such rules, so that uses of phonemic synthesizers have normally required extensive linguistics expertise or outstanding patience in trying out alternative phonemic sequences, until the resulting speech sounds somewhat natural and intelligible.

Text-to-speech synthesizers. Problems with the extensive hand-tailoring required for phonemic synthesis have prompted the development of complex rule sets for predicting the needed phonemic states directly from the input message and dictionary pronunciations. Such synthesis-by-rule permits virtually unlimited-vocabulary voice response. By providing automatic means to take a specification of any English text at the input and to generate a natural and intelligible acoustic speech signal at the output, a text-to-speech synthesizer represents the most ambitious form of voice response system listed in Fig. 3. Without the need for intervening human sequence selection such as a phonemic synthesizer needs, and with less storage requirement than other synthesizers, the text-to-speech synthesizer is probably the primary choice for large-vocabulary speech generation.

Figure 5 illustrates a typical structure for a text-to-speech synthesizer suitable for use in automatically reading books to the blind. An optical character recognizer can read typewritten

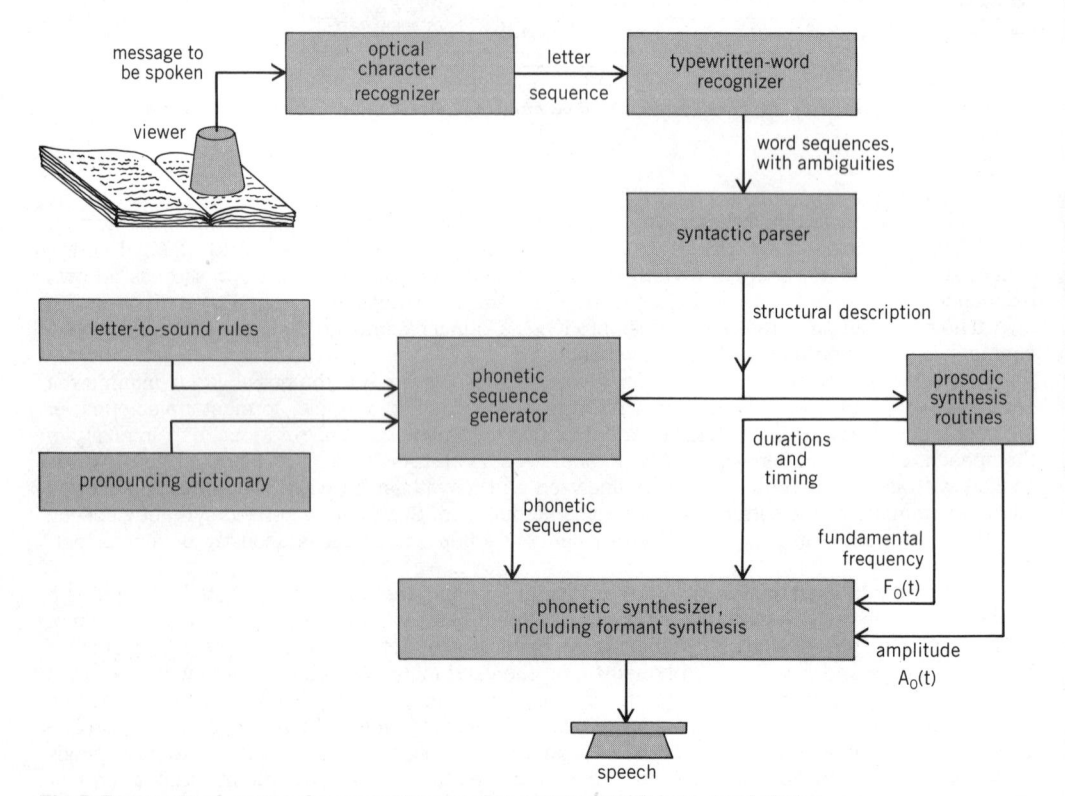

Fig. 5. Text-to-speech system for generating complex sentences with large vocabularies.

characters and produce a computer-readable specification of the spellings of words in the text. Next, words must be identified, and extensive text-to-sound rules must be used to provide the basic phonetic and prosodic instructions for controlling a speech synthesizer. Each common word is stored in a pronouncing dictionary, with its phonetic form, word stress pattern, and rudimentary syntax information such as whether it is a verb or noun. Unusual words like surnames can be generated by letter-to-sound rules. The parser examines the spelled input to determine the structural role of each word in the sentence, so that word ambiguities like the noun "con*v*ict" versus the verb "conv*ict*," or "*a*verage" as an adjective versus "aver*a*ge" as a verb, can be resolved. Also, homographs like "lead" (a metal) versus "lead" (to guide) can be distinguished by studying the syntactic structures in which they appear.

Parsing can also control the prosody of the synthesized speech, so that sound intensity, phonemic and syllabic durations, and pitch contours throughout utterances are determined by the phonemic sequence, the lexical stress pattern, the syntactic bracketing into phrases, the placement in sentence intonation and rhythm patterns, and so forth. Indeed, rule-governed control of prosody is one of the primary aspects of text-to-speech synthesis, since prosodies are the primary acoustic correlates of linguistic structures, and prosodies are critical to the achievement of natural flow, emphasis, and inflection in synthesized speech. Text-to-speech synthesizers must also adjust word pronunciations to take into account effects of neighboring words on expected forms of word-initial or word-final phonemes. Extensive research and rule testing are needed before text-to-speech synthesizers will be able to produce arbitrary English sentences without flaw in phonetic or prosodic details. *See* C*haracter recognition.*

Low-cost implementations. Speech output from machines has become much more commonplace since the development of single-chip microprocessors, digital signal processing chips, and a variety of fabrication technologies and integrated circuit architectures. The choices in voice output devices include: single-chip synthesizers (with a choice of algorithms); small circuit boards (offered as single evaluation boards or low-cost boards for incorporation into other manufacturers' products); stand-alone voice-generating boxes; and development systems that permit users to adapt voice response capabilities to specific applications with distinctive vocabularies. *See* I*ntegrated circuits;* M*icroprocessor.*

Time-domain methods. Generally, synthesis algorithms and the system architecture are more critical to the quality of the output speech than are hardware concerns such as speed and density of components on the chips or boards. Memory requirements are reduced with efficient speech encoding methods such as the Mozer time-domain methods (**Fig. 6**). Rather than performing complex spectral transforms involving digital filters and spectral feature selections, speech can be divided into short analysis periods, and the perceptually important features of the waveform within each period can be determined and stored as minimal representations of the sound to be produced. The complex speech waveform can be replaced by synthetic waveforms which do not even resemble the waveforms of actual speech in appearance, but which sound the same when heard by the phase-insensitive and linguistically categorical human ear.

Mozer time-domain methods replace each analysis period of human speech by time-symmetric waveforms, whose frequency spectrum is similar to that of speech, but whose phases are selected so that only a small number of bits are needed to represent the waveform. Characteristic of such synthetic waveforms are long silent portions, the need for only a small number of discrete (quantized) amplitude levels, and methods for repeating previous parameter patterns for successive analysis periods until the spectral changes are severe enough to warrant a new pattern. The synthetic waveform may be set equal to zero for half of the analysis period by neglect of low-amplitude portions of the speech waveform, and the pitch of the voice can be controlled by inserting different periods of silence between successive analysis frames. These synthetic waveforms are derived through complex speech analysis procedures at the manufacturer, and synthesis within the purchased device then consists of merely reading such stored data to produce a proper sequence of synthetic waveforms that sound like the desired speech.

Other time-domain methods use idealized speech segments which are stored and read out in fixed-rate or variable-rate controlled sequences during synthesis. For example, one single-chip sound-synthesis microcomputer has a read-only memory (ROM) containing the software synthesis program, the detailed parameter patterns for selected speech segments, parameters for representing the amplitude envelope of the speech, pitch data, and instructions for sequencing through

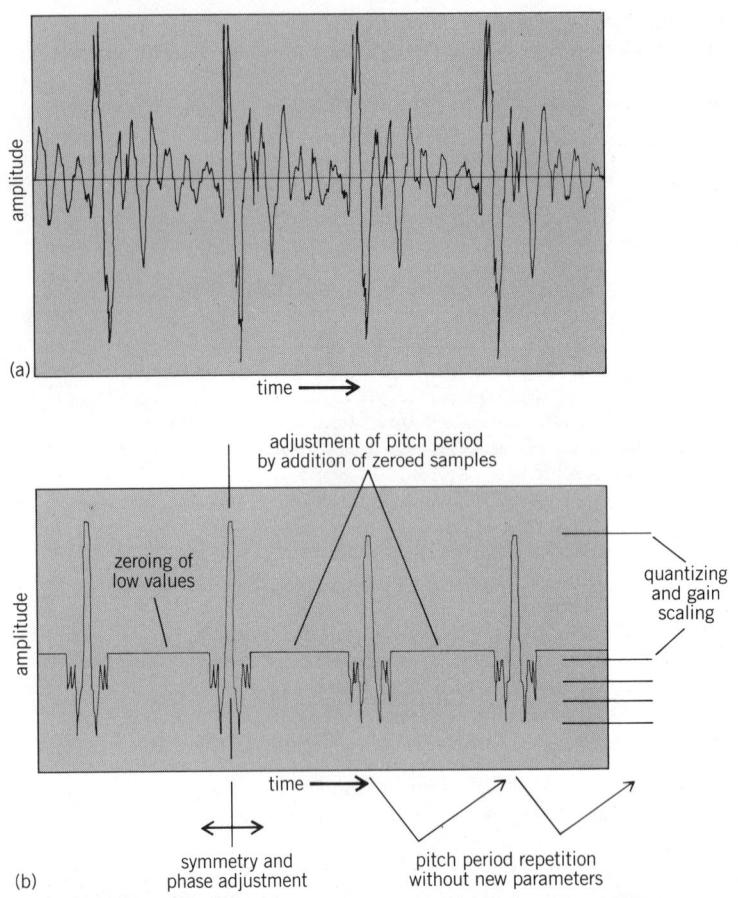

Fig. 6. Mozer methods of efficient time-domain coding for speech resynthesis. Complex speech waveforms are replaced with synthetic waveforms, whose phases and amplitude are adjusted for simplification while the amplitude frequency spectrum of the original speech is preserved. (a) A portion of vowellike human speech whose amplitude frequency spectrum must be preserved to assure human perception of the intended message. (b) A simplified waveform with a short-time frequency spectrum similar to that for a, but with several forms of data reduction before storage for resynthesis.

segments to produce utterances. The chip includes a processing unit that multiplies envelope and segment data, with pitch control of sampling rate. An on-chip digital-to-analog converter completes the production of speech through a speaker. A low-pass filter and amplifier may be needed in the speech production process.

System components. Speech output from a microcomputer can be achieved with a synthesizer, a digital-to-analog converter, a low-pass filter, and a speaker. Some synthesizer chips include the digital-to-analog converter and the filter, along with synthesis algorithms and read-only memory to store data for vocabularies to be synthesized. General-purpose digital signal processing chips can be used instead of synthesizer chips, to allow the synthesis algorithm to be readily changed, and otherwise permit flexibility in operation, but at slightly higher costs and usually with additional external circuitry such as that for digital-to-analog conversion, interfacing, and vocabulary-storing in read-only memory. Digital signal processors are particularly well suited to the prototyping of new synthesizers or new configurations for new applications.

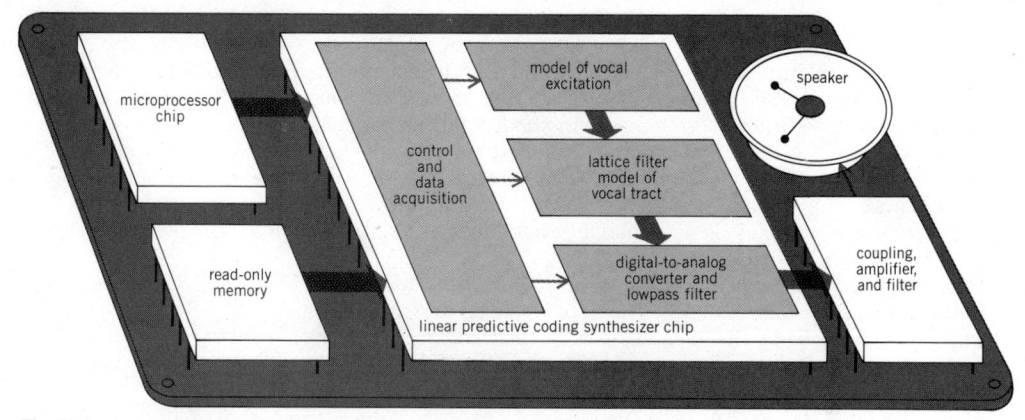

Fig. 7. Basic components of a single-circuit-board speech synthesizer, based on the linear predictive coding (LPC) method for modeling human vocal production processes.

Linear predictive coding. One of the most widely used low-cost speech synthesis methods is the linear predictive coding (LPC) method (**Fig. 7**). A single-chip microcomputer provides interfacing with keyboard inputs and other peripherals, and control of synthesis processes, while a read-only memory stores linear predictive coding data for the chosen vocabulary. The heart of the synthesizer is the dedicated large-scale integration (LSI) chip which has logic blocks for modeling the speech production processes of vocal-source excitation and acoustic-tube filtering, plus digital-to-analog processing, all supervised by a control and data acquisition interface. A typical filtering process involves a so-called two-multiply lattice which models successive short sections of an acoustic tube of varying cross-sectional area. Chips have been developed that can, through pipelining processes, perform the necessary hundreds of thousands of multiplications per second that are needed, and also can provide digital-to-analog conversion and filtering to produce outputs for coupling to the speaker.

Text-to-speech devices. The time-domain and linear predictive coding methods described above are among the parameterized voice response methods. More complex single-board speech synthesizers provide text-to-speech capabilities, which include text processing, dictionary look-up, letter-to-phoneme rules, stress and syntactic assignment, allophonic sequences, prosodic variables, generation of parameter patterns, and final synthesis of the speech. Some compromising of naturalness and intelligibility of speech results from low-cost text-to-speech devices, but the flexibility in producing any desired word sequences is very attractive for general-purpose applications.

Trends have developed toward low-power CMOS (complementary metal-oxide-semiconductor) fabrication, more memory and less demand for sophisticated algorithms, and improvement of the quality of voice output. Manufacturers offer services for the custom design, recording, and storage of a vocabulary for specific applications. However, many users desire the ability to develop their own vocabularies, so special vocabulary development systems have been devised. Improved performance can be achieved with software enhancements offered by speech service groups.

Assessment of systems. Parameterized voice response systems and text-to-speech synthesizers are expected to dominate most applications, since one provides high-quality speech in a reliable manner while the other permits unlimited vocabulary and fully automatic production of arbitrary English utterances. Critical to the assessment of any speech generator are the intelligibility and the quality (or naturalness) of the generated speech. Methods are needed for accurate measurement of the intelligibility of continuous speech and the subjective assessment of adequacies of machine-quality speech. In some applications, such as for cockput warnings, the machine-generated speech should sound robotic or distinctive to attract attention and be heard above noises, while in other situations, such as with bank-by-phone or consumer products, naturalness and good quality will be essential.

Since the cost of storage is decreasing rapidly, larger-vocabulary concatenation systems (with or without parameterization) are likely to be increasingly used, but the flexibility in sound construction and the unrestricted vocabulary and discourses permitted by text-to-speech systems will promote further work on them as well. As techniques advance, and the markets and uses expand, there will be a growing interest in methods for systematically evaluating the performances of all aspects of voice response systems. Standard tests for intelligibility and quality assessment will allow side-by-side comparisons of devices. Further research in phonetics, prosodics, syntax, and application of synthesized speech will contribute improved voice response capabilities, and those capabilities will provide informative assessment of abilities to model processes of human speech production. SEE SPEECH RECOGNITION.

Bibliography. G. Bristow, *Electronic Speech Synthesis*, 1984; J. L. Flanagan, *Speech Analysis, Synthesis and Perception*, 2d ed., 1972; J. L. Flanagan and L. R. Rabiner (eds.), *Speech Synthesis*, 1973; R. Linggard, *Electronic Synthesis of Speech*, 1985; I. H. Witten, *Making Computers Talk: An Introduction to Speech Synthesis*, 1986.

8

SYSTEMS APPLICATIONS

Data processing systems	286
Data processing management	294
Data-base management systems	295
Computer security	305
Cryptography	309
Real-time systems	321
Simulation	323
Word processing	327
Image processing	331
Robotics	334
Computer-aided engineering	340
Computer-aided design and manufacturing	346
Computer-integrated manufacturing	348

DATA PROCESSING SYSTEMS
Herbert Maisel

Electronic, electromechanical, or mechanical machines for transforming information into suitable forms in accordance with procedures planned in advance. The term data-processing system is also applied to the scheme, or procedure, that prescribes the sequence of operations to be performed in processing the information.

Typical business applications of data-processing systems include record keeping, financial accounting and planning, processing personnel information (including payroll processing), sales analysis, inventory control, production scheduling, operations research, and market research. Data-processing systems are also used to process correspondence and other information in business offices. These systems are called word processors. See Word processing.

In science and engineering, data-processing systems are used in data reduction, statistical analysis of experimental data, planning and design of engineering projects, and the display in tabular and graphic form of the results of research and development. Special-purpose computer systems, which also fall within the definition of data-processing systems, are used to monitor and control such things as chemical processes, machine tools, typesetting equipment, and power generation plants. See Data reduction.

Data-processing systems can be broadly classified as manual, semiautomatic, or automatic, depending on the degree of human effort required to control and execute the procedures. The trend is to reduce human effort, and automatic methods are becoming the dominant mode of processing. In a manual system the operations are performed by one or more individuals without the aid of mechanical devices. Varying degrees of mechanization can be introduced into manual systems through the use of machines such as calculators and bookkeeping machines. Semiautomatic systems use machines to a greater extent. The principal semiautomatic systems employ punched cards, and are referred to as a tabulating system or electronic accounting machine (EAM) systems. Automatic systems are usually built around electronic digital computers and termed electronic data-processing (EDP) systems. See Digital computer.

Data-processing functions. Virtually every data-processing system, regardless of the degree of automation, consists of six basic functions: recording, transmission, manipulation, reporting, storage, and retrieval—collectively termed the data-processing cycle.

Recording. Before information can be processed, it must be recorded in some form that is meaningful to a person or a machine. The information may be written or typed on a paper document, or it may be coded as a pattern of punched holes on a card, pulses on magnetic disk, or varying-width vertical dark bars on the product label (Universal Product Code, UPC). Many business machines, such as typewriters and cash registers, can be equipped to record data in a machine-readable form as a by-product of their normal function. Patterns of holes on cards or pulses on disks can be created by using a keyboard entry device. Optical scanners are used to record the sequence of bars in the UPC.

At one time the principal medium used to enter information into computers was the punched card. The principal device used to record information for processing by computers was the keypunch. Subsequently keyboards linked to magnetic tapes (key to tape) or to magnetic disk (key to disk) systems became widely used. The information is usually recorded on a small reel of tape or a small disk first and then entered into the computer system later. These recording systems are being replaced in turn by key entry devices that are linked directly to the computer via communication lines. Intermediate recording, whether on punched cards, tape, or disk, is no longer required.

Transmission. Once information has been recorded, it will usually need to be transmitted to another location for processing. The distance involved may range from a few feet to thousands of miles, and the information can be conveyed by personal delivery, mail, or wire. Where fast response is desirable and economically feasible, the data can be transmitted at high speeds by means of telephone or telegraph circuits, microwave links, or satellite channels. Numerous specialized business machines, such as airline reservation and credit authorization terminals, combine the recording and transmission functions by accepting data entered through a keyboard or read from credit cards or both and transmitting it directly to a distant computer system. See Data communications.

Manipulation. This is the stage in which most of the actual processing is performed. The operations involved can range from simple to highly complex. The most common types of operations are classifying, sorting, calculating, and summarizing. More specifically, the manipulation stage frequently involves (1) arrangement of the information into a sequence that will facilitate further processing; (2) determination of the exact procedure to be followed in processing each item of information; (3) references to files containing data that must be associated with the current information; (4) arithmetic operations upon the current information or file data or both; and (5) updating (changing) of the file data to reflect the current information.

Report preparation. After information has been processed, it is usually necessary to report the results in a meaningful form. Reports are the people-oriented products of the data-processing activity. They should be timely, complete, understandable, and in a convenient format. Checks, letters that are ready to be mailed, and lists of purchases at supermarket checkouts, as well as more routine summaries of the results of data processing, are commonly prepared. The routine summaries are frequently presented in graphical as well as tabular form, and include substantial amounts of text to make the report more understandable. Most reports are printed-paper documents, but other media, such as cathode-ray-tube displays or microfilm, are used.

Storage. Some or all of the processed information will need to be stored for future reference or retrieval. Information that is generated during one data-processing step frequently serves as a part of the input data for a later step, and must therefore be retained in a conveniently reusable form. The records of an organization may consist mainly of the contents of the storage generated by its data-processing system. Depending on the system, the information may be stored manually (as in ledgers or notebooks), electromechanically (as in punched cards or punched paper tape), or electronically (as in disk packs or magnetic tape).

Retrieval. The importance of the contents of storage and the availability of transmission facilities have resulted in many automatic data-processing systems providing immediate retrieval of stored information at work stations. Questions regarding the contents of storage can be posed at remote locations, and responses can be prepared and transmitted to these locations in a few seconds. This is called an on-line query facility. Special capabilities that permit retrieval of stored information based on a more time-consuming, complex sequence of searches through the stored information are also available.

Punched-card systems. The first successful punched-card data-processing equipment was developed by Herman Hollerith for the U.S. Bureau of the Census in the 1880s. By 1930, a full line of machines was available for processing data recorded in cards, and punched-card account-

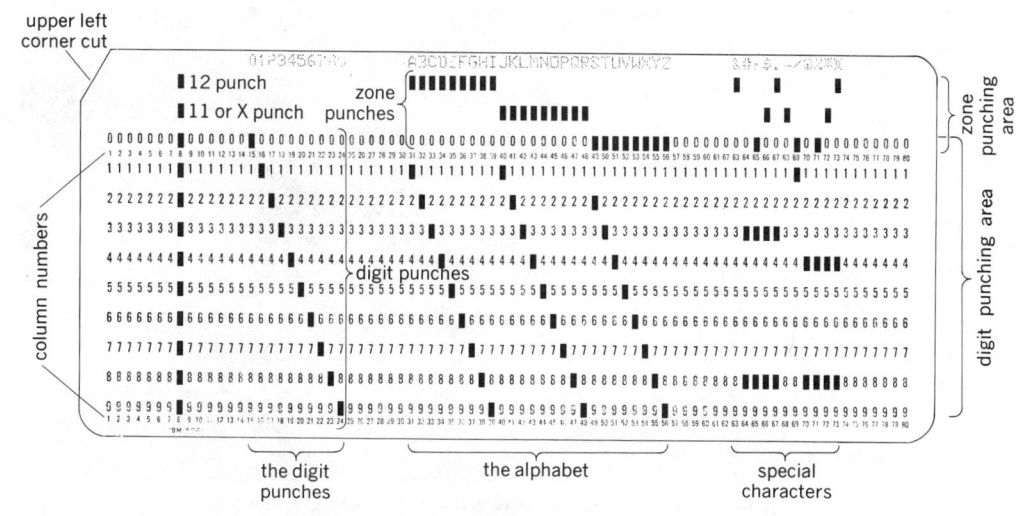

Fig. 1. An 80-column punched card showing the Hollerith coding for numeric and alphabetic information. (*After An Introduction to IBM Punched Card Data Processing, IBM Publ. F20-0074, November 1964*)

ing systems are in use around the world. Electronic data-processing systems, which offer greatly improved flexibility, speed, and economy, have been rapidly supplanting punched-card systems. The punched card itself, however, remains one of the principal means for recording data for entry into an EDP system.

The punched card is a piece of stiff paper in which data can be represented by punching holes in prescribed positions. The most commonly used type of card involves the Hollerith coding system and contains 80 vertical columns. Each column can represent a character (a digit, letter, or punctuation mark) by means of holes in 1, 2, or 3 of the 12 positions (**Fig. 1**). The card is 3¼ in. (81 mm) high, 7⅜ in. (184 mm) wide, and 0.07 in. (1.75 mm) thick. Each card normally holds the data describing a single transaction, account, or record.

Punched-card accounting systems generally contain a separate machine to perform each processing function. Though many of the machines can process hundreds of cards per minute, a fairly high degree of manual effort is required to load and unload each machine to the next. The operation of most punched-card machines is controlled by plugboards. These are perforated boards whose holes (termed hubs) are manually interconnected by wires (termed patchcords) in a manner that will cause the machine to perform the desired functions. This method of control is far less flexible than the internally stored programs used by most digital computers.

There are many types of punched-card machines, but a fully mechanized system can contain as few as three machines: a key punch to record the information in punched cards, sorter to arrange the cards in the proper sequence, and a tabulator to prepare and print the reports.

Electronic data-processing (EDP) systems. EDP systems (**Fig. 2**) take advantage of the great speed and versatility of stored-program digital computers to process large volumes of data with little or no need for human intervention. There is no fundamental difference between

Fig. 2. Large-scale electronic data-processing system. Disk drives are at the right, and tape drives at the left. Printers are in the foreground and to the right of the tape drives. The central processing unit and storage are in the center background. (*Sperry Univac Division, Sperry Rand Corp.*)

the computers currently used for business data processing and those used for scientific calculations; in fact, a single computer is often used for both types of applications. Scientific computers, however, tend to emphasize high computational speeds, while computers used for business data processing often place primary emphasis on fast, flexible input and output equipment.

Although large, high-performance computer systems cost hundreds of thousands or even millions of dollars, a wide variety of smaller systems is available at much lower prices for users with smaller volumes of data to be processed. These systems and others used in data communications take advantage of developments in microelectronics (**Fig. 3**) to deliver surprisingly high performance, along with compact dimensions and low prices (**Fig. 4**).

Every computer system has four basic functional parts: input equipment to permit data and instructions to be entered into the system; a storage unit to permit data and instructions to be stored until called for; a control unit, called the central processing unit (CPU), to interpret the stored instructions and direct their execution; and output equipment to permit the processed data to be removed from the system. SEE COMPUTER STORAGE TECHNOLOGY; DIGITAL COMPUTER PROGRAMMING.

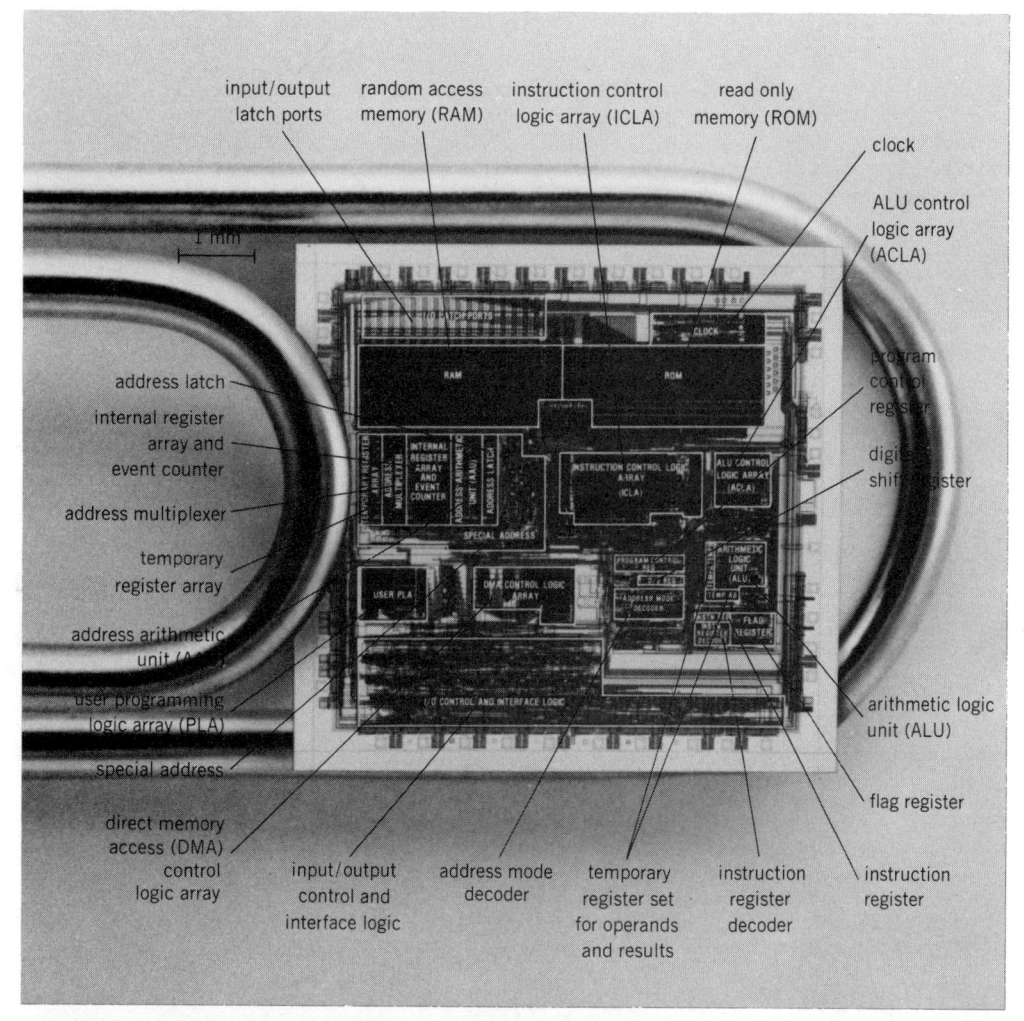

Fig. 3. MAC-4 one-chip computer, developed for a variety of telecommunications applications, compared to a standard-sized paper clip. (*Bell Laboratories*)

290 COMPUTER SCIENCE SOURCE BOOK

Fig. 4. Relatively low-cost EDP system. The system includes a keyboard, a cathode-ray-tube display, and a pair of diskette units. (*Digital Equipment Corp.*)

The remainder of this article discusses the input and output equipment used in EDP systems. The common types of input and output devices, their recording media, and their typical speeds are summarized in the **table**. Magnetic tape and disk can also be viewed as storage media that supplement the storage available in the computer itself. They have been termed auxiliary storage.

Disk pack units. Introduced in 1962, the disk pack has become the preeminent high-speed computer input/output medium. A disk pack typically consists of a stack of from 1 to 20 round stainless-steel plates mounted on a vertical spindle. Data are magnetically recorded on some or all of the surfaces of the disks. The disk pack can be conveniently mounted on a drive unit that spins it at 2400–3600 revolutions per minute. The drive unit also contains magnetic read/write heads mounted on a comblike access mechanism that moves horizontally between the disks in order to read and record information on them.

Disk packs have transfer rates from about 200,000 to nearly 2,000,000 characters per second and capacities of from about 10,000,000 to more than 600,000,000 characters per pack. The key

Input/output devices			
Unit	Medium	Input or output	Typical approximate transfer rate in characters per second
Disk pack unit	Magnetic disks housed in interchangeable cartridges	Both	200,000–2,000,000
Diskette unit	Flexible magnetic disks	Both	Tens of thousands
Magnetic tape unit	Plastic tape with magnetizable coating, housed on reels	Both	Thousands–1,250,000
Magnetic tape cartridge unit	Plastic tape with magnetizable coating, housed in cartridges	Both	Tens of thousands
Card reader	Punched cards	Input	20–2000
Card punch	Punched cards	Output	20–700
Paper tape reader	Perforated paper or plastic tape	Input	10–1000
Paper tape punch	Perforated paper or plastic tape	Output	10–200
Printer	Continuous paper forms	Output	10–20,000
Optical character reader	Paper or card documents	Input	10–3000
Magnetic ink character reader	Paper or card documents	Input	200–3000
Display unit	Cathode-ray tube or other display medium	Output*	10–100,000
Computer output microfilmer	Microfilm	Output	2000–60,000

*Input capabilities are usually provided by an associated keyboard or light pen.

advantage of disk packs that accounts for their preeminence is their rapid-access capability; any record stored in a disk pack can be located and read into the computer in a fraction of a second, whereas it may take as long as several minutes to locate a particular record stored in a reel of magnetic tape. Conversely, disk packs, on the basis of cost per character stored, currently cost several times as much as magnetic tape.

One development in magnetic disk technology deserves special mention. Flexible plastic disks, called diskettes or floppy disks, are widely used for applications in which low cost and ease of use are more important than high speeds and large data-storage capacities. Most diskettes are 8 in. (200 mm) or 5¼ in. (131 mm) in diameter, and may be housed in protective fiber-treated cardboard enclosures; the enclosure remains stationary while the drive unit spins the disk. Each diskette holds approximately 300,000 characters, and the data-transfer rate is about 30,000 characters per second.

Magnetic tape units. Magnetic tape is an important input/output medium for EDP systems because it permits large quantities of information to be stored in a highly compact, economical, and easily erasable form. The tape is usually made of plastic with a magnetizable oxide coating on which data can be recorded in the form of magnetic spots. The tape transports must be capable of moving the tape past the read/write heads at high speeds (up to 250 in./s or 6.25 m/s) and of starting and stopping the tape movement within a few milliseconds.

The magnetic tape currently in widest use with EDP systems is ½ in. (12.5 mm) wide, is supplied in 2400-ft (720-m) reels with a diameter of 10½ in. (256 mm), and is recorded with 9 parallel tracks across the tape at a density of 800, 1600, or 6250 frames per inch (32, 64, or 246 frames per millimeter). Each frame holds 9 bits (binary digits) and can represent one character of information. S*EE* B*IT*.

Transfer rates of magnetic tape units range from a few thousand to 1,250,000 characters per second. Though impressive, the transfer rates of both tape and disk fall far short of the internal processing speeds of the computer. As a result, the overall productivity of some data-processing systems are limited by the speed at which information can be entered into and removed from the system.

As an alternative to high-performance magnetic tape units, many EDP systems include smaller, less costly tape transports in which the data are recorded on shorter lengths of narrow magnetic tape, typically 0.15 or 0.25 in. (3.75 or 6 mm) wide, housed in conveniently interchangeable cartridges. The most commonly used type of cartridge is an adaptation of the Philips-type cassettes that are widely used in audio recording. The cartridge tape units have comparatively slow read/write speeds and small data-storage capacities; their offseting advantages are economy and convenience of use.

Magnetic tape is widely used to provide back-up for disk units and to permit the exchange of large volumes of information by sending reels of tape from one place to another. For example, computer programs that are purchased are often delivered on one or more reels of magnetic tape.

Card reader and punch. The fact that most early computers replaced or augmented punched-card systems gave the punched card a strong head start as a computer input/output medium, and it is still used. The punched card is a highly flexible medium that has many advantages for use as a source document and as a storage medium for permanent records. In EDP systems its principal drawbacks are the difficulty of correcting errors in the punched data, the fixed upper limit on the amount of data a card can hold (usually 80 or 96 characters), and the comparatively low speeds of even the fastest card readers and punches (see **table**).

Paper tape readers and punches. Paper tape can be punched and read by relatively simple, inexpensive equipment, making it practical to produce tape records as a direct by-product of the normal operations of many business machines, such as teletypewriters and cash registers.

Though generally called paper tape, the tape may be made of paper, plastic, metal, or laminated combinations of these materials. Data are recorded by punching round holes into the tape and read by sensing the holes either mechanically or photoelectrically. Nearly all paper tape in use at present is either 11/16, 7/8, or 1 in. (17, 22, or 25 mm) in width, and is recorded with 5, 7, or 8 data tracks at a density of 10 frames per inch (34 frames per centimeter). Each frame normally represents a single character using a code of 5–8 bits.

As with punched cards, the principal disadvantage of paper tape is the low speeds of the tape readers and punches available for use with computers. As a result, paper tape has been largely replaced by magnetic tape cassette units.

Printers. Electromechanical printing devices are the primary means for making information processed by computers available to people. However, display units are overtaking printers in this regard. Computer printers can be broadly classified as either serial or line printers and as either impact or nonimpact printers. A serial unit prints one character at a time in the manner of a conventional typewriter, whereas a line printer prints a full line, usually consisting of 80 to 132 characters, at the same time. An impact printer uses direct mechanical force to produce character images on the paper, whereas nonimpact printers utilize various electrical or chemical processes to form the characters.

Most high-speed computer printing is currently done by line printers using on-the-fly impact printing techniques. In these devices, multiple rapid-action print hammers press continuous paper forms against an inked ribbon and a moving type element at the precise instants when the selected characters are in the appropriate positions. The type element may be a rotating drum, a horizontally moving chain of type slugs (**Fig. 5**), or a horizontally oscillating typebar. Speeds of 300 to 2000 lines per minute are typical for line printers.

Matrix printers may be impact or nonimpact. The most successful are nonimpact and use thermal-chemical or electrostatic processes to create an image. Typically a 5-by-7 matrix of dots is used to print each character. The set of dots that is printed provides an image of the character (**Fig. 6**). A matrix printer that is widely used, especially in offices using word processing, is the ink jet printer.

A thermal matrix printer uses either heat-sensitive paper or wax-coated dark paper as the medium for printing. The head-sensitive paper undergoes a chemical change when subjected to heat, producing a visible image. Speeds of about 10 to 100 characters per second are common for thermal printers, and they are relatively inexpensive—costing from a few hundred to a few thousand dollars. However, the quality of the result is poor, and they may give off an offensive odor or accumulate wax debris.

Electrostatic printers are among the fastest and most versatile printers available. Speeds of several thousand characters per second can be achieved. The matrix printing approach accounts

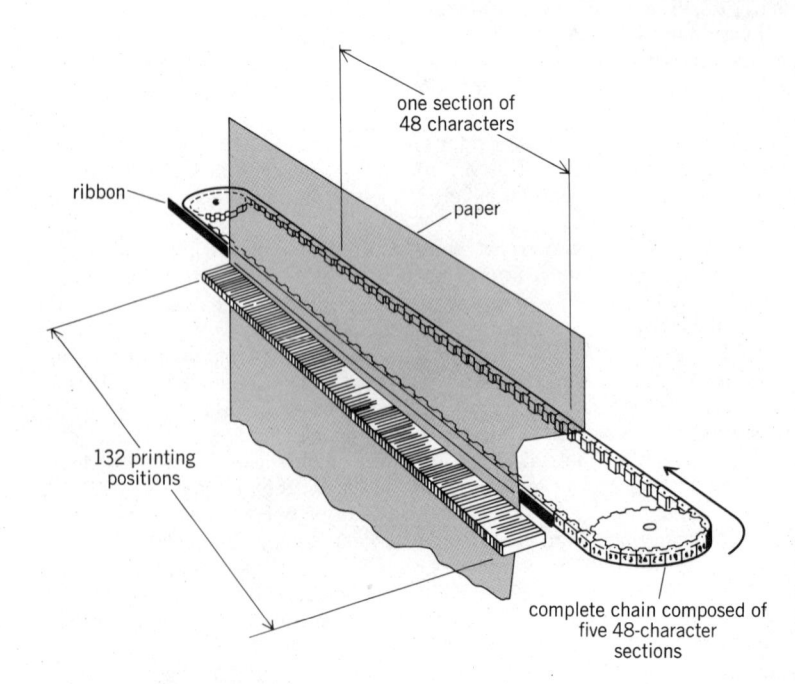

Fig. 5. Schematic representation of a chain printer. (*After H. Maisel, Computers: Programming and Applications, Science Research Associates, 1976*)

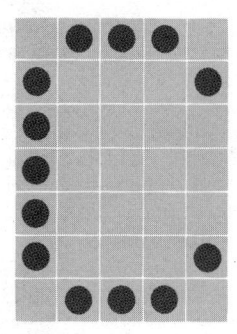

Fig. 6. Matrix of dots used to represent the letter C.

for their versatility. A 10-by-14 or even finger matrix can be used to obtain better printed images and a greater variety of characters.

A laser can be used to write the printed output on the light-sensitive surface of a drum. The image on this surface is then transferred to paper. Speeds of tens of thousands of characters per second can be realized by this type of printer.

Character reader. Optical character recognition (OCR) has been heralded as the solution to the great computer input bottleneck because it promises to reduce, and in some cases eliminate, the manual keystroke operations which are normally required in preparing the input data for machine processing. Machines capable of reading characters printed on paper documents by typewriters, cash registers, computer printers, and many other business machines are in use in applications such as utility billing and credit card processing. Moreover, machines that can read hand-printed characters are on the market, and extensive development work has been undertaken on machines to recognize ordinary handwriting. The principal barriers to wider use of optical character readers have been reliability problems and comparatively high costs.

Optical recognition techniques can also be used effectively to read hand-made pencil marks or printed bar codes. Optical mark readers and bar-code readers are considerably less costly than character readers and are widely used in applications such as test scoring, survey analysis, credit-card processing, and supermarket checkout.

Magnetic-ink character recognition (MICR), unlike OCR, requires that the characters be printed with a special magnetic ink. This requirement limits the flexibility and applicability of the MICR technique, though it permits reliable readers to be built at a lower cost. The banking field, which adopted magnetic-ink encoding as the common language for checks in 1959, remains virtually alone in preferring MICR to the more flexible optical techniques. S*EE* C*HARACTER RECOGNITION.*

Displays. Display units are widely used as "electronic blackboards" that provide rapid access to data stored in computer systems and facilitate human-machine communication. The great majority of current display units use cathode-ray tubes, but other technologies such as light-emitting diodes, liquid-crystal displays, and plasma (gaseous) displays are also used. The display units may be either connected directly to the computer or located remotely and connected by way of a data communications link. The displayed information may consist of characters or lines or both on the face of a cathode-ray tube. Most display units can also be used for input to the computer by means of either a keyboard or handheld light pen which the operator focuses upon particular points on the screen. S*EE* E*LECTRONIC DISPLAY.*

Two broad types of applications for which display units are particularly valuable are obtaining quick responses to inquiries (for example, about bank balances or airline reservations) through access to large, continually updated files of information; and providing convenient human-machine "conversations" which make it practical to construct programs and designs in step-by-step, trial-and-error fashion. Display units represent one of the most flexible and economical means for achieving communications between machines and people. Their most noteworthy weakness is their inability to produce permanent copies of the displayed information for future reference, and this can be overcome by equipping the display unit with an auxiliary printer.

Computer output microfilmers. Microfilm has two noteworthy advantages over the printed paper reports that serve as the principal output from most EDP systems: printing on microfilm can be performed at considerably higher speeds, and the microfilmed reports require far less storage space. Conversely, the acceptance of microfilm as a computer output medium has suffered because the information cannot be read by humans without the use of special microfilm readers. The advantages of microfilm clearly outweigh the drawbacks for many computer users, and equipment available that can record computer-generated reports on microfilm at speeds ranging from 1200 to 30,000 lines per minute.

Bibliography. E. M. Awad, *Business Data Processing*, 5th ed., 1980; G. B. Davis, *Computers and Information Processing*, 1978; W. Fuori and D. Tedesco, *Introduction to Information Processing*, 1983; M. R. Gore and J. W. Stubbe, *Computers and Information Systems*, 2d ed., 1984; L. S. Orilia, *Introduction to Business Data Processing*, 2d ed., 1982; B. Robichaud, E. Muscat, and A. M. Hall, *Introduction to Data Processing*, 3d ed., 1983; D. Sanders, *Computers Today*, 3d ed., 1988.

DATA PROCESSING MANAGEMENT
MICHAEL J. SAMEK

Managing the data-processing function, its people, and its equipment. This activity follows the well-recognized principles of planning, control, and operation. The basic prerequisites for data-processing management are therefore the same skills which are needed to manage any other enterprise.

Data processing is a continually evolving technology, and this fact differentiates data-processing management from many other managerial environments. Furthermore, data processing is most often a service function within an organization, and not an end product. Constant awareness of this aspect is essential to ensure successful discharge of data-processing managerial responsibilities.

Organization of people. Despite the apparently overwhelming and complex presence of computing equipment and its associated technology, the major and critical component in the data-processing function is people. To select, develop, and organize people for maximum effectiveness and efficiency should be the major concern. Many technical skills—if not experience—have been in short supply, making the organizational task more pressing. Providing an effective organizational environment which offers motivation through ongoing training and a competitive reward structure is one avenue to success. The other is to match the data-processing organization to the structure, the style, and the goals of the enterprise served. To achieve this, the products, the customers, the marketplace, even the politics and problems of the enterprise, must be understood by data-processing management. In turn, data-processing management must be a recognized, participating, and accepted part of the overall management structure of the enterprise.

Products of data processing. The products of the data-processing function are the developed application systems, which should be viewed as a portfolio of corporate assets, and the information output, processed efficiently through the computing equipment and often supported by telecommunications facilities.

Application systems. Effective application systems development again depends on knowledge and understanding of the business activity, which implies full participation by and interaction with the users. Methodology and structure, that is, standards, are necessary to make systems developers—analysts and programmers—optimally productive. A formal plan, spanning 1–3 years, is needed to give direction and priority to the development tasks.

Application software for a particular need may also be available from vendors. The decision process to purchase rather than develop software should, of course, take the cost difference into consideration, but equally important is the fit of vendor software to the particular requirements. However, added to the acquisition price of the application software is the inevitable cost of conversion, education, modification, and installation.

Information output. Converting input data into meaningful and relevant output is the real function of data-processing equipment. The technology employed, as well as the internal processes of the computer, are very complex. It is here that technical knowledge is paramount, making it very likely the most elusive area to manage. A high degree of reliance on a technically competent staff, either within or outside of the organization, is unavoidable. A fundamental knowledge of the technology on the part of data-processing management and frequent interaction with the technical staff are the best insurance that the technology stays within bounds and does not become the major driving force.

Managerial control. Continuous awareness of products offered by manufacturers and vendors, their capabilities, and their cost is a useful and effective means of maintaining the level of technical knowledge needed to exercise managerial control.

Inadequate control, manifested by failure to deliver output and projects within budget, is often cited as a problem of data-processing management. It is frequently unrecognized that the data-processing function contains an appreciable creativity factor, particularly in the development area. The inability to schedule creativity contributes to an on-time performance problem. The structuring of the work effort into manageable parts and clearly established responsibilities; keeping a constant watch on progress and work effort; immediately identifying problems; and determining resolutions can overcome this.

Demands of computer technology. Computer technology requires an unequivocal and exact representation of facts and figures. Its effective use makes particular demands on technicians and managers alike. Only what has been predetermined and planned will happen. Malfunctions aside, only that which has been programmed will be produced—no more, no less. Surprises can be minimized only by attention to detail and by exploration of "what if" consequences. Recognizing this is an essential ingredient of successful data-processing management. SEE DATA-PROCESSING SYSTEMS; DIGITAL COMPUTER.

DATA-BASE MANAGEMENT SYSTEMS
EDGAR H. SIBLEY

Special data-processing systems or parts of data-processing systems which are developed to aid in the storage, manipulation, reporting, and managing of data. They may be considered as building blocks constructing a data-processing system which also acts as a mechanism for the effective control of the data.

Cost of information systems. An information (or data-processing) system consists of such hardware or physical devices as computers, storage units and input/output media controllers; also software and the people who build, maintain, and use the system. In the early days of computing, the cost of the system was mainly in the hardware, but during the 1970s the cost of hardware dropped radically. The ratio of software-to-hardware cost now falls between 1 and 10 for most industrial and commercial operations. The cost of people has not dropped; thus the concept of "hardware is expensive and should be used sparingly" has become obsolete. Emphasis must be placed on reducing the cost of software, both in building the system and in maintaining it, that is, all parts of the so-called software life cycle. SEE SOFTWARE ENGINEERING.

Maintenance or modification occurs because of hardware changes, new ways of doing business, or different user orientation.

Software cost can be reduced in three ways:

1. While building the system, by using general system software. This spreads effort and cost over several applications. Early examples of this were such special packages or routines that took a square root, evaluated a trigonometric function, or even sorted (ordered) a set of data according to some numeric or alphabetic key.

2. When making modifications. This is achieved by making the system modular, such that only parts of it are affected by changes in the hardware configuration or by user-induced alterations. This modularity isolates system parts from one another, for example, the square-root routine need not be changed when its calling routine is modified.

3. By using a rapid-prototyping (RP) technique. This method involves the building of a model or "breadboard" of the system to be implemented. This is achieved relatively cheaply by use of a set of special interfaces provided in some commercial offerings. Such rapid-prototyping systems allow the users to "try out" their ideas before too much effort and resources have been

expended, thereby allowing the prototype to be testing in much the same way as an engineering prototype is built before its design is finalized and the production line is started.

The success of early packages gradually led to the adoption of more complex ones, or system software to perform management functions. The most complex set of such packages is an operating system.

Some common functions have been identified to help with management, manipulation, and control of the data itself. Such a set of packages is generally called a data-base management system (DBMS) by its manufacturers although their specific design and implementation may differ.

Management control of data. Without data, the process of controlling any system is impossible. Data are the physical representation interpreted through work orders, experimental results or analyses, costs of operation, or tax schedules. Data can provide information to a worker on what job to perform next and what special problems to expect; data help the engineer to see how to improve a design; for the manager data can highlight operational inefficiencies; data help the bureaucrat to decide how to govern and what new laws are needed.

The computer provides business, industry, and government with the means to improve the speed and efficiency of the collection, manipulation, storage, reporting, and dissemination of data, and this has been advantageous. However, the advent of the data-base concept constitutes both an advantage and a potential threat. The threat has several aspects which show why control or management of data is very important.

Organization of data. It has been estimated that a medium-sized corporation may need to retain 10^{10} characters of current important data in high-speed automated storage. By comparison, a book of 300 pages, 40 lines per page, and 12 words (each of about 6 characters) per line, contains about 10^6 characters (including spaces between words) and thus the 10^{10}-character "data base" could be stored in 10^4 books, which is indeed a good-sized library. However, the organization of a library makes it relatively easy to find any book, but imagine a library that had no catalog, no librarians and no one putting the books back on the shelves. The cost of a library staff is similar to that of organizing data in a corporate data base: it is necessary if data must be found and used effectively. The old systems, without well-organized data, suffered from the problem that people knew data existed, but could not find the data easily and became frustrated. One reason for the development of data-base management systems was to solve this need.

Data become truly available when a large cross section of potential users know of their existence, when their location and format are known, and when there is a mechanism for retrieving the data. If the mechanism to locate its format is used by humans, the location is normally termed a directory, while the format is stored in a dictionary. If the locating device is embedded in the data-base system, the mechanism is termed a schema.

A schema is therefore a machine-readable version of the location and format of the stored data. The difference between the schema and its instances or occurrences is shown in **Fig. 1**. This simple schema contains information about a person: name, date of birth, and salary. The representation is: name 10 characters in length, left justified with blanks appended for shorter names; date of birth as year, month, and day, with two decimal digits representing each; and salary of up to $9999.99 per month. The model is defined in the schema, while the data are recorded in each instance.

In order for the data-base management system to retrieve or store data about a person, it must consult the schema to determine its form as well as its location in machine storage. This means that a data-base management system with a query language interface can respond to a

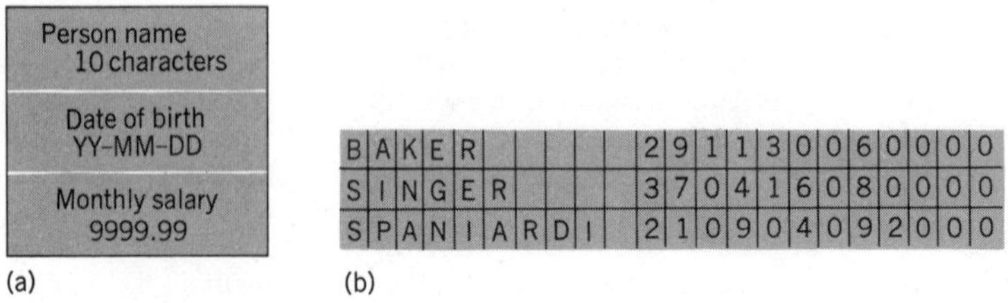

Fig. 1. Simple schema representing (a) a very simple record structure and (b) its stored data base of three instances.

request like FOR PERSON, FIND MONTHLY-SALARY, WHERE PERSON-NAME = "SINGER," or FOR PERSON, FIND PERSON-NAME AND DATE-OF-BIRTH, WHERE SALARY GREATER THAN 700.00

Data security. This powerful capability of the data-base management system enables a wide variety of potential users to obtain information that would otherwise be unavailable. However, this also creates some social problems, because access to the data may become too easy. SEE MULTIACCESS COMPUTER.

The concept of privacy has been defined as the right to be left alone. If anyone can obtain someone else's date of birth, that person's privacy has been violated. There must be some restriction on who can obtain what data under which conditions (and maybe when). A certain clerk may be allowed to look at salary data and read and update it during the working day (but not at night or during the weekend). This authority to access data must be vested in and controlled through the data-base management system; it is usually termed a security technique.

Typically, security may be enforced by insisting that users of the data-base management system identify themselves both by name or employee number and by some password. Other mechanisms may involve the insistence on use of particular terminal devices at predefined locations, allowance of only certain types of command or programs to be initiated, and hiding of sensitive parts of the data base except to certain highly privileged users. Thus the data may be screened from the general user through various levels of security, even to the extend of encoding them (requiring automated decoding routines to make them meaningful for the authorized user).

Integrity of data. Because the data are often stored in a device with moving parts they can be destroyed through mechanical or other failures. Data may also be lost through user carelessness or program malfunction. To protect the integrity of the data, several defensive steps may be taken. One major precaution is to take dumps, that is, copies of the data. This action is taken at regular intervals if the data are frequently changed; for example, the data may represent the quantity of various goods in a warehouse which changes every time an item is received or dispatched. In order to be able to restore a data base after it has been destroyed, it is merely necessary to get a copy of the last dump and update it. The updating makes use of an audit trail or log tape, which contains a history of the transactions affecting the data and generally also snapshots of data-base segments before and after a change. Thus by remaking all changes that were on the audit trail since the dump, the data base will be correctly restored to its most current image. The audit trail also allows the user to back-out an error (that is, to undo changes made in error) by going backward through the audit trail undoing all mistaken updates by using before-images of the data.

Improved performance. The introduction of a data-base management system changes also the system's orientation. The emphasis on programs (that is, programs using data), shifts to data (that is, data used by programs). A new measurement of efficiency determines how effectively the data are used and stored, and how readily available the data are. The data-base management system becomes the focal point from which such measurement may be taken. They allow the data administrator to determine how well the schema fits user needs, and how well the storage structuring of the instances reflects the needs. Thus the data-base management system measurements help improve performance.

In summary, the data-base management system provides a means for management of data by making available data to a large range of authorized users, while preserving the integrity of the data and improving the overall system performance.

Architecture. The somewhat simplified architecture of a data-base management system and its environment is shown in **Fig. 2**. It illustrates how a data request is satisfied. For example, consider the previous request for name and date of birth in the PERSON data base. An ad hoc user (that is, one who can query the system without having recourse to a previously coded program) goes to an input/output device with a keyboard or cathode-ray-tube (or both) combination. The person types in SIGNON JONES PASSWORD 51Z5QP, and then (after some response) AD HOC DBMS FOR PERSON, FIND NAME AND DATE-OF-BIRTH WHERE SALARY GREATER THAN 700.00

The following operations will be performed: (1) The word SIGNON is transmitted by the checking program to the scheduler program which rquests the SIGNON program from its library. (2) The SIGNON program is run by the scheduler program to check that Jones has given the correct password. (3) The AD HOC program is called from the library and starts to look for more inputs. (4) The word PERSON is taken by this program as the name of the schema. (5) The scheduler program

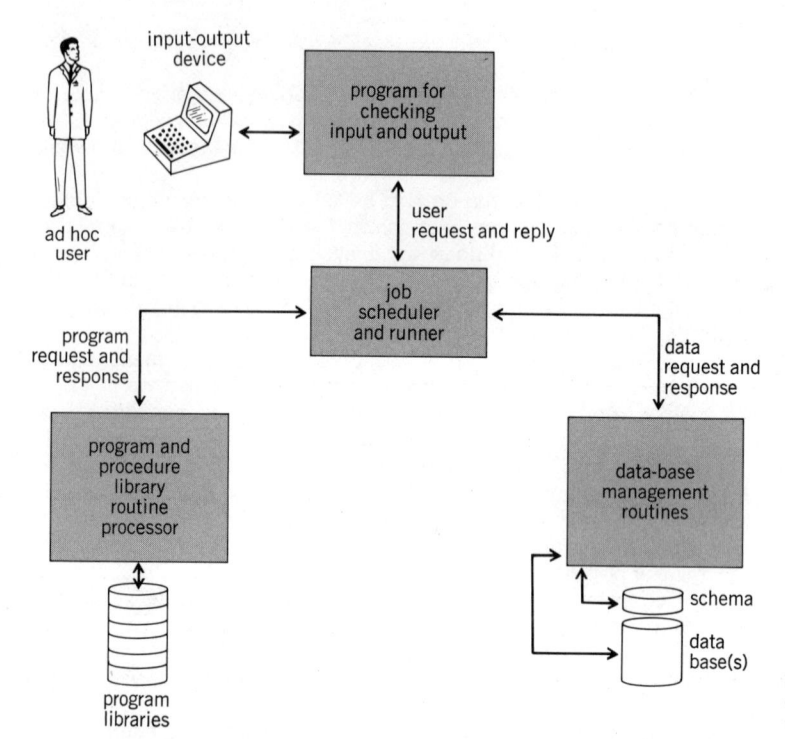

Fig. 2. Architecture of a data-base management system.

requests the data-base routine to load the PERSON schema from storage. (6) The next sentence is now checked to see whether NAME, DATE-OF-BIRTH, and SALARY are all valid words in the PERSON schema. (7) A search of the instances is made to determine which have a value of more than 700.00 in the SALARY item. In the above example, two people qualify. (8) The names and dates of birth of these two people are displayed for the user.

In this example, the authority of the user (Jones) to view any element (for example, date of birth) could be checked at step 6, if necessary.

This example demonstrates that the data-base management system consists of many routines that process data according to the schema. Many other special programs are associated with the data-base management system (such as the ad hoc query processor, the utilities to dump and restore the data base, and so forth). The data-base routines, in turn, use other operating system software such as access methods, input and output routines, and so forth. SEE COMPUTER SYSTEMS ARCHITECTURE.

Modeling data. Data can be used to represent important facts; a particular set of facts, with their relationships, are usage-dependent. For hiring a person, the attributes of importance (that is, the model needed) may be: date of birth, phone, address, sex, skills, and salary; however, for treating a person as a patient, the important model attributes are probably: date of birth, phone, address, sex, diseases, and so forth. Thus the important attributes represent the model of the entity under investigation.

Different data-base management systems model the data in different ways. The so-called relational system represents data as tables. The example in **Fig. 3** shows a unique identifier, or key, for a person (the Emp No, or employee number), and the person's date of birth, name, and salary. There must be only one line for each Emp No since this must be unique to a person. Moreover, the Education table, or Education relation, is linked to the person by the foreign key (Emp No) that has been added to the relation to identify which education relates to which person. The unique identifier for the Education relation is the concatenation of Emp No with School and

SYSTEMS APPLICATIONS **299**

Person

Emp No	Date of birth	Name	Salary ($)
204	29/11/30	BAKER	600.
193	37/04/16	SINGER	900.
067	21/09/04	SPANIARDI	920.

Education

Emp No	School	Degree	...
067	U OF MICH	BA	
193	HARVARD	BS	
204	OLD DOM	MS	
204	HARVARD	MS	
193	HARVARD	MS	

Fig. 3. Relational data base.

Degree, since the three are needed to distinguish a line for a person who has two same degrees from different schools or two different degrees from the same school. No entry in the table contains more than one elementary value (for example, it would be impossible to have two salaries for BAKER).

The hierarchical system allows more structure. In this type of system, groupings of elements are connected by parent-child relationships (**Fig. 4**). Here, a particular person may have one or several different educational categories (high school, bachelor's degree, and so forth), as well as several job histories (office assistant, clerk, manager, president).

The network system has more structure and complexity, because it uses named relationships and more complexity. In the example given in **Fig. 5**, there are four groups (or record types) with four relations (or sets). Because these three types of systems are structurally different, most current commercial data-base management systems service only one type; future systems are expected to be able to allow the users to choose the best system to suit their special needs.

Data-base administrator. In order to utilize a data-base management system effectively, there must be one person or group within the organization that looks after the system and makes decisions about its control. Typical questions are: What is a good schema (that is, one that is effective for a mix of users with different needs)? How often should the data be dumped? How well is the system operating (that is, monitoring the time and volume of the data accesses, and so forth)? Such control parameters suggest the need for special skills, other than programming and management skills that were prevalent in the "old" data-processing environment. The role of data-base administrator (DBA) has evolved to fill this need. The data-base administrator is a per-

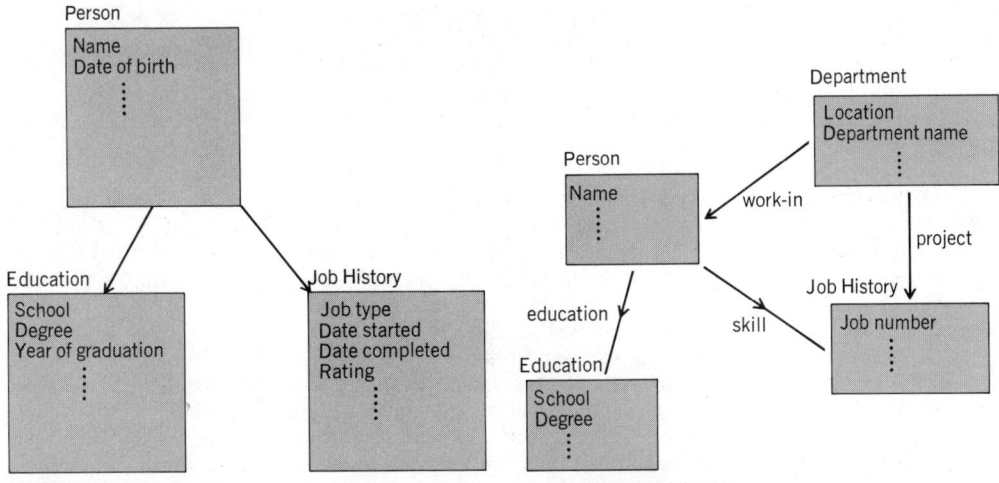

Fig. 4. Hierarchical schema.

Fig. 5. Network schema.

son or group that deals with corporate data, making decisions on the use, quality, access control, integrity needs, and so forth of all the data users of the organization.

Data administration. The management of the data in an organization involves both technical and administrative aspects, and implies more than a data-base administrator function, since the data-base administrator deals only with the technical part (for example, designing a data structure that is good for the set of organizational users). The more managerial role is assigned to a higher-level function, termed a data administrator (DA). This person is usually the manager of the data-base administrator.

The data administrator's position normally involves setting data policy, allocating resources in the data administrator group, and ensuring that the policies are carried out through control procedures enforced through the data administrator group. Naturally, because the data policy must mesh with the overall organizational policy, the data administrator acts as liaison officer with upper-level management in concerns affecting the data policy. The data administrator also acts as a liaison with user groups in all conflicts over data (such as ownership or sharing).

Data dictionary. Another essential function in a data-base management system is the recording of proper definitions of data entities. This implies some uniform way of storing and retrieving the information, and the software mechanism to achieve this is termed a data dictionary. The data dictionary requires a person or function termed the data dictionary administrator, reporting to the data administrator.

The data dictionary is like a schema; it records the names of data items and their structural relations, but it also carries definitions (in the form of a humanly understandable sentence or paragraph that describes the meaning or usage). This explanation aids in reducing misunderstanding due to homonyms and synonyms. A homonym occurs when two systems or users mean different things when they reference the same name (for example, a "full-time student" in an undergraduate school may differ from a "full-time student" in a medical school). A synonym occurs when two people give different names to the same entity (because neither knew that the other needed to use the same material). This may be an expensive problem because data may be unnecessarily collected and stored (when it already exists elsewhere), or it may be misused (when one user calls for it with the "wrong" name).

In addition, a data dictionary allows entitites other than data to be stored and manipulated, and relations may be defined between all entities. The implementor may ask: "What programs use the personnel file?" or "Which programmer wrote the accounts-receivable program?" This implies that there are entities like program, user, programmer, and so forth in the dictionary.

Rapid prototyping. As discussed above, the rapid-prototyping system is a means for easily defining a test system, so that users and implementers can try out their ideas and find if the requirements are being correctly stated or interpreted. The user of the rapid-prototyping system gives some input and output formats (generally through an interactive screen generator) and then relates the holes, or input positions, in the screen so generated to the data as defined in the schema and as recorded in the data dictionary. The user then provides the computational algorithms (usually in the form of a higher-level query language statement with parameters) and relates the algorithm/query to each screen, thereby showing which input screen triggers which algorithm and which screen is output from the data base using the algorithm. More complex control structures are normally allowed.

There are two somewhat different philosophies of rapid-prototyping systems:

1. Use the rapid-prototyping system as a proof of correctness of the original requirements specification; that is, ensure that the user will be satisfied if the ultimate system is designed and final-coded to the now approved specifications. The assumption here is that the inefficiencies of the rapid-prototyping–implemented system would be too great for a viable system, or that the prototype is a skeleton of the ultimate system. (Data validation and some batch transaction processing may be missing from the prototype.)

2. Iterate the rapid-prototyping system until it fully satisfies the customers and then freeze this as the production system. In this type of system, the user may be "paying" extra during running of the process, but have a good and sufficiently effective system to offset the added cost of a more efficient recoded system. Some systems are built with internal optimizers that allow the data administrator to improve the running by storage-device or schema adjustments and through a semicompilation step at the end of the rapid-prototyping system specification.

In the earliest use of this technique, in the late 1960s, users of the query-language interfaces of SYSTEM 2000 started to develop systems using the higher-level interface, and then (sometimes) made the implementation more efficient by coding the resulting system utilizing the COBOL or report generator interface. SYSTEM 2000 is a basically hierarchically modeled DBMS with any of the three possible means of data-base access (higher-level query language, report generator, and programming language, with the efficiency of the interface increasing in that order). Later, users of the NOMAD system (a combined hierarchical/relational DBMS) found also that it allowed them a fine rapid-prototyping capability. Some network models have sophisticated facilities for producing rapid-prototyping systems that are very efficient.

Design and implementation. The earliest commercially successful DBMS concentrated on the transaction processing market (which was the prime computing usage in the late 1960s). Possibly because of the preponderance of COBOL as a business programming language, estimated as the object language for 70% of all software systems, these systems often used a hierarchic approach. MARK IV and IMS (both having gone through many versions) are the major survivors from that era. The IMS system is essentially hierarchically structured, though it is possible to generate some internal structures that are networks, while retaining an essentially hierarchic programmer interface. The IMS system allows the data administrator to draw from four quite different accessing methods which have the indexed sequential access method (ISAM) and the direct (hashed) access method (DAM) as a general basis, but also allow the program to follow internal pointers that link repeating groups of the hierarchy.

The IDS (since upgraded as IDS II) was the earliest full data-base management system implementation on a commercial scale, and it introduced the network model. However, it was very effective as a transaction-processing system because the data administrator could choose the structures to have different accessing methods. For example, the Person record of Fig. 5 could be accessed by hashing (direct) accessing on the Emp No, while the Education record might be accessible only from the Person record by following pointers; meanwhile, the Department record might also be accessed by its name directly.)

Both the early hierarchic and network styles of data-base management systems where primarily used as transaction-processing systems to implement systems that were mainly sequential in nature. However, by being able to follow pointers (logical or physical) around the data base, the programmer could plan a good implementation. This way of implementing a system has been termed a navigational system.

Use of higher-level languages. The advent of systems that allowed the use of a higher-level language (such as SYSTEM 2000 and, later, the relational model) led to another type of system which had one major advantage: the user could formulate quite complex queries and present the answers in tabular or report form in a way well understood by most business and scientific personnel.

However, there was a potential disadvantage: there were possible inefficiencies in performing relatively complex operations, especially in handling large volumes of data in the interim (temporary) storage.

In practice, there are some difficulties in using a high-level language, because the user can be seduced into asking complex questions incorrectly (and getting the wrong answer but not knowing so). In fact, both SYSTEM 2000 and relational system users find it very easy for handling simple queries and some updates, but they often experience difficulties in formulating correct complex queries that involve quantifiers. On the other hand, the query languages are now driven by relatively sophisticated optimizers. These will generate a request for data that tries to minimize the volume of the data transferred while reducing the need for intermediate working storage.

Optimization. Relational data-base management systems, as introduced theoretically in 1970, have been particularly studied with respect to optimization needs, and some effective heuristic algorithms have been developed. As an example, suppose a request, as formulated in some higher-level language, is: FOR PERSON, FIND NAME WHERE SALARY GREATER THAN 700.00 AND SCHOOL IS "HARVARD" (AND WHERE EMP NO IN PERSON = EMP NO IN EDUCATION). The parenthesized clause may not be needed if the system can infer the joining of the Person and Education relations based on the common named key (Emp No); this clause would also not be needed in a hierarchic structured system, such as SYSTEM 2000, where the relationship is explicit in the structure.

One possible way to implement the solution to this query is to take each clause and extract the necessary data for its solution, as follows:

1. Search the Person table to produce a temporary table (A) with those lines where salary is greater than 700.00.
2. Search the Education table to give a temporary table (b) where "school = 'Harvard.' "
3. Join A and B by using the common column "Emp No"—the combined table (C).
4. Eliminate all columns except name, but remove any duplicates to give the answer.

Assuming the tables of Fig. 3, the process is illustrated in **Fig. 6**.

Other methods are possible, such as:

1. Search the Person table to produce a temporary table (A) with those lines where salary is greater than 700.00.
2. Search the Education table for the same Emp No as in temporary table A to give temporary table D.
3. Eliminate from D those schools not Harvard.
4. Join D and A.
5. Eliminate all columns except name, but remove any duplicates to give the answer.

This is obviously similar to but not the same as:

1. Search the Education table to give a temporary table (B) where "school = 'Harvard.' "
2. Search the Person table to obtain only those lines with the same Emp No.
3. Eliminate all columns except name, but remove any duplicates to give the answer.

In discussing these solutions, the size of the intemediate tables and the number of operations will be seen to depend on the statistics of the data base, as well as the type and complexity of the question. If the question is changed slightly, the best solution for the original question may not be the best for the new one. For example, suppose there are 2000 people in the data base

Table A

Emp No	Date of birth	Name	Salary ($)
204	37/04/16	SINGER	900.
193	21/09/04	SPANIARDI	920.

Table B

Emp No	School	Degree
193	HARVARD	BS
204	HARVARD	MS
193	HARVARD	MS

Table C

Emp No	Date of birth	Name	Salary ($)	School	Degree
204	37/04/16	SINGER	900.	HARVARD	MS
193	21/09/04	SPANIARDI	920.	HARVARD	BS
193	21/09/04	SPANIARDI	920.	HARVARD	MS

Answer table

Name
SINGER
SPANIARDI

Fig. 6. Solution method for a relational query.

who went to Harvard, but only 5 with a salary greater than $700.00. It is then best to start by finding the Emp No that have a high salary and then see whether these went to Harvard. In contradistinction, if only 5 went to Harvard, but 2000 earn more than $700.00, the best method is to find the Harvardians, and see if they have the salary qualification.

The dilemma of writing generalized software is therefore being replaced by heuristic optimizers in the query language. These mechanisms work on a set of algorithms and sometimes use the probabilities of occurrence of an element as the way of constructing the best-path solution. Many artificial intelligence and operations research techniques are being incorporated, and sampling and branch and bound methods are very popular. Storage structure techniques, such as the availability of inverted keys (hashed values) and internal links (because even relational systems may benefit from internally maintained nontable structure), can also be included in the algorithm, and the resulting process may be quite different because of this. SEE ARTIFICIAL INTELLIGENCE.

As a further example, the need for a search on school is greater if it is highly restrictive, yet some simple systems will always use an algorithm that selects on available inverted keys, thereby often giving large sets of possible intermediate values that are difficult to manipulate. For one large data base, the selection may be based on a person's nationality and date of birth. Now both of these columns have been inverted (their keys are in an inverted file structure), and a given nationality will produce several million possible answers while the date of birth gives only a hundred or so people. Unfortunately, the simple algorithm requires the two sets of selected records to be sorted and then merged: the consequent slow performance is not to user satisfaction.

In addition, a data dictionary allows entities other than data to be stored and manipulated, and relations may be defined between all entities. The implementor may ask: "What programs use the personnel file?" or "Which programmer wrote the accounts-receivable program?" This implies that there are entities like program, user, and programmer in dictionary.

Success factors. Although commercial offerings of data-base mangement systems have existed since the early 1960s, they have not always been successful. The degree of success depends on the expectations and resources, and often the expectations have been too high and the resources too low.

Many early failures were due to poor planning, lack of corporate commitment to the concept, or misapplication. The truly integrated data base requires a good management structure, as described for the data administrator and good technical support through the data-base administrator and systems programmers. If integration needs are not carefully assessed, unnecessarily large, monolithic data bases are formed, the result being poor performance and extra expense. Equally, the data-base management system should not be considered a new toy or merely a sophisticated access method. Thus good planning is needed to decide what is right for each organization. The degree of commitment of upper-level management is also critical to the success of a data-base management system. Data policy must not be changed rapidly or radically; otherwise the data-base structure and procedures will be forced to change just as quickly and problems will result. Thus, the major success factor in the implementation of the information system is a good, stable organizational plan for the management of data, with proper resource allocation, and structural change to allow for the new data administrator and data-base administrator roles in the organization.

The second success factor results from everyone understanding the meaning and use of the data. This strongly implies the use of a data dictionary. The third success factor is a good data structure. There are several design aids that have been developed for specific data-base management systems. They allow the data-base administrator to try various data structures for an anticipated usage, and thus they provide a means of tuning the structure for good performance. Such design aids have become the most important tools for the data-base administrator. The fourth success factor is programming good systems to access the data. This implies the use of a professional application systems group who know and understand the use of data-base management systems in general, and the selected system in particular.

The final success factor is providing user facilities, which might involve query language interfaces. These are available in many modern commercial data-base management systems, and they can be added on. Report generators (RPG) are also effective tools for the end user. The usefulness of these facilities depends on the education and support functions provided by the data administrator office so that noncomputer professionals can formulate simple queries and request reports without contacting the data-processing professionals. *See* DATA-PROCESSING SYSTEMS; DIGITAL COMPUTER.

Three-schema data-base methodology. The need to provide data to organizations in a controlled environment has led to the rapid adoption of the data-base technology, with still some distress on the part of users who need to have better access sooner. One of the problems that was addressed by a committee of the American National Standards Institute (ANSI), formed in 1972 to consider the need for standardization, was data independence. This is a somewhat misunderstood or ill-defined term; generally it is used to imply a minimum interaction between the way the user understands or "sees" the data and the way it is physically stored. However, as the above examples show, there is often a strange interaction between the logical and physical storage structure, and data independence is an attempt to reduce this. In particular, the relationships represented by the data and those relationships either explicitly stated or implied in the data are often very complex in an organization.

These considerations led to the idea that there were at least three kinds of schema needed by an organization:

1. External schema. This represented the data in the way that the users needed the data where users were considered as either programmers, transaction processing initiators (for example, airline ticket agents or bank tellers), computer-aided design/computer-aided manufacturing (CAD/CAM) system users, or ad hoc query system users. Needs of these classes of user will span the entire range of possibilities of data models, from tables for some clerks and managers to complex hierarchies or networks for the representation of parts and components in a CAM system. Though some commercial systems now have multiple interfaces (for example, IDMS has both network and relational interfaces to the same data base), some problems still arise in general. The idea of a multiplicity of different model views is, however, now being realized.

2. Internal schema. The use of a single schema to represent the way the system stores and relates the data is central to the data-base concept. Thus the idea of an internal schema allows the data-base administrator to decide what internal efficiencies and storage methods are appropriate for the organization and possibly also how they are mapped to the external schema.

3. Conceptual schema. Having realized that the real problems in data independence occurred because the relationship between the internal and external schema was neither simple nor stable, the committee decided that there was a need to isolate them, if possible, by making them both map to something that was more stable, the enterprise view of the data. Presumably this was not changing very fast, and thus if it could be captured in a new schema, it could form a more stable basis for design and modification of the system. The idea was therefore to relate the

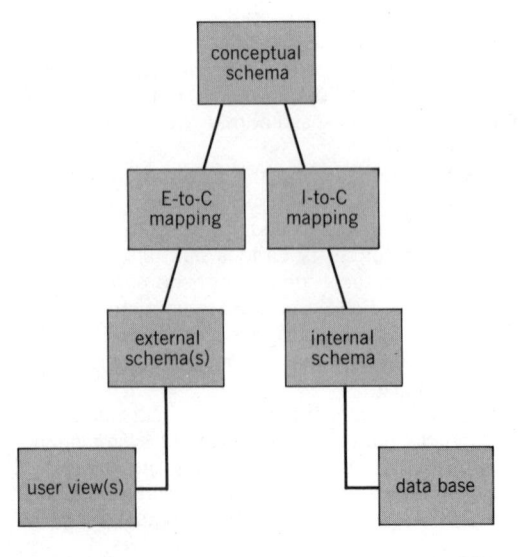

Fig. 7. Three-schema architecture. There will be as many user views as there are major classes of user. If there is a distributed data base, there may be several internal schema with consistency checks between them in the I-to-C mapping.

two other schemas through the conceptual schema (**Fig. 7**), mapping each to it so that the resulting mappings (I-to-C and E-to-C) could be changed independently of one another.

Since the three-schema architecture was proposed, there have been many research and development efforts aimed at exploiting the idea. In some of these, the conceptual schema is considered to be merely the agglomeration of all other schema presented in some slightly more consistent and palatable form. However, this somewhat subverts the intent of the original proposal: to provide a stable platform in a time of change. However, all systems that have tried to implement the concept are in a reserach (noncommercial) state, and thus the feasibility of the concept has not been tested.

Bibliography. S. Atre, *Data Base: Structured Techniques for Design, Performance, and Management*, 1980; *Database Engineering*, IEEE Computer Society Technical Committee, quarterly; G. C. Everest, *Database Management*, 1986; H. F. Korth and A. Silberschatz, *Database System Concepts*, 1986; H. C. Lefkovits, E. H. Sibley, and S. L. Lefkovits, *Information Resource/Data Dictionary Systems*, 1983; *Transactions on Database Systems*, Association for Computing Machinery, bimonthly; E. A. Unger, P. S. Fisher, and J. Slonim (eds.), *Advances in Data Base Management*, vol. 2, 1984.

COMPUTER SECURITY
H. Rex Hartson

The preservation of computing resources against abuse or unauthorized use, especially the protection of data from accidental or deliberate damage, disclosure, or modification. Safeguards are both technical and administrative. Threats are both external (physical) and internal (logical) to the computer system.

Computing systems provide powerful tools for the storage and use of information. They are equally powerful tools for the misuse of the same information. Because of the pervasiveness of computers in modern society, the potential for abuse has triggered public awareness of the need for computer security. Computer abuse, financial fraud, invasion of individual privacy, industrial espionage, and problems with national security, are primary concerns. The right of privacy is the right of individuals or organizations to determine the degree to which information about them is collected, stored, and shared with others. Protection of privacy is an ethical and legal issue rather than a technical one, and is not unique to computing systems; however, computer security mechanisms can be used to protect information for privacy as well. Protection of data integrity is assurance that stored data will be accurate and consistent.

Computer security policies are rules of access to computing resources. Security mechanisms are the means by which policies are implemented. Discretionary access-control policies support the concept of data ownership by individual users and their right to share the data with other users. Nondiscretionary policies, used primarily by the military, rely on a built-in hierarchy of security classifications used to make access decisions. Security based on classification hierarchies is also called multilevel security. Authorization is the process of granting access rights to, and revoking the access rights of, various users of a discretionary system. Enforcement is the process of ensuring that all accesses which occur are in accordance with the current state of authorization.

Maintaining computer security is a management responsibility involving both technical and administrative problems. Management tasks include policy formulation, arrangements for physical security, cost modeling, and auditing procedures to validate the security controls and keep a record of system transactions. The primary function of management is to evaluate security threats, risks, policies, and mechanisms.

Physical and logical security. Physical and logical security are two important parts of computer security. Physical security measures, external to the hardware and software, are intended to prevent, or to facilitate recovery from, physical disasters such as fire, floods, riots, sabotage, and theft of physical resources. Logical security mechanisms, internal to the computing system, are used to protect against internal misuse of computing resources, such as the theft of computing time and unauthorized access to data.

Physical security includes the control of physical access to computing resources. In order to make decisions about who can have access to each terminal and each user account, as well as to the computer room itself, the installation must have one or more mechanisms for authenticating personal identification. Some physical access-control mechanisms are based on something a person has, such as a key for a lock or a magnetically striped card; or something a person knows, such as a password or the correct answers to an authentication dialog. Keys and cards can be lost or stolen, and passwords copied or forgotten—or sometimes even guessed. Thus, some personal identification mechanisms are based on something a person is, such as dermatoglyphics (for example, fingerprints or lip prints) or anthropometrics (for example, individual hand or head geometry). Analysis of the dynamics of pen movement and pressure during the signing of a person's signature is a promising research direction. Cryptographic digital signatures provide unforgeable and verifiable user authentication. Most of the physical security mechanisms, of course, are not limited to computer security.

The problems of logical security, on the other hand, are more specific to computing. Logical computer security has several facets, including access controls, information flow controls, inference controls, and communication controls.

Logical access controls. All modern multiuser operating systems have some access controls for the sharing of resources, especially data. The objects protected by many systems are files. A coarse granularity of protection allows access to all of a file or none of it, and governs only a few access types, or operations on the objects, such as READ, WRITE, EXECUTE, or DELETE.

The access matrix (**Fig. 1**) is the basis for many methods of representing discretionary authorization information. The rows of the access matrix represent subjects, or users, of the system. The columns correspond to objects, or resources, of the system (mainly files). The authorization information contained in cell (x, y) of the table is a list of access types (allowable operations) that subject x may apply to object y. Access matrix entries are created, propagated, modified, and revoked as part of the authorization process. The enforcement process uses the matrix to determine whether to allow a request by a given subject to perform a specified operation on a certain object. A row of an access matrix is a capability list, which contains the access rights of a given subject to various objects. A column of a matrix is an access control list, which contains the access rights of various subjects to a given object.

The configuration of its access matrix at any point in time defines a system's protection state. The protection state is changed as a result of an authorization operation granting or revoking access rights, creating or deleting subjects or objects. These authorization operations are of course also subject to rights in the matrix. Theoretical results show that there is no general way to prove whether a given state of protection is safe, in the sense of whether it can leak an access

Objects / Subjects	File-1	File-2	...	SORT ROUTINE	...	File-*n*
SYSADMIN	--	--		OWN READ EXECUTE		--
USER 1	OWN READ	OWN READ WRITE		EXECUTE		--
SORT ROUTINE	READ	WRITE		--		--
...						
USER 17	--	READ		--		OWN READ WRITE

Fig. 1. Access matrix for representing discretionary authorization information.

SYSTEMS APPLICATIONS   307

right to an unauthorized cell in the access matrix. In practice, however, the safety question is trivially decidable for most real protection systems.

Access controls are also used in data-base management systems, but there are additional requirements. Data-base security needs a finer granularity (separate access decisions for small units of data). Access decisions must be based on a broader range of dependencies. For example, access might be conditional on data content, as in a policy which states that users in group X may not read any record from the personnel file for which the salary value is greater than $20,000. This policy cannot be implemented by the access matrix described above. Instead, the access condition (salary must be less than or equal to $20,000) is stored in the matrix and is evaluated at access time for each record that is about to be retrieved. This approach is called predicate-based protection. Procedural monitors, called formularies, have been used to evaluate access conditions. In another approach, called query modification, the access conditions are automatically combined with data-base queries before the data is retrieved. Queries thus modified cannot request unauthorized data. *See Data-base management systems.*

Information flow controls. While access controls protect access to data, they do not solve the problem of how to regulate what happens to the data after it is accessed. For example, someone authorized to read a top-secret file can make a copy of it. If access to the copy is not controlled as strictly as access to the original, the security of the information in the original can be compromised through the copy. Flow controls are concerned with labeling outputs of processes with authorization information consistent with the protection given the inputs. A multilevel protection policy called the star property expresses a flow restriction by not allowing information to flow from a given security classification to one that is lower (so that no one can later read the same information under a less strict access requirement). This property is extended in a lattice model of information flow, based on a hierarchy of security classes, which include both levels (for example, unclassified, confidential, secret, top secret) and sets of compartments (for example, NATO, nuclear, medical, financial) representing a need-to-know policy. Output from a program is not allowed to be sent to objects with security levels lower in the lattice than the highest level which has flowed from the inputs so far during the execution of the program. Alternatively, the security level of the file to which output is to be written can be raised, allowing the writing to proceed.

Security kernels. The difficulty of verifying a piece of software as large as an operating system had led to the concept of security kernels into which all security-related functions have been concentrated. An operating system kernel is a small, certifiably secure nucleus which is separate from the rest of the operating system. Nonkernel operating system software can then be allowed to run in a less protected environment. This new structure for operating systems, though achieved at the cost of a slight reduction in performance, has increased the trustworthiness of operating systems greatly over that of earlier systems with their defect-ridden, overly complicated patchworks of software. Most kernels implement multilevel, nondiscretionary security policies for access and flow controls. The simple security condition controls access by preventing a user operating at a given security level from reading data classified at a higher level. The star property controls flow by preventing the user from writing to a higher level. *See Operating systems.*

Inference controls. Statistical data bases are intended to provide statistical information (for example, demographic data) about groups of people without allowing access to data about specific individuals. However, it is often possible to infer data about an individual, given the statistical results for a group and some amount of prior knowledge about the individual. As an example, consider this query and its result:

COUNT (COLOR_EYES = GREEN AND
TOWN = LYONSDALE, NY) = 1

If it is known that a given individual fits this description, other details about that individual can illegally be deduced, for example, by:

COUNT (COLOR_EYES = GREEN AND
TOWN = LYONSDALE, NY
AND OCCUPATION = BOOKMAKER)

If this count is 1 also, that individual is a bookmaker. If small counts are not allowed in the responses, inference can still be made if information about the target individual is revealed in the difference between two large sets of people.

A mathematical device called a tracker provides a more general approach to inferring individual values. This approach is based on submitting statistical queries whose responses overlap. The overlapping process partitions the data base to form sets of records which act by inclusion and exclusion to isolate an individual record. Theoretical results indicate that very few statistical data bases can be made safe from all inference without becoming too restrictive for intended uses. For very large statistical data bases (for example, census data), it is effective to allow access only to randomly selected sample subsets of data which summarize the statistical characteristics of the full data base. Sometimes inference can be forestalled by introducing noise, in the form of slight random variations, into the data values.

Cryptographic controls. Cryptographic controls provide the means to encode data for storage or transmission so that even if an unauthorized person sees the data it will still be unreadable. Cryptographic controls thus protect transmitted data against electronic eavesdropping (for example, wiretapping). They also protect against the reading of data from tapes or disk packs that have been removed from their intended computers and therefore from access controls. Cryptographic controls protect the secrecy of the data and can provide proof of authenticity, so that a receiver of the data can be certain who sent it and that it is unmodified. Encryption is an encoding of the data, to be stored or transmitted, into a secret message by means of a key, which is the map to the encryption method. Decryption, also by a key, is necessary to return the data to its plainly readable form, called plaintext (**Fig. 2**). Transposition is a method of encryption that rearranges the symbols of the message. Substitution methods replace each message symbol with another symbol. Polyalphabetic substitution alternates between two or more sets of substitution alphabets for each plaintext symbol. If substitution is made from a table of symbols, the table is the key. Typically, the key is a parameter to an algorithm which computes the substitutions. For example, in a Caesar Cipher, for each letter in the alphabet the substitute is the letter which appears x letters later in the alphabet. Here, x is the key. If x is 1, substitute B for A. If x is 2, substitute C for A, and so on. The success of the system depends not on hiding the method of encryption, but on keeping the value of the key hidden. Thus, although the messages can be transmitted over open channels (channels susceptible to eavesdropping), the keys must be sent securely (perhaps hand-carried). Computer-generated pseudorandom sequences (sequences of nearly random numbers whose generation can be repeated) provide large, variable keys that are combined arithmetically (by multiplication, and so forth) with the numeric codes for the plaintext symbols to make encryptions which are very difficult to break.

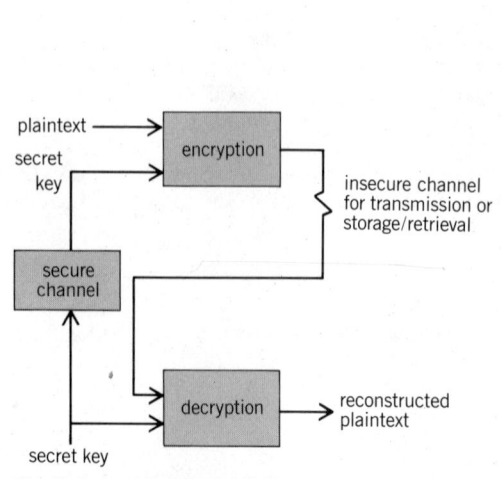

Fig. 2. Conventional encryption.

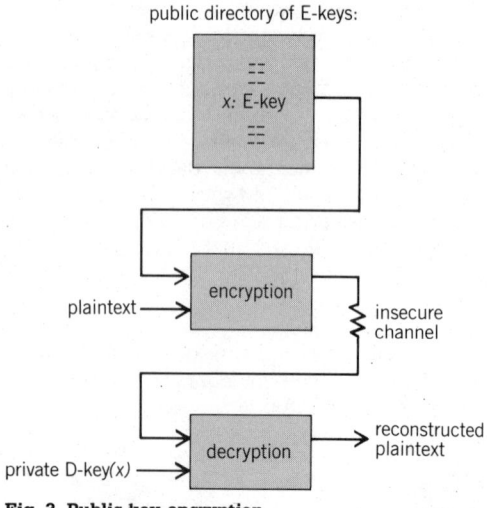

Fig. 3. Public key encryption.

In the interest of common hardware and communication interfaces, the National Bureau of Standards has produced a standard encryption algorithm, the Data Encryption Standard (DES), which has been mass-produced in integrated circuit microchips. The DES algorithm uses a combination of substitution and transposition and has been criticized for being too easy to break.

A recently developed method, called public-key encryption, uses two keys, one for encryption and a different one for decryption **(Fig. 3)**. The advantage is that the encryption key does not have to be transmitted in a secret way (for example, hand-carried). Anyone sending a message to party X uses X's encryption key, which is known publicly. The decryption key, however, is private to X. The two keys are related mathematically, but it is intended to be computationally too difficult to derive the decryption key from the public encryption key. SEE CRYPTOGRAPHY.

Bibliography. D. E. Denning, *Cryptography and Data Security*, 1982; E. B. Fernandez, R. C. Summers, and C. Wood, *Database Security and Integrity*, 1981; H. R. Hartson, Database security: Systems architecture, *Inform. Sys.*, 6:1–22, 1981; J. B. Grimson and H. J. Kugler (eds.), *Computer Security: The Practical Issues in a Troubled World*, 1986; L. J. Hoffman, *Modern Methods for Computer Security and Privacy*, 1977; R. T. Moulton, *Computer Security Handbook*, 1986.

CRYPTOGRAPHY

CARL H. MEYER, STEPHEN M. MATYAS, AND DON COPPERSMITH

The various methods for writing in secret code or cipher. As society becomes increasingly dependent upon computers, the vast amounts of data communicated, processed, and stored within computer systems and networks often have to be protected, and cryptography is a means of achieving this protection. It is the only practical method for protecting information transmitted through accessible communication networks such as telephone lines, satellites, or microwave systems. Furthermore, in certain cases, it may be the most economical way to protect stored data. Cryptographic procedures can also be used for message authentication, personal identification, and digital signature verification for electronic funds transfer and credit card transactions. SEE COMPUTER SECURITY; DATA-BASE MANAGEMENT SYSTEMS; DATA COMMUNICATIONS; DIGITAL COMPUTER.

Cryptographic algorithms. Cryptography must resist decoding or deciphering by unauthorized personnel; that is, messages (plaintext) transformed into cryptograms (codetext or ciphertext) have to be able to withstand intense cryptanalysis. Transformations can be done by using either code or cipher systems. Code systems rely on code books to transform the plaintext words, phrases, and sentences into codetext or code groups. To prevent cryptanalysis, there must be a great number of plaintext passages in the code book and the code group equivalents must be kept secret. To isolate users from each other, different codes must be used, making it difficult to utilize code books in electronic data-processing systems.

Cipher systems are more versatile. Messages are transformed through the use of two basic elements: a set of unchanging rules or steps called a cryptographic algorithm, and a set of variable cryptographic keys. The algorithm is composed of enciphering (**E**) and deciphering (**D**) procedures which usually are identical or simply consist of the same steps performed in reverse order, but which can be dissimilar. The keys, selected by the user, consist of a sequence of numbers or characters. An enciphering key (Ke) is used to encipher plaintext (X) into ciphertext (Y) as in Eq. (1), and a deciphering key (Kd) is used to decipher ciphertext (Y) into plaintext (X) as in Eq. (2).

$$\mathbf{E}_{Ke}(X) = Y \qquad (1) \qquad \mathbf{D}_{Kd}[\mathbf{E}_{Ke}(X)] = \mathbf{D}_{Kd}(Y) = X \qquad (2)$$

Algorithms are of two types—conventional and public-key (also referred to as symmetric and asymmetric). The enciphering and deciphering keys in a conventional algorithm either may be easily computed from each other or may be identical (Ke = Kd = K, denoting $\mathbf{E}_K(X) = Y$ for encipherment and $\mathbf{D}_K(Y) = X$ for decipherment). In a public-key algorithm, one key (usually the enciphering key) is made public, and a different key (usually the deciphering key) is kept private. In such an approach it must not be possible to deduce the private key from the public key.

When an algorithm is made public, for example, as a published encryption standard, cryptographic security completely depends on protecting those cryptographic keys specified as secret. SEE ALGORITHM.

Unbreakable ciphers. Unbreakable ciphers are possible. But the key must be randomly selected and used only once, and its length must be equal to or greater than that of the plaintext to be enciphered. Therefore such long keys, called one-time tapes, are not practical in data-processing applications.

To work well, a key must be of fixed length, relatively short, and capable of being repeatedly used without compromising security. In theory, any algorithm that uses such a finite key can be analyzed; in practice, the effort and resources necessary to break the algorithm would be unjustified.

Strong algorithms. Fortunately, to achieve effective data security, construction of an unbreakable algorithm is not necessary. However, the work factor (a measure, under a given set of assumptions, of the requirements necessary for a specific analysis or attack against a cryptographic algorithm) required to break the algorithm must be sufficiently great. Included in the set of assumptions is the type of information expected to be available for cryptanalysis. For example, this could be ciphertext only; plaintext (not chosen) and corresponding ciphertext; chosen plaintext and corresponding ciphertext; or chosen ciphertext and corresponding recovered plaintext.

A strong cryptographic algorithm must satisfy the following conditions: (1) The algorithm's mathematical complexity prevents, for all practical purposes, solution through analytical methods. (2) The cost or time necessary to unravel the message or key is too great when mathematically less complicated methods are used, because either too many computational steps are involved (for example, in trying one key after another) or because too much storage space is required (for example, in an analysis requiring data accumulations such as dictionaries and statistical tables).

To be strong, the algorithm must satisfy the above conditions even when the analyst has the following advantages: (1) Relatively large amounts of plaintext (specified by the analyst, if so desired) and corresponding ciphertext are available. (2) Relatively large amounts of ciphertext (specified by the analyst, if so desired) and corresponding recovered plaintext are available. (3) All details of the algorithm are available to the analyst; that is, cryptographic strength cannot depend on the algorithm remaining secret. (4) Large high-speed computers are available for cryptanalysis.

In summary, even with an unlimited amount of computational power, data storage, and calendar time, the message or key in an unbreakable algorithm cannot be obtained through cryptanalysis. On the other hand, although a strong algorithm may be breakable in theory, in practice it is not.

Computational complexity. The strength of a cryptographic scheme can be measured by the computational complexity of the task of cryptanalysis. The term complexity, when referring to a program or algorithm to accomplish a given task, means the number of elementary operations used by this program. The complexity of a task is the least possible number of elementary operations used by any program to accomplish this task. This is directly related to sequential time, or the time used by a conventional sequential computer. Of course, the time used by a faster computer will be less than that used by a slower computer. Other measures of importance are storage and parallel time, or the time used on a highly parallelized computer.

Given a particular algorithm (computer program) for solving a problem, analysis of the algorithm can involve probability theory, detailed knowledge of the problem at hand, and other disciplines, but meaningful estimates of the resource consumption of the algorithm can usually be provided. This gives an upper bound to the complexity of the given problem.

However, nontrivial lower bounds are very hard to obtain. This is a fundamental problem in the design of cryptographic systems: it is very difficult to ensure that a system is sufficiently hard to crack. Without a good lower bound, the possibility that someone will find a fast algorithm for cryptanalyzing a given scheme must always be anticipated.

Problem classes P and NP. An important direction of theoretical work concerns the consideration (from computer science) of P versus NP. The class P consists of those problems which can be solved in polynomial time. That is, there are constants c and k such that, if the input to the problem can be specified in N bits, the problem can be solved on a sequential machine in time $c \times N^k$. Roughly speaking, these are the tractable problems. They include multiplication of two large numbers, exponentiation modulo a large prime, running the Data Encryption Standard (discussed below), and roughly any straightforward problem which does not involve searching.

The class NP (nondeterministic polynomial time) consists of problems which can be solved by searching. Roughly speaking, a possible solution to a problem in NP is to guess in turn each of 2^N possible values of some N-bit quantity, do some polynomial-time work related to each guess, and if some guess turns out to be correct, report the answer.

An example of a problem in NP is the knapsack problem: Given a set of integers $\{A_1, A_2, \ldots, A_n\}$ and a target integer B, can a subset of the A_i be selected without repetition (say $\{A_1, A_3, A_8\}$) such that their sum $(A_1 + A_3 + A_8)$ is the target B? One algorithm for solution is to try all possible subsets and just see whether any has the desired property. This algorithm requires exponential time, so called because the size of the input (n) occurs in the exponent of the formula expressing the running time (in this case, roughly 2^n). In fact, all known algorithms for this problem require exponential time. But there may be an unknown algorithm which runs in polynomial time; no proof prohibiting this is currently known.

Certainly, any problem in P is also in NP. A major outstanding question in computer science is whether P equals NP or whether NP is strictly larger.

There is a particular collection of problems in NP, including the knapsack problem, which are termed NP-complete. These can be thought of as the hardest problems in NP. More precisely, either P = NP or P ≠ NP. If P = NP, then any problem in NP is also in P. If P ≠ NP, then there are problems that cannot be done in polynomial time on a conventional sequential computer but can be done in polynomial time on a nondeterministic computer. An important mathematical result states: if there are any such problems in NP but not in P, then each NP-complete problem is also in NP but not in P. This class has particular significance for cryptography.

In a good cryptographic system, certain operations (like decryption) are easy for those in possession of the key and difficult for those without the key. (In some public-key applications, encryption should be easy and decryption should be difficult.) The legitimate user, in possession of the key, should be able to easily decrypt messages, and this task should be polynomial-time on a conventional sequential machine. The cryptanalyst who could first guess and verify the correct key would be able to decrypt easily (in polynomial time). This could be done by searching over the space of possible keys and attempting to verify each one in polynomial time. Since the problem can be solved by searching, decryption is in NP.

If P = NP, then decryption would also be in P, and a good cryptographic system would most likely be difficult to design. Even if no way was seen to easily decrypt without the key, P = NP would guarantee the existence of an algorithm whereby the cryptanalyst could "easily" decrypt any message. Of course, this is not a proof, merely an intuitive argument. In particular, "easy" and "polynomial-time" are not exactly the same thing.

If P ≠ NP, then the NP-complete problems might form a good starting point for cryptographic system design. They are in NP, so that a machine endowed with fortunate guesses or inside information (that is, the key) can easily solve the problem (decrypt). But they are not in P, so that machines without such inside information would require time larger than any fixed polynomial (that is, the cryptanalyst's job would be "hard").

Unfortunately, mathematicians and cryptographers have not yet learned how to transform an NP-complete problem into a secure cryptographic system. In one attempt to do so, R. Merkle and M. Hellman devised a public-key scheme for encryption based on the knapsack problem. They showed how to choose a secret key K and generate from that key a set $\{A_i\}$ so that the legitimate user, knowing K, could easily solve a knapsack problem based on $\{A_i\}$, while the opponent, without K, would presumably have a difficult time. However, it turned out that the particular choice of $\{A_i\}$ prescribed in this scheme, chosen for ease of decoding by the legitimate user in possession of the key, rendered the scheme liable to attack by integer programming. Although some instances of knapsack problems are difficult, the special instances used by Merkle and Hellman were shown to be easy.

Even if an NP-complete problem is eventually transformed successfully into a cryptographic system, a proof of the difficulty of cryptanalysis of that system (or any other) can be expected to be taxing. Such a proof would probably also prove that P ≠ NP, and this conjecture has eluded computer scientists for several years. Thus, for now, the designers of cryptographic systems must rely on experience rather than rigorous proof of the difficulty of cryptanalysis.

Examples. Examples of the most efficient known attacks on several popular cryptographic systems are discussed below. The Data Encryption Standard (DES) apparently requires key exhaustion in order to break it. That is, no known method is faster than trying in turn each of the

$2^{56} \simeq 10^{17}$ keys, a task which would strain the largest computing facilities for years to come. An attack has been devised that allows this to be done in 2^{56} computations once and for all, storing a table of $2^{40} \simeq 10^{12}$ words, and using this table with a relatively modest amount of computation (2^{40} steps) to break a given key, under the assumption of chosen plaintext or chosen ciphertext. This attack fails when chaining techniques are employed [such as cipher block chaining (CBC) and cipher feedback (CFB) modes of encryption], so that DES is still safe. The attack also fails against repeated encipherment with three independent keys. There is no guarantee against a more efficient, analytic attack, although none is known at present.

The RSA algorithm, also discussed below, is based on the difficulty of factoring large numbers. However, a family of algorithms has been developed for factoring such numbers. Fifty-digit numbers are routinely factored in a matter of hours, and sixty- or seventy-digit numbers will be handled in a matter of days or months, respectively, before long. If the modulus involved has, say, 200 digits, then RSA should be secure in the foreseeable future.

Another proposed number-theoretic cryptographic scheme is based on the difficulty of solving the discrete logarithm problem. This problem involves modular arithmetic. Two integers a and b are congruent for the modulus m if their difference ($a - b$) is divisible by the integer m. This is expressed by the symbolic statement $a \equiv b \pmod{m}$, where mod is short for modulus. If P is a prime and E is an integer, E is a primitive element when E^0 mod P, E^1 mod P, E^2 mod P, ..., E^{P-2} mod P are all different, and take on each nonzero value mod P exactly once. Equivalently, if m is the least positive integer such that $E^m = 1$ mod P, E is primitive when $m = P - 1$. SEE NUMBER THEORY.

If P is a prime and E a primitive element mod P, then given X it is straightforward to compute Y such that Eq. (3) is satisfied, while it is more difficult to recover X given Y, E, and P.

$$E^X \equiv Y \bmod P \qquad (3)$$

But a modification of the factoring algorithm discussed above handles this discrete logarithm problem as well. This algorithm recovers X in a time given by expression (4) for some small

$$e^{c\sqrt{(\log P \log \log P)}} \qquad (4)$$

constant c; this is eventually smaller than any fixed fractional power of P such as $P^{1/6}$. Thus, this scheme also requires a large modulus P for security.

In summary, an outstanding problem in the field of computational complexity is to devise a provably secure cryptographic system. A second, perhaps easier, problem is to devise a cryptographic system which is provably at least NP-hard.

Privacy and authentication. Anyone can encipher data in a public-key cryptographic system (**Fig. 1**) by using the public enciphering key, but only the authorized user can decipher the data through possession of the secret deciphering key. Since anyone can encipher data, message authentication is necessary in order to identify a message's sender.

A message authentication procedure can be devised (**Fig. 2**) by keeping the enciphering key secret and making the deciphering key public, provided that the enciphering key cannot be obtained from the deciphering key. This makes it impossible for nondesignated personnel to encipher messages, that is, to produce $\mathbf{E}_{Ke}(X)$. By inserting prearranged information in all messages, such as originator identification, recipient identification, and message sequence number, the messages can be checked to determine if they are genuine. However, because the contents of the messages are available to anyone having the public deciphering key, privacy cannot be attained.

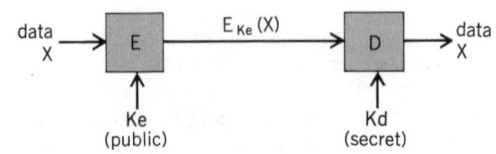

Fig. 1. Public-key cryptographic system used for privacy only.

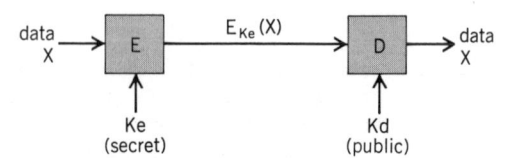

Fig. 2. Public-key cryptographic system used for message authentication only.

A public-key algorithm provides privacy as well as authentication (**Fig. 3**) if encipherment followed by decipherment, and decipherment followed by encipherment, produce the original plaintext, as in Eq. (5). A message to be authenticated is first deciphered by the sender (A) with

$$D_{Kd}[E_{Ke}(X)] = E_{Ke}[D_{Kd}(X)] = X \tag{5}$$

a secret deciphering key (KAd). Privacy is ensured by enciphering the result with the receiver's (B's) public enciphering key (KBe).

Effective data security with public-key algorithms demands that the correct public key be used, since otherwise the system is exposed to attack. For example, if A can be tricked into using C's instead of B's public key, C can decipher the secret communications sent from A to B and can transmit messages to A pretending to be B. Thus key secrecy and key integrity are two distinct and very important attributes of cryptographic keys. While the requirement for key secrecy is relaxed for one of the keys in a public-key algorithm, the requirement for key integrity is not.

In a conventional cryptographic system, data are effectively protected because only the sender and receiver of the message share a common secret key. Such a system automatically provides both privacy and authentication (**Fig. 4**).

Digital signatures. Digital signatures authenticate messages by ensuring that: the sender cannot later disavow messages; the receiver cannot forge messages or signatures; and the receiver can prove to others that the contents of a message are genuine and that the message originated with that particular sender. The digital signature is a function of the message, a secret key or keys possessed by the sender and sometimes data that are nonsecret or that may become nonsecret as part of the procedure (such as a secret key that is later made public).

Digital signatures are more easily obtained with public-key then with conventional algorithms. When a message is enciphered with a private key (known only to the originator), anyone deciphering the message with the public key can identify the originator. The originator cannot later deny having sent the message. Receivers cannot forge messages and signatures, since they do not possess the originator's private key.

Since enciphering and deciphering keys are identical in a conventional algorithm, digital signatures must be obtained in some other manner. One method is to use a set of keys to produce the signature. Some of the keys are made known to the receiver to permit signature verification, and the rest of the keys are retained by the originator in order to prevent forgery.

Data Encryption Standard. Regardless of the application, a cryptographic system must be based on a cryptographic algorithm of validated strength if it is to be acceptable. The DES is such a validated conventional algorithm already in the public domain. (Since public-key algorithms are relatively recent, their strength has yet to be validated.)

During 1968–1975, IBM developed a cryptographic procedure that enciphers a 64-bit block of plaintext into a 64-bit block of ciphertext under the control of a 56-bit key. The National Bureau of Standards accepted this algorithm as a standard, and it became effective on July 15, 1977.

Conceptually, the DES can be thought of as a huge key-controlled substitution box (S-box) with a 64-bit input and output. With such an S-box, 2^{64}! different transformations or functions

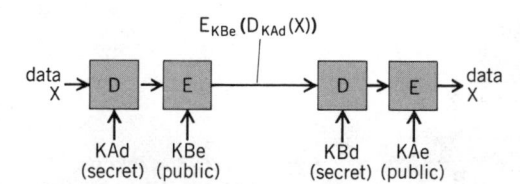

Fig. 3. Public-key cryptographic system used for both message authentication and privacy. KAe and KAd are enciphering and deciphering keys of the sender (A). KBe and KBd are enciphering and deciphering keys of the receiver (B).

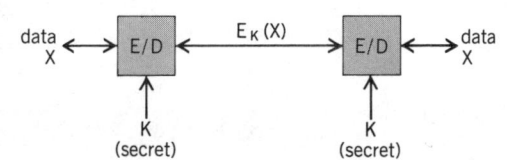

Fig. 4. Conventional cryptographic system in which message authentication and message privacy are provided simultaneously. K represents a common secret key.

from plaintext to ciphertext are possible. The 56-bit key used with DES thus limits the number of usable functions to 2^{56}.

A single huge S-box is impossible to construct. Therefore DES is implemented by using several smaller S-boxes (with a 6-bit input and a 4-bit output) and permuting their concatenated outputs. By repeating the substitution and permutation process several times, cryptographic strength "builds up." The DES encryption process consists of 16 iterations, called rounds. At each round a cipher function (f) is used with a 48-bit key. The function comprises the substitution and permutation. The 48-bit key, which is different for each round, is a subset of the bits in the externally supplied key.

The interaction of data, cryptographic key (K), and f is shown in **Fig. 5**. The externally supplied key consists of 64 bits (56 bits are used by the algorithm, and up to 8 bits may be used for parity checking). By shifting the original 56-bit key, a different subset of 48 key bits is selected for use in each round. These key bits are labeled $K_1, K_2, \ldots, K_{16}$. To decipher, the keys are used in reverse order (K_{16} is used in round one, K_{15} in round two, and so on).

At each round (either encipherment or decipherment), the input is split into a left half (designated L), and a right half (designated R), (Fig. 5). R is transformed with f, and the result is combined, using modulo 2 addition (also called the EXCLUSIVE OR operation; see **Table 1**), with L. This approach, as discussed below, ensures that encipher and decipher operations can be designed regardless of how f is defined.

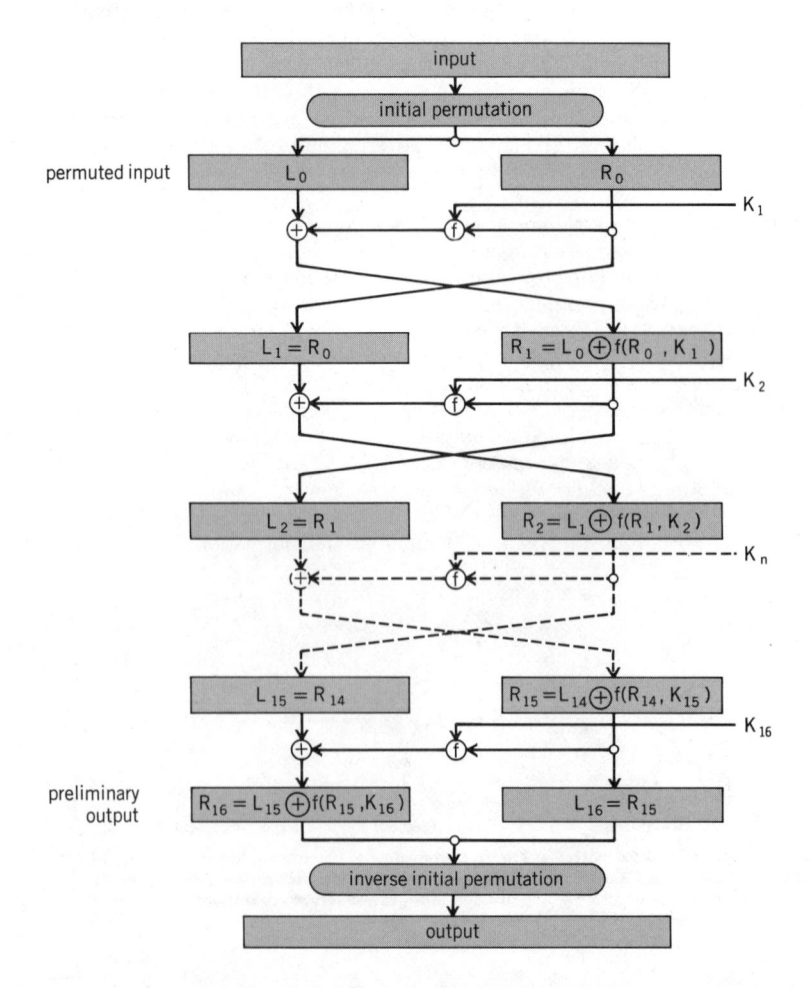

Fig. 5. Enciphering computation in the Data Encryption Standard. (*After Data Encryption Standard, FIPS Publ.46, National Bureau of Standards, 1977*)

SYSTEMS APPLICATIONS 315

Table 1. Modulo 2 addition

A	B	A ⊕ B
0	0	0
0	1	1
1	0	1
1	1	0

Consider the steps that occur during one round of encipherment (**Fig. 6**). Let the input block (X) be denoted $X = (L_0, R_0)$, where L_0 and R_0 are the left and right halves of X, respectively. Function f transforms R_0 into $f_{K_1}(R_0)$ under control of cipher key K_1. L_0 is then added (modulo 2) to $f_{K_1}(R_0)$ to obtain R_1, as in Eq. (6). The round is then completed by setting L_1 equal to R_0.

$$L_0 \oplus f_{K_1}(R_0) = R_1 \qquad (6)$$

The above steps are reversible without introducing any new parameters or requiring that f be a one-to-one function. The ciphertext contains L_1, which equals R_0, and therefore half of the original plaintext is immediately recovered (**Fig. 7**). The remaining half, L_0, is recovered by recreating $f_{K_1}(R_0)$ from $R_0 = L_1$ and adding it (modulo 2) to R_1, as in Eq. (7). However, to use the

$$R_1 \oplus f_{K_1}(R_0) = [L_0 \oplus f_{K_1}(R_0)] \oplus f_{K_1}(R_0) = L_0 \qquad (7)$$

procedure in Fig. 6 for encipherment as well as decipherment, the left and right halves of the output must be interchanged; that is, the ciphertext (Y) is defined by Eq. (8). This modified pro-

$$Y = [L_0 \oplus f_{K_1}(R_0)], R_0 \qquad (8)$$

cedure easily extends to n rounds, where the keys used for deciphering are $K_n, K_{n-1}, \ldots, K_1$.

RSA public-key algorithm. The RSA algorithm (named for the algorithm's inventors, R. L. Rivest, A. Shamir, and L. Adleman) is based on the fact that factoring large composite numbers into their prime factors involves an overwhelming amount of computation. (A prime number is an integer that is divisible only by 1 and itself. Otherwise, the number is said to be composite. Every

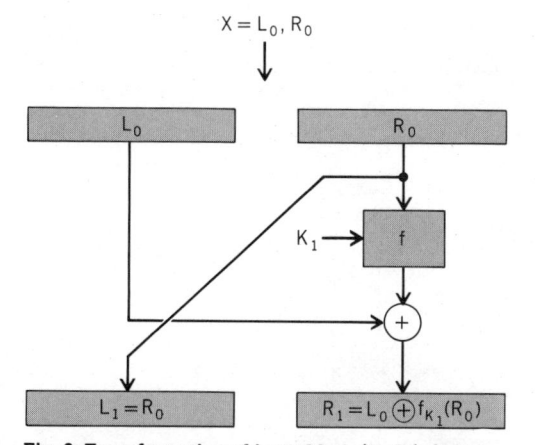

Fig. 6. Transformation of input block (L_0, R_0). (*After C. H. Meyer and S. M. Matyas. Cryptography: A New Dimension in Computer Data Security, John Wiley and Sons, 1980*)

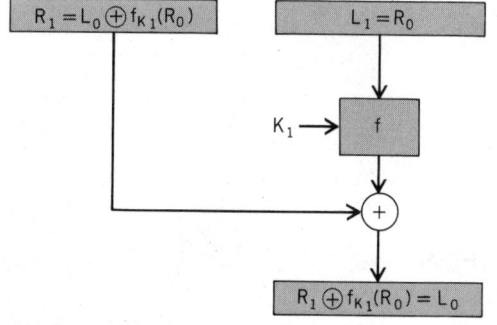

Fig. 7. Recovery of L_0. (*After C. H. Meyer and S. M. Matyas. Cryptography: A New Dimension in Computer Data Security, John Wiley and Sons, 1980*)

composite number can be factored uniquely into prime factors. For example, the composite number 999,999 is factored by the primes 3, 7, 11, 13, and 37, that is $999{,}999 = 3^3 \cdot 7 \cdot 11 \cdot 13 \cdot 37$).
To describe the RSA algorithm, the following quantities are defined:

p and q are primes	(secret)
$r = p \cdot q$	(nonsecret)
$\phi(r) = (p-1)(q-1)$	(secret)
Kd is the private key	(secret)
Ke is the public key	(nonsecret)
X is the plaintext	(secret)
Y is the ciphertext	(nonsecret)

Based on an extension of Euler's theorem, Eq. (9), the algorithm's public and private keys (Ke and

$$X^{m\phi(r)+1} \equiv X \pmod{r} \qquad (9)$$

Kd) are chosen so that Eq. (10) or, equivalently, Eq. (11) is satisfied. By selecting two secret prime

$$Kd \cdot Ke = m\phi(r) + 1 \qquad (10) \qquad Kd \cdot Ke \equiv 1[\bmod \phi(r)] \qquad (11)$$

numbers p and q, the user can calculate $r = p \cdot q$, which is made public, and $\phi(r) = (p-1)(q-1)$, which remains secret and is used to solve Eq. (11). (Tests are available to determine with a high level of confidence if a number is prime or not.) To obtain a unique solution for the public key (Ke), a random number, or secret key (Kd), is selected that is relatively prime to $\phi(r)$. (Integers a and b are relatively prime if their greatest common divisor is 1.) Ke is the multiplicative inverse of Kd, modulo $\phi(r)$, and Ke can be calculated from Kd and $\phi(r)$ by using Euclid's algorithm. Equation (9) can therefore be rewritten as Eq. (12), which holds true for any plaintext (X).

$$X^{Kd \cdot Ke} \equiv X \pmod{r} \qquad (12)$$

Encipherment and decipherment can now be interpreted as in Eqs. (13) and (14). Moreover,

$$\mathbf{E}_{Ke}(X) = Y \equiv X^{Ke} \pmod{r} \qquad (13)$$

$$\mathbf{D}_{Kd}(Y) \equiv Y^{Kd} \pmod{r}$$
$$\equiv X^{Ke \cdot Kd} \pmod{r} \equiv X \pmod{r} \qquad (14)$$

because multiplication is a commutative operation (Ke $\cdot$ Kd = Kd $\cdot$ Ke), encipherment followed by decipherment is the same as decipherment followed by encipherment [Eq. (5)]. Thus the RSA algorithm can be used for both privacy and digital signatures.

Finally, since $X^{Ke} \pmod{r} \equiv (X + mr)^{Ke} \pmod{r}$ for any integer m, $\mathbf{E}_{Ke}(X) = \mathbf{E}_{Ke}(X + mr)$. Thus the transformation from plaintext to ciphertext, which is many-to-one, is made one-to-one by restricting X to the set $\{0, 1, \ldots, r-1\}$.

Block ciphers. A block cipher (**Fig. 8**) transforms a string of input bits of fixed length (termed an input block) into a string of output bits of fixed length (termed an output block). In a

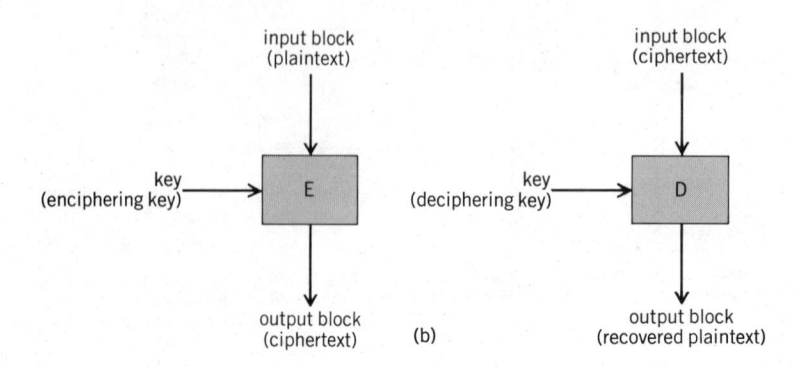

Fig. 8. Block cipher. (a) Enciphering. (b) Deciphering.

strong block cipher, the enciphering and deciphering functions are such that every bit in the output block jointly depends on every bit in the input block and on every bit in the key. This property is termed intersymbol dependence.

The following example (using DES) illustrates the marked change produced in a recovered plaintext when only one bit is changed in the ciphertext or key. Hexadecimal notation (**Table 2**) is used. If the plaintext 1000000000000001 is enciphered with a (56-bit) key 30000000000000, then the ciphertext 958E6E627A05557B is produced. The original plaintext is recovered if 958E6E627A05557B is now deciphered with 30000000000000. However, if the leading 9 in the ciphertext is changed to 8 (a one-bit change) and the ciphertext 858E6E627A05557B is now deciphered with key 30000000000000, the recovered plaintext is 8D4893C2966CC211, not 1000000000000001. On the other hand, if the leading 3 in the key is changed to 1 (another one-bit change) and the ciphertext 958E6E627A05557B is now deciphered with key 10000000000000, the recovered plaintext is 6D4B945376725395. (The same effect is also observed during encipherment.)

In the most basic implementation of DES, called block encryption or electronic codebook mode (ECB), each 64-bit block of data is enciphered and deciphered separately. Every bit in a given output block depends on every bit in its respective input block and on every bit in the key, but on no other bits.

As a rule, block encryption is used to protect keys. A different method, called chained block encryption, is used to protect data. In chaining, the process of enciphering and deciphering is made dependent on other (prior) data, plaintext, ciphertext, and the like, also available at the time enciphering and deciphering takes place. Thus every bit in a given output block depends not only on every bit in its respective input block and every bit in the key, but also on any or all prior data bits, either inputted to, or produced during, the enciphering or deciphering process.

Sometimes data to be enciphered contain patterns that extend beyond the cipher's block size. These patterns in the plaintext can then result in similar patterns in the ciphertext, which would indicate to a cryptanalyst something about the nature of the plaintext. Thus, chaining is useful because it significantly reduces the presence of repetitive patterns in the ciphertext. This is because two equal input blocks encipher into unequal output blocks.

A recommended technique for block chaining, referred to as cipher block chaining (CBC), uses a ciphertext feedback (**Fig. 9**). Let $X_1, X_2, \ldots, X_n$ denote blocks of plaintext to be chained using key K; let Y_0 be a nonsecret quantity defined as the initializing vector; and let $Y_1, Y_2, \ldots, Y_n$ denote the blocks of ciphertext produced. The ith block of ciphertext (Y_i) is produced by EXCLUSIVE ORing Y_{i-1} with X_i and enciphering the result with K, as in Eq. (15), where $\oplus$ denotes the

Table 2. Hexadecimal and binary notation

Hexadecimal digit	Binary digits
0	0000
1	0001
2	0010
3	0011
4	0100
5	0101
6	0110
7	0111
8	1000
9	1001
A	1010
B	1011
C	1100
D	1101
E	1110
F	1111

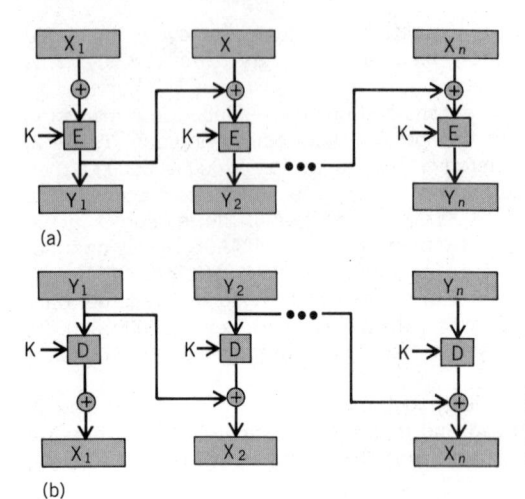

Fig. 9. Block chaining with ciphertext feedback. (a) Enciphering. (b) Deciphering. (*After C. H. Meyer and S. M. Matyas. Cryptography: A New Dimension in Computer Data Security, John Wiley and Sons, 1980*)

$$\mathbf{E}_K(X_i \oplus Y_{i-1}) = Y_i \quad i \geq 1 \tag{15}$$

EXCLUSIVE OR operation, or modulo 2 addition. Since every bit in Y_i depends on every bit in X_1 through X_i, patterns in the plaintext are not reflected in the ciphertext.

The ith block of plaintext (X_i) is recovered by deciphering Y_i with K and EXCLUSIVE ORing the result with Y_{i-1}, as in Eq. (16). Since the recovered plaintext X_i depends only on Y_i and Y_{i-1},

$$\mathbf{D}_K(Y_i) \oplus Y_{i-1} = X_1 \quad i \geq 1 \tag{16}$$

an error occurring in ciphertext Y_j affects only two blocks of recovered plaintext (X_j and X_{j+1}).

Stream ciphers. A stream cipher (**Fig. 10**) employs a bit-stream generator to produce a stream of binary digits (0's and 1's) called a cryptographic bit stream, which is then combined either with plaintext (via the $\boxplus$ operator) to produce ciphertext or with ciphertext (via the $\boxplus^{-1}$ operator) to recover plaintext. (Traditionally, the term key stream has been used to denote the bit stream produced by the bit-stream generator. The term cryptographic bit stream is used here to avoid possible confusion with a fixed-length cryptographic key in cases where a cryptographic algorithm is used as the bit-stream generator.)

Historically, G. S. Vernam was the first to recognize the merit of a cipher in which ciphertext (Y) was produced from plaintext (X) by combining it with a secret bit stream (R) via a simple and efficient operation. In his cipher, Vernam used an EXCLUSIVE OR operation, or modulo 2 addition (Table 1), to combine the respective bit streams. Thus encipherment and decipherment are defined by $X \oplus R = Y$ and $Y \oplus R = X$, respectively. Therefore $\boxplus = \boxplus^{-1} = \oplus$. Modulo 2 addition is the combining operation used in most stream ciphers, and for this reason it is used in the following discussion.

If the bit-stream generator were truly random, an unbreakable cipher could be obtained by EXCLUSIVE ORing the plaintext and cryptographic bit stream. The cryptographic bit stream would

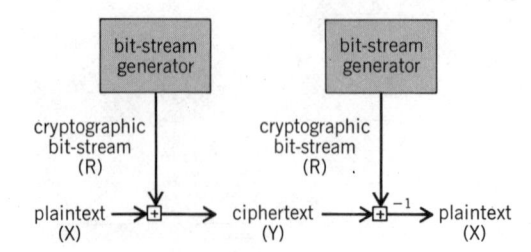

Fig. 10. Stream cipher concept. (*After C. H. Meyer and S. M. Matyas. Cryptography: A New Dimension in Computer Data Security, John Wiley and Sons, 1980*)

be used directly as the key, and would be equal in length to the message. But in that case the cryptographic bit stream must be provided in advance to the communicants via some independent and secure channel. This introduces insurmountable logistic problems for heavy data traffic. Hence, for practical reasons, the bit-stream generator must be implemented as an algorithmic procedure. Then both communicants can generate the same cryptographic bit stream—provided that their algorithms are identically initialized. **Figure 11** illustrates a cryptographic bit stream produced with a key-controlled algorithm.

When modulo 2 addition is used as the combining operation, each bit in the output ciphertext (recovered plaintext) is dependent only upon its corresponding bit in the input plaintext (ciphertext). This is in marked contrast to the block cipher which exhibits a much more complex relationship between bits in the plaintext (ciphertext) and bits in the ciphertext (recovered plaintext). Both approaches, however, have comparable strength.

In a stream cipher the algorithm may generate its bit stream on a bit-by-bit basis, or in blocks of bits. This is of no real consequence. All such systems are stream ciphers, or variations thereof. Moreover, since bit streams can be generated in blocks, it is always possible for a block cipher to be used to obtain a stream cipher. However, because both the sender and receiver must produce cryptographic bit streams that are equal and secret, their keys must also be equal and secret. Therefore public keys in confirmation with a public-key algorithm cannot be used in a stream-cipher mode of operation.

For security purposes, a stream cipher must never predictably start from the same initial condition, thereby producing the same cryptographic bit stream. This can be avoided by making the cryptographic bit stream dependent on a nonsecret quantity Z (known as seed, initializing vector, or fill), which is used as an input parameter to the ciphering algorithm (Fig. 11).

In a stream cipher, Z provides cryptographic strength and establishes synchronization between communicating cryptographic devices—it assures that the same cryptographic bit streams are generated for the sender and the receiver. Initialization may be accomplished by generating Z at the sending device and transmitting it in clear (plaintext) form to the receiver.

Cipher feedback. A general approach to producing cryptographic bit streams is the automatic modification of the algorithm's input using feedback methods. In a key auto-key cipher, the cryptographic bit stream generated at time $t = \tau$ is determined by the cryptographic bit stream generated at time $t < \tau$. In a ciphertext auto-key cipher the cryptographic bit stream generated at time $t = \tau$ is determined by the ciphertext generated at time $t < \tau$. A particular implementation of a ciphertext auto-key cipher, recommended by the National Bureau of Standards, is called cipher feedback (**Fig. 12**).

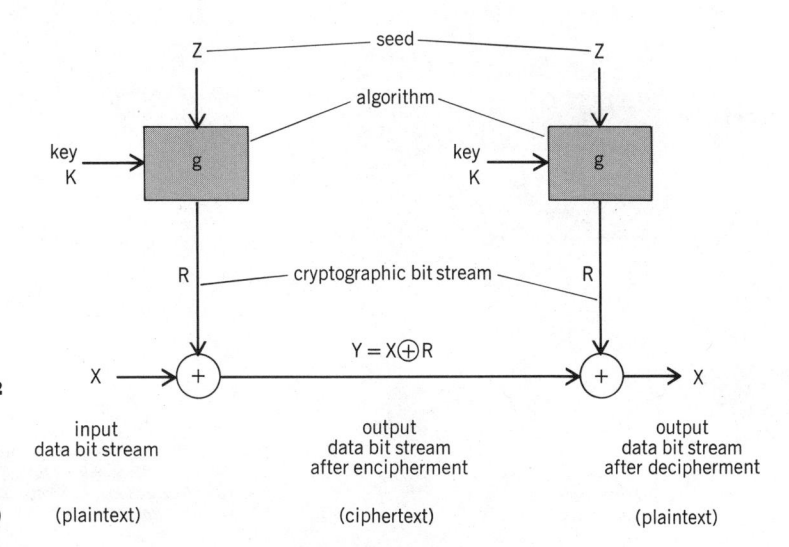

Fig. 11. Stream cipher using an algorithmic bit stream generator, modulo 2 addition, and seed. (*After C. H. Meyer and S. M. Matyas. Cryptography: A New Dimension in Computer Data Security, John Wiley and Sons, 1980*)

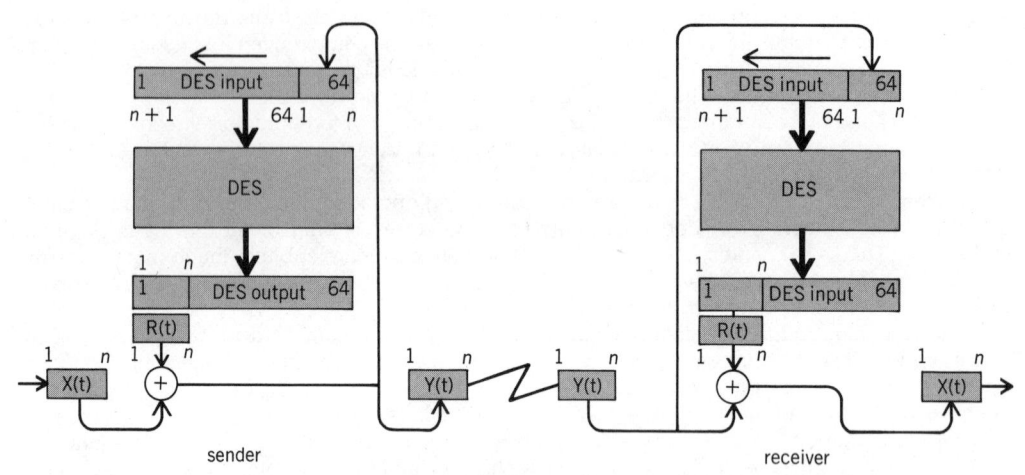

Fig. 12. Cipher feedback. (*After C. H. Meyer and S. M. Matyas. Cryptography: A New Dimension in Computer Data Security, John Wiley and Sons, 1980*)

In cipher feedback, the leftmost n bits of the DES output are EXCLUSIVE ORed with n bits of plaintext to produce n bits of ciphertext, where n is the number of bits enciphered at one time ($1 \leq n \leq 64$). These n bits of ciphertext are fed back into the algorithm by first shifting the current DES input n bits to the left, and then appending the n bits of ciphertext to the right-hand side of the shifted input to thus produce a new DES input used to the next iteration of the algorithm.

A seed value, which must be the same for both sender and receiver, is used as an initial input to the DES in order to generate the cryptographic bit stream. Federal Standard 1026 defines a 48-bit seed for all cipher feedback implementations, thus ensuring compatibility among users. The communicating nodes are synchronized by right-justifying the seed in the input to the DES and setting the remaining bits equal to 0.

One method to generate seed values with the DES is illustrated in **Fig. 13**. IC_0 (for initial condition) is a starting value supplied by the user and is placed in nonvolatile storage (where data remain permanent). IC_1 is produced by enciphering IC_0 with the (stored) cryptographic key, IC_2 is produced by enciphering IC_1, and so forth. At each iteration, IC_i replaces IC_{i-1}, and $seed_i$ is the left-most m bits ($m \leq 64$) of IC_i.

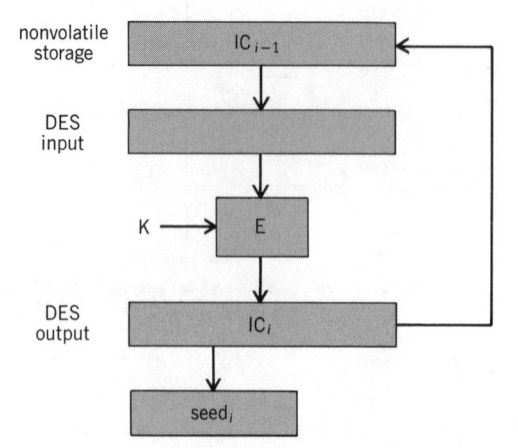

Fig. 13. Seed generation using the DES algorithm. (*After C. H. Meyer and S. M. Matyas. Cryptography: A New Dimension in Computer Data Security, John Wiley and Sons, 1980*)

iteration	DES input at sender							DES input at receiver						
0	0	0	0	S1	S2	S3	S4 S5	0	0	0	S1	S2	S3	S4 S5
1	0	0	S1	S2	S3	S4	S5 Y(t₁)	0	0	S1	S2	S3	S4	S5 Y(t₁)
2	0	S1	S2	S3	S4	S5	Y(t₁) Y(t₂)	0	S1	S2	S3	S4	S5	Y(t₁) Y(t₂)
3	S1	S2	S3	S4	S5	Y(t₁)	Y(t₂) Y(t₃)	S1	S2	S3	S4	S5	Y(t₁)	Y(t₂) Y(t₃)
4	S2	S3	S4	S5	Y(t₁)	Y(t₂)	Y(t₃) Y(t₄)	S2	S3	S4	S5	Y(t₁)	Y(t₂)	Y(t₃) Y(t₄)
5	S3	S4	S5	Y(t₁)	Y(t₂)	Y(t₃)	Y(t₄) Y(t₅)	S3	S4	S5	Y(t₁)	Y(t₂)	Y(t₃)	Y(t₄) Y(t₅)
6	S4	S5	Y(t₁)	Y(t₂)	Y(t₃)	Y(t₄)	Y(t₅) Y(t₆)	S4	S5	Y(t₁)	Y(t₂)	Y(t₃)	Y(t₄)	Y(t₅) Y(t₆)
7	S5	Y(t₁)	Y(t₂)	Y(t₃)	Y(t₄)	Y(t₅)	Y(t₆) Y(t₇)	S5	Y(t₁)	Y(t₂)	Y(t₃)	Y(t₄)	Y(t₅)	Y(t₆) Y(t₇)
8	Y(t₁)	Y(t₂)	Y(t₃)	Y(t₄)	Y(t₅)	Y(t₆)	Y(t₇) Y(t₈)	Y(t₁)	Y(t₂)	Y(t₃)	Y(t₄)	Y(t₅)	Y(t₆)	Y(t₇) Y(t₈)
9	Y(t₂)	Y(t₃)	Y(t₄)	Y(t₅)	Y(t₆)	Y(t₇)	Y(t₈) Y(t₉)	Y(t₂)	Y(t₃)	Y(t₄)	Y(t₅)	Y(t₆)	Y(t₇)	Y(t₈) Y(t₉)

Fig. 14. Self-synchronizing feature in cipher feedback. (*After C. H. Meyer and S. M. Matyas.* Cryptography: *A New Dimension in Computer Data Security, John Wiley and Sons, 1980*)

The cipher feedback approach is self-synchronizing, since any bit changes occurring in the ciphertext during transmission get shifted out of the DES input after 64 additional ciphertext bits are sent and received. If, for example, 8 bits are enciphered at one time, as shown in Fig. 12, and a bit is altered in $Y(t_1)$ changing it to $Y^*(t_1)$, then the sender's and receiver's inputs are as shown in **Fig. 14**, where the 40-bit seed is defined as S1, S2, . . . , S5. In this case, the blocks of ciphertext, given by $Y^*(t_1), Y(t_2), . . . , Y(t_8)$, can be correctly deciphered only at the receiver by chance since the DES input is incorrect in each case. After eight blocks of uncorrupted ciphertext have been received, given by $Y(t_2), Y(t_3), . . . , Y(t_9)$, both the sender's and receiver's cryptographic devices will have equal DES inputs again.

In general, any bit changes in an n-bit block of ciphertext can cause a change in any of the corresponding n bits of recovered plaintext and in any of the 64 bits of recovered plaintext immediately following. However, a permanent "out-of-sync" condition will result if a ciphertext bit is added or dropped, since the integrity of the block boundary is lost. To recover from such an error, the sender and receiver would have to establish the beginning and ending of blocks of bits that are enciphered at one time ($n = 8$ bits in the given example).

On the other hand, if enciphering takes place on a bit-by-bit basis ($n = 1$), then the property of self-synchronization is maintained even when bits are lost or added. This is because blocks are bits, and therefore the block boundary cannot be disturbed.

Bibliography. C. Deavours and L. Kruh, *Machine Cryptography and Modern Cryptanalysis*, 1985; M. R. Garey and D. S. Johnson, *Computers and Intractability: A Guide to the Theory of NP-Completeness*, 1979; M. Hellman, The mathematics of public-key cryptography, *Sci. Amer.*, 241(2):146–157, August 1979; A. G. Konheim, *Cryptography: A Primer*, 1981; E. Kranakis, *Primality and Cryptography*, 1986; C. H. Meyer and S. M. Matyas, *Cryptography: A New Dimension in Computer Data Security*, 1982.

REAL-TIME SYSTEMS
EARL C. JOSEPH

Computer systems in which the computer is required to perform its tasks within the time restraints of some process or simultaneously with the system it is assisting. Usually the computer must operate faster than the system assisted in order to be ready to intervene appropriately.

Types of systems. Real-time computer systems and applications span a number of different types.

Real-time control and real-time process control. In these applications the computer is required to process systems data (inputs) from sensors for the purpose of monitoring and computing system control parameters (outputs) required for the correct operation of a system or process. The type of monitoring and control functions provided by the computer for subsystem units ranges over a wide variety of tasks, such as turn-on and turn-off signals to switches; feedback signals to controllers (such as motors, servos, and potentiometers) to provide adjustments or corrections; steering signals; alarms; monitoring, evaluation, supervision, and management calculations; error detection, and out-of-tolerance and critical parameter detection operations; and processing of displays and outputs.

Real-time assistance. Here the computer is required to do its work fast enough to keep up with a person interacting with it (usually at a computer terminal device of some sort, for example, a screen and keyboard). These are people-amplifier-type real-time computer systems. The computer supports the person or persons interacting with it and provides access, retrieval, and storage functions, usually through some sort of data-base management system, as well as data processing and computational power. System access allows the individual to intervene (control, adjust, supply parameters, direct, and so forth) in the system's operation. The real-time computer also often provides monitoring or display information, or both. SEE DATA-BASE MANAGEMENT SYSTEMS; MULTIACCESS COMPUTER.

Real-time robotics. In this case the computer is a part of a robotic or self-contained machine. Often the computer is embedded in the machine, which then becomes a smart machine. If the smart machine also has access to, or has embedded within it, artificial intelligence functions (for example, a knowledge base and knowledge processing in an expert system fashion), it becomes an intelligent machine. SEE ARTIFICIAL INTELLIGENCE; EMBEDDED SYSTEMS; ROBOTICS.

Evolution. Real-time computer systems have been evolving constantly since the interrupt function, which allowed the computer to be synchronized with the external world, was invented. There are five primary paths along which real-time systems continue to advance:

First-generation real-time control systems comprise process control (for example, an oil refinery); guidance and control (for example, antiballistic missile and intercontinental ballistic missile systems); numerical control (for example, factory machine operations); dedicated (mini) computer systems; and store-and-forward message switching. SEE DATA COMMUNICATIONS.

Second-generation real-time computer systems comprise time-shared and multiprocessor computing; interactive computing; smart and intelligent terminals; and computer networks (distributed computers, distributed smart machines, and distributed intelligent machines). SEE MULTIPROCESSING.

Third-generation real-time assistance systems comprise operating systems; CAD (computer-aided design), CAM (computer-aided manufacturing), CAI (computer-assisted instruction), MIS (management information systems), and DSS (decision support systems); personal computers; word processing and work stations; and artificial intelligence expert systems. SEE COMPUTER-AIDED DESIGN AND MANUFACTURING; MICROCOMPUTER; OPERATING SYSTEM; WORD PROCESSING.

Fourth-generation real-time machines comprise smart machines with embedded computers; intelligent machines; and robots (dumb, smart, and intelligent).

Fifth-generation real-time integrated systems comprise the factory-of-the-future (totally automated factories); just-in-time (JIT) systems (in the factory and in distribution); computer utilities and knowledge utilities; and knowledge inference processing systems.

Artificial intelligence and experts systems. A new technology, artificial intelligence (AI), is rapidly advancing beyond the research stage into practical use by scientists, management, and many other areas of business and society. One branch is directed toward the development of real-time expert systems. Thus, widespread use of artificial intelligence, knowledge bases, expert systems, and people-amplifiers is expected to develop, and decision making will be amplified with real-time and intelligent computer systems. SEE ARTIFICIAL INTELLIGENCE; EXPERT SYSTEMS.

Real-time simulation. The real-time computer can serve as a tool allowing simulation of models of the real world. By coupling this tool with artificial-intelligence knowledge-base expertise, scientific experimentation becomes possible without cumbersome laboratory equipment and procedures. Scientists can play serious real-time experimental and mathematical games with the object of their research without first needing to learn sophisticated laboratory techniques or mathematics. The detailed mathematical and discipline-oriented experimental skills and procedures are embedded within the computerized model. Such robot simulators allow the scientist to concentrate upon the investigation, rather than the scientist becoming buried within the relevant mathematics and discipline crafts. However, the scientist must first learn his or her field plus the computer simulation/modeling language. Thus, robot simulator assistants increasingly do for the scientist what the calculator does for the average person: they remove the need to perform bulky, precise, and rote skill functions, allowing the researcher to get more quickly and easily to the core of scientific investigation.

With robot simulators the researcher can ask questions of a computer modeling system, and have simulated experiments performed that are otherwise nearly impossible or too time-consuming and costly. For example, the researcher can ask "What happens if . . .?" After performing the simulated experiment, the computer gives an answer, while the experimenter views the progress of the computerized experiment and intervenes when desired. Then the experimenter can ask "What happens if something else is done instead?" to arrive at a different comparable answer from the robot simulator. Through such real-time interactive simulations the researcher becomes directly involved in the experiment as a surrogate participant.

Future robot simulators are expected to take the form of advanced hand-held calculators with voice dialog and artificial intelligence capabilities, and to contain specialized expert knowledge making them capable of general decision making. Such smart robot simulators will be used as people-amplifiers or electronic assistants by managers, programmers, doctors, politicians, voters, and others. SEE DIGITAL COMPUTER; SIMULATION.

Bibliography. C. C. Foster, *Real-time Programming*, 1981; P. Heller, *Real Time Software Design*, 1986; H. J. Hindin, Minicomputer operating systems, *Comput. Des.*, 23(9):161–228, August 1984; H. J. Hindin and W. B. Rauch-Hindin, Real-time systems, *Systems & Software*, 2 (1):89–113, January 1983; E. L. Keller, Real-time systems, *Systems & Software*, vol. 4, no. 2, February 1985; P. D. Lawrence and K. Mauch, *Real-Time Microcomputer System Design: An Introduction*, 1987; J. Martin, *Design of Real-time Computer Systems*, 1967; D. A. Mellichamp, *Real-time Computing*, 1983.

SIMULATION
JOHN H. MCLEOD, JR.

The development and use of computer models for the study of actual or postulated dynamic systems. This definition, based on the current meaning of the word to the technological community, requires some interpretation.

The essential characteristic of simulation is the use of models for study and experimentation rather than the actual system modeled. In practice, it has come to mean the use of computer models because modern electronic computers are so much superior for most kinds of simulation that computer modeling dominates the field. "Systems," as used in the definition, refers to an interrelated set of elements, components, or subsystems. "Dynamic systems" are specified because the study of static systems seldom justifies the sophistication inherent in computer simulation. SEE ANALOG COMPUTER; DIGITAL COMPUTER.

"Postulated" systems as well as "actual" ones are included in the definition because of the importance of simulation for testing hypotheses, as well as designs of systems not yet in existence. The "development" as well as "use" of models is included because, in the empirical approach to system simulation, a simplified simulation of a hypothesized model is used to check educated guesses, and thus to develop a more sophisticated and more realistic simulation of the simuland. The simuland is that which is simulated, whether real or postulated.

The impracticality of developing intercontinental ballistic missiles and spacecraft by actual flight testing gave simulation its big impetus just after World War II. Since then the equipment and the techniques have been adopted by workers in other fields where the simuland does not exist or is intractable to experimental manipulation, or where experiments with the actual system would entail high cost, danger to the system or the experimenter, or both. Among these nonaerospace systems which have been simulated, in addition to those that are considered later, are chemical and other industrial processes; structural dynamics; physiological and biological systems; automobile, ship, and submarine dynamics; social, ecological, political, and economic systems; electrical, electronic, optical, and acoustic systems; and learning, thinking, and problem-solving systems.

Simulations may be classified according to (1) the kind of computer used (analog, digital, hybrid); (2) the nature of the simuland (spacecraft, chemical plant, economic system); (3) the signal flow in the simuland (continuous, discrete or mixed); or (4) the temporal relation of events in the simuland (faster-than-real-time, real-time, slower-than-real-time, with real-time being clock or simuland time). Thus, for example, one may have a continuous real-time analog spacecraft simulation, or a sampled-data (discrete) faster-than-real-time digital economic system simulation, though such complete classification is seldom spelled out.

Mathematical modeling. Mathematical modeling is a recognized and valuable adjunct, and usually a precursor, of computer simulation. In practice the mathematical equations describing the interrelation of components of the simuland are written in a form suitable for the computer. In true simulation the computer is programmed to retain an identifiable correspondence between computer functions and the dynamics of the simuland. If mathematical manipulations or computer characteristics obscure this relationship, the computer may be processing information relative to the simuland, but it cannot properly be said to be simulating it.

Mathematical modeling does not necessarily precede simulation, however; sometimes the simuland is not well enough understood to permit rigorous mathematical description. In such cases it is often possible to postulate a functional relationship of the elements of the simuland without specifying mathematically what that relationship is. This is the building-block approach, for which analog computers are particularly well suited. Parameters related to the function of the blocks can be adjusted intuitively, systematically, or according to some established technique for system identification until some functional criteria are met. Thus the mathematical model can be developed as the result of, rather than as a requirement for, simulation.

Analog simulation. Simulation, as defined here, has been developed since World War II. Analog computers, in which signals are continuous and are processed in parallel, were originally the most popular for simulation. Their modular design made it natural to retain the simulation-simuland correspondence, and their parallel operation gave them the speed required for real-time operation. The result was unsurpassed human-machine rapport.

Digital simulation. However, block-oriented digital simulation languages (such as MIDAS, CSMP, and their successors) were developed which allow a pseudo–simulation-simuland correspondence, and digital computer speeds have increased to a degree that allows real-time simulation of all but very fast or very complex systems. Inadequate input/output facilities degrade human-machine interaction in all but the most sophisticated digital systems which embody expensive input/output equipment; nevertheless, digital computers are better than analog for simulating certain kinds of systems, particularly those requiring high precision or extremely wide dynamic ranges. *See* DATA-PROCESSING SYSTEMS; DIGITAL COMPUTER PROGRAMMING; PROGRAMMING LANGUAGES.

Hybrid simulation. Hybrid simulation, in which both continuous and discrete signals are processed, both in parallel and serially, is the result of a desire to combine the speed and human-machine rapport of the analog computer with the precision, logic capability, and memory capacity of the digital computer. After years during which the weak points of each kind of computer seemed to combine more readily than their strengths, hybrid simulation now makes possible the simulation of a new array of systems which require combinations of computer characteristics unavailable in either all-analog or all-digital computers.

In the past, most hybrid simulation systems were engineered by connecting a general-purpose digital computer to one or more general-purpose analog computers through interface equipment consisting largely of digital-to-analog and analog-to-digital signal converters (**Fig. 1**). However, the practice of hybridizing analog computers by the addition of a complement of digital logic and the development of specialized digital hardware was followed by the development of powerful hybrid systems specifically designed for the simulation of large complicated simulands. The relatively high cost of such systems is more than justified for some types of problems, primarily by the speed derived from the parallel operation of the analog elements, particularly the integrators, which are so prominent in any computer simulation program. Such speed pays dividends when the simulation involves high frequencies or when many iterations of an experiment are required—for instance, when it is necessary to get a statistically significant number of simu-

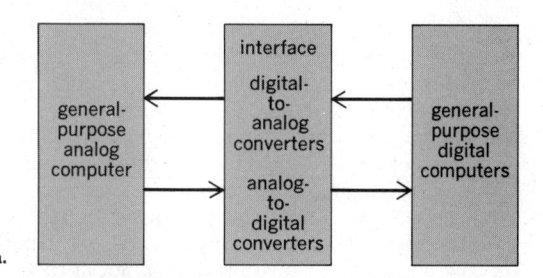

Fig. 1. Hybrid simulation system.

lation runs of a stochastic process. In such systems the digital processer can select and program analog elements and the interface equipment, and check out the simulation. SEE ANALOG-TO-DIGITAL CONVERTER; DIGITAL-TO-ANALOG CONVERTER.

As the digital computer is capable of determining which parts of the model are simulated in the central processor and which in the remote terminal, the operator need not know what parts of the simuland are being simulated digitally and what parts by analog components.

Trends. With the advent of still more powerful digital computers, indications were that large computation centers would be designed around extremely fast time-shared digital central processors, accessed through many different special-purpose remote terminals (**Fig. 2**), and this has indeed been the case in many instances. Terminals for business data-processing and purely mathematical computation by such systems can consist of digital alphanumeric input/output devices, sophisticated successors to the teletypewriter. Terminals for engineering design, however, usually have graphic input and output, and use programs to facilitate interactive human-machine discourse. Either of the above kinds of terminals may be used for computer-assisted instruction, but still more sophisticated special-purpose terminals, designed specifically for educational purposes such as those used with the PLATO system, are coming into use. SEE COMPUTER-AIDED DESIGN AND MANUFACTURING; COMPUTER-AIDED ENGINEERING; COMPUTER GRAPHICS; MULTIACCESS COMPUTER.

Some special-purpose remote terminals which are particularly well suited for simulation are functionally similar to a small- to medium-sized hybrid computer. These "intelligent terminals" contain elements to facilitate human-machine interaction and have a limited capability for independent computation under local control. Typically, however, these terminals are used for communication with a central processor.

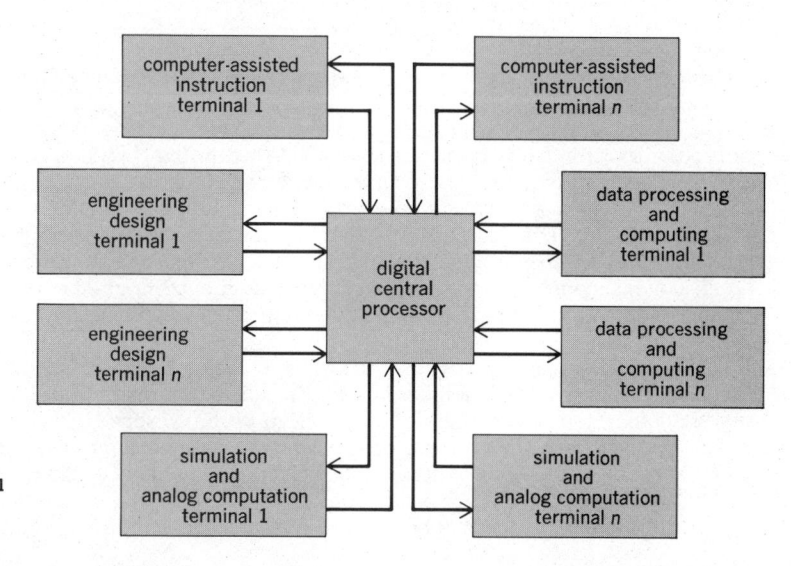

Fig. 2. Time-shared digital central processor with multiple inputs.

As the computing capacity of the remote terminals increases, they take on more of the character of satellite computers, and the overall system that of a computer network. The effect of such networks on simulation will be to provide access to more powerful simulation programs and to make more powerful equipment more widely and economically available. It should also discourage the practice of individuals who wish to simulate building their own model; ready-made models of many kinds can be accessed through the network.

The foregoing is a trend toward bigness; however, there is a countertrend. Started by the minicomputers and now getting a boost of unpredictable importance by the microcomputers, the current trend is such that it may not be long before all users can have as much computing power as they need in their own facility—if not at their own desk—so that the need to go to a network will be diminished if not eliminated. The exception may be the need for access to a large data bank, which becomes a communication, not a simulation problem. *See Microcomputer.*

Applications. Some simulationists have claimed that any system which can be adequately described in a natural language can be modeled on a computer, and thus simulated. Admittedly this seems to be an extremely broad statement, but it becomes credible if the meaning of "adequately" in this context is examined. A simulation study does not require that the simuland be completely described (an impractical if not impossible task in the case of many complicated systems). The simuland is adequately modeled when those factors—the parameters and the variables and their interrelationships which will significantly influence the results of a simulation experiment—are modeled and described with an accuracy commensurate with the accuracy required of the results.

The above is a qualitative description of adequacy as it applies to computer modeling for simulation. But computer modeling is completely quantitative; everything—parameters, variables, relationships, and even external influences—must be described by numbers. To do this, the modeler must be thoroughly familiar with the simuland and, having obtained the data required to assign the necessary numbers, must be able to program a computer to relate these factors. The modeler must also know the accuracy required of the results. Therefore most simulations of complicated systems are done by teams—an expert in the field of the simuland (economics, for example), a mathematician, a computer programmer, and an analyst working together to produce results useful to a decision maker (a business executive or a politician, for example).

Because simulation is a methodology for improving insight relative to complex issues in general, rather than in just certain fields, it has been used to investigate problems of all kinds. Only a few will be mentioned here.

Mental models of an economy have always been a tool of economic research. Three applications of simulation in economics are: (1) forecasting the effects on the economy (employment, production, consumption expenditure, inflation, balance of payments) of various policy changes (changes in government expenditure, tax rates, interest-rate ceilings, or the treatment of depreciation); (2) examining the behavior of the individual units in the economy (such as households, business firms, laborers); and (3) improving statistical tools used in estimating relationships among economic variables.

Management cannot be divorced from economics, and neither can be studied without regard to the social impacts involved. This is reflected in the computer simulation techniques that have been adopted by corporations in the advanced industrial countries. But with the increasing availability of low-cost microcomputers, simulation is also a tool for the management of small businesses. Their needs and problems are very similar to those of larger firms.

Traffic and transportation systems as well as business organizations require management, and effective management requires an understanding of the system of concern and, if possible, a means of studying the impact of alternative methods of controlling that system. Simulation fulfills these requirements.

Energy, however, has become the subject of the most intense simulation activity. Hundreds of models to support simulation studies of the generation, distribution, and use of electrical energy, triggered by the oil embargo of 1973, have been developed. The study of electrical energy systems has not been the only use of simulation to study energy-related problems. Another important application has been to study tradeoffs among the many existing and proposed sources of energy. *See Electric power systems engineering.*

Computer simulation has become an indispensible tool in the study of complex biological processes ranging from intracellular chemical reactions, through the behavior of various organ systems, to the evolution of entire ecosystems. For example, computer simulation is uniquely suited to the study of plant disease epidemics, complex biological phenomena in which growth and interaction of the pathogen and host are affected by environmental factors; and the crop manager, when intervening by means such as chemical treatment, can become a third interactive component. The simulation of ecosystems via numerical models is essential in studying the way in which these ecosystems operate normally, how resistant this operation is to the short- or long-term effects of perturbation, and how such effects can be predicted; all these questions are important in current ecological research as the pressures of human economic growth threaten to impair or even destroy the function of many natural ecosystems.

Bibliography. M. E. Johnson, *Multivariate Statistical Simulation*, 1987; J. McLeod (ed.), *Simulation in the Service of Society,* monthly; F. Neelam Karil, *Computer Simulation and Modelling*, 1987; *Proceedings of the Annual Summer Computer Simulation Conference; Proceedings of the Pittsburgh Modeling and Simulation Conference; Proceedings of the Simulation Symposium; Proceedings of the Winter Simulation Conference;* B. D. Ripley, *Stochastic Simulation*, 1987; *Simulation Councils Proceedings Series,* semiannual; J. M. Smith, *Mathematical Modelling and Digital Simulation for Engineers and Scientists*, 2d ed., 1987; Society for Computer Simulation, *Simulation,* monthly.

WORD PROCESSING
Eric A. Weiss

Writing and editing text by using computers or computerlike equipment. It may be thought of as writing with a typewriter that has some of the capabilities of a computer, and in most cases word processing uses a computer and a word processing program. It has become the preferred way to create text wherever large quantities of writing, rewriting, and editing are done. See Digital computer; Digital computer programming.

A typewriterlike keyboard is used (**Fig. 1**). The typed text is not immediately printed on paper but is displayed on a screen and simultaneously stored electronically. The displayed and stored text may be changed or corrected while it is being typed or after it is stored. At any time a copy of the text may be printed out on paper without destroying what is stored.

Thus the essential interconnected parts of a word processor are a keyboard, a display screen, a printer, and a computer or computerlike device both to electronically store what has been typed and to control the whole system (**Fig. 2**). These parts are available in many forms and different capabilities. Word processors are essentially personal computers that use word process-

Fig. 1. Typical word processing keyboard. (*IBM*)

Fig. 2. Essential parts of a personal computer word processor: keyboard, computer, display screen, and printer. (*IBM*)

ing programs. They range in size from a desk-top full of equipment to a unit that will fit in a briefcase and can be held on the lap (**Fig. 3**).

Word processing has two major advantages over typewriting: it simplifies the tasks of typing and editing, and it makes it possible to go from the first typed draft to the final copy without ever retyping, except for new material, corrections, and additions. The word processor continuously and automatically maintains a clean copy in its electronic storage ready to be printed.

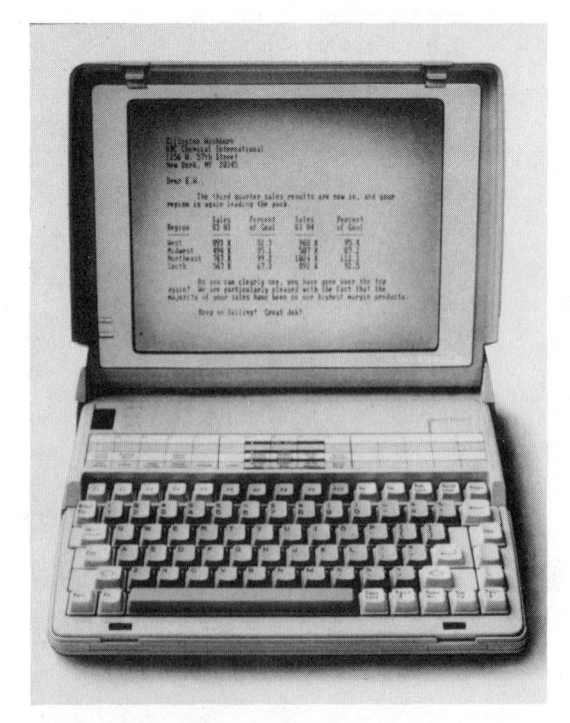

Fig. 3. Lap-size computer. (*Data General Corp.*)

Development. The designers and users of the first computers recognized in the late 1940s that they could manipulate text as well as numbers, but the machines were so large and expensive that it was inconceivable to use them as typewriters. By the late 1950s some text manipulation experiments were being made, chiefly in the academic world, using smaller computers and time-sharing arrangements. Over a period of about 15 years, these experiments devised and tested most of the techniques and features of today's word processing systems. The early configurations of hardware were usually called text editing systems. They performed so-called text processing to convey the notion of processing letters and words the way that electronic data processing handles numbers.

As technological advances increased the capability of electronic computing and storage equipment, two developments made obsolete the early word processing systems, involving magnetic storage typewriters and centralized typing centers. The first development was the stand-alone dedicated word processor, which combined in a fairly large desk-top unit the essential parts of keyboard, video display, high-speed printer, and electronic storage. The other development was an arrangement in which each typist had his or her own desk-top keyboard and video display unit. The separated units were connected by wires to a central point where the document printer, the magnetic storage facility, and the large controlling computer were shared by the separated users. SEE MULTIACCESS COMPUTER.

By the late 1970s technological developments had allowed the word processing function to go far beyond the simple preparation and printing of text to advanced levels of document editing, formatting, filing, and the electronic transmission of information. The next step was taken in the 1980s with the introduction of personal computers and word processing programs. SEE MICROCOMPUTER.

Functions. Word processing consists of five functions: writing, editing, formatting, printing, and sending and saving. Since the many word processing programs and systems are all different from each other, the following description is confined to the most common functions shared by most programs.

Writing. Writing is basically similar to typing except that nothing is printed on paper immediately. Pressing the keys on the keyboard causes letters, numbers, spaces, punctuation, and other common symbols to appear in lines on a display screen. Most displays show about 26 lines on a screen, each line being 80 characters long.

As typing proceeds, a cursor, which is a small blinking box or underline bar, moves across the screen and marks the place where the next letter will appear (**Fig. 4**). The processor auto-

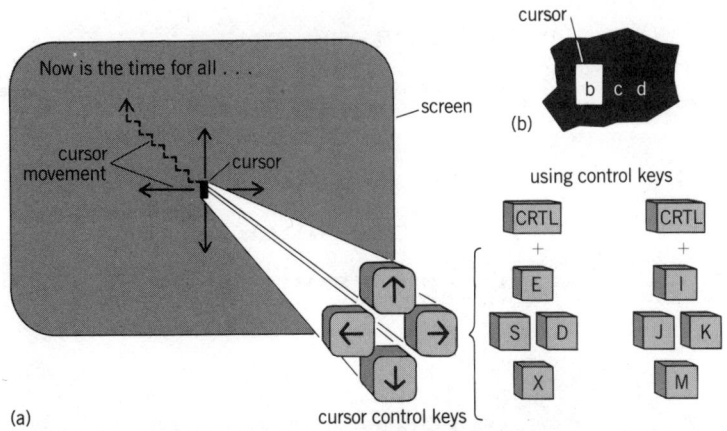

Fig. 4. Cursor. (a) Movement is usually controlled by pressing one of a set of four keys. On keyboards without cursor control keys, the cursor may be moved by pressing a control (CRTL) key along with various letter keys. (b) In the example shown, normal characters are white on black and, with the cursor over a character, the character becomes black on white. (On some screens, the cursor is an underline bar.) (*After M. Waite and J. Arca, Word Processing Primer, BYTE/McGraw-Hill, 1982*)

matically ends each line when it is full, and starts the next line with the next complete word, never breaking a word (automatic word wrap.) When the screen is full, the processor makes room for the next line by moving all the lines on the screen up (scrolling.) If the keys are depressed faster than the processor can put the letters on the screen, the letters are temporarily stored and the processor catches up at the typist's next pause, so nothing is lost and type-bar jams are not possible.

Editing. Editing consists of making corrections and changes in the text by deleting, changing, moving, or inserting characters. To edit, the cursor is moved to the place on the screen where the change is to be made. Usually the cursor movement is controlled by pressing one of a set of four keys (up, right, down, left; Fig. 4), but with some processors it can be controlled with a "mouse" or by touching the display screen at the desired location. The contents of the screen itself can be scrolled up or down by a single line, a screenful, or more, and the cursor can be moved to get to any part of the document.

The text at the cursor-marked spot may be changed by deleting or inserting. A block of text may be moved from one place in the document to another, even between parts of the document that are not visible at the same time on the screen, and from a previously stored document to the one being worked on. For insertions, deletions, or block moves, the processor automatically moves the text to make room or to take up any vacant space created, wrapping words as needed to make the lines correct.

Formatting. Formatting gives the finished document its desired appearance, and includes specifying the margins and the space between lines; making the right margin even (justification); adding headings and footings to each page; having the pages automatically counted and their numbers printed; and putting footnotes on the proper pages. Some word processors have formatting capabilities that allow printing with several different kinds of typefaces (**Fig. 5**). All of this is done by adding to the text various symbols or specially marked words which will not be printed out on the final copy.

Ideally, the display screen should show exactly what will be printed out and should look exactly like the printed page. Unfortunately there will always be some differences. For example, some of the formatting symbols and words should be displayed on the screen so that they can be checked, but of course they should not show on the printed page. Often a way is provided to "print preview" or "print to screen" to check on how the printed document will look.

Printing. When the document has been written, edited, and formatted, it may be printed out. With some programs the word processor can be used to work on another document while the

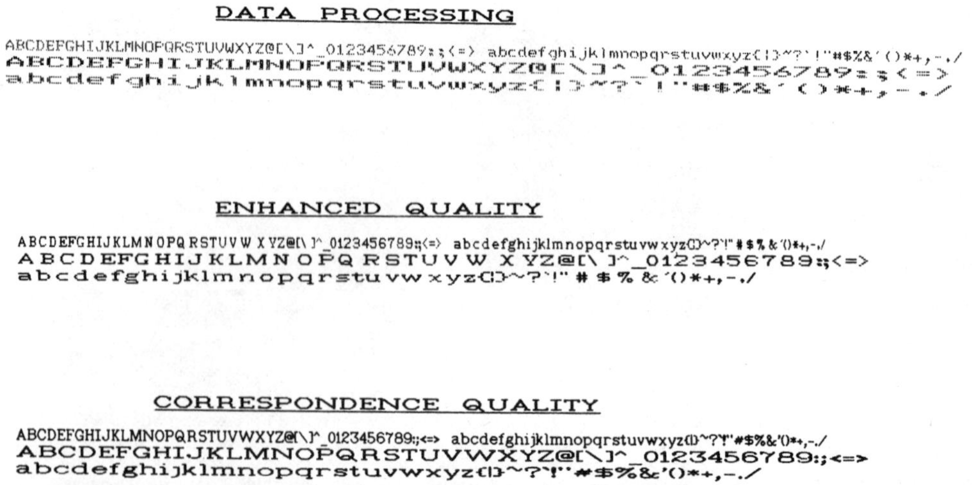

Fig. 5. Various kinds of typefaces, produced by a multimode dot-matrix printer. (*From W. Hession and M. Rubel, Performance Guide to Word Processing Software, McGraw-Hill, 1985*)

printing is going on. The quality of the printed product, some of the things that can be done in terms of formatting, and particularly the speed with which the document is printed, depend chiefly on the quality of the printer.

Sending and saving. These are the final steps in word processing and are the equivalent of sending out the finished document and filing a copy. If the document is to be sent electronically rather than as a paper copy, the word processor must be connected through a modem to a telephone line. After making this connection, the typist uses the keyboard to indicate the document's destination. On command, the word processor makes the call and, when the recipient's modem responds, transmits the document electronically over the telephone lines. The recipient may choose to have the document printed out as received or have it stored in his or her word processor, to be read later on the display screen. The sender may easily transmit the same document to many addresses or may send it to an electronic bulletin board, a central computer with which others may communicate. SEE DATA COMMUNICATIONS; ELECTRONIC MAIL.

In its most elementary form, saving is done by printing out an extra paper copy. However, with word processing, while the text is being typed it is also being temporarily saved electronically in the word processor. This copy is destroyed and lost when the processor is turned off or if there is an interruption in power. However, the typist can direct the word processor to save a copy of what is being written onto a disk. Some word processors save copies automatically.

Magnetic storage of text has advantages over paper files. For example, by using special programs, magnetic files can be sequenced in alphabetical order, added to, referred to, and retrieved from with little effort. They are far more compact; a 5¼-in. (133-mm) disk, for example, can store the equivalent of 50 to 100 typed pages. Most important, a magnetically stored copy need never be retyped, and can be used, in whole or in part, as the basis for creating other documents without any manual copying. SEE COMPUTER STORAGE TECHNOLOGY.

Advanced features. Some word processing programs can be used to check a document for spelling, punctuation, and simple grammatical errors. Others will automatically create indexes and tables of contents. Almost all will count the number of words in a document.

Bibliography. M. Bergerud and J. Gonzalez, *Word Processing*, 3d ed., 1987; S. Brand (ed.), *Whole Earth Software Catalog*, 1985; P. A. McWilliams, *The Word Processing Book: A Short Course in Computer Literacy*, 1984; M. K. Popyk, *Word Processing and Information Systems*, 2d ed., 1986; M. Waite and J. Arca, *Word Processing Primer*, 1982; W. Zinsser, *Writing with a Word Processor*, 1983.

IMAGE PROCESSING
WARREN E. SMITH

Manipulating data in the form of an image through several possible techniques. An image is usually interpreted as a two-dimensional array of brightness values, and is most familiarly represented by such patterns as those of a photographic print, slide, television screen, or movie screen. There are fundamentally two ways to process an image: optically, or digitally with a computer. This article focuses on digital processing of an image to perform one of three separate tasks: enhancement, restoration, or compression.

Digitization. To digitally process an image, it is first necessary to reduce the image to a series of numbers that can be manipulated by the computer. If the image is in the form of a photographic transparency, this digitization can be done by a scanning device that moves a spot of light over the transparency in a rasterlike fashion similar to a television scan. When the light falls on a particular area of the transparency, the amount of light transmitted at that point can be recorded by a photodetector, the signal digitized to, say, eight bits (yielding a possible 2^8, or 256, gray levels), and stored. The spot is then moved a distance equal to its width, and the process is repeated, recording the entire transparency in this way as a long string of numbers. The smaller the spot and the finer the scan (up to the limit of the film grain), the more accurate the description of the transparency will be. Each number representing the brightness value of the image at a particular location is called a picture element, or pixel. A typical digitized image may have 512 × 512 or roughly 250,000 pixels.

Once the image has been digitized, there are three basic operations that can be performed on it in the computer. For a point operation, a pixel value in the output image depends on a single pixel value in the input image. For local operations, several neighboring pixels in the input image determine the value of an output image pixel. In a global operation, all of the input image pixels contribute to an output image pixel value. These operations, taken singly or in combination, are the means by which the image is enhanced, restored, or compressed.

Enhancement. An image is enhanced when it is modified so that the information it contains is more clearly evident, but enhancement can also include making the image more visually appealing. An example is noise smoothing. Given the image of **Fig. 1**a, by replacing the value of randomly chosen pixels by 150 (bright gray) or 0 (black), the noisy image of Fig. 1b results. This kind of noise might be produced, for example, by a defective solid-state TV camera. To smooth the noisy image, median filtering can be applied with a 3 × 3 pixel window. This means that the value of every pixel in the noisy image is recorded, along with the values of its nearest eight neighbors. These nine numbers are then ordered according to size, and the number with as many numbers above it as below it (the median) is selected as the value for the pixel in the new image. The location of this pixel in the new image is the same as the location of the center of the 3 × 3 window in the old image. Eventually, as the window is moved one pixel at a time across the noisy image, the filtered image is formed, as in Fig. 1c. This is an example of a local operation, since the value of a pixel in the new image depends on the values of nine pixels in the old image.

Another example of enhancement is contrast manipulation, where each pixel's value in the new image depends solely on that pixel's value in the old image; in other words, this is a point operation. Contrast manipulation is commonly performed by adjusting the brightness and contrast controls on a television set, or by controlling the exposure and development time in printmaking. Another point operation is that of pseudocoloring a black-and-white image, by assigning arbitrary colors to the gray levels. This technique is popular in thermography (the imaging of heat), where hot objects (high pixel value) are assigned the color red, and cool objects (low pixel value) are assigned blue, with other colors assigned to intermediate values.

Restoration. The aim of restoration is also to improve the image, but unlike enhancement, knowledge of how the image was formed is used in an attempt to retrieve the ideal (uncorrupted) image. Any image-forming system is not perfect, and will introduce artifacts (for example, blurring, aberrations) into the final image that would not be present in an ideal image. To illustrate, the image of **Fig. 2**a is "imaged" on a computer that simulates an out-of-focus lens, producing Fig. 2b. The image of a point object through this system would look like Fig. 2c; this is called the point spread function of the system. Such blurring can be referred to as a local operation, in that the value of a pixel in the blurred image is an average of the values of the pixels around (and including) that pixel location in the original image. The averaging function is the blurring point spread function (Fig. 2c). The blurring process is mathematically referred to as a convolution of the original object with the point spread function.

Another point spread function, called a filter, can be constructed that "undoes" the blurring caused by the point spread function of Fig. 2c. Such a point spread function (not shown) has both positive and negative values, even though the blurring point spread function has only positive values. A general rule is that blurring point spread functions are positive, and sharpening point spread functions have both positive and negative values. By imaging Fig. 2b with the filter point

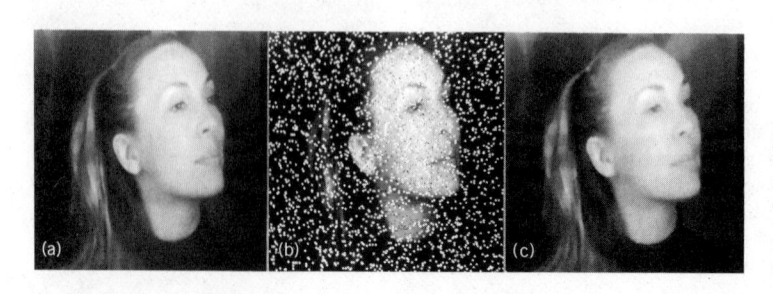

Fig. 1. Noise smoothing. (a) Original 256 × 256 pixel image. (b) Original image corrupted by spike noise. (c) Corrupted image filtered by a 3 × 3 pixel median filter.

Fig. 2. Example of restoration. (*a*) Original 256 × 256 pixel image (*courtesy of Richard Murphy*). (*b*) Blurred version of the original image. (*c*) The image of a point subject to the same blurring that produced the blurred version of the original image. (*d*) The results of the inverse filter applied to the blurred version of the original image.

spread function, the restored image of Fig. 2*d* results. The filter point spread function is spread out more than the blurring point spread function, bringing more pixels into the averaging process. This is an example of a global operation, since perhaps all of the pixels of the blurred image can contribute to the value of a single pixel in the restored image. This type of deblurring (called inverse filtering) will not work well if noise is added to the blurred image before the deblurring operation. A more sophisticated approach, modifying the deblurring filter according to the properties of the noise, is then required.

There exist mathematical transformations that can be performed on images to facilitate deblurring, as well as other operations. An extremely useful one in image processing is the Fourier transform, which decomposes the image into two-dimensional sine waves of varying frequency, direction, and phase. In fact, convolution of an image with a point spread function (the imaging process) can be carried out in the Fourier domain by simply multiplying the Fourier transform of the image by the Fourier transform of the point spread function, and taking the inverse Fourier transform of this product to get the final image. This process was used in the example of Fig. 2.

Compression. Compression of an image is a way of representing the image by fewer numbers, at the same time minimizing the degradation of the information contained in the image. There are two ways to perform compression: in the image space or in transform space (for example, Fourier). Compression in image space is discussed in the following example.

Figure 3*a*, representing the image to be compressed, contains 256 × 256 pixels, with each pixel having a possible 256 gray levels, so that 8 bits are required on a computer to store each pixel. Thus a total of roughly 500,000 bits is required to store or transmit the image. If the number of bits per pixel is reduced to 3 (8 gray levels), Fig. 3*b* results. The total number of bits

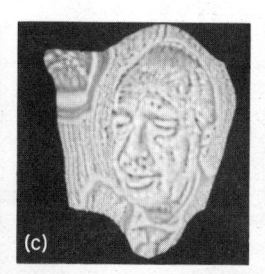

Fig. 3. Example of compression. (*a*) Original 256 × 256 pixel image, 8 bits per pixel (256 gray levels). (*b*) Original image, reduced to 3 bits per pixel (8 gray levels), for a bit reduction of 0.375. (*c*) Original image, with contrast and geometric transformations applied, followed by a reduction to 3 bits per pixel, for a total bit reduction of 0.188. (*d*) The inverse contrast and geometric transformation applied to *c*, to "decompress" the image. (*From R. N. Strickland and W. E. Smith, Stationary Transform Processing of Digital Images for Data Compression, Appl. Opt., 22:2161–2168, July 15, 1983*)

have been reduced by ⅜ or 0.375, but at the price of contouring the image. However, if a spatially variable contrast transformation is first applied to Fig. 3a with the resulting image then reduced to 3 bits, followed by a geometric distortion that shrinks areas of little variation (the wall and jacket) and leaves areas of large variation (the face) alone, Fig. 3c results. The geometric shrinking reduces the number of bits by a factor of 0.500, and the gray-level reduction to 3 bits further reduces the number by ⅜ to a total reduction of 0.188, or roughly ⅕ of the original number of bits required to represent the image. Applying the inverse geometric and contrast transformations to Fig. 3c results in Fig. 3d, an improvement over Fig. 3b, with a greater compression factor than Fig. 3b as well.

Applications. Due to its vast scope, image processing is an active area of research in such diverse fields as nuclear medicine, astronomy, electron microscopy, seismology, and many others. The concept of an image is expanding to include three-dimensional data sets (volume "images"), and even four-dimensional volume-time data sets. An example of the latter is a volume image of a beating heart, obtainable with computerized tomography. Advances in computer technology are making efficient processing of the huge data sets required in these problems possible, and such technology promises to bring sophisticated image processing into the home. SEE DIGITAL COMPUTER.

Bibliography. H. H. Barrett and W. Swindell, *Radiological Imaging: The Theory of Image Formation, Detection, and Processing*, 1981; E. R. Dougherty and C. R. Giardina, *Matrix Structured Image Processing*, 1987; R. C. Gonzalez and P. Wintz, *Digital Image Processing*, 1982; W. Niblack, *An Introduction to Digital Image Processing*, 1987.

ROBOTICS
ERNEST W. KENT

The study of problems associated with the design and application of robots and their control and sensory systems. The term robot has been loosely used historically, and has been applied to almost any feedback-controlled mechanical system. While the exact usage of "robot" is a matter of preference, the computer-controlled mechanical arm used in industrial applications probably represents a reasonable middle ground for definition by example (**Fig. 1**). Most of the concerns of practitioners of robotics can be present in such devices, and in turn much of the current work in robotics relates directly to them.

Robotics is also a broadly interpreted term; it is generally considered as covering research and engineering activities related to the design and construction of robots, but persons engaged in planning robot manufacturing or in studying the economic impact of robots might also consider themselves to be engaged in robotics. Much of this breadth of usage arises from the fact that robotics is a highly interdisciplinary field, involving mechanical engineering, computer science, artificial intelligence, biomechanics, control theory, cybernetics, and electrical engineering, to name only a few. SEE ARTIFICIAL INTELLIGENCE.

The emergence of robotics as a separate discipline has been given impetus by the developing complexity of robot systems. This has emphasized the fact that the design of the mechanical, electronic, and computational aspects of robots are interdependent. Previously it was possible for mechanical engineers to view a robot as just another numerically controlled machine tool, and for computer scientists to regard it as just another peripheral device. Although this viewpoint is possible for many simpler forms of robot, it is no longer a workable approach for current, complex, hierarchically controlled, sensory-interactive robots. In typical robotics research laboratories, specialists in many different areas work cooperatively on an integrated robot system.

Mechanical design. Almost all robots produce some sort of mechanical motion which, in most cases, has the purpose of manipulation or locomotion. For example, robot arms manipulate tools and parts to perform jobs such as welding, painting, and assembly; robot carts are used to transport materials. The design of the mechanical structures of robots is thus of great importance in robotics. Areas of concern in the mechanics of robots include degrees of freedom of movement, size and shape of the operating space, stiffness and strength of the structure, lifting capacity, velocity, and acceleration under load. In addition, good mechanical design is a factor in other

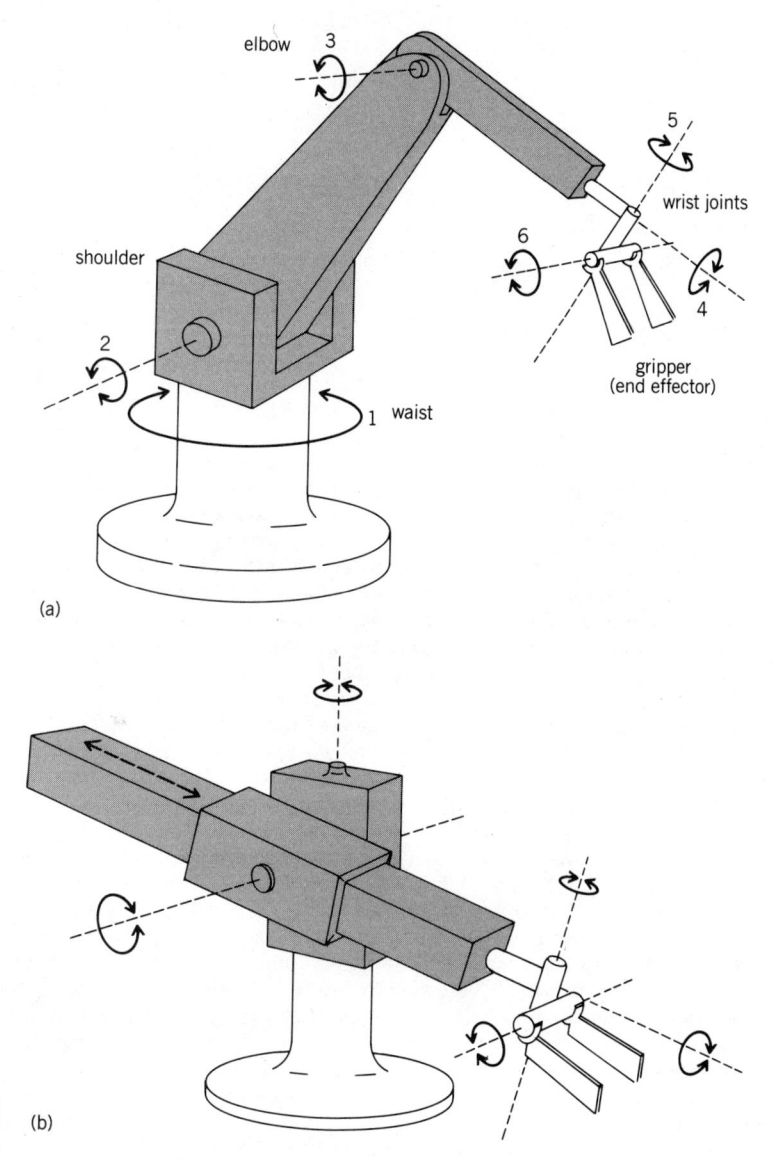

Fig. 1. Six-degree-of-freedom robot arms. (a) Arm with all rotational joints (numbered 1 to 6). (b) Arm with one sliding joint.

performance measures such as accuracy and repeatability of positioning, and freedom from oscillation and vibration.

Degrees of freedom. Some robots have very simple mechanical designs involving only a few degrees of freedom of movement. However, the design of robot manipulators can also be quite complex; in a typical industrial robot arm, six degrees of freedom of movement (exclusive of gripper closure) are required to enable the gripper to approach an object from any orientation. This is usually accomplished with three arm joints, which can position the "wrist" at any x, y, z coordinate in the working volume. The complex three-axis wrist joints can then orient the gripper attached to it by three independent motions (roll, pitch, yaw) around the x, y, z location of the wrist (**Fig. 2**). In effect, the wrist represents the origin of a three-axis coordinate system fixed to the gripper. Moving the first three joints of the arm translates this origin to any point in a three-

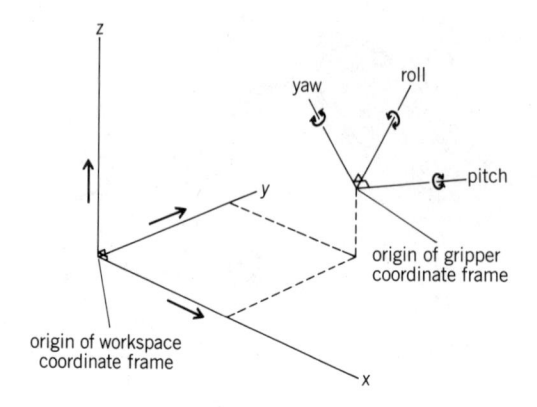

Fig. 2. Coordinate relations for a six-degree-of-freedom robot.

axis coordinate system fixed to the working volume; motion of the final three joints (in the wrist) orients the gripper coordinate system in rotation about an origin at the wrist point. For clarity, the robots in these figures have wrist-joint axes which do not all intersect at a single point. Some robots are constructed this way, but the mathematics of robot motion (kinematics) is considerably simplified if these axes do intersect at a single point. A wrist of this type is referred to as spherical, and the mechanical complexity of many robot wrists is due to this requirement.

Types of joints. Both sliding joints and rotational joints may be included in the robot's articulation (joint structure). Many robots use only rotational joints (as does the human arm), but only limited actions can be produced by using sliding joints alone (Fig. 1). Robot mobility usually involves adaptations of traditional devices such as wheels and treads, but walking robots, usually in some stable configuration such as a six-legged hexapod, have also been developed. The mechanical design problems of articulated legs are similar to those of robot arms.

Powering joints. The problem of powering the robot's joints is made difficult by the complex mechanical articulation. One approach is to place a prime mover (electrical, hydraulic, or pneumatic) at the joint itself. Power for these can be brought with relative ease through the joints and members of the arm. However, the weight and bulk of such motors and their associated gearing place constraints on the performance and mechanical design of the arm, particularly for joints in the wrist. A second approach is to place the prime movers in the immobile base of the robot and to transmit motion to the joints through mechanical linkages such as shafts, belts and cables, or gearing. This overcomes many of the problems associated with the first approach, but introduces a new set of problems in designing intricate backlash-free mechanical linkages which can transmit power effectively through the complex articulations of the arm in all of its positions. No one approach has clearly dominated the field.

End effectors. The purpose of the elaborate mechanical arm is to position an end effector (frequently a gripper) where it can perform some useful function. End effectors may be highly specialized for particular applications, or may be simple general-purpose pincers. Some robots change their own end effectors to suit the job at hand from a selection of special-purpose attachments. The development of more elaborate and dexterous general-purpose end effectors, including hands with humanlike fingers, is an area of intense study. The mechanical and control problems associated with such effectors are, however, exceedingly complex.

Control systems. A robot control system is the apparatus (usually electronic) which directs the activities of the mechanical parts. This may consist only of a sequencing device and a set of mechanical stops so that the mechanism moves in a repetitive pattern between selected positions, but more sophisticated systems employ servo-controlled positioning of the joints.

Servo systems. In this case, a measure of the actual joint position is obtained from a transducer such as an optical shaft encoder, and this is compared with the position specified for the joint. If the desired position and the measured position differ, the circuitry applies a correcting drive signal to the joint motor (**Fig. 3**). Such servo systems may be digital or analog, and in addition to position they may control joint velocity.

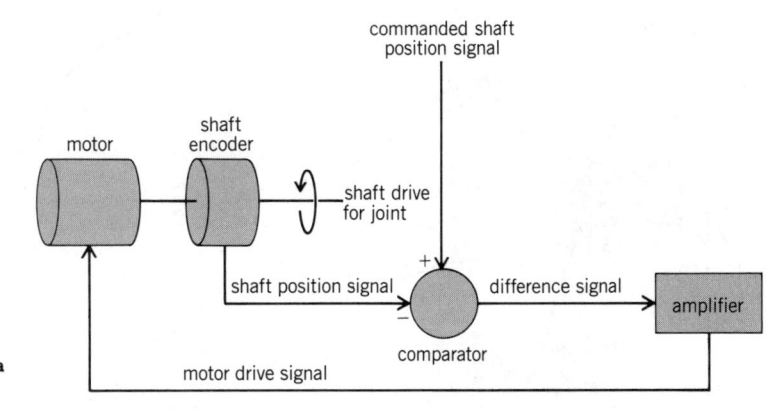

Fig. 3. Servo control for a single robot joint.

Servo devices allow the robot to be moved through any selected sequence of positions on command, without the necessity to preset mechanical stops. If the appropriate sequence of commands is generated, servo-controlled joints may be driven through continuous, smoothly varying paths. The sequence of positions defining the robot's trajectory may be preprogrammed by numerically specifying positions in the robot's coordinate frame, or they may be "taught" to the system by moving the robot to the desired point and recording the outputs of the joint position transducers. Such teaching methods allow a human to direct a complex action once, and to have the robot repeat it indefinitely thereafter.

Computer control. More sophisticated systems generate the robot's trajectory automatically by computer; such computations may be made on the basis of mathematical descriptions of work objects or tasks contained in the computer's data base. The computer may also generate trajectories for the robot which are are not fixed but vary with the state of the external world as reported by the robot's sensory system. This sensory-interactive type of control permits the robot to act appropriately in relation to conditions, rather than relying on assumptions about the world. For example, without expensive fixturing and timing of the work, the actual location of a part may vary from one instance to the next; without sensory-interactive control in such cases, the robot could proceed blindly through a set of actions at preprogrammed but incorrect positions.

Hierarchial control. The most advanced robot control systems make use of hierarchical control. In such systems each level of a hierarchy of control stages accepts, from its superior level, a statement of a goal to be achieved. The complexity of this goal will depend on the position of the level in the hierarchy; the lowest level is the joint position servo, where the goal is simply the next position commanded for that joint. Each higher level attempts to achieve its own current goal by issuing sequences of commands (subgoals) to its subordinate level. In selecting these subgoals, each level takes into account its own current goal, the current state of the external world as described by its sensory input, and the current status of its subordinate level. Thus, each level of the hierarchy acts as a servo control on the actions of the next lower level, giving it commands appropriate to reducing the difference between the current state of events and the state of events defined by its own goal (**Fig. 4**). Such systems are sensory-interactive, and constitute a task-decomposition hierarchy similar to that of many functions in the human nervous system. They allow the robot to be instructed with very general commands which define the goal at the highest level.

Sensory systems. The purpose of a robot sensory system is to gather specific information needed by the control system and, in more advanced systems, to maintain an internal model of the environment which has predictive power. The joint position transducers used in feedback control are in fact a minimal sensory system, but other sensors are usually included to gather data about the external environment. Visual, proximity, tactile, acoustic, and force-torque senses are all used.

Tactile sensors. Tactile (touch) sensors may be mounted in the robot gripper to detect contact with objects. These may take the form of simple switches, or may be analog transducers

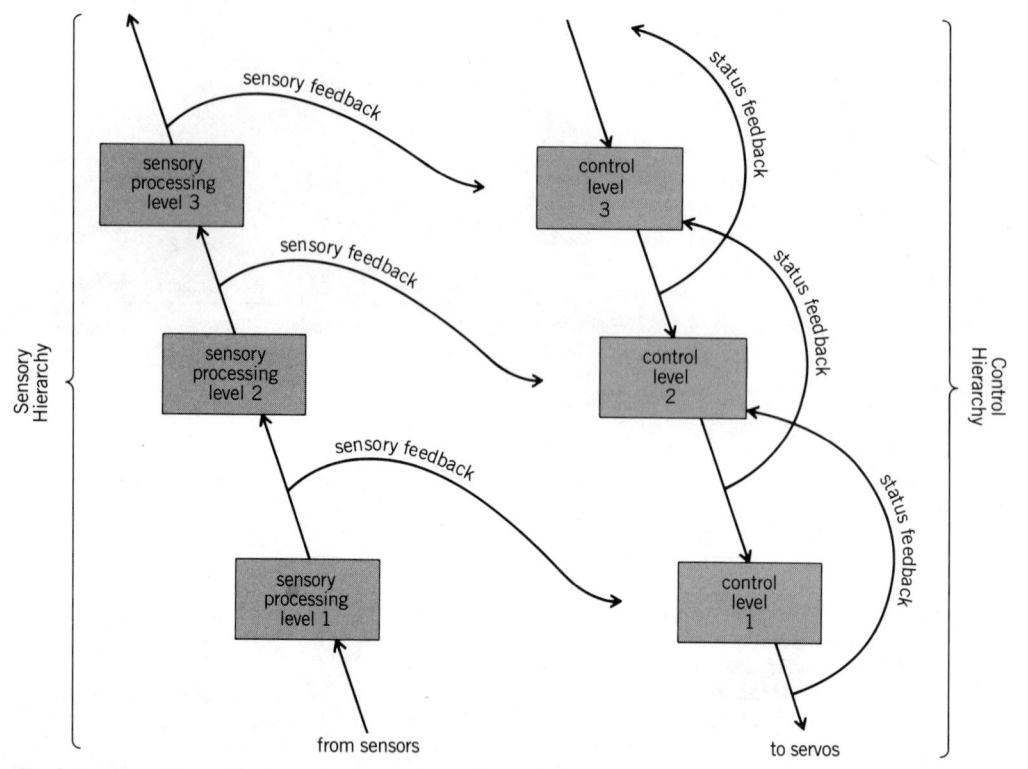

Fig. 4. Complex, hierarchical, sensory-interactive robot control system.

indicating degree and direction of pressure. Arrays of such transducers may be used to give a sense of patterned pressure which enables the robot to discriminate types and orientations of objects. Force and torque sensors, frequently mounted in the robot's wrist or fingers, are used to sense the degree and direction of resistance encountered by the gripper. These resistive forces may be due to the weight of the object being manipulated, or to contact with other objects or surfaces. Such sensors are used to adjust gripping pressure, to avoid applying destructive forces, and to guide proper mating of surfaces and parts. In combination, these senses allow a robot to feel the proper fit of work parts much as a human worker does.

Visual sensors. The most commonly used means of sensing objects at a distance is some form of visual sense. Usually this is done by computer analysis of an image from a television camera. Two important approaches are ambient light systems and structured light systems. Ambient light systems rely on normal sources of scene illumination, while structured light systems provide special patterns of illumination whose shape and orientation are known to the sensory system. The advantage of structured light is that the special patterns of illumination may be chosen to simplify and speed up the processing required to interpret the image. Procedures for determining depth in images rely fundamentally on triangulation, but in structured light systems the triangulation is between the camera and the light projector; in ambient light systems corresponding points in two images taken from different viewing positions must be triangulated, and this is much more difficult. Speed is important in robot vision because visual information is used by the control system to correct the robot's movements in real time, a process called visual servoing. SEE COMPUTER VISION.

Whatever the system of illumination used, the techniques of computer image processing are similar. At low levels, they include algorithms to do thresholding, and to find lines, edges, corners, and connected regions; these low-level vision processes are sufficient to perform many fundamental visual servoing operations. More complex systems include subsequent image-understanding operations which allow the robot to identify objects and to determine their orientation; this requires the robot to have some sort of previous knowledge about the kinds of objects in its environment. Such a knowledge base is used, together with the sensory data from vision (perhaps combined with other senses), to generate a world model describing the state of the environment.

Multimodal systems. The robot's world model can be continually updated, on the basis of new sensory input, and can also generate expectations about how the view will transform under movements in progress. The world model's hypotheses in turn aid in the interpretation of incoming sensory data. The most advanced robot sensory systems are multimodal (based on several senses), and are also hierarchically structured to generate successive levels of description, at increasing degrees of complexity and decreasing rates, suited to use by the successive levels of a hierarchical control system (Fig. 4).

Applications and forms of robots. The majority of robots are of the six-axis, jointed-arm variety, such as those depicted in Fig. 1. However, this basic type has been produced in a very large variety of sizes, shapes, and capacities which have been applied to a wide variety of tasks.

The initial impetus for robotics was to replace humans in heavy, repetitive labor, and to replace hard-automation (fixed-function) machinery with more flexible equipment which could be reprogrammed. Also, because of their initial limited sensory abilities, robots were best suited to those tasks with clearly prescribed paths of motion. Thus, the earliest applications of robots were found in tasks such as lifting parts to and from pallets and conveyors, loading automated machinery, and welding and spray-painting items traveling down assembly lines. By virtue of their earlier start, these applications numerically dominate the field of robotics.

The robots employed for these purposes range from small models with lifting capacities of several pounds to very large types which can lift many hundreds of pounds. In many lifting and placing tasks, less than six degrees of freedom are required, and many industrial robots have three, four, or five degrees of freedom. Designs also vary according to the size and shape of the work-volume required by the task; for example, many robots are designed to reach a full circle around themselves, because this enables them to achieve high productivity by tending several machines simultaneously.

With later developments in robotics, new industrial applications exploited the robot's speed and precision in such tasks as drilling and other light machining, gluing and fastening, simple assembly, packing and sealing, and testing and measuring. The machines developed for these tasks may have a repeatability of movement of better than 0.001 in. (25 micrometers), yet be able to move at high rates from one position to another; usually they are not adapted to heavy payloads. These robots are often fitted with highly specialized, changeable end-effectors which are actually automated tools in their own right. Robots of this sort are almost invariably of the continuous-path type because of the frequent necessity of following complex trajectories. Their control systems are correspondingly more elaborate, and frequently include sensory capability. Devices of this sort may, for example, place components into printed circuit boards, with very small clearances, after visually locating positioning marks on the circuit board.

Assembly tasks. Complex assembly tasks are prominent among the robot applications which have emerged with the more sophisticated sensory capabilities of robots. Such robots must be capable of locating and positioning complex three-dimensional parts, mating them to high tolerances, and then performing a variety of complex joining operations, such as screwing in bolts. Robot manipulators for assembly often have more than six degrees of freedom; this allows them to reach a given position and orientation in more than one way (for example, to avoid hitting an obstructing part). They are usually equipped with force-torque sensors or tactile sensors of some sort to enable them to feel, and adaptively respond to, insertion forces that would result in sticking and jamming of parts during positioning and mating. Since assembly usually implies a variety of parts present in the workspace, vision is often included to enable the robot to identify and locate parts for assembly; the alternative is complex or inflexible parts-presentation machinery. Vision capabilities required for assembly range in practice from simple to very complex. In many cases, parts have only a few stable positions in which they rest, and recognition and location of two-dimensional outlines is sufficient to acquire and orient them, particularly if they are separated.

The most complex tasks involve picking jumbled, mixed parts from bins, and this capability is not yet found in commercial robots.

Mobile robots. Simple mobile robots have long been employed for materials movement in factories, mail delivery within office buildings, and similar tasks requiring intelligent choice of path and a limited ability to avoid obstacles. Mobile robots for the home are available, although they have, as yet, little function other than novelty and entertainment. Developments in robot control and sensing, combined with advances in mechanisms for robot locomotion, promise to generate a significant expansion of applications for mobile robots. Among those applications are robots for guard and sentry duty and for commerical cleaning and vacuuming. Research and development has been undertaken on robots for agriculture, construction, mining, fire fighting, rescue, handling of hazardous materials, and undersea exploration. In some cases this involves the provision of sensory, world-modeling, and control devices for existing machines which already possess mobility and actuators, such as earth-moving equipment. In other cases, wholly new devices have been designed.

One of the principal problems in mobile robotics is the enhanced sensory requirement imposed by navigation in an unpredictable environment. For this reason, a truly autonomous mobile robot is not yet in sight for most outdoor uses. In many applications, however, semiautonomous robots can be employed to advantage. An interesting concept is robot ships which will have the capacity to deal with ordinary problems of ship operation, but which will be employed in convoys following a lead ship with a crew aboard. Similar concepts in land vehicles have also been considered.

Robot factory. Among the most complex applications of robotics is the robot factory. This is not a factory in which robots are used, even to the exclusion of human workers, but rather a factory which is itself a robot. That is, it is a collection of production machines, robot manipulators, materials handling systems, and other devices, all of which usually have their own local intelligence, but all of which are connected with, and coordinated and organized by a central control system which plans the operations and scheduling of production, and employs its resources in a flexible manner to accomplish its goals. Some commercial manufacturing systems are in place which trend strongly in this direction, without yet being fully self-sufficient. Experimental robotic factory systems, such as the Automated Manufacturing Research Facility at the U.S. National Bureau of Standards, are already fully automatic, although limited to simple machining. Research is expected to give such systems the ability to handle all phases of manufacturing, including process planning, scheduling, and production operations, when supplied with specifications for the desired product.

Emerging areas. As robots become more complex, they quickly exhaust the capacity of traditional computers. Computer science in robotics is focusing on the design of parallel multicomputer systems, and ultimately may evolve entirely special-purpose hardware for robot "brains." The robot factory presages the development of other robotic systems composed of multiple individual machines. The growth of robotic technology is also producing new disciplines concerned with the utilization, economics, and societal impact of robots. As robotics matures, these concerns can be expected to assume a major role in the field. SEE CONCURRENT PROCESSING; INTELLIGENT MACHINE; MULTIPROCESSING.

Bibliography. M. Brady et al. (eds.), *Robot Motion*, 1982; K. S. Fu, C. S. G. Lee, and R. Gonzalez, *Robotics: Control, Sensing, Vision, and Intelligence*, 1987; W. B. Gevarter, *Robotics: An Overview*, 1984; D. McCloy and D. M. J. Harris, *Robotics: An Introduction*, 1986; R. P. Paul, *Robot Manipulators: Mathematics, Programming, and Control*, 1981; W. E. Snyder, *Industrial Robots: Computer Interfacing and Control*, 1985.

COMPUTER-AIDED ENGINEERING
PETER A. MARKS

The use of computer-based tools to help solve engineering problems. Some use the term to describe those design activities which precede detailing and manufacturing, such as concept design and performance analysis. Others use computer-aided engineering as an all-encompassing term for computer-assisted engineering activities, including mechanical, electrical, civil, process, and manufacturing. Most, however, agree that the potential applications of computer tools to engineering will prove as revolutionary as the application of electrical power to manufacturing.

Computer-aided engineering can be considered as a set of four interrelated problem-solving aids: computer data bases and communications; computer graphics and modeling; computer simulations and analyses; and data acquisition and control of physical prototypes and production processes. The applications of computer-aided engineering range up to final production, at which time similar computer applications are usually described as computer-aided manufacturing (CAM) or computer-integrated manufacturing (CIM). S*ee* C*omputer-aided design and manufacturing.*

Although successful applications of computers to engineering problems were evident in the 1960s and before, it was not until the 1970s that computer aids emerged as a common factor in engineering. The computer-using engineer who once might have relied upon a large mainframe computer in a batch (noninteractive) environment often migrated to interactive minicomputer systems and then to microcomputers. While dramatic decreases in computer costs have made computer-aided engineering cost-effective, the real key is applications software, because computer-aided engineering is, in effect, an evolving kit of software tools which are used by engineers to help create and evaluate alternative designs. S*ee* M*icrocomputer.*

Engineers routinely use at least four kinds of "languages" to attack engineering problems. This approach is known as WRAP, an acronym for four modeling schemes: words, renderings, analyses, and prototypes. Various engineering disciplines bring special expertise to these four basic approaches: design engineers are particularly adept at graphical constructions, structural engineers at mathematical analyses, test engineers at acquiring data from physical prototypes, and so on.

Computers and computer software have revolutionized all four modes of problem solving, helping engineers to handle complex product development problems. There are, for example, specialized computers such as word processors and data-base machines to store and manipulate words. Similarly, there are graphics processors and computer-aided drafting systems; array processors and supercomputers dedicated to analytical simulations; and process computers dedicated to data acquisition and control of physical processes and prototypes.

Data-base and data communications technology. The complexity of many products outstrips the capacity of any single engineer to remember all the relevant information at any point in design. Access to the collective experience of the engineering team, as well as the experience embodied in references and standards, requires efficient organization of a project team, which may include hundreds of engineers.

Computers have emerged as a powerful aid to the management and communication of engineering information. For example, automobile manufacturers routinely make or purchase hundreds of different threaded fasteners. When a new component is being developed, it is usually much less expensive to order an additional quantity of an existing fastener than it is to design and procure a new one. Even so, manually sorting through the specifications for a thousand existing fasteners to find one that meets the new requirements (size, strength, corrosion resistance, and so forth) is so time-consuming that engineers rarely make the effort. However, a computer data base can be searched rapidly for appropriate existing fasteners and other items based on design requirements.

Other kinds of engineering information that companies have organized into computer data bases include test results, warranty reports, drawings, analysis results, cost and materials data, codes, design standards, component specifications, and documentation. Creating such a data base is a complex task. Furthermore, this information must often be organized in a way that takes into account all the future questions which engineers might want to ask. Thus, there is a possibility that a data base will become obsolete unless it is easy to update and retrieve information. There are several ways of organizing information in a computer. These include a simple file and increasingly flexible hierarchical, network, and relational data bases. The trade-off is generally future flexibility versus initial cost. However, as computer and memory costs have declined, more engineering information will be organized in relational data bases. This avoids the problem of having to predefine all possible questions. In addition, data management and control systems, essentially data-base programs to keep track of other data bases, have been developed. S*ee* D*ata-base management systems.*

Many of the greatest productivity improvements can come from taking people out of the loop when obvious decisions are involved. Thus a data base should be structured not only so that it is easy for people to use, but so that the information is in an unambiguous form which can be used directly by other computer programs. **Figure 1** shows the structure of an engineering data base. It would be ideal if the data base created on any drafting system could be used directly by any computer-controlled machine tool to manufacture that part. However, relatively few universally accepted standards in CAE exist today.

All the information in a data base is of limited value unless if is readily available to the user when needed. Advanced data communications technologies have become an important consideration in reducing overall project lead times, particularly for companies with engineers dispersed in many locations. Engineering applications often require both high bandwidths to handle the volume of information as well as multiple nodes to reach all those with a need for data-base access. *See Data communications; Data-processing systems.*

Computer graphics and modeling. The language of design engineers is in the form of graphical renderings, that is, sketches, drawings, plots, histograms, maps, vectors, schematics, graphs, and projections. Computer graphic systems, which have made it possible for engineers to create and manipulate graphic representations much faster, are almost invariably tied to an alphanumeric data-base program, which names drawings and parts for retrieval. A computer-aided drawing system might be considered to be a power tool to replace manual drafting (**Fig. 2**).

The use of computer graphics goes beyond automating manual drawing tasks. One class of application is the visualization of abstract or mathematical results. For example, the numerical output from mathematical simulations such as finite element analysis may be a dense printout several inches thick. However, most of this information can be better portrayed with graphic displays. There are many programs available to convert test data and analysis results into plots, histograms, surface displays, animations, color contour maps, and schematics. This potential of computer graphics may be compared to the power of a microscope or telescope. All of these instruments reveal information which was previously obscured by perceptual limitations, including, in the case of computer graphics, the limited ability of people to deal with vast quantities of alphanumeric data.

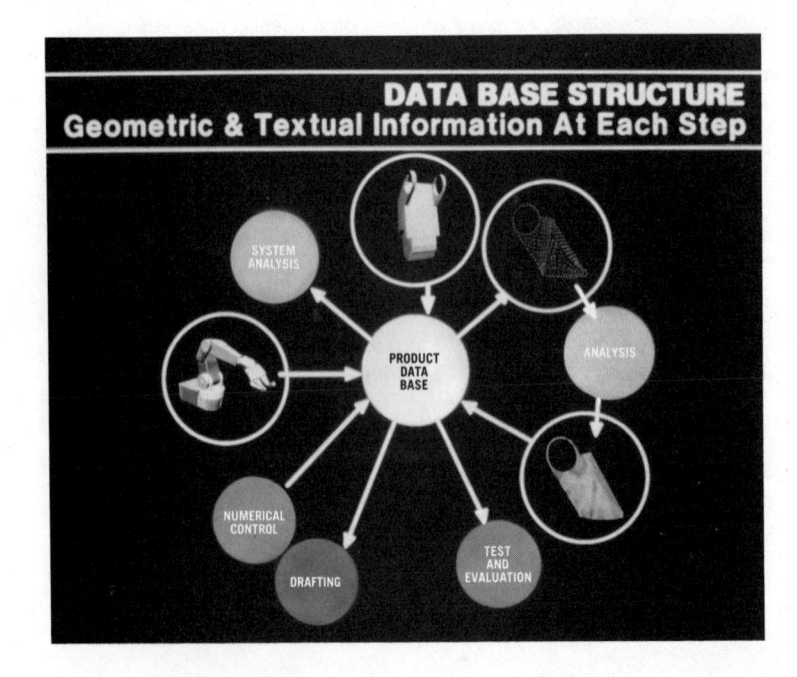

Fig. 1. Diagram of the structure of an engineering data base. (*Structural Dynamics Research Corp.*)

Fig. 2. Typical turn-key CAD/CAM system. The use of two screens improves operator access to both geometric and textual information. (*General Electric Co.*)

Perhaps the most important graphic technology for engineering is solid modeling. With a traditional drawing or blueprint, the actual three-dimensional object to be manufactured is as much in the mind's eye as it is on paper. This is also the case with the first generations of computer-aided drafting systems, which automated the process of producing drawings. It was still necessary to interpret the results before giving instructions to computer-controlled manufacturing machines. A complete solids modeling program, however, allows the engineer to build an unambiguous data base which can be used directly by other programs to calculate masses and mass properties, to prepare a model for mathematical analysis, to check for interferences, to manufacture the part, and so on. Thus a solids modeling program allows the engineer to work with a much more complete representation of the product early in the design process.

A logical assumption may be that solid modelers would simply set up a three-dimensional matrix of points and turn each one on or off to represent objects. However, with tolerances of 0.0001 in. (0.00025 cm) or so and geometrics which extend for many feet, or even miles in the case of mapping problems, this approach consumes far too much memory. Instead, the mathematical representation of a solid object typically follows one of two basic approaches. One approach is to build the object up out of a set of "primitives," much as with building blocks. The other approach is to represent the surfaces mathematically, and keep track of what is inside (solid) and what is outside. In order to make it easier for the engineer to create new geometries, hybrid methods have been developed. One program, for example, allows the user a great deal of flexibility in creating the geometry and keeps account of the results in a canonical form called rational B-splines.

The ability of some solid modeling programs to create free-form surfaces is very important, especially for cast, molded, and sculpted materials. **Figure 3** shows a model of a human face that was used in the design of face masks. The program also maintains a precise geometric data base which can be used for analysis and manufacturing functions. S*EE* C*OMPUTER GRAPHICS*.

Computer simulations and analyses. Engineers are trained to model real-world systems with more or less analogous equations. This use of simulations can be thought of as building a mathematical prototype, which is often faster and cheaper to create than building and testing the real thing. An added advantage of mathematical simulation is that it forces a better understanding of the system under investigation. Furthermore, it is relatively easy to try many variations in search of an optimal solution. However, not all problems are understood well enough to be modeled mathematically. Also, even with very powerful computers, some solvable problems, such as simulating aerodynamic flow around complex objects, require vast computing resources.

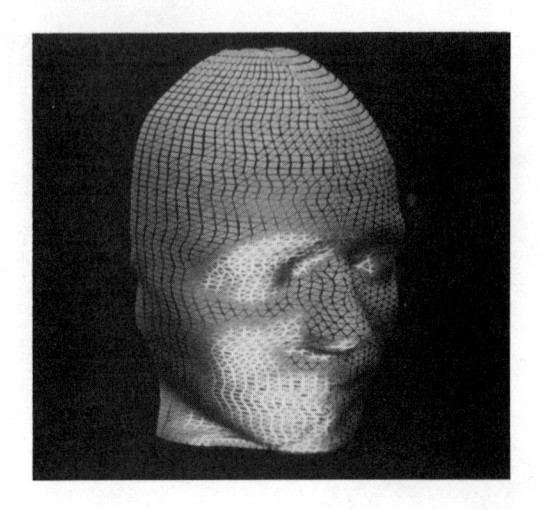

Fig. 3. Computer-generated solid model of a human face.

Finite element analysis techniques are an excellent example of the analytical applications of computer-aided engineering. The technique can be applied to any field problem, such as heat transfer, electrodynamics, and the behavior of structures. The response of a simple structure to loads, such as a single-degree-of-freedom spring, is easy to characterize mathematically. The response of a complex structure is far more difficult to characterize in a precise form. However, a reasonable approximation is possible by considering the structure as a network of interconnected finite elements, much as if it were a matrix of springs. Mathematically this results in a large number of linear equations, the solution of which is quite straightforward but much too time-consuming for manual methods. Finite element analysis software is well developed to solve these problems. *See* NUMERICAL ANALYSIS; SIMULATION.

Data acquisitions and control. Modeling with words, renderings, and analyses, even on the most powerful computers, rarely offers a complete understanding of product performance. Modern computer tools do allow far greater information to be understood in these forms, but there is still a role for building and testing prototypes prior to production. For example, computer finite element models require accurate input loads. Testing similar systems is a good way to determine these loads. The ideal, of course, is to have the best possible engineering design prior to building the first prototype of the product.

Computer tools have emerged to build prototypes faster through numerical control and computer-aided manufacturing techniques and to gain more insight into product performance through computer-aided testing techniques. In addition to general-purpose data acquisition and control programs, specialized testing techniques are well developed in the electronics industry and in the area of structural and vibrations testing (**Fig. 4**).

Computer hardware trends. Computer-assisted engineering applications use hardware similar to that in data processing, with input devices, central processors, main and auxiliary memory, and output devices. Some notable developments for engineering applications include very high-resolution graphic displays, a variety of easy-to-use graphic input devices, and specialized output devices such as plotters and machine controls. Robots might also be considered as specialized computer peripherals.

Another significant advancement has been the development of superminicomputers, which approach the performance of mainframe computers but at a much lower cost. Similarly, individual 32-bit microcomputers have been designed that approach the power of superminicomputers, but in desk-top work stations which can be networked to share resources and information (**Fig. 5**). The result is often a trend away from highly centralized computing to decentralized computing. *See* COMPUTER SYSTEMS ARCHITECTURE.

Computer software trends. Engineers orginally wrote many of their own programs to manipulate verbal, graphic, mathematical, and test data, often in the programming language FOR-

SYSTEMS APPLICATIONS **345**

Fig. 4. Computer-based testing system.

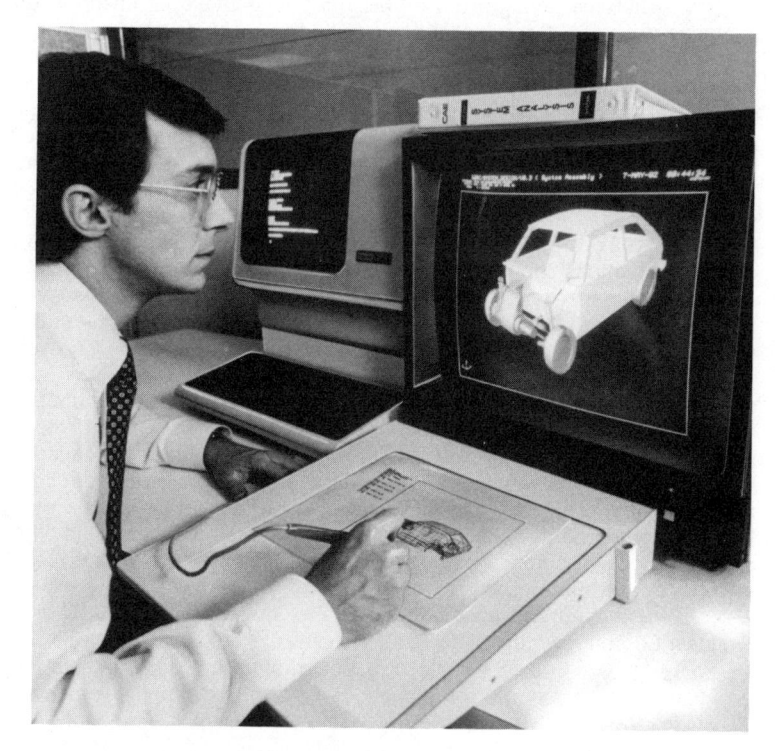

Fig. 5. Engineering work station with interactive access to data bases, solid models, analytical programs, and test results. (*Structural Dynamics Research Corp.*)

TRAN. Today, many programs that are used to solve engineering problems are purchased, since they are generally more comprehensive, better validated, and better supported than the programs an individual engineer might develop. These programs are often written in structured programming languages such as Ada and C, making them easier to maintain and upgrade. Greater attention is also being given to simplifying and easing user interactions with user-friendly help messages, step-by-step command menus, and so on. To the extent that artificial-intelligence programming methods become feasible, engineers can expect that working with a computer system will become increasingly like a dialog with a colleague. SEE ARTIFICIAL INTELLIGENCE; NONLINEAR PROGRAMMING; PROGRAMMING LANGUAGES; SOFTWARE ENGINEERING.

Implementation. Most users of computer-aided engineering techniques go through several stages of implementation. The first stage is often to automate some isolated task, such as drafting. Here the basic work tasks are unchanged, but there are some isolated productivity improvements. Once users are comfortable with the use of computers in a familiar task, a second step is often to replace a traditional modeling strategy such as prototype testing with a newer and more cost-effective strategy such as analytical simulation. This involves changes to the current process of engineering with new functions and responsibilities. The organizational issues surrounding change are often a stumbling block. A third step may be the integration of various automation and simulation activities in an overall engineering system, moving engineering toward a continuous process rather than a department-to-department batch process.

COMPUTER-AIDED DESIGN AND MANUFACTURING
LARRY D. MITCHELL

The use of computers in engineering design and manufacturing. Specifically, computer-aided design (CAD) refers to the use of computers to aid the designer from product conception to execution of engineering drawings. Computers can develop three-dimensional representations of engineering structures, analyze those structures, and make engineering drawings. Computer-aided manufacturing (CAM) refers to the use of computers to develop the optimum processing strategies for a given component. These strategies are converted to code for numerically controlled (N/C) machines which make the component. As more numerically controlled machines are installed, reorganization of the whole manufacturing process will occur, accompanied by increased plant productivity. In the early 1980s, the industrial robot became very important. Robotics and other high technologies are keys to a vastly more flexible and responsive manufacturing facility. SEE ROBOTICS.

The CAD/CAM technology provides a means of effectively using the computer-stored information for both CAD and CAM work in a common data base (data list). Thus the engineers need to input their ideas to the computer only once. SEE DATA-BASE MANAGEMENT SYSTEMS; DATA COMMUNICATIONS.

CAD. CAD/CAM was in its infancy in the early 1970s. The main developments were from industry, driven by the need to increase productivity of the engineering drawing process. Early CAD systems involved only basic automatic drafting; that is, the systems displayed the component in a line-type representation called a wire-frame model, on a televisionlike screen (cathode-ray tube). This provided a visual outline of the structure, but no detail of the interior of the component. Essentially, the representation was a natural selection because it had been used for many years for drafting. However, about the same time computer solids modeling was developed. With this capability, the design component is represented on the screen by the addition and subtraction of several primitive elements such as cylinders and cones. Even with the advantages of solids modeling, the wire-frame approach was selected, since this better met the industry goals of providing a basic drafting system.

Finite element analysis. After the introduction of CAD systems, a demand grew for engineering analysis capability. At this point finite element analysis (FEA) was introduced. This analysis technique takes a complex solid structure and breaks it into a large number of simpler elements so that the engineering characteristics of the simpler elements are known. The computer assembles the elements and solves for the internal displacements and later the stress distribution.

The engineer compares these stresses to the strength of the material. Redesign is carried out until all stress levels are acceptable. However, since the wire-frame model, with its lack of internal detail, was not a suitable data source for finite element analysis, other types of modeling capabilities were needed. Thus, CAD was expanded to include solids modeling, surface modeling (essentially the wire-frame model with surfaces hanging on the wire frame), and wire-frame capability.

CAE. All engineering design decisions are not made on the basis of stress levels alone. The large number of engineering constraints on any particular design has resulted in a large number of specialized engineering analysis programs. Moreover, in complex design problems there are a large number of design variables; the best values for them are derived by optimization, a method which attempts through numerical procedures to adjust the variables so that the design meets some objective, for example, a minimum-weight design. The collection of analysis and optimization capabilities along with CAD and finite element analysis is sometimes called computer-aided engineering (CAE).

CAT. In the late 1970s and early 1980s, computer-aided testing (CAT) was developed to satisfy the needs of testing and evaluation. In one application, automotive transmission life tests were automatically controlled by computers. Moreover, computer models of a newly designed automobile could be computationally crashed on the computer to predict the damage without actually crashing the prototype automobile. However, various automotive components still have to be statically tested to get enough data to complete the analysis.

Experimental modal analysis. Experimental modal analysis combines both computational testing and CAD. This involves measuring, nondestructively, the dynamic properties of a prototype structure with subsequent computer analysis to provide a wire-frame model on the cathode-ray tube. The model is animated in a way that corresponds to its motion at some troublesome vibration or noise frequency. The motion provides the engineer with ideas on how to modify the prototype to correct the problem. Next, the computer extracts a mathematical model from the experimental data. Using this model, the designed can ask "what if" questions; the computer makes the proposed modification in its mathematical model and displays the characteristics of the modified structure. The major advantage is that no modifications need be made to the very expensive prototype. This area of CAD is important in the design of structures so complex that they are beyond economical evaluation even on modern computers.

CAM. The first breakthrough occurred in the mid-1950s, when the first N/C machines were introduced: workers no longer were required to control the machine tools completely, since most control was done by a coded paper tape; in most cases, the workers still had to load and unload the workpieces from the machines. However, N/C machines still represent only about 4% of machine tool sales in the United States. A hindrance to the growth of N/C machines has been their programming complexity, although under CAM the programming is simplified. The computer has a N/C module that produces, from the geometry and the user-supplied tool sizes, speeds, feed rates, and tolerances, a programmed tool path needed to generate the part. This path is simulated on a color-graphics terminal screen in a different color from that of the component. **Figure 1** shows such a component. The cutter path is shown dotted at stations 1 and 2, with circles denoting the cutter positions. Once the path is verified by the user, the computer produces a N/C readable tape or disk file to be used in direct numerical control. **Figure 2** shows the N/C machine producing the component shown in Fig. 1. *See* COMPUTER GRAPHICS.

Robotics. A significant entry in the CAM field is the robot. The first industrial robot was installed by a large United States automobile firm in 1961. A robot is a programmable piece of flexible machinery that can do many varied tasks even in hostile environments. During one type of robot training, the robot records movements in its memory and then replays the action on command. The tasks that robots can do are limited; for example, a robot alone could not inspect a product for visible defects. Machine vision can be added to provide the robot with the capability of performing inspection and quality control checks. Moreover, machine vision can enable some trained robots to modify their actions through adaptive control. For example, the machine vision may determine that a bolt to be installed in a certain spot is coming to the robot upside down. Through the adaptive control function, the robot turns the bolt around and inserts it properly. As robots are given more and more senses they will become the flexible element in the production system that will allow rapid manufacturing reconfiguration to reduce manufacturing lead time. *See* ROBOTICS.

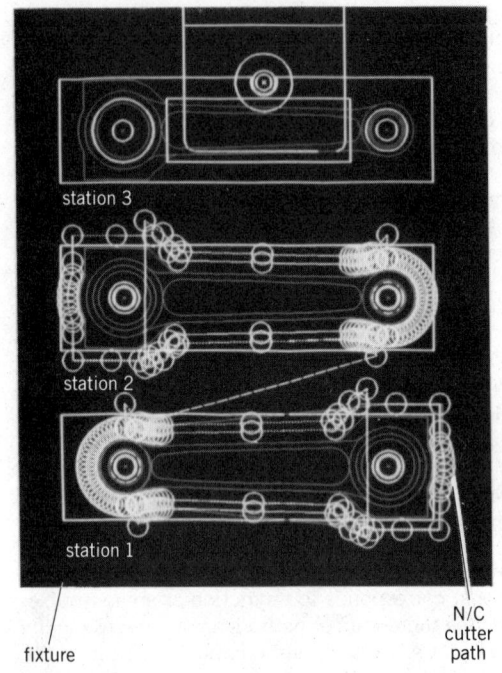

Fig. 1. Computer-aided design and manufacturing display on a system that allows the engineer to create a cutter location file and interactively preview the cutter path before machining. (*Control Data Corp.*)

Fig. 2. Numerically controlled machine in profiling operation using data generated by an integrated computer-aided engineering and manufacturing (ICEM) system. (*Control Data Corp.*)

Integrated CAD/CAM. The optimum results from CAD and CAM come from the combination of both technologies within the same facility. The CAD data base can be used for analysis, optimization, drafting, finite element analysis, interference checking, tool path definition, N/C tape generation, direct numerical control, inventory control, parts and service manual production, parts list, and many other things. In addition to the obvious efficiencies of the common data base, a data base that conforms to the International Graphics Engineering Standard (IGES) format provides data that can be assessed and used on entirely different CAD/CAM systems. The data may be supplied via computer to the potential job shops or suppliers that will bid on the production job, thus increasing response time and productivity. SEE COMPUTER-AIDED ENGINEERING; DIGITAL COMPUTER; DIGITAL COMPUTER PROGRAMMING; NONLINEAR PROGRAMMING.

Bibliography. Infotech, *Computer Aided Design and Manufacture*, 1985; J. R. Miller, Geometric modeling moves CAD one step closer to maturity, *Ind. Res. Develop.*, pp. 80–83, January 1983; A. P. Taylor, Getting a handle on factory automation, *Comput. Aided Eng.*, 2(3):74–80, May-June 1983; E. Teicholz, *CAD/CAM Handbook*, 1984.

COMPUTER-INTEGRATED MANUFACTURING
DENNIS WISNOSKY

A system in which individual engineering, production, and marketing and support functions of a manufacturing enterprise are organized into a computer-integrated system. Functional areas such as design, analysis, planning, purchasing, cost accounting, inventory control, and distribution are linked through the computer with factory floor functions such as materials handling and management, providing direct control and monitoring of all process operations.

Computer-integrated manufacturing (CIM) may be viewed as the successor technology which links computer-aided design (CAD), computer-aided manufacturing (CAM), robotics, numerically controlled machine tools (NCMT), automatic storage and retrieval systems (AS/RS), flexible manufacturing systems (FMS), and other computer-based manufacturing technology. Computer-integrated manufacturing is also known as integrated computer-aided manufacturing (ICAM). Autofacturing includes computer-integrated manufacturing, but also includes conventional machinery, human operators, and their relationships within a total system. SEE COMPUTER-AIDED DESIGN AND MANUFACTURING; ROBOTICS.

Factory of the future. The term computer-integrated manufacturing was first popularized by Joseph Harrington in 1975. He predicted that future manufacturing success would be based more on effective management of data and information flow rather than on how efficiently either piece parts or finished products were manufactured. He postulated that in the CIM factory of the future there would be areas of "departmentalized" decision making. "Departments" would be defined as being process ("hard technology") based, that is, involving processes such as milling, drilling, routing, and grinding. "Nondepartments" are defined as being information ("soft technology") based, such as design engineering, process planning, and inventory management, the basic premise being that they are generic throughout an organization. For example, process planning considered as the function "planning" applies equally to all processes in the factory, whether they be machining of metal or lay-up of composite material. Investment made to computerize the function of process planning based on the assumption that it is generic will result in reuse of this investment many times throughout the organization. The computer-based process planning function will not change at all; but the data on which it operates will be specific to the process of the moment. Computer-aided design systems are the best example of the concept.

The CIM factory of the future will integrate the traditional hard or process-based technology factory (departments) with emerging softward of systems-based technology (nondepartments). **Figure 1** shows such a factory concept. The goal of this factory is to be efficiently integrated and continuously flexible and economical in the face of change.

Effectiveness, efficiency, and economy. Efficiency is most often associated with transfer-line or assembly-line technology. The best-known developer of this technology was Henry Ford. His Model T factory could produce cars at an unprecedented rate, but the consumer had no choice at all about the specifications of the product. Flexibility is most often associated with robotics and other reprogrammable automation. Effectiveness is usually associated with the soft technology and organizational support structure of the enterprise.

Optimization of the CIM factory is based on specific criteria. By considering efficiency and flexibility and effectiveness, the CIM factory enables economy of scope. In economy of scope, flexibility is at least as important as efficiency, because the factory is seen to be an ever-changing dynamic environment which must always respond quickly to the needs of the marketplace, if not actually lead the need. The traditional factory with both rigid transfer-line technology and a rigid organizational structure cannot satisfy this objective; it strives for maximum volume of each product. In the ideal case, the CIM factory provides for profit with an order quantity of one, that is, when no two products are identical.

Organization. The CIM factory concept is illustrated in Fig. 1: hard technology is shown in the upper half and soft technology in the lower half. Soft technology can be thought of as the intellect or brains of the factory, and hard technology as the muscles of the factory. The type of hard technology employed depends upon the products or family of products made by the factory. For metalworking, typical processes would include milling, turning, forming, casting, grinding, forging, drilling, routing, inspecting, coating, moving, positioning, assembling, and packaging. More important than the list of processes is their organization.

The CIM factory is made up of a part fabrication center, a component assembly center, and a product assembly center (Fig. 1). Centers are subdivided into work cells, cells into stations, and stations into processes. Processes comprise the basic transformations of raw materials into parts which will be assembled into products. In order for the factory to achieve maximum efficiency, raw material must come into the factory at the left end and move smoothly and continuously

350 COMPUTER SCIENCE SOURCE BOOK

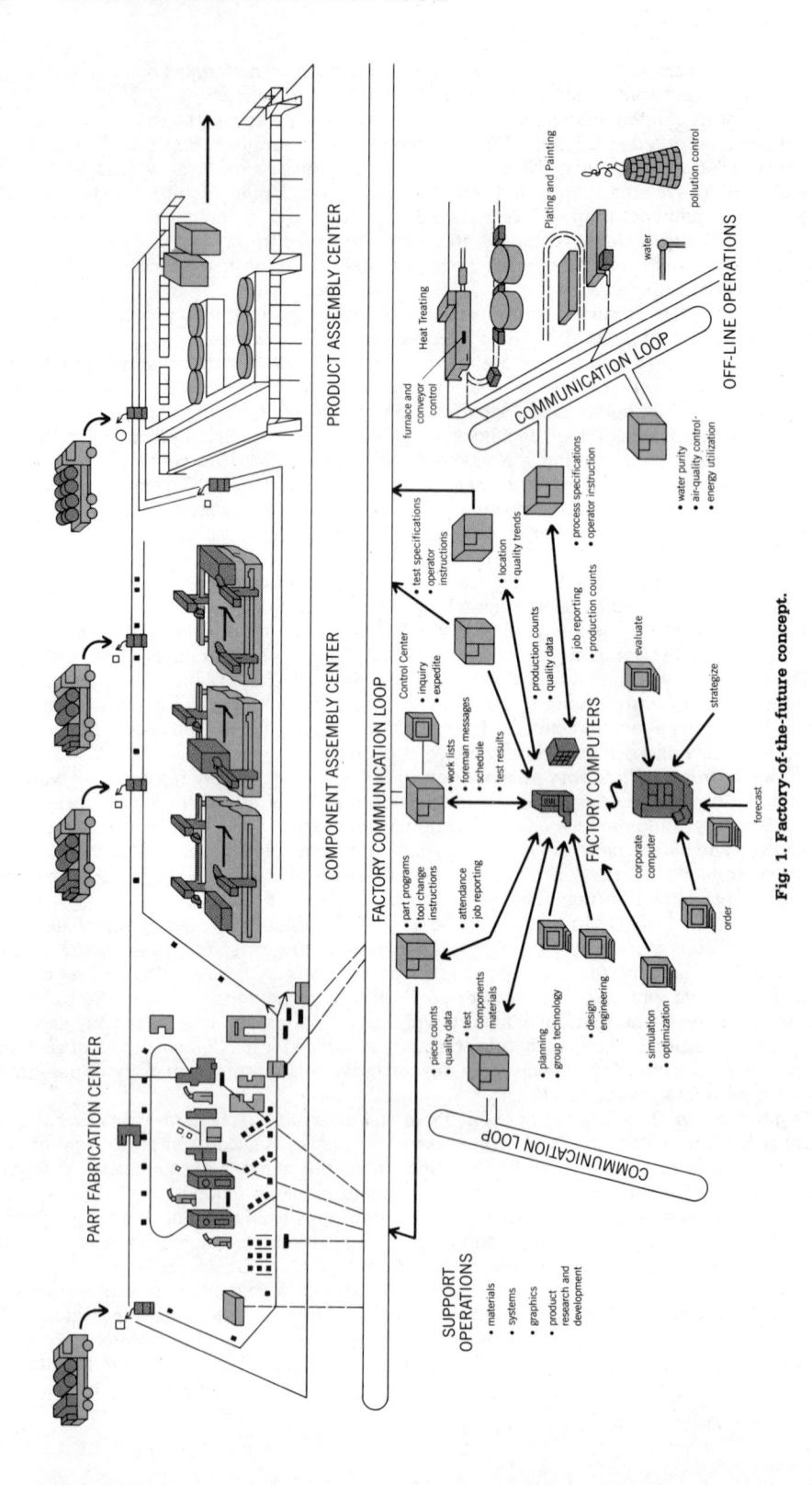

Fig. 1. Factory-of-the-future concept.

through the factory to emerge as a product at the right end. No part must ever be standing; each part is either being worked on or is on its way to the next work station. In conventional factories, a typical part is worked on about 5% of the time.

In the part fabrication center, raw material is transformed into piece parts. Some piece parts move by robot carrier or automatic guided vehicle (AGV) to the component fabrication center. Other piece parts (excess capacity) move out of the factory to sister factories for assembly. There is no storage of work in process and no warehousing in the CIM factory of the future. To accomplish this objective, part movement is handled by robots of various types. These robots serve as the focus or controlling element of work cells (**Fig. 2**) and work stations (**Fig. 3**). Each work cell contains a number of work stations. The station is where the piece part transformation occurs—from a raw material to a part, after being worked on by a particular process.

Components, also known as subassemblies, are created in the component assembly center. Here robots of various types, and other reprogrammable automation, put piece parts together. Components may then be transferred to the product assembly center, or out of the factory (excess capacity) to sister factories for final assembly operations there. Parts from other factories may come into the component assembly center of this factory, and components from other factories may come into the product assembly center of this factory. The final product moves out of the product assembly center to the end user.

Integration. The premise of CIM is that a network is created in which every part of the enterprise works for the maximum benefit of the whole enterprise. Independent of the degree of automation employed, whether it is robotic or not, the organization of computer hardware and software is essential (lower half of Fig. 1). The particular processes (upper half of Fig. 1) employed by the factory are specific to the product being made, but the functions performed (lower half of Fig. 1) can be virtually unchanged in the CIM factory of the future no matter what the product. These typical functions include forecasting, designing, predicting, controlling, inventorying, grouping, monitoring, releasing, planning, scheduling, ordering, changing, communicating, and analyzing.

It must be recognized that independent, optimum performance of the individual functions is not as important as their integration with one another, or their integration with the factory floor itself. This integration is brought about in two ways. The first is through an architecture of man-

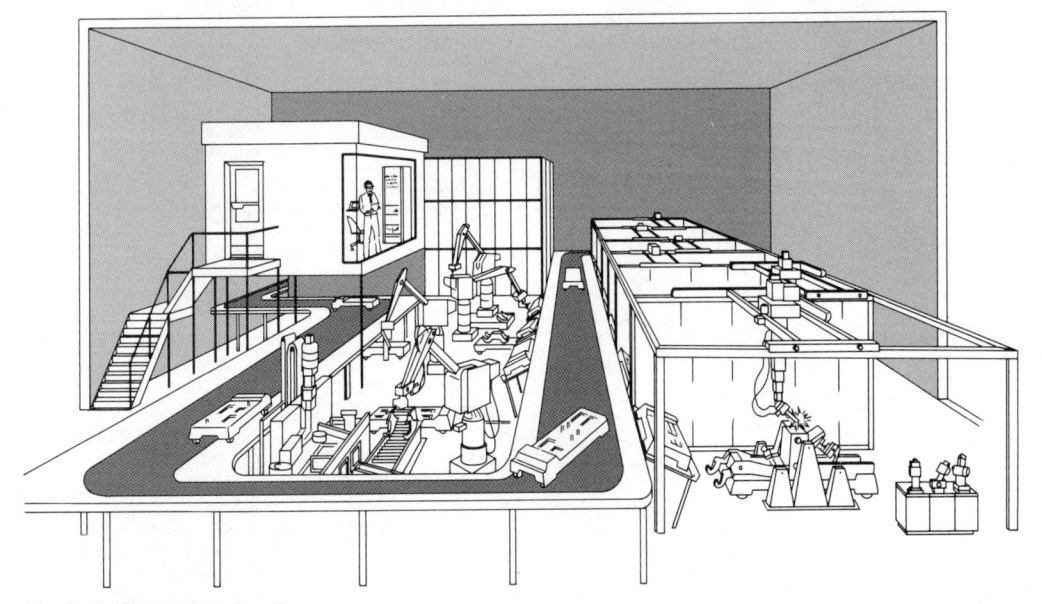

Fig. 2. Typical CIM work cell.

Fig. 3. Typical CIM work station.

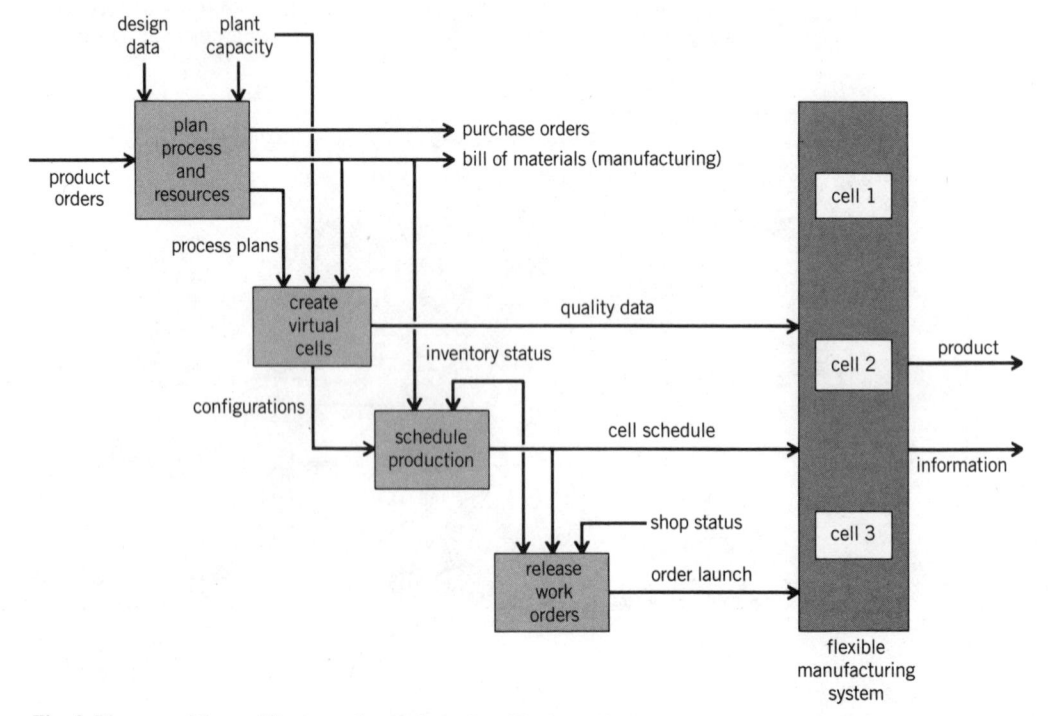

Fig. 4. Diagram of the architecture of manufacturing. (*Designed by D. Shunk, GCA Corp.*)

ufacturing which specifies precisely how and when each function is integrated with the other (**Fig. 4**). The second is through a cell controller and cell network.

The cell controller ensures integration of data between each machine, robot, automatic guided vehicle, and so forth, of the cell. The cell network (**Fig. 5**) actually performs this communication within the cell, and connects cells together into centers. In the cell network, communication is possible between each machine of the network and between different networks. The cell controller itself serves to perform such tasks as: downloading part programs from the CAD system to each machine in the cell, monitoring actual performance of each machine and comparing this performance to the plan, selecting alternate routing for a part if a machine is not operable, notifying operators of pending out-of-tolerance conditions, archiving historical performance of the cell, and transmitting to the center level on an exception basis the cell performance compared to plan. The center level of the CIM factory of the future is all of the policies and procedures that run the factory. These are embodied in computer software, which is in turn based upon an overintegration plan or architecture of manufacturing.

The purpose for the architecture of manufacturing is to provide a blueprint for employing CIM. While there are as many variations of the details of the architecture of the CIM factory of the future as there are factories, the structure of the architecture is generic. The focus is the flexible manufacturing system (FMS), which is made up of cells, stations, and processes. The information to be fed back to functions where decisions are made is more important than the product itself. In this example, the functions are defined very broadly and are used only to illustrate the absolute necessity for interaction between functions if the CIM factory is to be made to work efficiently, flexibly, and effectively.

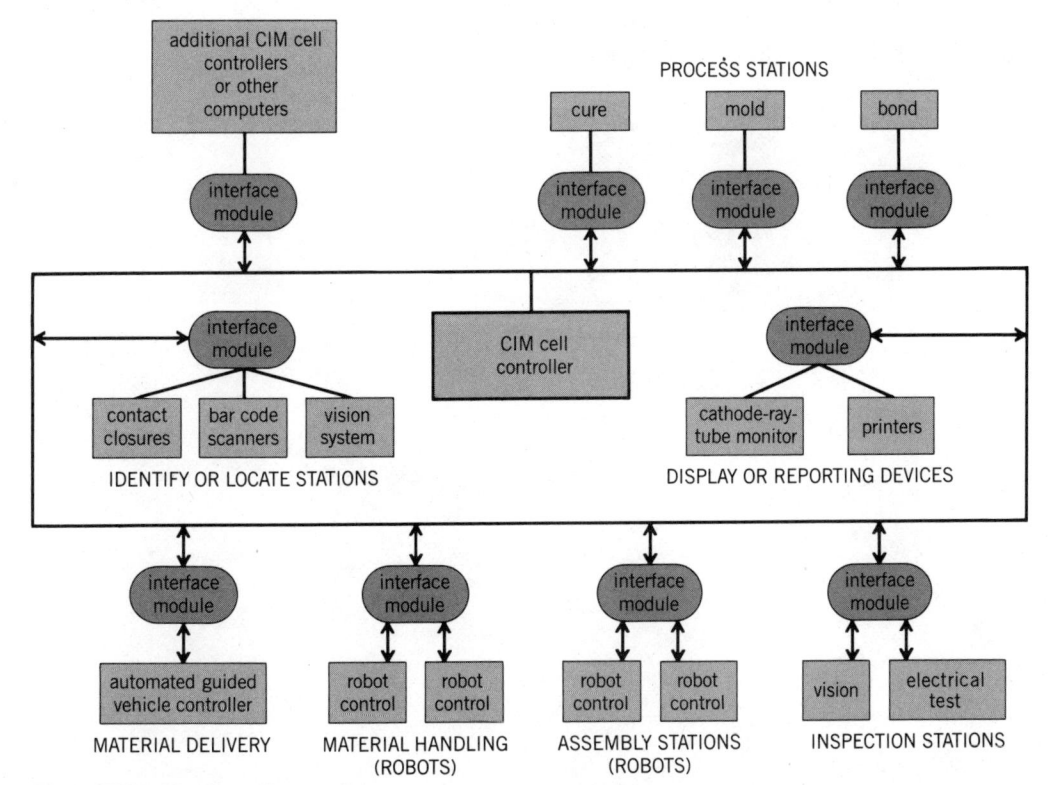

Fig. 5. CIM production cell network.

Analysis of the first block of Fig. 4 illustrates the idea. Here input to the model is product forecast. The input is changed into output depending upon the status of the controls coming into the top of the function box. In this case, one control is design data. It should not be possible for an order to be accepted when design does not exist. A second control is plant capacity; an order cannot be accepted if it cannot be filled by the plant within cost and schedule.

In the ideal CIM factory of the future, before any real decision is made, it is tested on a computerized model of the architecture to determine its feasibility. Thereby, any mistakes are made in theory, not in practice. Several simulation software packages are routinely used for this purpose. For the true CIM factory of the future to be realized, it will be necessary to build a complete simulation model.

Bibliography. A. A. B. Pritsker, *Introduction to Simulation and SLAM II*, 3d ed., 1986; V. Rembold et al., *Computer-Integrated Manufacturing*, 1985; C. M. Savage, Preparing for the factory of the future, *Mod. Mach. Shop*, October 1983.

CONTRIBUTORS

CONTRIBUTORS

Agerwala, Dr. Tilak. Manager, Architecture and System Design, IBM T. J. Watson Research Center, Yorktown Heights, New York.

Allan, Roger. Senior Editor, "Electronic Design Magazine," Rochelle Park, New Jersey.

Beaumont, Prof. Ross A. Department of Mathematics, University of Washington.

Berglund, C. Neil. Manager of Technology Development, Intel Corporation, Aloha, Oregon.

Birkhoff, Prof. Garrett. Department of Mathematics, Harvard University.

Boyd, Victor P. Deputy Director, International Electronic Message Systems, U.S. Postal Service, Washington, D.C.

Burghard, Ron. Intel Corporation, Aloha, Oregon.

Bursky, David. Associate Managing Editor, "Electronic Design," Sunnyvale, California.

Casasent, Prof. David. Department of Electrical and Computer Engineering, Carnegie-Mellon University.

Coppersmith, Dr. Don. IBM Corporation, Kingston, New York.

de Boor, Dr. Carl. Mathematical Research Center, University of Wisconsin.

El-Mansy, Youssef. Intel Corporation, Aloha, Oregon.

Enslow, Prof. Philip H., Jr. School of Information and Computer Science, Georgia Institute of Technology.

Frailey, Dr. Dennis J. Texas Instruments, Inc., Austin, Texas.

Gannon, J. D. Department of Computer Science, University of Maryland.

Gonzalez, Prof. R. C. Department of Electrical Engineering and Computer Science, University of Tennessee.

Gregory, Dr. Bob Lee. Sandia Laboratories, Albuquerque, New Mexico.

Greiling, Dr. Paul T. Hughes Research Laboratories, Malibu, California.

Gross, Prof. Jonathan L. Department of Mathematics, Columbia University.

Gruenberger, Prof. Fred J. Department of Computer Science, California State University, Northridge.

Grzymala-Busse, Prof. Jerzy W. Department of Computer Science, University of Kansas.

Hailpern, Dr. Brent T. IBM Research Laboratory, Yorktown Heights, New York.

Hartson, Prof. H. Rex. Department of Computer Science, Virginia Polytechnic Institute and State University.

Hayes-Roth, Dr. Frederick. Executive Vice President, Technology, Teknowledge, Inc., Palo Alto, California.

Helms, Harry L. Professional and Reference Book Division, McGraw-Hill Book Company, New York, New York.

Hoffman, Dr. Alan J. IBM Corporation, Yorktown Heights, New York.

Holst, Per A. Foxboro Company, Foxboro, Massachusetts.

Irene, Dr. Eugene A. Department of Chemistry, University of North Carolina.

Jarvis, Dr. John F. Robotics Systems Research Department, Bell Laboratories, Holmdel, New Jersey.

Joseph, Earl C. Sperry Univac, St. Paul, Minnesota.

Juliussen, Dr. J. Egil. Senior Member of Technical Staff, Texas Instruments Inc., Dallas.

Kanal, Dr. Laveen N. Department of Computer Science, University of Maryland.

Kent, Dr. Ernest W. National Bureau of Standards, Gaithersburg, Maryland.

King, Dr. Roger. Computer Science Department, University of Colorado.

Lea, Dr. Wayne A. Director, Speech Science Publications, Apple Valley, Minnesota.

Lee, Prof. Samuel C. Department of Electrical Engineering, University of Oklahoma.

Lehmer, Dr. Derrick H. Professor Emeritus, Department of Mathematics, University of California, Berkeley.

McLeod, John H., Jr. Professional Engineer, La Jolla, California.

Maisel, Dr. Herbert. Computer Science Program, Georgetown University.

Marks, Peter A. Director, Product Planning and Development, Milford, Ohio.

Matyas, Stephen M. IBM Systems Communication Division, Kingston, New York.

Meyer, Dr. Carl H. Advisory Engineer, IBM Systems, Communications Division, Kingston, New York.

Meyer, Dr. John F. Department of Computer and Communications Sciences, University of Michigan.

Mitchell, Prof. Larry D. Booke and Company, Inc., New York, New York.

Mizell, Dr. David W. Project Leader, University of Southern California/Information Sciences Institute, Marina del Rey.

Myers, Ware. Consultant, Temple City, California.

Nelson, Prof. Raymond J. Professor of Mathematics and Philosophy, Case Institute of Technology.

Newell, Dr. Allen. Department of Computer Science, Carnegie-Mellon University.

Patton, Peter C. Minnesota Supercomputer Institute, University of Minnesota.

Phister, Montgomery, Jr. Consultant, Santa Fe, New Mexico.

Plesset, Dr. Michael. Aerospace Corporation, Los Angeles, California.

Robinson, W. V. Processor Technology Research Group, Bell Laboratories, Whippany, New Jersey.

Rochkind, Mark M. Bell Laboratories, Holmdel, New Jersey.

Samek, Michael J. Director, Management Services, Celanese Corporation, New York, New York.

Schneidewind, Dr. Norman F. Computer Scientist, Computer Research, Pebble Beach, California.

Sheingold, Daniel H. Manager of Technical Marketing, Analog Devices, Inc., Norwood, Massachusetts.

Shively, R. R. Supervisor, Processor Technology Research Group, Bell Laboratories, Whippany, New Jersey.

Sibley, Dr. Edgar H. Department of Information Systems Management, University of Maryland.

Smith, Dr. Warren E. Optical Sciences Center, University of Arizona.

Tannas, Lawrence E., Jr. Consultant, Orange, California.
Tapia, Dr. Richard A. Department of Mathematical Sciences, Rice University.
Theis, Dr. Douglas J. Computer Systems Department, Aerospace Corporation, Los Angeles, California.
Thiess, Helmut E. Washington, D.C.
Tindell, Larry D. Senior Research Engineer, Artificial Intelligence Laboratory, Lockheed Missiles and Space Company, Austin, Texas.

Uhlig, Dr. Ronald P. Bell Northern Research, Ottawa, Ontario, Canada.

Verma, Dr. Pramode K. AT&T Information Systems, Morristown, New Jersey.
Ward, John E. Electronics Systems Laboratory, Massachusetts Institute of Technology.
Webber, Bonnie. Department of Computer and Information Science, Moore School, University of Pennsylvania.
Weiser, M. D. Department of Computer Science, University of Maryland.
Weiss, Eric A. Consultant, Springfield, Pennsylvania.
Wisnosky, Dennis E. Group Vice President, Industrial Systems Group, GCA Corporation, Naperville, Illinois.
Wright, Michael E. National Semiconductor Corporation, Santa Clara, California.

INDEX

INDEX

Asterisks indicate page references to article titles.

Abdank-Abakanowicz 8
Abstract data types 211–215*
  classification 212
  data structures and 211–212
  files and data bases 214–215
  primitive 212
  queues, lists, and stacks 212–213
  relation to algorithms 215
  sets 214
  trees and graphs 213–214
A/D converter *see* Analog-to-digital converter
ADA programming language 84–85, 209–211
Adleman, L. 315
ADT *see* Abstract data type
ALGOL 205–206
Algorithm 152–153*
  cryptographic 309–310
  hardware implementation 152–153
  programming languages 187–211*
  properties 152
  relation to abstract data types 215
Analog computer 6–26*
  applications 9
  components 10–16

Analog computer (*cont.*):
  description and uses 8–10
  digital equivalents 6–7
  digital multiprocessor analog systems 7–8
  history 8
  hybrid types 25–26
  inverse programming operations 19–20
  linear computing units 10–14
  multipliers 15–16
  nonlinear computing elements 14–15
  operation 23–25
  programming 16–23
  programming for use with calculus 21–22
  programming symbols 17
  programming to solve algebraic equations 20–21
  representation of programming variables 17–19
  signal-controlled programming 16
  types 6–8
  unique features 9–10
  use as simulator 22
Analog-to-digital converter 120–123*
  concepts and structure 120–121

Analog-to-digital converter (*cont.*):
  physical electronics 123
  techniques 121–123
AND logic element 109–110
APL (programming language) 207–208
Array processing: supercomputers 45–46
Artificial intelligence 246–250*
  architecture 246–247
  examples 247–249
  expert systems 248–249
  games 247–248
  knowledge 247
  perception 248
  problem-solving methods 246
  representation 246
  scope and implications 249–250
Asynchronous data transmission 231–232
Automata theory 153–156*
  finite-state machines 155–156
  Turing machines and intermediate automata 153–155
Auxiliary memory: architecture 51–52

Backus, J. 205
Bain, A. 243
BASIC 206
Binary digital counter 125–127
Binary number system 161–163
  bit 164–165*
Bipolar integrated circuits 88–91
  fabrication process 99–102
  linear 88–90
  semiconductor devices 90–91
Bit 164–165*
  microcomputer word size 39
Bit-sliced microprocessors 117
Boolean algebra 156–158*
  abstract relationships 157
  infinite relationships 157–158
  other forms 158
  set-theoretic interpretation 156–157
Boys, C.V. 8
Bubble memory see Magnetic bubble memory
Bush, V. 8

C programming language 209
Cache memory 57–58
CAD see Computer-aided design
CAE see Computer-aided engineering
CAM (computer-aided manufacturing) see Computer-aided design and manufacturing
Cartridge magnetic disks 63
Cartridge magnetic tapes 67
Cassette magnetic tapes 67
CAT see Computer-aided testing
Cathode-ray tube: electronic display 135–136

Central processing unit: microprocessor 115–117*
Character recognition 128–134*
  optical see Optical character recognition
  pattern recognition 129
CIM see Computer-integrated manufacturing
Circuit-switched communications 234
CMOS see Complementary metal oxide semiconductor
COBOL 206
Complementary metal oxide semiconductor 72
  fabrication process 102
  integrated circuits 93
Computer see Analog computer; Computer graphics; Computer security; Computer vision; Digital computer; Microcomputer; Multiaccess computer; Supercomputer
Computer graphics 143–150*
  applications 150
  CRT recorders 150
  cursive output 144–145
  DVST displays 150
  electronic tablets 147–148
  graphical input 146–147
  graphical output 144–146
  interactive input/output arrangements 147–150
  light pens 147
  mouse 148
  raster-scan output 145–146
  touch screen 148–150
Computer security 305–309*
  cryptographic controls 308–309
  inference controls 307–308
  information flow controls 307
  logical access controls 306–307
  physical and logical 305–306
  security kernels 307

Computer storage technology 55–68*
  auxiliary memory 51–52
  cache memory 57–58
  digital computer 30
  EEPROMs 60
  intelligent disk controller memory 58
  magnetic bubble see Magnetic bubble memory
  magnetic disk storage 61–64
  magnetic tape units 66–67
  main memory 50–51
  main semiconductor memory 58–60
  mass storage tape systems 67–68
  memory hierarchy 55–57
  memory mapping 52–54
  memory organization 57–58
  microcomputer data storage 39
  optical recording 64–65
  RAM chip types and technologies 59–60
  registers 50
  ROMs, PROMs, and EPROMs 60
  secondary memory 60–66
  semiconductor see Semiconductor memories
  supercomputer 44–45
  256K-bit RAM chips 58–59
  types of storage devices 50–54
Computer systems architecture 50–55*
  microcomputer 38
  peripherals and communication 54–55
  processing unit 54
  storage 50–54
  supercomputer 44–47
Computer vision 262–267*
  description problem 264
  intelligent machines 257–258

INDEX **365**

Computer vision (*cont.*):
  interpretation and models 265–267
  recognition techniques 265
  segmentation 263–264
  visual sensing 263
Computer-aided design and manufacturing 346–348*
  CAD 346–347
  CAM 347
  integrated CAD/CAM 348
  robotics 347
Computer-aided engineering 340–346*, 347
  computer graphics and modeling 342–343
  computer hardware trends 344
  computer simulations and analysis 343–344
  computer software trends 344–346
  data acquisition and control 344
  data-base and data communication technology 341–342
  implementation 346
Computer-aided testing 347
Computer-integrated manufacturing 348–354*
Concurrent processing 75–77*
  advantages and disadvantages 76
  communication and synchronization 76–77
  specifying concurrency 76
Control programs 186
Cryptography 309–321*
  algorithms 309–310
  block ciphers 316–318
  cipher feedback 319–321
  computational complexity 310–312
  Data Encryption Standard 313–315
  digital signatures 313
  privacy and authentication 312–313
  RSA public-key algorithm 315–316

Cryptography (*cont.*):
  security controls 308–309
  stream ciphers 318–319
  strong algorithms 310
  unbreakable ciphers 310

D/A converter *see* Digital-to-analog converter
Dantzig, G.B. 173
Data-base management systems 295–305*
  architecture 297–298
  control of data 296–297
  cost 295–296
  data administration 300
  data-base administrator 299–300
  data dictionary 300
  design and implementation 301–304
  modeling data 298–299
  rapid prototyping 300–301
  three-schema methodology 304–305
Data communications 228–233*
  communications processing 230–231
  media conversion 230
  teleprocessing 240–241*
  transmission 231–233
  types of applications 229–230
  videotext and teletext 241–243*
Data Encryption Standard 313–315
Data flow systems 79–82*
  advantages and limitations 82
  basic concepts 79–81
  comparison of conventional systems 81–82
Data processing management 294–295*
Data processing systems 286–294*
  electronic 288–294
  punched-card 287–288
  system functions 286–287

Data reduction 165*
Decimal counter 127
Decimal number system 158–161
Decision element: digital computers 27
Depletion-mode field-effect transistor 106
DFET *see* Depletion-mode field-effect transistor
Digital computer 26–38*
  codes 27
  efficiency 33
  evolution of capabilities 33–38
  fifth-generation 37
  first-generation 33–34
  fourth-generation 36–37
  hybrid types 25–26
  industry growth 38
  instructions for stored-program type 31–32
  logical circuit elements 27–29
  microcomputer *see* Microcomputer
  physical components 29
  programming *see* Digital computer programming
  second-generation 34–35
  stored program type 30–33
  stored-program computer characteristics 33
  system building blocks 29–30
  system fundamentals 26–30
  third-generation 35–36
Digital computer programming 182–185*
  addresses 182
  binary operations 182
  flow-charting 183–184
  instruction format 182–183
  languages 184–185
  notation 182
  number operations 182
Digital counter 125–128*
  applications 127–128
  specifications 128

Digital counter (cont.):
  types 125–127
Digital multiprocessor analog computer 7–8
Digital-to-analog converter 123–125*
  circuitry 123–125
  construction 125
  uses 123
Direct-access secondary storage device 52
Doping: integrated circuit fabrication 98
Dynamic random-access memory 68–69

E-JFET see Enhancement-mode junction field-effect transistor
Eckert, J.P. 57
EDP see Electronic data processing
EEPROM see Electrically erasable programmable read-only memory
Electrically erasable programmable read-only memory 70
  technologies 60
Electronic data-processing systems 287–294
  card reader and punch 291
  character reader 293
  computer output microfilmers 294
  disk pack units 290–291
  displays 293
  magnetic tape units 291
  paper tape reader and punch 291–292
  printers 292–293
Electronic display 134–143*
  applications 141–143
  categories 136
  cathode-ray tube 135–136
  color 138–140
  display electronic addressing 141
  flat-panel display 136

Electronic display (cont.):
  font 141
  special-purpose 136–138
  technique 140–141
Electronic mail 243–244*
  facsimile 243–244
  office automation systems 244
  small computers 243
  specially designed services 244
  telegraphy 244
Embedded systems 84–85*
ENFET see Enhancement-mode field-effect transistor
Enhancement-mode field-effect transistor 107
Enhancement-mode junction field-effect transistor 107
EPROM see Erasable programmable read-only memory
Erasable programmable read-only memory: semiconductor chips 60
Etching: integrated circuit fabrication 99
Expert systems 248–249, 250–254*
  components 252–254
  distinguishing characteristics 251
  importance of expert knowledge 250–251
  intelligent machines 258
  types 251–252

Fault-tolerant systems 82–83*
FET see Field-effect transistor
Field-effect transistor:
  depletion-mode 106
  gallium arsenide 104–105
FIFO see First-in first-out
Finite-state machine 155–156
First-in first-out buffers 60
Flat-panel electronic display 136

Flip-flop 29
Floppy disks 63
FORTRAN 205
Fuse-programmable read-only memory 70

Gallium arsenide: field-effect transistor 104–105
  integrated circuits 104–108
  memory chips 60
Goldberg, E. 8
Graph theory 177–180*
  definitions 178
  map coloring problems 178–179
  origin of 177–178
  planarity 179
  variations 179–180
Griswold, R. 208

Hartley, R.C. 165
High-availability multiprocessing 78–79
Hoare, C.A.R. 209
Hybrid computers 25–26

Ichbiah, J. 209
Image processing 331–334*
  applications 334
  compression 333–334
  digitization 331–332
  restoration 332–333
Integrated circuits 87–108*
  bipolar 88–91
  digital systems 29
  fabrication 95–104
  gallium arsenide circuits 104–108
  gallium arsenide FET 104–105
  integrated optical devices 94
  logic gate configurations 107–108
  microcomputer 38–42*, 94–95
  MOS 91–94
  types 88–94

Integrated optical devices 94
Intelligent disk controller memory 58
Intelligent machine 254–258*
 computer vision 257–258
 control hierarchy 257
 expert systems 258
 intelligent control 255–256
 intelligent robots 256–257
 interconnection of machines 258
Interleaved memory: architecture 51
 supercomputers 44–45
Iverson, K. 207

Kemeny, J.G. 206
Kurtz, T.E. 206

LAN *see* Local-area network
Last-in first-out buffers 60
LIFO *see* Last-in first-out
Linear circuits 88–90
Linear programming 173–175*
 applications 174–175
 general theory 173–174
 methods of calculation 174
LISP 208–209
Lithography: integrated circuit fabrication 98–99
Local-area networks 235–237*
 architecture 236–237
 purposes 235–236
Logic circuits 109–114*
 combinational and sequential logic 110–111
 digital computer elements 27–29
 embodiment 111–112
 gate configurations for GaAs circuits 107–108
 operation 109
 technology 112–114
 types of logic functions 109–110
Lovell, C.A. 8

Magnetic bubble memory 65–66, 72–75*
 devices 65–66
 information retrieval 73–74
 loop organization 73
 principles of operation 72–74
 storage locations 73
 technology status 74–75
Magnetic disk storage: average access time 62
 basic disk technology 62–63
 capacity 61
 cartridge disks 63
 floppy disks 63
 thin-film and vertical recording 63–64
 transfer rate 61
 cassettes and cartridges 67
 EDP systems 291
 half-inch tapes 66–67
 mass storage systems 67–68
Main memory: architecture 50–51
Mask-programmable read-only memory 70
Matrix theory 170–173
Mealy machine 125
Memory *see* Computer storage technology
Memory element: digital computer 27
Message switching 234
 data transmission 233
Metal oxide semiconductor 71–72
 integrated circuits 91–94
 logic circuit technology 112–114
Microcomputer 38–42*
 applications 41–42
 architecture 38
 clocks 39
 data bus 39
 data storage 39
 development system 86–87
 electronic mail 243
 embedded systems 84–85*
 hardware 38–40

Microcomputer (*cont.*):
 input and output 39–40
 integrated circuits 94–95
 microprocessors and computing power 40
 operating systems 187
 software 40–41
 speech synthesis components 282
 word size 39
Microcomputer development system 86–87*
Microprocessor 115–117*
 architecture and instruction set 115–116
 bit-sliced 117
 digital system design 117
 fundamentals of operation 116–117
 microcomputer computing power 40
Microprogramming: computer architecture 54
Minsky, M. 79
Moore machine 125
MOS *see* Metal oxide semiconductor
Multiaccess computer 226–227*
 software capabilities 227
 system components 226
 system operating requirements 226–227
Multiprocessing 77–79*
 classification 77–78
 high-availability 78–79
 response-oriented 79
 supercomputer 46–47
 throughput-oriented 78

NAND logic circuit 110
Natural language processing 258–262*
 contextual analysis 260–262
 natural language generation 262
 overall organization 262
 parsing 259
 semantic analysis 259–260

Nonlinear programming 175–177*
  computational methods 176–177
  general theory 175–176
  scope of applications 176
Nonvolatile static random-access memory 70
NOR logic circuit 110
NOT logic element 109–110
Number systems 158–164*
  binary system 161–163
  decimal system 158–161
  octal system 163–164
Numerical analysis 165–170*
  differential equations 169–170
  interpolation and approximation 166
  solution of linear systems 166–169
NV RAM see Nonvolatile static random-access memory

OCR see Optical character recognition
Octal number system 163–164
Op amp see Operational amplifier
Operating system 186–187*
  control programs 186
  microcomputer systems 187
  processing programs 186
  time-sharing applications 186–187
Operational amplifier: function in analog computer 11–12
Optical character recognition 129–134
  applications 132–134
  cursive writing 134
  different alphabets 134
  element design 131
  functional systems 129–131
  hand-printed characters 134
  postal address readers 132–133

Optical character recognition (cont.):
  stylized font characters 132
  typewritten and typeset characters 133–134
Optical computing 85–86*
Optical recording 64–65
OR logic element 109–110

Packet switching 233–235*
  applications 235
  data transmission 233
  packet format 234
  packet networks 234–235
  techniques 234
Parallel processing: array processing in supercomputers 45–46
  computer architecture 54
Parkinson, D.B. 8
PASCAL 209
Peripheral devices: computer architecture 54–55
Philbrick, G.A. 8
PL/1 (programming language) 206–207
Primitive abstract data types 212
Processing programs 186
Processing unit: architecture 54
  microprocessor 115–117*
  multiprocessing 77–79*
Programmable read-only memory: fuse PROM 70
  semiconductor chips 60
Programming: analog computer 16–23
  embedded systems 84–85*
  languages see Programming languages
  linear programming 173–175*
  nonlinear programming 175–177*
  software see Software engineering
Programming languages 187–211*
  ADA 209–211

Programming languages (cont.):
  aggregate types 193–195
  ALGOL 205–206
  APL 207–208
  applicative 202–203
  assignment statements 189
  BASIC 206
  binding attributes to variables 195–198
  C language 209
  COBOL 206
  compound statements 189
  concurrent programs 76
  conditional statements 189
  data types 196–197
  defining new data types 203–205
  digital computer programming 184–185
  expressions 189
  extent of a variable 197–198
  FORTRAN 205
  functions 200–202
  GOTO statements 190–191
  LISP 208–209
  name binding 199
  object-oriented 203
  objects, variables, and identifiers 188
  PASCAL 209
  PL/1 206–207
  procedure and function parameters 201–202
  procedures 191–192
  reference binding 199
  references 193
  repetitive statements 189–190
  result binding 199
  scalar types 192–193
  scope of an object 195–196
  side effects of procedures 201
  SNOBOL 208
  statements 189–191
  structure of 188–192
  value binding 199
PROM see Programmable read-only memory

Ragazini, J.R. 8
RAM *see* Random-access memory
Randall, R.H. 8
Random-access memory:
 capacity 69
 microcomputer 39
 read/write types 68–69
 redundancy 69
 256K-bit chips 58–59
Read-only memory 70
 microcomputer 39
 semiconductor chips 60
Real-time systems 321–323*
 artificial intelligence and expert systems 322
 evolution 322
 real-time simulation 322–323
 types 321–322
Register (storage unit) 50
Reprogrammable semiconductor memories 70–71
Response-oriented multiprocessing 79
Ritchie, D. 209
Rivest, L. 315
Robotics 334–340*
 applications and forms of robots 339–340
 control systems 336–339
 emerging areas 340
 intelligent robots 256–257
 mechanical design 334–336
 use in computer-aided manufacturing 347
ROM *see* Read-only memory
RSA public-key algorithm (cryptography) 315–316
Russell, F.A. 8
Russell, J.B. 8

Secondary memory 60–66
 bubble memory devices 65–66
 magnetic disk storage 61–64
 optical recording 64–65

Secondary storage *see* Auxiliary memory
Semiconductor memories 60, 68–72*
 fuse PROM 70
 main memory 58–60
 nonvolatile memories 69–71
 read/write RAMs 68–69
 reprogrammable 70–71
 ROM 70
 semiconductor technology 71–72
Sequential-access secondary storage device 51–52
Shamir, A. 315
Shannon, C.E. 165
Simulation 323–327*
 analog 324
 digital 324
 hybrid 324–325
 mathematical modeling 324
 trends 325–326
SNOBOL 208
Software engineering 215–224*
 design data representation 220–222
 design of software 216–217
 functional specification 216
 program implementation 217
 program testing 217–218
 requirements definition 216
 software management 223
 software piracy 224
 software portability 224
 structured design 218–220
 structured programming 222–223
Speech recognition 267–275*
 accuracy 269
 difficulty 267–269
 operation of speech recognizers 269–273
 practical implementations 273–275
Static random-access memory 68–69
Store-and-forward communication 234

Stored-program digital computer 30–33
 characteristics 33
 instructions 31–32
Supercomputer 42–47*
 architecture 44–47
 array processing 45–46
 circuitry 45
 interleaved memory 44–45
 multiprocessing 46–47
 pipelining 44
 scientific applications 42–44
 vector processing 46
Synchronous data transmission 231–232

Teleprocessing 240–241*
 hardware 240–241
 logical communications support 240
 software 241
Teletext *see* Videotext and teletext
Thin-film magnetic recording technology 63–64
Thonson, W. 8
Throughput-oriented multiprocessing 78
Transistor 90–91
Turing machine 153–155

Ultraviolet-erasable programmable read-only memory 70
UV EPROM *see* Ultraviolet-erasable programmable read-only memory

Vector processing: supercomputers 46
Vertical magnetic recording technology 64
VHSIC program 84
Videotext and teletext 241–243*
 display alternatives 242

Videotext and teletext (cont.):
    services 242–243
Virtual memory 51
Voice response 276–284*
    assessment of systems 283–284
    linear predictive coding 283
    parameterized systems 278–279
    phonemic synthesizers 279–280

Voice response (cont.):
    reproduction of stored speech 276
    system components 282
    text-to-speech devices 283
    text-to-speech synthesizers 280–281
    time-domain methods 281–282
    word concatenation systems 276–278

Von Neumann, J. 40, 164

WAN see Wide-area network
Wide-area networks 238–239*
    architecture 239
    purposes 238–239
Wiener, N 164
Wirth, N. 209
Word processing 327–331*